The ⊂
Living Image

New World in the Atlantic World

Jack P. Greene and Amy Turner Bushnell, Series Editors

Tropical Versailles: Empire, Monarchy, and the Portuguese Royal Court in Rio de Janeiro, 1808–1821
By Kirsten Schultz

Creole Gentlemen: The Maryland Elite, 1691–1776
By Trevor Burnard

Within Her Power: Propertied Women in Colonial Virginia
By Linda L. Sturtz

Naked Tropics: Essays on Empire and Other Rogues
By Kenneth Maxwell

The King's Living Image

XXX

THE CULTURE AND POLITICS OF VICEREGAL POWER IN COLONIAL MEXICO

Alejandro Cañeque

Routledge

New York • London

Published in 2004 by
Routledge
270 Madison Avenue
New York, NY 10016
www.routledge-ny.com

Published in Great Britain by
Routledge
2 Park Square
Milton Park, Abingdon
Oxon OX14 4RN U.K.
www.routledge.co.uk

Routledge is an imprint of the Taylor & Francis Group.
Printed in the United States of America on acid-free paper.

10 9 8 7 6 5 4 3 2 1

Library of Congress Cataloging-in-Publication Data

Cañeque, Alejandro
    The king's living image : the culture and politics of viceregal power
in Colonial Mexico/ by Alejandro Cañeque.
        p. cm. — (New World in the Atlantic World)
    Includes bibliographical references and index.
    ISBN 0-415-94444-9 (hardcover : alk. paper)
    ISBN 0-415-94445-7 (paper : alk. paper)
    1. Mexico—Politics and government—1540–1810. 2. Viceroys—
Mexico—History—17th century. 3. Political culture—Mexico—
History—17th century. 4. Power (Social sciences)—Mexico—
History—17th century. 5. Spain—Politics and government—17th
century. I. Title. II. Series.
    F1231.C25 2004
    972'.02—dc22
                                                        2003026844

Acknowledgments

It was that quintessentially Spanish character, Don Quixote, who at some point in his troubled career declared, "It is fitting that those who are well-born should give thanks for the benefits they have received." I cannot but agree with Don Quixote's dictum even if the nobility of my ancestors can be questioned. Because, in addition, I believe with Seneca that ingratitude is the worst form of human iniquity, it is not possible for me to escape the moral obligation of thanking the many people from whom I have received intellectual and material benefits during the years that it took me to complete this book. In the first place, I would like to thank Antonio Feros, who, first as my dissertation advisor, then as a colleague, and always as a friend, has read countless versions of this book and offered invaluable advice. His vast knowledge of the political intricacies of the early modern Spanish world has helped shape this study in decisive ways. Last, but not least, he has always supported and endorsed all my intellectual and academic endeavors with great enthusiasm and generosity, and for that I am deeply grateful. His patronage, no doubt, has been worthy of a seventeenth-century Spanish *valido*.

Because this book is based on my doctoral dissertation, I feel obliged to thank all those who participated, in one way or another, in its elaboration. In particular, I would like to thank Ronnie Hsia, Brooke Larson, Gene Lebovics, Barbara Weinstein, and Kathleen Wilson for their invaluable contributions to the shaping of the original idea that gave birth to this book. I am also very grateful to Sir John Elliott, Solange Alberro, and Fernando Bouza, who carefully read my dissertation after it was completed and offered many helpful suggestions to improve it. Many thanks also to Angela Dillard, Víctor Peralta Ruiz, and Sinclair Thomson who read different drafts of the last two chapters of this book and, with their comments, helped me sharpen and refine my arguments and ideas.

I owe a very special debt of gratitude to Nicolás Sánchez-Albornoz, who first convinced me that, despite all my hesitation and many doubts, I was qualified to undertake doctoral studies and who then has supported me throughout my academic career with his encouragement and friendship. My gratitude also to Clara Lida, who generously offered her help when I first went to Mexico City to initiate the research that would lead to this book and whose friendship and advice I have continued to enjoy afterwards. I also wish to express my indebtedness to the late Warren Dean, who, at the initial stages of my career, was always ready to give me his unconditional support.

My deepest appreciation goes to Magdalena Chocano Mena, Linda Curcio-Nagy, Jordana Dym, Alejandra Osorio, Pedro Guibovich Pérez, and Kirsten Schultz, who have read and commented upon many different versions of this study. From the very beginnings of this project, I have been very fortunate to count on their friendship, and their help has made possible, in many different ways, the completion of this book. Heartfelt thanks also go to Raquel Díez, who not only has helped me get a hold of some most rare and esoteric materials but also, with her unfailing enthusiasm, has very often provided me with the energy needed to carry out this project. To her I am indebted in more ways than are possible to express with words.

At various stages of the writing of this book, I benefited from the advice and support of many friends and colleagues. I also had the opportunity to present portions of it in different venues and countries. I wish to thank all those who invited me to these presentations and those with whom I had the opportunity to exchange ideas and opinions on a variety of subjects. Many warm thanks in particular to Christian Büschges, Jesús Bustamante, Joan Casanovas, Nancy Fee, Carlos Gálvez, Marta Irurozqui, Oscar Mazín Gómez, José de la Puente Brunke, Mónica Quijada, José Antonio Rodríguez Garrido, Christoph Rosenmüller, Nelly Sigaut, and Margarita Suárez.

The archivists and librarians in Mexico City, Seville, Madrid, and New York, who, at some point or another, made my life easier with their invaluable help also deserve my gratitude. Especially, I would like to thank Jesús Camargo from the Archivo General de Indias, for all his help with the digitized documents housed in that repository, and Liborio Villagómez, from the Fondo Reservado of the Biblioteca Nacional in Mexico City, for providing me with microfilms of many rare publications of the colonial period. A very special thanks as well goes to Marsha Ostroff, who patiently and carefully read and made sure that successive drafts of this book were written in good, conventional English instead of a form of "Spanglish." Her help has been priceless. I am also grateful to Rosario Páez for her inestimable assistance in locating several illustrations for the book. Finally, I am indebted to the Program for Cultural Cooperation Between Spain's Ministry of Culture and United States' Universities for the research grant I was awarded, which enabled me to start research in Spain; to the Department of History of New York University, for a fellowship that funded a substantial portion of the writing of this manuscript; and to the Gallatin School of New York University, for two Faculty Enrichment grants that allowed me to complete my research.

List of Illustrations

Fig. 1 Diego Rivera, *The History of Mexico* (1929–1935) 2

Fig. 2 Frontispiece, Juan de Solórzano Pereira, *Política indiana* (1647) 33

Fig. 3 Cristóbal de Villalpando, *Aparición de San Miguel* (ca. 1684) 44

Fig. 4 Frontispiece, Francisco Aguado, *Sumo sacramento de la Fe. Tesoro del nombre christiano* (1640) 47

Fig. 5 "Philip IV's devotion to the Holy Sacrament," from Isidro Sariñana, *Llanto del Occidente en el ocaso del más claro sol de las Españas* (1666) 48

Fig. 6 "Charles II's devotion to the Holy Sacrament," from Agustín de Mora, *El sol eclipsado antes de llegar al cenit* (1700) 49

Fig. 7 Seventeenth-century Mexican monstrance 50

Fig. 8 Cristóbal de Villalpando, *Triunfo de la Santa Iglesia Católica*, also known as *La Iglesia militante y triunfante* (1684) 106

Fig. 9 Miguel and Juan González, *Moctezuma's Entry* (1698) 126

Fig. 10 Melchor Pérez de Holguín, *The Entry of Archbishop–Viceroy Morcillo in Potosí* (1716) 128

Fig. 11 "Catafalque of Philip IV in the cathedral of Mexico City," from Isidro Sariñana, *Llanto del Occidente en el ocaso del más claro sol de las Españas* (1666) 130

Fig. 12 Anonymous, *San Hipólito* (eighteenth century) 147

ix

Fig. 13   "The liberality of King Charles II," from Agustín
de Mora, *El sol eclipsado antes de llegar al cenit* (1700)   160

Fig. 14   "The love and care of the Spanish kings for their Indian
subjects," from Isidro Sariñana, *Llanto del Occidente
en el ocaso del más claro sol de las Españas* (1666)   188

Fig. 15   Indian labor services performed by order of the viceroy,
from *Códice Osuna*   202

Fig. 16   Labor services performed by the Indians in the viceregal
palace, from *Códice Osuna*   203

Fig. 17   The appointment of Indian magistrates by the viceroy,
from *Códice Osuna*   217

Contents

Introduction: Rethinking the Spanish Empire in America   1

    The Invention of the State   7
    Seeing the Viceroy   11

1   Imagining the Viceroy   17

    The Rule of One   19
    The Image in the Mirror   26
    The Mystery of Power   36

2   The Pillars of Government   51

    The Viceroy's Companions   53
    The Realm's Head   65

3   In the Service of Two Majesties   79

    A Tale of Two Knives   80
    One Body, Two Heads   93
    A Remedy from Heaven   106

4   Performing Power   119

    The Politics of the Viceroy's Body   120
    Ritual Challenges   132
    The Preeminence of the Body   141

5   The Economy of Favor   157

    On Favors and Rewards   159
    The Crown's Dilemma   165
    The Specter of Corruption   175

6   The Political Culture of Colonialism   185

The Rhetoric of Wretchedness   186
The Civilizing Mission   192
To Serve Is To Be Civilized   201

7   Colonial Rhetoric and Indian Rebellion   213

Two Republics and One Viceroy   214
A Republic Without Rhyme or Reason   222
The Return of the Wretched Indian   230

Conclusion: The Power of the King's Image   237

Appendix   247

The Viceroys of New Spain in the 16th and 17th Centuries   247
The Archbishops of Mexico in the 16th and 17th Centuries   249

Glossary of Spanish Terms   251

List of Abbreviations   255

Archives and Libraries   255
Other Abbreviations   255

Endnotes   257

Introduction   257
Chapter 1   264
Chapter 2   277
Chapter 3   291
Chapter 4   311
Chapter 5   327
Chapter 6   341
Chapter 7   355
Conclusion   367

Bibliography   371

Manuscript Sources   371
Printed Sources   372
Secondary Sources   379

Index   395

Introduction: Rethinking the Spanish Empire in America

The figure of the colonial viceroy, who ruled New Spain in the name of the Spanish Crown, has made a lasting impression on the Mexican historical imagination. Generally portrayed as an absolute and despotic ruler, the specter of the viceroy continues to shape contemporary political culture. Perhaps one of the most familiar images of viceregal authority is Diego Rivera's famous mural in the National Palace in Mexico City that depicts the Spanish conquest and colonial rule. In this painting, the figure of a dour viceroy, standing under a canopy and surrounded by other members of the colonial ruling elite, is juxtaposed against the terrifying depiction of the burning at the stake of two victims of the Inquisition to reinforce the connection between Spanish despotism and cruelty and viceregal authority (see Figure 1). More recently, the haunting image of the viceroy has appeared in the writings of *Subcomandante* Marcos, the internationally known leader of the *Ejército Zapatista de Liberación Nacional* (EZLN). A few weeks after the outbreak of the indigenous uprising in the southern Mexican state of Chiapas on New Year's day, 1994, the "Department of Press and Propaganda" of the EZLN released a document written by Marcos in 1992 intended "to awaken the consciousness of several comrades" who were starting to sympathize with the *Zapatista* cause. The document, filled with irony and bitter sarcasm, was a damning indictment of the poverty and dire living conditions of the indigenous population of Chiapas, one of the poorest and most neglected areas of the entire country. Marcos, nevertheless, reserved his most corrosive criticisms for the main representative of the Mexican state in Chiapas — that is, the Governor of the state, who, according to Marcos, was an utterly greedy and corrupt politician. Interestingly enough, Marcos always refers to the Governor as the "viceroy" or, in an even more derogatory way, the "apprentice of viceroy." He explains how the Indians had to walk over 1000 kilometers to the nation's capital just to ask for the central government

Fig. 1 Diego Rivera, *The History of Mexico*, 1929–1935, National Palace, Mexico City.

to arrange an interview between them and the "viceroy." "They arrived," says Marcos, "in the capital of the former New Spain, today's Mexico, in the year 500 after the darkness of the foreign nightmare descended upon this land." Marcos concludes his document in a prophetic, almost Biblical way, by telling us the terrible destiny that awaits the "viceroy," a destiny that has been dreamt of by the "viceroy" himself:

> The viceroy dreams that his land is being shaken by a terrible wind which uproots everything; he dreams that everything that he stole has been taken away from him; he dreams that his house is destroyed and that the kingdom he ruled is tumbling down. He dreams and he cannot sleep. The viceroy calls on the feudal lords, and they tell him that they have dreamt the same things. The viceroy does not have a moment's rest; he meets with his doctors and they all decide that it is Indian witchcraft, and they all decide that only with blood will the viceroy get rid of the spell. And the viceroy gives orders to kill and to jail, and he builds more prisons and barracks, and the dream still keeps him awake.[1]

It is quite clear from these passages that, in order to portray the Governor in the most negative way possible, Marcos has chosen a term to refer to him that, almost 200 years after the last viceroy stepped on Mexican soil, still conjures up visions of absolute and corrupt power. Of course, in the case of Marcos, his use of the figure of the viceroy as a political weapon, which allows him to convey in a forceful way the abusive nature of the Chiapas Governor's power, is almost natural. After all, he sees the history of Mexico as an uninterrupted line that starts with Hernán Cortés and ends up with Carlos Salinas de Gortari, the President of the Mexican Republic at the time of the insurrection. It is not by accident that the famous "Proclamation of the Lacandon Forest," issued by the rebels on January 2, 1994, and addressed to the people of Mexico, begins by declaring, "We are the product of 500 years of struggle." In this regard, it makes sense to see the present-day governor of the state of Chiapas as the reincarnation of the colonial viceroy. After all, the former is thought to be the direct descendant of the latter.

This kind of "anti-viceregal" rhetoric is not exclusive to leftist artists and guerrillas. Writing a few days before the legislative elections of July 1997 that brought defeat to the ruling *Partido Revolucionario Institucional* for the first time in almost seven decades, one of today's prominent Mexican historians argued that the 63 viceroys who ruled New Spain between 1521 and 1821 on behalf of a distant king who never once crossed the ocean created a tradition (already incarnated in the Aztec *tlatoanis*) of "centralized, divinely sanctioned power that has lasted, under different forms, almost to the present day." Under these circumstances, he concluded, it was not difficult to be cynical about democracy in Mexico,[2] nor is this anti-viceregal rhetoric peculiar to Mexicans. According to one prominent North American scholar of colonial Mexico,

> … inherent in the colonial order was an arbitrary, monolithic state headed by a vice-sovereign with nearly absolute authority who functioned essentially as an overseer of the enormous estate of its absentee owner. …[H]is Majesty's representatives often were little less than unrestrained despots. …[T]heir will took on the semblance of statutes and their persons an aura of infallibility. …This haughty importance, so gratifying to vanity, fostered a tradition of personalism and dictatorship fated to haunt the political life of the later republic.[3]

But, was this the real nature of viceregal power? Were the viceroys who ruled New Spain in the sixteenth and seventeenth centuries "tyrants" who governed in a despotic way? No doubt, one can understand how tempting it is to see the figure of the viceroy through the prism of a modern governor or president of the republic, but we should be very careful when making broad comparisons that ignore the great gulf of historical experience and cultural transformation that separates twentieth-century Mexican rulers from their supposed colonial predecessors. Thus, the main aim of this study is to recover the colonial political culture that explains the existence of the viceroys and, at the same time, distinguishes them from modern rulers.

Despite the political significance of the viceregal figure, little is known about the mechanisms of viceregal power. Traditionally, studies of the viceregal post in the Habsburg period have been biographical and descriptive, focusing on the two or three more "important" viceroys — those who are thought to have decisively contributed to establishing royal authority in the American territories, especially in the sixteenth century — and ignoring the rest.[4] Those historians who have examined the structure of Spanish colonial administration have usually seen the viceroy as a prominent figure in the effort to build a colonial state. Concentrating on the legal and institutional aspects, some scholars have approached the study of the viceregal figure as an instrument of absolutism and of the expanding royal state in its struggle against corporate privileges and the network of patron–client relationships.[5] On the other hand, the absence of major open challenges to the Crown has been explained as a result of the development in Habsburg Spain of a strong bureaucratic structure and an administrative class of *letrados* (law graduates) to staff it. These *letrados* were the ones who really held the Spanish monarchy and empire together.[6] Accordingly, some scholars have argued that the viceroys were just administrators (the coordinators of the various administrative hierarchies) and imperial agents, charged with imposing royal authority in the New World.[7] In this administrative structure, the viceroys constituted the political layer of the imperial bureaucracy, while the justices of the High Court formed the professional echelon. Both viceroys and justices constituted the highest model of an exemplary administrative order, one on which the Habsburg state was based.[8]

In the case of colonial Spanish America, the "state" is probably one of the most frequently used terms and, at the same time, one of the least investigated. In this study, however, I will argue that the state as the normal form of political organization is a highly problematic concept when applied to the study of the sixteenth and seventeenth centuries and, thus, not very useful in understanding viceregal power. Moreover, we should get beyond the state-building metaphor with its teleological implications. Because the state is so often taken for granted, it will be necessary to explain in detail why, then, we should avoid the use of this term. The identification of the viceroy as one of the fundamental agents in the construction of the colonial state should not be a surprise if one bears in mind that, at least until recently, one of the main preoccupations of historians of the sixteenth and seventeenth centuries has been the study of the emergence of the "modern state," considered by many the fundamental protagonist of the political process from the sixteenth century onward. According to this view, the state becomes the essential element of modernity, which cannot be understood without this concept. In the Spanish case, the state as a form of political organization would not have been born suddenly but over the course of a long historical process initiated in the thirteenth century, though it was not until the end of the fifteenth century, during the reign of the Catholic Monarchs, that the "advent of a true state" is located in time. This "true state" is defined as a superior power concentrated around the person of the monarch, whose power operates through a series of institutions — diplomacy, the bureaucracy, the army, the treasury — whose main characteristic is a unity of command and decision.[9]

Some authors, however, believe that the concept of the "modern state" is too general, thus it is more appropriate to speak of the "absolutist state," as this term defines with greater precision the type of state that appears at the end of the fifteenth century. This approach views absolutism as a conscious tendency of the monarchy whereby it progressively liberated itself, during the course of the Middle Ages, from any kind of control or institutional limits. One of the main characteristics of the early modern period, thereby, would have been the advance of an authoritarian conception of power (which concentrated on the monarch) to the detriment of a "pactist" conception, which maintained that power lay not only in the king but also in the realm (understood as estate assemblies). Although the king appears as the embodiment of the state, in reality the state enjoys relative autonomy as an apparatus of power, an institutional complex interpolated between the monarch and his subjects. According to this view, the history of the Spanish absolutist state may be divided into three different phases: The first, which can be defined as that of emerging absolutism, represents the phase of state consolidation and would go from the beginning of the reign of the Catholic Monarchs up to the crushing of the urban revolts of the 1520s; the second phase, that of an increasing absolutism (albeit one facing opposition), would extend up to the death of Charles II in 1700; and, finally, a phase of mature or full absolutism corresponded to the entire eighteenth century.[10]

For their part, historians of colonial Spanish America have not shown an excessive interest in recent decades in the study of the political history of the Spanish empire in America (and much less in the figure of the viceroy). Originally, this constituted, in many ways, a welcome reaction against the previous emphasis on the institutional and legal aspects of the Spanish dominion in America. As a result, the emphasis shifted to the social, economic, and ethnic aspects of the local colonial societies. In these studies, nonetheless, the colonial state is always a given, the only dispute being whether the state created by the Spaniards in the New World was "strong" or "weak." A few historians have examined this matter, some of them emphasizing the importance and relative autonomy of the state in colonial society. According to these scholars, the Spanish monarchy erected a modern state apparatus in colonial Spanish America that pioneered new procedures of bureaucratic control, establishing a centralized and rationalized model of exploitation of the Indian communities. It foreshadowed the Weberian model of legal domination that did not become triumphant in the West until the nineteenth century. Thus, the power of the colonial bureaucracy was, by the standards of the time, tight and efficient. By imposing this heavy bureaucratic apparatus in order to avoid the formation of dominant social groups, the colonial state would achieve a hegemonic role.[11] Other studies have argued that colonial power was in fact "diluted" among the different institutions that comprised the colonial state (king and council in Spain; viceroys, high courts, and regional officials in America). The colonial state before 1750 should be characterized not as an "absolutist state" but as a "consensus state," in which the colonial bureaucrats, rather than acting as executives of the imperial government, became mediators between the Crown and the colonists.[12]

Despite these studies, the investigation of the politics of imperial rule has been neglected by most historians in favor of the study of the colonial economy and society. In 1985, William B. Taylor published a critique of what he thought had become the two most common approaches to the study of colonial Latin America. He criticized the "dependency approach" for its excessive concentration on economics and its lack of attention to politics. In the *dependentista* approach, the role played by the institutions of the state was generally minimized, and the state was treated as little more than a vehicle of coercion in the economic interests of a ruling class.[13] He was equally critical of social historians for eschewing the study of formal institutions and political events, a practice that encouraged its adherents to treat societies as things, seeing both the rulers and the ruled as forming two distinct closed worlds without many relations existing between them. Taylor made a case for the importance of the study of the state in colonial Latin America if we were ever to understand how power and social change worked. He argued that we should set aside dichotomies such as ruler/ruled, omnipotent state/weak state, outside world/local community, and secular/religious and see the state, following E.P. Thompson, as the "institutional expression of social relationships"; in other words, we should think of state institutions and communities in a very broad sense:

> … as bundles of relationships among people rather than as things or units that lead lives of their own, interacting with other units but not bound to them except perhaps one-to-one. In this way, it is easier to see that most people are in some sense both rulers and ruled and that power relationships may be intermittent, incomplete, and complicated by many conflicting obligations and loyalties; and to recognize that a single, unified, coherent ruling class did not exist.[14]

I certainly agree with Taylor's approach to the study of power relations and the ruling class. By and large, this is my approach to the study of viceregal and colonial power. I also subscribe to Taylor's critiques of dependency history for not paying enough attention to local factors and of social history for focusing on localities or groups and losing sight of systems; however, I cannot share his insistence on using the "state" as a useful category for the analysis of colonial society, at least in the sixteenth and seventeenth centuries. While he contends, for example, that "it makes little sense to speak generally of a Latin American working class in a capitalist system much before 1900," he sees no problem in affirming that "one of the peculiarities of early Latin American history is that the state became important before thoroughgoing mercantilism or industrial capitalism from Europe had much effect."[15] While he is probably right in his first assertion, I disagree with the second one, and I would argue that, paraphrasing Taylor, it makes little sense to speak generally of a colonial state existing much before 1800. Interpolating the state into the study of power relations in colonial Spanish America obscures more than illuminates these relations. This assertion, of course, merits some explanation, as the "state" is a concept so deeply entrenched in the historical imagination.[16]

The Invention of the State

As Philip Abrams affirms, "We have come to take the state for granted as an object of political practice and political analysis while remaining quite spectacularly unclear as to what the state is." Abrams contends that the state, in fact, is a spurious object of sociological concern, as the state is not a thing that exists as a real entity with will, power, and activity of its own. Rather, it is agencies and actors — the government, the administration, the military and the police, the judicial branch, regional governments, and parliamentary assemblies — that make up the "state." Abrams proposes to "abandon the state as a material object of study whether concrete or abstract while continuing to take the *idea* of the state extremely seriously." This is so because, since the seventeenth century, the idea of the state has been an essential feature of the process of subjection. For this reason, we should move beyond Hegel, Marx, and Weber, from an analysis of the state to a "concern with the actualities of social subordination" or "politically organized subjection." The "state" is an ideological project, an exercise in legitimatization, a mystification of this process of subjection, because political institutions conspicuously fail to display a unity of practice and are divided against one another. For Abrams, it is this actual disunity above all that the state conceals. The state is the unified symbol of an actual disunity; thus, our aim should be not the study of the "state" but of political beliefs and practices.[17]

While I agree with Abrams on what our ultimate aim should be (thus, this book is designed not as a study of viceregal power as an embodiment of the Spanish colonial or imperial "state" but as an investigation of the political beliefs and practices that constituted viceregal power and the Spanish imperial system of rule), I believe that in the sixteenth and seventeenth centuries the idea of the "state" as the essential concept that unified and gave cohesion to the political community had not yet entered the political imagination of the Spanish polity. Spanish domination was based on different principles, and it is the main purpose of this study to uncover those principles. My approach to the study of the colonial political system, in general, and viceregal power, in particular, is thus grounded in the idea that we can understand the workings of the system only if we make an attempt to understand it according to its own principles, not ours.

Since the Enlightenment, the Western mind has seen the past primarily as the progenitor of the present, overemphasizing the evolutionary element in history;[18] thus, the predominance of the "genetic approach" has made the study of the beginnings of the modern centralized state and the emergence of a competitive state system a favorite theme for historians.[19] Not infrequently, this approach has been related to the belief that "inferior" or "inadequate" stages have been left behind.[20] In the case of the Spanish monarchy, for example, the "statist paradigm" has been used to explain its failure, the failure being its supposed inability to fully establish a centralized and bureaucratic government; in other words, the inadequacy of the Spanish monarchy lay in its incapacity to become a "true state." Such a reasoning, however, has a serious flaw. By adopting a conceptualization of the political order that had not yet been formulated, it is assessing the political system of the Spanish monarchy using assumptions and principles that were not those on which it was built. In that regard, it attributes to the Spanish monarchy deficiencies that only make sense if they are seen from our current viewpoint.[21] This is a crucial point if we are to understand why a study of Spanish colonial and viceregal power cannot be framed within the narrow and historically determined boundaries of the state paradigm.

The fact is that the modern concept of the state — an entity with a life of its own, distinct from both rulers and ruled, and able, in consequence, to call upon the allegiances of both parties — had not yet come into reality in the early modern period. When Hobbes introduced the term "state" around the middle of the seventeenth century to denote the highest form of authority in matters of civil government, it was still a relatively new and contentious term; so were the notions that the duties of subjects were owed to the state, rather than to the person of a ruler or to a multiplicity of jurisdictional authorities (local or national as well as ecclesiastical or secular). Renaissance and early modern political theorists certainly use the term "state" or the Latin *status*, but they mean something quite different. For example, when they refer to the "state of the king," they simply mean the standing of the king or his kingdom, not the modern idea of the state as a separate apparatus of government. Even when Machiavelli, who is seen as one of the principal theorists of the early modern state, talks about the *stato*, he employs the term to refer either to different forms of government or to the prevailing regime. He also frequently uses the term to denote the lands or territories of a prince. His most important innovation is, no doubt, the distinction he makes between the institutions of *lo stato* (the institutions of government and the means of coercive control that serve to organize and preserve order) and those who have charge of them. Although Machiavelli and other theorists of classical republicanism (Contarini, Guicciardini) begin to speak of the *status* or *stato* as the name of that apparatus of government that rulers are said to have a duty to maintain, the power structure in question is not viewed as independent from those who have charge of it. The ruler or chief magistrate, far from being distinguishable from the institutions of the state, is said to possess and even embody those institutions himself. Thus, the belief that the powers of government should be treated as essentially personal was still very much alive in the sixteenth century.[22]

The same can be said of the Spanish world, where the political community and the government were understood in the same manner and where these assumptions appear to have survived, as will be shown in this study, at least until the end of the seventeenth century. If a sure sign that a society has entered into the self-conscious possession of a new concept is that a new vocabulary comes to be developed to describe it, then, in the Spanish world of that time, the modern meaning of the concept of the state as a locus of power distinct from either the ruler or the body of the people was not yet part of the political imagination, as it had not entered the Spanish language by the end of the seventeenth century. For example, in order to define the word *estado*, Sebastian de Covarrubias, in his *Tesoro de la lengua castellana* (published in 1611), explains that, "In the republic, there are different estates, some secular, some ecclesiastical, … some are knights, some are citizens, some craftsmen, some peasants, etc." That is to say, instead of the *Estado* (state), we should speak of the *estados* (estates). Next, Covarrubias adds that the term *estado* "in another way is taken to mean the government of the royal person and his realm, for the purpose of its preservation, reputation, and augmentation."[23] On the one hand, then, the term *estados* refers to the social estates into which the community was divided, but on the other it is also used to describe the "matters of state," which are all those that have to do with the maintenance or increase of the "state of the monarch" — that is, the different dominions of the Crown. Thus, the Crown is comprised of many "states" (one of them being the "state of the Indies"), and that is why the Council of State (like the Secretary of State later on) is the one that deals with "state affairs" (i.e., foreign affairs). A century later, the first dictionary of the Spanish language, published by the Royal Academy between the years 1726 and 1739, repeats the definition of Covarrubias that referred to the different estates of society and defines *estado* as the "country and dominion of a king, a republic, or a lord." Nothing else is added; that is to say, not even at the beginning of the eighteenth century had the impersonal concept of the state entered the Spanish language. At most, we find reference to what constitutes a "matter of state," which, according to the authors of the dictionary, "is all that which belongs to the government and the preservation, increase, and reputation of the state of the realm and of the prince."[24]

Early modern society was populated by "imaginary persons" (*personae fictae*, in the terminology of the law) such as the estates or the corporations of diverse rank, which were the exclusive subjects of the system. The "individual" as an "indivisible" person, as a unitary subject of rights, was nonexistent. This way of conceiving the political community had one fundamental implication: The multiplicity of *estados* (estates) and the absence of individuals made the existence of the *Estado* (state) as the only depositary of the subjects' loyalties impossible. In other words, as long as the political and juridical assumptions were not altered in a radical way, it was not possible to conceive of the modern idea of the state.[25] The political logic of early modern European or American societies was then very different from that of a strict "statism." In that regard, the "Renaissance" should not be seen as a precursor of "modernity" as no fundamental break with the "medieval" past had in fact occurred. The princes had not yet been replaced by the states and Europe had not yet taken the place of Christendom. Similarly, the consolidation of the "dynastic monarchies" should not be equated with the consolidation of the national state. The medieval institutional structure remained in place and Renaissance ideas penetrated the aristocratic–hierarchical world without really transforming it. If early modern European monarchs tended to consolidate power in their own hands, especially in regard to judicial, fiscal, and military matters, this should not be taken to mean that autonomous self-sustaining centralized administrative structures came into existence.[26] Indeed, the notion of a centralizing state was literally inconceivable, and its use as a category of analysis for understanding this period should be avoided. To use the term "state," with all the characteristics commonly attributed to it, is evidently a projection of categories that belong to the political order of our time on the political formations existing before the liberal revolution. Among other reasons, this is so because the polity still revolved, to a great extent, around the idea of empire (understood in the medieval sense as a Christian and universal monarchy), and the concept of "nation–state" was still marginal in the political discourse of the time. Thus, the consolidation of the so-called "national monarchies" at the end of the fifteenth century was not followed by the disappearance of the notion of "universal power" that characterized the Middle Ages.[27]

In the Spanish case, these ideas would be reformulated in such a way as to transform the Spanish monarchy into a "Catholic monarchy," the idea of universalism being one of the constituent elements of its own identity. In this rethinking and renovation of the Spanish monarchy, the American possessions played a decisive role, because the conquest of the New World was seen as the fulfillment of the providential destiny of the Spanish monarchy, destined to become a universal monarchy. In the mid-seventeenth century, Juan de Solórzano could still assert that the prophecies announcing that the "kingdom would be one everywhere in the world and that remote peoples and their gold and silver would be brought in its service" had been fulfilled in the Spanish monarchs.[28] On the other hand, the Spanish monarchy, like all the early modern monarchies, was built on the base of a profound respect for corporate structures and for the traditional rights, privileges, and customs of the different territories that made up the monarchy. Unions as well as acquisition of territories did not mean a submersion into a larger entity. The rights and privileges of the individual region remained intact, and whenever a ruler violated them he was suspected of turning from a rightful prince into a tyrant. No one conceived of a government that did not count on the collaboration and recognition of the powers of those territories in those spheres that by right belonged to them (estate assemblies and law courts became the guardians of local and regional rights and privileges).[29] That is, the logic of the Spanish monarchy was not one of centralization and uniformity but of a loose association of all its territories, a logic very different from that of the centralizing sovereign nation–state.

Seeing the Viceroy

In order to reconstruct the logic of Spanish rule in colonial Mexico, it is essential to examine the politics of viceregal authority, as the appointment of viceroys was a key mechanism in the imposition of royal authority in New Spain, but I do not approach the study of viceregal power as a study in the history of colonial state-building for the reasons that have been shown above. If we are to understand the nature of viceregal power (and, by extension, of Spanish colonial rule) most fully and without the constraints imposed by the state paradigm, we must learn to "see" a viceroy as contemporaries would have done, and the way to this end is the study of the viceregal institution as both image and ritual;[30] in other words, we must start looking at the political culture of the Spanish monarchy, a culture whose principles were very different from those of the state paradigm.[31] Although the subject of my study is politics, specific policies, partisan conflicts, and formal institutions will only be studied to the degree they give us access to the more fundamental bases of the culture of authority. Instead, I draw attention to the images and distinctive political languages used to define and refer to viceregal power, to the operation of viceregal symbols, and to the pervasive concern with ritual and gesture. This allows me to understand how viceregal power was constituted, sustained, and contested.

When ruling their vast American territories, the Spanish monarchs tried to establish a system of government that reproduced as closely as possible the idea of kingship prevailing at the time. It was a conception in which power was conceived of in a personal way: It was embodied in the person of the sovereign, from whom it was inseparable, and did not signify a separate and transcendent entity. Therefore, I examine in Chapter 1 how the idea of kingship was incarnated in the viceroy, analyzing the different ways in which contemporaries imagined the public person of the viceroy and to what extent this viceregal person was identified with that of the monarch. The aim of this chapter is to elucidate the nature of a viceroy's power and how accurate it is to define the viceroy as simply the head of the colonial bureaucracy. To answer this question I first explain the advantages contemporaries saw in the rule of viceroys. Then I examine the political rhetoric of the viceregal arch (the triumphal arches erected to welcome every new viceroy). Finally, I study certain recurrent images, mostly of a religious nature, used to describe and refer to royal and viceregal power.

In order to reconstruct the system of rule created by the Spanish monarchy in the New World, besides examining how the political discourse constructs the viceregal figure as the manifest center of power that he was, we must investigate the limits of viceregal power. In this regard, the different social and political bodies that constituted a highly decentralized polity such as the early modern Spanish monarchy were the depositories of a series of rights that invested them with a high degree of autonomy. Chapter 2 analyzes the ideological foundations on which the two main secular corporations of colonial society — the *Real Audiencia*, or High Court, and the *cabildo secular*, or municipal council — based their power and how these ideologies shaped in a particular way the relations of these two institutions with the viceroys. Similarly, Chapter 3 examines the discourses that legitimized the power of the Church and the Inquisition, analyzing in detail the relationships of the viceroys with the ecclesiastical hierarchy in order to explain the high level of conflict that existed between viceroys and prelates in sixteenth- and seventeenth-century New Spain.

Another way of "seeing" viceregal power as contemporaries would have done is through ritual. As Quentin Skinner has argued, the emergence of the modern concept of the state as both a supreme and an impersonal form of authority brought the displacement of the charismatic elements of political leadership and with it the belief that sovereignty is intimately connected with display, that the presence of majesty serves in itself as an "ordering force." The connection between the presence of majesty and the exercise of power could not thus survive the transfer of public authority to the purely impersonal agency of the modern state.[32] In sixteenth- and seventeenth-century New Spain this transfer had not yet occurred, thus the belief that authority is intimately connected with display was still very much alive. On the other hand, one intrinsic aspect of early modern society was the lack of physical force available to local rulers. In that regard, Michel Foucault has contended that the theory of the absolute monarchy "enables power to be founded in the physical existence of the sovereign, but not in continuous and permanent systems of surveillance." That is why the authority of the absolute sovereign was based on "spectacular and discontinuous interventions of power, the most violent form of which was the 'exemplary,' because exceptional, punishment."[33] This would explain the importance attributed by contemporaries to indirect enforcement, above all exemplary punishment, and the almost metaphysical belief in the value of authority's presence, based on the assumption that society was essentially disorderly and authority had to be regularly and visibly manifested. This led to a sensitivity concerning all aspects of symbolic authority, as the populace was seen as being highly responsive to nuances detected in public appearances and ceremonies.[34] It is also connected with the fact that, in a society where most of its members were not literate, the symbolic representations of power reached a critical importance: It was the language of power that everybody understood. These are crucial arguments if we are to understand why the rituals of rulers and government by ritual played such an extraordinary role in New Spain in the sixteenth and seventeenth centuries.

Thus, Chapter 4 examines how the Spanish rulers constructed their authority through ritual, focusing on the all-important role that the public display of viceregal power played in the grammar of imperial rule and explaining the significance of the viceroy's extreme visibility, in opposition to the "invisibility" of the Spanish king. In addition, it studies how the tensions and conflicts existing among the different institutions of colonial rule were acted out on the public stage of the streets and churches of Mexico City. The overarching argument is that imperial authority depended on the continuous public display of the rulers.

To fully grasp the political nature of colonial society and viceregal rule, certain features that traditionally have been labeled as "private" must also be examined. In fact, much that was labeled private according to interpretive categories used to discuss the foundation of the modern state has now been shown to be constitutive of the political structures of the *ancien régime* (e.g., kinship groups, factions, patronage, clientelism, brokerage, favoritism, nepotism). In that sense, it has been contended that if the "state" is understood to mean a power that functions in the name of abstract sovereignty and public interest, above any "private" purposes and forces, it is pointless to study a state that never existed.[35] Patronage, in fact, was one of the fundamental mechanisms of rule of the Spanish monarchs, a mechanism that was transmitted to the viceroys. Chapter 3, therefore, focuses on viceregal patronage and how viceregal power was mobilized through networks of personal loyalties and the distribution of offices. In addition, it examines the dilemma faced by the Crown when trying to curtail the abuse of the system of patronage by the viceroys and discusses the meaning and significance of corruption in colonial society. My main argument is that patronage and clientelism should not be seen as widespread corruption but as part of a system of government in which networks of personal loyalty and institutional lines of authority were interconnected, affecting the very nature of political power.

In the last instance, the ones who bore the brunt of the viceregal abuses of the system of royal patronage were the members of the indigenous communities, the producers of the material wealth that allowed the economy of patronage to function. It was precisely the existence of this population that lent the American dominions their specificity and peculiarity, setting them apart from the rest of the monarchy's possessions and conferring upon the American territories their colonial condition. The last two chapters, therefore, examine the viceroys' relationship with the indigenous population of New Spain and the discourses and practices of the Spanish Crown in relation to the natives. My analysis is strongly influenced by the idea that language and the written word (the rhetorical devices, the figures of speech, the discursive formations) not only reflect the practices of a given society but also contribute to their creation and constitution. In other words, the argument is that the indigenous population was constituted as the object of empire and as colonial subject through discourse. Thus, the general aim of

Chapters 6 and 7 is to analyze the specific colonial discourse in which the Spanish monarchy and the New Spanish ruling elite engaged.[36] More specifically, Chapter 6 focuses on the "rhetoric of wretchedness," which dominated from very early on every approach of the Spanish rulers to the indigenous population. Through it, a very peculiar identity for the indigenous population was constructed. The chapter also discusses the specificities of the civilizing mission of the Spanish monarchy and the interplay between the rhetoric of wretchedness and the civilizing project. Chapter 7 further elaborates on the political culture of Spanish colonialism, focusing on the role of the viceregal figure in relation to the native population and how Spanish colonial discourse moved beyond the rhetoric of wretchedness to endow this population with two different and contradictory identities: the idealized rural Indian as opposed to the demonized urban Indian. It also examines how these two contrasting identities shaped the reactions and behavior of the Spanish authorities on both sides of the Atlantic in the face of two rebellions: the Tehuantepec indigenous uprising of 1660 and the Mexico City riot of 1692.

The use of the concept of "colonial discourse" applied to the Spanish experience in the New World, however, has been criticized because of the many differences that existed between the Spanish empire of the sixteenth and seventeenth centuries and the colonial empires formed by the Europeans in the nineteenth and twentieth centuries, on which that concept is based. By this logic, we should speak of the existence of "colonial discourses" in Spanish America only in the eighteenth century, as the practices of the Habsburg monarchy were very different from those that this paradigm analyzes. Thus, Spain and its possessions in the sixteenth and seventeenth centuries would be irrelevant, chronologically as well as geographically and culturally.[37] No doubt these arguments have some validity. To begin with, it is necessary to be prudent when using the term "colonial," as the Habsburg monarchy never considered the American territories to be colonies, but "viceroyalties" or even "kingdoms." This was an important difference, as it endowed those territories with rights and privileges, which, to a great extent, assimilated them to the Crown's European possessions;[38] however, in practice, this conceptualization applied only to the population of Spanish descent, both peninsular and Creole. In this sense, it is certainly incorrect to speak of colonialism to refer to the non-indigenous sectors of the population of Spanish America before independence. For the majority of these sectors, the cultural and ideological model always remained the imperial motherland.[39]

At the same time, it is undeniable that there always existed a qualitative difference between the European territories of the Monarchy and its New World possessions, as it was generally argued that they had been united to the crown of Castile *accesoriamente* — that is, in a position of subordination, Castile being the principal entity in this union and the kingdoms of the Indies being considered in many ways dependent on the Castilian realm. As the members of the Council of Castile would emphatically contend in 1641 in the course of a dispute with the president of the Council of the Indies over a matter of ceremonial precedence, "The inferiority of the Council of the Indies is so obvious that the Council does not want to waste any time considering it, since in all fundamental matters it depends on the Council…, and this is based on sound arguments, because the Indies were conquered by Castile, [and] they are provinces united to it in an accessorial way (*accesoriamente*), being ruled by the same laws."[40]

Moreover, if we focus our attention on the way the Spaniards saw and ruled the indigenous population, the picture we get is very different, and many points of contact can be identified between the discourses and practices of the Spanish monarchy and those of the nineteenth-century colonial powers. As Mark Thurner has recently observed, the early precedent of Iberian "old colonialism" or "first imperialism" provided bearings and language for the emerging "new colonialism" or "second imperialism."[41] In this respect, José Rabasa has argued that Spanish colonization was just a rehearsal of the categories deployed by the northern European powers in India, Africa, or the Middle East three centuries later.[42] I do not think, however, that this term is a fortunate one, as it presupposes a fundamental identity between both types of colonialism. Although it is possible to identify, as Rabasa has suggested, those aspects of the sixteenth- and seventeenth-century colonial enterprise that constituted prototypes and inaugurated power relations that remained in force during the second phase of European expansionism, we nevertheless need to insist upon the historical alterity of Spanish colonialism in relation to eighteenth-century colonialism and, above all, the one that came into existence after the Industrial Revolution.

The period covered by this study extends from the last third of the sixteenth century to the end of the Habsburg dynasty in 1700. I concentrate on this period because my aim is to analyze not how the system of viceregal power was created but how it worked when all the structures of colonial rule were completely established. Though the emphasis will be on the seventeenth century, my study includes the period that starts around the end of the 1560s, when Philip II, determined to strengthen royal authority and the interests of the Crown in the New World, appointed Martín Enríquez and Francisco de Toledo as viceroys of New Spain and Peru, respectively. They were two energetic personages who governed their viceroyalties for long periods of time, twelve years each, the former from 1568 to 1580 and the latter between 1569 and 1581. When their terms of office had ended, the political, administrative, and ecclesiastic structure of the American dominions would be completely and perfectly defined. It was also in the 1570s when some of the most conspicuous actors and institutions of colonial rule made their appearance in the New World: The Inquisition was established in Peru in 1569 and in Mexico in 1571; the Society of Jesus, which was destined to play a fundamental role in the history of the New

World, arrived in Peru in 1568 and in Mexico in 1572; and, finally, the ecclesiastic *Patronato Real*, which governed the relations between the Church and the Crown, acquired its definitive form in 1574. Thus, after the 1570s, the viceregal system created by the Spanish Crown in New Spain would remain unchanged, except for minor adjustments, for almost 200 years.

1

Imagining the Viceroy

Speaking of the figure of the viceroy in his *magnum opus* on the government of the Indies, Juan de Solórzano Pereira, one of the most eminent of seventeenth-century Spanish legal writers, asserted that the "highly honored and preeminent" office of viceroy had been created "so that those vassals who live and reside in such remote provinces need not go seek their king, who is so far away, having his vicar nearby to ask for and get all those things they could expect and get from their king." For this reason, added Solórzano, the viceroys had to be obeyed and respected as persons who stood in place of the king, even when they committed some wrongdoing or exceeded their powers and instructions (even though the king might punish them afterwards), and this was so because it always had to be presumed that anything done by the viceroys had to be judged as done by the king who appointed them.[1] These words by Solórzano sum up perfectly the way in which the Spanish Crown conceived of the rule of its remote American possessions and the privileged position that viceroys occupied in the power structure of a political formation of an imperial nature such as the *Monarquía Hispánica*, as the Spanish empire was known by contemporaries.[2]

More specifically, and according to the laws of the realm and the royal titles issued to them, the viceroys appointed to rule New Spain were to be the "governors" of the provinces entrusted to them. In this capacity, they were allowed to grant the favors and rewards that they considered appropriate. Also, they could distribute those government and judicial offices that were customarily assigned to them and not under any specific prohibition. In addition to their titles of viceroys and governors, those chosen for these positions received two other separate appointments as *capitanes generales* (commanders in chief) and presidents of the *audiencia* of Mexico.[3] In

17

the sixteenth century, the viceroys were appointed for an indeterminate number of years, according to the monarch's will (the first two viceroys ruled for 15 years each, although the average term of office was 5 or 6 years). After 1629, viceroys would be appointed for only 3 years, usually with an extension of their term for another 3 years.[4] The viceroys were entrusted with several missions. First of all, they were to procure the expansion of religion. Second, they were to keep those provinces in "peace, tranquility, and calm." Third, the viceroys were to take any necessary steps to ensure the administration of justice. Fourth, they were in charge of the defense of the viceroyalty. Fifth, they were responsible for rewarding the descendants of the conquerors and first settlers. Sixth, they had to be especially careful in ensuring the "good treatment, conservation, and augmentation" of the Indians. Finally, the viceroys were in charge of protecting the interests of the Royal Treasury.[5]

In his *Política indiana*, Juan de Solórzano devoted an entire chapter to the things the viceroys of the Indies could and could not do.[6] Solórzano contended that the viceroys could do in their provinces everything the king who appointed them could do if he were present in those provinces. Solórzano goes on to enumerate the things that the viceroys "can do." They can order anything necessary to ensure the security, tranquility, and good government of the provinces under their charge, especially anything related to the conversion and well-being of the Indians. They can give Indians in *encomienda* (only in Peru). They can allocate Indians to work in the mines, ranches, and haciendas. In the case of New Spain, they can directly administer justice to the Indians or call upon the help of an *oidor* (civil judge) or *asesor letrado* (legal advisor). They appoint all the offices and benefices of their districts, except those specifically reserved to be provided by the king. In the case of a vacancy in any of the offices provided by the king, they can appoint someone temporarily — except in the offices of *oidores, alcaldes del crimen* (criminal judges), and cathedral prebendaries. They can also confirm city ordinances. Finally, they are in charge of the royal treasury and the defense of the viceroyalty.[7] Solórzano observed that the viceroys had been awarded all these powers as a sign of respect for their great authority; however, he warned that the viceroys had no absolute power, as they were subject to the king's orders and laws. In his opinion, the most they could do was suspend the execution of some royal decree, "replying again and again," if they truly believed that serious harm to the republic or the king himself would occur by executing that decree. Solórzano contended that in such cases the viceroys were not committing a crime nor could they be accused of disobedience. They were just complying with the royal will, "which is always presumed to wish only that which is appropriate."[8]

But, one could ask, to what extent did all this power and authority vested upon the American viceroys turn them into the despots of popular — and not so popular — images? When trying to answer this question, historians have usually ignored the fact that, when royal councilors and officials wrote all those laws and royal decrees dealing with the viceregal figure, and on which the understanding of viceregal power has traditionally been based, they did not have the need to overtly state many assumptions of the political culture of the time, assumptions that they took for granted and for which the meaning and significance may be lost to modern readers. In this regard, it is then necessary to examine the political vocabulary of the period in a systematic way: the concepts, the images, and the metaphors used in both Spain and Mexico to refer to and deal with the figure and power of the viceroy, a vocabulary that does not necessarily show up in laws and decrees. In doing this, we must situate the works dealing with this matter in its general ideological context — the context of inherited assumptions.

An ideology, according to Quentin Skinner, is "a language of politics defined by its conventions and employed by a number of writers."[9] Thus, my aim here is to examine the shared vocabulary, the principles, and the assumptions uniting a number of texts, in order to identify "the constitutive and regulative conventions" of the reigning ideology. This, in turn, will allow us to understand the function of language in the theory and practice of viceregal power. In this approach, political ideas and principles are given a central role in shaping political behavior, because "in recovering the terms of the normative vocabulary available to any given agent for the descriptions of his political behavior," Skinner has argued, "we are at the same time indicating one of the constraints upon his behavior itself." In other words, we cannot expect a political agent "to have meant or done something which he could never be brought to accept as a correct description of what he had meant or done."[10] Therefore, the aim of this chapter will be to examine how a viceroy was imagined by his contemporaries and to determine the nature and the reach of viceregal power through the examination of its ideological foundations.

The Rule of One

On the evening of July 21, 1668, a very unusual occurrence took place on the Island of Sardinia, one of the kingdoms under the rule of the Spanish monarch. On his way back to the viceregal palace after paying a visit to a church, the marquis of Camarasa, viceroy of Sardinia, was murdered by several Sardinians who fired three gunshots at him.[11] This "atrocity," in which not even "the virtue and dignity" of the viceroy could halt the "sacrilegious hands" of the aggressors, prompted Rafael de Vilosa, a member of the Council of Aragon, to write a treatise on whether murdering a viceroy was a crime of *lesa majestad*. He was stunned to hear some Sardinians argue that, although the crime of killing a viceroy was a serious offense, it could not be considered one of *lese majesty*.[12] One of the arguments Vilosa utilizes to show the enormity of the crime of killing a viceroy is that the king and the *ministros superiores* constitute one and the same person, as the latter are considered to be members of the body of the prince and the prince's majesty and royal splendor are communicated to them. The viceroy, then, is part of the prince's body and, as someone who serves the king in a position of the highest rank, is considered to be his relative (*colateral*).[13] The ruler and the realm together constituting one body, the greatness of the prince's ministers can be recognized, Vilosa contends, in that "being so immediate to the person of the prince, they are considered to be his limbs," and therefore "they cannot be offended without affronting the one with whom they are united." For Vilosa, it was an established principle in all confederacies that the offense made to one confederate is also made to the other members of the confederacy. Vilosa then goes on to argue:

> Thus if confederates who form a mystical body establish that one member of the body cannot be offended without the whole body being injured, since the prince is the head of the mystical body which is composed of him and his ministers and since the viceroy is united to the royal person with a closer link than the one uniting the confederates themselves, two inevitable consequences will follow. …The first is that, being the link of the representation with which the persons of the prince and his lieutenant general are united closer than that of the confederates, the offense done to the latter will be considered to be the same as that done to the former. The second one is that, being the viceroy such a superior minister, whether we wish to consider him as head of that magistracy in which the person of the king is represented, or we wish to consider him as a limb of that universal body of the monarchy whose head is the prince, it cannot be comprehended that it could be wounded without injuring the head.[14]

The notion of "mystical body" used by Vilosa to describe the kind of relation that exists between the king and his *ministros superiores* is fundamental to understanding the nature of viceregal power. The idea of a political community endowed with a "mystical" character had its origins in medieval thought and was common to all European countries. It had originally been articulated by the Church, although it was not part of the biblical tradition. *Corpus mysticum* originally designated the Sacrament of the Altar (that is, Christ's body), but after the twelfth century it served to describe the body politic or *corpus iuridicum* of the Church — the Church as a supernatural (mystical) body of which Christ was its head. This notion then was used by the jurists to describe the secular commonwealth, in an attempt to transfer to it some of the transcendental values usually possessed by the Church. It came into being in the twelfth century, at that moment when the doctrines of corporate and organic structure of society began to pervade political theory. Society or, to be more precise, the commonwealth was conceived of as a living organism and thus systematically compared with the human body. This organic metaphor was similarly applied to both the Church and the secular body politic. On the other hand, the attribution to each part of the community of the role of a specific part of the organic totality contributed to create a sense of community among all its members, high and low.[15]

This organic notion of the body politic had one fundamental implication, still prevalent in seventeenth-century Spanish political thought. In this conception, no separation existed between the king and the "state," as an entity in its own right. The "state" was the collective body of the prince, as the Church was the collective body of Christ. This "bodification" of the "state" helps, therefore, to explain the absence of any conception of the "state" as an abstract personification beyond its members. The "state" was an organic whole. It did not exist apart from its members nor was the "state" some superior being beyond its head and members or beyond moral values and the law. As Ernest Kantorowicz has argued, "This organic oneness of head and limbs in the body politic should prevent us from rashly replacing it by the abstraction of the impersonal state."[16] Images such as those of the "mystical body" or the "body politic" are not simply metaphors used to describe the state; they are images that provide a sense of a political community conceived in terms essentially different from that of the state. They suggest that individuals are neither solitary nor distinct but exist only as members of a body and that the hierarchical organization of the political community is as natural and well ordered as that of a human body, which, in turn, is a reflection of the perfect ordering and harmony of the celestial bodies. In short, they constitute a symbolic system that sets limits to thought, supporting certain ideas and making others almost inconceivable.[17]

This mystical body would, of course, be incomplete without a head, the king. Thus, this organic unity of head and limbs in the political community is always used as the main argument to justify the advantages of monarchical rule or, in other words, the rule of one. The rationale already appears in the *Partidas*, the legal code compiled by Alfonso X in the thirteenth century. In the Thomist variant of scholastic political theory that dominated medieval and early modern Spanish political thought, the king is not only the "head" of the realm but also the "soul." This is a consequence of the fact that this philosophical system was erected on the twin foundations of classical and Christian thought. According to the *Partidas*, the "prophets and saints" had said that kings were vicars of God on earth who ruled over the people to keep them in justice. In the same way as the soul resides in the heart and gives life and unity to the whole body, justice, which is what keeps the people alive, resides in the king, who, being one, forms a whole or unity with the inhabitants of the realm. That is why they called the king "heart and soul of the people." On the other hand, the "learned men" said that the king was the head of the realm, because, in the same way as the senses, which are found in the head, are the ones which command all the limbs, the king's commands must be obeyed by all, as the king is "lord and head of everyone in the realm."[18]

These are the same ideas expressed by Thomas Aquinas in his treatise on the rule of princes. Quoting Aristotle, Aquinas maintains that "political happiness" consists of the "perfect rule of the republic," and a commonwealth is perfect when each one occupies the appropriate place so as to avoid any "repugnance" among the members of the community. When this happens, a harmony is created in the commonwealth that is similar to the harmony of the celestial bodies, which, due to their orderly and perfect movements, produce a certain melody and softness. Thus, if the perfect republic resembles the harmony of the celestial spheres, similarly it must resemble the harmony of a well-proportioned body:

> It is the same with a true and perfect commonwealth as it is with a well-proportioned body in which the organic forces enjoy perfect vigor. And if the supreme virtue, which is reason, directs the rest of the inferior faculties, making them follow its commands, then as a result a certain softness and perfect delectation of the forces among themselves is produced, which we call harmony. Thus for a true political government to exist it is required that the limbs be in conformity with the head and not be discordant among themselves...

For Aquinas, the main obligation of the ruler is to attain the well-being of those who are under his rule. This well-being consists of maintaining the peace or, in other words, preserving unity and agreement among all the inhabitants. If this unity is missing, then the usefulness of living in the company of other men is lost; therefore, for Aquinas, the rule of one is better than the rule of many, as the unity toward which any good government must tend is easier to achieve with the "rule of only one." Aquinas resorts to the example of nature in search of support for his arguments, as "natural things are made perfectly and in each one nature does which is better; thus every natural government is of one." Only one heart is in charge of moving all the limbs, while only one force, reason, presides over the soul. What better example, asks Aquinas, than the existence of only one God, "the maker and ruler of everything?" For him, this conforms to reason, as art (that is, those things created by man's hand) imitates nature, and the more these things imitate nature, the more perfect they are. From this, Aquinas concludes that, of necessity, he who rules must be only one.[19]

In Scholastic thought, then, the attainment of peace and concord represents the highest value in political life. A division of power among the rulers or the prevalence of factions among the people is the greatest danger that threatens the tranquility and security of the republic. Where there is confusion there cannot be justice. Hence, the government of a single ruler is the only one that can guarantee to bring peace to the commonwealth.[20] These recurring ideas appear several centuries later in one of the most influential works of seventeenth-century Spanish political thought, Juan de Santa María's treatise on the Christian commonwealth, published in 1615. Quoting St. Augustine, St. Thomas, Aristotle, and Plato, the author contends that:

> The most excellent government is that which recognizes one supe-rior, one king, and one head, because every natural and good gov-ernment proceeds from one [source], and that which is closer to the number one (*la unidad*) has by far more similitude with the divine and is more perfect, which brings with it great advantages. Kings reign through God … and being God one and most simple in His being and nature, head of the entire universe, through whom everything is ruled with admirable and ineffable providence, and since He is the idea of every good and wise government, there can be no doubt that the best government for us is that one which most conforms to His being.[21]

In his defense of the monarchy, Santa María does not hesitate to resort, like many others did before him, to the metaphor of the human body, a body that, we must not forget, in the scholastic thought that dominates early modern Spanish political theory is the perfect and harmonious work of both God and nature:

> If the limbs, being many and with different functions, are governed by one head, and this is God's and nature's order, what would be the wisest?…Would it not be a great monstrosity if a body had two heads? Then it would be a much greater one if a kingdom were ruled by two people or more, independent one from the other. Oneness (*la unidad*) is the origin of many a benefit, whereas plural-ity causes many an evil. (pp. 8–9)

The metaphor of the human body allows Santa María to explain the place and obligations that everyone must have in the commonwealth, including the "mystical head of this body of the republic," the king. Kings, then, are supposed to do in their kingdoms all that a good head does with its body (p. 47). In fact, the book is a treatise on the figure of the king and how he must conduct himself in government. Thus, the different faculties and senses of the human body — understanding, sight, hearing, smell, taste, and touch — have, for Santa María, their correspondence with one or more of all the qualities the good ruler must have — good counselors, per-sonal rule, justice, prudence, magnanimity, clemency, good faith, temper-ance, etc. The most important and noble "offices" of the body are evidently located in the head. Here, the soul exercises its main operations through the faculties of understanding and will. Here, the "imperial faculty," the will, commands and rules over all the other faculties, which obey it and are subject to it. Also, here resides, like the king at his court, the faculty of understanding, for as "the will is called emperor, because it reigns and commands, understanding is called king, because it governs and rules all of man's operations, guiding them towards their proper ends" (pp. 35–37). The perfect commonwealth and its government, therefore, must be structured in the same way as the different parts of the human body, each one attending to their trade and occupation without forcing either the rules of nature or the rules of government.[22]

These are the same political conventions that the anonymous author of a manuscript of the early seventeenth century utilized to argue in favor of the rule by viceroys in the kingdom of Portugal, at a time when some voices were defending the desirability that the kingdom be ruled, again, by three or more governors.[23] To show that the rule of one person (i.e., a viceroy) is better than that of three or more persons, the author begins with the idea that "the number one is more perfect than the other numbers," because "all numbers are born from the number one." (*Así como la unidad es más perfecta que los otros números, donde todos ellos nacen, así el gobierno de uno es mejor.*) Anything that is one, not divided and separated, is always better and firmer; thus, the more a commonwealth imitates and reaches oneness, the more it prevails and thrives and the more firmly it is sustained and ruled. The author goes on to give numerous reasons, based on human experience and the example of nature, to prove that viceregal rule is the natural and logical way of ruling. To begin with, all things are ruled by only one God. Likewise, the soul (*el ánimo*) is ruled only by the faculty of understanding and the limbs by the head. Besides, nature teaches us that the "republic of bees" has only one ruling head. Similarly, there is only one lord of the household or one pilot to steer the ship. A ship with more than one pilot, like a kingdom with more than one ruler, would cause confusion and the creation of factions and divisions. The different actions of government require a certain unity that cannot be achieved with more than one head. The author concludes that the existence of many governors ruling equally and at the same time in the place where only one head should be is something as monstrous as having one body with two or three heads.[24]

Solórzano Pereira also deals with this question in his treatise on the government of the Indies. He devoted Book V of *Política indiana* to the discussion of secular government. Written in perfect hierarchical order, it starts with an examination of the bottom of that hierarchy of rule, the *cabildos* and *alcaldes mayores*, followed by the *audiencias*, and then the viceroys, to end on the top of the ruling scale with "The Royal and Supreme Council of the Indies." He starts his discussion in the first of several chapters dealing with the figure of the viceroy by declaring that, with the increase in the population and importance of Peru and New Spain, it was necessary to appoint "governors of more distinguished bearing with the title of viceroys." Solórzano points out that at the beginning of the Spanish domination both the viceroy and the *audiencia* were in charge of conducting the business of government, but this divided government brought with it many an inconvenience, for which reason it was decided that matters of government would be the exclusive domain of the viceroy. According to Solórzano, this only proved what every writer had previously noted, that the rule of only one person was better. Solórzano adds another reason why it was decided to appoint viceroys. Due to the remoteness separating the Indies from Spain, it was even more necessary than in the other provinces of the monarchy for the kings to appoint "these images of theirs to represent them closely and efficaciously" and to keep the inhabitants of those territories in peace and tranquility. In this way, possessing such great dignity and authority, the viceroys would be able to restrain and keep in check the sometimes unruly inhabitants of the New World.

Solórzano maintains that the viceroys' authority and power are so great that they can only be compared to the same kings who have appointed them as their "vicars" to represent their persons. That is exactly what the Latin word *proreges* means, and that is why in Catalonia and other places they called the viceroys *Alter Nos*, because of "this absolute similarity of representation." According to Solórzano, this is why, in general, in the provinces ruled by them, and with the exception of those cases in which the contrary is indicated, the viceroys "have and exercise the same power, influence, and jurisdiction as the king who appoints them." Solórzano cites a royal decree of 1614 in which all the inhabitants of the Indies, including the *audiencias*, are ordered to obey and respect the viceroys in the same way as the king is obeyed and respected. For him, all this makes much sense, because:

> Wherever there is an image of someone, there is a true representation of that one whose image is brought or represented ... and ordinarily this representation is even the more brilliant the farther removed the viceroys and magistrates are from the masters who influence it and communicate it to them, as Plutarch rightly noticed with the example of the moon, which gradually gets bigger and more resplendent the more she is separated from the sun, which lends its splendor to her.[25]

This passage makes clear that for Solórzano as for many other political writers of the period the concept of the viceroy as the king's image was essential for grasping the true nature of viceregal power. By being the monarch's image and alter ego, the viceroy was held to be in possession of all the majesty, power, and authority of the king. Being the king's image ultimately meant that a viceroy was expected to rule following the same political principles and adopt the same behavior as his original. Indeed, no self-respecting viceroy, although always acknowledging his subordination to the king, would have thought of himself as a mere royal agent or as an administrator or bureaucrat. As will be shown in the course of this study, this way of understanding viceregal power had important implications that fundamentally affected the way colonial Mexico was ruled.

The Image in the Mirror

Keeping in mind how central the viceregal position was supposed to be in the Spanish American system of rule, it comes at first as something of a surprise to realize how little was published in the sixteenth and seventeenth centuries specifically and directly dealing with this figure. But, in looking a little deeper, it is soon realized that, in fact, an entire series of treatises on viceregal power was published in New Spain in the seventeenth century. I am referring concretely to the printed descriptions of the triumphal arches that were erected every time a viceroy entered the city of Mexico for the first time.[26] Traditionally, these accounts have been ignored by historians on the grounds that they were just bad literature (they were unbearably hyperbolic "baroque" pieces of court flattery) or lacked any historical interest. Of course, this did not explain why the most prominent writers of New Spain (including Sor Juana Inés de la Cruz, the foremost writer of colonial Mexico) seemed to have no qualms about contributing to the task of designing some of these arches.[27] At most, these tracts have been used, mostly by art historians, as sources to describe viceregal entries and the arches that were erected to welcome the new viceroys.[28] These works are, however, of great significance for the purposes of this study, for in them was embedded a theory of viceregal power, repeated time and time again, on which the whole system of government of New Spain was based.

The arches were erected by both the municipal council and the ecclesiastical chapter, and both were very similar in concept or design. The viceroys or the peninsular authorities did not intervene, at least in theory, in their elaboration. In that sense, they were a public and baroque display of the ways in which rulers and government were conceptualized by the secular and religious elite of New Spain, but these descriptions contain barely any references or allusions to the concrete reality of the viceroyalty. They were essentially visual treatises on good government as understood in the seventeenth-century Hispanic world. In that regard, these descriptions can be ascribed to the well-known and rather old genre of advice books for rulers, known as "mirrors for princes." The elaborate arches that welcomed every viceroy were then visual "mirrors for princes," or, more exactly, "mirrors for viceroys."[29]

That the viceregal arch was a mirror was clearly asserted by the Jesuit Alonso de Medina, who designed the arch erected by the cathedral chapter to welcome the count of Salvatierra in 1642, when he entitled its description *Espejo de príncipes católicos* (Mirror of Catholic Princes).[30] The interest of this arch lies in its being the only occasion in the seventeenth century in which a biblical figure was used — that of Joseph in Egypt — as a reflection of the viceroy and as an image of the good prince reflected in the arch; however, the resort to classical antiquity is not absent from the iconography of the arch. Joseph, "his face a living portrait of our prince," appears in the main painting triumphantly seated on the throne, after the pharaoh had appointed him "viceroy" of Egypt as a reward for having revealed his dreams to him. Curiously, Joseph is dressed "in Roman garb."[31] That these allegorical images had to appear in classical guise was a consequence of the humanist recovery of classical values and images, and the designers of the Mexican arches, with all their Counter Reformation Catholicism, were the direct heirs of this inheritance. As many of them observed, the mythological "fables" could be a source of political knowledge and moral wisdom, as long as they were tempered by religion, for, even among the shadows of these fictions, one may discern the light of the true heroic virtues;[32] hence, the apparent contradiction of representing Joseph, "the Egyptian," dressed like a Roman. The author of *Espejo de príncipes católicos* concludes the description of the arch with a romance, in which the specular character of the arch can be noticed clearly. For Medina, the meaning of the arch designed for the contemplation of the viceroy is quite apparent. It is a "clear mirror" in which the viceroy looks and sees his majestic image reflected.[33]

As a positive instrument of knowledge, the mirror allows us to know ideal images; thus, we can use the mirror for its clarity and to consult what we are and what we ought to be. Although the mirror reflects the image of what we are longing for and can be used to assess our defects, awakening our consciousness of the ideal by translating it into sensible images,[34] the mirror/arch offers no place for introspection — the object is always superior to the image. Although the author of *Espejo de príncipes católicos* recognizes that we use mirrors to assess our possible physical and psychological weaknesses before we step into the presence of the "supreme majesty," the viceroy, as the embodiment of that majesty and power, must be immaculate and, therefore, without the need of a mirror. The viceroy must look in the mirror, not to see an ideal image that is better than himself, an image that can be used to correct his own defects, but to behold an image that is perfect in a double sense: because it is a faithful copy of the viceroy and, at the same time, because it is a reflection of an abstract idea, that of the perfect prince. The mirror images have a fundamental ambivalence, however. Because they are visions of something higher, of an ideal reality, they do not have independent existence; they are by their very nature inferior to what they reflect,[35] hence the insistence on the part of the arch designers on making clear that the heroes in the arches were just mere sketches of the individuals they were a reflection of, whereas the viceroys were finished models, whose virtues were always superior to those of the mythological personages. That is why, in the description of the arch conceived by Sor Juana, she asserts that, when she tried to find among the heroes of antiquity any one whose deeds could be compared with the virtues of the new viceroy, she could find no one who "even in appearance resembled his incomparable qualities."[36]

Nevertheless, if we agree that the image is always ambivalent, we must conclude that the figure of the viceroy must be an ambivalent one, too, as he himself is an image of a superior and invisible reality — the king. As will be shown in the course of this study, this specular condition helps explain the fundamentally ambiguous nature of viceregal power and the unstable position in which the viceroys always found themselves. On the one hand, as ideal images, they should be treated — at least in a conceptual way — correspondingly (hence, the language and rituals of majesty used when dealing with them); on the other hand, the inhabitants of New Spain never allowed them to forget that they were no more than a mere reflection, explicitly distinguished from a reality far greater and more stable. This same kind of ambiguity was expressed in the very terms used to conceptualize the position of viceroy. On the one hand, he was called "prince" (i.e., supreme ruler) as kings were; on the other hand, he was often referred to as "*ministro superior*,"[37] but a *ministro* is, after all, "someone who serves somebody."[38] He was then the king's servant, an all too apparent contradiction with his position as "supreme ruler," as someone who admits no superior.[39] All this notwithstanding, the viceregal entries meant a momentary suspension of this intrinsic ambivalence, as there was always the hope that the viceroys would closely resemble the Idea of the perfect prince. This is the true meaning of the rhetoric of hope and joy for the arrival of a new viceroy with which all arches were infused.[40]

The authors of "mirror for princes" books always illustrated their teachings with examples of venerable, heroic, and virtuous figures from the Bible or antiquity. The images materialized in the triumphal arches were the equivalent of these sacred and (mostly) classical exempla. In other words, the text being "written" on the arches was reduced to a minimum in the form of exempla. Each painting on the arch can thus be read as a whole "chapter" dealing with some of the conventional topics in the advice literature. This economy of language found, in the seventeenth century, its most perfected expression in the literature of emblems and devices that was commonplace in political books; however, emblems and hieroglyphs were used not only for practical reasons (they were appropriate to convey an idea within a limited physical space) but also for a much more fundamental one, the belief that these images in the form of emblems and devices were symbols that hid in some mysterious way a deeper truth. The symbol was seen as the mysterious language of the divine. It was commonly accepted that God had spoken to man in riddles, these riddles being embodied in the Scriptures and also in pagan myths. Thus, the mission of the political writer of emblems was to unravel these enigmas again and again to provide answers to the questions of history and nature.[41]

Quoting the German Jesuit Athanasius Kircher, who was highly influential in the cultural world of New Spain, Carlos de Sigüenza y Góngora affirmed that "devices, hieroglyphs, and symbols [are] like animated artifacts, whose material body is the painting, to which the epigraph gives spirit,"[42] but it is Sor Juana Inés de la Cruz in her *Neptuno alegórico* who puts forward these ideas in total clarity when explaining in the introduction the reasons why allegories are utilized in triumphal arches. In her opinion, the custom among the ancients, and above all among the Egyptians, to represent their gods in the form of hieroglyphs was due to the deities' lack of visible form. This made it impossible to show them to men with only the help of their eyes. That is why "it was necessary to seek out hieroglyphs that, though they were not perfect images, at least could represent them through similitude." Moreover, this was a sign of reverence to the deities, so as not to "vulgarize their mysteries to the common and ignorant people." Sor Juana points out that the same happens in the Christian religion, as Christ Himself spoke in parables to his followers,[43] and the Holy Scriptures were not translated into the vulgar languages as a sign of respect and reverence, so that "the frequent relation does not diminish their veneration" (*el mucho trato no menoscabe la veneracion*). Sor Juana concludes that, because the deeds of the viceroy are so great, "the mind is not able to comprehend them, nor can the pen express them, it is not an unreasonable thing to seek out ideas and hieroglyphs that symbolically represent [them]."[44]

In other words, the power that the viceroy represents and embodies is so incommensurable and mysterious that human intelligence cannot comprehend it; therefore, it is necessary to resort to symbolic images that, as the purely visual embodiment of an idea, allow us at least to glimpse that superior reality. This is the same reasoning used to refer to God, whom we can only know through analogies. As shall be explained in the last part of this chapter, in these lines Sor Juana implicitly states that the nature of royal (or viceregal) power is so extraordinary that it can only be explained as a mystery.

Probably the two best known arches of the seventeenth century were those erected in 1680 to welcome the count of Paredes, marquis of La Laguna, because their authors were the already mentioned Sor Juana Inés de la Cruz and Carlos de Sigüenza y Góngora, two outstanding figures in the cultural world of New Spain. Following a well-established tradition, for her commission from the ecclesiastical chapter Sor Juana chose a mythological figure, Neptune, as the incarnation of a good ruler and also as the figure that best resembled the virtues of the new viceroy. As for the arch designed by Carlos de Sigüenza, it has been much discussed, because, for the first time ever, the author utilized Aztec rather than classical mythology as the source of exempla to illustrate the idea of the good ruler. This, in turn, has been seen as a sign of some sort of proto-nationalism or creole patriotism.[45] Nevertheless, from the standpoint of the political doctrine being conveyed by those Aztec figures, Sigüenza's design was by no means a radical departure from all the previous ones, inasmuch as, in Anthony Pagden's words, "the vehicle for the expression of the classical virtues may have been American Indians, but the virtues remained classical."[46]

In the printed explanation of the arch conceived by him, Sigüenza includes a prelude in which he discusses the reasons why cities erect triumphal arches to receive their rulers. For him, to celebrate rulers in such a way is proof not only of the respect and veneration owed to them, but also of the gratitude felt by their inferiors for their rulers, because cities and kingdoms would not survive without these "political souls," who as such give life to them. Following this, Sigüenza resorts to the mirror metaphor in order to explain the meaning of these arches. According to him, their aim is to serve princes "as a mirror where to mind the virtues with which they must adorn themselves," and from which their power and authority can take example and aspire to emulate that which is symbolized in them. It is then very appropriate, concludes Sigüenza, that in these arches, which in fact are the first gates that the cities open to their rulers, be represented the heroic virtues that the prince must possess when he begins his rule, making him an exemplary ruler. Later in the description, Sigüenza clearly reveals the exact political nature of the arch. In defending himself from some critics who criticized him for including citations from the Holy Scriptures in a secular arch, he argues that his goal in designing the arch had been to propose to the new viceroy a compendium of political virtues that he could use as a mirror. He then adds that because the "ethnic" virtues (i.e., the "Indian" virtues) were deficient for lacking the light of knowledge of the true religion, they had to be supplemented with the virtues that, of necessity, princes must possess. For Sigüenza, these virtues are "those cultivated by the gentiles and those that the Scriptures teach us much improved with the florid voices of their examples."[47]

In these mirrors/arches, therefore, the viceroy is always addressed as "prince," in the sense of sovereign or supreme ruler of the land. This was not just a matter of grandiose rhetoric or typical courtier adulation, but also the expression of how the power of the viceroy was conceived. In New Spain, the viceroy was the supreme ruler of a kingdom — the kingdom of New Spain — and he was expected to rule, not as the head of a bureaucracy, but as a monarch. Thus, in the viceregal arches, we find materialized a theory of viceregal power that closely follows the theory of monarchical power, as it was understood in early modern Spain. In the literature of "mirrors for princes," as it was established by the humanists in the sixteenth century and became the mainstream political thought in Spain, the essential business of government was to maintain the people in security and peace, and the main aim of a ruler was to avoid factions in the republic.[48] The Jesuit Matías de Bocanegra, one of the main literary figures of seventeenth-century New Spain, commissioned in 1642 by the municipal council to design the arch that was to welcome the count of Salvatierra as viceroy, is no doubt in agreement with this idea when he asserts that the best government "has as its enterprise to banish from the republic internal discords and civil enmities, because they are the poison that most pitifully corrupts monarchies."[49]

According to the writers of advice books, the ideal prince was to have heroic qualities, and his main ambition was to be the pursuit of fame and glory. This heroic figure, however, must fight against fortune to prevent his quest for honor and glory from becoming an unsuccessful enterprise. Accordingly, one of the paintings of *Astro mitológico político*, the arch designed by Alavés Pinelo in 1650, depicted the hero Perseus (the viceroy) flying on Pegasus (the fame). It signified the virtue or effort so characteristic of princes who, transported on the wings of fame, triumph over the vices. Alavés concluded his description of the story of Perseus as symbol and hieroglyph of a prince's heroic virtues with a painting that depicted Perseus' transformation into a star or constellation. Alavés contends that this was a special favor awarded Perseus by the gods because of the fame that his virtues had reached.[50] Similarly, the anonymous author of the arch commissioned in 1653 by the municipal council to receive the duke of Alburquerque chose the figure of Ulysses as the duke's image reflected in the arch/mirror and, at the same time, as the personification of the idea of the good ruler. Ulysses, always helped by Zephyr and Aeolus, represents the prince favored by fortune, because no matter how courageous and enterprising a ruler may be, if he is not fortunate he will not be able to get his rule safely into port. But, the author observes, because fortune is variable, the good ruler, like Ulysses, must know how to face the adversities of fortune with his wisdom and prudence. That is why Ulysses is also the personification of the prudent prince, as prudence and courage are the two pillars on which success in government is based.[51]

The only quality that could help a prince overcome the capricious power of fortune was virtue. This virtue of the ruler consisted of a series of individual moral qualities which, in the prince, were transformed into a creative force that set him apart from the rest of the people. Only these qualities allowed the prince to maintain his position. To Bocanegra, for example, the effects of the virtuous prince were almost magical and miraculous, because his rule not only gave life and fertility to the land but also communicated vitality and harmony to the kingdom.[52] No ruler could be considered a man of true virtue unless he was in possession of all the leading Christian virtues. In Spanish and Spanish–American thought, these virtues were the ones that really distinguished a Catholic prince from a heretical or atheistic one.[53] The two fundamental virtues of the Catholic ruler were thought to be prudence or wisdom and justice. For Sor Juana, as for so many writers of the period, wisdom was the most important of all princely virtues, because it was the "root and source from which all the others emanate; and more in a prince, who so much needs it to direct the government, for the republic could well suffer that the prince were not liberal, not pious, not strong, not noble, but the only thing that cannot be made up for is his not being wise because wisdom, not gold, is what crowns princes."[54] Likewise, Sigüenza believes that prudence is so necessary a virtue for rulers that it would not be easy for them to maintain power without possessing it. To him, prudence is the virtue that must shine the most in princes, as it is an aggregate of all the virtues.[55] As for justice, this is the virtue on which the selection by the prince of skillful ministers of justice, suitable for government, depends. This is also what Bocanegra hopes the count of Salvatierra will do.[56]

Other Christian virtues, indispensable for kings and viceroys, are fortitude, clemency, liberality, and magnificence. According to Bocanegra, fortitude is the sister of prudence, as "it would be of little use to the prince to be wise if he were not also strong, able to sustain upon his shoulders the very machine that he rules." The ruler, therefore, must be strong and generous, because his mission is to shield the helpless and to protect the destitute.[57] Clemency is another fundamental virtue, because, in Sor Juana's words, "princes must put pity before strictness."[58] For his part, Sigüenza notes that the virtue of clemency "must be the most estimable thing in all princes." For him, "there is no more powerful weapon to defeat human wickedness than clemency, because, with the assistance of gentleness and rewards, it introduces into men's spirits what is laid down by the law for their own utility."[59] Liberality and magnificence are also very important princely virtues. Sigüenza, for example, argues that the greatness of princes will not be lessened by being liberal and splendid, as "princes have more than enough to be able to benefit the worthy (*los beneméritos*)."[60]

All these qualities, however, would be of no consequence if the prince did not show the fundamental virtues of piety and religion (Figure 2). These are the virtues that, in the words of the author of *Portada alegórica*, "suit a Catholic prince most." The Spanish monarchy will be secure, warns his author, as long as it leans on a viceroy observant of the Christian religion. Also, he must show his piety by fomenting divine worship and recognizing that he must subordinate his power to the superior one.[61] The virtue of piety also had a place in the arch created by Sor Juana. She designed an emblem in which a vessel on the sea was steered by Neptune, who was staring north. With this painting, claimed Sor Juana, she wanted to represent the virtue of religion, as "there can be no wise government if the supreme prince who controls it does not implore the supreme wisdom of God to make him successful." For Sor Juana, religion and piety not only serve as an example to everyone, but "establish and secure the state" as well.[62] For his part, Sigüenza begins his enumeration of the different virtues personified by the Aztec emperors with none other than Huitzilopochtli himself, the god of war to whom those human sacrifices that so

Fig. 2 Frontispiece, Juan de Solórzano Pereira, *Política indiana*, 1647. For Solórzano, piety and religion are the two pillars upon which the transatlantic empire of Philip IV is founded. The king, who is wearing the royal insignia typical of the Spanish monarchs (the scepter, the sword, and the crown), steps on a globe that rests upon Neptune's body to indicate the universal character of his monarchy, whose dominion depends on the control of the seas. (Courtesy of the Hispanic Society of America, New York.)

disgusted Spaniards and creoles alike were offered. In this god, Sigüenza sees the personification of "the need that princes have to begin their actions with God," as no power (*imperio*) exists that does not immediately proceed from God.[63]

At this point, the true nature of the viceregal arch should be evident. It can be best understood as an exemplary mirror in which the viceroys can gaze at the personification of an idea, the Christian prince, who, at the same time, was a reflection of the viceroy's own image. This allows us to see the arch designers in a very different light from the traditional view, for they were playing not the role of flatterers and sycophants but one that was most dignified and important, that of counselors of the prince. The mirror-for-princes writers often argued that any man of learning who acted as a counselor to his prince was performing a service of the highest public importance, as he was contributing to the preservation of the monarchy. And, if everyone obeyed a virtuous ruler who was advised by virtuous councilors, these councilors would be helping preserve the best form of rule, under which the people would be able to prosper.[64] A wise ruler is then one who never makes a decision without listening first to his advisors. For that reason, Alavés Pinelo had asserted that "princes must surround themselves with wise men," for a good soldier should not be armed only with his sword, but with advice as well.[65]

Similarly, in one of the paintings of the arch erected in 1653 by the municipal council to welcome the duke of Alburquerque, Ulysses appears spreading grains of salt on a sown field. He is depicted with a parrot on his shoulder and a heart hanging from his chest. For the anonymous arch designer, the heart signifies advice, as this was the way it was represented in antiquity. The salt is the symbol of the wisdom and knowledge with which the ruler must sow all his opinions, so that they will be fruitful. Finally, the parrot represents the eloquence that must characterize every ruler, because it is always better to govern through persuasion than through imposition. The author reminds the reader that a ruler cannot decide efficiently if he does not understand the matter he is dealing with, for which reason he must not be hasty in making decisions.[66] In the same way, Sigüenza shows in the arch designed by him how the emperor Ahuitzotl, by making a hasty decision, provoked the flood of Tenochtitlán. He concludes that "the prince runs the risk of these calamities when he throws himself into big enterprises without getting advice beforehand, because God is the only one who does everything right without advice."[67] It is in this light that we come to understand the act of designing a viceregal arch, not as an act of flattery or as simply an opportunity to further one's personal career,[68] but as the realization of one of the most important functions any seventeenth-century educated person could aspire to, that of giving advice to his or her prince.[69]

One last factor in the theory of the viceregal arch, not mentioned so far, explains why the arches/mirrors were not only reflections, in classical garb, of the idea of the ruler, but also magnificent reflections of each individual viceroy. One recurring aspect of all the arches is the emphasis on the noble parentage of the viceroys. Matías de Bocanegra, for instance, argued that his parents' "nobility and luster" and "the equality in the ties and relationships of marriage" were very important to the general esteem in which a prince was held.[70] For his part, Alonso de Medina compares the viceroy/sun to the vicereine/moon, as "the president of the stars" is only inferior to the "monarch of the planets." That is why "the heroic noble ancestry of his most noble wife" makes the count of Salvatierra's works "more splendid and proven than gold."[71] But, it is the author of *Marte católico* who expresses these ideas in the most eloquent way. For this writer, equality in marriage is a common care of the great nobility. Part of the splendor and magnificence of the duke of Alburquerque was due, according to this author, to his having the duchess by his side. She was his equal "in greatness of heart, generosity of spirit, perspicacity of the mind, the qualities of the soul, and the perfections of the body." As a result, the kingdom of New Spain had taken on "a certain luster and splendor" with the presence of the duchess.[72]

This emphasis on the nobility and excellence of the viceroys and their wives was the logical consequence of the theory of viceregal power. If, in the political thought of the time, the viceroy was the living image of the king, ambiguous though that image might be, it was necessary that the image be endowed with the same majestic power and virtuosity as the object of which it was a reflection. The author of *Marte católico* noted that Mars' virtuosity had merited him a place among the seven celestial gods. He went on to explain that, in the skies, Mars occupied the fifth sphere, which was necessarily brighter than the others, because of its closeness to the fourth sphere, the sun. This closeness made Mars so luminous and radiant that many among the ancients thought it was the sun itself. It is little wonder then that, referring to the viceroy, the writer exclaimed:

> It is an augury of great happiness for Mexico to know that its Mars is linked so closely to the sun of the fourth sphere, which is the fourth Philip of Spain, whose shining light sends him to this kingdom like another sun, a virtue of the sun and a virtue of God, to rule over and govern it with as much influence as if in the Most Excellent Lord, the duke of Alburquerque, the king himself were present in this land, being a matter of pride for this Western world to have as its superior and ascendant a prince so illustrious that he ranks as a star of the first order among the most sublime of Spain's grandees. (fo. 8)

Spanish political imagery had concluded that kings realized on earth the same function as the sun did in the sky. The king–sun's rays (the acts of government) had to have the same beneficial effects on men and on the body politic as the rays of the sun–king of the stars and planets had on earth.[73] Hence, the viceroy, as the king's image and reflection, must possess the same brightness and luminosity as the monarch in order to be able to effectively realize that beneficial mission. For this same reason, Sigüenza calls the count and countess of Paredes *luminaria magna* not only "because their lights stand out so much in the sky of nobility," but, above all, "because they have the same post that gave that title [*luminaria magna*] to the sun and the moon, that is, they ascend to the government to brighten us all." Because the sun is considered to be a great king, concludes Sigüenza, "therefore kings, superiors, and princes will be regarded as luminaries and respected like suns."[74] As Roy Strong has argued, because the planets actually revolved around the sun in a post-Copernican universe, this emphasis on solar imagery can be viewed as an expression of an increasing political reality — the move of monarchs toward absolutism.[75] As I have tried to show so far, we should not underestimate the significance of this world of analogies and correspondences, as they had transcendental implications. Their transcendence lay in the fact that they were treated not as human constructions, simple images, or metaphors, but as objective, self-evident realities. Thus, as Peter Burke has observed, the analogy between the king and the sun performed "the important function of 'naturalizing' the political order, in order words of making it seem as inevitable and unquestionable as nature itself."[76]

The Mystery of Power

When the construction of the cathedral of Mexico City, which had lasted for over a century, was about to be completed, its designers faced a difficult task: where to place the high altar. Because there were different opinions, on July 22, 1668, the marquis of Mancera, viceroy of New Spain at that time, wrote a letter to the queen regent asking for instructions, as he thought he should not make a decision without first consulting with her. Not until June 1670 did the viceroy receive a *cédula real* (royal order) with the answer to his question. In the royal letter he was informed that the matter had been forwarded to Sebastián de Herrera Barnuevo, chief master of royal works, and Francisco Bautista, the Society of Jesus' architect, for them to give their opinions on this subject. In a letter written to the president of the Council of the Indies and forwarded to the viceroy, both argued that after having considered examples of the most famous ancient and modern churches, in Spain, Italy, and other places, plus what religious and secular authors had written on this subject, they came to the following conclusion:

> We believe that, for the greater decorum of the divine cult, in the palaces of princes the lord should not be seen from the door, for respect increases the greater the diligence required in seeking him,

taking increasing pleasure from the atrium to the place of adoration, the retreat of the Sancta Sanctorum, and the more both curtains conceal the deity, the greater the veneration becomes.[77]

I consider this passage truly exceptional because encapsulated in these few lines we find two fundamental principles of seventeenth-century Spanish political culture. The first refers to the king's invisibility, for, as we are told, the more difficult it is to see the "lord," the greater the veneration we feel for him. Since the times of Philip II, the invisibility and inaccessibility of the king had been turned into an enduring Spanish political axiom. At the same time, this was the same kind of reasoning used to emphasize the veneration due to the Holy Sacrament, as it was argued that the Sacred Host should not be publicly exposed at all times because such exhibition would result in a loss of respect and reverence.[78] The second and most striking aspect of this passage is the total conflation of the language of divinity and the language of princely rule. When the authors of the report declare that "the lord" should not be seen from the door, to whom are they actually referring: God or the prince? The answer is that it is not possible for us to know because at this point the two languages have been fused to such a degree that no clear distinction exists between one or the other. Thus, encapsulated in this passage we find one essential trait of Spanish political culture — that is, the identification of divine and human power. This identification was so complete that the language used to deal with God was almost exactly the same as the language utilized to address the king, and vice versa.

No better example proves this than the way the Spanish king was addressed in writing. In an edict issued in 1586, Philip II ordered that, when writing to him, he should be addressed simply as "lord" (*señor*).[79] Knowing the superlative and elaborate titles that were used, for instance, to address viceroys and bishops, this extreme simplicity seems a little surprising,[80] but the initial surprise dissipates as soon as it is realized that this is exactly the same title used to address God. Thus, references to "God Our Lord" or the "King Our Lord" are found again and again in the documentation.[81] Similarly, the word "majesty" is used indistinctly to refer to both God and the king. In fact, public servants and especially clerics considered themselves to be serving God and the king at the same time, or, to use an expression common at that time, they were "in the service of two majesties." In this sense, the king's "invisibility" mentioned earlier was part of this identification of Heaven and earth because in so many ways the Spanish king was as invisible as God, and his power as mysterious and inexplicable. The world below was a reflection of the world above as much as heavenly politics was a replica of its earthly counterpart. In this regard, theology was inseparable from political concerns, as the language of human politics furnished the natural vocabulary for talking about God's power and vice versa.[82]

A good example of this is a work on the nature of the earthly and heavenly Churches titled *Jerarquía celestial y terrena* that was published in the Spanish city of Cuenca in 1603. What is of interest in this work and what gives it its power comes from its familiarity with the world of politics, even when it deals with a subject that, by definition, is otherworldly. As its author, the Augustinian friar Jerónimo de Saona, explains, all creatures are graded in a hierarchy, with some being "purged and illuminated, and guided, and governed by others, from the lowest and the lowliest up to the highest seraph, the one closest to God."[83] For Saona, the concept of hierarchy is a sort of gravitational force that makes the denizens of the universe organize themselves in such a way that all of them tend toward unity — that is, toward resembling God. Because of this ordering force of the cosmos, some beings are closer to God than others. The closer to divinity, the more they resemble God and, therefore, the higher they will be in the hierarchy. From this, Saona concludes that:

> It was fitting for the beauty and order of the universe that some creatures were more important and presided over others because in the same manner as some numbers are far from the number one, which is their origin, and others are close, and some are derived from and in a way ruled by others, thus in a similar way some creatures are closer to God, while others are farther removed from Him.[84]

This hierarchy in fact creates the "beauty" of the universe. It is divided into the supracelestial (the Trinity, which has no hierarchies), the celestial (the angels), and the subcelestial (human beings). In Saona's opinion, God created the angels to serve as "pages of His household," granting more nobility and favors to those who were more noble and eminent. That is why the archangels possess more "glory" than the angels proper.[85] The amount of glory progressively increases until it reaches the seraphim, who, according to Saona's explanation:

> Just as they are the supreme ones, those closest to God, those with the best nature, those belonging to the chamber of the great King of Glory, those members of the Secret and Supreme Council of God, those who open the room and enter the chamber without knocking because they are in possession of the golden key, those who possess the Golden Fleece, those who have the king's seal ... in the same way, they are the ones with the greatest glory.[86]

It is quite apparent that, for Saona, Heaven is structured in the same way and inhabited by the same personages as the Spanish royal palace.[87] The seraphim, for instance, seem to fulfill the same functions in Heaven as the gentlemen of the chamber in the royal palace.[88] Further on, Saona notes that, despite the different angelic hierarchies, all of them are called angels, for *angel* means the same as nuncio, messenger, or ambassador because "all are ministers sent by God for the salvation of believers." The difference between them is that the angels of the supreme hierarchy — the seraphim — are those "to whom His sovereign majesty and greatness first reveals His will." These superior angels, in turn, transmit God's will to their most immediate inferiors, and so on down.[89] In this world of analogies and mutual correspondences between the world above and the world below, it is not difficult to find a certain similarity between angels and viceroys. For it is the case that the majority of the viceroys appointed to rule New Spain in the seventeenth century were either gentlemen of the king's chamber or members of his Council of the Indies. As such, they were individuals who had had direct contact with the monarch — that invisible and remote figure — enjoying the extraordinary privilege of seeing him in person. In this sense, they belonged to the inner circle of those closest to the king. The king, in turn, had sent them to Mexico as his representatives or "ambassadors" to govern and "illuminate" his vassals.

According to Saona, "all creatures are bound and linked together with God" through the power of love, which is what unites and "makes the lover and the loved one, one and the same" (*hace unos al amante con el amado*). It is through the seraphim (whose name means "ardent" or "lover"), that the other creatures are united with God. The seraphim have, in Saona's view, three jobs: They purge, they illuminate, and they perfect the hierarchy levels below them, while they are purged, illuminated, and perfected only by God. This is the same task that the sun carries out in relation to the moon because the sun illuminates the moon but itself is not illuminated by any other planet. When the sun rises, the first thing it does is to purge or clean the air, as God cleans with His goodness all that is imperfect in the supreme hierarchy. The sun also illuminates with its rays, which is the same thing that God does with His wisdom, by illuminating our minds. Finally, with its light and glow, the sun perfects or warms the air, which was "without luster or beauty" because of the night cold, in the same way as God forms or perfects the seraphim with His love. The seraphim, for their part, bathe in that "great sea of love, soaking their wings in that sacred liquid." There the seraphim enjoy the "ray and glow of the vehement light of the eternal sun ... There they are left deified, transformed, and stamped with that most beautiful image of God." This proximity to and intimacy with God is what allows the superiors to illuminate the inferiors and reveal to them "the mysteries that they hear and receive immediately from God." From all this, Saona concludes that it is appropriate that "he who illuminates and he who purges others of imperfections be magnificent and perfect."[90]

These same reasonings lay behind all the pomp and circumstance that surrounded the viceroys, as well as the viceregal arch designers' insistence, as we have seen, on showing at all costs the viceroys' excellence, merits, virtues, and unblemished nobility. As "superiors" whose mission it was "to illuminate" their "inferiors" and "reveal" to them the "mysteries" directly received from the king, the viceroys had to appear, in their subjects' eyes, "deified" and "stamped" with the royal image and glow. Likewise, we cannot ignore the significance of the language of love, so profusely used by Saona, in understanding the nature of royal and viceregal power, as it was quite common among political theorists to argue that the political bond that kept the commonwealth united was mutual love between the ruler and the ruled.[91] For Alonso de Medina, for instance, the fact that the king had granted to Mexico a prince so excellent as the count of Salvatierra, to rule over and protect it, was a clear sign that he loved Mexico "with tenderness." In turn, Mexico, as proof of gratitude for the great favor being done to it, had to return the king's love by showing "all the abundance of its affection" toward the viceroy. In a similar vein, Matías de Bocanegra asserted that "the prince must love his people so much that he feels his subjects' injuries as if they were bites that pricked and drilled his chest."[92]

In Saona's study, God, the monarch of Heaven, rules His dominions in the same way as the Spanish monarch, God on earth, rules his: He rewards the good (allowing them to progressively ascend in the hierarchy) and punishes the bad (who sink more and more into the depths of Hell).[93] Those who gradually ascend more and more resemble God, acting as "presidents and governors" of those below. Their job consists of purging, instructing, illuminating, and perfecting their "subjects" (those below them in the hierarchy), in the same way as God instructs and illuminates the superior angels.[94] From this, it is not difficult to realize that God and the seraphim have in Heaven the same mission as the king and his viceroys have on earth in relation to their vassals: They must serve as an example to their subjects, enlightening them and guiding them along the right road. It was rather common among political writers of the period to point out the great political force that could be found in the imitation of the ruler by his subjects. Thus, kings and princes had to rule more by example (i.e., by their subjects imitating those virtues that their rulers possessed) than by imposition and the use of force.[95]

Celestial government possesses an uncanny similitude with the peculiar way in which the Spanish monarchy was ruled through the system of *consultas* (consultations) of the royal councils.[96] Saona observes that in spite of the fact that angels formed a perfect union with God, it is possible for discords and differences to exist among them because, until God informs them of His will, the angels hesitate, and some ask God for one thing and others for another. This happens not because their opinions are false but because of their *nesciencia*, their not knowing what the divine purpose is. All of them, no doubt, have good intentions. Once the divine will is known, the disputes cease, and neither does the victor boast his triumph nor does the vanquished take offense at the defeat. This is the reason why a hierarchy exists among angels, so that the superior ones, to whom God makes His wishes known directly, can transmit them to the inferiors because, as Saona concludes:[97]

> Wherever there is an ordered priority (*prelacía*) and a well-arranged government, neither differences nor contrary [ideas or opinions] are to be found because it would be against reason if the inferior defied the superior. There are not even two angels one of whom is not subordinated to the other; therefore, there cannot be two angels between whom there is discord.[97]

Such a perfect hierarchy, therefore, is the only thing that can prevent the creation of factions in the heavenly republic. Although God always has the last word, a diversity of opinions is a completely legitimate thing. Angels in Heaven then have to face the same problem as the members of the different royal councils on earth: to ascertain the divine (royal) will. This is the reason why royal councilors, after presenting their views, always conclude their *consultas* to the king by declaring, "Your Majesty will order as he likes" (*V. M. ordenará lo que mejor pareciere*).

Among the angels is one in particular whose job in Heaven seems extraordinarily similar to that of an earthly viceroy. A book published in Mexico in 1643 and devoted to extolling the excellence of the "prince of angels" and "great governor of the celestial republic," the archangel Saint Michael, confirms this argument. This book is a consummate example of the intertwining of theological and political concerns because its subject is by definition otherworldly, but its language so strikingly worldly. To the author, the Jesuit Juan Eusebio Nieremberg, St. Michael is superior to every other spirit in God's court and kingdom because he commands the nine choirs of angels. St. Michael is second only to God and third in power, sanctity, and majesty after God and the Virgin, "Queen of Heaven."[98] According to Nieremberg, the Church calls St. Michael *prepósito del paraíso* (president of paradise), which is the same as calling him *prefecto pretorio* (praetor), who was, among the Romans, a provincial governor whose dignity and powers were enormous. The office of St. Michael is also very similar to the one that Joseph had in Egypt, who was so respected that "he was revered as king, although he was no king." That is why Nieremberg declares that "similarly, the other angels greatly revere St. Michael because, *although he is not God, he is vested with divine power. Thus they venerate God in him*, in the creature, they venerate the creator. So much honor is due to such a great prince of Heaven, so much veneration and respect!" (pp. 52–54) [emphasis added].

Here, St. Michael clearly appears characterized in the likeness of a viceroy. Like the archangel, viceroys were usually compared to the praetors of the Roman empire.[99] On the other hand, it has already been shown how the figure of Joseph was also utilized as a model of the perfect viceroy. Finally, like St. Michael, the viceroys, although they were not kings, were vested with royal power, and it was for this reason that vassals had to venerate in their figure that of the king. All this notwithstanding, in this world of hierarchical correspondences, the viceroy/archangel cannot be at the same level as the archangel/viceroy. That is why Nieremberg, although calling St. Michael "vicegod" and "vicar and lieutenant (*lugarteniente*) of Jesus Christ," asserts that the authority of "this prince of Heaven" is so great that sometimes he receives the name of God, and this is something, the author adds, that does not even happen with the viceroys, for, although they represent the royal person and handle affairs with his authority and in his name, it has never been seen that a viceroy is called king or that he signs his decrees by writing *Yo el Rey* (pp. 67–69). At the same time that he makes this clear, however, Nieremberg beseeches the reader to obey and respect the archangel, because his greatness, dignity, and power make him worthy of it:

> Let us obey him, obeying the Lord. Let us not despise him. …Let us revere and honor him as the Lord's vicar … inasmuch as He has been so kind as to give this glorious spirit a great part in the government of His sacred monarchy, accepting our petitions and supplications through him. (p. 74)

The language Nieremberg uses in his plea is similar to the language constantly employed in the letters of the king and the councilors of the Indies to request that the inhabitants of New Spain respect and obey the viceroys. Angels feel great love and respect for St. Michael "not only because of his princely authority, but also for being a benevolent benefactor, which adds to the respect they feel as subjects and the affection of grateful people," because thanks to him the republic of angels was preserved when Lucifer rebelled against God. Thus, in St. Michael, angels have "a most perfect example to imitate, as he imitates and resembles God" (pp. 77–81).

The occupations and privileges of St. Michael in Heaven are, likewise, very similar to those of a viceroy on earth. St. Michael is "commander in chief of God's armies" (*capitán general de los ejércitos de Dios*) at whose head he accomplished the great deed of defeating Lucifer. He fulfills among Christians the same role as Mars did among the gentiles (p. 65). He is also "God's chief magistrate" (*el justicia mayor de Dios*) because "this post so characteristic of Christ is communicated and delegated to this sovereign spirit." Like Christ, he is not only just but also merciful. On the Last Judgment Day, he will be in charge of executing the sentences pronounced by Jesus Christ, in the same way as "kings do justice and pass sentences through their superior ministers" (pp. 113–117). In his capacity as "Chancellor of Heaven," St. Michael is also in possession of "God's seal," with which he marks Christians with the grace he imprints in their souls (pp. 145–148). St. Michael's privilege of "presenting the predestined to Heaven until they take possession of glory" is, for Nieremberg, proof of the authority and confidence God has entrusted to His archangel (p. 150).[100] Finally, Nieremberg notes that the authority this angel has in Heaven is so great that he is in charge of distributing guardian angels among men and nations. This prerogative belongs to St. Michael because he is "the prince and superior of angels and *God's vicar*, and thus it is up to him to rule the angels and set them in their *offices*, in conformity with God's service and will" (p. 128) [emphasis added].[101]

Similarly, the manner in which St. Michael rules and takes care of the public affairs of Heaven has a remarkable similitude with the way viceroys conduct the business of government. St. Michael "incessantly" gives orders to the angels, and everything the inferior angels do is as if he himself had done it, as it was done following his orders. He also assists the guardian angels with instructions and advice, so they will be better informed about their obligations. That is why the guardian angels come to him, asking him what to do, awaiting his orders, "and consulting the Lord through him, so everything weighs down on this sublime spirit who attends to everything with great charity for humankind." St. Michael also holds meetings (*juntas*) with the guardian angels, in which the other angels "consult" him. Because he is "president" of this "senate and council" of angels, everything is resolved and dealt with in his name and decrees and sentences are issued in favor of or against some kingdoms or kings. That is to say, Nieremberg makes clear, in these consultations the angels ask St. Michael "as someone who was served as God and held His supreme authority" (pp. 130–136).[102]

When, more than 20 years after the publication of Nieremberg's book, Bernardo de Frías, canon of the Guadalajara cathedral, delivered a sermon to commemorate Saint Michael's day, he began his eulogy by asserting that the most precise way to refer to the greatness of this angel was to call him "image or likeness of God." This was so because of "the greater virtue, power, and sovereignty that was communicated to him by God, so as to more closely represent His majesty."[103] Moving forward, the canon explains that the excellence of this prince of angels is due to God's authority having been communicated to him, which makes him "sovereign ambassador of the supreme God" and "vicegod on earth" (fos. 8–9). Frías marvels at the fact that "this authority, so great that it is inexplicable," is granted by God only to St. Michael. He sometimes is even called God, something that does not even happen with the viceroys, because, although "they represent so closely the royal person and handle things with communicated royal authority, and resolve in the same royal name, nevertheless the excellence never comes to be called majesty or king, but *prorex, prorege*, viceroy, he who is in place of the king." The figure of St. Michael is also very appropriate to remind forgetful viceroys that, no matter how powerful, they must be humble, because after all they are not the king. "The profound humility" of St. Michael makes him recognize that nobody can be like God. This led him to confront "that immoderate insolent Lucifer," who pretended to be like

Fig. 3 Cristóbal de Villalpando, *Aparición de San Miguel*, ca. 1684. Sacristy in the Cathedral of Mexico City. In this epiphany of St. Michael, the archangel manifests himself to mortals with all the majesty, brilliance, and magnificence that befit God's viceroy.

God (fo. 9). Frías concludes his sermon by assuring us that God appreciates this archangel so much for being His image that on the Last Judgment Day he will carry "the royal banner" in his capacity as "royal standard-bearer of the militia of Christ" (*Alférez Real de la milicia de Cristo*) because St. Michael is "the beautiful lamp of Heaven which dignifies and illuminates the Holy Trinity" (fos. 11 and 13).

One of the main characteristics, therefore, of the archangel St. Michael as an image of God is his "inexplicable authority" and "sovereign majesty" (Figure 3). In this regard, Nieremberg had already pointed out that this archangel's majesty was so great that it made people shudder in his presence, in the same way as "some emperors and kings are of such a great majesty that those who go to speak in their presence become disturbed and speechless and shake."[104] This is the same majesty in which the viceroys participate as images of the king. This is what Alavés Pinelo was referring to when he stated that the greatness of the viceroy he was welcoming, though benign, instilled respect and admiration and left people speechless.[105] Likewise, one of the main arguments of the treatise on the crime of *lese majesty* perpetrated against viceroys that, as we have seen, Rafael de Vilosa wrote around the same time as Bernardo de Frías delivered his sermon was that the sovereign majesty that resides in the king is effectively communicated to the viceroy. In order to reach this conclusion, Vilosa had first made an attempt to define the concept of majesty, but, apart from quoting Aquinas, for whom majesty was the supreme power, he ended up acknowledging that it was not easy to explain such an idea. Vilosa admits that it is "a hidden thing from which veneration is born," like the majesty in Moses' face after God had spoken to him. This is the same majesty that can be noticed in princes from the moment they are born, the majesty that "warns us of the veneration with which we must treat them" and that compels us to obey "those whom we know were born to command." From this Vilosa deduces that "some hidden virtue" must be possessed by those who are born to the purple. This concept of majesty is so mysterious and inexplicable, points out Vilosa, that, in reality, the only thing that can explain it is the name itself,

> … which contains everything in itself, and that which is more than everything cannot receive more or less. It is not circumscribed with limits nor is it closed in by time, and what the soul is to the body, majesty is to power (*imperio*). In the same way as the soul permeates the body … so majesty does influence everything it has under its dominion. It is an indivisible thing and, because it is sacred, it can be neither profaned nor mixed with that which is not.

In his attempt to explain what for him is inexplicable — and, we could add, to make a little clearer a rather abstruse explanation — Vilosa goes on to say that no majesty is superior to another majesty, because that which is supreme and the highest does not admit an equal; otherwise, it would not be supreme. That is why, if to a supreme power is added another that is its equal, "neither one nor the other will be supreme, because it would be the same as saying that there are two infinites." On the verge of conceptual confusion, Vilosa exclaims, almost in desperation, that "wanting to illustrate things like these is to make them even more obscure." However, there is one thing the author has no doubts about: While reminding us that Plato had already said that the king was a human God, he asserts that kings possess this majesty because they are images of God.[106]

From this conception of majesty as mystery, as a concept that the human mind can hardly apprehend, an identification between the monarch (and his image, the viceroy) and the *Santísimo Sacramento* (Holy Eucharist) developed in the seventeenth century, as the main aspects that defined the figure of the sovereign converged in this cult. In the cult of the Sacred Host, the Habsburg monarchy found the perfect metaphor for its concept of kingship. To begin with, this sacrament is as mysterious and difficult to explain as the concept of majesty itself. Those clerics who preached sermons exalting the sacrament constantly referred to the "divine and sovereign mystery" of the Holy Eucharist. Similarly, the cult of the Holy Eucharist, through its association with the Habsburg monarchy, in both its Spanish and Austrian branches, was what allowed the different territories of the monarchy to remain united. In this sense, the sacred Host was the heart of the Catholic monarchy and was what gave it life (Figure 4). In the words of one preacher, all "the apostates and rebels to the two majesties" would have to pull it up first to be able to finish off the monarchy's life.[107] According to one Mexican version, this identification between the Habsburg dynasty and the Holy Sacrament originated in the time of archduke Rudolf I, whose devotion to the Sacred Host reached a high point one rainy night when he ceded his horse to a priest who was carrying the Sacrament to an ill person and accompanied him on foot.[108] This gesture would become a central element in the rhetoric of Spanish kingship. Thus, Philip II, Philip IV, and Charles II all were said to have shown their devotion to the Holy Sacrament with gestures and in circumstances that replicated very closely Rudolf's story (Figure 5).[109]

In the seventeenth century, the cult of the Holy Sacrament attained a special significance in the American territories, especially from the year 1626, when Philip IV decided to establish the annual celebration of the Holy Eucharist to give thanks to God for having salvaged the fleet of the Indies (which was on its way back to Spain) from an ambush by Dutch corsairs.[110] In the 1650s, the viceroy, the duke of Alburquerque, ever conscious of royal prerogatives, decided to promote this cult by asking both the secular and the regular clergy to keep the Holy Eucharist "uncovered" for a period of 40 hours consecutively in each of their churches.[111] The sermon preached in the Mexico City cathedral by Jacinto de la Serna to signal the beginning of this celebration is a consummate example of the fusion of the languages of divinity and kingship (and its viceregal image). The manner in which the preacher addresses the viceroy at the beginning of the sermon clearly shows this:

> Most Excellent Lord: The Supreme Maker, Our Lord God, creator of all things, who was kind enough to create that most beautiful creature, the sun, placing it in the middle of the heavens in order to imprint His government on it, very vividly imprinted Himself on the kings and princes He put on earth. ...The sun is an image of God in the sky and our Catholic monarch, Philip IV the Great, vividly represents Him in his monarchy. And Your Excellency is image and sun of both majesties in this New World.[112]

Kingship and divinity are blended here in a play of multiple images and reflections, the sun being the main protagonist (Figure 6). It is not at all surprising for a sermon devoted to the Holy Eucharist to appear brimming with solar images. We have already seen how the effects of the prince's

Fig. 4 Frontispiece, Francisco Aguado, *Sumo sacramento de la Fe. Tesoro del nombre christiano*, 1640. The refulgent brilliance of a monstrance containing the Sacred Host illuminates and affirms the imperial rule of Philip IV over the four corners of the world. The Catholic Monarchy is guarded by the allegories of Power and Piety. (National Library, Madrid, Spain.)

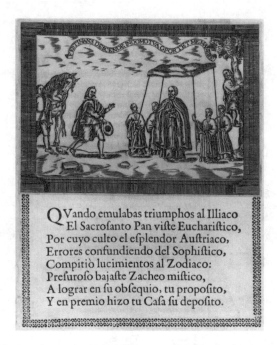

QVando emulabas triumphos al Illiaco
El Sacrofanto Pan vifte Euchariftico,
Por cuyo culto el efplendor Auftriaco,
Errores confundiendo del Sophiftico,
Compitiò lucimientos al Zodiaco:
Prefurofo bajafte Zacheo miftico,
A lograr en fu obfequio, tu propofito,
Y en premio hizo tu Cafa fu depofito.

Fig. 5 "Philip IV's devotion to the Holy Sacrament," from Isidro Sariñana, *Llanto del Occidente en el ocaso del más claro sol de las Españas*, 1666. In this image taken from Philip IV's catafalque on display in Mexico City's cathedral, the king is depicted reenacting an incident from the life of Rudolf I, the founder of the Habsburg dynasty. Upon encountering a priest who is carrying the viaticum, the king quickly gets off his horse, steps into the mud to adore the Holy Sacrament, then gives his horse to the priest and accompanies him on foot. (Courtesy of the Hispanic Society of America, New York.)

power are similar to those of the sun over the earth and the planets. In the case of the consecrated wafer, the solar metaphor is even more accurate. The Host is a sphere as perfect and resplendent in its whiteness as its solar counterpart. Like the sun and the king, it is the center of all attention, and the monstrances where this precious spiritual food is kept are designed in the shape of radiant suns, enveloped in rays all around (Figure 7).[113] Like the sun, which appears every day only to hide again at night, the Holy Sacrament is not always visible, and here lies the special significance of the duke of Alburquerque's gesture in requesting that the consecrated Host be constantly in sight for 40 hours. Such a request was like asking the sun to shine continuously for almost two days or, still more significant from the political point of view, like allowing vassals to gaze at their king for a long time, something quite unusual. Thus, in his sermon, Jacinto de la Serna refers to the Host as "this divine Lord [who] is granting a public audience

Fig. 6 "Charles II's devotion to the Holy Sacrament," from Agustín de Mora, *El sol eclipsado antes de llegar al cenit*, 1700. Among many images eulogizing the deceased king, this one from Charles II's catafalque establishes a perfect correspondence between kingship, divinity, and solar imagery. Just as the reflection of the sun's rays on a mirror produces a burning flame, the luminosity irradiated by the Sacred Host strikes Charles II's heart and produces a burning love for the Sacrament. (Benson Latin American Collection, General Libraries, The University of Texas at Austin.)

in this sacred palace of St. Peter in its Audiencia room which is this Tabernacle."[114] One basic political assumption of the time was that the just monarch who loves his people is the one who grants an audience easily, so that he may listen to the wrongs done to his vassals and hear their petitions.[115] In New Spain, the king may not be available at all, but that is why he sends his viceroy, who will fulfill this royal duty as someone who is the embodiment of the absent king, and this is one explanation of the high visibility of viceroys.

The effects of the Sacred Host are also the same as those of the sun, and it is here where a complete confluence of meaning between viceregal power and the power of the Host takes place. As de la Serna asserts in addressing the viceroy:

> All creatures wish to come face to face with the sun; all need its light; all look upon it as their soul that gives them life, movement, heat, refuge, and shelter....Who does not see Your Excellency vividly

Fig. 7 Seventeenth-century gilded monstrance. (Franz Mayer Museum, Mexico City.)

represented in these properties of the sun, for in all of this New Spain ... everyone desires your presence, everyone needs your light; you are the soul of this republic, giving life to it with the wise movements of your government.[116]

The viceroy's mission, then, is the same as that of the sun and the Holy Eucharist. They all exist to remind us, by means of their brightness and mysterious majesty, of the existence of both an invisible God and an invisible king. If gazing at the Host was like anticipating the face-to-face vision of Christ in paradise — from which vision the faithful hoped to obtain spiritual and temporal favors — gazing at the viceroy was like contemplating the king himself in all his splendor and glorious majesty — from whom the Mexican vassals expected to obtain favors and rewards. This is why the public exhibition of the consecrated Host produced the same effects among the faithful as the viceroy's public appearance among the king's vassals because, as de la Serna puts it, "Whenever Your Excellency appears in public, with the royal majesty of what you represent ... you honor and dignify everything."[117]

2

The Pillars of Government

On the 12th of January of 1624, the viceroy of New Spain, the marquis of Gelves, with the approval of the Mexican *audiencia* (High Court), ordered the expulsion of the archbishop of Mexico from New Spain. This act of force on the part of the viceroy against the highest religious authority of the viceroyalty would ultimately provoke a riot in Mexico City three days later. In the course of this riot, the High Court, with the help of the municipal council, would decide to depose the viceroy and take over the government of the viceroyalty. Years later, in 1647, Juan de Palafox, bishop of Puebla and *visitador general* of New Spain, after a long and bitter history of clashes with the Society of Jesus and with the count of Salvatierra, the viceroy at that time, was forced to flee his diocese and take refuge in the mountains when the viceroy made the decision to send troops to Puebla to eliminate the opposition of Palafox and his supporters.[1] In an extreme way, these occurrences sum up perfectly the tensions and constant conflicts that engulfed New Spain in the seventeenth century and which constitute the most remarkable aspect of its political history in that period. Such tensions and confrontations clearly belie the traditional image of a colonial society dominated by a unified and coherent ruling elite with common goals. All this makes necessary a more nuanced approach to the study of the Spanish ruling class, one in which colonial political agendas are not considered to be self-evident.

Some years ago, Jonathan Israel argued that the high level of conflict that characterized New Spain in this period was due to the cumulative effects of three factors: the serious economic crisis that Mexico experienced in the seventeenth century, the constant fiscal pressure exerted by the monarchy between 1620 and 1665, and the movement of reform against bureaucratic corruption and wasteful use of resources, exemplified

51

by the reform program of the count-duke of Olivares and his protégés in Mexico, Gelves and Palafox. Spain, locked in conflict with its enemies for the hegemony of Europe, was driven to intensify its exploitation of the empire, introducing an exacting program of tax increases, tighter regulation of trade, and strengthening of the fiscal machinery, which exacerbated the problems arising in Mexico and the resentment of the Creole population. This, in turn, caused a weakening of viceregal authority in the seventeenth century that contrasted with the remarkably tight and efficient grip of the colonial bureaucracy that, by the standards of the time, had characterized colonial rule during the reign of Philip II.[2] But, as shall be shown in this and the following chapters, no clear evidence exists that economic or fiscal matters played any important or decisive role in the disturbances of New Spain. What the evidence does suggest is that these disturbances were mainly driven by political motivations, by the competition for power among different segments of the ruling elite. In order to understand the power play that created the Mexican turmoil, we must look at the political culture of the Spanish monarchy and, more specifically, at the culture of viceregal authority.

As the king's image and alter ego, a viceroy was expected to rule with the same guiding principles as the monarch. In practice, the power of a viceroy depended largely upon his force of character and his political skills to chart his way through the complexities of colonial society. In the case of New Spain, it was right before he made his solemn entry into Mexico City that he had the opportunity to grasp a sense of the political forces with which he would be interacting. These forces were represented by various corporate bodies: The royal *audiencia*, the *cabildo secular* (municipal council), the *cabildo eclesiástico* (ecclesiastical chapter), and the Inquisition all sent their representatives to welcome the new viceroy before he was publicly received on the city streets a few days later.[3] This meant much more than simple courtesy on the part of the principal institutions of colonial society, as it allowed the new viceroy to meet, for the first time, the representatives of those forces he would have to reckon with in the course of his term of office.

It has been argued that when a government lacks a standing army and a police force (as colonial society in the sixteenth and seventeenth centuries did), its power rests on the way authority is articulated and perceived, and all political life derives its legitimacy from a set of authorizing languages. In other words, language participates in authority.[4] As Pierre Bourdieu has observed, in the struggle of social groups to impose a certain vision of the world, "agents possess power in proportion to their symbolic capital, i.e., in proportion to the recognition they receive from a group." Thus, those agents who are invested with the monopoly of the legitimate use of an "authorized language" (that is, a language uttered by the person legitimately licensed to do so, spoken in a legitimate situation, and enunciated according to the legitimate forms), as "authorized representatives" (they have been invested with the power to use such a language), are in possession of a significant amount of "linguistic capital" and, consequently, of symbolic power.[5] Thus, in order to reconstruct the logic of Spanish colonial rule, it is necessary to recover the different political discourses that endowed these bodies with identity and authority. My main aim in this chapter is, therefore, to uncover the political discourses that gave the *audiencia* and the *cabildo* their authority (due to its complexities, the relations between secular and ecclesiastical power, including the Inquisition, will be studied in the next chapter), in order to establish the legitimacy of their claims as holders of political rights and determine what kinds of limits these discourses imposed upon royal and viceregal power. This, on the other hand, will allow me to explain the tensions and conflicts that existed among the different institutions of colonial rule, tensions that in Mexico were heightened by the absence of the monarch. As we shall see, though the mission of the viceroy, like that of the king, was to represent the unity of the body politic and to guarantee that harmony existed among all its members, his authority was often contested by other institutions of colonial rule.

The Viceroy's Companions

In his classic institutional history of the Spanish possessions in America, C.H. Haring argued that two principles were characteristic of Spanish imperial government in America: "a division of authority and responsibility, and a deep distrust by the Crown of initiative on the part of its colonial officials." Haring goes on to contend that, in spite of the apparent centralization of authority in the hands of the viceroys, they found their power considerably restricted both in theory and in practice. In larger matters of policy — not routine administration — the viceroy was reduced to playing the role of a mere royal agent charged with the execution of royal orders. Moreover, the viceroys had to share virtually all their powers with the *audiencia* as a council of state, and all the more important offices were appointed and removed by the king; consequently, he could exercise little effective control over subordinates. For Haring, therefore, the conflicts over matters of jurisdiction originated in the division of authority among different individuals or tribunals exercising the same powers (executive, legislative, judicial). For him, "Spanish imperial government was one of checks and balances," secured by a deliberate overlapping of jurisdictions.[6] At the same time, the political role of the *audiencias* has led historians to argue that the *audiencia* was the most important and characteristic institution in the government of the Spanish possessions in America. While José Ignacio Rubio Mañé indicated that the *audiencia* was the main instrument kings had for limiting the powers of the viceroys, other historians have usually emphasized that, in practice, the viceroys had to share their power with the *audiencia*, so much so that it made Haring wonder where the ultimate authority in the colony rested, in the viceroy or in the *audiencia*.[7]

John Parry also was puzzled by the difficulty of determining where, in the Indies, real authority lay. He contended that the entire system was devised deliberately to prevent the growth of a strong colonial government.[8]

These ideas have proved extremely popular among historians of colonial Spanish America (interestingly enough, they also belie the popular image of the viceroys as despotic rulers); however, these ideas have also contributed, in many important ways, to obscuring the political nature of the Spanish imperial polity, thus baffling many historians with regard to the real nature of colonial power. Regarding the role of the *audiencia* in the government of New Spain, although its importance in limiting viceregal power has been rightly pointed out, I will argue that this happened not because the Crown deliberately pitted the *audiencia* against the viceroys as a way to prevent the latter from accumulating too much power but because the nature of the political system itself made it inevitable. A look at some key political concepts in the period under study may help us illuminate the question of colonial authority which has so much puzzled institutional historians. In this sense, the *cartilla política* (political first reader) that one of the canons of the cathedral of Cartagena, Spain, presented in 1666 to the child king Charles II may serve as a helpful guide to identify some of these concepts. In alphabetical order, the first reader described and explained a series of concepts and ideas which the author considered to be essential for good government. Thus, with this little book, the canon declared, the king would be able to learn, very early in his life, the basics of government. For the letter "c" he chose the word *consejo* (counsel), for the letter "j" he used the word *justicia* (justice), and for the letter "p" he selected the word *prudencia* (prudence).[9] As will be demonstrated below, it was almost inevitable for the canon to make such a selection.

Traditionally, the Spanish kings of the sixteenth and seventeenth centuries have been seen as quintessential "absolute monarchs." Strongly influenced by the ideas of the Enlightenment and nineteenth-century liberalism, many historians tended to identify the concept of "absolute monarchy" with "despotic" government.[10] In the Spanish case, this was translated — with a little help from the black legend — into the pervasive idea that the Spanish kings ruled their dominions arbitrarily and almost without limitations. It was this kind of background that allowed one modern historian to contend that the directing principles of government of the Spanish imperial system were "those of arbitrary patrimonial power, legitimized by the notion of the divine right of kings."[11] But, the truth is that the Spanish monarchy was never shaped by the theory of Divine Right, and a majority of Spanish political thinkers rejected it. According to this theory, the king drew his authority from God alone. Because God alone was the king's superior, the king was under no obligation to account to his subjects for his actions. The king was subject only to divine law, and subjects could never actively resist their king.[12] In the Spanish case, although everybody accepted the idea that all power came from God, a majority of legal and political writers argued that, contrary to the contention of the supporters of the Divine Right of Kings, power was transmitted from God to the community. Then, the people, for the sake of preserving their society, had transferred their power to the monarch. As explained by Juan de Santa María, due to the discord and violence that originally existed among humans,

> ... men were obligated and forced to seek a manner of living in which every one could quietly and peacefully enjoy that which was theirs. Thus, they determined to live together and subject themselves to laws and a king who also kept [these laws] and, with justice, all the other virtues necessary for the augmentation and preservation of any republic. And, to this end, kings were awarded their great power, as they have the scales of justice in one hand and the sword of power in the other, ... because there cannot exist a republic without justice nor a king worth his title if he does not keep and uphold justice.[13]

What separates the Spanish monarchy from the theory of the Divine Right of Kings is the idea that the people originally participated in the constitution of the monarchy; in other words, kings were created by the people.[14] The fundamental consequence of the premise that power came from the people is the idea that the monarch's interests were not above those of the community; therefore, the monarch had the inescapable obligation of ruling for the benefit of the common good. In other words, the king's chief mission was to administer justice, procuring the security and well-being of his subjects.[15]

This did not mean that the power of the king could not be "absolute," because, as many authors sustained, once the people had surrendered their power to the king, they could not impose their will upon the sovereign or any limitations to his power. Other writers, however, followed a more constitutionalist and less absolutist approach and argued that, though the king might be superior to each individual of the community, his power was never above the power of the community as a whole.[16] It was not a Spaniard, however, but the Frenchman Jean Bodin who best expressed, at the end of the sixteenth century, the idea of the king's "absolute power." For him, the main trait distinguishing the absolute monarch was condensed in the Latin formula *princeps legibus solutus* (i.e., the king was free from any legal constraints). For Bodin, the essence of the king's power was his capacity to promulgate and abrogate laws, as opposed to the traditional mission of kings as givers of justice. Thus, in Bodin's conception, the legislative function replaced the judicial one as the defining characteristic of royal power, but not even in this construct was the king's power supposed to be totally unrestrained. In the medieval and scholastic traditions to which Bodin still belonged, above the king's power and desires were always the laws of God and the laws of nature, which the monarch should observe at all times. Nor did his "absolute power" mean that the monarch should fail to observe the "constitutional" and customary laws of the realm. In the last instance, the absolute monarchy was based in the belief that the fundamental aim of government had to be to secure order rather than liberty, because order and harmony in any commonwealth were extremely fragile. Any political society required a sovereign who was absolute in the sense that he commanded but was never commanded, thus preventing the creation of parties or factions, which always created disorder. Thus, the absolute power of the king was the very foundation of political stability.[17]

Although certainly influenced by the ideas about royal power expressed by Bodin, the Spanish monarchy never abandoned the notion that the main reason that justified the existence of kings was their obligation to administer justice. Spanish political thinkers continued to see the king as a judge, and, in particular, as a reflection of God's justice. In the words of Juan de Santa María, for instance, justice is a fitting virtue for kings "since it is incumbent in their office and is what makes them sovereigns and lords — lacking in justice they cannot serve in this capacity." Besides, justice is what sustains kingdoms, and a just king is loved, respected, and voluntarily obeyed by his subjects. That is why, adds Santa María, the ancient kings of Egypt made their magistrates swear that they would not obey their commands or execute their orders and decrees if they believed that they were contrary to justice or the laws of the kingdom.[18]

This principle of not obeying unjust royal orders is the basis of the famous formula "I obey but do not execute," which is how those royal decrees, the application of which was thought to produce harmful results, were responded to. Traditional historiography has thought that this principle is ultimately responsible for the lack of respect for law that characterized the colonial period and whose consequences are even extended up to the present to explain the inefficiency of the law and the absence of the rule of law in many Latin American countries.[19] It is necessary to point out, nevertheless, that this was a legal principle, included in law collections such as the *Recopilación de Indias* and developed by political writers.[20] As Jerónimo Castillo de Bobadilla, for example, explains with precision, royal mandates were not to be obeyed when they ordered something that went against conscience, faith, natural law, or the laws and privileges of the different kingdoms.[21] Needless to say, this principle lent itself to abuse, but that in no way means that it gave free rein to a lack of respect for established laws. This principle, however, had a major and transcendental effect: By permitting royal officials to delay the execution of orders from their superiors indefinitely, it drastically reduced the possibility for the monarch to establish an effective chain of command.

If justice was the foundation of the Commonwealth, then the extraordinary relevance that the *audiencias* acquired in the Spanish monarchy seems only logical. For Juan de Madariaga, the influential Carthusian monk and political writer, the *audiencias* and *chancillerías* were created through the "piety and clemency" of the kings so their vassals would have near their homes a person who could hear their grievances and complaints, and they would not have to travel to the Court to receive justice from the king.[22] That is to say, the justice handed out by the *audiencias* is an extension of the justice that the king was supposed to administer directly. In this sense, the *audiencias*, as such, are the image of the king–judge. When Juan de Solórzano examined the placed occupied by the royal *audiencias* in the structure of government of the Spanish possessions in the New World, he declared that the Spanish kings should be thanked very much for the great benefit that their vassals in the Indies had been granted with the foundation of the *audiencias*. As he explained:

> …in the places where kings and princes can neither intervene nor reign and govern the republic by themselves, there is nothing better they can do to secure it agreeable benefits than to give it ministers to reign in their name and place, to protect it, to administer and distribute justice in a right, fair and saintly fashion, something without which kingdoms cannot exist or be preserved, just as without souls human bodies are unable to exercise some vital, animal or natural functions.[23]

For Solórzano, then, justice is the foundation of any commonwealth, which explains why the inhabitants of the Indies should be so grateful for the existence of these courts. Their mere existence ensures the peace and tranquility of the land, because the king, in creating them, is ensuring that he rules according to divine and human law. As Charles V put it himself when he decided to establish an *audiencia* in New Spain, he was obliged to God and his vassals in New Spain to do so in order to comply with his duties as king.[24] In creating the *audiencia*, therefore, he was simply doing that which a good king should always do: making sure that his subjects had a place near them where they could seek justice.

If the *audiencias* occupied such a preeminent place in the Spanish monarchy, what, then, was to be the relation between *audiencia* and viceroy, and what did it really mean for a viceroy of New Spain to be president of the *audiencia*? No doubt, of all the institutions of colonial rule, the viceroys had the closest relationship with the royal *audiencia* of Mexico (in New Spain, two *audiencias* were established, one in Mexico City and one in Guadalajara). The *audiencia* of Mexico City had two main functions. As a court of law, it was the highest royal court of appeal within its district, also serving as a tribunal of first instance in criminal cases that arose within Mexico City and within five leagues around it. The *audiencia* of Mexico City served at the same time as the viceroy's consultative council, deliberating with him on certain days of the week on matters of political administration. These administrative sessions were called *Acuerdos*.[25] Whereas the viceroy as such had the sovereign representation of the royal person, in his capacity as president of the *audiencia* he represented the king as the font of justice; however, the viceroy, unless he was trained as a lawyer, had no voice or vote in the determination of judicial decisions, and he was expressly forbidden to intervene in matters concerning the administration of justice.[26] The viceroy, nonetheless, had the responsibility of general supervision to see that justice was administered with integrity.[27] Although they were not permitted to intervene directly in the administration of justice, the viceroys had at their disposal mechanisms by which they could manipulate judicial decisions. One of them was the authority to grant pardons in criminal cases, which caused the judges to complain that in this way the viceroys were in a position to alter and revoke sentences.[28] As could be expected, this and other examples of viceregal interference created a certain tension between viceroys and *oidores*, the former always trying to enhance their power *vis-à-vis* the latter and the *oidores* attempting to defend their independence, with the Crown generally supporting the judges' claims, at least in strictly judicial matters.[29]

The fact that the best government, as we saw in Chapter 1, was the rule of only one did not mean, in the view of many authors, that kings should rule by always having their own way. Kings and princes, like other mortals, are imperfect beings, maintained Juan de Madariaga, and all the errors that man commits are due to a lack of advice. The problem with a monarch is that "the foolish things" that he does by not accepting advice harm the entire republic. Madariaga infers from this idea that the king, therefore, cannot govern the kingdom as he pleases, but he needs the aid of his council.[30] That is why, for Juan de Salazar, the best form of government is a "mixed" government (at the same time monarchical and republican or aristocratic), like the one that exists in Spain, in which the king rules with the help of many councils.[31] According to Madariaga, so that a sovereign be able to submit all his subjects, an "extremely boisterous and very discordant" crowd of people, to his will:

> ...he must be endowed with three royal virtues, *power, wisdom,* and *justice.* The first, which is the supreme power, should not reside in equal measure in many others, but only in the royal person, since that is what is essential to the monarchy. But with the other two, wisdom and justice, which can be advantageously found in other men, he is always aided by his councillors, who *with him form one body in the senate*; these same councillors receive part of the supreme power through his royal graciousness, some over certain kingdoms and others over others, to aid the government with this communication of virtues.[32]

While the supreme power is concentrated in the hands of the monarch, he makes use of the members of the royal councils and of the *audiencias* to better govern and administer justice, without this meaning that the source of all governmental actions as well as all acts of justice does not originate with the monarch. In New Spain, this system is reproduced in a very similar way: The viceroy is the main repository of royal authority, but he governs and imparts justice with the help of the *audiencia.* As the king's image, the viceroy had to rule in the same way as the king would; hence, the *audiencia* was bound to play in America the same political role as the different councils that assisted the king at the court.[33] The *audiencia*, then, must not be seen as an independent institution but as a political body always subordinated to the viceroy.[34] In Madariaga's fragment, therefore, we can find the explanation of an apparent contradiction, one that has intrigued historians: A viceroy, a supreme governor and direct representative of the king, is deprived of the capacity to impart justice, while the *audiencia*, apparently, had wrenched away an important portion of the viceroy's authority by acquiring responsibilities of a political nature.[35]

The political writers of the seventeenth century saw no contradiction in the monarch or the viceroy administering justice through qualified members of the republic; on the contrary, it was a sign of their virtue as good rulers. According to the conciliar structure characteristic of the Spanish monarchy, it was left to the prince to "execute" and "command" but when carrying out his fundamental task, the administration of justice, it was the councils and tribunals who made the decisions (although, of course, the king always had the last word). It was at this moment that the councilors left off being "consultants" and turned themselves into "judges." It was on this metamorphosis that the fundamental importance of their office was based.[36] Diego Pérez de Mesa explained it clearly at the beginning of the seventeenth century:

> … and because the supreme prince is not a letrado [law graduate] and the councilors of justice are able to adequately decide what is juridical, the prince grants them the authority to make decrees and command, because he is not able to interpret the laws by which the councilors make decrees, pardoning or sentencing. And thus the writs and edicts of the courts command with royal authority, which is not true of the other councils, in which the decree or consulta is returned to the king and he chooses and orders what seems best to him.[37]

The specific reason why the viceroys of the Indies were not permitted to vote on the lawsuits heard in the *audiencias* was because they were not *letrados.* Logically, if the king himself, because he was not a *letrado*, did not participate directly in the administration of justice, it does not appear possible that his "image" in America would realize a duty that he himself did not exercise. That the *audiencia* was the personification of the king–judge is clearly demonstrated in the language used, for instance, by the bishop of Puebla in a *consulta* presented to the *audiencia* of Mexico in 1664 during the course of one of the many conflicts that the viceroys had with the bishops:

> It is quite surprising that Your Most Excellent Viceroy by himself alone should issue a royal writ for which there is no law or royal order issued by Your Royal Person that permits or concedes to him a similar prerogative. Only the royal courts enjoy such a special concession and privilege ... [and His Majesty] orders that the viceroys do not issue writs in the name of the king but rather with the *audiencia* ... because it is prohibited that [they] use Your Royal Name and Seal.[38]

What is of interest here for our theme is not the conflicts between the secular and ecclesiastical powers, an aspect that will be analyzed in the next chapter, but, primarily, to point out the language used by the bishop. We could ask ourselves: To whom, exactly, is the bishop directing himself — the king or the *audiencia*? The answer is that, in reality, both of them, because although physically the bishop is talking to the *oidores* of the *audiencia* of Mexico, "politically" he is talking to the king himself, which is seen by the fact that the *audiencia* is referred to by the expression "Your Royal Person." Second, the fact that a viceroy could not issue royal writs on his own, because he needed the signature of the *oidores*, is directly related to the privilege that the *audiencias* possessed to promulgate decrees, not in the name of the king but as if the king himself were issuing them — something that not even a viceroy could do, because his decrees were emitted only in his name and with his name.[39]

The discourse of justice and counsel constructed the justices of the *audiencia* as indispensable figures of the body politic, ready to assert their authority whenever the viceroys attempted to diminish it. That is the way we can read a long letter sent to the king by three Mexican *oidores* in 1620. The *oidores* frame their discourse with the idea that, if they are to execute their transcendental mission (to administer justice), they must be surrounded with much the same authority and dignity as the king or the viceroy. The *oidores* complain that the viceroy, the marquis of Gualdalcázar, has a low opinion of and even despises the *audiencia*, treating the *oidores* "as if they were his servants and not His Majesty's." The viceroy also creates divisions in the *audiencia* as two of the *oidores* and the *fiscal* are his partisans. Among the wrongs the viceroy has done them is included, first, the way he treats them both in speech and in writing without the courtesy and respect due them and which are suited to the authority of their office, in an attempt to monopolize all of the royal authority, ignoring the orders of the monarch that instruct the viceroys to treat them as his "colleagues." Another wrong committed against the *oidores* is that the viceroy keeps them from writing to the king without his previous knowledge.[40] They also complain that the viceroy calls the *oidores*, *alcaldes*, and *fiscales* to his chambers when he has to reproach them for some act, instead of doing it, as he is obliged to, in the *Acuerdo*. In this way, he takes advantage of the fact that he is in his own chambers and among his servants to insult and demean them.[41] Besides, the viceroy issues writs "in the name of Don Felipe and under the royal seal," without having the authority to do so on his own, without the *audiencia*. For all of these reasons, the *oidores* beg that the monarch order the viceroy to treat in an appropriate manner those persons "who have supreme jurisdiction of justice in this kingdom in the name of His Majesty, and who represent the royal person so directly."[42]

According to the *oidores*, the viceroy justifies his abuses of power by means of two royal *cédulas*. The first authorizes him to try criminal cases involving the *oidores*, *alcaldes*, and *fiscales*, but to the *oidores* this lends itself to abuses on the part of the viceroy, as it permits him to put any of them on trial for petty reasons. Thus, they conclude that for the administration of justice — "which is what preserves kingdoms and states" — to be effective, it would be better that he not be able to proceed against them or, in any case, proceed in a very limited way (for serious crimes such as *lese majesty*, the unspeakable sin, embezzlement of the royal treasury, or for marrying without the king's permission). The second *cédula* orders that, when differences of opinion exist between the viceroy and the *audiencia*, they present to him their point of view, but if the viceroy persists in his opinion then it should be done as he thinks it should be.[43] The problem for the *oidores* is that the viceroy wants to control not only the governmental affairs that fall to him, but also those having to do with the administration of justice that exclusively belong to the judges of the *audiencia*. The *oidores* argue that the *audiencia* exists precisely to remedy the injustices that viceroys may commit. For all these reasons, the *oidores* ask the monarch to order the viceroys not to interfere in those government affairs that are being appealed to the *audiencia*. In addition, they request that the second decree be revoked. The *oidores* base their petition on the fact that the king himself has given an order that, whenever a royal decree is issued that could prove to be harmful, it should be obeyed but not complied with; therefore, it would not be logical that the same should not be done with the orders of a viceroy.[44]

The king responded to these claims by reaffirming the right of the viceroys to proceed against *oidores* accused of crimes and to sentence them if they were found guilty, although they could not carry out the sentence or deprive them of or suspend them from their position without consulting first with the Council of the Indies. This measure, in practice, was not very effective, being above all a symbolic reaffirmation of the superiority of the viceroy over the *oidores*.[45] At the same time, the viceroy was reminded that he was to treat the *oidores* with respect and deference. The viceroy should understand that the *oidores* were his *compañeros* (companions) and that the honor that he possessed due to his high position was the same bestowed on the *oidores*, with the pertinent differences. All these honors and courtesies, concluded the monarch in his missive, were necessary so that the *oidores* were respected and enjoyed the esteem that was needed for them to discharge the responsibilities of their offices. For all of these reasons, the viceroy, "as head, father, president and protector" of his "companions and ministers," was more obligated than anyone to respect and honor them.[46]

Among the political languages available to early modern political writers, the language of friendship was often utilized to explain the relationship between rulers and their advisors. Influenced by Aristotelian and Ciceronian ideas, contemporaries believed that friendship gave rise to and sustained the most lasting political bonds.[47] Friendship was found not only among equals but among unequals as well. For example, for Juan de Madariaga, the king's councilors, in addition to forming a whole or mystical body with the monarch, are "faithful friends" of the king who, although inferior to him with regard to dignity and estate, are his equals with regard to reason and intelligence.[48]

Writing in his *Política indiana* of the virtues a good viceroy must have, Solórzano advises them to avoid being too self-confident and believing that they know everything, thus the viceroys should not disdain the advice of the *oidores* they have at their side and over whom they preside. Solórzano recalls that, besides, many royal decrees order the viceroys, in all serious cases brought before them, to ask for advice from the *oidores*.[49] Solórzano advises the viceroys to treat the *oidores* as "their colleagues and companions" (although this, of course, does not mean that he considers them to actually be their equal), not only because of the importance and high status of their positions but also because the viceroy is "their head," in such a way that the *oidores* share in the authority the viceroy enjoys. By honoring and showing great respect for the *oidores*, especially in public, the viceroy helps to heighten his own authority because, in a certain sense, the viceroy is honoring himself. In addition, this has the added advantage that, following the example of the viceroy, the people will respect and revere these magistrates even more, which, adds Solórzano, "is extremely important for the tranquility and preservation of the republic."[50]

Similarly, Juan de Palafox, bishop of Puebla and acting viceroy of New Spain, maintains that a viceroy, in matters of grave importance, should always depend on the opinion of the *Acuerdo* and, if necessary, on that of experienced persons. In the opinion of Palafox, one of the principal duties of the viceroy is that of serving as president of the *audiencia*, because, as such, he is in charge of matters concerned with justice, and, although in his capacity as viceroy and *capitán general* he is independent of the *audiencia*, as president "he is one and the same with it, since he is the head of the tribunal." For all of these reasons, the way in which the viceroy relates to the *oidores* is very important:

It is well to treat the *oidores* and ministers with love and esteem, and although one must always preserve the authority and *superiority of the head*, it is necessary that this not be done in a way that seems to divide the group, and thus His Majesty orders in his decrees that they [the viceroys] have them for *friends and companions* and as assistants in the hardships and labors of government. It is a courtesy to address them as *Vuestra Merced* and *Señor* in both their presence and absence, and although he does not accompany them [to the door] when they leave nor goes to greet them when they enter [his chamber], he treats them with more decorum and more affability than he does anyone else in general.[51]

While these ideas probably constituted the majority opinion in Spanish political thought, in the late sixteenth and seventeenth centuries an ideological debate developed between two broadly defined political currents regarding the role of the ruler's counselors, and it was in this respect that the idea of prudence became a key concept to understanding the political practices of the Spanish rulers. Yet, what exactly constituted a ruler's prudence was a controversial matter. While for some authors — theorists of the reason of state such as Giovanni Botero, Justus Lipsius, or Jean Bodin — prudence lay in identifying that which was most "useful" for the preservation of the commonwealth (and to determine that the ruler, as head of the republic, was the one most qualified to decide what was best for its preservation, although he could always consult with his advisors), for others — the uncompromising critics of Machiavelli and Bodin and the defenders of the "true" Catholic reason of state such as Madariaga, Rivadeneira, Santa María, or Juan de Mariana, as well as — prudence lay in identifying that which was "honest and truthful" and which served to distinguish good from evil (and to decide that the participation of the ruler's advisors was indispensable). For these authors, monarchical power had limits that were established through a covenant between the king and the kingdom and those who wanted to eliminate them aimed at making royal power absolute and transforming the king into a tyrant. Translated in terms of the Spanish monarchy, it was a question of determining whether the king was obligated to rule his kingdoms through the mediation of his councils or whether he alone was sufficient for such a task. In this regard, the English expression "King in Parliament" can be compared to the Spanish "King in Council," thus the opinion of many political writers who saw as tyrannical the rule of a king without his council.[52]

This ideological debate at the center of the monarchy would be reflected in political practices in New Spain as seen in the conflicting discourses of viceroys and *oidores*. The viceroys generally defended a "pure" monarchical government, in which the viceroy was able to take political action independent of the control of the Justices of the High Court, while the *audiencia* defended a "mixed" monarchical system, in which the *oidores* actively intervened in the functioning of the government.[53] It is within the context of these debates that the grievances of the *oidores* against viceroy Guadalcázar, examined above, acquire all its significance. It is also in this context that we should place the confrontation between the *audiencia* of Mexico and the marquis of Gelves who would eventually bring about the viceroy's downfall. The *oidores* had complained very early on in his government that Gelves, besides meddling with the administration of justice and impeding the appeal of his decisions to the *audiencia*, had been ruling without consulting with them. For his part, Gelves, in rejecting the accusations of the *oidores*, had emphasized that, for the viceroys to be able to rule effectively, they should not be subjected to the constant supervision of the judges, something that contributed to their authority being diminished.[54]

Many of these ideas constitute the ideological background of an anonymous pamphlet written to justify an unprecedented action: the overthrow by the *audiencia* of viceroy Gelves after the outbreak of a riot in Mexico City on January 15, 1624. In a revealing way, the author or authors of the pamphlet, while accepting that the viceroy's intentions had been to serve God and the monarch, blamed the viceroy's advisors for not giving him prudent counsel. Among the long list of accusations presented in the pamphlet against the viceroy, several familiar ones stand out: He had not permitted his decisions to be appealed to the *audiencia*; he had impeded several *oidores* to exercise their office, and, as a consequence, the entire kingdom had been wronged because justice had not been administered; he had gone against what the law established in the hearing of cases; he had scorned the *oidores* and *alcaldes del crimen*; and he had held back letters written for the king. In addition, he had violated ecclesiastical immunity; he had banished several *regidores* without permitting them to be heard in the *audiencia*; and he had burdened the inhabitants of Mexico, without their consent, with a new tax. Because according to divine, natural, and positive law, one can "resist the prince that obviously violates the law," the *audiencia*, the document contended, was authorized to depose the viceroy. Furthermore, "the judge that proceeds against the law with manifest injustice and causing irreparable damage … denying appellations which must be admitted according to the law, can be resisted." Even the pope may be resisted, although he has no judge or prince above him, except God, because "natural law is so strong that should … the Sovereign Pontiff commit flagrant violence or injustice in manifest damage of other sovereign princes or the Church, he can be resisted and kept in check." Finally, the pamphlet argued that when the royal *cédula* established that, in cases of conflict between the viceroy and the *audiencia*, what the viceroy ordered had to be carried out, in reality it affirmed that this procedure should be followed as long as it did not cause unrest or a commotion in the land. As was clear to everyone, the viceroy's commands had wronged so many inhabitants of Mexico that they eventually caused the tumult of January 15, for which reason the commands of the viceroy should not be obeyed, as it was totally justified for the *audiencia* to take over the government because as long as the marquis of Gelves remained in office "neither would the *audiencia* be able to hear the cases with freedom nor would the kingdom have the freedom granted by His Majesty to seek justice."[55]

In order to explain the continual bickering among the different sections of the ruling elite that characterized New Spain, especially during the seventeenth century, Jonathan Israel centered his analysis on the rivalries between Creoles and *peninsulares*. In these confrontations, the viceroy, along with the regular clergy, represented the peninsular, bureaucratic, and imperial faction, while the archbishop of Mexico City, along with the *audiencia* and the *cabildo*, led the Creole and "Mexican" party.[56] It does not seem, nevertheless, that the concept of Creole or Mexican identity played any significant role in the minds of the *oidores*. First, above all, the *oidores* as well as the viceroys saw themselves as servants (*criados*) of the king to whom they were united by a close personal dependence, one that left little room for loyalties to impersonal entities such as the "state" or the "nation." If the *oidores* were willing to join with other sectors of the New Spanish elite to oppose or confront the viceroy, it was, basically, because they saw themselves as the privileged defenders of the "constitutional" principles of the Spanish polity. And, if any viceroy chose to rule against these principles, it was their obligation to resist such a "tyrannical" ruler. This is precisely what the pamphlet examined above argues: If the marquis of Gelves, with his actions, ruled as a tyrant by impeding the administration of justice and violating the rights and liberties of the various bodies that comprised the colonial polity, it was not only justified but licit, as well, to depose him. The extraordinary importance that the discourse of justice and counsel had in Spanish political culture endowed the *oidores*, in their double role as judges and advisors, with the preeminent position that they occupied in the structure of colonial power. In the opinion of many political commentators, the stability of the monarchy and the defense of royal authority were based on these two fundamental principles (along with that of religion). And this discourse was the one that endowed the *audiencia* with the power to oppose the viceroys.

The Realm's Head

Most historians agree that the *cabildo* or municipality was the cornerstone of Spanish rule and settlement in America and that this institution was of extreme importance because it was the only one in which the Creole population was largely represented.[57] Regarding the social and political nature of the Spanish–American municipal council, the traditional narrative maintains that, at first, the Spanish–American *cabildos*, heirs to the powerful city councils of late medieval Castile, had been truly representative of the towns, as they were elected democratically by the white citizenry in annual elections. But, this "democratic complexion" of the Castilian municipality that had been transplanted in the New World came to an end with the crushing of the revolt of the Castilian towns by Charles V in 1521. Thus, by the seventeenth century, with appointed *corregidores* (the first one in Mexico City was appointed in 1573), the sale of town council positions, and closed elections (only members of the council were entitled to vote), the city government had become the preserve of a narrow circle of wealthy and influential families, an "oligarchy" in which the private interests of the *regidores* did not always coincide with the general interests of the community they represented.[58]

Furthermore, if the Spanish municipalities in America lost their popular character early on, they also increasingly lost their autonomy through the increasing centralization of the Crown's authority, with *corregidores* or, in the case of Mexico City and Lima, viceroys interfering in their affairs. Any elections of members of the *cabildo* that still occurred (of *alcaldes ordinarios*, for example) were generally subject to the approval of the *corregidor* or viceroy. This made Haring conclude that "as the cabildos were gradually deprived of whatever initiative and independence they may have possessed in the beginning, the office of regidor became politically of less and less consequence."[59] However, Jonathan Israel, more recently has argued that in New Spain municipal councils, especially the *cabildos* of Mexico City and Puebla, provided positive political leadership for a broad combination of Creole groups. The *cabildo*, in fact, represented local interests and was the principal political and representative institution of the Creole population. The *cabildo* of Mexico City claimed a special preeminence among the Mexican *cabildos*, considering itself the representative of all Mexican Creoles, a claim hotly contested by Puebla. The *cabildo* of Mexico City supported the Creole line in all the major political issues of the early and mid-seventeenth century, even when this brought the *cabildo* directly into collision with viceregal policy. The viceroys, for their part, recognized the political importance of the *cabildos* while trying to neutralize them by interfering in the elections as much as they could. In short, Israel concludes that, when the viceroys were fully in control of the political situation, the *cabildos* could be stifled; however, in the seventeenth century, the viceroys had less than complete control.[60]

To truly understand the political role and power of Mexico City's *cabildo*, we must take a look at the broader context of the place that cities and city councils occupied in the structure of the Spanish monarchy. Traditional historiography has generally argued that by the seventeenth century royal absolutism had triumphed in Spain. Few limitations and little organized opposition to Habsburg rule were offered. The Castilian aristocracy had been neutralized by the use of royal patronage and the toleration accorded to its prerogatives. Of equal importance, the Castilian *Cortes*, or parliament, from which the aristocracy had been excluded, had been reduced to total submissiveness. The eradication at the beginning of the sixteenth century of a militant, urban-based opposition to Habsburg rule and the consolidation of a firm alliance between the Crown and the aristocracy removed all barriers to the advance of monarchical authoritarianism.[61]

These ideas have been subjected to close scrutiny in the last two decades, resulting in a fundamental revision of the history of the Castilian *Cortes* in the Habsburg period. For the revisionist historians, the *Cortes* was far from being politically inconsequential during this period; in fact, it was the most active of all the parliamentary institutions of any monarchy in Europe. It had the right to approve extraordinary taxes, thus depriving the Crown of fiscal autonomy — something normally considered to have been essential to royal absolutism. The principle of no taxation without consent gave the *Cortes* and the 18 cities it represented the ability to block and thus frustrate the interests of the Crown, placing them in a strong position to negotiate tax agreements favorable to their own interests. Between 1600 and 1664, when the *Cortes* ceased to be summoned, the relationship between the Crown and the *Cortes* was put on an explicitly contractual basis, which was perhaps not totally dissimilar from the one usually associated with the Crown of Aragon: No new services were allowed without the vote of the *Cortes*, and no vote of the *Cortes* could take place without the prior consent of the cities. The real strength the *Cortes* derived from these contracts, however, was not political but administrative, and it gave the *Cortes*, in the name of the kingdom, a great part of the financial administration of the state. Not even Philip IV and his chief minister, the count-duke of Olivares, who was determined to weaken the powerful position that the *Reino* (meaning both the *Cortes* and the cities) had acquired, felt able to dispense with the *Cortes* entirely or with the need for its consent for taxation.[62]

One crucial aspect of the way the *Cortes* functioned was that the powers provided to the *procuradores* (deputies) by their cities were limited, sometimes explicitly through the issuance of special instructions and oaths of obedience. Consequently, monarchs went to extraordinary lengths to placate, persuade, favor, bribe, and influence first the *procuradores* (deputies) and then the urban *regidores* to accept the tax agreements (here, the *corregidores* played a crucial role in order to talk the *regidores* into approving the *Cortes* resolutions). All this contradicts the image of a servile and pliable *Cortes*.[63] Interestingly, the most prominent political writers of the sixteenth and seventeenth centuries rarely mentioned the role played by the *Cortes* in the political structure of the monarchy, while instead highlighting the different "senates" that served to govern the republic, from town councils to royal courts (*audiencias* and *chancillerías*) and royal councils. In the Castilian constitutional tradition, the realm was comprised of a series of municipal "senates," which constituted the base of the commonwealth. Between the town councils and the court councils existed an entire structure of "senates," perfectly articulated and which constituted the monarchy materially.[64] The *Cortes* was but just another part in this conciliar structure, its model being precisely that of the municipal councils of the realm. Because in Castile the cities constituted the institutional foundation of the body politic, consulting them directly was therefore as acceptable and "constitutional" a procedure as that of summoning the *Cortes*.[65]

Historians have tended to judge the performance of the Castilian *Cortes* according to modern liberal, democratic principles (e.g., it lacked legislative power, its members were not democratically elected, it refused to adopt an openly adversarial position toward the Crown), but the *Cortes* never considered its duty to be the detailed scrutiny of government policies; its main function was to *cooperate* with the monarchy by conceding subsidies.[66] To serve the king was an opportunity to show "fidelity and love." For the good vassal, obedience to a loving lord was a primary duty. If the king sacrificed his own well-being in defense of his vassals, he could expect in return their loving and grateful obedience. This rhetoric of fidelity and love helps explain the repetitious and almost universal expressions of pride in a tradition of family and corporate service to the king voiced by the gentry of the cities and why among the most insistent arguments of the *corregidores* was that their city should not fail in the honor of always being first in the king's service. That did not mean that they complied with the law, but they obeyed the king.[67]

The relationship between *corregidores* and *cabildos* was very similar to the one that existed between the viceroy and the *audiencia*, which, in turn, was, as we have already seen, a reflection of the relation between king and councils.[68] At the end of the sixteenth century, Castillo de Bobadilla expressed this with clarity in his treatise on the figure of the *corregidor* which, through numerous reprints, was to become the standard reference on the subject for almost two centuries. Bobadilla uses the image of the body to explain the type of relationship that exists between the different members of a city council. The *corregidor* forms a mystical body with the *regidores* and, for that reason, Bobadilla maintains, if the *corregidor* does not agree with some of the *regidores*' resolutions, he must not allow it to be written in the *cabildo* minutes that the "the city" adopted this or that resolution, because "the *corregidor* is the head and the *regidores* the members of the body of the city council … and the said *regidores* without the said head … would make up an acephalous body, which is a headless monster."[69] As for the *regidores*, they are, in Bobadilla's opinion, the city, or more precisely, the head of the city, and for that reason they have the same power as a group as do all the people collectively. This makes the office of *regidor* one of great dignity, for which reason the *corregidor*, although he is their superior and the royal majesty resides in him, must treat them with deference.[70]

In order to describe the relationship between *corregidor* and *regidores*, Bobadilla also refers to the example of Rome (a model for him of good political government) and to the same theory on the origins of political society utilized to explain the monarch's power: Although originally the power to command resided in the Roman people, when they transferred all their power and jurisdiction to the emperor they became subordinated to the prince. As a result, the people, and with them the *regidores* who represented them, lost all their power to command.[71] That is why city councils (or "senates of the republic," according to Bobadilla's terminology) exist: to give advice to those who have "the supreme authority," and that is also why the *corregidor* is the only one who can execute the resolutions of the *cabildo*, as he is the only one who possesses "the power and authority to command."[72] This is clearly the same language used to explain the power and authority of the monarch. Its main implication is that the *corregidor* must act in his *cabildo* in the same way as the king does in his palace with his councilors or the viceroy with the *oidores* in the *Acuerdo*: Although power, undivided, resides in the *corregidor*, he, like the king or the viceroy, should not take any resolutions without consulting with the *regidores*. As Bobadilla explains:

> The consideration of whether it is a good idea to reform the old ordinances or create new ones is only up to the corregidor, but the act, manner, form and order of doing it corresponds jointly to the corregidor and regidores, and not to some without the others, since the king, although he has the power, does not make laws alone but with the advice of his wise councillors.[73]

The Spanish monarchy was structured in such a way that any site of power was always a reflection of a higher site (the end of this hierarchy of power being God and His celestial court).[74] Thus, municipal councils and *corregidores* occupied the base of the Spanish monarchy's political hierarchy, while reproducing at the local level the same structure represented at the top by the king and his council and, at the intermediate level, by the viceroy and the *audiencia*.

In the case of Mexico, we have already seen that traditionally it has been thought that the absolute monarchy and the imperial bureaucracy had reduced the cities to the role of mere followers of the dictates of the Crown and its representatives, but in light of the ideas presented above, it can be affirmed convincingly that the *cabildo* of Mexico City in fact fulfilled a role very similar to that of the Castilian cities represented in the *Cortes*. From the start, the political nature of the city of Mexico was assimilated to that of those cities. At its foundation, the Crown awarded Mexico City the title of "metropolis" or "head" of the kingdom of New Spain.[75] This is of great significance, for among the privileges these cities were entitled to was the right to send their deputies to the *Cortes*. In fact, Mexico City never exercised this right, one of the reasons being the distance between Mexico and the peninsula, as the *fiscal* of the Council of the Indies pointed out at the end of the seventeenth century.[76] This does not mean, however, that the Mexican *regidores* or the Crown were not conscious of the position that the Mexican *cabildo* occupied in the monarchy's "constitutional order."

When levying new taxes, the Mexican *cabildo* fulfilled the same role as the cities of Castile that voted in the *Cortes*: The Crown had to ask the city for its consent, without which it could not proceed. On the other hand, and similarly to the Castilian *Cortes*, the predominant political discourse of the Mexican aldermen, in relation to the monarch, was one of cooperation, love, and loyalty. This, nevertheless, did not mean that the *regidores* did not show a high degree of independence and, occasionally, even of obstruction of the king's wishes.

The decisive role of the Mexican *cabildo* in the concession of subsidies can be clearly appreciated in the period extending from 1620 to 1650, when the Crown requested a substantial increase in the fiscal contributions of Mexico City in order to help defray the expenses of the monarchy. So, in October 1628, the viceroy, the marquis of Cerralvo, presented to the Mexican city council a letter from the king that requested that the city contribute 250,000 ducats every year for 15 years for the Union of Arms. This was a plan devised by the count-duke of Olivares, the king's favorite, according to which each kingdom of the monarchy would be responsible for the maintenance of a force of soldiers. A part of this force would be available to go to the support of any part of the monarchy under attack by an enemy. Needless to say, in the case of the New World, the plan would be reduced to no more than another demand for money.[77]

Utilizing the best arguments from the theory of monarchical power, Cerralvo, addressing the *cabildo*, argued that "the pleasure of the prince has the force of law," while at the same time declaring that the benignity of the king was the reason why "what he could order as king he wants to justify to his vassals with reasons." In any case, the viceroy hoped that Mexico City would carry out the king's wishes as soon as possible because as "the realm's head" it was obligated to set an example for the other cities of New Spain.[78] When several weeks later the *cabildo* again met to make a decision, six *regidores* (out of a total of 17) voted for the summoning of the *Cortes* in New Spain, when the representatives of all the cities of the kingdom would decide whether to approve the requested subsidy. To this attempt, the viceroy responded quickly and categorically with the following words:

> [This vote] looks more like a king's decree than like aldermen's votes, since I do not know whether there is anyone who may be unaware that the summoning of cities is exclusively a royal prerogative, and no vassal has the right to vote such a thing in a cabildo, nor even to imagine it. If I, who act as His Majesty in this kingdom, would consider it an excessive thing to summon it without him having expressly ordered it, how can those who judge themselves with the authority to do such a thing dream of it? And what amazes me the most is that the excess is so great that a regidor, in a particular vote, dares to say that, although a cédula of His Majesty forbids it, it should be done. Moreover, I cannot fail to find it extremely irregular

that there being in the cabildo a person holding the staff of His Majesty in his hand in his capacity as corregidor of this city, he did not send the one who said such a thing from this very cabildo to where … he would receive the appropriate punishment.[79]

The *regidores'* proposal for the *Cortes* to be summoned in New Spain was doomed to failure from the beginning, because not even a majority of the *cabildo* had requested it. The viceroy very likely was aware that, insofar as there was no *Cortes* tradition in New Spain, an immediate and categorical answer would be enough to keep the situation under control and eradicate any parliamentary claims, without provoking the *regidores'* opposition.[80] As long as no attempt was made to impose any new contributions without the *cabildo*'s approval, the Mexican *regidores* had no reason for an outright rejection of the new subsidy. This is what happened with the Union of Arms, for just a few days after the viceroy's response the *cabildo*, apparently unanimously, decided to approve the concession of the contribution.[81]

Mexican *regidores*, like their Castilian counterparts, would use all kinds of obstructionist and dilatory practices when the time came to vote new subsidies, at the same time using the opportunity to strengthen their preeminent position or obtain material benefits. In the case of Mexico, there is probably no better example of this in the entire seventeenth century than the protracted and extremely complicated negotiations that took place to create the *armada de Barlovento*. In 1635, facing an increase in attacks from pirates and corsairs, the government in Madrid decided to create a permanent fleet to defend the Caribbean and the coast of the Gulf of Mexico. This naval squadron was to consist of 12 galleons and two smaller vessels and was to be financed by new taxes to be raised in the Mexican viceroyalty. Accordingly, in February 1636, the marquis of Cadereita, the newly appointed viceroy, sent the *cabildo* of Mexico City a letter informing it of the decision to create this fleet. After reminding the city of the care with which the king attended to the "defense of the faith and the punishment of heretics," the "great benignity" with which he treated his vassals, the "honors and rewards that with the utmost generosity" he distributed among them, and how certain he was of the loyalty with which the city had always served its king, the viceroy concluded his letter by ordering the *cabildo* to meet in order to deliberate on the way the city was going to contribute to the financing of the new fleet. He added that besides distributing the rewards and honors he had brought from "the royal hand" he hoped to get greater ones from the king's liberality.[82]

In its response to the viceroy, while recognizing how necessary the squadron was and its obligation to serve the king, the *cabildo* declared it had no doubt that the monarch and the viceroy, in his name, were going to help the city with rewards that would give its residents the strength necessary to serve the king well on such an occasion. After reminding the viceroy that the city was in dire straits because of a long series of extraordinary expenses it had had to face in previous years, the *cabildo* asked the viceroy to specify the amount of money the royal treasury was going to contribute to the creation of the squadron.[83] When the viceroy did so, the *cabildo* responded by enumerating a long list of "concessions" it expected to extract from the monarch in return for their approval of the subsidy. The most important one was, no doubt, the request to allow again trade with Peru, something that the Seville merchant guild strongly opposed. In addition, the city also requested, among many other petitions, that the post of *corregidor* be eliminated (offering to pay a certain amount of money for it); that the territory under its jurisdiction be increased; that the city of Mexico be awarded the title of "lordship"; that Creoles were appointed by the viceroy to the posts of *alcaldes mayores* and *corregidores*; that the *encomiendas* be given for life or, at least, extended for two more lifetimes; that the inhabitants of New Spain be rewarded with half of the positions of *oidores*, *alcaldes*, and *fiscales* for the *audiencias* of New Spain and Peru; that the number of *familiares* of the Inquisition in Mexico City be increased to 100; and that the administration of the new subsidy with which the *armada de Barlovento* was going to be financed should be given to the city. In turn, the city, whose residents had always proved to be "such loyal, loving, and obedient vassals," committed itself to contribute a subsidy of 200,000 pesos a year, provided that these rewards were granted.[84]

Over the next six months, a long series of proposals and counterproposals were exchanged between the viceroy and the *regidores*. Finally, after the viceroy had accepted most of the conditions imposed by the city, the *regidores* signed the deed that granted the 200,000 pesos.[85] In any case, this did not mean the end of the give and take between viceroy and *regidores*, as the agreement had to be confirmed by the monarch. The city councilors, growing impatient, threatened to suspend the collection of the subsidy because the viceroy had not respected some of the terms of the agreement and, as time went by, the confirmation of the contract by the monarch did not arrive. When the royal confirmation at last arrived, the *regidores* were very disappointed, as the king had ignored many of the concessions requested (for example, the legalization of trade between Mexico and Peru).[86] As a result, more negotiations between the *regidores* and the viceroy followed, in which the former tried to convince the latter to support their claims, while the viceroy negotiated with the *cabildo* the best means to obtain the money for the subsidy. The final outcome was clearly negative for the claims of the city. A few years later, in 1643, the city was forced to renounce one of the most important concessions it had gotten from the Crown — the administration of the subsidy by the *cabildo* itself — because municipal finances were bankrupt (the Mexican merchant guild subsequently would take over its administration).[87]

The long and protracted negotiations for the concession of the *armada de Barlovento* subsidy illustrate very well where the real power of the Mexican *cabildo* resided. Although this occasion was an unmatchable opportunity for the seventeenth-century Creole oligarchy of New Spain to assert their economic interests and their social and political preeminence, the power derived from their capacity to sign contracts with the Crown (like the one subscribed at the end of 1636) was not political but administrative, as it gave them the faculty to administer a very significant part of New Spain's income.[88] This explains the lack of success of the Mexican *cabildo* when negotiating more general concessions, such as the legalization of trade between Mexico and Peru or the extension of the *encomiendas*.

As has been shown, in these negotiations the viceroy played a fundamental role. If, in the Castilian cities with representation in the *Cortes*, the *corregidor* was the one charged with the mission of convincing the *regidores*, often after arduous negotiations, to vote the new subsidies, in Mexico a "political sliding" took place, as here it was the viceroy who always negotiated the new subsidies and taxes with the city councilors, while the *corregidor* moved into the background or even identified himself with the position of the *regidores* (recall the angry remarks of the marquis of Cerralvo concerning the "invisibility" of the *corregidor* of Mexico City when the time came to defend the Crown's interests). It was almost inevitable that the viceroy would try to exert his influence on the *cabildo*, in a way becoming the *de facto corregidor* of Mexico City and pushing the official *corregidor* into the background. The count of Salvatierra would make this explicit in an account he wrote in 1645 on the state of New Spain. After reporting the sorry state in which he had found the municipal finances and explaining all the measures he had taken to straighten up the city government, he concluded: "I shall very willingly take care of the republic as *corregidor* while protecting it as viceroy."[89]

This is something that does not seem to have escaped the perception of the *regidores* themselves. When the *cabildo*, as we saw, proposed to the king to eliminate the post of *corregidor* in exchange for a certain amount of money to be used in the creation of the *armada de Barlovento*, it justified its proposal with the argument that such an office was not necessary in a place where there was an *audiencia* with four *alcaldes de corte* and a *cabildo* with two *alcaldes ordinarios*, plus a viceroy who oversaw everything. To strengthen its argument, the city council also contended that Lima, the other viceregal capital, had no *corregidor*, being governed by *alcaldes ordinarios*. The city's arguments seemed to convince the Crown, as it accepted the proposal immediately, on condition that the *regidores* would not be elected *alcaldes ordinarios*.[90] With this decision, the monarch was implicitly acknowledging that a "viceroy–*corregidor*" was more than enough to convey his wishes and commands to the Mexican *cabildo*. Alvarado Morales has argued that with the abolition of the office of *corregidor* of Mexico City, the city councilors were seeking to consolidate an autonomous Creole power *vis-à-vis* the Crown. This, however, seems to contradict his further argument that the ultimate reason for the subsequent insistence of the Crown on getting rid of the post was to weaken the *cabildo* politically and economically.[91] Knowing that a *corregidor* was not really necessary, the Crown was above all interested in collecting the money offered by the city. This explains why the Crown and four successive viceroys insisted, between 1636 and 1650, on eliminating the post of *corregidor* even when the city council ran into trouble trying to get the resources necessary to pay for the 200,000 pesos it had offered for its abolition.[92]

The constant interference and the effective control often exerted by the viceroys on Mexico City's *cabildo* in the course of the seventeenth century appear to contradict the supposed "state crisis" that took place in that century and was part of Spain's unstoppable process of decline. According to this argument, starting in the late sixteenth century, a chronic degeneration of effective state power occurred, as well as a liquidation of the capital of royal authority by the end of the century. This was apparent especially in the relations of the Crown with its own bureaucracy: Royal policy had to be filtered through what the councils and the officials saw as their own interests, and the king himself failed to impose his will on his servants. The control of the Crown over the apparatus of the state was also weakened by the increasing privatization of the administration with the spread of venality and the patrimonialization of office holding. The hold of the central agencies of the Crown on the government of the country became fragmented and diffused across a multitude of local seigniorial and municipal authorities. In this regard, the disappearance of the *Cortes* after 1664 is seen not as part of a victory of the centralizing, absolutist monarchy over the traditional dualism of king and kingdom, but as one aspect of a general process of "devolution" or decentralization of the machinery of consent to each individual city with representation in the *Cortes*. In addition, the transformation of municipal offices into hereditary brought about as a consequence the transformation of the municipal ruling bodies into increasingly closed and mutually supportive oligarchies. The *corregidores*, the vital points of contact between the municipalities and Madrid, increasingly appear less as agents of the Crown than as allies of the *regidores*. The entire chain of authority in Castile, so the argument goes, was being ruptured from top to bottom. This fragmentation of central authority was paralleled by a process described by some historians with the term "refeudalization." Crown and aristocracy were enmeshed in a web of mutual dependence. The aristocracy, whose rents were shrinking, needed, for instance, the lucrative viceregal government offices, while the Crown needed the prestige of the *grandees* in the great state and military offices and their influence and followers in local government.[93]

In the case of New Spain, it has been assumed that a similar breakdown of the centralized ruling institutions took place in the seventeenth century. In this connection, it has been possible to argue that the hacienda owners "progressively became masters, legislators, judges, and magistrates over the hacienda residents," to the detriment of the power of the Crown.[94] It has also been contended that between the late seventeenth and the mid-eighteenth centuries "an age of royal impotence" was caused by the sale of many positions in the American *audiencias*, something that illustrates an increase in the weakness of the Crown.[95] This weakness at the center, in turn, caused an increase in the autonomy of the Spanish colonies in America. Between 1650 and 1750, it has been claimed, Spanish America experienced a greater degree of autonomous growth and freedom from metropolitan control. Colonial revenue was employed in colonial administration and defense rather than being sent to the mother country.[96]

This seems to be hardly an accurate assessment, especially if we keep in mind that judicial powers firmly remained in the hands of the king's judges.[97] Furthermore, for the entire seventeenth century only a few posts of *oidor* were sold. It happened at the very end of the century and, in the case of New Spain at least, met a determined resistance from both viceroys and *oidores*, so much so that, on one occasion, they denied the beneficiary the possession of his office, while at the same time they wrote the king to inform him of the negative effects that such a move would bring about.[98] On the other hand, Jonathan Israel has argued that the bulk of Mexico's public revenues continued to be shipped to Spain, the Philippines, and the Caribbean garrisons and that Mexico and Peru, like the Spanish dependencies in Europe, were the victims of "a vigorous, sustained and massive" fiscal drive that coincided with the reign of Philip IV (1621–1665).[99] Finally, the idea of a breakdown of royal authority in the seventeenth century seems difficult to reconcile with the situation of the *cabildo* of Mexico City in the last decades of the century, when its power and prestige seemed to be in its nadir, so much so that in 1693 the viceroy wrote to the king to inform him that, because the Mexican *cabildo* had only three *regidores* and it had been impossible to find anybody who wanted to buy or rent a post in the municipal council, he had appointed eight *regidores* who would become members of the city council without having to buy their offices. Apparently, the Creole population no longer found these posts attractive, which is not surprising given the fact that between 1668 and 1670 half of the *regidores* were imprisoned, accused of defrauding the Royal Treasury, or that, since 1652, one *oidor*, appointed by the viceroy, had been in charge of supervising municipal revenues.[100] Seen from the perspective of the Mexican *cabildo*, then, it does not appear that royal authority had diminished in any significant way by the end of the seventeenth century.

In reality, the phenomenon that took place in the Spanish monarchy in the seventeenth century was not the struggle of the forces of centralism against those of decentralization, but a struggle between the monarch's authority and the power of the realm, between the "constitutionalists," who argued that the power of the commonwealth resided both in the king and in the realm (the latter understood as the cities gathered in the *Cortes*), and the "pro-absolutists," who contended that the sovereignty of the king was absolute and that the *Cortes* only possessed the power to advise the monarch, not to overrule him.[101] In this struggle, relations between the monarchy and the cities played a decisive role, but these relations should not be seen in the context of the history of the opposition between central-ization and the construction of the "modern state," on the one hand, and the autonomous urban powers, on the other. What really preoccupied the urban oligarchies was to secure and reproduce their municipal power rather than to fight for their supposed autonomy. In addition, by identify-ing the absolute monarchy as the decisive factor in the construction of the "modern state," we are ascribing to the monarch a statist program that seems to be most alien to his political conceptions.

From its origins, the "absolute monarchy" was never a centralized sys-tem of government with a bureaucracy that faithfully followed the king's orders. Political power was dispersed into an array of relatively autono-mous centers, whose unity was maintained, more in a symbolic than in an effective way, by reference to a single "head." This dispersion corresponded to the dispersion and relative autonomy of the vital functions and organs of the human body, which, as we have seen, served as the model for social and political organization. This vision made impossible the existence of a completely centralized political government — a society in which all power was concentrated in the sovereign would be as monstrous as a body that consisted only of a head. The function of the head of the body politic (that is, the king) was not, therefore, to destroy the autonomy of each of its members but to represent, on the one hand, the unity of the body politic and, on the other, to maintain harmony among all its members. To accom-plish this, the head was to guarantee the rights and privileges of every member of the body politic. This is the paradox, from the modern stand-point, of the political system that existed before the modern state: "Abso-lute" monarchical power was compatible with the existence of other powers endowed with ample autonomy, without the center demanding the elimination of the peripheral powers.[102] In relation to this, it should be noted that "centralization," a term that belongs to the nineteenth and twentieth centuries, implies a complete bureaucratic hierarchy, a fully organized system of government with an unbroken chain of command; however, the "absolutist" hierarchy was incomplete at the lower end, and monarchic authority at the local level continued to be problematic. At the local level, the Crown was able to exercise effective control only extraordi-narily and erratically (the *corregidores* were an example of this in Spanish America, as they were often less than reliable instruments of royal author-ity). This was the paradox, so common of absolute monarchy everywhere in Europe, of "absolute authority and limited power" or, in the words of Jaime Vicens Vives, "the maximum concentration of authority at the sum-mit and the minimum irradiation of that power downward," which in Castilian terms would translate as "absolute obedience and limited com-pliance."[103]

As a fundamental member of the body politic, the *cabildo* of Mexico City possessed a power that it did not hesitate to exert whenever the opportunity arose. This opportunity presented itself in the seventeenth century because of the Crown's financial hardships. In the give and take that took place between viceroys and *regidores*, it seemed, for a moment, that the latter were going to have the last word, but the abandonment of an active European imperial policy, especially after the death of Philip IV in 1665, greatly reduced the financial needs of the Crown and, with it, the fiscal pressure on its subjects. This would explain the absence of tension or significant clashes between the viceroys and the Mexican city council in the last third of the century. In any case, this does not justify the idea that the monarch's authority had evaporated; it simply remained as limited at the local level as it had been one century before.

3

In the Service of
Two Majesties

On January 12, 1624, after a long and protracted confrontation between the viceroy of New Spain, the marquis of Gelves, and the archbishop of Mexico, Juan Pérez de la Serna, the *audiencia* issued an unprecedented writ ordering the archbishop's expulsion from the kingdom of New Spain. That same day, Pérez de la Serna was placed in a carriage and escorted by troops to Veracruz, but, defying the viceroy's orders, the cortege stopped at San Juan de Teotihuacán, a mere 20 miles or so from Mexico City. On the morning of January 14, Lorenzo de Terrones, *alcalde del crimen* of the *audiencia* of Mexico, who was in Teotihuacán, received orders from the viceroy to force the archbishop to continue his journey to Veracruz. In order to execute the viceroy's orders, the magistrate, accompanied by the chief constable of the *audiencia*, a notary, and several soldiers, went to the convent of San Francisco where he had been informed he would be able to find the prelate. That morning, Pérez de la Serna had declared that because he had no intention of leaving Teotihuacán, he would have to be dragged out of town. The *alcalde* and his party found the archbishop in the church of the convent. He was standing by the high altar, "covered with a cape embroidered in gold and with the monstrance of the Holy Sacrament uncovered." On seeing them, the archbishop took one Host in his hands and showed it to the newcomers. Faced with this gesture, the *alcalde* begged the archbishop not to consume the consecrated Host. The prelate answered that he would not, but when the *alcalde* ordered the soldiers to take the archbishop to the carriage that was awaiting him, he again took the Host in his hands, forcing the soldiers to stop dead. According to the account of the notary, the archbishop then sat on a chair that was next to the altar "and with great

79

sorrow and shedding tears, he begged everyone to consider the state this affair had reached, pondering in Latin and Romance how His Excellency the said viceroy, the marquis of Gelves, without justification, had forced the *oidores* to issue the writ that banned him from the kingdom. And among other reasons, he asserted that the said marquis of Gelves was the greatest tyrant in the world." Faced with the archbishop's determination to utilize the Sacred Host as weapon and shield to prevent his deportation, the *alcalde* had no alternative other than to send the notary back to the capital to inform the viceroy of what had happened. The following day, a riot would break out in Mexico City that would end with the overthrow of the viceroy, an occurrence, likewise, without precedent in the history of New Spain.[1]

The Teotihuacán incident probably sums up better than any other the relations between the secular and ecclesiastical powers in seventeenth-century Mexico, relations that can be defined as stormy at the least, because the conflicts and clashes at the highest level between viceroys and prelates were constant and unabated. It is necessary, therefore, to ask how this situation came about, especially because it so much contradicts the usual image of the Church as a loyal instrument of the colonial state. Although the role of the Church is essential for understanding the system of rule established in America by the Spanish monarchy, we do not know much about it, as the few historians who have dealt with this subject have focused their attention on the crisis created in the colonial Church by the Bourbon reforms of the second half of the eighteenth century.[2] But, if we are to comprehend the nature of the relationship between the Church and civil power (more specifically, the viceroys), we first of all need to examine how contemporaries viewed the role of the Church in the commonwealth and analyze the political–religious discourse that endowed it with power and identity. By doing so, we will be able not only to get a better grasp of the place of the Church in colonial society but also to help explain the high level of antagonism and opposition between civil and religious power. I concentrate my study on the upper echelons of the ecclesiastical hierarchy (archbishops and bishops) and on the inquisitors, as they were the ones who could most effectively challenge and question viceregal authority, although these same tensions were reproduced at the local level between priests and civil magistrates.

A Tale of Two Knives

The greatest difficulty found in studying the Church and its relations with colonial power is perhaps the traditional tendency to reduce these relations to the binary opposition of Church and State. In addition, it is common to argue that the Spanish king was in a very real sense the secular head of the Church in colonial Spanish America, the Church having simply become an administrative branch of royal government.[3] A more elaborate argument maintains that the Church constituted an ideological state apparatus and that the fundamental relationship between the Church and the state was characterized by a sharing of the functions of hegemony (consent) and domination (coercion), although the state always retained the upper hand.[4] Against these arguments, however, it could be argued that had the Church been subject to the Crown's power so thoroughly, the level of conflict and antagonism between Church and secular authorities would have never been so high and widespread. As an example, suffice it to say that had some careless inhabitant of New Spain maintained the aforementioned affirmation that the monarch was the effective head of the American Church, he or she would have in all likelihood ended up before the Inquisition, accused of heresy.[5] Understanding the colonial power structure requires, therefore, that we avoid easy reductionisms. We need to complicate our image of the colonial ruling elite, as neither was colonial power, as has already been argued, organized along "statist" principles, nor did the Church constitute a monolithic structure, as it was profoundly divided, especially in Mexico, by a prolonged conflict between the secular and the regular clergy, which made it very difficult to impose, in any effective way, the dictates of the ecclesiastical hierarchy.[6]

The fact that, in the sixteenth and seventeenth centuries (especially before the system created by the Peace of Westphalia), the global political order was still conceived of in terms of "Christendom" rather than in terms of independent "states" and that the universalism of the "imperial idea" was actively present in the Spanish monarchy as a "catholic (universal) monarchy" will help us understand that in seventeenth-century New Spain the relation between the "Church" and the "colonial state" cannot be conceived of as simply a relation of subordination of the Church to the power of the "state." This is not to deny that the monarchs always tried to exert the greatest possible control over the clergy of their kingdoms, but to emphasize that the relations between civil power and spiritual authority took place in a context in which canon law enjoyed great preeminence (still far from the statist concept of the law, which conceives the state as the only true sovereign entity). These relations, therefore, could only be understood as relations between the "civil power" and the "spiritual power." While in the international order these two powers were represented by the figures of the monarch and the pope, in the context of New Spain they were embodied in the figures of the archbishop (and the bishops) and the viceroy. The fundamental implication of this would be that, by preventing the establishment of fully secular principles of government, this dual constitution of power represented an insurmountable obstacle in the creation of a political organization of a state nature.[7]

The political writers of the period resorted to a series of images to represent this intrinsic dual nature of power. Castillo de Bobadilla, who was, as we have seen, an author of great influence, described it in the following manner:

> Two great luminaries were created by God in the firmament ... *the sun*, which is the greater one, to illuminate by day, and *the moon*, which is the lesser one, to shine at night. And in the same way, as firmament of the universal Church, He created these two great luminaries, which are two dignities, one the *pontifical authority*, which is the greater, to preside over the day's things, which are the spiritual ones, and the other the *royal power*, which is the lesser, to preside over the night's, which are the temporal ones. And these two powers are also signified by those *two knives* which, according to Saint Luke, were shown to Christ, Our Lord, by the disciples, one meaning the temporal and the other the spiritual power.[8]

Francisco Ugarte, a seventeenth-century author, explained how this dual power worked:

> With these two powers God rules the world because in the same way as the kings preside over worldly things, the high priest does over the godly ones. And, in the same way as the punishment of the body corresponds to kings, the punishment of the spirit belongs to the Church, for which reason ... the king brings the sword to punish the evil and defend the good, and the pontiff, the keys to close the doors of the kingdom of Heaven on the excommunicated and to open them up to the penitents. ...And when the Church is unable to correct the infidels and those who oppose it or persecute it, Saint Isidore says that Christian kings and princes have the obligation to defend it and protect it and to persecute and humble those who are disobedient and show insolence and disrespect toward the Church.[9]

Power, therefore, is conceived of in a dual way and expressed in the form of jurisdictions, but this duality has nothing to do with the modern idea of the separation of Church and state, as the ideal was a close cooperation of both powers in the government of the republic, each one within its own sphere or "jurisdiction," the temporal or secular, whose head was the monarch, and the spiritual or ecclesiastical, whose ultimate authority resided with the pope. The concept of jurisdiction is crucial to understanding relations between the members of the ruling elite because it implies the political–juridical autonomy of the different social bodies. In the juridical and political language of the time, power is always designed and understood as "jurisdiction," and this is so because the activity of the authorities is mainly oriented toward the resolution of conflicts among different spheres of interest, conflicts that the authorities solve "doing justice."[10]

On the other hand, according to the doctrine of the "two knives" or the two powers, Church and clerics were exempt from the prince's jurisdiction, as the prince lacked spiritual power and could not impose temporal power over non-temporal institutions. Although some writers maintained that this exemption originated in divine law, thereby being irrevocable by any human power (including the pope), the predominant view in the seventeenth century was that this exemption had its origin in human law, for which reason it could be diminished or altered. In any event, the Church was governed by its own set of rules and regulations — known as canon law — which were completely independent from the temporal laws of the realm. This allowed a very small margin of influence of the secular powers over Church law. Though never attempting to suppress Church autonomy, royal power would try to limit it through different means (by demanding, for instance, the royal approval of all papal decrees, by asserting the subjects' right to appeal to the king the sentences of the ecclesiastical courts, or by imposing royal patronage). While this regalism served to recognize symbolically the preeminence of the Crown as head of the body politic, at the less apparent but not less effective jurisdictional level (that is, in the everyday practice of power), Church autonomy was still of enormous significance in the seventeenth century.[11]

While all political writers shared the view that all power, whether spiritual or temporal, came from God, opinions were divided as to how God transmitted His power to men. In the seventeenth century, a majority of Spanish authors sustained that God's power was transmitted through a single person — the pope. Even so influential a lay author as Castillo de Bobadilla admits this. Speaking of the dual nature of power, he notes that "it is very controversial whether both these knives reside in the Church and the Roman pontiff and in which way." In principle, it seems clear that the "material knife" (that is, the temporal jurisdiction) does not belong to the Church, as "these two powers are different." Moreover, if the pope occupies Christ's place on earth, it appears to be evident that he must only take care of spiritual affairs. In addition, Bobadilla quotes different authors who contend that royal power comes from the people, as they transferred it to the monarch, for which reason it does not seem that the pope possesses this kind of power. All these opinions notwithstanding, Bobadilla asserts that the contrary opinion — temporal power also resides in the pope and from him it is transmitted to the monarchs — it is the "surest and most followed" opinion (though he recognizes that, regarding this matter, not even the Church has a definite view). Bobadilla, nevertheless, qualifies his assertion by arguing that, even if the pope has "the two powers and the two knives," temporal power resides in the pope only "potentially but not in actuality" (*en hábito y potencia y no en acto*), because the exercise of this power is transferred to the monarchs by the pope.[12] Other authors, however, such as the influential Jesuit Francisco Suárez, while arguing that the pope's jurisdiction was superior to that of temporal rulers, would outrightly dismiss the notion that the pope had the temporal jurisdiction *in habitu*, being able to reclaim it from rulers or exercise it by himself whenever he deemed it pertinent. For Suárez, this was simply nonsense, something impossible to prove and contrary to reason and experience.[13]

This assertion of the superiority of the pope's power did not prevent the Spanish monarchs from doing everything possible to limit papal intrusions into their kingdoms. This would be the cause of numerous conflicts with the Holy See.[14] The theoretical supremacy of the pope, in reality, played a crucial role in the conceptualization of the Spanish monarchy as a catholic and universal monarchy. By the seventeenth century, after all the debates and controversies of the sixteenth century, the idea was already perfectly crystalized that the Spanish Crown owned its American possessions legally through a papal donation and on the condition that it had to undertake responsibility for the propagation of the Catholic faith.[15] This, in addition, had a very important consequence for the development of royal power in America. Because the pope donated the American territories to the Spanish monarchs in exchange for the foundation and maintenance of the churches of those territories (something the papacy could not undertake for lack of resources), the Spanish monarch became the great patron of the American Church. This ecclesiastical patronage, however, was not something new. Its ideology went back to the *Reconquista*, having been incorporated into *Las Siete Partidas*, where Church patronage appeared as a right and an honor that corresponded to the Spanish monarchs for having conquered so many lands that had belonged to the Moors.[16] The model followed in America, however, was the system of royal patronage created after the conquest of Granada (the papal bulls of 1486 and 1493 had awarded the monarchs the right of presentation to benefices of all the churches of the kingdom of Granada and the Canary Islands).[17] The king's ecclesiastical patronage was defined by early modern writers as an honorific, onerous, and useful right. The main honor was the right of presentation of the Church servants; its greater responsibility, the obligation to defend the Church and maintain its servants; and its main utility, the income that the churches gave to their patron (in the way, for example, of a share of the tithes). This right of patronage was inalienable and, though it was confirmed by numerous apostolic titles, these titles were accessory, for which reason only the kingdom and its representatives — the kingdom in Cortes — could exonerate the monarch from this patronage.[18]

After the conquest of America, the *Patronato Real* (as the ecclesiastical patronage of the Spanish monarchs was known) would be transplanted to the new territories being established by the papal bulls of 1501 (which donated the tithes of the Indies to the kings of Castile in exchange for their commitment to support and maintain the churches and the clergy) and of 1508 (which granted to the monarchs the patronage of all churches, as well as the presentation to all benefices).[19] This right to patronage, moreover, would be interpreted by the Crown in an extensive way, having already become common in the seventeenth century the idea that the popes, despite being the ones who had ceded the American territories to the Spanish monarchs, governed the American Church through the mediation of the latter, thus escaping their direct control.

Solórzano, for whom the *Patronato* was one of "the jewels that shines the most in the diadem of the Spanish monarchy," was the one who best expressed this evolution in favor of royal interests. As he made clear, the protection of churches and especially cathedrals belonged, by right, to all "absolute princes of Christendom," as they were the sole owners of the soil on which the churches of their dominions were founded and built. That is to say, for Solórzano, the *Patronato* had ceased to be a papal concession to become the monarch's right. Furthermore, pointed out Solórzano, in those lands taken from the infidels, the right to patronage likewise belonged to the monarchs who conquered them, without the need of a papal privilege. But, in case any further doubts lingered regarding the American *Patronato*, the Catholic Kings had also requested from the pope the concession of the *Patronato* privilege, in the same way as it had been granted to them after the conquest of Granada. Thus, the Spanish monarchs had become "vicars of the Roman pontiff" and "apostolic delegates in the Indies," with authority over not only temporal but spiritual matters as well.[20] Moreover, Solórzano asserted that this *Patronato Real* right had been incorporated into the Crown, becoming a *regalía* (royal privilege), for which reason not even the sovereign could alienate it or renounce it. Thus, because it was a patrimonial asset of the Crown, those conflicts raised in relation with the *Patronato* had to be resolved by the secular, not ecclesiastical, courts.[21] Of course, this regalist view of the *Patronato Real*, according to which the popes had "delegated" (meaning "renounced") their powers of government over the Indies in favor of the Spanish monarchs, was never accepted by the pontiffs, and the price Solórzano paid for advancing it was his inclusion in the Roman Index.[22]

The regalist view is perfectly summarized in a dispute that took place in Mexico in 1665 that was the result of the claims of the bishop of Oaxaca that, during the Mass and after praying for the pope, prayers should be said first for the prelate and then for the monarch, as the new Roman ritual established and was done in the churches of Spain. To this, the *fiscal* of the *audiencia* responded with an attack on the attempt to place a bishop before the monarch, as that prelate was, after all, the king's vassal and beneficiary, the king being, "the universal head and the only one that must be recognized by all in temporal matters." The Crown attorney concluded that, though the new ritual established that, after the pope, the bishop should be mentioned before the king, it would be highly problematic to change "the ancient custom of mentioning ... the kings before the bishops," especially "in such distant lands ... where it is most necessary to keep the greatness and majesty of the king's name." The fact that in the Indies prayers for the monarch were said before praying for the bishop was also, in the opinion of the *fiscal*, a matter of gratitude, which was acknowledged by all the ecclesiastics for the largesse shown by the monarch in his patronage of the churches. Furthermore, contended the *fiscal*, according to papal bulls "the kings were regarded, in ecclesiastical matters, as the vicars and legates of the apostolic see, [and these were] dignities that surpassed that of prelate."[23]

No doubt, the most important prerogative of the *Patronato* was the presentation of bishops. It was the prerogative of the monarchs "to elect and present the prelates and all the prebends, benefices, and ministers of the churches ... down to the lowest office of sacristan." Yet, the "collation and canonical institution" of the prelates (that is, their confirmation) was reserved to the popes, whereas that of the prebendaries, beneficiaries, and other Church officials was left to the prelate of each diocese.[24] Here, the dual nature of episcopal authority can be clearly appreciated: While the king selected the bishops and "presented" them to the pope, it was the pontiff who appointed them. This prerogative of selecting the bishops has traditionally been interpreted as the best proof of the tight control exercised by the Crown over the American Church, converting the Church, in this way, into a vast and loyal bureaucracy.[25] Although it is true that the presentation of bishops can be seen as an attempt by the Crown to control the clergy, the problem with seeing the Church as part of the royal bureaucracy or with regarding the king as the head of the American Church is that it ignores the dual notion of power on which the Spanish commonwealth was founded. Although the Crown would always try to assert its right of ecclesiastical patronage, at the same time it would never attempt to dispossess the clergy of its autonomy.[26]

All this endowed the highest representatives of ecclesiastical power with a great deal of independence. Whereas in the peninsula this independence was in many respects lessened by the presence of the monarch, in New Spain this check did not exist, and the bishops, though considering themselves loyal vassals of the king, also saw themselves as the equals of the viceroys. In this regard, the system of ecclesiastical patronage may be seen as one of the mechanisms established by the Crown to secure the obedience and loyalty of the clergy, particularly the bishops, of whom it does not seem that the Crown was totally sure that they would always execute the king's orders with exact fidelity. So it was expressed by the count-duke of Olivares in a memorial that he presented to Philip IV in 1624, in which he declared that the ecclesiastics should be treated with cunning and artifice, making sure they were "content and pleased, since they are people who have and admit so much dependence on the Sovereign Pontiffs, even in temporal matters ... so that they will not oppose any negotiations undertaken with the Sovereign Pontiffs."[27] So it was also believed by Solórzano when he stated that, "It is of the utmost importance that the kings possess this right of presentation in the cathedrals of their kingdoms, and especially in the remote regions of the Indies, so that they will know the prelates and the prelates will be more obligated to them."[28]

In order to comprehend the relationship between the viceroys and the ecclesiastical hierarchy, it is indispensable to examine how contemporaries imagined the figure of the bishop (the archbishop was, in practice, just a *primus inter pares*) and what the ultimate origin of his authority was. The eminent role of bishops had been pointed out by Francisco Suárez when discussing whether secular princes had any power to rule the Church. While acknowledging that kings were God's vicars, he observed this was only in regard to temporal matters, because in the spiritual realm, God's vicars were the bishops (and the pope). In that sense, the "Catholic truth" was that kings had no spiritual power whatsoever over the Church, which meant that the king's power could not be above that of the bishops.[29] For his part, Pedro de Reina Maldonado, a canon from the cathedral of Trujillo, Peru, and the author of a treatise on the figure of the bishop, describes the prelate in terms very similar to those used to depict a viceroy. The perfect prelate must be characterized by his prudence, as this is a virtue peculiar to princes and rulers. He must seek advice, because he did not acquire the "science of government" by just becoming a bishop. Moreover, because "all those who rule by themselves" and "whose office is to be heads" cannot do everything, they need to select some "companions" to help them with the many different matters of government. He also needs to grant public audiences in order to administer justice and provide in the affairs of government. In that regard, justice and clemency are the two virtues that are the most important for a bishop to be able to keep his rule, because they cause fear and love in his subjects. He must strive to maintain his reputation and credit, which will give him authority, something so necessary for those who occupy public posts and deal with matters of government. Finally, in matters of favors and rewards, he must be extremely liberal.[30] This kind of language and the constant use of words such as "government," "rule," or "subjects" emphasized the political aspects of the episcopal office and contributed to place bishops at the same level as viceroys and *audiencia* presidents.

In a work published around the middle of the seventeenth century, Gaspar de Villarroel, bishop first of Santiago de Chile and later of Arequipa, also analyzed in detail the figure of the bishop. Villarroel presented the bishop as a personage of great power, as a "prince of the Church," yet he was quick to make clear that this ecclesiastical primacy had to be understood as not being detrimental to royal jurisdiction. As a prince, the bishop possessed the extraordinary power, peculiar to kings and sovereign princes, of being able to dispense "graciously" the penalties imposed by his own sentences. Besides, he could excommunicate kings, if they did not have a papal privilege excluding them from such a penalty.[31] To emphasize the greatness of the post of bishop, Villarroel utilized the same concept used to describe the figure of the viceroy, declaring that the bishops formed part of their prince's body. Bishops, moreover, could not be summoned to appear before any judges except before the pope himself. That is why, observed Villarroel, the monarch could only summon the bishops to ask them for advice.[32] Villarroel presented the bishop as a figure whose power and preeminence were such that he could be compared to kings and popes (in fact, noted Villarroel, the election of the pope corresponded to the bishops but, because of the inconvenience of congregating so many bishops who resided far away from Rome, this privilege had been transferred to the College of Cardinals).[33] Villarroel, however, recognized that because the Church was a monarchy, "it would be reduced to a confused aristocracy" if it were governed only by the bishops without having a ruling head.[34] Aware of the great power that this language bestowed upon bishops, Villarroel deemed it necessary for these prelates to bridle their own power, yet he did not hesitate to assert that bishops had the same power in their dioceses as the pope in the universal Church.[35]

As in the case of kings, Villarroel wrote, one must kneel in front of a bishop, the residence of the bishop is also called a palace, and the first entry of the bishop into his diocese is done "in the manner of a triumph and can compete with the king's entry."[36] Thus, in the entries of the archbishops of Mexico, just as in the viceregal entries, a triumphal arch in which the archbishop was usually depicted as a god or hero of Antiquity was erected in front of the cathedral. Although this may seem surprising at first, it was not so for contemporaries, as bishops were seen as "governors" of their dioceses and the faithful as their "subjects" (after all, the pope was the "monarch" of the Church). Understood in this way, it was almost natural that the same visual rhetoric was used with archbishops as with viceroys. As governors, both had to look at themselves in the mirror of classical heroes — the model for good rulers. For example, the anonymous author of the description of the arch erected in Mexico City in 1653 to welcome the new archbishop used the image of Apollo to depict him and declared that the mission of a prelate had to be "to rule his subjects in such a way that, abandoning the dangerous path of sin, they shall follow the true and certain [path] of virtue."[37] Similarly, the two authors of the arch built in 1670 to receive archbishop Enríquez de Rivera depicted him as the Greek god Pan and pointed out that the symbols of a prelate, prince, and governor were the miter, the staff, and the pallium, which signified his authority, power, and jurisdiction, respectively.[38]

Like the viceregal arches, the archepiscopal arch may be viewed as a "mirror of prelates" in which the virtues that must characterize a good prince of the Church were represented. The rhetoric of the archepiscopal arches is practically the same as that used in the viceregal arch. The archbishop as prince must be guided in his government by the virtues of wisdom, piety, and liberality. As judge, he must be just; as father, he must be clement. If he rules virtuously, this exerts a positive influence on his subjects, something that contributes to keeping them at peace. This must be the ultimate goal of his rule, as this is what brings happiness to the commonwealth (here an explicit reference is usually made to how peace and tranquility are achieved whenever the secular and ecclesiastical princes join hands to rule in harmony). Perhaps the only discernible difference from the language of the viceregal arch is that the archbishop, in addition, is represented as shepherd and husband. As shepherd, he protects his sheep with love, illuminating them with his teachings (that is why the affable side of a prelate is always highlighted, because he must rule his subjects with gentleness as is appropriate to a member of the Church); as husband, the archbishop was imagined as married to his church (bishops were appointed for life), and, like husband and wife, only death could separate him from his church.[39]

As governors of their dioceses, archbishops and bishops are likewise conceived of in a very similar way to that of the viceroy. The bishop forms a body with the ecclesiastical or cathedral chapter, of which he is the head, whereas the chapter constitutes a "senate" whose main responsibility is the administration of the diocese, especially when the episcopal see is vacant. The canons, in particular, play the role of the bishop's advisors. He is obliged to listen to their opinions, yet he has no obligation to follow them, because the bishop is the one who possesses the power to command and execute (*mero imperio* and *gobierno monárquico*), and his power cannot be communicated to the chapter (this argument clearly conceptualizes the bishop's power along lines that are extremely similar to those used to explain the power of the king himself or of the viceroys). However, without the chapter's consent, the bishop cannot alienate his church's property.[40] The bishop, like the viceroy, surrounds himself with his *familia* (retinue), through which he exercises his authority and patronage. In this regard, Villarroel affirms that no one questions that a bishop must have a great retinue, because "ecclesiastical pomp and greatness" are of much importance in preserving the dignity of the post, and besides "the bishop's house must be a hospital for the needy." But, he castigates those who maintain that the only way to preserve a bishop's authority is by surrounding himself with great pomp and a large entourage. Villaroel also dissents from those authors who contend that a bishop's servants must wear rich and costly vestments as a way to increase their master's authority. Although they are allowed to have a large retinue, bishops, because of the modesty that must characterize them, should not overdo their pomp and display, as "great pomp does not further personal credit," which in a bishop must come from his charitable deeds with the poor. Likewise, the bishop's servants and retainers must dress in a dignified way but without excess because, in the words of Villarroel, "every servant is a portable image of his master."[41] Like a viceroy, a bishop is also a dispenser of favors and rewards, because, in the words of Reina Maldonado, the distribution of offices was peculiar to prelates and princes. If, as we shall see in Chapter 5, viceroys exercised their patronage primarily through the distribution of the posts of *corregidores* and *alcaldes mayores*, in the case of bishops their patronage was manifested through the distribution of benefices and *doctrinas*. The distribution of these posts was informed by the same principles that guided the granting of secular offices by either the king or the viceroys (it should be guided by the laws of distributive justice — that is, they should be used to reward the worthy rather than the members of the bishop's entourage).[42]

The fact that bishops were endowed with so great a power and that the monarch was not the source of this power led the authors who dealt with the subject to examine the question of whether bishops were obligated to obey the monarch. The question of the bishops' fidelity did not escape Solórzano, who, despite his reputation as a regalist writer, begins the chapter in which he discusses the matter by stating that bishops, before taking possession of their bishoprics, are obligated to take "a special oath of staying faithful to the Roman pontiff." Solórzano adds that bishops cannot delegate this oath to anyone; however, in the case of the New World bishops, because of the great difficulties and inconveniences of having to go personally to Rome, they are allowed to take the oath before another bishop.[43] Having made this point clear, Solórzano further on declares that he still has to say "something about another oath whereby bishops are to swear to our lord, the king, that they shall not usurp his jurisdiction and income, let alone his ecclesiastical patronage in the Indies." Clearly, this is not the language of subordination one would expect to find when referring to the royal bureaucracy. In reality, it is a declaration of ecclesiastical autonomy and, in many ways, a confession of the limits imposed on royal authority by that autonomy. What is remarkable here is that whereas it is clearly expressed that bishops owe fidelity to the pope, in the case of the monarch, it is only expected from them not to call the *Patronato* into question. Moreover, it took almost a century for the Crown to be able to impose this oath, when a *cédula* in 1629 established its definitive form.[44] From the above, it seems clear that the monarch could not request an oath of fidelity from the bishops; the only thing available to him was to ensure that he or his representatives keep the *Patronato* under their control. This Solórzano acknowledges when he confesses that prelates cannot be obligated to take this oath because their bishoprics belong to the spiritual sphere, at the same time trying to explain, with all kinds of arguments, that this oath is neither an encroachment upon the bishops' rights nor an attempt to demean ecclesiastical liberty. With it, the king only tries to preserve his prerogatives and rents. In the end, Solórzano brings up his regalism by asserting that, in any event, bishops are obligated to "revere and obey the king because of his superiority in all temporal matters, and thus not only must they take the said oath but also come before him whenever they are notified and summoned."[45]

Villarroel also examines the question of the bishops' fidelity, wondering whether "when they are dressed as bishops they are stripped of their vassalage." The very fact that Villarroel is asking this question is an indication that the doubt still existed in the seventeenth century and that the monarchs could not take for granted the imposition of their authority on the clergy (this question would have never been asked of a viceroy or *oidor* because there was no doubt as to whom they owed their loyalty). In fact, Villarroel begins by asserting that a bishop cannot be the king's vassal because he is completely exempt from royal jurisdiction, both civil and criminal, and without the power to judge and command no vassalage can exist. This was the only possible conclusion if one looked at the juridical nature of episcopal authority. In order to explain the obedience owed to the monarch by the bishops, Villarroel resorts to the same argument utilized by most of the writers who deal with this matter: Although the monarch has no "contentious" jurisdiction over the bishops, he does have "political or economic" jurisdiction over them, because they reside in his kingdoms.

This is the same authority that the father possesses over the members of his family.[46] Thus, if the paterfamilias, for instance, can throw whoever causes a disturbance out of the house, the monarch, as the mystical head of the realm, likewise can expel from his kingdoms any cleric who may cause a breach of the peace.[47] Villarroel adds still another reason why bishops owe fidelity to the monarch, a reason not written down in the legal codes but equally important in seventeenth-century society and already mentioned above: By granting the bishops benefices, they remain obliged to the king for the favor; these benefices, says Villarroel, "induce a just subjection in the prelates, which I should dare to call vassalage." This great honor received from the king's hand must be reciprocated with equal greatness. Thus, the great liberality of the Spanish monarchs, who had returned to the cathedrals the tithes ceded to them by the popes at the beginning of the conquest and who supported with their own treasury those churches who lacked tithes, had to engender in the bishops, concludes Villarroel, "gratitude and subjection."[48]

If it was generally accepted that bishops owed fidelity to the monarch and had to obey his commands, this did not mean that bishops were stripped of their power by this fidelity and obedience. One could be a loyal vassal of the king and, at the same time, vigorously defend episcopal authority, even if that meant constantly clashing with the monarch's representatives; after all, the king himself accepted as one of his obligations the defense of the liberties and immunities of the Church. This apparent contradiction was superbly expressed in the episcopal rhetoric with its constant references to the fact that all the prelates' actions were aimed at "the service of both majesties" (*al servicio de ambas majestades*), the divine and the human,[49] but the defense of episcopal authority was often viewed as an attack upon royal authority as embodied in the king's representatives, who likewise had to defend their authority at all costs. The end result was constant clashes among the members of the ruling elite. The ideal was that both powers helped each other in a mutual and reciprocal way.[50] In Bobadilla's view, "neither must the Church disturb temporal jurisdiction nor the secular judges, the ecclesiastical, as the said jurisdictions are distinct and separate." Nevertheless, conscious of the unending conflicts between both powers, Bobadilla recognized that this matter constituted a "delicate subject."[51] If at some point Bobadilla asserted that a bishop might have an "armed retinue" and be able to use the "temporal knife" to defend himself from those lay persons who might attack the ecclesiastical jurisdiction, this assertion was no obstacle for him to advise the *corregidores* — as the king's representatives at the local level — to "courageously" defend royal jurisdiction. In so doing, they would be favoring and protecting justice from the abuses of ecclesiastical immunity, to which many wrongdoers resorted to avoid being prosecuted for their crimes. It was for this reason, Bobadilla averred, that the representatives of royal authority should not let themselves be afraid if the ecclesiastical judges excommunicated them, as they could always appeal to the Royal Council (to the *audiencias* in the case of the Indies) to be absolved from their excommunications.[52]

Because their authority did not proceed from the king, bishops had the obligation to defend their autonomy — the "liberty" of the Church in the juridical–religious discourse of the time — in the face of any interference from royal authorities. This obligation was so ingrained on the ecclesiastical mind that even a dying archbishop would not forget to entrust the persons congregated around his deathbed with "the defense of the Church's authority and jurisdiction."[53] Likewise, Reina Maldonado would assert that vicars and ecclesiastical judges should strive to keep the immunities of the Church, so that its authority and jurisdiction were not violated.[54] As was contended by the Jesuit Francisco Núñez de Cepeda, "It is a worthy thing to love and seek peace but not with so little discretion that to not disturb it, the bishop will violate the obligations of his post."[55] For this reason, sometimes feuds were necessary and obligatory in order to defend the Church's dignity, as when the prelate defended the immunity, the property, or the jurisdiction of the Church. Núñez de Cepeda added that:

> It is not up to the bishop to look only to the luster and decorum of the Church but to defend, at the same time, its immunity, an enterprise both dangerous and difficult because he has to navigate between the two jurisdictions, the ecclesiastical and the secular, as he would between Scylla and Charybdis, ... it being more than likely that by siding with the Church, something he is obligated to because of his office, he should incur the disfavor of the temporal prince, and if he does not defend [the immunity of the Church], maybe because he wants to please [the prince] or because he fears him, he is sure to incur the indignation of the eternal king and his vicar.

Núñez de Cepeda expressed in militaristic and categorical terms the prelate's obligation to defend the immunity of the churches, of the clerics, and of ecclesiastical property, immunity that was based upon natural and divine law:

> Since the hearts of princes are variable and fickle, their passions vehement, and their courtiers always strive after their favors, ... a

bloody war may be stirred up against the bishop. That is why it is advisable to summon one's courage and be prepared to face the opponent with speed ... and be in the vanguard of the Lord in resisting His enemies. ...Nor is it advisable or allowed that ... the bishop let go the smallest matter. He shall rather lose his life than to consent that the authority with which the Lord has ennobled his principality be diminished.[56]

To this, Núñez de Cepeda added that "to make war on vices and to make the faithful respect it and obey it, the Savior gave complete power and jurisdiction to the Church," and, when pleading and other gentler means were not sufficient, the prelate should use the more effective and powerful means of censures. But Núñez de Cepeda warned that "one must not use these weapons at all times or have them always drawn," because "experience has shown that though they are the sinews of ecclesiastical discipline, ... if they are wielded inconsiderately or for trivial causes, instead of causing fear they prompt scorn." The prelate, therefore, should show that "he has weapons that may injure, but without urgent necessity he should not draw them."[57] As will be examined next, if bishops framed the defense of their authority in such terms, it is easy to see that the clash between archbishops and viceroys in Mexico was practically inevitable, because the viceroys, imbued with the charisma bestowed upon them by their acting as the king's image, could not permit any bishop to diminish their power, even though they might be perfectly aware of how difficult it was to impose their authority upon someone who claimed to have a power and jurisdiction independent from that of the king's.

One Body, Two Heads

In a not exactly positive assessment of the role played by the bishops in New Spain, viceroy Alburquerque informed the monarch in 1656 that:

> ...in these provinces the miters are the ones that trample on everything, to Your Majesty's detriment, and cause innovations and embroilments, as [is the case] in the kingdoms of Europe with the neighboring secular princes, it being necessary that Your Majesty and his Royal Council apply all the attention and care that is required to handle [those princes] to the bishops of these kingdoms because here there are no others who provoke distrust and cause innovations and embroilments than the bishops.[58]

In a similar vein, at the beginning of his term in office in 1665, meditating on the turbulent history of the relations between the representatives of secular and ecclesiastical power in New Spain, the marquis of Mancera pointed out to the king that:

> ...the discord between viceroys and archbishops in this kingdom is so old and continuous that it seems to be congenital to both posts, with irreparable damage to the cause of God, Your Majesty, and your people and vassals following from this lack of conformity between the heads.[59]

Both Alburquerque and Mancera were pointing to a problem that every viceroy always had to confront. The viceroys could not approach their relations with the archbishops of Mexico from a position of theoretical superiority, as was the case with the *oidores*, but from one of equality, as they both had to compete with another head of the body politic, making it much more difficult for one or the other to argue in favor of his superior power. In New Spain, while the viceroy was the head of the secular arm of the republic, the archbishop was the head of the ecclesiastical arm, which made it extremely difficult, if not impossible, for the viceroys to impose their authority on him. We have already mentioned that the dual conception of power provoked constant jurisdictional conflicts. In the case of Mexico, because of the monarch's distance and absence, this duality of power was manifested without mitigating circumstances. The bishops of New Spain, in general, and the archbishops of Mexico City, in particular, were well aware that as members of the body politic, whose supreme head was the king, they were expected to collaborate with the viceroy and the other civil authorities. Nevertheless, as heads of the "ecclesiastical republic," the archbishops possessed a power which in many ways could be deemed similar to that of the viceroys. Thus, I will argue that the capacity of the viceroys to impose their decisions without the archbishops' consent was practically zero; in cases of conflict with the archbishops, the viceroys had no other alternative than to turn to the ultimate authority of the monarch.[60]

If bishops accepted (at least in theory) that they had to obey the monarch inasmuch as they were his subjects, that did not necessarily mean that they also had to obey the viceroys. So it was expressed in 1666, in a plain and straightforward way, by Diego Osorio, bishop of Puebla, on receiving a writ issued by the marquis of Mancera and the *audiencia*, "requesting and asking" him to comply with the king's order to reside in a place in his diocese, the farthest from Mexico City (Osorio had received this order as a result of his clashes with the count of Baños, Mancera's predecessor). The bishop, without denying his willingness to obey the king's commands, rejected the viceroy's writ on the allegation that he was exempt, by divine, natural, and positive law, from the viceroy's jurisdiction.[61] Coming out in defense of viceregal authority with the help of Villarroel and other authors, the *fiscal* of the *audiencia* retorted that the bishops could be rightfully considered vassals of the king, and when the king "requested and asked" something from the bishops, he did so as a courtesy and to honor them, not because he was not able to give them orders (something he could do because he had political and economic jurisdiction over them). Because

"His Majesty communicates to the viceroys the high jurisdiction that they exercise and he has stipulated that their commands be obeyed as if they were given by his royal person," the *fiscal* argued that the viceroy possessed authority over the bishop. The crown attorney closed his argument by asserting that entire volumes could be written about all the cases in which the bishops had to obey royal commands, many of these commands being those contained in the *Patronato* instructions, which the bishops were obligated to follow "precisely and inviolably under the oath they take before taking possession of their pastoral offices."[62]

In the report on the government of New Spain that he submitted to his successor, the marquis of Mancera developed his ideas about the problems that a viceroy had to face when trying to govern the clergy.[63] To Mancera, "the economic governance of the secular clerics has always been the cause of great preoccupation for the viceroys because of their large numbers, their methods, and the excessive indulgence of some prelates." He criticizes the bishops above all for their continuous attempts to interfere with *Patronato* matters. Viceroys were obligated to defend this royal prerogative because, according to Mancera, "the Royal Patronato of the Indies, which the kings of Spain enjoy by right and by papal privilege and through apostolic bulls of the Sovereign Pontiffs Alexander VI and Julius II, is without any doubt the jewel that shines the most in their royal diadem," but the bishops systematically violated the *Patronato* instructions as to nominations, presentations, and removal from benefices and Indian parishes. It being established, for instance, that prelates had to propose to the viceroy, as vicepatron, three candidates for the appointment of parish priests so he could choose one of those three, the bishops usually presented only one candidate, thus hindering the viceroy's freedom of election.[64] The same thing happened with the many interim priests appointed by the bishops, as these priests remained in their parishes for many years.[65] Mancera also complained that, very often, no evidence existed that the bishops had taken the oath that obligated them to respect the *Patronato*; furthermore, they also implemented papal briefs that had not been approved by the Council of the Indies. The bishops were not satisfied with all these infringements of the royal *Patronato*, trying in addition to extend their power over juridical, governmental, and even military matters. Mancera finally regretted that, on top of all this, the viceroys also had to deal with the lack of courtesy toward them of the bishops.[66]

This difficulty in imposing viceregal authority upon the prelates had its origin, as we have already seen, in the particular way power was conceived of in the Spanish polity. This was to cause endless clashes between the civil and religious authorities. When in 1603, the newly appointed archbishop, Fray García de Santa María, tried to introduce a new ceremonial for the mass recently established by Rome, he ran into the determined opposition of the viceroy, the count of Monterrey, who did not like some of the new ceremonies because they tended to emphasize the preeminence of the episcopal figure *vis-à-vis* the viceroy. Monterrey tried to stop its implementation by arguing that this new ceremonial had not been approved by the Council of the Indies, to which the archbishop astutely responded by making use of the Crown's own religious rhetoric: He contended that this ceremonial was not really new, it had only fallen into disuse, and that he had personally heard the king insist that some of these ceremonies be performed in his presence because "he appreciated more being an obedient son of the Church than being king," always regarding the ecclesiastical arm as his superior. When the viceroy insisted that the implementation of the new ceremonial be suspended until he and the *audiencia* could confirm that it was already in effect in Spain, García de Santa María replied that he marveled at this request, because the viceroy very well knew the archbishop was obliged by different oaths to obey the pope's commands as the universal head of the Church, especially in matters so removed from the jurisdiction of an *audiencia* as how to pray or the way mass was celebrated. One year later, writing to the monarch on board the ship that would take him to Peru to take over the viceregal government there, Monterrey would vent his frustration with the archbishop's attitude by insisting that, as viceroy, he had had the power and authority to banish from the viceroyalty any prelate who would not submit to royal authority. If he had not done that, it was only because the Council of the Indies had prevented him from such a determination.[67]

In the course of the clashes between secular and religious authorities, attitudes tended to become more radical and arguments to be presented in a much blunter way. This can be clearly appreciated in the opinions advanced by both sides as a result of the excommunication lay down by archbishop Pérez de la Serna against the marquis of Gelves in the course of the conflict that brought both of them face to face. While the viceroy presented all kinds of arguments to justify his supposed authority over the prelate (and by extension over the clergy in general), the archbishop advanced a theory of episcopal power in which this power appears as totally independent from royal and viceregal authority. The viceroy tried to establish his authority over the archbishop by asserting that ecclesiastics were obliged to obey their temporal kings, as was instructed by Saint Peter and Saint Paul in their epistles, for which reason they had to appear at Court whenever they were summoned by their monarchs. Gelves also added that the king could, through the "political and economic power" he possessed, expel from his kingdom anyone who might cause disturbances. Because viceroys had the same authority in the provinces under their rule as the king did in his kingdom, reasoned Gelves, viceroys could therefore expel any rebellious cleric from their domains. In his response to Gelves, the archbishop adopted a radical attitude, replying that the obedience due to kings and secular princes referred only to those cases in which they possessed the necessary power. As clerics enjoyed a special *fuero* (they were governed by laws other than royal law), they were not subject to the king's authority, which fell under another *fuero*. Pérez de la Serna added that "to affirm that clerics are subject to secular power is the opinion of condemned heretics," and even if they committed some serious crime secular judges could not prosecute them. Because "no secular prince has power over clerics," the cleric who did not obey the viceroy's orders could not be accused of being disobedient, as "the act of disobedience entails subjection in the subject and power in the person who commands." If a cleric, for example, were to receive two opposing orders, concluded Pérez de la Serna, one from the archbishop and another from the king, he had to obey the prelate because "the archbishop is his natural judge and his superior and has jurisdiction over him, while the king does not. And, although the king may be his economic head, ... [the cleric] has a greater obligation to obey his ecclesiastical and jurisdictional head."[68]

In an attempt to strengthen his claimed ascendancy over the archbishop, Gelves maintained that his authority was not only secular but ecclesiastical as well, because the popes had delegated their authority in the Indies to the Spanish kings. For this reason, should the viceroy take legal action against an ecclesiastic who was disobedient, he would not incur the censures established by the bull *In Coena Domini* against those lay officials who usurped ecclesiastical jurisdiction.[69] To this, Pérez de la Serna responded that, in order to take proceedings against an ecclesiastic, the license of the pontiff's delegate (i.e., the monarch) was not enough. Although the pope, "because of the sovereignty and fullness of his power," was able to delegate ecclesiastical cases to a lay person, this lay person (the monarch) could not delegate them to another person (the viceroy), without express order of the pope. Furthermore, contended the archbishop, even when an ecclesiastic was appointed viceroy, if he ordered the arrest of some cleric using the secular power and jurisdiction that belonged to a viceroy, he would be excommunicated anyway, as in such an instance he would have been exercising his secular office and would have given the order as a layperson. Gelves also asserted that, through the presentation of ecclesiastics by virtue of the *Patronato*, the king became their superior and the clerics subject to the monarch. To that, Pérez de la Serna retorted that the patron had no jurisdiction to punish clerics, nor could he try their crimes because, though a layman could exercise ecclesiastical patronage, this did not give him jurisdiction over the clerics.[70]

Finally, the viceroy contended that, because monarchs could not be excommunicated, neither could viceroys;[71] however, for the archbishop this point was doubtful and questionable. To begin with, he argued, those kings who did not enjoy a special privilege from the pope could certainly be excommunicated, and in case they did that privilege was personal and nontransferable. Besides, a monarch did not transfer all his sovereignty to the viceroys, as they had no authority over judicial matters and their decisions in matters of governance could be appealed to the *audiencia*. For all these reasons, averred Pérez de la Serna, those rulers who did not have such a privilege could be excommunicated by the prelate "as they are his subjects in spiritual matters."[72] This was "the crown and greatness" of the episcopal dignity, its greatest burden and obligation, reflected the archbishop by way of a conclusion; because it was his obligation to ensure the spiritual welfare of his subjects, he should not be afraid of opposing the powerful. To that end he had to use "the excellence, greatness, and majesty of his office" to censure those who were unworthy of belonging to the Church. That is why the viceroy, by impeding the use of the ecclesiastical jurisdiction with threats and deeds, "had excommunicated himself with the censures of the bull, from which no one escapes."[73]

Proof of the viceregal impotence that all too often characterized the relations of the viceroys with the clergy is an incident that occurred during the rule of the marquis of Cerralvo, the successor of viceroy Gelves, and was provoked by a sermon preached by one of the cathedral prebendaries. In that sermon, the prebendary had asserted that whenever the monarch was in need the vassals had to come to his aid with their property and their lives, but levies and taxes were justified only if they were applied to the well-being of the vassals, not to give out rewards to those who did not need them. When these views reached the marquis of Cerralvo, he reacted quickly, asking the archbishop, Francisco de Manso, to punish what, according to the viceroy, had been an act of contempt toward the king's person by banning the impudent cleric from the pulpit. In Cerralvo's view, the pulpit should be utilized only to interpret the Gospel and castigate vices in general, not in any specific way. Bearing in mind the long history of conflict that had marred the relations between the viceroy and the archbishop, it was rather unlikely that Cerralvo could succeed.[74] The archbishop responded to the petition in the usual way, assuring the viceroy that as "loyal servant of His Majesty and so zealous of the royal service" he would punish the prebendary appropriately, but nevertheless putting off the matter and permitting the prebendary to continue to preach. Faced with the archbishop's lack of cooperation, Cerralvo considered the possibility of "requesting and asking" (i.e., ordering) the prelate to take legal action against the prebendary, but he dropped that idea faced with the certainty that the archbishop would not comply with the "request," with the result that royal authority would be slighted. He also considered directly ordering the expulsion of the cleric, but he likewise abandoned the idea, certain that the archbishop would excommunicate him for that. Cerralvo had no other alternative, therefore, than to refer the matter to the monarch, lamenting the great "mortification" to which he was being subjected.[75]

In his relations with the monarch and the Council, an archbishop could permit himself to use language of such liberty and candor that would have been unthinkable in the case of a viceroy. At least this was the case with Francisco Manso who, referring to his confrontations with viceroy Cerralvo, complained bitterly in a series of letters to the monarch that "I have spent my strength in a constant struggle that has lasted already three years trying to resist the usual outrages and tyrannies of this governor, without having gotten help or an answer ... from Your Majesty," and he added,

"Your Majesty should not complain about anybody later on, or say that you were deceived, nor should you excuse yourself by saying that you were advised in this or that way because you were told so in a timely fashion," to conclude, "Sire, I am already exhausted from shouting for three years without being heard. I have fulfilled my duties to God, Your Majesty, and my conscience."[76] Such drastic language, however, was not, in general, utilized by prelates when addressing the Crown, although the basic arguments were always the same: Conflicts with the viceroys arose whenever a prelate's attempts to serve the king, by protecting his vassals and redressing their grievances, clashed with the private interests of the viceroy. In these situations, the latter always accused the former of creating factions and being seditious, believing that any opposition to his dictates was an attempt to disturb the peace.[77]

If a bishop's authority was in and of itself elevated and exalted, when in addition he was a member of the Council of the Indies and was appointed *visitador* of the kingdom, he became a formidable figure, as he could claim for himself not only ecclesiastical but secular authority as well.[78] The marquis of Cerralvo had the opportunity to confirm this when the Crown decided, in 1627, to appoint the councilor of the Indies, Francisco de Manso y Zúñiga, as archbishop of Mexico, besides commissioning him to grant a general pardon for the 1624 riot and to continue the investigation that was being carried out on that matter.[79] For Cerralvo, the presence in Mexico of an individual with so much power was detrimental to the office of viceroy. For example, some treasury officials did not recognize the viceroy but rather the archbishop as their superior. This was, in his opinion, "the greatest offense that may be committed in the Indies" and a matter that damaged the monarch's "reason of state" in the Indies. Cerralvo sardonically observed that it was only fair that, if the viceroy did not attempt to be archbishop, then the archbishop should not attempt to be viceroy. He further advised the monarch that, in the Indies, ecclesiastics should not be appointed to royal offices and that the monarch should make it clear to them that their exclusive obligation was to attend to spiritual matters.[80] In his comments, Cerralvo again and again insisted on what radically differentiated him from the archbishop: He represented the king's person; he was, in fact, the king's shadow and image, forming part of the monarch's own body. It was, therefore, inadmissible that some treasury officials obeyed the archbishop instead of the viceroy.[81]

Because (as will be discussed in Chapter 4) a ruler's authority and his ability to exercise that authority were in great part based upon his credit and reputation, the attacks of the archbishop, another figure who enjoyed great respect and authority (it was not the same thing to be criticized by the archbishop as by the "plebs"), impaired the viceroy's reputation not only in the eyes of the monarch but also in those of the people in general.[82] This was an extremely serious matter, for if, on the one hand, it could make the viceroy lose royal favor, arduously earned after many years of service (at least, this was Cerralvo's argument), it could also make the people lose their respect for the viceroy and cause a grave disturbance of the peace (according to Cerralvo, this was exactly what had happened to viceroy Gelves during the riot of 1624).[83] The solution was for the king "to greatly stretch out the viceroy's hand, reforming all those things that weaken his authority" and for the prelates to devote themselves to being prelates, to looking after souls, without usurping temporal authority. Thus, Cerralvo concluded, "God shall have what belongs to God and Your Majesty what is his."[84]

If this was the view from Mexico, on the other side of the Atlantic, the monarch and the Council of the Indies had to weigh all kinds of matters when solving disputes between viceroys and bishops. When things would get to the point that an outbreak of violence might be feared, then the only solution was to remove one of the two or both from their posts, but this was not an easy decision to make. It was extremely difficult to remove a bishop from his diocese, because he was, as already mentioned, appointed for life or, in the episcopal rhetoric, married to his church, for which reason it was not so easy to break the bonds that united a prelate to his church if he did not want this to happen.[85] The only alternative was to appoint him bishop to some diocese in Spain or to summon him to the Court with the excuse that the monarch wished to consult with him on matters of the highest importance. In the case of the viceroys, the Crown always attempted to preserve their authority, doing nothing that could be interpreted as diminishing their power *vis-à-vis* that of the bishops. When archbishop Manso wrote the king accusing the viceroy of being implicated in less than honest business transactions, the Council pointed out to the monarch that, if some of the accusations were true, "it is in accordance with the law and with the principles of good government that he who has a post as great as that of viceroy should not be placed under suspicion while he is in office, so as not to diminish his authority or his subjects' respect, something that is generally observed in these kingdoms with any corregidor, as any cases that may arise against him are withheld until his *residencia*."[86]

In the view of the Council of the Indies, disputes between an archbishop and a viceroy constituted a matter of enormous seriousness because they always led to the creation of factions, which made some "popular commotion" very probable (the specter of the revolt of 1624, which had cost the viceroy his office, was always present in the discussions of the Council, especially in the years immediately following the revolt). In addition, the councilors believed that the greater the authority of the persons in conflict, the more critical and dangerous their dissension became. In the case of Cerralvo and Manso, the root of the problem was, in the Council's opinion, the meddling of the archbishop with temporal government. As a consequence, the authority and standing of the viceroy had been impaired, with the government ending up in the hands of two persons. Although accepting that both the viceroy and the archbishop directed all their actions to the service of the king, the councilors believed that it was inevitable that some disturbance would follow from this state of affairs, as the devotion and affection of the people would be divided between the two heads of government. The councilors, therefore, contended that the archbishop should not deal with temporal matters, not even if he did so in his capacity as councilor of the Indies, because, as the monarch himself had observed, the archbishop as councilor was not the viceroy's superior. While the Council as such was effectively the viceroy's superior, individually each councilor was not. Moreover, the archbishop had to understand, declared the councilors, that New Spain had only one viceroy, that he was the one who represented the royal person, and that he, not the archbishop, was the one who gave the orders.[87]

When the monarch and the Council became convinced that the confrontation had reached such proportions that it could not be remedied, they saw as the only solution the appointment of a new viceroy and the presentation of the archbishop to the bishopric of Badajoz, Spain, thus forcing him to leave Mexico. The archbishop, however, would take almost five years to obey this order, giving as an excuse that when he received the news he had just begun the *visita* of his diocese, something that had not been done in almost 20 years. Thus, between 1631 and 1633, Manso wrote to the monarch letter after letter from the wildest and remotest parts of his archbishopric to inform him of the progress of his *visita* and also of his inability to leave for Spain as he first had to meet his diocesan obligations.[88] Faced with the archbishop's apparent intention of not abandoning Mexico and with the fact that their confrontations had become ever more fierce and bitter, the marquis of Cerralvo decided to request permission from the king to expel the prelate by force. Cerralvo was well aware of what had happened when viceroy Gelves decided to deport archbishop Pérez de la Serna, and for that reason he preferred not to make such a move without the express order of the monarch.[89]

This petition caused a division of opinions among the members of the Council, which shows how problematic it was to employ royal authority against an archbishop. For example, the count of Castrillo, president of the Council of the Indies at the time, while affirming that it was not necessary for a prelate to be accused of sedition to be recalled to the court (as the law permitted such an action), noted that the difficulty consisted in knowing what to do should the archbishop, ignoring the repeated orders of the monarch, refuse to abandon Mexico, as "royal authority would be very much weakened," if such a thing were to be tolerated. Here, Castrillo dissented from the majority of his colleagues at the Council, who argued that the viceroy should avoid expelling the prelate by force. Although Cerralvo maintained that this would not cause any disturbance, the councilors were not so sure of the consequences of such a rigorous measure "against the greatest prelate of those provinces," nor were they certain of how "a populace comprised of so many humors, wills and conditions" would react on seeing that "their archbishop" was being taken away. The councilors, though recognizing that the obedience of the archbishop to the monarch should be placed before their doubts and fears, were nevertheless confident that the prelate would eventually comply with the order. For that reason, they believed it would suffice to write him, "using severe and strong words but which show no distrust," to let him know that the Council awaited his arrival. The count of Castrillo, for his part, contended that, if this had been the first or second time that the archbishop was ordered to come to Spain, he would have agreed with the rest of the Council, as it was always better to use less rigorous methods first. Because that was not the case, however, the only way to make the archbishop understand that he had to obey the monarch was to inform him that, if he did not embark in the first fleet that was to depart for Spain, the successor of viceroy Cerralvo would bring with him an order of expulsion. By so doing, no one would think that Cerralvo had expelled the archbishop because of personal animosity. The monarch decided to follow the recommendations of the president of the Council, thus the marquis of Cadereita, who was to succeed Cerralvo in the government of New Spain, was given a royal letter whereby he was to deport the archbishop if he could not convince him to leave. Cadereita, however, did not need to use the letter, as at the beginning of 1635 Manso at last boarded a ship and went on his way to the peninsula.[90]

Clashes between archbishops and viceroys followed one another, uninterrupted, until 1673, when the archbishop Payo Enríquez de Rivera was appointed interim viceroy. Practically the only peaceful moments were those during which the episcopal see was vacant.[91] Yet, the endemic antagonism between the highest representatives of royal and ecclesiastical authority in New Spain did not prevent the Crown from appointing bishops and archbishops as acting viceroys, one more proof that, in sixteenth- and seventeenth-century Mexico, besides the viceroy, no figure was more powerful than the prelate, who was considered perfectly qualified to exercise the functions of government (after all, his office was that of ruler of souls). Although the *audiencia* was also qualified to exercise those functions, and would have been the logical choice for those periods when the post of viceroy was vacant, one can observe a preference for the appointment of prelates as acting viceroys and an avoidance of the *audiencia* ruling by itself.[92] In many ways, this preference was in accordance with the monarchical ideology examined in Chapter 1 and its emphasis on the rule of "only one," with all the advantages that such a rule was thought to have. This appears to have weighed much more than any kind of distrust the Crown might have felt toward the bishops because of the latter's tendency to put the interests of the Church before those of the Crown. In addition, the political culture of the Spanish monarchy assumed that prelates, because of their virtue and wisdom, ought to form part of the prince's councils, thus better helping to preserve the republic.[93]

In this regard, it is of great interest to examine the arguments utilized to keep archbishop Enríquez de Rivera as acting viceroy of New Spain for seven long years, when the usual thing would have been for him to occupy the post for no more than a year. Following the Crown's instructions, Enríquez de Rivera took over the government of the viceroyalty after the duke of Veragua's death on December 13, 1673, only a few days after he had taken office. When some months later, as the Council was discussing whether a new viceroy should be appointed or the archbishop be left at the helm of the civil government, it was pointed out that the decision to appoint the archbishop viceroy had been made with great deliberation and knowing the qualities of virtue, learning, prudence, experience, and almsgiving that characterized him. For all these reasons, he had been judged as highly fitted to be entrusted with a government as important as that of New Spain. To this, the Council added that in the months the archbishop had been in office, he had acted with skill and moderation in all those matters of a temporal nature, which was what should be expected from "his blood and his obligations as son of the duke of Alcalá." The councilors were clearly in favor of letting the archbishop keep his post of viceroy for the time being. To lend more weight to their opinion, the councilors pointed out how well other prelates had ruled the viceroyalty in previous occasions, specifically citing the names of Juan de Palafox, Marcos de Torres, and Diego Osorio. Though acknowledging the conflicts with the viceroys in which all of these prelates had been involved, the councilors argued that this problem did not exist in the case of Enríquez de Rivera, because the marquis of Mancera, with whom he had had a conflictive relationship, had already abandoned Mexico. To reinforce their argument that it was not unusual for an archbishop to be the head of government, the councilors recalled the times of the Conquest when an ecclesiastic, Pedro de la Gasca, had eventually reestablished order in Peru, "using his breviary as his sword," adding that in Spain, Italy, and other territories it was common for archbishops and bishops to take over viceroyalties temporarily.

Without a doubt, the most interesting comments made by the councilors regarding this matter were those referring to viceregal patronage. The councilors contended that the greatest advantage of letting the archbishop govern for a time was that during that time the viceroyalty would experience some relief from the onerous burdens ordinarily imposed upon its inhabitants by the viceroys who arrived from Spain. The entries of these viceroys, plus the large retinues they brought with them, were a great expense; besides, they usually took the honors and rewards that should be distributed among the deserving inhabitants of New Spain to give them to their retainers. The councilors added that Enríquez de Rivera would not pay so much attention to his private interests as would a secular viceroy, among other reasons, because all of his retainers were ecclesiastics and they would not hamper his government seeking offices and favors, which was usual with the retainers of the viceroys. Furthermore, the archbishop had already shown signs of impartiality in the distribution of offices (including the distribution of some among the retainers of the duke of Veragua, who had been left helpless after their patron's death), as the principles that had guided this distribution, asserted the councilors, had been none other than "equity and commiseration, for which reason all the worthy individuals of that kingdom were left consoled, each one awaiting the reward of his merits and needing no other means than justice, it being true that in the Indies this relief is experienced rarely." For all these reasons and some others of a practical nature (the fleet was not sailing that year), the Council believed that it would be better to postpone the appointment of a new viceroy until the following year.[94]

When the matter was again discussed one year later, the Council proposed that Enríquez de Rivera remain as viceroy, thus showing its satisfaction with the good that had resulted from his rule; among other reasons (and not the least important, certainly), the councilors mentioned that the archbishop, in only six months, had doubled the amount of the remittances sent to the royal treasury. To strengthen their proposal, the councilors presented some very interesting opinions about viceregal government. They began by insisting on the advantage of having as viceroy someone such as the archbishop who had no wife, children, or relatives to look after; neither did he have to worry about maintaining his retainers, as he supported them with the archbishopric's rents. The councilors then went on to reject the arguments that a cleric was not qualified to take charge of military matters or that he would always try to call the *Patronato* into question. The councilors again brought up the case of Pedro de la Gasca to indicate that it would not be the first time that a cleric had acted effectively in military matters. As for the *Patronato*, the Council gave a key to understanding the behavior of the prelates as viceroys and as to why the Crown never had problems in this regard. For the councilors, the *Patronato* was safe with Enríquez de Rivera because he was a virtuous individual and the son of the duke of Alcalá, but also, above all, because he owed the archbishopric and the post of viceroy to the king, for which reasons it was difficult to believe, contended the councilors, that "having such bonds, he might wish to take away from the post of viceroy that which belongs to it." As a member of the nobility who had been favored by royal liberality, the archbishop was bonded to the monarch by ties of loyalty and gratitude strong enough to reassure the councilors about his behavior as viceroy.[95]

Eventually, the count of Paredes would be appointed viceroy in 1680, thus putting an end to the "temporary" government of the archbishop. The successor to Enríquez de Rivera in the archbishopric, Francisco de Aguiar y Seijas, was archbishop of Mexico between 1681 and 1698, an unusually long period of time (many archbishops died soon after their appointments because they were usually nominated for this post at an old age). During this time, no disputes occurred between the archbishop and four successive viceroys worth mentioning. This seems to be a striking development given the turbulent history of the relationship between viceroys and prelates since the sixteenth century. Although with the available documentation it is not possible to assert, in any categorical way, the reasons for the peace of the last quarter of the seventeenth century, it seems very plausible that the political instability that characterized the center of the monarchy during the minority and reign of Charles II, with the constant quarreling of court factions and the frequent shifting of political alliances, would have contributed to give a great degree of uncertainty to the political careers of the viceroys appointed to rule the dominions of the monarchy. As a consequence, in New Spain the viceroys would have shied away from any direct confrontation with the archbishop to prevent their position from becoming even more unstable.[96] To this it should be added that Aguiar y Seijas, who enjoyed a great moral authority, seems to have been exclusively concerned with Church matters, without being much interested in political affairs.[97] In addition, Oscar Mazín has argued that in the final decades of the seventeenth century the Church in New Spain, besides being dominated by three powerful figures — Aguiar y Seijas; Manuel Fernández de Santa Cruz, bishop of Puebla; and Juan de Ortega y Montañés, bishop of Michoacán — saw the economic, social, and political consolidation of the New Spanish cathedrals. This consolidation would have allowed the bishops and the cathedral chapters to enjoy, in general, a position of predominance *vis-à-vis* the viceroys (Figure 8).[98]

It is, then, something of a paradox that political instability at the center of the monarchy would bring a long period of relative peace and tranquility to the viceroyalty (relative because this was also the time when the attacks of pirates and corsairs on the coasts of New Spain reached their peak). Yet, before the reign of Charles II, the high level of conflict that existed among the members of New Spain's political and religious elite can only be explained by the dual conception of power typical of early modern Spanish political culture. In Spain, this duality became blurred because everyone acknowledged the supremacy of the king, and the only figure who could have questioned that supremacy, the pope, was far enough away to prevent the conflicts between both powers from reaching high intensity, although it certainly did not prevent confrontations in those provincial capitals in the peninsula which had episcopal sees. In Mexico, on the other hand, the absence of the monarch and the enormous distance that separated him from his New Spanish vassals allowed the bishops to bolster their power and authority in such a way as to be able to challenge the supremacy of viceregal power. The confrontations were endless, especially with the archbishops, as they resided in the same city as the viceroy, making the opportunities for conflict much more frequent.[99] In a way, it could be argued that the history of the relations between New Spain's archbishops and viceroys in the sixteenth and seventeenth centuries, with its endemic conflicts and antagonism, proved the veracity of one of the main arguments advanced by

Fig. 8 Cristóbal de Villalpando, *Triunfo de la Santa Iglesia Católica*, also known as *La Iglesia militante y triunfante*, 1684. Sacristy in the Cathedral of Mexico City. This painting, commissioned by the ecclesiastical chapter, depicts the Catholic Church in all its power and glory. The Church, represented as a female figure holding a monstrance and wearing the papal tiara, is guarded by two figures, which can be seen as symbolizing the secular and ecclesiastical heads of the New Spanish body politic: St. Michael, prince of Heaven and God's viceroy, and St. Peter, prince of the Church and bishop of Rome.

contemporary political writers: The rule of one was the best kind of government because a commonwealth with more than one person at the helm was as great a monstrosity as a body with two heads.

A Remedy from Heaven

On November 16, 1666, the marquis of Mancera joined the *audiencia* of Mexico in writing a letter to the queen regent in which they complained bitterly of abuses on the part of Mexico's Inquisition. Among the inquisitors' many outrages, alleged the viceroy and the *oidores*, were stealing money from the Royal Treasury of Guadalajara, under the pretext that an *oficial real* (as the officials of the Royal Treasury were known) of that city was indebted to someone punished by the Holy Office, and forcing the *oficiales reales* of Zacatecas to provide them with the mercury they needed for some mines of their property. Of course, the inquisitors had achieved their goals by laying down censures and excommunications right and left. To force the inquisitors to return the money they had taken from the treasury of Guadalajara, the *audiencia* served the inquisitors with a royal writ.

When the inquisitors failed to comply, the *audiencia* issued a second order. This time the inquisitors responded by presenting the viceroy with an opinion that accused the *oidores* of preventing them from carrying out their duties. Though this was punishable by excommunication, for the moment they decided not to proceed in that direction.[100] As if this were not enough, the inquisitors had used the same methods to snatch away all manners of trials and proceedings under the *audiencia*'s jurisdiction by availing themselves of the privileges of the *fuero inquisitorial* (the Inquisition's legal code and privileges).[101] The inquisitors behaved, the viceroy and *oidores* claimed, as though they were the sole and absolute judges of the realm, "paying no attention to the viceroy or the *audiencia*, not even to show them the courtesy and civility of informing them of a single proceeding, judging themselves to be fully sovereign and considering licit whatever they do, using the pretext and excuse of their holy ministry." The viceroy and the *audiencia* pointed out that they had tolerated such abuses from the inquisitors in the interest of public peace, but that if no remedy were enacted matters would worsen and they would continue "suffering and tolerating new acts of disrespect every day, knowing [the inquisitors] that nothing is remedied while everything is allowed to them." The letter concluded by advising the queen that, though previous similar complaints made to her had received no response, the gravity of these matters required an urgent remedy; otherwise, the authority of the viceroy and the *oidores* would be seriously impaired, putting at risk, as a consequence, the obedience of the populace to royal authority.[102]

Such was the state of relations between the representatives of royal authority and the Inquisition of Mexico around the mid-seventeenth century. The *audiencia*'s letter offers an excellent summary of the role the Holy Office had come to play in the Spanish monarchy, as well as of the problems and dilemmas the representatives of royal authority had to face in their relations with the tribunal; however, the complaints of the viceroy and the *audiencia* were nothing new. Since its creation in 1571, the Mexican Inquisition was continually embroiled in conflicts with the other institutions of colonial power. In these conflicts, the Mexican tribunal appears as a corporate body that behaves in an autonomous way, sometimes collaborating with the Crown and its representatives, but more often than not opposing them in order to further their own interests. But, why would an institution thought to be an essential part of the Spanish monarchy and that on which its security rested behave in such an unpredictable way?

Much ink has been spent on trying to define the true nature of inquisitorial authority. Was the Inquisition an ecclesiastical tribunal or an essentially secular tribunal in the service of the monarchy? Many historians have insisted that the Inquisition was the instrument of royal absolutism. For example, Bartolomé Bennassar has written that the Inquisition was "the monarchy's absolute weapon."[103] Jaime Contreras believed the Inquisition was "an ideological instrument whose political efficacy served to lay the foundations of the authoritarian principles that shaped the modern state."[104] According to Domínguez Ortiz, the king would have imposed his will on the tribunal while at the same time respecting the institution's ecclesiastical character. Royal control would have focused on three aspects: naming the inquisitor general, financing the tribunal, and resolving the many jurisdictional conflicts that arose as much with secular courts as with their ecclesiastical counterparts.[105] However, Henry Kamen has argued that it would be difficult to demonstrate that, thanks to the Inquisition, royal power was strengthened in any way. In Kamen's view, the fact that opposition to the Inquisition in Castile was normally led by representatives of royal authority (*corregidores*, high courts, and the royal councils) seems to confirm that "the tribunal was often seen as an obstacle rather than an asset to royal power." Furthermore, he contends that the Inquisition "rarely took any action that was nakedly political, and it would consequently be mistaken to regard it as an instrument of state."[106] Similarly, I.A.A. Thompson has argued that the Inquisition was only rarely an instrument of royal absolutism, more often acting in pursuit of its own interests.[107] Some historians have emphasized a certain ambiguity in the nature of inquisitorial power. On the one hand, the Holy Office was an ecclesiastical tribunal because any authority and jurisdiction exercised by the inquisitors came from Rome, but the Inquisition was also a secular tribunal, exercising power delegated by the Crown (the Crown always supported this contention). In that sense, it was a "somewhat ambiguous mixed entity."[108] The fact is, as Kamen has observed, that the Inquisition itself always claimed dual jurisdiction, because they represented both pope and king.[109]

This peculiar dual nature of inquisitorial power allowed the tribunal to claim that neither the Crown nor the Church courts could go against its papal privileges. This constitutive ambiguity also gave the tribunal a lot of room for political maneuvering, allowing it to tilt its power toward the pope or the king according to its own interests. On the one hand, the Inquisition always enjoyed a high degree of autonomy from Rome. Very early on, the monarchy had managed to prevent the pope or any other ecclesiastical judges from hearing appeals of cases in which the Inquisition was involved; these cases would be heard only before the inquisitor general. This prerogative is what gave the Inquisition its independence from Rome, autonomy that the monarchy always tried to increase, perhaps believing that the more independent from the papacy the Spanish Inquisition became, the easier it would be to put pressure on it. On the other hand, the power received from the pope gave the tribunal a high degree of autonomy from the Crown. Because the official authority of the inquisitor general came from the pope and not from the king, he was under no legal obligation to obey the monarch's commands, attending to the king's wishes only voluntarily. However, the Inquisition documents always refer to the king as its "protector and patron." This was no mere formula; as in the case of the cathedrals, the king, as patron of the Holy Office, possessed the right to nominate its highest official, the inquisitor general. Formally, no other official of the Inquisition could be nominated by the king for his appointment by the Holy See. Although it is true that the members of the Council of the Inquisition were appointed by the king, this appointment was in a certain way conditioned to the will of the inquisitor general, as the monarch had to choose the councilors from a list of three candidates submitted by the latter. Except for the treasury officials, the rest of the officials of the Inquisition, including the inquisitors of the different tribunals, were appointed exclusively by the inquisitor general. The king was expected to ensure the correct functioning of the institution, having the obligation, as its patron, to provide the economic resources necessary for its sustenance, but this gave him no right to interfere with the activities of the Inquisition. Moreover, the secular privileges awarded to the Inquisition had the effect of increasing the jurisdiction of the Holy Office but not the possibilities of the Crown of intervening in its affairs.[110]

This dual nature of inquisitorial power led to endless clashes between the Inquisition and the civil authorities, something that can be clearly appreciated in the history of the relations of the Mexican tribunal with the royal authorities during the course of the seventeenth century. Here, the enormous distance from the monarch would increase the tendency of the inquisitors to act autonomously from secular power. In an attempt to solve such conflicts, a *concordia* (covenant) was established in 1610 between the Holy Office and the royal authorities in order to clearly delimit their respective fields of competence and also to limit the number of *familiares*.[111] Also established was the procedure to follow in cases of jurisdictional conflict between the inquisitors and secular justice whenever nonreligious crimes were committed by the *familiares* of the Inquisition. This procedure was of a highly ritualistic character and would remain a permanent source of conflict. According to this *concordia*, in case of jurisdictional conflict, the senior *oidor* was to meet with the senior inquisitor to try to reach an agreement. Should this fail, the viceroy was to choose a cleric from a list of three candidates presented to him by the inquisitors who was to meet with the senior *oidor* and the senior inquisitor to vote for a proposal that had to be approved by a majority of votes. Should the three votes be cast in favor of three different proposals, the viceroy would cast the decisive vote for one of the three.[112]

This *concordia*, nevertheless, meant the beginning and not the end of a prolonged conflict between the inquisitors, on one side, and the *oidores* and the viceroys, on the other. At stake was the reach and importance of inquisitorial power. The dispute began because it was not clear from the wording of the *concordia* whether the senior *oidor* and the senior inquisitor had to meet in the *audiencia* or in the seat of the Inquisition, or whether the *oidor* should precede the inquisitor in his sitting and voting (as shown in the next chapter, this was not exactly a petty detail). To solve the problem, a *cédula* was issued in 1618 instructing that the junta should take place in the *audiencia* and the *oidor* should precede the inquisitor, but the inquisitors refused to obey this and other *cédulas* — in which the precedence of the *oidores* over the inquisitors in all public ceremonies was established — with the allegation that none of these *cédulas* had been approved by the Council of the Inquisition.[113] This argument is of great transcendence and the key to understanding the difficulties encountered by the monarch, the viceroys, or the *oidores* when imposing their authority on the Inquisition. It also clearly contradicts the opinions of those who maintain that the tribunal was simply an instrument of monarchical absolutism. The fundamental question is that neither the inquisitors nor the other officials of the Inquisition were ministers of the king, nor did their appointment fall under the king's prerogative.[114] This is a decisive difference in a system of government in which both viceroys and *oidores* considered themselves to be the king's servants. The Inquisition was ruled by a council (*Consejo de la Suprema y General Inquisición*) which was presided over by the inquisitor general. Although it is usually emphasized that the Council of the Inquisition was part of the conciliar system of the monarchy, it is not sufficiently emphasized that the inquisitor general was appointed by the pope, while the inquisitors were directly appointed by the inquisitor general, without the king's intervention. The inquisitor general, therefore, received his authority — the apostolical jurisdiction — from the pope, not from the king, which endowed him with a level of autonomy unmatched by other council presidents.[115]

An indicator of this autonomy is the fact that the inquisitors were not supposed to inform the monarch regularly about their affairs, like other royal officials did. Instead, they usually wrote to the inquisitor general or to the Council of the Inquisition, as the Council of the Indies had no authority over the American inquisitors.[116] This autonomy can also be appreciated in the language utilized in the discussions of the Council of the Indies regarding the question of precedence and the exact place the Inquisition should occupy in the public theater of power. In a *consulta* in 1629, the councilors pointed out that the councils, *chancillerías*, and *audiencias* always preceded the Inquisition in public ceremonies. This was something that had to be more strictly observed in the Indies because, being so far away from the king, it was highly advisable that the royal authority embodied by the viceroy and the *audiencia* always be kept in a prominent place. While recognizing that the Holy Office should always be helped and favored, the councilors affirmed that those officials who "strictly and immediately" represented the king must have preference over all the others.[117] In a new *consulta* to the king about the same issue written in the following year, the councilors reaffirmed their previous assertions that the *oidores* had precedence over the inquisitors. In addition, they noted that whenever a jurisdictional conflict had to be settled at the court, the councilor of Castile always preceded that of the Inquisition, for which reason the same should be observed in Mexico and Lima, because, due to the great distance that separated them from the court, the *audiencia*s often fulfilled the same functions as the councils. Finally, they added that,

> …though the jurisdiction of the inquisitors in all affairs concerning the faith is apostolic and ecclesiastic, and most deserving of being venerated and favored, in those affairs regarding conflicts of jurisdiction it is only royal and awarded voluntarily to them by privilege of Your Majesty, who has allowed them to hear some civil and criminal cases involving its own ministers and familiares. …This being assumed, it seems to be an intolerable thing that the oidor who is to defend the royal and ordinary jurisdiction, which always has to be extended, helped, and favored as is stipulated by the laws which deal with this, does not precede the inquisitor.[118]

For the councilors of the Indies it was clear that the inquisitors were not associated with the figure and power of the monarch as ostensibly and closely as were the *oidores*. No matter how many prerogatives the king had given them, the monarch was not the ultimate source of their power. Furthermore, the fact that the Crown had to establish agreements such as the *concordias* with the Inquisition was another clear indication that the monarchs were dealing with a separate power, a power that only arduously and in a limited way were they able to control; however, this does not mean that the power of the Inquisition was completely separate from the king's power. As another corporate member of the commonwealth, it owed loyalty and obedience to the king, the head of the body politic. Its power was separate in the same sense as one arm is separate from the other while still belonging to the same body and following the commands of one single head. The problem here was that the Inquisition, because of its special nature, could follow the commands of two different heads.

In view of the lack of compliance by the inquisitors of Mexico and Lima with the previous *cédulas*, a new royal order adopting a middle-of-the-road solution was issued in 1635, whereby the jurisdictional conflict juntas were to take place in the viceregal palace and in the presence of the viceroy, precedence now being given to the one who was the most senior.[119] Nevertheless, the Council of the Inquisition still disagreed with this decision, alleging that the custom heretofore followed in the Indies favored the claims of the inquisitors. Finally, in 1640, the monarch ceded to the pretensions of the Inquisition, dispatching an order by which, thenceforth, the senior *oidor* should go to the Inquisition palace to solve any disputes over jurisdiction with the senior inquisitor. Also, the meeting would be presided over by the inquisitor.[120] It is not clear why the Crown gave in to the Inquisition's pretensions. It is likely that it believed that by satisfying the Inquisition's desires, it would be able to achieve, once and for all, harmony between royal and inquisitorial authorities. Solórzano, however, resorts to what, as we shall see below, was the Spanish monarchy's usual rhetoric regarding the Inquisition to justify this decision. For him, such a decision was taken because the councilors who intervened in its deliberations (two for each royal council) were extremely conscious of how important it was to "favor and authorize" the "Holy Inquisition."[121]

If this decision had been taken in order to end the disputes, that was something it did not accomplish at all, as conflicts went on for the rest of the century. The *audiencia* of Mexico, with the assent of the viceroys, would continually request that the 1640 *cédula* be repealed, constantly using the discourse of authority to defend its position. In 1645, for example, it wrote a letter to the king (also signed by the viceroy) requesting that the custom not be altered and that the *oidor* not be forced to go to the inquisitorial palace, on the grounds that "in such remote and isolated places" it was essential to preserve the authority and respect of the royal officials, because that would make them be obeyed promptly. In the eyes of the viceroy and the *oidores*, this was far more necessary in a place where there was no army ready to repress any disturbances.[122] Here, the *audiencia* is implicitly recognizing the fundamental importance of the symbolic nature of its power and that any gesture that could diminish that symbolic power, no matter how insignificant, would put its authority at risk. This same argument, now in relation to the viceroy, was also brought up years later in a letter sent to the king in 1662, in which the viceroy and the *oidores* observed that, because the meetings to resolve conflicts of jurisdiction had to take place in the seat of the Inquisition and in the presence of the viceroy, it would not be "in accordance with the authority and representation of such a great minister, who so closely represents Your Majesty, to have to go to the court of the Inquisition, giving in to the sovereignty notoriously feigned by the inquisitors, … and there being no one to prevent it."[123]

In their relations with the Inquisition, the Spanish monarchs always had to face a serious dilemma, which generally resulted in political paralysis whenever the Inquisition became the subject of any decision. On the one hand, the rulers were aware of the wide-ranging abuses and excesses committed by the tribunals (and we should point out that most of the time the abuses had nothing to do with heresies or religious matters). On the other hand, their own political–religious discourse kept them from confronting the Inquisition decisively. To the Spanish monarchs — so it was declared by Philip III in a royal *cédula* sent to the viceroys of New Spain and Peru in1603 — the Inquisition's mission consisted of serving and glorifying the Catholic faith. The creation of the tribunal had meant a considerable benefit for the Church and for the diverse kingdoms of Spain's monarchy, because the Inquisition had "cleansed [them] of an infinite number of heretics" by holding "great and celebrated autos de fe," that had caused heretics "great fear and confusion, [while giving] Catholics singular joy, tranquility and consolation." One of the principal arguments used to justify the existence of the Inquisition was that the Spanish monarchy had freed itself of the disturbances and civil wars that religious differences had caused in many European nations. (France during the second half of the sixteenth century would be a case in point.) For all the aforementioned reasons, Spain's rulers had great "devotion for and attachment to" the Holy Office. That is why the monarchs always instructed the American viceroys to honor and favor the inquisitors and their officials and servants as much as they could and to respect and cause to be respected "all the privileges, exemptions and liberties" granted to them. The viceroys were obligated to do so not only because they were good Catholics, but also because their position of eminence would cause others to follow their example.[124]

If one of the main duties of the Spanish monarchs was to ensure peace and unity among all their subjects, no more dangerous cause for conflict in the commonwealth could be found than religious divisions. This horror of "heresy," which had a religious as well as a political component, is well reflected in Juan de Solórzano's opinions when examining the role of the Inquisition in his treatise on the government of the Indies. He opens the chapter with these words:

> Heresy, the nature and perversity of those who follow it is such that, if it is not checked and completely eradicated as soon as it is born, not only will be harmful to religion but also will totally pervert or subvert the political order (*estado político*) of kingdoms. ... Thus, any Catholic and well-governed republic must not allow even the discussion of which some foolishly presumptuous statesmen have tried.

For Solórzano, the Inquisition is "a remedy come from Heaven against the many evils, sects, errors and horrors in which we see many provinces burn" and should be thanked for having helped to preserve the purity of faith enjoyed by the Hispanic kingdoms. According to him, the Spanish kings are such zealous defenders of the Inquisition because they very well know that "the cause of religion must be the first one in any well-founded republic, and its purity and defense is the greatest support and the firmest foundation of empires."[125] The idea that the Spanish monarchs should be enormously grateful to the Inquisition for all it had done to prevent religious divisions in their realms was a principle firmly engraved on the minds of sixteenth- and seventeenth-century rulers. This may help explain why, when facing the abuses of the Inquisition, the monarchs' only choice was to act with tepidity and in contradictory ways.

In the case of the viceroys, they not only had to deal with the autonomous power of the Inquisition but also with the ambiguity of the Crown in its approach to the problem of inquisitorial power. On the one hand, they always could be recriminated by the monarch if they did not show enough authority and determination before the inquisitors. This is what happened to the count of Alba de Liste when, in 1651, he faced a threat of excommunication by the Mexican inquisitors if he refused to turn over to the inquisitors some documents that had been entrusted to him by a person who was being prosecuted by the Inquisition.[126] At first, the viceroy tried to keep the documents in his possession, but the inquisitors, with their usual diligence in such cases, threatened to excommunicate all those persons "of any estate, quality or condition" who had in their possession any documents belonging to the accused man and who did not turn them over within six hours. In the face of such expeditious methods, the viceroy consulted with several persons as to whether he should submit the documents to the Inquisition, as he only intended to send them to the king. The advisors' opinion was that Alba de Liste should submit the papers, because some of them referred to matters of faith, and in these matters even the king was subject to the dictates of the Inquisition; consequently, the viceroy turned the papers over. When this incident was examined by the Council of the Indies, however, it was decided that a letter should be sent to the viceroy recriminating him for having consented to the inquisitors' demands: first of all, because the documents contained information regarding possible unlawful activities of the inquisitors and other things that affected the public good, but also because the Inquisition could not excommunicate a viceroy.[127] Interestingly enough, the monarch concluded his letter by indicating to the viceroy that at least he should have kept copies of the documents.[128] With this last sentence, the monarch was implicitly acknowledging the difficulty of imposing his own authority on the inquisitors, as he was well aware that, once in the hands of the inquisitors, it would be next to impossible to recover the documents, hence the suggestion that the viceroy should have kept a copy.

A viceroy could also be recriminated for not being cooperative and forthcoming enough in his relation with the Inquisition. This is what happened to the marquis of Mancera, a viceroy who had an elevated concept of his post and who did not appear to be inclined to allow the Inquisition to interfere in the exclusive affairs of the royal authorities, but on this occasion the firmness of the viceroy did not seem to have the blessings of the queen regent and the Council, and he was sent a letter instructing him not to hinder the activities of the tribunal. In her letter, the queen justified her decision with these words:

> [T]he preeminence of the office and affairs of the tribunal of the Inquisition causes it to be of such a dignity that the examples of other tribunals do not apply to it, it being true that I receive a particular service when all the ministers, and more those who are as principal as you are, set an example to the subjects of whatever quality or condition, so that they shall not lack in the observance and respect with which the Holy Office of the Inquisition must be treated.[129]

The kind of contradictory language utilized by the monarchs, with which they attempted to defend both royal jurisdiction from inquisitorial intrusions and inquisitorial authority from any royal official determined to assert his authority over the Holy Office, made it almost impossible to solve the endemic confrontations that had always existed between the representatives of royal authority and the Inquisition. These clashes reached their climax at the end of the seventeenth century, when the Spanish Inquisition had become a real headache for the monarchy. By this time, the tribunal had reached the conclusion that the jurisdiction awarded by the king to the Inquisition had become thoroughly ecclesiastical and thus could not be modified or taken away. This idea, which tended to turn the Inquisition into a totally ecclesiastic organ, thus possessing a high degree of autonomy from royal power, would be widely challenged by the councils of the monarchy.[130]

The problem the Crown had to face can be clearly appreciated in a long report sent to Charles II by the Council of the Indies around 1696 regarding the excesses of the American Inquisitions, in general, and that of Mexico, in particular. The Council started by recounting a complaint received, not from the viceroy or any other civil authority, but from the bishop of Puebla in relation to the abuses committed by the Mexican tribunal in appointing an excessive number of officials and *familiares* (whose credentials left a lot to be desired). To the bishop, this was just an easy way for the Inquisition to extend its jurisdiction. He also affirmed that the abuses of the Inquisition went unpunished because its decisions and sentences, even if they were about temporal matters, could not be appealed to the *audiencia*.[131] Finally, the bishop observed that he had refrained himself from invoking his ecclesiastical jurisdiction because the "despotic" disposition of the tribunal was well known.[132] Further on in their report, the councilors described what, in their view, was the *raison d'etre* of the Inquisition: The Catholic kings had created the tribunal to preserve their kingdoms from the contagion of Judaism and "other sects." To this end, they had considered it appropriate "to communicate the royal and secular jurisdiction" to the Inquisition's tribunals in order to augment the authority and reverence that the inquisitors needed to carry out their mission.

In the face of the Inquisition's claims that its power was autonomous from that of the king because its jurisdiction was exclusively ecclesiastical, the councilors insisted that the Inquisition had to submit to the Crown's authority in those temporal affairs in which it had jurisdiction, as the monarch might eliminate, if he wished, that privilege previously awarded to the Holy Office. In the councilors' view, the pretensions of the Inquisition had extremely serious consequences because the administration of justice to those who sought it was impeded when the Inquisition meddled with royal jurisdiction, and this put the monarch's authority and his dominion over his possessions at risk, as it was the good administration of justice that kept the public peace. For a government to function adequately, this is how, in the opinion of the councilors, the relations between the different jurisdictions should be:

> It is an elementary proposition that each one of the two jurisdictions, ecclesiastic and secular, has a different sword for its use in the administration of justice, it being well-known the incapacity of one jurisdiction to use the sword of the other. That is the reason for the existence of the bond that unites both jurisdictions, mutually supporting each other, so that what cannot be done by the spiritual sword will be executed by the temporal one. Because if these two distinct jurisdictions were not to fraternize with each other, ... the body of the republic would be maimed, if the ecclesiastic arm were not joined to the secular one. That is why supreme kings and princes are called ministers of God, to Whom they must give account of the defense and conservation of their churches and of the observance of His divine precepts.

It is for that reason that the Inquisition, when it used its temporal jurisdiction, should not utilize the weapons that canon law had put at its disposal, such as censures and excommunications. Behaving with great prudence and restraint — according to the councilors — both prelates and governors of the Indies renounced the exercise of their powers so as to avoid disturbances; yet, the consequence, compounded by the abusive use of its power by the Inquisition, had been the transformation of that tribunal into a "monarchy" (*un imperio monárquico*). The councilors observe that, because "love [is] the impregnable fortress of authority," the Inquisition's abuses had surely provoked a great hatred among those inhabitants of the Indies who had been subjected to such abuses, as it was love and respect that made authority venerated (i.e., to be obeyed), not servile fear, such as that prompted by the inquisitors' methods and abuses. In the councilors' minds, therefore, the conduct of the inquisitors put at risk the king's authority over his American dominions, where his authority needed to be revered more, due to the great distance that separated those lands from the monarch.[133]

This was the predicament of the Crown in its relations with the Holy Office, and the quandary seemed to have no solution, as the Crown's own politico–religious discourse prevented it from proceeding in any effective way against inquisitorial power. But, even if the rhetoric would have been different, the juridical nature of the tribunal (rooted in the same dual conception of power that allowed us to explain the clashes between viceroys and bishops) would have meant an insurmountable obstacle, decisively limiting the king's power to make the inquisitor general and, through him, the inquisitors comply with his orders. In their confrontations with royal officials, the inquisitors knew how to use skillfully their own legitimating discourse which endowed them with a great amount of "symbolic capital," as they presented themselves as representatives of the two greatest authorities: the pope and the king. If the king's power was limited, that of the viceroy was much more so, the inquisitors being well aware of the scarce authority of the viceroys over them.[134] Ultimately, the representatives of both royal and ecclesiastical power were those who constantly felt the intrusions of the Inquisition in their respective spheres of influence. It could be concluded, then, that the inquisitors, rather than being a tool utilized by the monarchs to impose their authority, turned out to be trying and irritating rivals of that same royal authority.[135]

This seems to be a rather paradoxical conclusion, accustomed as we are to the Inquisition's conventional image as an institution created to instill fear in the population and, in that way, ensure control over it.[136] While the popular image of the Holy Office may be that of an agency that functioned as some sort of secret police in the service of the absolutist state, recent investigations of the activity of this tribunal have shown that, in fact, its effectiveness very often was confined to the radius of the city where the inquisitors resided.[137] If, in the peninsula, the supposed long hand of the Inquisition never reached much farther than the big cities, what can be argued of the Mexican case, where one single tribunal and three inquisitors were supposed to control a territory that was six times bigger than the peninsula (with sixteen tribunals) and where the immense majority of the population was not subject to its jurisdiction?[138] No doubt, its capacity to instill terror in the general population was rather limited.[139] Furthermore, the Inquisition was not an institution isolated from the rest of society, entirely devoted to its repressive work; rather, it was enmeshed in relationships of kinship, friendship, and clientelism that closely linked it to New Spanish society. What is more, one often gets the impression that the inquisitors were more interested in administering their private businesses than in systematically repressing the inhabitants of New Spain, as they spent more time utilizing inquisitorial power to obtain economic benefits for themselves than to secure a strict orthodoxy among the populace. The paradox, therefore, lies in the fact that an institution that has generally been seen as an instrument of the dictates of the colonial state or the imperial monarchy more often made its presence felt in the lives and activities of the representatives of that same power of which it was supposed to be an instrument of repression.

4

Performing Power

In the letter mentioned in Chapter 2 that the *oidores* of the *audiencia* of Mexico sent to the king in 1620 to complain about the authoritarian practices of the viceroy, the judges devoted a great deal of space to what, at first sight, may seem to be anecdotal matters in the relations between the viceroy and the *audiencia*. For example, the *oidores* contended that the viceroy had clearly shown his intent to snatch away their power and authority by forbidding them to place black velvet cushions on the floor in front of their seats when they attended church services whenever the viceroy was not present (this being, according to the *oidores*, the usual custom everywhere in the Indies).[1] Ironically, it would be a viceroy, the count of Salvatierra, who, years later, would complain to the king because the *visitador* inspecting the viceroyalty at that time, the bishop Juan de Palafox, argued that the viceroy could not put a cushion on his seat while sitting in the *audiencia* with the *oidores*. Whereas the *visitador* thought that the viceroy should not be sitting high up, lest he differentiate himself from the *oidores*, the viceroy contended that the cushion, having been used by the viceroys since time immemorial, simply served "to differentiate himself with this little sign from the other ministers."[2]

Although most historians have been aware of the ceremonial, complicated protocol and frequent disputes over matters of precedence that surrounded the viceroys, they have generally dismissed them as simply amusing episodes, as vestigial medieval customs designed to please the vanity of the vice-sovereigns, or as utterly irrelevant no matter how "colorful" they were.[3] In my investigation of colonial politics in the Habsburg period, however, I take seriously the study of the rituals of power and the power of rituals. Pomp and pageantry, spectacle, and splendor are treated as integral parts of the political process and the structure of colonial power. I ground my study

119

in the conviction that the rituals of rulers, the "symbolics of power," were not mere incidental ephemera but, indeed, were central to the structure and working of colonial society. Here, I part company with those who, following a functionalist point of view (public rituals serve, for example, as a safety valve, to reinforce social hierarchy, to express community or contention), argue that these spectacles were just the mask of power.[4] In my approach, I see pomp and ceremony as neither the exercise of power by cosmetic means nor the mask of power, but as integral parts of power and politics. In this sense, political rituals embody the very production and negotiation of power relations and are not merely the instrument of power, politics, or social control (which are usually seen as existing before or outside the ritual activities).[5] Moreover, I avoid seeing the rituals of colonial power as simply a reflection of the social structure, because they, like language, were endowed with a capacity to construct social reality.[6] The rituals that were acted out in Mexico in the sixteenth and seventeenth centuries shaped colonial society as much as they were a reflection of it, allowing for a variety of often unpredictable responses; therefore, the theater of colonial politics, constitutive as well as representative of power, was by no means inconsequential in elaborating the rapport of forces in the colonial power play. This approach allows me to understand more completely how viceregal power, in particular, and Spanish imperial power, more generally, were constituted.

The Politics of the Viceroy's Body

Throughout the early modern period, the Spanish monarchy created or adapted an extraordinarily rich repertoire of rituals devoted to creating what can be considered a true "theater state." These rituals were mostly borrowed from the ritual vocabulary of the Church. In Catholic thought as elaborated in the Middle Ages, rituals had the ability to enact, to bring something into being, to make something present (the consecrated Host did not represent the body of Christ; it *was* the body of Christ).[7] It should be no surprise, then, that in the quintessential Catholic monarchy, the Spanish monarchy, power was thought to be enacted through ceremonial performances. This is clearly appreciated, for example, in the rituals surrounding the reception in New Spain of the royal seal. The royal seal was stamped on all the writs (*reales provisiónes*) issued by the *audiencias*. Every time a new monarch ascended the throne, a new seal with the king's coat of arms would be sent to Mexico, the old one being melted down and the silver sent back to Spain. On its arrival in Mexico City, the seal was received in the same way as the king or the viceroy was: The *audiencia* and the *cabildo* would go to meet it and ride back to the city with the seal, placed on a horse or mule, between the president of the *audiencia* and the senior *oidor*.[8] Thus, the ritual of reception of the seal made the king "present" at the same time that it reactivated his power. Just as happened with the Host, the seal did not represent or symbolize the king — it *was* the king.

In this regard, the same can be argued in relation to the figure of the viceroy. He was a "symbol" of royalty who, as such, reenacted the king's power every time he was displayed in the theater of colonial politics. In his analysis of the rituals of justice in *ancien régime* France, Michel Foucault argued that in early modern society "power was what was seen, what was shown and what was manifested," and in the absence of continual supervision power sought a renewal of its effects through the spectacle of cruelty and torture, so as to make everyone aware, through the body of the criminal, of the unrestrained presence of the sovereign.[9] In New Spain, this "liturgy of punishment" through which royal power was manifested also played its role, with public executions of criminals and *autos de fe* taking place regularly.[10] But, a "liturgy of magnificence" also existed in Mexico that likewise revealed royal power periodically and sought a renewal of its effects. Here, to paraphrase Foucault, it was the viceroy's body, rather than the criminal's, that played the main role. On his displayed body, exhibited in processions, surrounded with brilliance and splendor, royal authority was legible to all. This production of magnificence was perfectly regulated and formed part of a ritual, a "viceregal epiphany," that met two demands: It marked the viceroy, not with infamy, as in the case of the criminal, but with majesty, by the many symbols that accompanied him. Also, it was spectacular and had to be seen by all as the triumph of the sovereign power that had sent the viceroy; his body, constantly exhibited through the streets of Mexico City, was made a visible announcement of the king's power.

Because the viceroy's body played such a transcendental role in proclaiming royal authority, his exhibition in public was regulated to the smallest detail. That is why, among the recommendations given by the president of the Council of the Indies to the marquis of Montesclaros to make certain his success as viceroy of New Spain, he included a piece of advice on how he should "govern his person." For the president, every viceroy ought to follow the general rule that nothing said to him should disturb or upset him. He then went on to add that,

> [a viceroy's] person and actions must be of great demeanor, modesty and gravity. ...He must dress in a decorous way, the cape long rather than short, his traveling clothes should be of grave and dignified colors, he should wear no feathers in his hats, and in all these matters and in everything else he must always look older rather than younger. He must always walk very slowly, in a orderly manner, calmly and showing authority. In churches and on the street, he must never look directly at the people, although ... he will try to see and notice everything. ...He should utter few words, [and] those in a grave and soft-spoken manner. Whenever he gets irritated, he must not lose his temper, one single word or look being sufficient as punishment.[11]

This way of exhibiting himself in public highlighted the viceroy's majesty, as gravity and impassivity were thought to be characteristics peculiar to monarchs (the Spanish kings were famous for their impassivity).[12] This regulation of the publicly displayed body was applied not only to the viceroys but also to any magistrate whose public appearance meant a manifestation of royal power. Thus, any royal magistrate was expected to adopt the same body language as the monarch who had given him his power.[13] In this regard, the body of the ruler must not only be well proportioned and display an austere appearance (to walk in a solemn and sober way, for instance, shows a judicious intellect) but must also be, in Castillo de Bobadilla's words, a "splendorous and adorned" body as well. Rulers and magistrates must dress with greatness and distinction, not for their own sake but because of the authority they represent, as their offices are imbued with the majesty of the prince and "for that reason the populace esteems them more and fears them more, because they cause fright with their greatness." The dignity and decorum of the office of viceroy, therefore, demand that his body be covered with great magnificence. Likewise, this need to dress splendidly must be extended to his retainers and servants.[14] Because of all this, argues Bobadilla, "the luster and splendid treatment of the ruler's person and retinue should not be censured but praised, because ... beauty and greatness inspire admiration."[15] Although the practice of "conspicuous consumption" may not be governed by a strictly economic logic (i.e., may not be oriented toward financial gain), it nevertheless contributes to an increase in another sort of capital, one as important as economic capital in early modern societies: the symbolic capital that was accumulated through the public recognition of honor and prestige.[16] Magnificence, therefore, was one of the essential mechanisms through which a viceroy's authority was constituted and sustained.

In this regard, it is interesting to note that the same arguments were advanced by Pedro de Reina Maldonado in relation to bishops. For him, it was not illicit, superfluous, or a sin for a bishop to dress "with beautiful and splendid clothes," for, in that way, the office was more exalted. More interesting still, in light of the usual conflicting relations between civil and religious authorities, is the author's comment that in those cities where viceroys and *audiencias* resided it was even more necessary for a bishop to show "luster and magnificence." With this comment, Reina is asserting the importance of the public display of the bishops' power as a way to affirm and sustain ecclesiastical authority *vis-à-vis* the secular authorities, but this was not the only reason why a New World bishop should dress with magnificence, for through the splendor of a prelate's clothes the Indians would be able to appreciate God's majesty and, by instilling fear and reverence in the Indians, it would help make the person of the bishop more respected among the natives.[17]

Just as the external appearance of the viceroy's body was perfectly regulated, both his public and private gestures were highly ritualized. As the king's image, he repeated directly the "sacred center" of political authority in New Spain.[18] As such, colonial rituals always revolved around his figure. In the theater of power the viceroy, like his original, the king, occupied the focal point. Platforms, curtains, rugs, and armchairs marked the viceroy's place. In this geometry of authority, the viceroy was also the center and axis of a lateral symbolics of power in which the viceroy's right side signified preeminence or deference and his left indicated inferiority. Similarly, proximity or distance from the viceroy's body were used to codify rank and privilege. In this regard, it has been argued that protocol was used as a weapon to enhance royal authority,[19] but court etiquette was much more than a weapon. It was the substance of the king or, in our case, the viceroy, as the viceroy's movements, dress, and language objectified the essence of his power: They were unavoidable, obligatory, and imperative. He was not simply the viceroy; he had to act as such. His post depended on his representing his office with dignity. Viceregal ceremonial and ritual thereby re-presented his power every day and in every formal act; they constructed viceregal power.[20]

This could be appreciated from the moment he landed in Veracruz and in his progress toward the capital. Through the viceregal progress, the viceroy, like the king himself would have done, took symbolic possession of his realm. His public processions and attendance at festivals stamped the territory with ritual signs of dominance, marking it as though it were physically part of him.[21] In the case of Mexico, Octavio Paz has pointed out that the itinerary followed by the viceroys from Veracruz to the capital city was a "ritual voyage which can be seen as political allegory." Thus, before arriving in Mexico City, the new viceroy made public entries in three cities: the port city of Veracruz, associated with the landing of Cortes and the beginnings of the conquest; Tlaxcala, the capital of the Indian republic allied with the *conquistadores*; and Puebla, a city founded by the Spaniards and the rival of Mexico City, which in the symbolic geography of New Spain represented the Creole center, while Tlaxcala signified the Indian one. In addition, in Otumba, where a decisive victory of Cortes' army had taken place, the outgoing and the incoming viceroys met for the transfer of power.[22]

The public entry of every new viceroy into these cities in his progress toward the capital was a ritual with a very precise political meaning, whereby the viceroy was assimilated in a symbolic and ritual way with the absent monarch. Every public gesture of the viceroy was modeled after the royal entry, which always began with a gesture of loyalty on the part of the city: handing over the keys of the city to the ruler on his arrival at the city gates. The ruler, in turn, guaranteed the rights and privileges of the city residents.[23] The official procession that welcomed the new viceroy at the entrance of the city constituted, from the political point of view, a very important aspect of the ceremony of the viceregal entry. At the head of the procession were the constables with kettledrums and bugles, followed by numerous knights. After them (in hierarchical order, from lesser to greater and indicative of the distribution of power in the body politic) came the university professors, the *audiencia* reporters and clerks, the city councilors, the *alcaldes ordinarios*, the *corregidor*, the members of the tribunal of accounts, the *alcaldes del crimen*, and, finally, the *oidores*, with the senior *oidor* bringing up the rear of the procession. After meeting him, the viceroy rode in procession on a horse offered to him by the city for this special occasion towards the triumphal arch erected by the city council. There, the city clerk, in the presence of the *audiencia*, had the viceroy swear an oath that he would defend the kingdom and maintain the city's privileges. Once this ceremony had been performed, the doors of the arch were opened so the viceroy could pass through, after which the *regidores* placed the viceroy under the royal canopy (*palio*). Then, with the two *alcaldes ordinarios* holding the bridle of the viceroy's horse, the procession headed toward the cathedral, where another arch had been erected. There, the ecclesiastical chapter, holding a cross and a canopy and singing the *Te Deum Laudamus*, went to meet the viceroy. Finally, after the cathedral ceremonies were concluded, the viceroy proceeded to the viceregal palace.[24]

While the realities of political life were often disorderly and contentious, the procession expressed an ideal image of the political community. In the procession the city was put in order; it was an occasion when the ideal of a society both hierarchical and harmonious, both stratified and unified, attained a momentary reality. But, the procession also embodied a fundamental tension between the rules that ideally governed its staging and the actual behavior of its participants. The processional order lent itself to different interpretations that reflected the diverse views of power and society held by the different sectors of colonial society. If the procession can be understood as a theatrical performance, there was always the risk that the participants would fail or refuse to perform as scripted. In fact, processions were regularly disrupted by their participants.[25] It has been argued that royal entries were a fusion of two distinct processional rites: the royal progress and the civic procession. The former was framed by the assumption that the size and quality of a great man's entourage directly reflected his status. In the latter, the frame consisted of the view of urban society as an organic hierarchy, in which the guilds played a very important role.[26] The viceregal entry, however, was designed to highlight political authority above all;[27] thus, it had no room for civic or popular displays (although native participation in the festivities was always prominent, they did not take part in the viceregal procession, nor did any confraternities[28]). Few things expressed, therefore, the majesty of viceregal authority more vividly than the sight of so many brilliantly dressed men, walking or riding with solemn dignity around an even more resplendent viceroy.

In addition, during the procession a series of symbols associated with royalty highlighted the close bond that existed between the absent and invisible monarch and the present and visible-to-all viceroy. Foremost among these symbols was the horse presented to the viceroy by the *cabildo* and on which he paraded in every city that celebrated a formal entry — the horse had been a royal symbol at least since medieval times.[29] Also impressive was the oath and the handing over of the keys, a ceremony that emphasized not only the king's sovereignty over the city but his obligation to respect its privileges as well. Similarly, the cathedral chapter meeting the viceroy with cross and canopy while singing the *Te Deum* was a ceremony reserved for monarchs on the occasion of their first entry into a city. In relation to this, the right to sit under a canopy or baldachin (*dosel*) in the main chapel of any church when attending services was another privilege of kings that was also reserved for viceroys,[30] but above all else it was the use of the *palio* that most underlined the viceroy's power and his condition as a surrogate monarch, for two reasons. First, for the Spanish monarchy the *palio* was probably the most important marker of royalty, more important than even the crown, because the Spanish monarchy was conspicuous for the absence of a coronation ceremony (Figure 9).[31] Second, in an intrinsically Catholic monarchy in which the language used to refer to and address the monarch was the same as that used to refer to God, it was almost inevitable that the same marker be utilized to denote the monarch's sovereignty as to signify divine power. To parade under the canopy was a privilege that the monarch shared solely with the Sacred Host, something that comes as no surprise if we bear in mind the identification that existed in the seventeenth century between the Holy Sacrament and the Habsburg monarchs, as was shown in the first chapter.[32]

In this regard, the debate that took place in the 1630s as to whether viceroys had a right to be received under the canopy shows us in a precise way the transcendent importance attributed to the symbols of power and how such symbols were thought to be endowed with a constitutive force. Ever since the first viceroys had been appointed to rule New Spain, it had been customary to receive them under the *palio* whenever they celebrated an official entry, until the use of the *palio* was prohibited in 1620 because of the many expenses it caused.[33] But, in 1632, when a grandee, the duke of Escalona, was appointed viceroy of New Spain for the first time, he solicited permission to be received under the canopy for two reasons: one, on account of his status as grandee and two, because of the geographical distance that lay between the viceroy and the monarch any prerogative that increased the dignity of the former's post would greatly contribute to making his time in office more effective. The effects attributed to this quintessential symbol of Spanish royalty were such that the duke of Escalona maintained in his petition that one of the reasons why the marquis of Gelves had lost control of his government in the 1624 riot was because he had not been allowed to parade under the canopy during his official entry into Mexico City, something that, in Escalona's view, had enormously impaired his authority.[34] Although it could be adduced that these arguments were simply shallow rhetoric presented by Escalona to reinforce his

Fig. 9 Miguel and Juan González, *Moctezuma's Entry*, 1698. As a way to enhance the significance of the Spanish conquest, this painting, part of a series that depicts the conquest of Mexico for a transatlantic, imperial audience, portrays Moctezuma as a powerful king and emphasizes the sovereignty of Moctezuma's rule (which, according to the Spanish legal fiction, had been legitimately transferred to the Spanish Crown) by anachronistically representing him under the quintessential marker of Spanish kingship, the *palio*. (Museo de América, Madrid, Spain.)

request, it is interesting to note that a majority of the councilors of the Indies who examined his petition agreed with him, that the authority of viceroy Gelves had been seriously affected by the absence of such an important marker of royal sovereignty.[35]

In 1638, when the brother of the deceased duke of Escalona was selected as viceroy of New Spain, he requested to be awarded the same privilege as his brother — that is, the use of the *palio*. In the subsequent debate that took place in the Council over this petition, the majority opinion, including that of Juan de Palafox, argued that because the current duke of Escalona had the same qualities as his late brother he should also be allowed to use the canopy for his entry; however, they added to their opinion that the prerogative of the canopy was awarded because viceroys represented the king's person, and no matter how great the difference of rank between a grandee and the "titled nobility" (dukes, counts, and marquises), it was not so great as to allow such an inequality between viceroys. They all occupied the same post, contended the councilors, and they all, therefore, ought to possess the same esteem and authority, especially "in such remote provinces where so much attention is paid to outward appearances."[36] With this last sentence, the councilors were not saying that the utilization of the *palio* by the viceroys was just a decorative matter, which was allowed to satisfy the fancy of New Spain's inhabitants. What they were really arguing was that the distance of those lands from Spain made it far more necessary to associate the viceroys with the symbols of royalty.

Nonetheless, this debate in the council did not end the discussion over the *palio*. That same year a *cédula* was issued that allowed the viceroys to parade under the *palio*, provided that no more than 8000 pesos were spent on their entries into Mexico City (and 12,000 in Lima),[37] but complaints about the excessive expenses caused by this ceremony forced the Crown to come up with a peculiar solution to solve the problem. From the 1640s onward, and utilizing the pretext that the duke of Escalona, in spite of the royal *cédula* that allowed him to be received under the canopy, had renounced this privilege when the Mexican *regidores* presented him with the canopy, it became customary to give two royal letters to the viceroys before their departure for the Indies. The first was a public one, by which the viceroys were allowed to be received under the canopy in consideration of their personal status and the eminence of the post of viceroy. The second was a secret one, whereby the king ordered the viceroys not to use the *palio* ceremony, even though they had been authorized to do so by the previous *cédula*.[38] This ingenious formula solved the problem of excessive expense while, at the same time, safeguarding the viceroy's authority by explicitly acknowledging that it was right for the viceroy, as the king's living image, to use so fundamental a symbol of royalty. He was not denied this use; it was only postponed, due to "the poverty of the present times," until the situation improved. Such a solution clearly shows the transcendent importance that contemporaries attributed to certain objects, which

Fig. 10 Melchor Pérez de Holguín, *The Entry of Archbishop–Viceroy Morcillo in Potosí*, 1716. As this painting from the viceroyalty of Peru shows, viceroys were still being received under the *palio* in the early eighteenth century. (Museo de América, Madrid, Spain.)

rather than being mere adornments of power were its very embodiment (Figure 10).

In his study of the English royal entry, R. Malcom Smuts has argued that the Stuart kings' dislike for public ritual, especially the royal entry, contributed to the collapse of royal authority in the 1640s. Instead of a visible symbol of the values that united England, Charles I ruled as a remote source of authority. Thus, by failing to project an effective public image, he found it increasingly difficult to inspire loyalty.[39] This is something that the Spanish monarchs and their viceroys appeared to have always had in mind, despite the very serious financial difficulties experienced in the seventeenth century and the many criticisms made against the excessive costs of the viceregal entries. In the Mexican case, for example, the king was always a remote source of authority but, contrary to the English monarch, he never lost his powerful public image thanks to his viceroys, who were living and constant reminders of his existence, hence the ambivalence in restricting the use of the symbols and marks of royal sovereignty by the viceroys. For their part, the viceroys always attempted to emphasize their power symbolically, conscious as they were that their power could be seriously compromised if their public image as the supreme authority of the viceroyalty was not clearly transmitted to the populace. As the marquis of Villamanrique would put it, "In those parts where the Royal Person of Your Majesty is so far away it is much advisable that every estate everywhere keep the decorum and reverence due to those who represent you."[40]

This might explain the fact that ritual entries of rulers never went out of style in New Spain, as they had elsewhere by the late seventeenth century, when monarchs emancipated themselves from old royal ceremonials that had brought the ruler together with his subjects in public forums, creating in their stead "rites of personality" carried out inside the walls of their palaces.[41] In the case of Mexico, not until the second half of the eighteenth century can these trends be discerned, although viceregal arches continued to be erected as late as 1783, when the practice was discontinued,[42] nor does New Spain's elite appear to have experienced any changes in their attitude toward the kind of conspicuous consumption exemplified by viceregal entries, in spite of the enormous debt accumulated by the *cabildo*. Throughout the seventeenth century, the Mexican *regidores* never failed to comply with their obligation of paying for the expenses of the entries, even if that meant having to mortgage every single piece of property owned by the *cabildo*.[43] This attitude on the part of the *regidores* could have been caused, as Colin MacLachlan has argued, by the Mexican elite's interest in giving the monarch's representative a vivid image of their status and power.[44] But, it may have also been motivated simply because, in the world of New Spain, the belief that the exercise of power is intimately connected with display was still very much alive.

The inhabitants of Mexico City were constantly being reminded of the idea that the viceroy was a surrogate king through a series of ritual ceremonies that made him the center of the rites of passage of the monarch and his family. Every time a member of the royal family was born, married, or died, or whenever the king's or the queen's birthday was celebrated, all the representatives of the principal institutions of New Spanish society went to the viceregal palace to offer congratulations or express their condolences to the viceroy. There, the viceroy, seated under a canopy (which certainly highlighted the idea of majesty whose embodiment he was) would receive these corporations with great solemnity, separately, and in strict hierarchical order, beginning with the lesser ones and concluding with the *oidores*.[45]

Along with viceregal entries, probably no ceremony in New Spain was more solemn and impressive than the funeral for the king's death (the funeral rites of any member of the royal family were usually equally splendid). Indeed, it has been argued that the fact that the exemplary ritual center of the Spanish monarchy — the palace and monastery of El Escorial — was a monument to death lent an extraordinary significance to the rituals of death.[46] If, in the viceregal entry, the culminating moment of all the ceremonies and festivities was the procession that led the viceroy to the triumphal arch (symbol and compendium of royal government), in the obsequies the culminating moment was the solemn and funereal procession that made its way from the viceregal palace to the cathedral and the catafalque erected there (symbol and compendium, likewise, of royal power) (Figure 11).[47] If the viceregal procession had no room for the clergy or the common people, almost everyone participated in the funeral procession. It was a perfect microcosm of colonial Mexican society, with

Fig. 11 "Catafalque of Philip IV in the Cathedral of Mexico City," from Isidro Sariñana, *Llanto del Occidente en el ocaso del más claro sol de las Españas*, 1666. The statue of Philip IV (in the second body of the catafalque) is shown in the company of four statues of king Solomon, whose virtues make him the perfect model for the Catholic monarch, who always must place religion and piety before anything else. In the lower body, the royal insignia appear surrounded by statues of great rulers (Constantine, Charlemagne, Alexander), gods and heroes of Antiquity (Theseus, Jason, Prometheus, Janus), and four female figures representing Spain. The catafalque is crowned with an image of Faith, who carries a cross in one hand and a chalice and the host in the other. The base of the funerary monument is replete with emblems and devices that illustrate (as in the case of the triumphal arch) all the virtues a good ruler must have, all of which were embodied, according to the author, in the person of king Philip IV. (Courtesy of The Hispanic Society of America, New York.)

the lowest members of society heading the procession and the representatives of royal power bringing up the rear. As one chronicler would exclaim, it manifested a "wonderful harmony."[48] The procession, therefore, presented an idea of the community as harmonious and hierarchical as that of a mystical body. The funeral procession for King Philip IV's death, celebrated in Mexico City in 1666, is probably the most refined example of this form of processional order. If we are to believe the chronicler, thousands of people participated in the procession, which was headed by the black and mulatto confraternities, followed by the Indian and then the Spanish brotherhoods. After these, came the colleges and seminaries, the religious orders (in strict order of seniority, starting with the most modern, the Society of Jesus, and concluding with the oldest, the Dominicans), the clergy, and the ecclesiastical chapter. The royal tribunals marched after the clerics. In first place came the *Protomedicato* (board of medical doctors) followed by the *Consulado* (merchant's guild), the university, and the city council. After them, came the royal insignia (the scepter, the sword, and the crown), escorted by members of the military orders. The chancellor of the *audiencia*, the tribunal of accounts, and the *audiencia*, in this order, marched behind the royal insignia. Finally, the viceroy appeared, as expressed by the chronicler, "crowning the cortege with his greatness." He marched with the senior *oidor* at his left. In addition, the viceregal guard escorted the viceroy and the *audiencia*, while the city battalion brought up the rear of the cortege.[49]

From the political standpoint, it is necessary to underscore several aspects of the processional order. First, while the procession that welcomed the viceroy was exclusive, the funeral procession was inclusive. They constituted different ritual "genres," so to speak. In the procession that welcomed the viceroy, as mentioned earlier, if the common people were formally absent, it was because, in a procession devised to emphasize political power, it was not necessary to include the people who lacked such power. By including blacks, mulattos, mestizos, and Indians, the funeral procession, on the contrary, showed that, although the common people's mission was not to rule the community, they were nevertheless rightful members of the body politic (in the language of the period, they were not the head but the feet of the body politic[50]). That is, the physical space they occupied at the procession reflected the position they occupied in the political community: They were literally performing their place in the body politic.

In this regard, it should be noted that the tribunal of the Inquisition was the only institution of colonial Mexico to be absent from the funeral procession. Still more interesting is the fact that the Holy Office celebrated its own funeral for the king.[51] The reason for the Inquisition's behavior was in all likelihood the peculiar status of the tribunal and its pretension of independence from both viceregal and episcopal jurisdiction. Furthermore, its absence from the procession was, no doubt, the best way to avoid being placed in a position of inferiority in relation to royal or even ecclesiastical authority, for the processional order was an assertion of royal power, with the "king's living image" being the "crown" of the procession and its apex. It may be argued that, in a way, the entire procession was an extremely long introduction to the viceroy's appearance. Moreover, the procession proclaimed the preeminence of secular over ecclesiastical power (although not the latter's separation or independence from the former) by having the clergy march before the royal tribunals (in the processions, the order of precedence was always established from front to back). Finally, the fact that the viceroy marched with the senior *oidor* at his side was also a political statement, with which he was affirming his will to cooperate with the *audiencia*. Marching alone, behind the *oidores*, separating himself from the *audiencia*, would have meant that the viceroy desired to assert his power as independent from that of the *audiencia*. Thus, the procession provided a continuous discourse on the constitutional order of the community. As Edward Muir has argued, the procession was, in fact, the constitution, because one of the defining characteristics of the period was that political constitutions were ceremonial as well as textual in nature.[52] As will be shown below, that is why any change in the processional order was considered a grave matter and created continuous confrontations among the different institutions of colonial rule.

Ritual Challenges

As we have seen, in colonial society only the *oidores* and bishops could seriously question viceregal authority. In the case of the former, it was more a question of establishing the limits of viceregal power within a relationship of subordination (at least in theory) than an open challenge to viceregal power. In the case of the latter, the problem was far more serious, especially in Mexico City, where the archbishop constituted another powerful center of power, often challenging viceregal authority. These confrontations very frequently were played out on the public stage. That is why the public appearances of viceroys and archbishops were potentially charged with conflict, their gestures and those of their subordinates being carefully scrutinized in order to detect any attempt to assert the authority of one to the detriment of the other. In a highly ritualized society, the power of viceroys and archbishops was constantly tested on the public stage of the streets and churches of Mexico City.

The public image of the archbishop was constructed in a very similar way to that of the viceroy. Both were conceived of as "princes of the republic," the one secular, the other ecclesiastical. Ideally, both the viceroy and the archbishop should cooperate in the ruling of the commonwealth, without attempting to extend their respective jurisdictions beyond the established limits. Whenever cooperation between both of them was achieved, the peace and harmony of the community was guaranteed.[53] The archbishop surrounded himself with the same pomp and circumstance as the viceroy, his retinue being equally large. While the viceroy was escorted by the *audiencia* at all public occasions, the archbishop always appeared in public accompanied by the ecclesiastical chapter, as he was their "head." It comes as no surprise, then, that the same public gestures were used with him as with the viceroy. For instance, archbishops also staged ceremonial entries when they first arrived in Mexico City.[54] As with the viceroy, the municipal council was in charge of the episcopal entry, organizing the festivities and setting up illuminations.[55] Even more relevant to our argument is the fact that triumphal arches were also erected on which archbishops were represented as classical heroes or gods.[56] Likewise, the funeral ceremonies for archbishops resembled closely not just those of viceroys but those celebrated to honor the king himself. As in the funeral for the king's death, the ceremony included a solemn procession, in which all the institutions and corporations of colonial society participated from the viceroy on down to the confraternities. The procession concluded at the cathedral, where a sumptuous catafalque, complete with emblems and hieroglyphs, was erected to honor the deceased prelate.[57] It should not be surprising, therefore, that the archbishops also tried to appropriate certain markers of sovereignty — the *palio* and the *dosel* — which were intimately associated with royal and viceregal power. The paradox here is that during the course of the Middle Ages, the monarchs had appropriated these markers, which had originally belonged to the Church, in an attempt to reinforce their own power. By the seventeenth century, such markers had become completely associated with royal power, though the American archbishops and bishops would still insist on using them to mark their authority. This attitude would create tensions and clashes with the viceroys throughout the century.

Around the end of the sixteenth century and the beginning of the seventeenth, a more determined attitude on the part of the Crown to prevent the prelates from utilizing the *palio* — the quintessential royal symbol — can be clearly appreciated. It seems that cities heretofore had customarily received prelates under the canopy.[58] Now, the monarch, alleging that this was a ceremony reserved only for him and his viceroys, forbade the prelates, in a straightforward way, to use it and requested that the pope scrap this privilege for the bishops.[59] Evidence suggests, however, that in the mid-1600s some bishops (especially those of Puebla) were still received under the canopy. So was Juan de Palafox received in 1640,[60] and so was the new bishop, Diego Osorio de Escobar, received in 1656. The difference between the two entries is that Bishop Osorio was received under the canopy in express contravention of the viceroy's orders. When the viceroy was informed, he flared up and in a long and repetitive letter begged the king to punish the bishop's audacity, reminding the monarch that the *palio* was a sacred object and his "greatest royal privilege." In a peremptory tone, he also pointed out to the king that the viceroys' orders "must be obeyed blindly," especially in the Indies because of its remoteness; otherwise, he argued, viceroys would not be necessary, nor could the monarch preserve his possessions.[61]

As for the *dosel*, this was a ticklish matter because the viceroys had tried, from very early on, to prevent the bishops from using it when the former were present in places — the churches — that fell under the exclusive jurisdiction of the latter. Archbishops and bishops, for their part, insisted that they had every right to sit under a baldachin placed on an elevated platform in their churches, whether the viceroy was present or not. An early example of these attitudes was the opposition by viceroy Martín Enríquez to archbishop Moya de Contreras' use of the baldachin, an opposition that came as no surprise, as this viceroy's rule was characterized by a determined reassertion of royal authority in New Spain.[62] For similar reasons, a conflict arose at the beginning of the seventeenth century between the count of Monterrey and archbishop García de Santa María when the latter tried to introduce a new church ceremonial that called for the use of the *dosel* by the archbishop at all times. Monterrey vigorously opposed this in the name of the royal authority that he represented, while Santa María vehemently defended its use with the argument that the authority and dignity of a prelate required the use of the dosel.[63] By the mid-seventeenth century, it appears that some sort of compromise had been reached. The archbishop could not sit under a canopy if the viceroy and the *audiencia* were present (with this, the preeminence of royal over ecclesiastical power was acknowledged), unless he was celebrating mass in pontifical dress — that is, he was wearing all of the archbishop's liturgical vestments and insignia (in this way, the equality between archbishop and viceroy was being recognized).[64] This compromise solution, however, did not solve the problem entirely, as it could lend itself to different interpretations. The archbishops could try to affirm their right to use a baldachin whether the viceroy was present or not, especially as a means of asserting their power when they were embroiled in some confrontation with the viceroys. The viceroys, for their part, could opt for tolerating the practice or asserting the preeminence of royal power, depending on how their relations with the archbishops were at that precise moment.

The royalist arguments in defense of viceregal primacy are presented in all clarity by Juan Francisco de Montemayor, one of the *oidores* of the *audiencia* of Mexico, whose opinion viceroy Baños had solicited concerning the decision by Diego Osorio, archbishop elect, to sit under a baldachin even when he was not in pontifical dress.[65] Montemayor begins his report by recognizing that without a doubt the pope has the authority to determine all kinds of ecclesiastical ceremonies, but he goes on to affirm that whenever the viceroy attends a ceremony with the archbishop the former has precedence because he represents the king. For that same reason, the archbishop cannot use a *dosel* in the presence of the viceroy unless he is wearing the pontifical dress. After wondering how it is possible to think that "before the king" (that is, before the viceroy) anybody, even a prelate, might sit under a canopy, Montemayor launches an all-out defense of royal authority. In his view, the clergy must be subordinated in all aspects to secular authority, except in questions of religious doctrine, and bishops, no matter how great their dignity may be, are not exempt from the "obedience and vassalage they owe His Majesty as their natural king and lord."[66] Not all the *oidores*, however, shared such "regalist" ideas. While for Francisco Calderón, for instance, the archbishop might use the baldachin — which, in his words, was the "seat and throne" of archbishops and bishops — as long as the viceroy was not present, even if he was not in pontifical dress, for Antonio de Lara, the majority of jurists who dealt with this matter argued that bishops might sit under a canopy in the churches, even if the viceroy was present (although he recognized that his examples did not refer to the Indies).[67] For his part, archbishop Osorio contended that the use of a *dosel* was an honor owed to prelates as proof of veneration, as ecclesiastical jurisdiction, the distribution of the sacraments, and the spiritual government of souls resided in them.[68] It is clear that in the archbishop's mind the viceregal and archiepiscopal figures were parallel, seeing both as rulers, though one was a ruler of bodies and the other of souls.

This tug-of-war between the secular and ecclesiastical powers necessarily would manifest itself during the celebrations of Corpus Christi, the most important of all the annual rituals in New Spain, jointly attended by viceroy and archbishop. After the viceregal entry, it was the costliest festivity paid for by the city council. The culminating moment of the festivities was the solemn procession that paraded the Sacred Host throughout the streets of Mexico City.[69] Although it was in theory a strictly religious celebration, the identification that existed in the Spanish monarchy between the body of Christ (the Sacred Host) and the body of the king made this festivity a celebration full of political significance. In the course of the seventeenth century, the presence of the Spanish monarchs at the Corpus procession celebrated in Madrid became customary and the viceroys would replicate that presence across the ocean, becoming indispensable figures in the Mexican celebration. In the Madrid procession, the existence of two ritual centers (the Host and the monarch) was indisputable, but in Mexico things became more problematic, as the religious authorities would always insist that the Holy Sacrament and themselves were the exclusive protagonists of the ceremonies.[70]

For example, in 1663, the viceroy, the count of Baños, tried to alter the customary route of the Corpus procession to make it pass in front of the viceregal palace so that the vicereine could see it without having to leave the palace, but the symbolic meaning of such a gesture was too evident for the archbishop to ignore.[71] Defending the right given to him by the Council of Trent to decide all matters affecting the order and route of any religious procession, archbishop Osorio rejected the change. The archbishop was further driven to oppose the viceroy because the latter had alleged that by virtue of the *Royal patronato* he had the authority to decide the route of a procession, though the *oidores* convinced him that that was not the case. The archbishop also alleged that in Madrid the queen herself left the palace to see the procession from the residence balcony of some member of the nobility, without seeking to divert the procession. With all the more reason, therefore, the archbishop contended, the vicereine should "seek His Divine Majesty to adore Him, not permitting Him, because of the authority and power of [her] post, to go seek her at her house." All this notwithstanding, the archbishop decided to compromise on this occasion and accept the proposed change because the preparations for the procession had almost been completed. In return, however, the archbishop got snubbed by the vicereine during the procession, as she appeared on the balcony of the palace only after the archbishop and the cathedral chapter, who were accompanying the monstrance, had walked by. Only then, as the viceroy and the *oidores* were passing by the palace, did the vicereine show up on the balcony. This very visible gesture left no doubt as to whom the vicereine was "adoring."[72]

In the viceregal entry procession, the viceroy was welcomed separately by the representatives of the city and the clergy, but the Corpus procession featured a fusion of all sectors of society around its central symbol: the consecrated Host.[73] For that reason, the position of a person or corporation in relation to the monstrance was of the utmost importance, becoming a frequent object of contention.[74] This "politics of proximity" was not peculiar to the Corpus procession. In fact, it was a defining characteristic of all processions, which always revolved around a "sacred center," be it the king or the Host, the viceroy or the archbishop. We have already seen how their proximity to God or the monarch endowed certain angels (the seraphim) and certain noblemen (the gentlemen of the chamber) with a special and almost mystical kind of prestige and power. This translated into the arrangement of processions in such a way that the marching order always revolved around a center or focal point, a symbol of power and authority. In New Spain, in most processions this was the viceroy, whereas in the Corpus procession it was the monstrance displaying the Sacred Host that constituted the core of the ritual parade. Thus, maintaining proximity to the "ritual center" of the procession was a public declaration of power, for which reason the viceroys always strived to find a way to have themselves seen as close as possible to the Host. As a result, the monstrance displaying the Host could become, quite literally, an object of contention between the secular and the ecclesiastical powers.

Perhaps the most notorious example of this in seventeenth-century Mexico was a dispute over the exact position of the viceroy's pages in the 1651 Corpus procession that brought the viceroy, the count of Alba de Liste, and the *cabildo eclesiástico* (the archiepiscopal see was vacant at the time) face to face.[75] The viceroy claimed that, because that was the position occupied by the king's pages in the Corpus procession in Madrid, his pages should march right before the monstrance, forming two rows and flanked by the members of the cathedral chapter, marching likewise in two rows, or, as an alternative, the chapter could process before the viceroy's pages. But, for the prebendaries, the distance that the viceroy wanted to put between them and the monstrance or the interjection of alien bodies — the pages — in the body of the *cabildo* was something totally inadmissible. The day of the procession the viceroy rejected the prebendaries' last-minute offer to walk behind the Sacred Host (which happened to be the position that the viceroy took in the procession) and left the cathedral to draw up a *real provisión* with which to make the *cabildo* comply with his orders. Then, some clerics tried to take the monstrance with them so that the procession could begin, but the *corregidor* and the *alcaldes del crimen*, standing in front of the monstrance and following the viceroy's orders, tried to impede them. In the ensuing brawl that erupted in the cathedral the clerics argued that only the archbishop had the power to give orders in the cathedral and that the Corpus was just a religious not a secular festivity, to which the secular officials replied by accusing the clerics of rejecting the jurisdiction of the *Royal patronato* and the authority of the viceroy, to whom they owed obedience as the king's vassals. When the viceroy and the *audiencia* returned to the cathedral with the *real provisión*, the chapter decided to obey it, but when the procession finally started off, after a delay of several hours, the members of the cathedral chapter decided not to march "in the form of a *cabildo*" and to mingle instead with other clerics.[76] With this gesture, the ecclesiastical chapter disappeared from public view, thus avoiding being seen in a position of inferiority in relation to the ritual center of the procession.

The behavior of viceroys and archbishops when they met in public constituted an entire poetics of power. For example, in processions the archbishop was to march in front of the viceroy and was never to mingle with the *audiencia*. Whenever the viceroy attended a public ceremony other than a procession with the archbishop, the viceroy had to march on the right side of the archbishop.[77] When the viceroy was attending services at the cathedral, whenever the archbishop walked from the choir to the altar and back again, the viceroy would rise from his seat and walk forward two or three steps to receive the prelate's blessing. Similarly, whenever the archbishop walked past the viceroy or the vicereine, the page who was carrying the train of his cape had to release it. Also, when the archbishop paid the viceroy a visit, the latter would go to meet him at the door of the first antechamber and, on leaving, the viceroy would accompany him to the first step of the main stairway. When the viceroy was the visitor, the archbishop would greet and say goodbye to him in the middle of the staircase of his residence, and sometimes he even accompanied him to his carriage.[78]

Each member of New-Spanish society was the carrier of a capital of honor, according to his or her respective position in the social hierarchy, which, in the last instance, declared an individual's power. This power, in turn, was staged in different spaces, the viceregal palace (or rather "royal" as it was called by contemporaries) being one of the privileged stages of power in Mexico.[79] Here, the leading actor was, no doubt, the viceroy, his movements and those of the rest of the actors who swarmed about the palace being perfectly regulated by court etiquette. This etiquette provided the inhabitants of the palace with a mental map for guiding their behavior. The regulating etiquettes and ceremonies were necessary above all among people of similar but not equal status. It was imperative that one's status not be confused with that of another, much less that of the viceroy, who in theory presided over everything from the summit of the hierarchical pyramid. Thus, in the case of visits to the viceroy, the higher the rank of the visitor, the farther he was permitted to penetrate into the palace, whereas the viceroy moved in the opposite direction, walking from his chamber to the appropriate place to welcome the visitor, according to the latter's rank and position.[80] In this spatial code the stairs were critical points of formal contact. Stairs were critical locations for measuring the relations between powers and a way to lessen the status of the visitor, depending on where the host chose to meet him.[81] That the archbishop usually accompanied the viceroy to the middle of the stairway or to his carriage was an indication of the primacy of royal power, just as keeping him to his right side was. It was enough that the archbishop awaited the viceroy high up on the stairway instead of going to meet him farther down for the viceroy to clearly understand the message.

In the constant confrontations between viceroys and bishops, which very often were manifested in ritual form, this liturgy of courtesy played a central role. Any variation of its precepts could indicate a declaration of war or a sign of good will.[82] This is precisely what happened in the clash between the marquis of Mancera and archbishop Enríquez de Rivera. The conflict originated in Mancera'a solid support of the religious orders in their customary disputes with the archbishop concerning the Indian doctrines, support that the archbishop believed to be an unacceptable encroachment upon his jurisdiction.[83] As a result, Enríquez decided to use the "symbolic" weapons at his disposal to respond to this intrusion. Thus, he stopped visiting the viceroy for a long time (these courtesy calls were one of the main forms of communication among the members of the ruling elite, a means of securing harmony and cooperation among them). This action caused, in the words of the viceroy, "the astonishment and even the scandal of the populace." In addition, the archbishop began to manipulate the rituals of deference in a subtle way in order to ritually attack the viceroy.[84] An excellent occasion to do this was the solemn Mass celebrated for the Corpus octave, when the cathedral was packed with people. As recounted by the notary who was assisting the viceroy that day:

> The High Mass having come to an end and the procession begun, His Excellency along with the Royal Audiencia and the other tribunals followed the most sacred monstrance along the transept and

towards the choir, at whose entrance His Lordship was standing accompanied by the rest of the prebendaries. On the arrival of the monstrance, he descended to the church floor, and when it passed in front of him, His Lordship genuflected to the Holy Sacrament. Then he proceeded towards his seat, exchanging courtesies with His Excellency and all the ministers, and His Excellency and everyone else corresponded with the appropriate reverences, ... his train bearer carrying the train without releasing it from his hand. ...This I saw and very carefully took note thereof...[85]

The gesture of the archbishop was beyond doubt. By prostrating himself before the Holy Sacrament and refusing to release the train of the cape, a courtesy owed to the viceroy because of the preeminence of his post, he was refusing to recognize the supremacy of viceregal over episcopal power. At stake was the preeminence of viceregal power, which a little gesture, executed by the archbishop in front of New Spain's entire ruling elite, had questioned.[86] As the *Acuerdo* reminded Enríquez de Rivera in a note that it sent to him soon after the cathedral incident, "the train on the prelates' vestments was introduced because of the gravity and dignity of their persons, and not releasing it when exchanging courtesies denotes *superiority*, which is something tolerable and allowed when done before those who do not have an equal or greater [dignity]."[87]

The viceroy would have considered the continual discourtesies the archbishop directed at him as demonstrating a mere lack of urbanity had they not become public knowledge, but when they took place during a public ceremony, for all the populace to see, then it became a matter of being disrespectful not only to the person of the marquis of Mancera but also to the viceroy of New Spain and, by extension, to the monarch himself. Then, Mancera contended, it was no longer possible to practice "dissimulation."[88] These same ideas had been forcefully expressed by the *fiscal* of the *audiencia* when answering a request made of him to give his opinion on this matter:

The preservation of monarchies consists in ... preserving the authority and esteem of the offices, and that is why everyone is obliged to give them special consideration and respect for the greater interest of the common good. ... This is so because this obligation emanates from natural, divine, human, canon, civil, and political law, and he who does not comply with this reverence in all places ... commits a great and despicable crime, such that he who occupies the office cannot pretend not to notice when those prerogatives owed him because of [his post] are omitted. Furthermore, being the above general and common rules that apply to the courtesy owed to any magistrates, the present case has other qualities of much greater consideration, as the Most Excellent Viceroys of the

> Indies are the living representation of His Majesty who sends them, on whose authority and preeminence there are many statements aimed at maintaining in all its luster such a great post.[89]

The political elite both in Madrid and in Mexico saw the exercise and maintenance of authority as highly problematic and always uncertain; authority was understood to be something fragile and delicate that was constructed and maintained with great effort and care. As William Beik has observed, the problem of authority is one of the most fascinating aspects of early modern political society. This is a world in which the establishment of authority depended greatly on such things as prestige, reputation, or public appearances much more than on the use of force. Thus, the way in which legitimate authority was constructed and perceived was fundamental for the establishment of the bases of power. Furthermore, the authority of the king was predicated on an ideology of personal loyalty, not of impersonal service. In this regard, authority was always personal and was privately owned, although it was exercised in the name of the king.[90] The importance of personal prestige and *crédito*, therefore, was essential to the effective exercise of authority.[91] In 1643, one of the *oidores* of the *audiencia* of Mexico complained to the king that his credit had been impaired by the viceroy who had accused him, during a public hearing, of having accepted a bribe. In response, the Council of the Indies decided to write to the viceroy to let him know how unbecoming to his position such a behavior was, as he should be well aware of the importance of preserving the credit of the *oidores* as the best way to maintain royal authority.[92] No wonder, then, that, in the Spanish world, authority was defined as the "credit of majesty" and was seen as a more effective instrument of rule than physical coercion. This invisible force called "authority" also signified "esteem, faith, truth, and regard," and "ostentation, pomp, display, majesty, stateliness, and gravity, both in one's behavior and in one's standards of decorum and representation."[93] The authority of the Spanish monarchy, then, was predicated upon the personal credit of its officials and the pomp and circumstance surrounding them.

This was certainly the view of the marquis of Mancera. As a result of an unexpected event — the sudden death of the duke of Veragua, Mancera's successor, a few days after he took possession — he found himself in a position of inferiority in relation to the archbishop, because Enríquez de Rivera, according to the king's orders, had become the acting viceroy of New Spain. The now archbishop–viceroy wasted no time in asserting his superiority over the former viceroy. The unwritten protocol that regulated relations between the incoming and the outgoing viceroys established that, as a sign of deference, the outgoing viceroy should be at the right side of the incoming one on all the visits and occasions in which both appeared together (as we have seen, the right side always indicated preeminence and superiority).[94] Thus, when Mancera went to visit the archbishop to congratulate him for the queen's birthday, Enríquez de Rivera went to meet him, as was customary, at the first antechamber; however, when he took Mancera back to his chamber, the archbishop took the ex-viceroy's right side, and once there he also insisted on sitting on his right side. Mancera later on would contend that this "outrage," executed in front of all the people present in the palace, could seriously damage his credit and mean the loss of the good opinion created by all his work as viceroy, especially at so delicate a moment, when he was going through the proceedings of his *residencia* (judicial review).[95]

The ritual battles between viceroys and archbishops, far from being odd anecdotes lacking in meaning, were the embodiment itself of the production and negotiation of the relations between the secular and the ecclesiastical powers, relations that even in a specifically Catholic monarchy such as the Spanish monarchy could be characterized as stormy. Ultimately, what was at stake in the broader context was the degree of control that the monarch would be able to exert upon the clergy of his kingdoms.

The Preeminence of the Body

During the official celebrations of the feast of the Assumption on August 15, 1663, the two *oidores* who had attended Mass in the cathedral of Mexico City (the viceroy was absent due to illness) asked the *corregidor* and the *regidores* to escort them formally on their way back to the *audiencia* palace. According to the *regidores*, they had no obligation to escort the *audiencia* if the viceroy was not present; however, they decided to do so to avoid a public incident with the *oidores*. Once they arrived in the Justices' chambers, the *corregidor* could not help saying to the *oidores* that it had been a great pleasure for the city to accompany them, albeit that was not the custom. To this, one of the *oidores*, in an irate way, asked the *corregidor*: "Where is the king?" "Here, my lord," answered the *corregidor*. "Then," the *oidor* replied, "if the king is here, here he must be accompanied." Although the description of the incident by the witnesses is very similar, it is interesting to note the one point of contention: All the *audiencia* witnesses emphasized the fact that the *oidores* "made up a tribunal," wearing their hats but not their capes, while the witnesses for the *cabildo* made it clear that the *oidores* had already taken their hats off and put their capes on.[96] The emphasis the witnesses placed on the hats and capes of the *oidores* was not just anecdotal but was also full of political meaning. The hats donned by the *oidores* during public ceremonies were the mark of their investiture as royal judges and the visible and ceremonial sign that they were constituted in a "body" endowed with royal power. This was a crucial point. By insisting on the fact that they were still wearing their hats, the *oidores* were reinforcing their image as depositaries of the king's power, while the *cabildo*, by denying this fact, was divesting them of much of that power. It was clear to everybody that when the *oidores* were ceremonially congregated together as an *audiencia*, they experienced a symbolic transformation of an extraordinary nature: Rather than representing the king, the *oidores* as a group became the king himself.

The "language of bodies" is fundamental for understanding the relations among the institutions of colonial rule and their public behavior. To the extent that they were constituted as "bodies," their members represented royal power in its fullness. Although as individuals each member certainly possessed a measure of royal power, it was never to the same degree as when they were congregated together and *en forma* (forming or in the shape of a body). It was seen as natural that, according to the organicist view of the political community prevalent at the time, a political body or corporation was endowed with a personality and power that an individual, separated and isolated from such a corporation, could never enjoy, in much the same way as an arm, separated from the body, was an inert member, unable to realize any of its natural functions.[97] This goes a long way toward explaining the behavior in public of New Spain's ruling institutions. The *audiencia*, the municipal *cabildo*, and the tribunal of the Inquisition were leading characters on the public stage of Mexico City, but their participation, as in the case of viceroys and archbishops, was characterized by constant disputes that marked the tensions and ambiguities of the colonial structure of power.

In the case of the *audiencia*, the viceroys would insist on always being accompanied by the *oidores* wherever they went. They would also be opposed to the appearance of the *oidores* in public forming a *cuerpo de audiencia* when the viceroy was not present.[98] If the viceroy and the *audiencia* were seen, not as separate institutions, but as just one organic whole, a mystical body, then the power of a viceroy should be more apparent and visible when he appeared surrounded by "his" *oidores* and "forming a body" with them. For their part, the *oidores* usually resisted what they saw as the ceremonial abuses of the viceroys. When the marquis of Guadalcázar insisted that the members of the cathedral chapter refrain from going to meet and welcome the *oidores* whenever they went to the cathedral if he did not go with them, the judges contended that the prebendaries should still meet the *oidores* ceremonially because the *audiencia* represented the monarch whether or not the viceroy went with them.[99] In 1674, they would write to the queen regent to complain about the custom introduced by the viceroys (in a gesture that clearly assimilated them to the monarch) of having the *audiencia* visit them for their birthdays or those of the vicereines, or whenever they were ill. Furthermore, the viceroys insisted upon being escorted by the *audiencia* with all accustomed pomp and circumstance (the *oidores* had to go "with hats and without capes," keeping their "seniority and order of precedence") on certain occasions when, according to the *oidores*, they were not really obliged to do so, as these occasions were not *fiestas de tabla* (those feast days on which it was mandatory for the viceroy and the *audiencia* to participate in the processions and celebrations in the cathedral).[100] The *oidores*, in reality, did not deny the viceroy's superiority, inasmuch as he was their "head." What they criticized was the viceroys' attempt to make the *oidores* completely subordinate to their power, ignoring the fact that the *oidores* also partook of the king's authority, for which reason it was indispensable for them to have enough "credit" to be able to carry out their duties.[101]

It was a well-established political principle that harmony between the *oidores* and the viceroy was an indispensable condition for maintaining the authority of each, hence the continuous reminders of the Crown to the *oidores* that, in case the viceroy interfered with matters reserved for the *audiencia*, the pertinent observations should be conveyed to him but without the general population finding out. Should the viceroy persist in this interference, the *oidores* had no choice but to obey him (provided that it would not cause a public uproar) and to notify the king about what was happening. In this way, royal authority, which had to be preserved at all costs, was saved.[102] The same principle had to be applied to the *oidores*, as they shared equally in royal authority and majesty. As Juan de Solórzano observed, whenever the viceroy had to reprimand an *oidor*, he should do it in secret, so that "he does not weaken the esteem which he [the *oidor*] enjoys."[103] In a world in which order and social peace were considered to be very fragile, nothing would upset this delicate equilibrium more than the sight of a divided and quarreling ruling class, as it was always possible that the common people might take advantage of the ruling elite's divisions to riot or stage a rebellion. As the ruling heads of the community, invested with the charisma of royal authority, it was supposed that the viceroy and the *oidores* (and bishops and archbishops for that matter) wielded great influence on the rest of the population; hence, the insistence on preserving peace between them at all costs.

In viceregal thinking, both the viceroy and *oidores* were depositories of royal authority, but because the viceroy was imagined as the king's *living image*, while the *oidores* were simply *images* of the king, the viceroy's authority should be superior to that of the judges. For example, concerning the squabble about the viceroy's cushion mentioned at the beginning of this chapter, the count of Salvatierra had no doubts about two things: First, his power and authority were superior to that of the *oidores* because he represented royal power more closely (*más inmediatamente*); that is, the power of a viceroy resembled that of the king more closely than did the power of the *oidores*.[104] Second, this superior power of the viceroy had to be acknowledged in public by the *oidores* (that is, during all public ceremonies and rituals), as only in this way could the authority necessary to guarantee the subjects' obedience and love be established.[105]

The gesture of Salvatierra can be better understood if we keep in mind that it was performed in the *Sala del Acuerdo*, a space filled with political symbolism. It was there, under the king's portrait and with all solemnity, that the royal letters were opened, read, and obeyed by kissing and placing them upon the magistrates' heads. It was also the chamber in which the viceroy was sworn in to his office.[106] Moreover, Salvatierra's gesture, which may seem to us to be so insignificant, had, in the context of seventeenth-century New Spain, a deeper meaning: the strengthening of the viceroy's and, by extension, the king's power, in opposition to those who wanted to limit it. As we saw in Chapter 2, while the viceroys very often attempted to conduct their political activity independently from the control of the *audiencia*, the *oidores* always insisted that the only possible good government was that in which the viceroy ruled in cooperation with the High Court. Thus, the disputes between viceroys and *oidores* regarding ceremonial matters were but the most visible aspect — and, in the opinion of many of its protagonists, the most decisive one, given the effects attributed to the public exhibition of rulers — of these conflicting views of viceregal power.

Yet, the Crown did not always agree with some of the viceroys' ceremonial excesses. In 1619, it decided to fine the marquis of Guadalcázar 4000 ducats (and 300 to each *oidor* for having consented to it) for a series of ceremonial abuses he had committed during the obsequies for the death of the vicereine. He had permitted his retainers to march mingled with the body of the *audiencia* during the funeral procession, he had forced the *oidores* to wear ceremonial mourning clothes while they heard cases in the courtrooms (something reserved for the death of royal persons only), and, last but not least, he had allowed a catafalque to be erected in the cathedral that was an improved version of the same one that had been raised to honor the passing of the queen. The viceroy defended his actions by arguing that all these ceremonies had been done not to honor the deceased person but to show respect for the dignity of the viceregal office, especially because in a place so remote and where the natives were so inclined to ceremonies it was much more necessary to display pomp and magnificence. In this way, the viceroy contended, the natives would be able to learn of the Spanish monarch's greatness by seeing that of the person who ruled them in his name.[107] Although the Crown would have normally agreed with Guadalcázar's arguments, this being to a large extent the reason why viceroys existed, it did not seem to be convinced on this occasion. Clearly, the viceroy had gone too far, for, to the Crown, it was one thing to foster the figure of the viceroy as the living image of the king (or the vicereine as the queen's image) and quite another to make that image appear to be larger or more powerful than the original.

In deciding the outcome of the give and take between viceroys and *oidores*, it is evident that a viceroy's determination to defend his power and prerogatives as well as his connections with the court could be decisive factors. For example, it seems to be more than a mere coincidence that the Mexican *oidores* had decided to express their complaints in 1674, at a time in which the viceregal post was temporarily filled by the archbishop of Mexico, Enríquez de Rivera. During the archbishop's long time in office as acting viceroy (from 1673 to 1680), the *oidores* were able to limit their image of subordination to the viceroy, securing royal *cédulas* that upheld their views, but when the archbishop's successor, the count of Paredes, arrived in Mexico he wasted no time in soliciting the king to have all the *cédulas* issued in 1674 revoked. The success of Paredes — the *cédulas* favoring the position of the *oidores* were abrogated by a royal order in 1681 — was determined, in all likelihood, by the powerful connections of the viceroy at the Madrid court, as he was the duke of Medinaceli's brother, who, besides being one of the wealthiest and most powerful noblemen of Castile, was the monarch's chief minister at the time.[108]

While the *oidores* had to deal with the "ceremonial abuses" of the viceroys, they, for their part, tried the same methods with their colleagues in the *audiencia* of Mexico, the *alcaldes del crimen*. In 1672, for example, the criminal judges decided to no longer take part in the Saturday *visitas de cárcel* (jail inspections), which they used to do with the *oidores*.[109] The reason was because, once the inspection was concluded, the *alcaldes*, wearing their hats, carrying their staffs, and without their capes (that is, marching ceremonially and "forming a chamber" [*en forma de sala*]), had to escort the *oidores* through the corridors of the *audiencia* palace and downstairs to the *oidores'* carriages. For the *alcaldes*, this resulted in grave damage to their offices and decreasing their authority, as it was clear proof of the inferior place the *oidores* wished to assign them. The *oidores* always contended that their office was of greater importance and rank than that of the *alcaldes*. In a way, this was ceremonially recognized, because in the processions they always marched behind the *alcaldes* and just before the viceroy; that is, they were the closest to the processional center. To justify their pretensions, the *oidores* asserted that the jurisdiction of the criminal chamber had been "picked out" of that of the *audiencia* and was limited to criminal matters. For this reason, the *alcaldes* could not have the same authority as the *audiencia* (i.e., the *oidores*). Moreover, contended the *oidores*, the inspection of the prisons was a "royal ceremony," as royal power was "vividly represented" in it, for which reason it was necessary to dignify it with certain ceremonies that made the tribunal respected and revered, ceremonies that were the more necessary the farther away the monarch was. That was why the two inspecting *oidores* used to go "forming a body and with their hats on" (*en forma, en cuerpo y con gorras*) — that is, representing the royal *audiencia*.[110]

To these arguments, the *alcaldes* responded that they could not possibly be subordinate to the *oidores* because, in criminal cases, they represented the king "vividly and closely," without any limitation or possibility of appeal to another court. For this reason, the monarch had given them a jurisdiction that was "separate, independent, and divided" from that of the civil chamber, with the *oidores* having no authority to interfere with the affairs of the criminal chamber. Moreover, their authority, the *alcaldes* asserted, was equal to that of the *oidores*, as they could issue writs by themselves in the king's name and with the royal seal, and they could be commanded only by the king, the Council of the Indies, and the viceroy. The *alcaldes* argued that, according to the royal *cédulas*, the prison inspections were not carried out by the *oidores* accompanied by the *alcaldes* as their inferiors, but by all together forming a body. The *alcaldes*, therefore, did not understand how the *oidores* could pretend to represent royal power alone because, though constituting a separate chamber that enjoyed the same authority as the civil chamber, the *alcaldes* would always be a part of the "body of the *audiencia*." The *alcaldes* added that, if some of them had sometimes accompanied the *oidores* after the inspections, it had been done as a courtesy or because of friendship, it being one thing "to go incorporated in a voluntary manner" and another "to go out as inferiors, accompanying by obligation." The *alcaldes*, in a petition addressed to the viceroy, summarized their position in the following way:

> The superior ministers can neither yield nor subordinate themselves to such ceremonies and attentions without knowing the will of His Majesty, whose post they represent, and the cédulas of His Majesty command us only to assist and accompany Your Excellency with all due attention because of your being our head and that of the entire royal audiencia, and because of the royal authority which vividly shines in the person of Your Excellency, in which we are always venerating, irrespective of ceremony, time, or place, the royal person of His Majesty, … it being an irregular and strange thing for the body to wish for itself alone those attentions which are only due to the head and that these attentions be rendered by the same members who comprise it.[111]

Ultimately, what was at stake was the judicial autonomy of the *alcaldes*, which the *oidores* usually encroached upon during the jail visits. The dispute between *alcaldes* and *oidores* was resolved by the Council of the Indies in favor of the *alcaldes*. The Council considered that the pretensions of the *oidores* were "exorbitant and against the authority of the *alcaldes*," because the representation of both the civil and criminal chambers was equal. Thus, the *alcaldes* ought to escort the *oidores* only to the door of the criminal chamber.[112] A certain irony can be found in the fact that, some years before, the *oidores* had been involved in a similar dispute with the *regidores* of Mexico City, although back then the *oidores* had been the ones forced to defend themselves against the claims of the *regidores*. In 1660, the *audiencia* wrote to the king requesting the elimination of the feast of San Hipólito, which had been celebrated every year since 1530 on August 13 to commemorate the conquest of Mexico. Besides the Mass in the cathedral, the most important ceremony was the parading on horseback of the city banner, in which the viceroy and the *audiencia* escorted the city's *alférez mayor* (banner bearer) and the *regidores* throughout the streets of Mexico City (Figure 12).[113] The *oidores* initially justified their petition as a means

Fig. 12 Anonymous, *San Hipólito*, eighteenth century. Because the final conquest of Tenochtitlán occurred on San Hipólito's feast day, here the saint is represented as a triumphal Hernán Cortés astride the Mexican eagle, which, in turn, is standing on a prickly pear cactus. The two praying figures are Moctezuma, who is leading the indigenous population, and Pedro de Alvarado, who leads the *conquistadores*. He was one of Cortés' captains, the one who was said to have completed the capture of Tenochtitlan. (Franz Mayer Museum, Mexico City.)

to eliminate superfluous expenses, but they soon revealed the true reason: They thought it was "unseemly" that the two junior *oidores* had to pick up the *alférez mayor* at his home and, from there, ride with him in their midst to the city hall, where the *alférez* was to pick up the banner before the procession began. To the *audiencia*, having to escort the *alférez* in this way, when he was not bearing the royal banner, was an abuse that impaired the authority of the *oidores* (as we have seen, for someone to ride or march between two others was a public declaration of the superiority of that person). In the view of the *oidores*, this was justifiable only when the *alférez* was carrying the royal insignia.[114] The *regidores*, on the contrary, argued that this was an honor and a favor done to them by the king to augment their authority. Besides, it was due to them because they were the "head of all the provinces of this New World." In the opinion of the *regidores*, the *audiencia*, instead of fomenting the city's authority, was trying to lessen its "luster and authority."[115]

Years later, during the celebration of San Hipólito in 1676, the *regidores* attempted another gesture that greatly upset the *oidores*. Now (the *oidores* informed the monarch) the *regidores* did not think it was enough that two *oidores* had to escort the *alférez* from and to his home, even though he was not bearing the banner; now they wanted the *oidores* to dismount from their horses and go up to his chamber. For the *audiencia*, having "to do with a *regidor*, already without any representation, that which Your Majesty does not allow done with your viceroy, who is the living image of Your Royal Person in these kingdoms," not only was an "indecorous and unseemly" pretension but also a "monstrosity."[116] If at times they had gone upstairs to the chamber of the *alférez*, the *oidores* argued, it had been as a courtesy and because the *alférez* had invited them to "some refreshments, sweets and chocolate"; however, it was one thing to do this voluntarily and another very different one to be obligated to do so, for which reason they had no choice other than to defend their authority — something very necessary in such a remote place, they added — in the face of the *regidores'* pretensions. The *audiencia* also took this opportunity to remind the monarch that if the *alférez* marched at the viceroy's left during the parade it was because he was bearing the royal banner; thus, it did not seem to be fair that the *oidores* had to escort him when he was not carrying it. In the words of the *fiscal* of the *audiencia*, the *alférez* was at that moment "already stripped of the royal insignia and with no other representation than that of his private person, to whom no such veneration is due, nor is it fair that by doing so the authority and reputation of the post of *oidor* be wasted."[117]

We have already seen the prominent place occupied by the cities — especially those with representation in the Cortes — in the political constitution of the Spanish monarchy, among which was Mexico City as head of the kingdom of New Spain. Throughout the seventeenth century, Mexico City's *cabildo* insisted on defending its authority in public — that is to say, its place in the processional order as well as its association with specific markers of power. If, in the case of the viceroy and the *audiencia*, their ceremonial place was undisputed (they always constituted the "head" of the procession), the situation was not so well defined for the rest of the institutions of colonial government. This created constant disputes about exactly where to place them in the processions and how they should display themselves in public. The *cabildo* always tried to preserve its identity as a body differentiated from the other bodies that comprised the commonwealth. This would make the *regidores* demand that at public ceremonies no extraneous person could be introduced into the body formed by the *cabildo*; that is, no one besides the *corregidor* or the *regidores* could march or be seated with them. That was the function of the *maceros* (mace bearers), who always marched before the city, marking with their presence the boundaries of the body formed by the *corregidor* and *regidores*.[118] To allow outsiders to mix with the *cabildo* during a public ceremony contributed to blurring its public presence as a corporation endowed with authority and privileges. For this reason, the *regidores* always rejected the appearance of the *corregidor* behind the *superintendente de propios* (superintendent of city property) at public ceremonies. This post was always filled by an *oidor*, who, not surprisingly, always tried to have precedence over the *corregidor*. The *regidores*, however, contended that to allow the head of the *cabildo* to be in an inferior place was a "monstrous deformity."[119]

If cushions as signs of power and superiority were objects of contention between viceroys and *oidores*, in the case of the municipal council, chairs similarly constituted an essential element in the semiotics of power. To be allowed to sit on a chair at public ceremonies was a privilege reserved in New Spain for viceroys, bishops, and the judges of the *audiencia*, while *cabildo* members sat on a bench.[120] An easy way for a *corregidor* to stand out from the rest of the *cabildo*, therefore, was to sit on a chair separated from the bench of the *regidores*.[121] This custom must have been very widespread because in 1652 the monarch was forced to issue an order prohibiting the *alcaldes mayores* (as the *corregidores* were known in New Spain) from sitting on a chair, with a cushion and a rug, apart from his town council. Their only distinguishing sign was to be the occupation of the first place in the bench by the *alcalde mayor*, as he was the "head of the body" of the town council.[122] Toward the end of the seventeenth century, an emphasis by the Mexican *cabildo* on enhancing its symbolic status can be observed. To that end, the *cabildo* repeatedly requested to be allowed to sit on chairs at public ceremonies.[123] This, however, was not a new development. As early as 1625 the *regidores* regretted that when attending church services they were not allowed to sit on chairs next to the Epistle. According to them, this had caused such a loss of reputation to the *cabildo* (as their place in the churches was "obscure and without distinction from the rest of the populace") that no one could be found who wished to buy one of the six vacant posts of *regidor*, something that, in the words of the *regidores*, had never been seen before in a city as wealthy and important as Mexico. The ultimate reason for this lack of buyers, they said, was that the many expenses occasioned by the office did not offer the compensation of a "preeminent and safe place" in churches and at public ceremonies.[124] It was evident for the *regidores* that the place and manner in which one appeared in public had all kinds of repercussions.

With regard to the Inquisition, the very ambiguous place that it occupied in the power structure of New Spain was constantly reflected in the ceremonial order. This caused the inquisitors to get embroiled in continual ceremonial disputes with everybody else. As Francisco Bethencourt has observed, the history of the Spanish Inquisition is, in fact, a history of constant battles to maintain its power and prestige *vis-à-vis* the rest of the institutions, being quite evident that the discords on matters of etiquette hid in reality political and institutional conflicts.[125] The same can be said with respect to processional prerogatives, which the Inquisition was always keen to defend, especially in those moments of triumph when its power glowed more than ever (i.e., during the celebration of the *autos de fe*). In these ceremonies, the inquisitors were preceded only by the viceroy, albeit this had not always been the case. By the end of the sixteenth century, the Inquisition had been successful in making the viceroys appear during the celebration of the *autos* in a position of inferiority (i.e., the senior inquisitor marching between the viceroy and the second most senior inquisitor or having the inquisitors sit between the viceroy and the senior *oidor*). The viceroys vigorously opposed this, in time succeeding in asserting their right to precede the inquisitors — that is, marching between the two senior inquisitors.[126] During the *auto de fe* procession, then, the inquisitors had no alternative other than to recognize the viceroy's primacy, but in his absence they could not miss the opportunity to become the absolute protagonists of the ceremony. This is clearly appreciated in the controversy that arose in regard to the processional order of the great *auto de fe* celebrated in Mexico City in 1649. Because the bishop of Yucatan, who was ruling in place of a viceroy at the time, could not attend because of the illness that would take him to his grave, the *audiencia* requested, as was instructed in the royal *cédulas*, that the senior *oidor*, replacing the absent viceroy, should take the leading position in the ceremonies. The inquisitors responded that this position belonged to the archbishop — in his capacity as *visitador* of the Mexican tribunal — and the inquisitors. To this the *fiscal* of the *audiencia* replied, in a report solicited by the *oidores*, that if the senior *oidor* — acting as president of the *audiencia* — did not occupy the leading position:

> He would be denied the first place and precedence that ... belongs and is due to Your Royal Person, closely and vividly represented in this royal audiencia, not only as monarch and lord of all temporal things and matters in these provinces and patron of the spiritual ones, but especially of those matters of the faith and similar ceremonies which look to its exaltation and defense as his only and

principal instigator and defender. ...And it would be very much against [His Majesty's] intention and wish that, in the present auto, this royal audiencia failed to give [the Catholic faith], with its representation and royal name, the favor and assistance that he wants it to be given.[127]

Here, the *audiencia*, to uphold its supremacy over the Inquisition, utilizes the same politico–religious discourse with which the Crown had constructed the identity of the Inquisition as the quintessential defender of the Catholic faith and the religious unity of the monarchy. According to the reasoning of the *fiscal*, because the monarch was the main defender and supporter of Catholicism and the Inquisition (whose main mission was to defend the Catholic faith), it was only natural for the senior *oidor*, as the monarch's main representative in Mexico (in the absence of the viceroy), to preside over the *auto de fe*. The inquisitors, however, did not seem very impressed by these affirmations of royal power, replying that the *oidores*, or any other secular judges, lacked jurisdictional power over the affairs of the Inquisition. For that reason, they summoned the *oidores*, "in the name of the Holy Apostolic See and of His Catholic Majesty," to attend the *auto* and occupy the place they had been assigned by the inquisitors; otherwise, the inquisitors would respond with the usual penalties and censures (i.e., excommunication), which were reserved for those who obstructed the Inquisition. Faced with inquisitorial inflexibility, the *oidores* decided to attend the *auto de fe* to avoid further complications, albeit informing the king about this incident and asking him to punish the inquisitors in a fitting way, as they had shown with their behavior that they had no respect whatsoever for the "king's name." For the *oidores*, all this was just another example of the inquisitors' intrusions into matters that were not within their jurisdiction, in an attempt "not only to oppose but to prevail over the authority and jurisdiction of the judges and courts of Your Majesty."[128] For the *fiscal* of the Council of the Indies, who wrote a report for the councilors on this incident, the relation of subordination that should exist between the *audiencia* and the Inquisition and the place that the senior *oidor* should have in the *auto de fe* was clear enough:

[T]his should be the procedure [to follow], with all the more reason in the Indies, [because] the principal representative of royal authority has precedence in all the ceremonies and functions, since all those conquests belong to the Real Patronato, and the salaries of all the ministers who exercise royal or pontifical jurisdiction are paid for by the royal treasury. Thus, the viceroy being the one who represents [royal authority] and [this royal authority] being transferred, because of absence or illness or any other impediment, to the audiencia, and by the audiencia to the senior oidor, in the autos de fe he must have the same place as the viceroy would because the display of precedence looks to the office of the king, which is represented by the senior oidor who is its image.[129]

This view notwithstanding, Juan de Solórzano, whose opinion the Council had asked for on this matter because of his extensive knowledge of the government of the Indies, appears to be rather skeptical about the possible acceptance by the inquisitors of the opinions of the *fiscal*. He very much doubts that the inquisitors will be willing to give the first place to the senior *oidor*, especially knowing that at times they had even quarreled with the viceroy about it, although in general they accepted the viceroy's precedence, as he represented the king "closely" (*inmediatamente*), whereas this representation was not "so close" (*tan viva*) in the senior *oidor*. Furthermore, Solórzano adds, the government was not really transferred to the senior *oidor* but to the entire *audiencia*, nor was he allowed to appropriate those ceremonials which were reserved exclusively for the kings or their viceroys because an *oidor* acting as president of the *audiencia* did not become the equal of the viceroy. For all these reasons, Solórzano concludes that the Mexican inquisitors were not far wrong when they refused to give the principal place to the *oidor*. At the same time, he warns that, should the Council contradict this opinion, it could not issue a *cédula* without first being approved by the Council of the Inquisition; otherwise, the inquisitors would refuse to obey such an order.[130]

The Inquisition often quarreled with the municipal council of Mexico City because the tribunal usually contended that its lower officials should precede the *corregidor* and *regidores* at public ceremonies or be incorporated into the "city's body." In 1650, when the inquisitors notified the *cabildo* that, in the procession previous to the proclamation of the Edict of Faith that was going to take place in the cathedral, the *corregidor* was to march right behind the inquisitors and with the Inquisition's chief constable at his right, the *corregidor* refused to attend the ceremony, with the excuse that he was ill. The inquisitors reacted to his refusal by threatening to excommunicate him and fine him 2000 pesos. Although the *corregidor* gave in and did attend the procession, he subsequently sued the inquisitors in the *audiencia* to make sure that his privileges and those of the *cabildo* were protected. In the view of the *corregidor*, incorporation of the officials of the Inquisition into the "city's body" was a "despicable and ugly act in the eyes of the people," which had been carried out only because of the "irresistible violence" with which the Inquisition used to impose its resolutions. He justified his decision to sue the inquisitors on the grounds that,

> The most serious concern of magistrates must be to preserve the authority of their offices and the decorum of the royal jurisdiction that they exercise, since if these are tarnished or impaired, there follows the worrisome problem that the populace, following the

example of the show of force made by others against the magistrates, fails in their obligation to venerate and respect them. Thus, not only is it inevitable that the magistrates must see to the defense of the honors and prerogatives of their offices and to the satisfaction of the insults made to royal authority and jurisdiction, but neither are they free to remit or excuse them.[131]

In the eyes of the *corregidor*, to allow such a low-status figure as the chief constable of the Inquisition to walk publicly at his right (a sign of deference and preeminence) was to allow his reputation and "credit" to be damaged and diminished. The *corregidor*, therefore, had no choice other than to defend the decorum of his post, which, in the last analysis, was what gave him the moral authority to have his orders complied with. That is why it was impossible to ignore these public examples of disrespect and contempt.[132] But, as we have seen before, the Inquisition was not easily intimidated. A few years later, in 1655, the city presented the inquisitors with a royal letter favorable to its claims, which stated that the city could not be forced to admit into its "body" any officials of the Inquisition during the procession of the Edict of Faith, as such a thing was against "the luster and authority" of the city. This royal *cédula* notwithstanding, the inquisitors replied that only the Council of the Inquisition had the authority to regulate anything related to the tribunal.[133]

The visits of the inquisitors to the viceroy, as in the case of other institutions, were highly ritualized, every gesture being measured carefully. It was an elaborate liturgy in which the power relations between the viceroy and the Holy Office were acted out on the public stage. Here, the limits of viceregal and inquisitorial power were continuously negotiated through rites of preeminence and deference. It was a delicate matter because of the autonomous power demanded by the Inquisition.[134] The elevated concept that the inquisitors had of themselves and their power, which had reached new heights by the end of the seventeenth century (as shown in Chapter 3), is revealed in a letter written to the *audiencia* in 1696 to complain about the lack of deference of the viceroys toward the Inquisition. The immediate reason for their complaint was that the newly arrived viceroys visited the establishments of the religious orders before paying their respects to the Holy Office. According to the inquisitors,

> … being this tribunal the ecclesiastical community that has the greatest authority and the esteem of this city and kingdom, and, *in many ways, being all the other [religious communities] its subjects,* … it is objectionable that the residents of this city usually consider and think that the post of prelate of any of the said convents is of greater importance [than is the Inquisition], … and this is something that, in view of the great diversity of peoples in this city, damages the esteem and authority of the Holy Office, which *in no*

matter whatsoever depends on or is subordinated to the viceroys, while the said convents and their prelates depend on them, through the Patronato Real, for their nominations of curas doctrineros and for the salaries that they receive as such priests from His Majesty.[135]

For the Inquisition it was clear that the greater autonomy from royal power that it was claiming for itself at the end of the seventeenth century should likewise be manifested on the public stage. This attitude is what made the inquisitors, on their first visit to the newly appointed viceroy, the count of Moctezuma, seek to have the new viceroy meet them at the entrance to the antechamber and say goodbye to them in the middle of that same room (traditionally, the viceroy received the inquisitors in his chamber, rising from his seat under the baldachin and walking forward three or four steps to meet the inquisitors only as the latter walked into the room). The inquisitors did not hesitate to inform the viceroy that if he did not do so, they would not go to the palace to welcome him. Taking their claims a step further, the inquisitors maintained that, in fact, they should be received in the same manner as the archbishop was, though, for the time being, they were willing to compromise with the former proposal. The viceroy, not surprisingly, rejected the inquisitors' pretensions, albeit offering a solution that tells us much about the importance of the language of public gestures as one of the fundamental mechanisms through which power relations were negotiated among New Spain's ruling elite. The count of Moctezuma proposed to the inquisitors that he receive them while in bed, with the excuse that he had become indisposed after the long journey, a proposal that they accepted.[136] While the inquisitors would be able, with this gesture, to comply with their obligation toward the viceroy without having to give in to their pretensions, in the eyes of the residents of Mexico City the viceroy's authority would not be discredited and questioned by the inquisitors' highly visible gesture of refusing to welcome the count of Moctezuma (which would have amounted to a refusal to recognize the viceroy's authority).

In his study of seventeenth-century court society, Norbert Elias noted that gestures like the one described above and all the others presented in this chapter were not "mere externals" but "literal documentations of social existence." To Elias, these formalities are externals only in societies where money or profession are taken as the "reality of social existence."[137] In seventeenth-century society, the theatricalization of body movements (to take off one's hat, to alight, to remain standing or seated, etc.), the chance of preceding another, the way someone was greeted, and so on presented in a symbolic way the difference of status, one's own depreciation, and the acknowledgment of the other's superiority. Everyone knew this vocabulary and grammar of gestured signs. If gestures such as the count of Moctezuma's may look ridiculous from the modern point of view, they were of an almost ontological seriousness for the members of the Mexican ruling elite. If contemporaries attributed such a great transcendence to all kinds of public rituals, it was because their effects were far from negligible. They were much more than a disguise with which to make their power more palatable. Their power depended on these rituals because their power was constituted through them; in other words, it was not ritual in the service of colonial power but colonial power in the service of ritual.

5

The Economy of Favor

When in 1680 the count of Paredes arrived in Mexico City to become the new viceroy of New Spain he was welcomed by two triumphal arches erected by the municipal council and the cathedral chapter in which both of their creators, Carlos de Sigüenza y Góngora and Sor Juana Inés de la Cruz, respectively, had included paintings that allegorized the virtue of liberality as being peculiar to rulers. As Sigüenza put it, "princes have nothing better to immortalize themselves than liberality and magnificence. ...With nothing better than the bestowing of rewards do the hands of princes shine." To illustrate these ideas, he used an image of the Aztec ruler Motecohçuma Xocoyotzin, who, according to him, had been characterized by his generosity. Quoting Seneca, Sor Juana, for her part, contended that "he who honors the worthy man gains a reputation for himself." She designed a painting in which Neptune, as the image of the good ruler, was shown rewarding a dolphin for the services he had rendered to the monarch of the seas.[1] With these words and images both Sigüenza and Sor Juana were expressing one of the basic political principles of the time: The union between a ruler and his subjects required the ruler's bounty. This was something that all political writers of the period agreed upon: The ruler, whether the king or the viceroy, had to be liberal.[2] As the ruler of the New Spanish polity, the viceroy was expected to show his generosity with the inhabitants of the kingdom, although, as a matter of fact, viceregal munificence was only an extension of royal liberality, the king being the ultimate source of the favors and rewards bestowed upon the inhabitants of New Spain by the viceroys. Liberality, or the need for the monarch to be generous with his vassals, rewarding all those who had rendered him any services, becomes, therefore, a key term to understanding the transatlantic political practices of the Spanish monarchy.

A clear parallel existed between the practice of royal liberality and the constitution of a network of loyalty to the monarch. It was in the seventeenth century when the power of the Spanish monarchs reached its greatest development, and one of the mechanisms through which that power was sustained was the utilization of client networks as a means to strengthen the king's authority.[3] This mechanism was likewise utilized by the Spanish kings to establish and maintain their authority over their transatlantic dominions and as a way to ensure the loyalty of their American subjects. While the Spanish Crown attempted to symbolically and ritually reproduce in Mexico the figure of the king in the person of the viceroys as a means to sustain its power, it tried something similar with the creation and reproduction of systems of patronage on the other side of the Atlantic. Here, the viceroy, in the name of the king, became the main source of patronage, as he was in charge of distributing rewards among the inhabitants of New Spain worthy of them (in New Spain, royal and viceregal bounty took the form of the distribution of, above all, the posts of *alcaldes mayores* and *corregidores*). With this, two goals were accomplished in theory: On the one hand, the viceroy would be able to secure a more effective control of the viceroyalty with the establishment of networks of personal loyalty between him and the district officials, who were spread out all over the territory, and, on the other hand, the monarch would secure the loyalty of his New Spanish subjects, who were obligated to the sovereign by a debt of gratitude, as the viceroy's distribution of rewards was made in the king's name. Viceregal and royal power and patronage, therefore, were tightly chained together; yet, this situation presented the monarchy with a serious difficulty that would become a reality in the seventeenth century. The viceroys' power to distribute honors and rewards could seriously reduce the monarch's ability to control his American subjects, inasmuch as the viceroys could use these rewards for their own benefit. As will be shown in this chapter, this situation would create a difficult dilemma for the Crown, still unresolved by the end of the century: On the one hand, the Crown always believed that the upholding of the viceroys' power and authority was indissolubly tied to the distribution of favors and rewards, because it was something that so closely identified them with the monarch, while, on the other, the Crown was well aware that the wrong use of this prerogative could contribute to a weakening of royal power in the remote lands across the ocean. In other words, rightly used, viceregal patronage could strengthen the power of the monarchy; wrongly used, it could weaken it.

Although relations of patronage and clientage were central to the functioning of colonial society, these are, however, aspects that have hardly been studied by historians, although one always finds references in passing to the system of patronage on which colonial government was based and, above all, to the corruption that characterized that system of government.[4] The study of patronage can certainly be elusive, because patronage, as Mario

Biagioli has pointed out, is "an institution without walls, its reality made of etiquette-bound rituals," and thus difficult for the historian to grasp.[5] In fact, the word *patronage* itself is a modern concept used by historians to explain a particular form of social binding and hierarchical organization. Patron–client relationships in the early modern period were reciprocal exchanges in which the patron gave material benefits, advancement, and protection in return for a client's loyalty and service, demonstrations of respect and esteem, information and advice. Patron–client ties and networks were a way of organizing and regulating power relationships in a society where the distribution of power was not completely institutionalized. They were informal structures operating within the existing formal institutional framework. In other words, personal ties and loyalties were what provided "substance" to the "form" of the institutions, suggesting that sixteenth- and seventeenth-century institutions were qualitatively different from modern ones.[6] This makes it necessary, therefore, to question the nature of the "colonial state" as an autonomous entity with independent goals and programs by emphasizing the many ways that it was infiltrated by society and how its political institutions were dominated by networks of clients. Thus, the nature of colonial society can be better understood by examining how viceregal power was mobilized, not through the agency of the purely impersonal state, but through client systems and personal ties and loyalties.

On Favors and Rewards

In a memorial presented to king Philip IV, his favorite, the count-duke of Olivares, declared that "liberality and magnificence are virtues that belong naturally to kings and those virtues which are the most necessary appear to be the ones that most naturally belong to the greatness of kings, who with favors tie the vassals' hearts in love and obedience."[7] Similarly, Juan de Solórzano asserted that nothing exalted kings and contributed to defend kingdoms and estates more than a monarch's benignity and liberality toward his subjects, especially toward those who had helped him conquer his dominions.[8] Royal liberality thereby conferred vitality, strength, and virtue to the members of the body politic, transforming royal subjects into perfect servants of the *res publica*. Thus, the monarch appeared as the great patron of his subjects, with no one being able to advance socially or politically without the assistance of royal patronage.[9] No other monarch had more to give than the Spanish monarch: Clerics were offered archbishoprics, bishoprics, abbeys, and other prebends; the laity, membership in the military orders, *encomiendas*, and public offices (besides all the court offices).[10] The effects of royal liberality were decisive, because, through it, the prince became the "vassals' master" because of the gratitude they felt for the favor granted. That is why it was important for the prince to begin his rule with liberal measures and in this way ensure his subjects' loyalty.[11]

Fig. 13 "The liberality of King Charles II," from Agustín de Mora, *El sol eclipsado antes de llegar al cenit*, 1700. This image from the catafalque of Charles II depicts him as a liberal and magnanimous king, virtues that characterize any good ruler. The king's liberality must be like that of the sun, king of the stars, which spreads its beneficial rays over all creatures, without showing distinctions or favoritism. (Benson Latin American Collection, General Libraries, The University of Texas at Austin.)

As the author of the arch commissioned in 1660 by the ecclesiastical chapter of Mexico City to receive the count of Baños would put it, all the liberality that the city hoped the new viceroy would show during his rule by generously distributing favors and rewards among its worthy inhabitants "would be repaid with their love" (Figure 13).[12]

The basic idea behind royal patronage was that, in any well-governed commonwealth, the ruler never failed to reward good subjects and punish the bad ones. In his influential political treatise published in 1595, the Jesuit Pedro de Rivadeneira asserted that true justice — that which the prince ought to achieve in his government — consisted of "two things mainly: first, distributing the rewards and levies of the republic with equality; second, punishing the criminals and doing justice between the parties." According to Rivadeneira, the just prince must not allow any service to go unrewarded or any crime, unpunished, because "reward and punishment are the two weights that keep the clock of the republic at the correct time."[13]

The virtue of liberality is, therefore, closely associated with the virtue of justice. Political writers always point out that the king's liberality can be voluntary or obligatory. "Obligatory liberality" is a matter of justice, as it obligates the king, by virtue of "distributive justice," to reward those services rendered by his vassals, giving to each one according to his merits. Because the royal bounty is limited, the king is advised not to be extremely generous with the voluntary rewards so that he will be able to meet the obligations imposed by distributive justice.[14]

This economy of favor and reward was profoundly influenced by Seneca's ideas, whose reputation and influence were at their highest in this period. For him, "to give gladly, to take gladly, to give gladly back" (that is, granting favors) is "a matter which, more than anything else, holds human society together."[15] Perhaps the chief characteristic of this economy of giving is that, although it may seem paradoxical, it leaves no room for spontaneity in the act of granting a favor or giving a gift: Both the one who gives and the one who receives are caught up in a network of mutual obligations, as the favor, by the imperative of gratitude, demands to be returned accordingly. Nothing is as despicable as ingratitude. This was an idea that completely permeated Spanish society at the time, as is shown in Don Quixote's admonition to the chain of galley slaves whom he had just granted the "grace" of setting them free: "It is fitting that those who are wellborn should give thanks for the benefits they have received, and one of the sins with which God is most offended is that of ingratitude."[16] In a similar vein, captain Alonso de Contreras, in many respects the archetypal Spanish soldier of the seventeenth century, would declare that, even though he had lost the favor of his patron, the count of Monterrey, he would rather remain as his servant in disgrace than look for the favor of another patron, because he would never be ungrateful to him for the rewards he had received from him.[17] Gratitude, in turn, sets in motion, once more, the mechanism of liberality, all causing a spiral of mutual social relationships of favor or beneficence and gratitude or an inclination to serve. This "economy of grace" is never driven by a commercial logic in which the obligation to return the favor received is settled by paying back the debt in the same amount that was given; on the contrary, it is driven by a usurious logic that obligates one to return more than what was received.[18] It is also not driven by a juridical logic in which the granting of a favor originates a contractual bond binding both parties; otherwise, the spontaneity and liberty that characterize gratitude would be lost.[19] These unwritten principles permeated society, turning the granting of favors into a fundamental agent of political relations. Thus, in the distribution of rewards and favors, royal power was limited by the non-codified laws of liberality (or the obligation to give) and gratitude (or the obligation to give back).

As Pierre Bourdieu has noted, in societies that are not driven by the logic of modern capitalism, "a man possesses in order to give. But he also possesses by giving." The moral obligations and emotional attachments created and maintained by these acts of giving are one of two ways of getting and keeping a lasting hold over somebody (the other is debt). Thus, trust, obligation, personal loyalty, gifts, and all the virtues of the ethic of honor become the defining elements of power. In presenting itself "as the most economical mode of domination because it best corresponds to the economy of the system," this "symbolic power" is much more effective than overt violence (besides being the only possible way of exercising domination in societies where it is difficult to exercise direct domination).[20] This applies well to a society such as that of New Spain in the sixteenth and seventeenth centuries in which objectified institutions were not completely developed, and symbolic mechanisms for sustaining domination through interpersonal relations were far more important.

This royal economy of favor was transmitted for the most part to the viceroys. The ethics of giving and the relations of patronage subjected the powerful figure of the viceroy to a series of obligations toward his *familia* (the retainers and members of his household in the broadest sense). Among a viceroy's retainers were relatives who were united to him not only by ties of kinship but also by a patron–client relationship and who depended on the viceroy for their social promotion (and for their enrichment, the critics of the viceregal system of patronage would add),[21] as well as an indeterminate number of *obligaciones* — that is, persons who had been recommended to the viceroy by influential courtiers (as could be the case with the councilors of the Indies themselves).[22]

The viceroys set off for America surrounded by an entourage, which in most ways exactly reproduced the king's court, although on a lesser scale. So, among the required members of any viceroy's retinue were the confessor, the chaplain, the *caballerizo mayor* (master of the horse), the *mayordomo mayor* (lord high steward), the secretary, the captain of the guard, and the physician, as well as a multitude of *gentileshombres de la cámara* (gentlemen of the chamber), pages, and valets (in addition to other more menial servants such as wardrobe keepers, cooks, coachmen, and lackeys).[23] The existence of this viceregal court was indispensable insofar as it was one more manifestation of the conception of the viceroy as the king's image. In this regard, Xavier Gil Pujol has argued that the creation of viceregal courts in the different dominions of the Spanish Monarchy was one of the mechanisms utilized by the Crown to compensate for an absent king. By helping create a provincial court culture that fomented among the local ruling elites patterns of behavior and sociability that mimicked those at the center of the Monarchy, these viceregal courts contributed, in a powerful way, to the cohesion of a highly heterogeneous polity.[24] Though Gil Pujol bases his arguments on European viceregal courts such as Valencia, Naples, Barcelona, or Lisbon, they no doubt also apply to the American territories, where two distinct viceregal courts, one in Mexico and the other in Lima, were created. All this notwithstanding, Gil Pujol argues that viceregal courts had important political liabilities, the most noticeable one being the fact that the real source of favor and patronage was not located at the viceregal but at the royal court; thus, viceregal patronage was reduced to distributing minor offices and rewards.[25] As we will see, this may have been the case of the European viceregal courts, but was not so in New Spain, where the distribution of public offices was never a minor affair. Because of the geographic, economic, social, and political conditions of the Mexican viceroyalty, this distribution acquired an extraordinary relevance and was always a contentious matter. As Luis de Velasco had already asserted in the 1550s, the major preoccupation of a viceroy in New Spain was the provision of *corregimientos* and *alcaldías mayores*, and this was so because it was impossible to accommodate everybody.[26]

As patron, the viceroy was obliged to reward his clientele, and in Mexico the easiest way to do so was the granting of an *alcaldía mayor*. In New Spain, then, the main manifestation of viceregal patronage was the distribution of public offices.[27] Although officially the provision of these offices belonged to the king as "natural and sovereign lord" of the Indies, its distribution was left to the viceroys to obviate the inconvenience of the great distance from the metropolis.[28] Thus, in the instructions given by the monarch to each viceroy before his departure, it was explicitly stated that it was the responsibility of the viceroy to fill these posts. Although it was pointed out to him the convenience of consulting on this matter with the *oidores*, as they would know who the best candidates would be, the viceroy was not obliged to follow their advice.[29] In any case, the monarchs remind the viceroys in the instructions that it is their wish that the rewards and favors be distributed among those inhabitants of New Spain who have performed services for the Crown. To this end, the monarchs instructed the viceroys to find out who were the worthiest persons, both clergy and laymen (known in Spanish as *beneméritos de Indias*), in the district under their jurisdiction so they could send a list of the names and merits of each one to the king every year.[30]

Ever since the conquest, the Spanish monarchs always wanted the descendants of the conquerors and first settlers to be included among the *beneméritos* of the Indies.[31] This was the logical consequence of the royal economy of favor because, as Fernando Pizarro, the grandson of the conqueror of Peru, argued in the seventeenth century, distributive justice and the laws of gratitude obligated kings to reward their vassals's services, both in their own persons and in that of their descendants. And, who had performed greater services to the Crown, asked Pizarro, than the *conquistadores* who had contributed to the enlargement of the monarchy with their conquests? When liberally distributing his property, Pizarro contended, the monarch might grant a favor to whomever he wished (even his relatives), but, when the great services performed by the *conquistadores* for the Crown were rewarded, those who had performed the greatest services and their descendants should be preferred to the other candidates, as the dignity acquired by the father for the services rendered to the republic is inherited in the same way as blood is inherited. To do the opposite would be to commit an act against distributive justice, which demands that rewards be distributed in accordance with the services given.[32] Similar arguments had already been advanced a few decades earlier by another Mexican descendant of *conquistadores*, Gonzalo Gómez de Cervantes, who in a memorial sent in 1599 to one of the members of the Council of the Indies contended that the descendants of the discoverers and conquerors of the New World deserved to be the recipients of the king's bounty, because not only had they given the Spanish monarchs so many good kingdoms but also, most importantly, they had brought countless heathen souls to the Church.[33]

The viceroys always objected to the king's wishes, their main contention being that these descendants very often were not qualified to serve in public offices. They further contended that, because so many aspired to one of these posts, it was impossible to satisfy everyone, while it was politically advisable that not only the descendants of the *conquistadores* but also all of the inhabitants of New Spain as well should expect to have their merits rewarded.[34] Writing at the beginning of the seventeenth century, the marquis of Montesclaros disapproved of the many legal complaints lodged by these descendants against the viceroys for not rewarding them with public offices. The marquis saw this attitude as a sign of contempt of viceregal authority. Moreover, Montesclaros believed it was inappropriate to put any descendant of conquistadors before the other candidates for a post; by doing so it was assumed that the "carpenter who made the brigantines, or the blacksmith who made the nails, or the one who paved the streets of Mexico, all of them being paid their day's wages, were as worthy as the marquis del Valle who had conquered it." In case this was not enough, the viceroy reminded the monarch that, due to the lack of Spanish women at the beginning of the conquest, many descendants of *conquistadores* were mestizos and mulattos, something that made them "incapable of being upright and honest men."[35] Montesclaros also believed that the poverty of these descendants disqualified them for these offices that required persons of property.[36] For all these reasons, he requested that, when providing these offices, "each one's virtue be taken into account, without making conquistadores and corregidores two correlative terms. This will encourage them to seek rewards because of their personal merits, instead of thinking they belong to them by birthright. In this way, the viceroy will be revered and respected as is fitting."[37]

Doubtless, this defense of a "pure" economy of favor on the part of a member of the nobility was paradoxical (it was common to argue that the nobles, simply for having been born nobles, were to be preferred in the distribution of offices[38]), but it was also self-interested. Should a viceroy be forced to distribute offices among the *conquistadores*' descendants, he would be deprived of the discretionary power that allowed viceroys to grant such rewards to their retainers or any other persons with whom they wanted to establish a relation of dependency. This clearly meant a loss of power for the viceroys, because by giving an office to a descendant of conquistadors who deserved it by birthright, he would not be bound to the viceroy by any debt of gratitude and submission, hence the connection Montesclaros made between the obligation to grant these offices to the offspring of *conquistadores* and his loss of authority. This is also why Luis de Velasco II would always insist that these individuals should understand that the granting of one of these offices was a royal favor, not a matter of justice, thus the authority of the viceroys should not be limited by their claims.[39] Some viceroys, nevertheless, did not appear to have any qualms about how to distribute offices. The marquis of Villena, for example, advised his successor, the count of Salvatierra, to give the most important offices to "his own obligations" (that is, the members of his clientele), while the medium-range offices should be for the Creole nobility; the rest should be distributed among the descendants of *conquistadores* and those persons for whom the viceroy's retainers or any other prominent person had interceded with the viceroy. Finally, Villena recommended that his successor always have something to give, as it makes for "a crafty government that causes some to keep their hopes and others to fear to lose what they possess."[40] As can be appreciated from these words, the descendants of *conquistadores* occupied a very small corner in the marquis of Villena's scheme.

The Crown's Dilemma

Reflecting on the figure of the viceroy, Juan de Palafox y Mendoza, councilor of the Indies, bishop of Puebla, and *visitador general* (inspector general) of New Spain between 1640 and 1649, affirmed that if a monarch was to reign with happiness he must not "tolerate that anyone be as revered and worshiped as he, nor be more esteemed or feared in all his kingdoms than he himself." In so doing the sovereign would avoid an extremely pernicious evil, that of "political idolatry in which the image receives the homage due to the original, ... with the viceroy's precepts being more revered than those of the king," this being far more dangerous in remote places where its inhabitants were always more predisposed to sedition. To avoid this danger, Palafox saw only two solutions. The first one was to deprive the viceroys of their post as soon as they committed some serious disobedience. With such a resolution, the inhabitants of the kingdom would be warned that "there is someone else who is more powerful than the image who rules them, the latter being just a shadow of the former." The second solution was to divide the granting of rewards in such a way as to make vassals and nobility more dependent on the king than on the viceroy, "because," Palafox adds, "the subjects' love goes to wherever they believe the reward is."[41] Here Palafox is expressing in a very concise way the dilemma regarding viceregal patronage that the Crown had to face throughout the entire seventeenth century: to attempt to eliminate viceregal abuses of the system of patronage and, at the same time, always to assert the close relation that existed between the viceroys' power and their appointment of *alcaldes mayores*.

Already in 1618 the monarch had issued a *cédula* instructing the viceroy of Mexico to inquire about the origin of the great sums of money that the *alcaldes mayores* used to remit to Spain. Because these remittances could not proceed from their salaries, the monarch had had no other choice but to conclude that the money proceeded either from his royal treasury or from the "work and blood of the Indians." The king instructed the viceroy to find out, secretly and with the help of the *audiencia*, the best way to put a stop to such profits.[42] In 1619, the Crown would issue a detailed *cédula* with which it tried to put order into the distribution of offices. The Crown acknowledged that the viceroys awarded these offices to the members of their entourage (*allegados, criados y familiares*), among whom some had been "entrusted to the viceroys by powerful persons to whom the viceroys were obliged" (the viceroys' retainers are defined as all those "who came from these kingdoms, or move from one province to another, in the company of the viceroys and under their protection"). This *cédula* orders once again that both the descendants of *conquistadores* and those born in the Indies must be preferred when distributing the offices. Furthermore, it is expressly forbidden to appoint to these offices any relatives (within the fourth degree) or retainers of the viceroys (or the vicereines, because, as is expressed in the *cédula*, the "relatives of these ministers' wives are usually more annoying and of greater harm to public government than the relatives of the husbands themselves"). In addition, the obligation is established that, before taking over their posts, all those appointed must appear before the senior *oidor* and the fiscal of the *audiencia* to verify whether they are relatives or retainers of the viceroy.[43]

In one of the many letters Palafox wrote to the king at the beginning of his *visita* in 1641, he lamented that, "In the high courts some justice is done, but the alcaldes mayores do little justice or none at all. ...The alcaldes mayores, who are those who represent Your Majesty immediately after the audiencia, are the ruin of these provinces and their least necessary magistrates."[44] Palafox went on to assert that even the most honest of viceroys always filled the posts of *alcaldes mayores* with their servants and relatives, and this eliminated one of the benefits of these posts: They served "to give a little pension to the conquistadores." But, in the present state of affairs, Palafox argued, they only served to anger them "when they see that a viceroy's chamber servant, who rose to this post from less than page, has precedence over the grandchildren and heirs of those who participated in the conquest." If a Creole obtained one of these posts, added Palafox, he had to pay dearly for it.[45] Another serious problem Palafox saw with the *alcaldes mayores* was that they all were in the business of trading with their subjects, taking advantage of their privileged position to exploit both the Indians and the Spaniards who lived in their districts. Palafox recognized that some theologians accepted these commercial transactions, even though they were forbidden, on the grounds that the salaries of the *alcaldes mayores* (between 300 and 500 pesos per year) were not sufficient to meet their material needs and natural law allowed them to find the means to secure their survival.[46]

Palafox, however, believed that the harm caused by the system was too great to allow its existence. He concluded that the only solution was to eliminate the *alcaldes mayores* and substitute them with *alcaldes ordinarios*, whose posts would be appointed every year from among the residents of the towns and villages. Palafox, nevertheless, added that he was aware of the strong opposition this measure would meet on the part of the viceroys and that they would never implement it on the grounds that their office would be discredited if these appointments were taken away from them. To this, Palafox responded that the office of viceroy "is so commanding in these provinces, and so many fear and respect its image, that the original [the king] could be jealous, … so forcefully do the rays of royal dignity reverberate in those who represent it at such a distance." Palafox was convinced that should the prerogative of distributing offices be taken away from the viceroys, their position was so preeminent that their authority would not suffer at all. "If an oidor, a fiscal or an alcalde de corte, none of whom distributes offices," asked Palafox, "is still highly respected and feared, how much more shall be a viceroy, even without the right to appoint these offices?"[47]

This letter from Palafox signals, in a way, the beginning of one of the most bitter controversies ever to take place in seventeenth-century New Spain. Although the disputes in which the bishop was involved during his stay in Mexico between 1640 and 1649 are well known, what has generally been emphasized are his clashes with the regular clergy, above all with the Franciscans, because of the Indian parishes (Palafox insisted that the friars should be replaced by members of the secular clergy) and with the Jesuits, because of the tithe he insisted was due to the episcopal authority (which the Jesuits refused to pay). On the other hand, Jonathan Israel attributed the confrontation between Palafox and the viceroy, the count of Salvatierra, to the fact that the viceroys usually led the imperial and bureaucratic faction, to which the majority of the regular clergy belonged, while Palafox had become, in Israel's opinion, the "most genuinely popular leader of the Creoles not only of his own time, but of the whole seventeenth century." In such a role, he would be helped by the *audiencia* and the municipal council.[48] In his analysis of Palafox's thought, David Brading, however, reaches the opposite conclusion by arguing that the bishop was "an imperial visitor in the New World." In his view, the root of Palafox's conflicts lies in his challenging of the vested interests of the colonial establishment, both secular and clerical, and his failure was a sign of the weakness and decay of the Spanish monarchy, as the Crown was unable to defend his own minister in his confrontation with an ecclesiastical corporation.[49] In Brading's account, the figure of the viceroy is almost invisible, and no explanation is provided as to why he clashed with Palafox. This comes as no surprise, as it is unclear in Brading's view whether the viceroy belonged to the "colonial establishment" or whether he was another "imperial visitor."

The main problem with these two views stems from their attempt to reduce all the actors in Spanish colonial society into two opposing but well-defined categories — the imperial–bureaucratic and the Creole — but this attempt runs against the much more complicated realities of the politics of seventeenth-century New Spain. Social actors operated, to a great extent, according to political interests and conceptions very different from their identification with imperial or Creole and protonationalistic concerns. One of the motivations (and not a minor one) that induced these actors to a specific political behavior was the patron–client relationships in which many of them were enmeshed and which were an essential part of the armature of their society. It is with respect to this aspect that the controversy regarding the *alcaldes mayores* acquires all its relevance. Interestingly, this controversy is mentioned just at the beginning or in passing by both Israel and Brading and then quickly disappears from the narrative or moves to the background. However, those involved in the dispute at the time, including the Council of the Indies, would attribute the spark that ignited the conflict that engulfed New Spain in the 1640s to the bitter confrontation between Palafox and Salvatierra regarding the *alcaldes mayores*.

So it was asserted by the Council of the Indies when recognizing that, although the conflicts between Palafox and Salvatierra were due to several causes, the immediate cause had been a royal order issued on October 17, 1645, that gave Palafox, in his capacity as *visitador general*, the authority to intervene in any lawsuits brought forth against the *alcaldes mayores*. In view of the serious problems this decision had caused, however, the Council ordered Palafox to suspend any proceedings he might have initiated against the *alcaldes mayores*.[50] Palafox saw his clash with Salvatierra as a consequence of trying to impose the royal will — which he represented as *visitador* — over the private interests of the viceroy. According to Palafox, the viceroy had rushed to the defense of the *alcaldes mayores* for a simple reason: He was secretly selling office appointments, something that brought him fat profits every year. It was only logical, he reasoned, that if the *alcaldes mayores* had to pay large sums (far above their annual salaries) to get these posts, then once they got them they had to earn back the money they had spent as quickly as possible. Palafox also points out that the viceroy was accustomed to granting some of these lucrative offices to the *oidores* as a way to secure their collaboration and compliance. In the view of Palafox, the viceroy, by taking advantage of his great power, was defending his own private interests rather than those of the king. As a result, in Mexico the viceroy's orders were more obeyed than the orders of the king himself.[51]

For the count of Salvatierra, however, it was clear that, ultimately, he was trying to defend his authority from Palafox's intrusions. (The best way to interfere with a viceroy's capacity to control the territory under his jurisdiction was to meddle with the activities of the *alcaldes mayores*, who constituted a key element in the network of viceregal power.) The same argument is utilized by all the influential personages whose support the viceroy was able to get. Their arguments consistently insist on stressing the bond that closely unites the viceroy with the monarch (something that was lacking in the *visitador*, as he was not so closely assimilated to the king's figure as was the viceroy), implying with this that, when obeying the viceroy, one was obeying the king, thus neutralizing Palafox's argument that to obey the viceroy was to disobey the king.[52] For the superior of the Dominicans, for example, public peace depended on the viceroy being revered and respected, as he was the "main head of the secular estate," and, for the Mercedarian superior, the person of the viceroy was sacred, as in it the person of the king was "vividly" venerated.[53]

This view of the preeminent power of the viceroy was likewise shared by the Council of the Indies. As the Council reported to the king, although Palafox, as *visitador*, had been granted the authority to punish those who did not obey his orders, this power could not include the viceroy because he was the "representation and living image of Your Majesty, who is superior to everyone in the provinces under his rule and whose authority and jurisdiction must be maintained unimpaired as is fitting to the one who acts as Your Majesty and is your deputy." At the same time, the Council, agreeing with Palafox's opinions about the *alcaldes mayores*, requested the king to send a reliable official to New Spain to undertake the *residencia* of these *alcaldes*. Moreover, the Council requested that the count of Salvatierra's successor be instructed in detail "on how much viceroys abuse their power and sovereignty when they grant offices in an unjust way … and when they allow and conceal the many extortions done to their subjects for their private advantage by the *alcaldes mayores* appointed by them."[54]

Echoing the opinions of the Council, the monarch decided to appoint the bishop of Yucatan as acting governor of New Spain until the arrival of a new viceroy and, in this way, to force Salvatierra to leave Mexico as soon as possible. Salvatierra was appointed viceroy of Peru, while Palafox, for his part, was to return to Spain as soon as a bishopric became vacant — to get them out of Mexico appeared to be the only possible solution to the conflict. The monarch, in addition, ordered that the person who was to be sent to continue Palafox's *visita* not conduct any *residencias* of *alcaldes mayores*, as it was against the law to conduct *residencias* of those who had already been subjected to one. The interesting thing about the appointment of a provisional governor is that, in order to differentiate him from a viceroy, the governor was forbidden to appoint any offices (except those whose term in office had expired) nor was he allowed to dismiss any one who had been appointed by his predecessor. The monarch justified his decision by pointing out that "since the appointment of *alcaldes mayores* and the rest of offices is what most disturbs the free will of the people, and the time [the bishop of Yucatan] is going to be in office is limited, it is considered right for him not to have this responsibility, and thus avoid the formation of factions that this matter might give rise to."[55]

The Crown, in general, seemed to agree with Palafox's diagnosis that the *alcaldes mayores* acted in an abusive manner, and, in the course of the following decades, it would attempt to solve the problem, always in a hesitant way, by adopting various measures but never of a radical nature. For instance, in 1645, and as a result of the reports sent by Palafox, a 1000-ducat fine was imposed on the count of Salvatierra for having distributed several posts of *alcalde mayor* among close relations of the members of the *audiencia* and the tribunal of accounts of Mexico, something that was forbidden by the *cédula* of 1619. In addition, and in a gesture more symbolic than effective, the monarch was to appoint five *beneméritos* of the Indies in place of the five relatives of the *oidores* who had been appointed *alcaldes mayores* by Salvatierra.[56] Around the same time, the Council, in a gesture indicative of the road that was to be followed if royal authority was to be imposed, suggested to the king that it would be desirable for him to appoint the *corregidor* of Veracruz, a key place in the system of colonial power because it was the gateway to New Spain, where the annual fleets arrived and departed. The Council was aware of the many frauds committed against the royal treasury by the *alcaldes mayores* of Veracruz, who usually took advantage of their connections with the viceroys. Due to the wealth that usually circulated in the city, this post was one of the most profitable, for which reason the viceroys always appointed a member of their clientele to fill the post.[57] The king agreed with their councilors' opinion; thenceforth the king himself would appoint the *corregidor* of Veracruz, and his salary would be substantially increased — from 250 pesos to 1000. This move was not something new, for in 1629 the king had already claimed for himself the appointment of the governors of the fortresses of San Juan de Ulúa, in Veracruz, and Acapulco, which previously had been the responsibility of the viceroys.[58] Something similar had also happened with the appointment of the *alcaldes mayores* of important cities such as Puebla or San Luis Potosí.[59]

In this regard, it is of interest to examine the arguments utilized by the count of Alba de Liste, who had just been appointed viceroy, to oppose this measure. First of all, he contended (and he was probably quite right) that the same frauds could be committed by a person appointed by the king as one named by the viceroy. On the contrary, he reasoned, the one appointed by the king would enjoy more freedom to do as he wished because of the great distance that would separate him from the monarch. Furthermore, he would be more prone to try to profit from the post at any price to make up the great expenses that he would have incurred when moving from Spain to the Indies. But, above all, to take the appointment of such an important post away from the viceroys would have negative repercussions on their power, as "they would be divested of the authority, love, and respect that there, more than anywhere else in the world, they must have and retain," and their commands to the *corregidor* of Veracruz would not have the "strength which is required."[60] Although this may appear as a self-interested opinion, what Alba de Liste is really insinuating is that it was indispensable that a place as important as Veracruz, where the fleets were organized and received, had to be under the command of someone who would follow the orders of the viceroy — who was in charge of dispatching the fleets — faithfully and reliably. The only sure way to secure this obedience, in a society in which the chain of command was imperfect and where, by and large, no one could be sure that the king's or the viceroy's orders would be carried out in an exact way, was to place in that post somebody who would follow viceregal instructions more because of patron–client obligations than because of an abstract and often nonexistent bureaucratic chain of command. The patron–client ties and networks established between viceroys and *alcaldes mayores* were thereby a flexible way of attaching provincial officials to a central government too distant to enforce tighter attachments, in an age when more impersonal or abstract allegiances would have been difficult to maintain.[61]

The events of Tehuantepec (in the present-day state of Oaxaca) in 1660 brought home again the problem of the appointment of *alcaldes mayores* by the viceroys. That year several indigenous uprisings took place, resulting in the killing of the *alcalde mayor* of Tehuantepec — a retainer of the viceroy, the duke of Alburquerque — at the hands of the Indians.[62] This occurrence was unusual enough to make the Crown launch an inquiry to establish the ultimate causes of the uprising. From the start, the Council acknowledged that these kinds of disturbances were caused by the abuses to which the indigenous population was subjected by the *alcaldes mayores*. In the opinion of the Council, these abuses took place above all because the viceroys appointed their retainers to these positions instead of choosing "persons of experience, zeal, and Christianity."[63] In this situation, the Council had to face an apparently unsolvable dilemma. On the one hand, it was aware that this order would not be implemented, as had been the case with the previous ones, and the viceroys would keep appointing persons without merit, for which reason more radical measures were called for — such as eliminating the post of *alcalde mayor* or depriving the viceroys of this prerogative. On the other hand, the Council rejected taking these measures on several grounds. First of all, if *alcaldes ordinarios* were to be elected instead of *alcaldes mayores* (as Palafox had suggested back in 1641), there was no reason to believe that the former would not commit the same abuses as the latter. Likewise, it was recognized that should all the *alcaldes mayores* be appointed by the king, this would not prevent them from committing abuses, but, above all, such a measure would have negative repercussions on the viceroys' authority:

> [This Council] strongly objects to taking away from the viceroys the power of awarding offices because this power *gives them their greatest authority*, as everyone who aspires to fill them, because of their perquisites, becomes dependent on them [the viceroys]. Moreover, if the viceroys make appropriate use of this power, the importance of their having it cannot be denied because, with it, they more closely resemble the supreme authority and the royal prerogative of Your Majesty, preserving the respect that the post of viceroy must inspire in political and military government. And this is more so in kingdoms and provinces so far away from the royal influence of Your Majesty, where all this is considered very necessary for obedience to the Crown to be maintained.[64]

To the Council, it was essential that the powers of the viceroy, who was the image of royal power, be closely associated with this economy of favor, which was one of the fundamental mechanisms through which monarchical power was constituted. In the face of such a dilemma, the Crown was only able to resolve that, before taking any drastic measures, reports and opinions were to be requested from several prelates who were well acquainted with this matter.[65] When the reports were received in the Council, all of them suggested that the *alcaldes mayores* should be either replaced by *alcaldes ordinarios* or eliminated completely, leaving the Indians to be governed by themselves.[66] In view of these opinions and recognizing that abuses would always be committed as long as the viceroys appointed the *alcaldes mayores*, the *fiscal* of the Council of the Indies requested in 1663 that the monarch, at the proposal of the Council, thenceforth appoint the most important *alcaldes mayores*, with the rest being replaced by *alcaldes ordinarios* elected annually;[67] however, no action appears to have been taken in this regard in the following years.

In these years, no better example than the government of the count of Baños illustrates the dilemma the Crown had to face: having to defend viceregal authority while at the same time being aware of the need to take more radical measures if the lack of control in the distribution of offices was to be remedied. The count of Baños was probably one of the most controversial viceroys of the seventeenth century, as he antagonized practically all the sectors of colonial society, in particular Diego Osorio, bishop of Puebla. One of the main reasons for complaints about him was precisely his bad distribution of offices, shamelessly favoring his relatives (including his own sons) and marginalizing the Creole candidates. In view of the many conflicts caused by his controversial rule, the monarch decided not to extend his term of office for another three years (which was the custom), not even until the arrival of his successor, and so the bishop of Puebla was appointed acting viceroy.[68] One of the measures taken by the bishop–viceroy during his three months in office, with the agreement of the *oidores*, was to declare vacant all the offices filled by the count of Baños and to use them to reward the worthy. The bishop justified his position by contending that the viceroy had infringed royal orders by distributing the offices among his retainers, without being certain of the merits or services of many of them.[69] Although the bishop apparently had only followed the royal *cédulas* to the letter, the monarch frowned upon his actions, castigating him for having attacked, with his actions, the viceroy's authority and recriminating both the bishop and the *oidores* for not having had in mind "how much the authority of my viceroys must be upheld as they so much resemble my royal person."[70]

It would not be until 1678 that the monarch would decide to take radical measures, although he did so without following the recommendations of the 1662 informants, concisely instructing that "for just causes and other considerations appropriate to my service and the public good of the Indies" from then on he himself would appoint all the *corregidores* and *alcaldes mayores*.[71] It is not clear why it was then that the Council of the Indies changed its mind and recommended a measure it had previously opposed. It seems that the immediate motive was the complaints received in Madrid regarding the abuses committed in the appointment of offices by the count of Castellar, viceroy of Peru.[72] Also influencing this decision might have been the fact that, at the time, two clerics — Payo Enríquez de Rivera, archbishop of México and acting viceroy of New Spain between 1673 and 1680, and Melchor de Liñán y Cisneros, archbishop of Lima and acting viceroy of Peru from 1678 to 1681 — were provisionally at the head of the two American viceroyalties, not members of the nobility, who would have probably offered much more resistance to such a measure. In the case of New Spain, what can be mentioned is the decision made by the monarch in 1676, at the suggestion of the Council, that the *alcaldía* of Villa Alta de San Ildefonso, in the district of Oaxaca and one of the richest in Mexico, which during his government the count of Baños had awarded to one of his sons, revert to the king.[73] This decision had been made in the wake of a report sent by Enríquez de Rivera confirming that those appointed to this *alcaldía* gave to the viceroys, as a gift and a sign of gratitude, the amount of 24,000 pesos the first year and, afterwards, 1500 pesos for each month their appointment was extended.[74] (In 1676, the annual salary of this *alcalde mayor* was 350 pesos.[75])

Nevertheless, this crucial change lasted for barely two years. In 1680, the monarch revoked the *cédula* of 1678 and restored to the viceroys the "royal prerogative" of appointing *corregidores* and *alcaldes mayores*. The king justified his decision by pointing out how inconvenient it was for the inhabitants of the Indies to have to turn to the Council to request one of these positions. More interestingly, however, the sovereign argued that "being so far apart from my royal influence, ministers of the highest rank such as my viceroys, presidents, and governors *need the utmost authority*, for which reason, ever since the discovery of both provinces, the appointment of offices has been left to them."[76] In these words the connection between power and patronage can be clearly appreciated. The distribution of offices and benefices was a royal prerogative, one of the markers of the sovereign power of the king and one of the most effective mechanisms with which to affirm his power and secure the loyalty of his vassals. Nothing assimilated viceregal power to royal power, while at the same time reinforcing the viceroy's power, as much as the invisible bonds of dependency created by the economy of favor.

This was also the way the count of Paredes understood his power, as can be appreciated in a letter he sent to the king in 1681, in which he expressed his opposition to the distribution of offices among the descendants of *conquistadores* only for being such descendants. As he contended, the "loss of authority to my post that follows when this distribution is not left to my discretion should be carefully considered, because neither will the Spaniards show respect for a viceroy who cannot appoint them to any posts whatsoever nor will the Creoles have any reason to respect someone who, of necessity, is going to employ them for the mere fact of being Creoles."[77] In the opinion of Paredes, therefore, a viceroy must have total freedom when conceding favors as his authority depends on it. The reason was simple: The viceroy's discretionary power in the distribution of offices allowed him to meet his obligations as patron of the members of his entourage (which guaranteed their loyalty), and at the same time it gave him enough room to establish bonds of dependency with those members of Creole society that he saw fit.

The change of attitude of the Crown in 1680 showed an interesting development. Now, not only was the power to appoint those *alcaldes mayores* (whose appointment had reverted to the Crown before 1678) returned to the viceroys, but, for the first time, it was also accepted that viceroys could grant offices to their retainers. The duke of La Palata, viceroy of Peru at the time, had suggested that, instead of choosing between total prohibition and the general abuse of giving offices to every viceregal retainer, a happy medium of allowing the viceroys to appoint twelve offices among their retainers could be reached. This would satisfy everyone without doing wrong to the Creole population.[78] The king accepted the proposal, but, to avoid appointments being made to only the twelve best offices, the condition was imposed that only two of these posts were to be of the "first class" (the *alcaldía mayor* of Tepeaca and the *corregimiento* of Oaxaca), while five offices would belong to the "second class" (Tehuacan, Miaguatlan, Chalco, Guanajuato, and Xochimilco) and another five to the "third class" (Mestitlan, Veracruz Vieja, Huatulco, Tonalá, and Sultepec).[79]

This decision, however, might have been made to compensate the viceroys for the fact that in these years the Crown, as an emergency measure to solve the financial needs of the monarchy, had begun "to benefit" (that is, to sell) many of the offices that previously had been distributed by the viceroys.[80] The attitude of the viceroys regarding these sales is well represented by the opinions of the count of Galve, viceroy of New Spain between 1688 and 1696, expressed in several letters he wrote to his brother, the duke of the Infantado. The viceroy, referring to the complications he had to face for not being able to distribute the offices at his discretion because many of them had been "benefited," accused the members of the Council of the Indies of being interested only in obtaining money by any means available, without taking into account the realities of a place such as Mexico and the bad consequences that their resolutions brought about. For these reasons, the viceroy was unwilling to remove from their posts, at least until they had completed their terms of office, those *alcaldes mayores* who had been appointed by him and whose positions had been sold in Madrid to someone else.[81] The accusations of Galve against the councilors of the Indies, however, do not seem warranted, as the councilors themselves strongly opposed the sale of those offices that administered justice. Though the councilors based their rejection on the harm that the administration of justice would experience as a result of these sales, the fact cannot be ignored that, as in the case of the viceroys, these sales could mean an important diminution in the power of patronage exercised by the members of the Council.[82] As a result of this opposition, the Crown would only in a hesitant way continue to sell these posts. In the Crown's opinion, the sale of offices of *alcaldes mayores* and *corregidores* was only a temporary measure, more tolerated than accepted (hence the notion of "benefit" instead of "sale," which indicated that the buyer did not become the owner of the office).

The sale of offices has traditionally been seen as a manifestation of the decline of the Spanish monarchy in the seventeenth century, as it contributed to the weakening of royal authority in the Indies,[83] but these sales should not be seen as just another aspect of the "impotence" or "devolution of power" of the Spanish Crown at the end of the seventeenth century; rather, this limitation or "impotence" should be understood more as an intrinsic characteristic of *ancien régime* government than as an indication of the inexorable decline of the Spanish monarchy. Moreover, if the Crown always hesitated to take from the viceroys the power of granting favors, it was not for lack of authority but because it conceived viceregal power as being tightly chained to the power of distributing rewards. Ultimately, however, the pressing fiscal needs of the monarchy would be, to a great extent, what would take from the viceroys their power to appoint local offices.

The Specter of Corruption

The methods used by the viceroys for the distribution of offices and the behavior of the *alcaldes mayores* in their districts have been pointed out by colonial historians as clear indicators of the existence of a general state of corruption in colonial Spanish America. John Leddy Phelan, for example, has contended that Spanish bureaucrats in the seventeenth century became morally decayed. For him, the basic cause for the prevalence of graft at all levels was the lack of professionalism of the provincial bureaucracy (the *corregidores* and *alcaldes mayores*) and the inadequate and rigid salary scale. Both the Council of the Indies and the viceroys virtually ignored professional considerations in selecting provincial magistrates. The *corregidores*, moreover, lacked the legal training and the professional *esprit de corps* of the *oidores*. If the *oidores* were not as corrupt, it was precisely because of their semiprofessional character. As for the inadequacy of the salary scale, not even an embryonic system of merit raises existed by which magistrates might hope to receive periodic increments, nor were sustained efforts made to adjust salaries to changing economic conditions, such as inflation. All this made corruption rampant. Phelan points out that the solution that might have yielded substantial results — that is, to raise the salaries of the *corregidores* — was never proposed by anybody.[84]

Horst Pietschmann, for his part, believes that the existence of corruption would have been the principal manifestation of a more or less permanent tension among the Spanish state, the colonial bureaucracy, and colonial society. Pietschmann asserts that corruption in Latin America was not simply a more or less frequent abuse, but it was present in a consistent way in every region and in all periods. In this regard, corruption was more widespread here than in Europe. According to him, the four main types of corruption in colonial Spanish America were illegal trade, bribery, favoritism and clientelism, and, finally, sales of offices and bureaucratic services. The fact that corruption was not limited to the bureaucracy and that the transgression of legal, religious, and moral norms was widespread in the society at large is interpreted by Pietschmann as a manifestation of "a more or less permanent crisis of conscience and also as an acute crisis of state power."[85]

These kinds of arguments — which have become the received wisdom — are the logical conclusion of a teleological approach to the study of colonial and early modern history, based on the idea that all the defining characteristics of the "modern state" can already be found in the sixteenth and seventeenth centuries, besides ascribing to the absolute monarchy a full consciousness and a leading role in the creation of such a "modern state." According to this view, while the Spanish overseas empire could be defined as "a centralized bureaucratic empire," the colonial state created in Latin America in the sixteenth century would have lacked many of the traditional elements that still existed in the peninsula (a feudal nobility, for example). This system was "entirely modern" and "aimed toward the future," in the direction of the "modern rational-bureaucratic ideal" as expressed by Max Weber. The decline of the Spanish monarchy in the seventeenth century, whose chief manifestations in the colonial state would have been an acute increase of corruption, patronage, and the sale of offices and a decrease of royal authority, would have then represented a step backwards in the unstoppable march toward political modernity.[86]

However, the most recent historiography has shown that the European monarchies of the *ancien régime* were neither as "absolute" nor as "modern" as traditionally had been thought, their level of "centralization" and "bureaucratization" leaving a lot to be desired. Roger Mettam, for example, has argued that the successes of Louis XIV and his ministers rested more on their skillful exploitation of the traditional values of French society than on the modernization of the administrative machinery and the creation of a new kind of royal official. "There was scarcely anything," Mettam concludes, "which could meaningfully be called 'modern' in the France of Louis XIV."[87] In the case of the Spanish monarchy, the construction of a centralized state or the creation of a professional bureaucracy was not clearly among the priorities of the monarch or his councilors.

When discussing the problem of corruption, two caveats are in order. In the first place, there was nothing specifically Spanish or Spanish American in the fact that corruption existed in colonial Spanish America, as this was a problem with which all early modern societies had to deal. Second, as Sharon Kettering has pointed out, "Great care must be taken in applying the concept of corruption backward in time. …By modern standards, seventeenth-century officials were corrupted by patron–client demands and by low salaries, ill-defined duties, a confusion of public and private funds, and an absence of inspections, systematic bookkeeping, and regular accounts."[88] In this respect, it could be argued that most of the types of graft enumerated by Pietschmann were not seen as illicit at the time. In general, some confusion arose between what was considered proper and improper, as patron–client obligations made it difficult to distinguish, for instance, between a "gift" and a "bribe."[89] This does not mean, however, that in early modern societies the norms governing public office holders were not clearly articulated or were nonexistent. In fact, corruption among judges or dishonesty among accountants was considered by public authorities to be shocking and reprehensible.[90]

In the case of the sale of offices, despite Pietschmann's opinions, it is quite clear that they cannot be considered as a corrupt practice whatsoever. Of course, the existence of abuses cannot be denied, but the sale of offices in itself was legitimate, although not everybody agreed on this matter. Those who defended the legality of these sales contended that they could be allowed as long as the offices were sold to capable and suitable persons, at moderate prices, because of need of the republic or the monarch (this is the argument with which the sale of *alcaldías mayores* will be justified at the end of the century), and as long as the offices of judge and councilor were never sold. The opposing view maintained that the monarch could not sell the offices under any circumstances because he was not the owner, just the administrator. Furthermore, he had the obligation to appoint officials for the purpose of ruling and administering justice fairly, not for his own advantage or profit.[91] That the sale of offices was a controversial matter was publicly acknowledged at the very end of the seventeenth century by Pedro

Portocarrero, chaplain of Charles II and Patriarch of the Indies, in the treatise on monarchical government he wrote in the 1690s. As we have seen, the sale of offices became an important issue at the end of the century, as the Crown started to sell offices it had never sold before. This was reflected in Portocarrero's work, as he devoted several chapters to discuss the matter. Although Portocarrero was against the sale of offices, especially those that entailed the administration of justice, he nevertheless pointed out that it was licit to resort to these sales in case of urgent need, for which reason those rulers who took such measures should not be censured. This argument did not prevent him, however, from adding that, although such an expedient might be lawful, it did not follow that it was necessarily appropriate or beneficial for the monarchy, thus rulers should avoid it at all costs.[92]

For his part, Hernando de Mendoza, the confessor of the viceroy of Naples and author of a tract on favors written at the beginning of the seventeenth century, attacked the idea that the viceroy might accept money in return for the concession of a favor, as the true favor must always be given altruistically. For Mendoza, the king's purpose when making the viceroys his *alter nos* was not to give them "such a vile authority that can be sold like bread or meat but to give them a most dignified and honest authority with which to administer justice and grant favors and rewards to all his vassals." To this, Mendoza added that the authority possessed by the viceroy to award favors was not his but the monarch's. The viceroy, in reality, was but a "salaried servant," whose office consisted of administering the kingdom, for which reason he was not allowed to sell other people's property, as the monarch did not wish favors to be sold. If the king stipulated the opposite he would be committing an extremely grave sin because he did not have the authority to destroy the republic, which was the inevitable consequence of the selling of rewards. Nevertheless, Mendoza did not deny that public offices might be sold, though a viceroy, as mere administrator of the king's property, could not do such a thing unless he had expressly been given license by the monarch to do so. Mendoza saw no problem in the sale of offices distributed by the viceroy if that had always been the custom, provided the holders of these offices did not administer justice; however, those offices that administered justice, Mendoza strongly argued, could not be sold by the viceroy under any circumstance, as doing so was forbidden by the king. That the viceroy was authorized to award these offices, concluded Mendoza, did not mean that he was permitted to sell them.[93]

From these words we can start to understand what type of relationship existed between corruption and patronage in the eyes of contemporaries. Royal patronage was a legitimate mechanism of power and an integral part of a society that, unlike modern societies, did not automatically identify the concepts of "patron" and "client" with corruption. It was evident to all that everyone's destiny depended on having patrons and benefactors. The monarch, in turn, transmitted this mechanism to his viceroys, who were expected to use it as a means to strengthen royal power, but if the viceroys employed this system of patronage for their own private interests instead of the king's then a "corruption" of the system occurred. This was the meaning contemporaries attached to the word "corruption" and this was what Palafox had in mind when he relentlessly attacked viceregal patronage, because, according to him, the viceroys utilized patronage not as a mechanism to cement royal authority but as a way to promote their private interests.

On the other hand, to argue, as Phelan does, that the solution to corruption was to increase the salaries of the *corregidores* is not realistic. The chronic near-bankruptcy of the monarchy and the inadequacies of the tax system meant that royal officials would have to be paid low salaries during the entire Old Regime.[94] Officials therefore were expected to supplement their salaries by accepting gifts, favors, and perquisites. In the case of New Spain's *alcaldes mayores*, this supplement came from their commercial activities. At the end of the seventeenth century, the viceroy, the count of Galve, explained quite straightforwardly in a letter sent to his sister-in-law, the duchess of the Infantado, how the system worked. He related to her that he had tried to appoint a person recommended by the duchess as *alcalde mayor*, but this person was forced to give up the appointment because he did not have *avío* available. As the viceroy explained to the duchess, "these offices [of alcaldes mayores] do not yield enough to support oneself unless one takes to the post what they call *avío*, which are goods and cash used to exchange and trade with the goods produced in the province where they have been appointed alcaldes mayores."[95] Society accepted the use of positions for private gain as long as it did not become too excessive. The problem was that, as Colin MacLachlan has pointed out, in the New World, the "line between private entrepreneurship and exploitive greed could easily be crossed."[96]

Another equally important reason for why the *alcaldes mayores* were not paid sufficient salaries at the same time explains the apparent paradox of the endless prohibitions by the Crown of the commercial activities of the *alcaldes*.[97] In the political discourse of the Spanish monarchy, the granting of an office was an honor that implied a will to serve the public and procure the common good; it was not a means to get rich. These ideas were profoundly influenced by the Ciceronian concept of public office as a duty. As Cicero argued:

> In general those who are about to take charge of public affairs should hold fast to Plato's two pieces of advice: first to fix their gaze so firmly on what is beneficial to the citizens that whatever they do, they do with that in mind, forgetful of their own advantage. Secondly, let them care for the whole body of the republic rather than protect one part and neglect the rest. The management of the republic is like a guardianship, and must be conducted in the light

of what is beneficial not to the guardians, but to those who are put in their charge. ...For to use public affairs for one's profit is not only dishonourable, but criminal and wicked too.[98]

Cicero's ideas can be seen in the way in which the office of king was understood among most political writers of the seventeenth century. According to this, the institution of monarchy had been created not only for the use and advantage of the king, but also for the benefit of all his realm. To be king, therefore, was a great honor, but it was also a heavy burden. In the words of Juan de Santa María:

> [Kings] were not created or introduced into the world for their own convenience and pleasure ... (if that were the case, no one would freely accept to be subjected to them), but for the benefit and common good of all their vassals, for their advancement, for their self-preservation, to rule them, to protect them, and to serve them, ... because although the scepter and the Crown seem to have a commanding and domineering face, strictly speaking it is a servant's office. ...Thus, to reign and command is a mixture of a small amount of honor and much responsibility.[99]

If this was the way the office of king was understood, the office of his representatives in the towns and villages should be understood in a similar way. This can be appreciated clearly in the royal order of 1618 that was mentioned earlier, in which the viceroy of Mexico was ordered to investigate the sources of the exorbitant profits of the *alcaldes mayores*. In one of the few instances in which this idea is explicitly expressed, the monarch points out that it is his wish to make clear that the "ministers who serve or go to serve in those kingdoms do not go to earn property or get rich, but to serve God Our Lord and the royal estate, considering themselves paid with their salaries."[100] Because being *alcalde mayor* was an honor but, at the same time, a burden that forced the appointee to take care of the common good, the salary should be sufficient to live honestly, although without luxury. Nothing was more remote from this ideal of public service than the business enterprises of the *alcaldes mayores*, and as long as the way in which this office was conceived did not change it comes as no surprise that the censures of the Crown followed one after the other uninterruptedly.[101] This was also the reason why Diego de Avendaño, while contending that no doubt the sale of offices was licit (including offices that administered justice if that were to bring some utility to the republic), rejected the legality of selling those offices that included administering justice to the Indians, because, for him, it was clear that the buyers of such offices were not seeking a greater reputation but just an economic benefit.[102]

This same conception of public office also helps to explain the supposed lack of professionalism of the colonial "bureaucracy," as nothing was more alien to the Ciceronian concept of office than the Weberian idea of the professional bureaucrat. The office was understood as a "reward" and "honor," not as a "profession" with a well-defined mission and salary scale, nor did a well-defined administrative career exist with a clear system of promotions, not even among the *letrados*, as promotion was not automatic. Professional advancement always depended on royal favor. If a bureaucracy, according to the Weberian definition, is characterized by a set of consistent and impersonal rules, where rational standards regulate performance without personal considerations and employment is based on technical and professional qualifications, then the Spanish colonial bureaucracy was not a bureaucracy at all. Though it could be admitted that some bureaucratization occurred in the Weberian sense, New Spain's colonial government had many of the characteristics of the older system that Weber called "patrimonialism."[103]

In this regard, it is not surprising that the *alcaldes mayores* appointed by the viceroys were their own clients who owed them personal loyalty and service, because in this type of society patronage was the main mode of administrative recruitment and advancement, nor should it be surprising that the viceroys and *oidores* were not always impartial, impersonal bureaucrats acting in the best interests of the state. They sought to advance their own financial and career interests, those of their families and clients, and those of their patrons, and they profited personally from their offices.[104] Even such an unrelenting critic as Hernando de Mendoza, who thought that allowing favors to be awarded for money was "one of the greatest rogueries that can be committed in relation to this matter, and the viceroy who would do such a thing or consent to it would deserve to be dishonorably deprived of his office," is perfectly aware of the principles on which the society of the time was based. He acknowledges that it would be "an unbearable curtness and tyranny" not to allow the viceroy's servants and relatives to solicit the concession of some favor for themselves or their friends, as "God's law does not oblige so much, nor have we ever seen an ecclesiastical or secular prince who sometimes does not give in to the entreaties of servants and friends."[105] All this did not mean a lack of loyalty to the king. They all spoke in the king's name and they all acted in the king's service, but once this was made clear they all proceeded to take care of their own private interests. These aspects of colonial administration, therefore, should not be explained as manifestations of a general corruption of colonial society but as constitutive aspects of a society that was very different from ours. It was a society that had no clear division between the "institutions" and the "public." The real division lay not in the formal political structures but in the networks of social relationships, thus the common idea that sees colonial society made up of well-defined and separate entities such as the "state," the "bureaucracy," or the "society" should be rejected, along with the views of a generalized corruption and a crisis of the authority of the state.

Pietschmann is surprised because, in a journal written in the middle of the seventeenth century, Gregorio Martín de Guijo, presbyter of the cathedral of Mexico City, mentions without censuring a series of occurrences (e.g., viceroys who are showered with attentions by other functionaries, members of the *audiencia* who become godfathers of wealthy residents, secretaries of viceroys and other agencies of government who earn enormous illicit profits, sales of offices, all kinds of bribery, favoritism) that for Pietschmann constitute "an excellent source on the transgressions of state functionaries around the middle of the seventeenth century."[106] Besides the inappropriateness of referring to individuals such as the viceroys and the *oidores* as "state functionaries," one could ask if Martín de Guijo's lack of censure would not be the best proof that, when judging seventeenth-century New Spanish society, our traditional ideas are not very useful and what in our eyes constitutes flagrant cases of corruption might have been taken as something else at that time.[107] Take, for example, the case of the viceroys themselves. For over a century and a half, when they left Spain to take up their posts they were allowed to take with them tax-exempt merchandise, worth thousands of ducats, to trade with in the Indies. This clearly contradicted the concept of office presented previously, but initially it had been justified by the lack of all kinds of goods at the beginning of colonialization. In time, however, the viceroys would use this license to make big profits, greatly exceeding the authorized amounts of goods to be traded. Around the middle of the seventeenth century, the Council of the Indies even insinuated that the viceroys, with their commercial transactions, had contributed to an increase in contraband, besides engaging in unfair competition with the rest of the merchants. For these reasons, the Council suggested to the king that viceroys should thenceforth be appointed on the condition that they could not carry any type of merchandise to the Indies.[108] It is not clear whether this prohibition was ever implemented, but what is significant here is how a public post was regularly used to obtain a private profit, without the legality or illegality of the action being clear at all (it certainly was not clear when it took the Council more than 100 years to finally bring up the issue).[109]

As Michel Foucault has observed with regard to *ancien régime* societies, "By placing on the side of the sovereign the additional burden of a spectacular, unlimited, personal, irregular, and discontinuous power, the form of monarchical sovereignty left the subjects free to practise a constant illegality." As he explains, the non-application of the rule and the non-observance of numerous edicts and ordinances were conditions of the political and economic functioning of society. Illegality was so deeply rooted and so necessary to the life of each social stratum that it had in a sense its own coherence and economy. That meant that, for decades, ordinances could be published and constantly renewed without ever being implemented.[110] Very often, the perception of corruption depended upon the individual, his activities, and the political situation at the time. In the Mexican case, a skillful viceroy who distributed favors in an even-handed way would not usually raise unfavorable opinions among New Spain's inhabitants. In this way, the distribution of offices became a complex political game. If a viceroy was politically adept, he would be able to balance the distribution of offices and benefices among his retainers and the inhabitants of New Spain. Conversely, whenever a politically inept viceroy monopolized the distribution of offices among his clients, then the grievances and discontent of the Creole population became louder, provoking, at least as it was seen from Madrid, a weakening of the bonds of loyalty that tied the Creole population to the monarch.[111]

This system was tolerated as long as its positive aspects (it supplemented, for example, the low salaries) outweighed the negative ones and did not negatively influence the judgment of royal officials. Even among the critics of the system, some saw the deals and transactions of the *alcaldes mayores* as legitimate only if they did not commit very many abuses and extortions.[112] But, when the activities of certain *alcaldes mayores* caused disturbances as serious as the Tehuantepec uprising of 1660 or the censures of the Creoles regarding viceregal patronage became general, as in the case of the count of Baños, then more drastic measures could be taken, such as not extending a viceroy's term of office or launching a special investigation. As long as the deals and transactions of viceroys and *alcaldes mayores* were kept within certain limits and their profits were not outrageous or their practices clearly abusive, then in the eyes of the majority of their contemporaries no corruption had occurred, even though in our eyes it might seem otherwise. In the case of the distribution of offices, patronage was considered corrupt only when it resulted in the appointment of men of decidedly inferior ability. This certainly was one of the main accusations brought forward against many *alcaldes mayores*. In addition, many *alcaldes* came to their posts with an attitude that could only be defined as one of trying to squeeze the golden goose as fast and exhaustively as possible. Although the Crown was aware of this state of affairs, we have already seen that it was only at the end of the century that it decided to take more radical measures, although always in a hesitant way.

6
The Political Culture
of Colonialism

Undoubtedly, the members of the indigenous population — the producers of the material wealth that allowed the functioning of the economy of favor — were the ones who bore the brunt of the abuses of the system of clientage examined in the previous chapter, and it was precisely the existence of this population that gave its peculiarity to the possessions of the Spanish monarchy in the New World and distinguished them from the other dominions of the Crown. How, then, did the viceroys of New Spain approach and relate to the indigenous inhabitants of the viceroyalty? How did they rule them? In order to answer these questions, we first need to look at the ways in which the natives of the New World, in general, and those of New Spain, in particular, were incorporated into the discourse of the Catholic Monarchy and integrated into its "body." Such an analysis must include not only the discourses and practices of the Crown officials in relation to the native population, but also those of the Creole elites, because in the sixteenth and seventeenth centuries their members were considered Spaniards, enjoying, at least in theory, the same rights, privileges, and obligations as their peninsular counterparts.

Although in many respects the Spanish exploits in the New World contributed to the creation of modern colonialism, it should be noted that Spanish society created the colonial project very often by drawing from the past (if a model existed for the theorists of the Spanish monarchy, it was that of imperial Rome), trying to adapt certain elements from that past to a novel contemporary situation.[1] Another characteristic of that project was that, despite the dominating presence of certain elements, it was never monolithic. Different and very often opposing ideas contributed to the

185

Spanish colonial project, and it was perhaps this diversity of approaches that endowed Spanish colonialism with an ambiguous and even contradictory nature. In that sense, the colonial project was constantly debated and called into question. The heated debates that took place in the first half of the sixteenth century as regards the indigenous inhabitants of the New World are well known,[2] but once the dust settled and two basic principles were accepted by everyone — the intrinsic humanity and right to liberty of the Indians — many other unresolved questions of a more practical nature remained: How should these peoples be incorporated into the Spanish polity? How were they to be ruled? What kinds of rights and obligations should they have? Should they be assimilated completely, or should they preserve their traditional ways? Some of these questions provoked equally heated debates and controversies, and examining the ways in which they were answered is the aim of this chapter. As will be shown in the following pages, the discursive practices of the Spanish monarchy constructed the Indians as rightful members of the body politic who were subject to numerous obligations because of their subordinated position, but, at the same time, were endowed with certain rights to which they were entitled as vassals of the Spanish monarch. The central point of my analysis will be what I have termed the "rhetoric of wretchedness," which, from very early on, dominated every approach of the Spanish rulers to the indigenous population, at least to those living in the central areas. This rhetoric, in turn, would play a fundamental role in shaping and defining the civilizing mission of the Spanish monarchy. The importance of this mission should not be overlooked, as the entire Spanish colonial venture was predicated upon it.

The Rhetoric of Wretchedness

"Our main concern and that to which one should attend in the first place and that which we indeed wish and procure," declared the Spanish monarch in a letter sent in 1619 to the marquis of Guadalcázar, viceroy of New Spain, is "the preservation, protection, and good treatment of the Indians, and that they be rightly governed and kept in peace and administered justice as vassals of this Crown." Unfortunately, the king asserted, the royal officials in the Indies were only interested in getting rich and reaping profit from the Indians' sweat and toil, but the Indians, "as sad and wretched persons of little worth and great subjection and obedience, do not resist anything, enduring vexations and harassments in their properties and persons until they lose their lives," for which reason they were particularly in need of protection and relief, something that, as the monarch affirmed in the letter, was especially entrusted to himself. Because there was not much the king could do to right these wrongs because he was so far away, it was the responsibility of the viceroy to ensure that the Indians were treated well. As he told Guadalcázar: "I wanted to make sure you understand that this is my royal will and the cause I wish to be attended to in the first place and above everything else, and that in this way I relieve my royal conscience … leaving in charge of yours the execution of everything, since this belongs to your care and the posts you exercise."[3]

The idea of the native as a "wretched person" (*persona miserable*) is the defining element of the Spanish Crown's discourse on the Indian. It was permanently inscribed in the *Recopilación* of 1680, but it had taken shape long before. In a royal decree from the time of Philip II, which later would be incorporated into the *Recopilación*, it is plainly acknowledged that "the Indians receive in their persons and properties great harm and many wrongs and oppressions from some Spaniards, *corregidores*, members of the religious orders, and clerics." The decree goes on to explain that these Indians, "as wretched persons, neither resist nor defend themselves, abiding by everything they are ordered." For this reason, the viceroys were instructed to investigate and punish these abuses, though they had to make sure that the Indians did not utilize this as an excuse to "stop serving."[4] Similarly, in another law of the *Recopilación* that reproduces royal *cédulas* from both Philip II and Philip IV, the bishops of the Indies are asked, because "the Indians are wretched people of such a weak nature that they are easily harassed and oppressed," to try to prevent, by any means necessary, these abuses, making sure that the Indians are treated with the leniency and moderation that had so many times been ordered (Figure 14).[5]

Two fundamental ideas are intertwined in the royal discourse. On the one hand is the obligation to ensure the well-being of the indigenous population; on the other, the idea that this population is basically made of "wretched" beings who need special protection. The origin of these ideas can be found, no doubt, in the discourse of the religious orders, above all the Franciscans, who from the beginnings of their presence in the New World would be responsible for transmitting to the metropolis certain images and concepts about the native population.[6] Although historians have generally emphasized the friars' loss of influence *vis-à-vis* the secular authorities over the course of the sixteenth century, the reality is that the ideas conveyed by the Franciscans would profoundly shape the Crown's discourse and its behavior regarding the Indians. Both the monarch and the members of the Council of the Indies were constantly bombarded with letters and all kinds of memorials in which, while denouncing colonial realities, the friars explained their views on the character and nature of the natives. In addition, the monarch was reminded, time and again, of his duties and obligations to his vassals from across the Atlantic. These obligations had originated from a belief in the providential destiny of the Hispanic monarchy. The Spanish monarchs, it was argued, had been chosen from among all the princes of the world by Divine Providence, through His vicar, the pope, to expand the Christian faith throughout the world and,

LA Aguila Real expelle vitoriofa
Del nido à la baftarda; mas piadofa
Los polluelos, que dexa, le alimenta,
Y adoptandolos hijos, los fomenta.
De efte modo tambien Reyes Hifpanos
Con los Indios, polluelos Mexicanos,
Piadofos, y clementes fiempre fueron;
Pero todos, Philippo, te cedieron;
Pues fegun tus afectos paternales,
De adoptivos, fe vieron naturales.

Fig. 14 "The love and care of the Spanish kings for their Indian subjects," from Isidro Sariñana, *Llanto del Occidente en el ocaso del más claro sol de las Españas*, 1666. In this emblem from Philip IV's catafalque, the Spanish royal eagle has expelled the illegitimate Mexican eagle from his nest, but instead of abandoning the "humble Mexican chickens" (the "wretched Indians") to their own devices, he protects them and, showing great pity and compassion, accepts them as his own natural children. (Courtesy of the Hispanic Society of America, New York.)

especially, in the New World. This providential destiny compelled them to ensure the spiritual and corporal welfare of their new vassals. The reward for their dedication would be the "rule of all the world."[7]

In a memorial written in 1587, Gerónimo de Mendieta, the influential Franciscan friar, did not fail to remind the king that he was obliged to look after both the spiritual and the temporal welfare of the Indians with more care and watchfulness than any other of his vassals. This was so not only because that was why the pope had ceded him dominion over the Indies, but also because both natural and divine law obliged "the one who rules and governs to look more after the poor than after the rich, more after the weak and feeble than after the mighty." No one could ignore, added Mendieta, that the Indians were "the poorest, the weakest, the feeblest, and the most ignorant of all nations," as they did not even know how to present their needs to their king, for which reason it was necessary that others spoke for them. In the opinion of Mendieta, however, the monarch had not only the same obligations toward the Indians as a king had toward his vassals, but also those of a tutor toward his pupils, of a teacher toward his disciples, and of a father toward his children. Because the talents and abilities of the Indians were those of young children of no more than ten or twelve years of age, they were easily deceived and exploited, and thus in particular need of royal protection. This lack of ability meant that the natives could be ruled as easily as schoolchildren; when they committed some transgression, a dozen lashes were sufficient punishment for the Indians to learn their lesson, for they needed the lashes as much as they needed their bread, "the lash being so natural to them that they cannot live without it, and they themselves recognize that lacking it they go astray like children."[8]

Along with their childlike nature, the natives possessed many other qualities — positive ones, in Mendieta's view — that differentiated them from the Spaniards:

> They are gentle, domestic, and peaceful, so much so that irrational animals come near them and accompany them more than with any other nation, and there are hardly any quarrels among them except when they drink wine, which usually turns them violent. They are *humble*, neglectful of their own interests [*despreciados de sí mismos*], *obedient*, and of incredible *patience*. They are liberal with the little they have and *not at all greedy*; thus they care neither to amass properties, nor to build sumptuous houses, nor to leave entailments, nor about the dowry they will give to their daughters, … which is *a most suitable quality for a Christian and apostolic life*. They are ceremonious, because of their nature or because that was the ancient custom of their ancestors. They are inclined to religious things and all those matters which pertain to divine worship.[9]

What makes this passage so interesting is the manner in which Mendieta represents the Indians as ideal Franciscan friars, something which, of course, fits perfectly in the Franciscan New World utopia.[10] Mendieta, nevertheless, points out that all these qualities will only come to light if the Indians have someone to appropriately guide them (e.g., the friars in their *doctrinas*), because if they were to follow their own free will, they would be worse than any other people.[11] This was not always the case, however. Mendieta argues that before the conquest the Indians were able to rule themselves with "great prudence, order, and discretion," but after their conquest by the Spaniards, the Indians:

> … lost their nerve and got frightened, losing their style of government without adopting that of the Spaniards, … and they were left in the state and with the ability and talent of children of nine or

twelve years of age, in need of being governed like minors by guardians or tutors, ... for a ten-year-old Spanish or mestizo boy will
take on any Indian, no matter how big ... and this happens because
the Indians are usually of little strength and weak, besides being
naturally timid and pusillanimous.

It is precisely because of this weakness and pusillanimity that the Castilian
kings are obliged to defend and protect the Indians "with great diligence
and vigilance, as with sheep surrounded by hungry wolves wishing to
suck their blood."[12] Mendieta's arguments certainly justified the predominant role of the friars in New Spain. At the same time, let us not forget
that, as Georges Baudot has observed, for the Franciscans extreme poverty, meekness, the absence of social and material ambition, and eternal
childhood were necessary images in the construction of the Indians as
instruments for the salvation of the Old World. Thus, freed by the conquest from "Satanic" political and religious leaders, the American Indians
were endowed with an entire gamut of images that made them acceptable
instruments of the eschatological destiny of humankind.[13] Mendieta
could not understand that his own evangelizing project, which implied
the subordination of the natives, tended to favor the existence of coloniz-
ers (those "hungry wolves") and colonized (the "sheep"). For him, the
relations of power created by the colonial regime amounted simply to a
matter of pusillanimity, brought about by the infantilization experienced
by the Indian as a result of the conquest.

Although this idealization of the native, whose foundation was the concept of the wretched Indian, is typical of the utopian view of the Franciscans, it became a conventional image in the religious and political
discourse of the Spanish monarchy. Writing in the 1560s, Juan de Matienzo,
the influential *oidor* of the *audiencia* of Charcas, whose experience with the
indigenous population of the Americas happened not in Mexico but in the
Andean world, did not hesitate to assert that "all the Indians of every nation
so far discovered [are] pusillanimous and timid." He concluded, with the
help of Aristotle, that the natives, due to their melancholic nature, were
"timorous, weak, and ignorant" besides being characterized by their
patience, humility, and obedience (and, of course, also by their idleness and
drinking excesses).[14] These ideas, similarly, run through many of the
decrees issued by the Third Mexican Provincial Council, celebrated in 1585
to adapt the Church of New Spain to the mandates of the Council of Trent.
The Third Council was probably the most important of the colonial era,
another council not being celebrated until almost two centuries later, in
1771. One of its most important resolutions was the approval of a universal
catechism to be used in the Christian instruction of "children, slaves, Indians, and other persons of little capacity." Such catechism should be translated into the chief indigenous languages. Another decree declared that
"being the Indians of a timid and pusillanimous nature, it is most necessary

that the priests treat them with gentleness and affability and not with harshness and threats." The "natural gentleness and subjection" of the natives should move the priests to pity them and to defend and protect them from ill treatment. This did not mean that they could not discipline them when necessary, but the priests should punish the Indians with moderation and never in person, but through their assistants. Moreover, the Council forbade the imposition of fines on the Indians; all punishment should be corporal, as was befitting their condition of being poor and miserable people.[15]

Around the middle of the seventeenth century, Juan de Palafox wrote a memorial to the king on the Indians of New Spain, which represents one more turn of the screw in the process of idealization inaugurated by the Franciscans. Yet, if Mendieta presented an image of the native that was a faithful replica of the good Franciscan, we should not forget that Palafox, as bishop of Puebla, was a prominent member of the secular clergy and was immersed in a protracted battle with the religious orders on account of his attempt at replacing the friars of the Indian parishes with members of the secular clergy. It should also be recalled that Palafox was inspector general of New Spain and, before arriving in Mexico, had been a member of the Council of the Indies, first as the Crown's attorney and later as a councilor. Finally, while in Mexico he became the acting viceroy for almost a year. It should come as no surprise, therefore, that Palafox was more interested in presenting an image of the Indian as the perfect vassal of the Spanish monarch. He argues that the Indians had placed themselves voluntarily under the dominion of the Spanish Crown, never having tried to rebel; rather, "they obey it and serve it with the most submissive obedience and loyalty." In addition, they were good and fervent Christians who treated their priests with humility and respect (something that mirrored the pious behavior of the Spanish Crown, showing in this way that the Indians, as good vassals, followed their king's example).[16]

This image of the good vassal does not eliminate that of the good Christian constructed by the Franciscans. To Palafox, the natives are not driven by greed or envy; they are free from any ambition (according to him, very few aspire to the posts of governor or *alcalde*); they are humble ("like extremely gentle lambs do they humble themselves or abide by and do all they are commanded"); they live frugally (they make do with just a mat to sleep on the floor, their dress is comprised of a simple shirt and a pair of cotton trousers without any need for hats or shoes, and they feed on a few corn tortillas and chiles); and many voluntarily choose to live in poverty, living in happiness and frugality. The Indians, moreover, are patient, long suffering, resigned, and peaceful, because, no matter how many and how great their wrongs are, "most rarely do they show anger or a desire for revenge, … nor do they worry, get angry, or are upset."[17] After examining all these virtues, which are very similar to those described by Mendieta, Palafox insists again upon the virtue of obedience (which is, in the last analysis, what characterizes the good vassal) and concludes that for no other virtue are the Indians more admirable. They are such good vassals and so obedient to royal orders that they never protest when tributes are imposed on them or when they are sent to the labor drafts, nor did they complain when they were forced to resettle in towns, as they allow themselves to be taken to and fro "like so many herds of gentle sheep."[18] The Palafoxian discourse unites, therefore, the Franciscan political–religious utopia with the more pragmatic imperial vision of the Spanish monarchy. To Palafox, the natives are in essence useful vassals of the Crown, who have contributed enormously to its enrichment, while costing very little. Thanks to the treasures from the Indies, the monarch has been able to keep his power and authority, thus he should show special gratitude to the Indians and try to protect them by all possible means.[19]

For his part, Juan de Solórzano Pereira permanently inscribed the rhetoric of the wretched Indian in imperial discourse by dedicating two complete chapters of his *magnum opus* to a discussion of the concept. According to Solórzano, the Indians are characterized by their "imbecility, rusticity, poverty, pusillanimity, constant labors, and services."[20] It is this wretchedness that has prompted the monarchs to earnestly instruct the viceroys, *audiencias*, and prelates to procure their well-being and good treatment. Likewise, this condition entitles the natives to all the favors and privileges granted to minors, rustics, and the poor. Thus, their lawsuits should be conducted summarily, without too much attention being paid to legalisms. No ecclesiastical censures are to be imposed on them, and corporal punishments should be administered more with the moderation of a father than with the rigor of a judge, because, Solórzano contends, "they are more in need of forgiveness because of their little capacity."[21] The Indians, concludes Solórzano, are to be considered "wretched persons because those are deemed as such who cannot govern themselves and need others to direct them, govern them, and assist them," which is why they are usually compared to minors and women.[22] In this way, the discursive strategy initiated by the Franciscans reaches here its political perfection. If Mendieta utilized the infantilization of the Indians, a concept with a clear Christian echo (the special devotion of Christ for children, etc.), to justify the evangelizing project of the Franciscan order, Solórzano, and with him the royal discourse, appropriated the rhetoric of infantilization and wretchedness to justify political control over the New World peoples. If the natives were incapable of governing themselves, was it not clear that the imposition of Spanish authority upon them was totally justified?

The Civilizing Mission

The construction of the Indians as wretched persons and its corollary, the obligation of the authorities to protect them, has been utilized to contend that the Spanish colonization was always characterized by a lofty ethical content,[23] but in reality this kind of argument ignores the project of domination hidden behind the discourse of protection. The rhetoric of wretchedness, which constituted an integral part of Spanish colonial discourse, was used to justify the domination and exploitation of the natives. Indeed, the Spanish Crown was expected to ensure the welfare of the Indians because they were the king's vassals, and securing the well-being of his subjects was one of the main obligations of the monarch. In securing this welfare, however, the king would also be fulfilling the "civilizing mission" of the Spanish monarchy, as the conquest was carried out for the good of the Indians themselves. Thanks to that violent encounter, they had been delivered from the "tyranny and servitude in which they formerly lived."[24] As will be shown, the civilizing drive constituted one of the fundamental principles of conduct of the Spanish Crown in the New World. In this regard, the Spanish colonial project, with its emphasis on the need to civilize the natives, would contribute to inventing modern colonialism.[25]

The rhetoric of wretchedness was closely intertwined with a civilizing ideology to justify the collection of tribute from the indigenous population. Juan de Matienzo, for example, affirmed that given the Indians' "limited intelligence and pusillanimity," they were in need of an overlord to defend them and instruct them; the Indians were to pay the king a "salary" for such a service. Matienzo wonders with great aplomb who owes more to whom: the Spaniards, who, besides instructing the Indians in the true religion, teach them "to live like humans," or the Indians, who give them silver, gold, and other material things, which are but "stones and sludge" when compared to invaluable things such as the ones the Spaniards have given to the Indians. Because, according to Matienzo, the Indians do not own property with which to pay the tribute, they will have to use "their labor and sweat." Moreover, having to work to be able to meet their tax obligations will produce a salutary civilizing effect among the natives: "This will make them take a liking to working and acquiring property, and they will begin to leave their servitude and tyranny and to know what liberty is." That is to say, work will make them free, and through it they will discover the virtues of private property. The Indians will understand they are no longer their *caciques*' slaves and will begin to like the idea of possessing things.[26]

Not everybody, however, would agree with Matienzo's ideas. For the influential José de Acosta, it was objectionable to justify the exaction of tribute from the Indians with the argument that it was done in exchange for the religious instruction they received. It would look like the Gospel was being auctioned to the highest bidder. "Christ commands us," Acosta contended, "to give gratis what gratis we have received."[27] This notwithstanding, Acosta believed that the Indians were obliged to compensate the Spaniards (either the king or the *encomenderos*) in some way for the work they performed in governing them.[28] Acosta also saw the payment of tribute as a civilizing tool. Because the "barbarians" from the Indies were "an indolent and lazy nation," it would be very advantageous for them to be forced to work to be able to pay their tributes, as long as, Acosta clarifies, this work was done for their own benefit and not for the gain of the Spaniards; otherwise, what was supposed to be just tribute would just become robbery.[29]

A parallel question that arose after the conquest was whether the Indians should also pay the tithe to the Church. On principle, the answer seemed to be very simple: If the Indians should pay the tribute to the king (or to the *encomenderos* in his name) in acknowledgment of his dominion, they should also "pay the tithe to God, who is the King of Kings,"[30] but the matter was never that simple. From the start, the religious orders, particularly the Franciscans, were opposed to making those Indians converted to Christianity pay the tithe that traditionally all Christians were obliged to contribute to the diocesan clergy. They contended that the Indians were in fact already paying the tithe when they paid their tributes, for these were paid to the monarch so that he, as "King and Lord" of the Indians, would administer justice to them and provide them with religious instruction and priests. The Indians, therefore, were already contributing to maintenance of the Church (which was the reason why all Christians had to pay the tithe). Moreover, the religious orders argued, the clergy could be perfectly supported with the tithe paid by the Spaniards. Given their extreme poverty, the Indians would not be able to deal with a new imposition, which would increase their exploitation; because of their condition as "a wretched and timid people of little courage," they would not offer any resistance to a new contribution. For the friars, to insist on making the Indians pay the tithe was just another link in the campaign mounted by the secular clergy to dispossess them of the administration of the Indian parishes.[31] It appears that the arguments used by the religious orders had the desired effect. Although being poor was not a sufficient excuse not to pay the tithe, it was decided that, in view of the poverty of the Indians and their condition of neophytes, the tithes were to be included with the tributes, from which the former would be paid, and in that way the contributions of the Indians would not be increased.[32]

Along with the collection of tribute, another much more difficult matter the Spanish Crown had to deal with after the conquest was how to control the indigenous population to ensure their utilization as a labor force. Antonio de Mendoza, the first viceroy of New Spain, already complained that if the Indians were allowed to move from one town to another (something that, in theory, they could do because they were free persons) they would take advantage of such freedom to avoid paying tribute or being drafted for public works.[33] On the other hand, the geographical dispersion that characterized the native settlements did not favor in the least the task of control. At the same time, the extraordinary importance that the conversion of the natives had for the Spanish colonizing project gave a special urgency to this problem. Very early on, members of the religious orders requested the monarch to order all that was necessary to ensure that the Indians lived "congregated" in towns, something that would greatly facilitate their labor of indoctrination.[34] The clerics were, therefore, the ones who, from the beginning, most insisted upon this question, but in this insistence lay more than just an evangelizing interest. Incorporated into it we find an entire civilizing program for the Indian. As was straightforwardly declared in one of the resolutions of the First Mexican Council, celebrated in 1555:

> It is a great hindrance that the Indians live scattered and isolated from one another throughout the fields and mountains, many of them living more like beasts than like rational and political men, whence it follows that only with great difficulty are they instructed and taught in the things of our Holy Catholic Faith and in those human and politic, ... because in order for them to be truly Christian and political, like the rational men that they are, it is necessary that they be congregated, subdued, and converted (*congregados y reducidos*) into towns and villages that are comfortable and suitable, and not live scattered and dispersed in the mountains and sierras, so that they shall not be deprived of every spiritual and temporal benefit.[35]

For the clerics gathered at the Council, the only possible and acceptable form of life for the rational man, and that which distinguishes him from the animals, is life in the company of other men — that is, to be part of a "polis," which makes him into a "politic" man. Outside of the *polis* is only barbarism, and what characterizes the "barbarian" is his lack of civility (*policía*) and hence humanity,[36] but, in sixteenth-century New Spain, the rational man had to be Christian as well as civil or political. One concept cannot be understood without the other, as the "politicization" of the Indian contributes, at the same time, to his Christianization. As the clerics attending the 1555 Council contended, it is more appropriate "to make men politic and human first rather than to establish the faith upon ferine customs."[37] This civilizing program becomes explicit in very concrete ways: The Indians will have to abandon "their feral and wild old customs" and adopt those of "politic men" — namely, "to have tables to eat and beds to sleep high up and not on the floor, ... and the houses with so much cleanliness and neatness that they will look like the dwellings of men, and not the huts or pigsties of filthy animals."[38] Nevertheless, it may be counterproductive to force the Indians to change all their customs too suddenly, which is why those customs that are good or indifferent may be tolerated, but certain customs (real or imagined) are peculiar to the Indians that define them as barbarians and which must be eradicated by any means: incest, sodomy, idolatry, nakedness, idleness, and drunkenness.[39] All of these "vices" are closely related, as idleness, which is the root of all evil, leads to drunkenness, and this to all kinds of aberrations, both physical and spiritual (i.e., incest, sodomy, and idolatry). For the count of Monterrey (who, as viceroy of New Spain between 1595 and 1603, would play a decisive role in the process of resettlement of the indigenous population), the congregation of the Indians in towns would be the only means to reform the vices of "these wretched ones." What is more, by concentrating the Indians in towns, it would be easier to make them work, something that, no doubt, would increase their level of civility (*policía*).[40]

The first concern of the ruler, therefore, must be to attract the barbarian or savage to the "political" or "civil" life. From this, a commentator such as Solórzano deduces that rulers have every right to force such people to live in towns, an argument that justified the policy of the Spanish monarchy of resettling the indigenous population. As reasoned by Solórzano, the Indians "were accustomed to living in many places like beasts in the fields, without trace and knowledge of a sociable and political life," for which reason they had to be concentrated in towns so that "they could start living like men, and by abandoning their old and feral customs they could become more fit to receive our Holy Faith and Christian Religion." The prince or the republic, concludes Solórzano, can therefore compel his vassals, even though they are free, as long as it is for the benefit of the common good.[41] It is important to note here that the civilizing discourse was not directed exclusively to the peoples of the New World. Regarding the inhabitants of certain regions of Galicia in northwestern Spain, it was said at the end of the sixteenth century that "would His Majesty order to reduce them to towns ... it would be the greatest possible service to God and also to His Majesty [because] these barbaric people would become politic and domestic and taught the Christian doctrine, something impossible if they keep living in the way they do."[42] This kind of language is exactly the same as that used to refer to the natives of New Spain. As Nicholas Thomas has observed, the stigmatization of particular populations may be energized as much by analogies with subaltern domestic groups as by their race. Although colonial discourse theory has usually assumed that race is the basis for representing others (almost always in a negative way), that was not the case in premodern European discourses, which tended to characterize non-Western peoples as a lack or poorer form of the values of the center — that is, as barbarians who lacked civility or religion or clothes.[43]

Taking this civilizing discourse as a point of departure, throughout the second half of the sixteenth century the Spanish viceroys were repeatedly instructed by the Crown to try to concentrate the indigenous population in towns, slowly but without interruption;[44] however, this policy of resettlement or congregation does not seem to have caused a massive movement of people. The reason may be simple: Despite all the insistence on the fact that the Indians of New Spain were living like beasts scattered throughout the mountains, the reality was that Mesoamerican civilization was characterized by a high rate of urbanization, which is why after the conquest the Spaniards did not feel a great need to regroup the native population. In fact, they based their new territorial divisions on the existing indigenous territorial units (known as *altepetl* or, in an approximate translation, city-states or local ethnic states, which would become the *pueblos de indios* of the colonial era).[45] To this it should be added that the Spaniards never had at their disposal the means or the organization required to carry out such an undertaking. Viceroy Luis de Velasco II, who took a particular interest in the process of resettlement, would repeatedly complain that the congregations could not be carried out for lack of money, and by the end of his term in office in 1596 he would inform his successor that the congregations had been halted for lack of resources.[46]

One of the greatest defenders of the resettlement policy happened to be Gerónimo de Mendieta, who had written to the monarch in 1589 asking for implementation of the congregation program. In his case, of course, this policy fully coincided with his evangelizing project that required the radical separation of Spaniards and Indians. Mendieta could only see advantages in the resettlements: By being concentrated in well-defined towns, each one with its priest and secular magistrate, the Indians could be counted more easily. Knowing who and where they were, it would be easier to prevent them from going back to their former practices. Moreover, with the greater human contact that would exist in these towns, the natives would become more "civilized." Mendieta, the great defender of the Indians, rejects the idea that forcing them to abandon the houses where they had been born and raised would become a great trauma for them, for everyone knew, says he, how common it was for the Indians to move from one place to another, and "how easily they build their little houses, which always require little work, and their little trees and plants are redone in a short time," because the majority did not possess anything of great value.[47] The rhetoric of wretchedness functions smoothly here to justify the uprooting of the indigenous population.

It is not clear to what extent Mendieta's letters had an effect on the Court, although we know that in 1585 the Third Mexican Council had admonished the New Spanish authorities for doing little to implement the royal orders regarding the concentration of the Indians in large towns.[48] We also know that viceroy Velasco II often reminded the monarch of the importance of carrying out the concentration of the native population. For him, the congregations were very necessary, because the inclination of the Indians to dwell in "hidden, inaccessible, and isolated places, and all by themselves" rendered it very difficult to teach them the Catholic doctrine and "reduce them to a politic life."[49] The Crown seemed to be responsive to Velasco's requests and decided to give a new impulse to the resettlement policy.[50] In all probability, the fact that, after several decades of severe population loss, many of the *calpolli* or subdistricts that constituted each *altepetl* had ceased to be viable must have had a significant influence on this decision;[51] however, this fact is nowhere mentioned, as the Crown resorted instead to a civilizing rhetoric to explain this decision. In the *cédula* sent to viceroy Velasco II in 1595 instructing him to carry on with the concentration of Indians in towns, it is affirmed that "by congregating the Indians in towns, they are better and more easily taught about our Holy Catholic Faith and how to live with the civility (*policía*) and intercourse of men of reason, as seen in those already concentrated."[52] Likewise, the count of Monterrey, during whose rule the majority of the new resettlements were carried out, told the marquis of Montesclaros, his successor, that the basis for the "general concentration" of the Indians was the need "to concentrate them in large towns and, with that, to bring them to a Christian and politic life." For Monterrey, these resettlements were the most important thing ever done in the Indies after the conquest and conversion of the Indians. It was also the most difficult, not only because the life and property of numerous vassals of the king or the royal income were dependent upon it, but also, and above all, because the Christianization and civilization (*policía*) of so many souls depended on its success. Because God himself, Monterrey asserted, had trusted the Royal Crown with the "conversion, direction, and protection of this barbaric and timid nation," the monarch should consider as well spent all the money necessary for this enterprise.[53]

In order to ensure the success of the resettlement program, the Crown this time decided to increase the resources earmarked for it.[54] The program was most active approximately between 1595 and 1605 and was developed under the direct supervision of the viceroy, who organized it in a precise manner, appointing two different types of officials: those in charge of indicating the places where the Indians were to be resettled and those in charge of carrying out the removal and transfer.[55] These officials were charged with making sure that the new towns always had streets and a central square, where the church as well as the city hall, the community house, and the jail were to be located.[56] Every official in charge of a transfer was to gather all the Indians affected by the removal and, through an interpreter, was to make them understand His Majesty's decision to carry out a "general concentration" because of the great benefits of living "together and in a civil manner (*en policía*), as is usual among all the nations of the world." In this way, besides being able to help one another, they would enjoy spiritual solace, thanks to the presence of a priest, and access to justice, because a magistrate would always be nearby. The priest was also to be present when this speech was given, and in his sermons he was expected to energetically persuade the Indians of the many advantages of such removal.[57]

It is not easy to discern to what extent this attempt at concentrating the indigenous population was successful.[58] From the beginning, the protests of the Indians followed one after the other, and they were not alone in their resistance to the removals. Despite Mendieta's enthusiasm, it seems that many of his coreligionists were opposed to these resettlements, probably because they were not under their control.[59] This was an undertaking essentially carried out by the secular authorities, under the direction of the viceroy, though, as has been seen, the cooperation of the religious authorities was always to be sought. Juan de Torquemada, among others, was a harsh critic of the resettlements carried out during the administration of the count of Monterrey, but it was the abuses committed with this pretext that he criticized; he did not contradict the main principle that guided the program — that is, the necessity of forcing the Indians who lived scattered throughout the mountains, "in disarray and without civility" (*sin concierto ni policía*) to live "with order and in well-formed towns."[60] On the other hand, given the limitations of the Spanish colonial regime and despite the grandiosity of the resettlement program, it was all but impossible to control the population in a systematic way.[61] Thus, in addition to the legal complaints constantly being lodged by the natives, which contributed a great deal to delay and hamper the regrouping of the population, there was also added the direct resistance of many Indians who would flee from the new settlements shortly after being transferred to them.[62]

At any rate, by the end of the first decade of the seventeenth century, the process of resettlement had been brought almost completely to a halt;[63] yet, all the viceroys appointed until the end of the seventeenth century would continue to be instructed to carry on with the congregation program. When, in 1696, the count of Moctezuma, the last viceroy of New Spain appointed by the Habsburg dynasty, received his Instruction, he was ordered, like all of his predecessors, to continue to finish the process of resettlement begun in 1595, while procuring the "preservation of the Indians" and their "edification in our Holy Catholic Faith."[64] It could be argued, and this would probably be the conventional explanation, that this was just one more instance of the negligence and bureaucratic routine in which the decadent Spanish monarchy had become entrenched in the time of the equally degenerate Charles II; however, I think that a different kind of argument can be offered. To begin with, it would be erroneous to read many of these Instructions literally: Instructing the viceroy to continue the resettlement of the population in an age in which no one no longer paid any attention to the matter was an acknowledgment on the part of the Crown that the civilizing of the Indians — of which the program of resettlement was such a fundamental element — was an unfinished business, first of all because the congregations were by far never complete, an incompleteness that, for example, was painfully highlighted with every instance of alleged Indian idolatry. With the inclusion of such an instruction, the viceroy was simply being reminded of the civilizing mission of the Spanish monarchy, a mission that, let us not forget, was indissolubly united to the Christianization of the inhabitants of the New World.

These two aspects, civilizing mission and Christianization, were also closely intertwined in what has been termed by historians the policy of

"Castilianization" of the Indians — that is, their learning the Spanish language. We have already mentioned the importance of language as a mechanism of power and as a fundamental instrument of colonization. In this regard, no doubt the theorists of the Spanish monarchy were well aware of the value of language as a political tool. As Solórzano observed, the conquerors always imposed their language and customs upon the vanquished to show their dominion and superiority;[65] yet, the Spanish colonizing project was always characterized by a great ambiguity regarding the use of Spanish as an imperial language and whether it should be imposed upon the Indians. In the first place, the superiority of the Spanish language was not all that clear as Latin was considered superior to Spanish.[66] Moreover, a conflict always existed between the work of Christianizing the native population, on the one hand, and its gradual assimilation into the dominant culture, on the other. The imperative to expand the Christian faith was of such great importance for the Spanish colonial project that, in fact, it became an obstacle to the expansion of the Spanish language, although it is true that, from the beginning, the Crown saw the expansion of Spanish across the Atlantic as an instrument of its civilizing program. The learning of Spanish, it was argued, would facilitate the comprehension of Christian doctrine by the natives, as not even the most perfect of the indigenous languages was able to express the mysteries of the Christian religion in all of its complexity.[67] It was also contended that maintaining the use of the native languages would only serve to preserve Indian idolatry. Castilianization of the Indians, on the other hand, would serve "to direct them towards the good manners and politic life with which they need to live" and to learn how "to rule and govern themselves as men of reason."[68] That is, in much the same way as the "mysteries" of Christianity could not be appropriately expressed in the indigenous languages, it was not possible for the "politic man" to communicate in a language that was "barbaric and without any *policía*," incapable of expressing the complexities of a civil and political life.[69]

Nevertheless, faced with the certainty that waiting for the natives to learn the language of their conquerors would be to prolong their conversion indefinitely, the first friars had already decided that a much easier and faster method would be to learn the indigenous languages themselves. It was even proposed that the use of Nahuatl as a *lingua franca* be expanded to cover all of New Spain, as it was thought to be a language understood by many of the natives who belonged to other linguistic groups.[70] When the Council of the Indies proposed in 1596 that *caciques* who spoke or allowed their Indians to speak their own language be removed from their posts, the monarch not only did not approve this proposal, but ordered that, as had already been mandated, no parish priests should be appointed who did not know the language of the natives, adding that teachers should be appointed for those who voluntarily wanted to learn Spanish.[71] For almost a century, this would be the policy followed by the Crown: to recommend, on the one hand, that the authorities do everything possible to make the Indians learn Spanish, as this would facilitate the civilizing project of the monarchy, while, on the other, insisting on the idea that Indian parishes and benefices should be granted only to those clerics who knew the indigenous language of their charges, as Christian indoctrination was a priority. If we add to this the perennial lack of the resources needed to create schools or to pay for Spanish language teachers, it should not come as a surprise that by the end of the seventeenth century the Castilianization of the natives had made very little progress.[72]

At the end of this century, nonetheless, a new attempt by the Crown to revive the question of the Castilianization of the Indians took place. The motives are not all that clear, but they could have been influenced by a certain pessimism in relation to Indian Christianity, which became widespread in the second half of the seventeenth century. In the case of Mexico, a series of treatises was written in this period to denounce the survival of idolatrous practices among the Indians.[73] Thus, the idea that, by learning Spanish, the natives could be instructed in the Christian dogma in a much more profound way was manifested in a series of *cédulas* issued in the last two decades of the century. As the king declared in one issued in 1691, the order given to establish in every Indian town schools where Spanish would be taught had no other aim than the "greater honor and glory of God, because by knowing the Spanish language the Indians will be instructed radically and fundamentally in the mysteries of our Holy Catholic Faith, which is my main object in this business."[74] As a result, the impulse toward Castilianization became more systematic and better organized, although it does not appear to have been much more successful in the long run, if we are to judge it by the renewed efforts at Castilianization that were carried out in the second half of the eighteenth century.[75]

To Serve Is To Be Civilized

From the very beginnings of their settlement of the New World, the Spaniards, through the *encomienda* system, started to use the indigenous population in all sorts of work,[76] but the numerous complaints that this type of exploitation raised, because of the many subsequent abuses, made the Crown decide to prohibit all personal service performed not only to the *encomenderos* but to any private person, as well, including viceroys and *oidores* (Figures 15 and 16).[77] A different question, however, was what to do with forced labor of a public nature, or, as Solórzano would say, those services "that concern the public sustenance, the government and political adornment of the entire republic."[78] Since the 1550s, for example, the viceroys had started to recruit the population of the valley of Mexico to carry out agricultural work (especially to grow wheat, which the Spaniards preferred over the corn cultivated by the natives), to participate in the building of the new capital city, and to work in the mines. This recruitment of

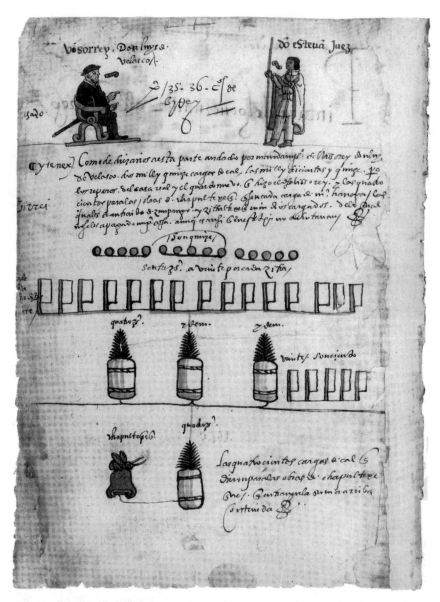

Fig. 15 Indian labor services performed by order of the viceroy, from *Códice Osuna*. This indigenous document, part of the legal record of a *visita* undertaken in 1565, combines the pictorial tradition of pre-Hispanic records with a Spanish text. It registers a complaint about the lack of payment to the Indians for certain repairs and other work done in the viceregal palace. The viceroy Luis de Velasco I is depicted in the company of don Esteban de Guzmán, an Indian magistrate. (Biblioteca Nacional, Madrid.)

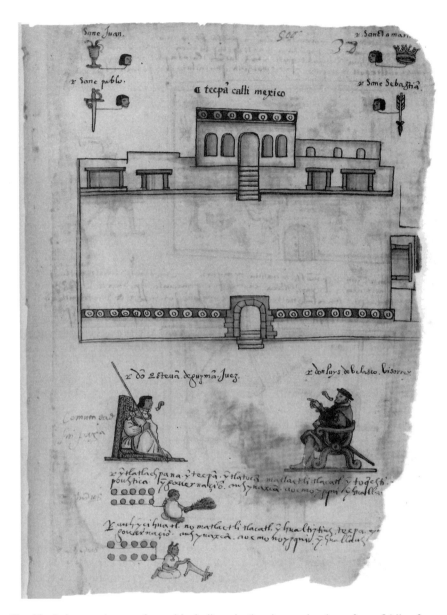

Fig. 16 Labor services performed by Indians in the viceregal palace, from *Códice Osuna*. This document, which includes a written Nahuatl text that uses the Latin alphabet, depicts Luis de Velasco I and don Esteban de Guzmán and relates how ten men and ten women from the four Indian parishes of Mexico City who formerly were obliged to perform labor in the viceregal palace (the men to sweep and the women to mill) no longer do so. (Biblioteca Nacional, Madrid.)

labor was based on the principles of rotation and compulsion and would be known in Mexico as *repartimiento*. This system of forced labor had pre-Hispanic antecedents, of which the Spaniards had been quick to take advantage for their own purposes, although that aspect of community work that had characterized the pre-Hispanic modality rapidly disappeared to become a more or less efficient system of exploitation of native labor for the benefit of the population of European descent.[79]

Nevertheless, given the particular characteristics of the Spanish colonial project, it was not easy to justify the existence of such a compulsion. Over the years, this would cause continual "pangs of conscience" for the Crown, especially because it had to deal with the fierce opposition of the Franciscans. The system of *repartimiento* had worked without too many problems until the 1570s, and the native communities were able to meet the demands for labor without much difficulty, but this situation came to an end when a series of epidemics between 1576 and 1591 caused a notable decrease in the indigenous population. The system of forced labor began to exert an excessive pressure upon the Indian communities, which observed that they still had to contribute the same number of workers even though the population of many of their communities had been dramatically reduced.[80] This would lead the Franciscans, with Gerónimo de Mendieta at their front, to develop an intense campaign to abolish the *repartimiento*, which they saw as being responsible for the exacerbation of the indigenous death rate. Unlike the resettlement program, in which he saw nothing negative, Mendieta showed a constant opposition to the labor draft. His voice was heard everywhere, and he wrote countless letters to the king, the Council, the archbishop of Mexico, and successive viceroys of New Spain to denounce the horrors of forced labor. When, in his *Historia eclesiástica indiana*, Mendieta examined all the epidemics and diseases that had afflicted the Indians since the arrival of the Spaniards, he concluded that, in fact, "the greatest and most harmful pestilence of the Indians" had been the *repartimiento*.[81]

According to the Franciscan friars, the Indians could not be forced to cultivate the Spaniards' fields nor work in the construction of their buildings, let alone to serve in their houses, for they were as free as the Spaniards themselves, and, because Spaniards and Indians constituted "two independent republics," it would be unfair to make one serve the other. Even if it were accepted that they all formed just one republic, no reason existed to make the Indians serve the Spaniards, as they were not their slaves. Moreover, they contended, it was unheard of in Christendom to force plowmen or workers of any trade to work; they offered themselves for hire whenever they saw fit and for a wage freely agreed upon with their employers.[82] Although these arguments were consistent with the evangelizing project of the Franciscans, what makes them so interesting is that they constitute, in many ways, a counter-discourse that goes against the exploitative dynamic of colonialism that characterized social relations in the New World. In an implicit way, the Franciscans were denying this dynamic because, for them, no distinction should be made between the indigenous peasants and workers of New Spain and those of the rest of the monarchy.

To be sure, the Franciscans do not deny the existence of social hierarchies. In any well-ordered republic, they contend, people must help one another, because, as Aristotle and Saint Thomas explained, the "lesser and less noble things" must serve the "greater and more noble ones," but this cannot be applied to the current case, maintain the friars, because "for the same reason that there cannot exist a good manner of republic and friendship between wolves and sheep, there cannot exist a good manner of republic, confederation, and league between Indians and Spaniards, because they are of the most different humors and conditions: the Spaniards, insolent and extremely proud and [fond] of great pomp; … the Indians, the opposite, fainthearted and miserable, spending their lives with almost nothing." Furthermore, the Indians are sufficiently able to govern themselves, as they proved before the conquest, for which reason the Spaniards should abstain from meddling in their affairs. If the Spaniards want the Indians to help them, they should pay them for their work in the same way as they would pay any Spaniard.[83] And, if the Indians do not want to help them, that is what mestizos and blacks are for. To Mendieta, it was difficult to believe that the Indians were forced to work when New Spain had a "rabble of so many stray and useless people, comprised of Spaniards, mestizos, mulattos, and free blacks." It would be a very healthy measure to make all these people work in the *repartimientos*, he adds caustically, if only as a way to make the highways safe and to put order in the republic of the Spaniards.[84] This antipathy toward the mestizos, mulattos, and blacks was not peculiar to Mendieta. Another Franciscan, Juan de Silva, was incensed because none of these groups, who were the "most vile and low" of the population and the "scum and rubbish of all the earth," was compelled to serve in the labor draft.[85] The ideal society that the Franciscans wished to establish in New Spain allowed no room for groups of people who were difficult to assign to either one of the two republics of Indians and Spaniards, hence their loathing for them.

For the Franciscans, it is not a legitimate argument to say that the mystical body every community forms must have a head and feet and that, therefore, the Indians, because of their nature, are to be the feet of the commonwealth, as they are better endowed for physical work than the Spaniards. It is not a legitimate argument, because the kingdoms of the Indies were not ceded to the Spanish kings by the pontiffs "to make them the feet of the Spaniards, but to raise them from the mud of idolatry to the riches of Heaven." Even if we were to accept that the Indians are the feet of the republic, this republic would be a disproportionate one, as all its members from the knees up would profit without sharing anything with the feet. It would be the same as "seeing a man go out to the square fabulously dressed, wearing a rich hat, a feather and a medallion, a white and tidy collar, a rich cape, jerkin and gloves perfumed with ambergris, ... but being barelegged, barefooted, his feet covered with mud and sores, and bleeding."[86] Although it is true, reason the Franciscans, that in order to procure the good of some, rulers may have to harm others for the sake of the public good, in the Indies the common good of the Indians should take precedence over that of the Spaniards. After all, the Indians were the "natural lords" of those lands, not the Spaniards, who were just "parvenus who tyrannically went in and conquered these lands." Furthermore, those "infernal repartimientos" did not even redound to the temporal or spiritual benefit of the Indians, and, if some authors defended the legality of forced labor with all sorts of justifications, that did not mean they were true, because it was the easiest thing to find suitable arguments to prove the biggest lie, "as all heretics do."[87] The *repartimientos*, therefore, were illicit, because they were unjust and pernicious, being the equivalent of enslaving those whom God and nature had made free. Only that which was just and honest was licit.[88]

Mendieta contended that if the *repartimientos* were not eliminated they would end up destroying the Indians, and then the Spaniards would be ruined and impotent because they needed the help of the Indians for everything. Moreover, Mendieta argued, if the Indians were to disappear, the loyalty of New Spain would be at risk, as it would be left at the mercy of mestizos, mulattos, and blacks, who would incite one another to rob and riot, and the peace and tranquility that had characterized a land inhabited by people as gentle and peaceful as the Indians would be destroyed. Nevertheless, Mendieta conceded that, to avoid further trouble, the *repartimiento* should not be eliminated suddenly (as colonial society already depended heavily on the system), although certain measures at least should be taken in order to make it more tolerable: No free Indians should be compelled to work in the mines;[89] no Indians should be forced to work outside their municipal district; towns should not contribute an excessive number of Indians; for every day of service, the Indians should be paid one *real* (up to then they were paid only half a *real*, which was not worth much); and, finally, the labor draft should not impede the Indians from attending Sunday mass.[90]

Although the labor draft was criticized by the majority of New Spain's clergy, the Franciscans' opposition was, no doubt, the most radical of all. Although the matter was widely debated in the sessions of the Third Mexican Council, celebrated in 1585, no decree condemning forced labor was issued. All the religious orders and numerous university professors presented a joint resolution that declared that the *repartimientos* "in the way they are done, are unjust, detrimental, and harmful for the souls, properties, salvation and life of the Indians." That is, they criticize the abuses of the system but do not ask for its total abolition (with the exception of the draft for the mines, which has no justification whatsoever, as the good it achieves — the increase in the extraction of silver — is not above the public good, because such a draft means the extermination of the Indians). In the same way, most of the bishops of the viceroyalty presented resolutions condemning forced labor in the mines, but none of them asked for the abolition of the agricultural or public works draft, just a reform of its abuses and an increase in the remuneration of the Indians.[91] Probably the most interesting opinion and the one most illustrative of the official discourse on forced labor was offered by archbishop Pedro Moya de Contreras, under whose presidency the Council took place.[92] Moya de Contreras presented a resolution in which he declared that, given the nature of the Indians, it seemed advisable "to try to make them interested in work and even to compel them to it with just means, because they are naturally inclined to idleness, which gives rise to all kinds of vices." For this reason, concluded the archbishop, the labor draft, as long as it was done in the appropriate manner, should not be condemned, because it was not unjust in and of itself; on the contrary, it was "good Christian and politic government.[93]

As we have already seen, one of the aspects that defined the New World natives as barbarians in Spanish colonial discourse was their inclination to "idleness." We have also seen that certain writers who were highly influential at the Court — Matienzo and Acosta — contended that obligating the Indians to work was part of the civilizing mission of the Spanish monarchy. Thus, since the moment the first viceroy of New Spain was appointed, he was instructed to make the natives cultivate the land and work at diverse "mechanical trades."[94] Years later, Martín Enríquez was told in his Instruction that, "The Indians by their nature and inclination are given to idleness, from whence there follows much harm, ... idleness being the cause of many vices." Nevertheless, the Spaniards were forbidden to force the Indians to work; the viceroy was to just order the latter to "hire themselves out" as workers in the fields or in the cities.[95] Even the Franciscans agreed on this point; although they condemned all kinds of forced labor, they accepted the idea that the Indians could be forced to hire themselves out to work, thus satisfying the needs of the commonwealth;[96] however, the Dominicans, or at least Juan Ramírez de Arellano, their most visible voice in the debate over the draft, even rejected that the viceroys could compel the Indians to offer themselves for hire.[97]

The line of argumentation followed by the Jesuits, led by José de Acosta, differed greatly from that of the Franciscans and the Dominicans, being closer to the arguments advanced by Moya de Contreras. In his famous treatise on the Indian that he presented to Philip II only a few years after the conclusion of the Mexican Council, Acosta criticizes the Franciscans (without explicitly mentioning them) for seeking to abolish the labor draft. That was something, according to him, that seemed very generous in theory but, all things considered, would be a foolish thing to do, as Spanish dominion could not be maintained without this kind of work. Against the Franciscan insistence on the existence of two separate republics, Acosta affirms that Indians and Spaniards form a single and identical political community, as all have the same king and are subjected to the same laws. As Aristotle would have said, Acosta adds, in any commonwealth those who have the ability to do manual labor should serve, whereas those who stand out for their intellectual talent have been born to lead. For that reason, and bearing in mind that the Indians already had been forced to serve in labor drafts before the Spanish conquest, Acosta does not see any injustice or wrong being done to them if they continue to serve under the Spaniards, as long as they are paid a just salary, nor does Acosta think that utilizing the Indians as beasts of burden is unjust or pernicious, because they were used to doing it since time immemorial, and when "one is used to doing a thing, not only does it not seem hard, but one even likes it." And, if they refuse to do this work willfully (which would not be surprising given their idle nature), then the Spaniards have no other choice than to compel them to do it.[98]

On the other hand, Acosta utilizes a definitely twisted argument (which resonates with the idea of providential destiny) to defend forced labor in the mines. After acknowledging the horrors of such work, he goes on to assert how much we must admire God's goodness and providence because, "in order to bring such remote and barbaric peoples to the Gospel, He provided these lands so copiously with gold and silver metals so as to awaken the greed of our people." The Spaniards' thirst for precious metals had made possible the evangelization of the Indians by leading them to the New World; in other words, Christian avarice had brought about Indian conversion. For that reason, it is necessary to be tolerant with the miners, argues Acosta, to make sure the commerce in precious metals keeps going so the conversion of the Indians can continue.[99] To him, clearly, the end justifies the means and, in the name of Christianity, the Indians may be thrown, without too many pangs of Christian conscience, into the hell of the mines, if by so doing we ensure that the work of Christianization will be preserved: Better a dead but Christian Indian than one who is alive and pagan.

Viceregal discourse in the late sixteenth and early seventeenth centuries closely follows arguments like those advanced by Acosta. The viceroys played a crucial role in all matters regarding the labor draft, as it was left in their hands to decide how to organize it or even, possibly, how to eliminate it.[100] Indeed, one of the reasons given to justify its abolition was that the draft had been established by the viceroys and that no royal order authorized it.[101] All the viceroys who ruled New Spain during that time (that is, when the debates over the *repartimiento* became very heated) dealt with the matter in a similar way: lamenting all the hardship and suffering that it caused to the natives while at the same time invoking a certain "reason of state" that forced them to preserve the labor draft, because otherwise it would be impossible to preserve the benefits the monarchy obtained from its American dominions. Regretting the many hardships that forced labor in the mines caused to the Indians, the marquis of Villamanrique would write in 1590 that, in spite of everything, he could not abolish it because it was evident that, should this personal service be eliminated, "the exploitation of the mines, which are the main nerve from whence all the wealth of this land comes, would cease."[102]

The viceroys always stressed that they tried to moderate the system as much as possible, while compensating the Indians for their work in a just way,[103] but, in the last analysis, it was the civilizing mission that allowed the viceroys to have a clear conscience in matters such as the forced labor of the Indians. As Luis de Velasco II would say to Mendieta in a letter written in response to one the friar had sent to him denouncing the excesses of the *repartimiento*, "May Your Reverence believe that if it were up to me and if it were possible to relieve the natives from the personal service, I would do it with much ease," adding immediately after that "we do not proceed in this matter as blindly as some people would think, for there are many expert opinions from learned and conscientious persons who do not condemn it absolutely; rather, they affirm that it is inevitable, because the republic could not be preserved without it, and being moderate they agree that in it there is no wrong or offense done to the natives, assuming their humble and servile nature."[104] In some "pieces of advice" that he left to his successor, Velasco makes his argument still more explicit: The nature of the Indians and the little inclination they have for work are such that "it has always been necessary to compel them to do that which they would do had they the capacity and *policía* to bring themselves to serve."[105] In other words, the barbarism of the Indians, their lack of civility, did not permit them to comprehend that in every well-ordered community some ruled and others were ruled, some served and others were served, hence the necessity of the Spaniards' civilizing mission, for the day the American natives understood that, given their capacities, they had been born to serve and that through hard work they would become truly human, then forced labor would no longer be necessary.[106]

When in the mid-seventeenth century Solórzano discussed the question of Indian forced labor in his *Política indiana*, the heated debates of the turn of the century had already died down; yet, it was still a matter that could not be eluded, and that caused a major ideological conflict for theorists of the imperial monarchy, such as Solórzano himself. Thus, he dedicates many pages of his work to the topic, discussing in minute detail every aspect of the subject. His method consists of examining the arguments in favor of and against forced labor before advancing his own opinion, although he often seems unable to reach a definite conclusion. In many ways, this was a reflection of the same doubts that assailed the Crown with regard to this matter. Solórzano begins his examination by asserting that the Indians, as free vassals of the king, cannot be compelled to carry out personal services to private individuals. That is why it is quite clear that the *encomenderos* cannot force their Indians to serve them nor can the Indians be drafted to serve any Spaniards, not even the viceroy himself,[107] but to be drafted to do work for the benefit of the common good is a different and much more problematic matter. After carefully and thoroughly examining all the arguments in favor of and against the "personal services" of the Indians, Solórzano concedes that the best thing would be to substitute voluntary for coerced labor, but he immediately calls on the rhetoric of wretchedness to affirm that experience has shown that very few Indians would do that work voluntarily, because "they are very lazy and given to idleness and drunkenness and lewdness and other vices, … and since they have little greed and content themselves with so little in order to eat and clothe themselves, many spending their lives like beasts, … some force and compulsion are necessary to make them abandon that state."[108] Solórzano hopes things will change in the future so it will not be necessary to coerce the Indians into working. In the meantime, they have no other alternative than "to tolerate" these labor drafts, because that is what the good of the republic requires.[109]

That was precisely what the Crown had decided to do at the beginning of the seventeenth century, after much hesitation and many discussions. After years of criticism and attacks on the *repartimiento*, the Crown had ordered its suspension in 1601 and that the Indians should voluntarily offer themselves for hire in the public squares,[110] but this decision did not last for long. In 1609, another *cédula* was issued whereby the draft for agricultural work, cattle raising, and work in the mines was allowed again, given the "repugnance the Indians show as regards to work and the fact that compelling them is unavoidable." It was also added that, if, in the course of time, the Indians improved their nature and a sufficient number of them wanted to do this work in a voluntary way, then the draft should gradually be eliminated.[111] In 1632, however, when the marquis of Cerralvo, the viceroy of New Spain at the time, decided to suppress all the *repartimientos* except those used in the mines and in the *desagüe* (the drainage of the lakes surrounding Mexico City), he was probably moved by a series of royal *cédulas* in which the monarch had complained that, despite his strict orders, the labor draft still subjected the Indians to all kinds of abuses.[112] Moreover, Solórzano's hesitation did not disappear in the case of forced labor for the mines (perhaps because, as inspector of the mercury mine of Huancavélica, he had had the opportunity to see first hand the extreme nature of work in the mines). Carefully weighing up all the arguments used by the supporters and detractors of such labor, he came to the conclusion that more licit and tolerable means than forcing the Indians should be sought — namely, using slaves, criminals, or voluntary workers, whether Indians, mestizos, free blacks, or even Spaniards.[113]

By the end of the seventeenth century, the civilizing mission of the Spanish monarchy did not seem to have had the desired effect, for the official discourse still continued to defend the civilizing capacity and disciplinary effects of forced labor. In the detailed account of his government that he wrote for his successor in 1698, Juan de Ortega y Montañés, archbishop of Mexico and acting viceroy, declared the following:

> I admit with certainty that the laziness of these natives makes it necessary to exhort them to work in their own *milpas* [cornfields] and little orchards as well as in the haciendas and mines, and that the repartimientos are necessary for the mines and haciendas as well as for making them cultivate their milpas. …Thus I consider that the diligence of the viceroys, working hard to this end with their characteristic dedication, will in this way make sure that the Indians do not submit to their own laziness, … thus putting a stop to their own native inclination to not work, … and *moving them away a great deal from the vices of drunkenness and theft* to which they are inclined … by their own nature.[114]

In the mind of Ortega y Montañés, as for Solórzano some decades before, no doubt existed that forced labor contributed to the civilizing of the Indians. By obligating them to work, they would avoid giving themselves over to alcoholism, idolatry, and other vices, something that characterized those populations who lived in a state of barbarism and to which they would, without a doubt, give in were they allowed to live in sloth. The rhetoric of idleness reaches here its greatest expression: The Indians are so little given to working that they have to be forced to labor not only in the mines or in the fields of the Spaniards but also on their own plots of land because otherwise they would not do it. This was the logical conclusion to which the rhetoric of the wretched Indian would lead: If the native is construed as an extremely frugal individual, for whom a few tortillas are enough, then it must be assumed that he hardly needs to break his back toiling the land. If the native is also seen as lacking any material ambition, then it is clear that he must lack the motivation to grow an agricultural surplus. It is not surprising, therefore, that the existence of an indigenous agriculture which, to a great extent, was not guided by principles of commercial exploitation of surpluses but by the growing of only that which was necessary to preserve the existence of the community, would be interpreted by the Spaniards as negligence and laziness on the part of the Indians and a lack of interest in cultivating their own lands. In the remarks by Ortega y Montañés, we can also appreciate the "civilizing" role that had been attributed to the viceroys. As the supreme representatives of the Spanish monarchy in New Spain, it was their special responsibility to force the natives to overcome their torpor. Finally, another aspect to the archbishop's comments should be stressed. In his account, he perceives the Indian not only as a drunkard but as a thief as well. This kind of perception does not fit well with the image of the miserable Indian that we have been examining up to this point. As I will argue in the next chapter, the view of the archbishop was no doubt influenced by the image of the urban Indian, which, by the end of the seventeenth century, had developed quite differently from that of the rural Indian.

7

Colonial Rhetoric and Indian Rebellion

"As Your Lordship probably knows," viceroy Martín Enríquez told his successor in 1580, "in this land there are two republics to govern, one of Indians and one of Spaniards, and His Majesty sent us here mainly [to take care of] all that concerns the Indians and their protection, and this has to be attended to with the utmost care because, as the weakest part, the Indians are such a wretched people that any Christian heart is obliged to feel much pity for them."[1] Similarly, but half a century later, another viceroy, the marquis of Cadereita, would assert at the end of his rule that he had always concerned himself with the "preservation and increase of the wretched Indian natives, who so much need the protection of the viceroys in the name of His Majesty," never consenting to "any excesses of the powerful who badly use the sweat and blood of these people."[2] It is clear from these remarks that viceregal discourse fully shared in the rhetoric of wretchedness. In that sense, the comments by these two viceroys reflected faithfully the language of the Instructions given by the monarch to every viceroy before leaving for the New World. In them, the king would always instruct the viceroys that, "One of the things about which you must show the greatest care is the good treatment of the natives, because the safe preservation of those kingdoms and provinces depends upon it, as you will realize by the *cédulas* which have been issued for their good treatment and the moderation in the use of their services and work, for which they must be rewarded sufficiently."[3]

Nevertheless, we must ask to what extent this rhetoric shaped viceregal practice. To what extent did the presence of a viceroy affect the natives of New Spain? Did the viceroys intervene actively in the lives of the latter? In

213

order to respond to these questions, it is necessary to examine not only the daily routine of government but also those moments in which that routine broke down. As is well known, the revolts and rebellions staged by subaltern groups are privileged moments that allow us to appreciate with greater clarity the political ideas of these segments of the population, something that, under normal circumstances, is usually much more difficult to determine. In the same manner, it is during such moments of rupture that the dominant groups make many ideas and feelings explicit that in everyday life are not revealed with the same transparency. Such an analysis will allow us to ascertain a distinction in the discursive practices of the colonial elite (both peninsular and Creole) between those referring to the rural indigenous population and those directed at the urban common people, particularly the inhabitants of Mexico City. As we shall see, these practices contributed to the creation of two very different kinds of "Indian."

Two Republics and One Viceroy

In 1565, Gerónimo de Mendieta wrote a long letter to Philip II in which he detailed, in a tone of great urgency, the many things needed in New Spain to protect the indigenous population from the infinite abuses that were committed against them. Among the measures proposed by Mendieta, one dealt specifically with the viceregal figure. He recommended that the power and authority of the viceroys be reinforced *vis-à-vis* that of the *oidores*, "because in a world like this, it is necessary that someone truly represent the royal person of Your Majesty, who can only be represented properly by an illustrious person," because "the nature of the Indians requires only one and not many heads for their government; and this head must have prudence and good judgment more than knowledge of Digests and Codes, which have brought them more harm than benefit; and the said viceroy, to this end, being of such a quality, should have absolute power in all matters concerning the rule of the natives without the oidores being able to curb him."[4]

In a letter written to the commissary general of the Franciscan order three years before, Mendieta had made many of these ideas even more explicit. He clearly showed no sympathy for the *oidores*. For him, the ones who were appointed to New Spain were just those who had been rejected by the Spanish *audiencias* and, once they got to their posts, they were only good at thwarting the viceroys. He wondered how it was possible to put the opinion of a humble licentiate, only because he had studied some laws in Salamanca, before that of a viceroy. The ideal world imagined by Mendieta, therefore, allowed no room for legalisms and judicial processes in the European style, as the *oidores* complicated everything with their legalisms. Moreover, the Indians did not need them, because their problems and conflicts should be resolved by following native customs, without having recourse to laws whose juridical subtleties they would not be able to comprehend.[5] In Mendieta's view, the viceregal figure was to play a fundamental role in the revitalization of what modern historians have termed the "utopia" of the Franciscans in the New World — that is, the construction of a society in which the indigenous population (the *república de indios*), completely separated from that of European origin (the *república de españoles*), would be ruled by the mendicant friars, with the help of the indigenous ruling elite. As the supreme authority, the viceroy would govern the native population without the interference of *oidores* or bishops (who would devote all their energies to ruling the Spaniards). Thus, in the ideal vision of Mendieta, New Spain (at least the indigenous part of it) would become a vast school where the Indians/children would be instructed by the friars/teachers, all under the stern but benevolent gaze of the viceroy/ "supreme father" of the Indians.

With his argument about the ruling of New Spain with an "absolute" viceroy, Mendieta was, in reality, contributing to the shaping of the viceregal figure. In his words, we can detect some of the central ideas that defined the figure of the viceroy and that have been already examined in this study:

> Since His Majesty is absent [from New Spain], which is what causes its agitation, he should at least have here a person representing him, instead of having a divided kingdom with many heads. …What I mean is that his viceroy must become a de facto viceroy, for this name and title denote that he is the king's image, acting as the king, in the king's place, and no one other than the king himself should be able to subject him or diminish him or undo what he does.[6]

Because the king could not be present in the American lands, and he was the only one, in Mendieta's opinion, who could put a stop to the abuses committed by the Spaniards, it was utterly necessary to send there a ruler endowed with the same authority and power as the monarch to make sure that the royal orders, always just and sensible, be abided by. That is why a viceroy had to be a person with such qualities — noble, prudent, experienced, virtuous — that he could be entrusted, if it were necessary, with the government of half the world. Thus, in a way, the Franciscan utopia contributed to the shaping of an imperial political post the characteristics of which set it radically apart from that utopia, but still another reason exists as to why, in the view of Mendieta, the viceroy should have "absolute" power over the indigenous population. As he explains, the Indians are of such a quality that they need to have a "supreme and absolute leader," so that they understand that everything they are ordered to do emanates from his will and command; otherwise, the Indians will take advantage of the discords that always arise in those communities ruled by two or more heads, "because they are naturally given to unrestrained freedom, not knowing how to take advantage of such freedom."[7] In other words, the Indians/children do not know how to distinguish between liberty and licentiousness, for which reason they need a viceroy endowed with great authority and highly respected and whom the Indians will obey as naturally as children obey and respect their fathers. That is why legalisms and judicial processes are completely unnecessary, in the same way as a father does not need the law to make himself obeyed.

Mendieta's missives were written in the 1560s, a time of transition in the history of the Spanish–American territories, when the Spanish dominion was already definitely established, but the political–administrative structure was not yet completely defined. It is for this reason that Mendieta, despite his extremely pessimistic view of the general situation in the viceroyalty, still could argue for a predominant role of the religious orders in the life of New Spain. This pessimism notwithstanding, he insisted that they still had time to remedy the disastrous situation and return to the golden age of the first years of the conquest, when the friars occupied a preeminent place in the society of New Spain.[8] But, at the end of the decade, Philip II was determined to strengthen royal authority and the interests of the Crown in the New World so he appointed Martín Enríquez and Francisco de Toledo as viceroys of New Spain and Peru, respectively. The viceregal figure would emerge greatly reinforced after the rule of both viceroys, with all the political imagery that exalted and identified that figure with the sovereign perfectly developed. Speaking of Martín Enríquez, the Franciscan Juan de Torquemada would assert in the early seventeenth century that "he had much raised the dignity of the office of viceroy, which up to his time had been a little more informal and approachable."[9]

In this regard, it could be argued that the monarch seemed to have followed Mendieta's recommendations to strengthen the viceregal post as the best way to ensure the welfare of the natives, but the reasons that led to this bolstering of viceregal authority did not necessarily coincide with those advocated by Mendieta. As a matter of fact, he showed little sympathy for viceroy Enríquez, contending that the Indians' state of prostration was due to the fact that the new viceroys were not like the first two — Antonio de Mendoza and Luis de Velasco I — who had been "fathers and tutors" to the Indians and whose rule had constituted a "golden time" for New Spain (Figure 17).[10] Almost a century later, Juan de Palafox, in his already-mentioned memorial on the Indian, asserted that the viceroys, because of the supremacy of their post, were far removed from Indian realities and thus ill-equipped to understand their sufferings.[11] In a way, Palafox was not far off the mark. In a highly hierarchized society such as that of New Spain, the social distance that existed between a viceroy and the indigenous population was unbridgeable. To the viceroys, this population was reduced to a shapeless mass — the "Indians" or "*los naturales*" — for whom one had to worry rhetorically, because their preservation and

Fig. 17 The appointment of Indian magistrates by the viceroy, from *Códice Osuna*. According to this document, written in both Spanish and Nahuatl, during the ceremony in which the viceroy Luis de Velasco I handed over their staffs (symbols of legitimate authority) to the Indian *alcaldes* and *alguaciles*, he entrusted the newly appointed magistrates with the "religious instruction, policía, and good treatment of their Indian charges." These words closely replicate the instructions given by the Crown to the viceroys regarding their obligations with respect to the indigenous population. (Biblioteca Nacional, Madrid.)

increase was, as we have seen, one of their obligations. No doubt, the preoccupations of the viceroys lay elsewhere.

If we were to utilize the viceregal correspondence to establish what these priorities were, it would be quite clear that in the period covered by this study the priorities and preoccupations of the viceroys did not focus principally on the natives (with the exception of the last years of the sixteenth and the early years of the seventeenth centuries, when the viceroys played an active role in the resolution of three matters that directly affected the indigenous population: congregations, *repartimiento*, and the establishment of the Indian court). We see that a great proportion of the viceregal correspondence was devoted to economic matters. No doubt fiscal matters — or, to put it another way, maximization of the resources of the colony — created many headaches for the viceroys.[12] Another large segment of that correspondence dealt with the viceroy's relationship and frequent conflicts with members of New Spain's political elite, both secular and ecclesiastic. To a great extent this was a logical outcome, as a viceroy was much more worried about and affected by what his hierarchical equals or quasi-equals (mainly the *oidores*, bishops, and inquisitors) could say or write about him than by what those who were at the bottom of the social and political ladder thought of him.[13]

The district magistrates and parish priests were the ones who took care of everyday Indian "trifles," which is why the language used by the viceroys' chief subordinates (the *alcaldes mayores* and *corregidores* spread out throughout the territory), whose contact with the indigenous population was continuous and on a daily basis, could never be the same as that of a viceroy. As an example, we can mention what an *alcalde mayor* wrote to the count of Salvatierra in 1646, against the background of the disputes (examined in Chapter 5) that brought the viceroy face to face with bishop Palafox. Several *alcaldes mayores* had written to the viceroy to complain about Palafox's actions as *visitador general*. They pointed out that their authority had been impaired not only because he backed the parish priests, who always tried to obstruct their jurisdiction by persuading the Indians to disobey them, but especially because it had been made public that Palafox was going to take an active part in the legal suits brought against them by the Indians. All this would hamper the collection of tribute and the *alcabala* in their districts, as the Indians knew they would be protected by Palafox if they decided to confront their magistrates. In the words of one of these *alcaldes*:

> Without the help of Your Excellency, it is hard, my lord, to resist, these idolatrous barbarians, to whom the faith has taken their fancy, as they observe how much the clerics are supported and defended by their prelate, while the magistrates are so much insulted. Your Excellency, my lord, since you have His Majesty's powers, show by punishing that you closely represent him, and this will serve as a new conquest in these environs, which are tyrannized by a bishop from whom may God free me.[14]

This kind of bellicose language is almost nonexistent in viceregal discourse, which is characterized by a certain paternalism in keeping with the benevolent image that corresponded to a viceroy as the king's living image. Representative of this language is what the marquis of Cerralvo wrote at the end of his term in office: "As something of great importance, His Majesty most justly entrusts his viceroys with the preservation of the Indians, and we all take the greatest care in it," immediately adding that "I have done my best to prevent the alcaldes mayores, doctrineros, and encomenderos from vexing them, and in their disputes (*pleitos*) and businesses I have always been their advocate."[15] Though certainly such an assertion could be seen as a rhetorical device, by affirming that he had always been the protector of the Indians in their disputes or lawsuits, Cerralvo in all probability had in mind something very concrete: the General Indian Court, which was established in New Spain at the end of the sixteenth century. Presided over by the viceroy, this court heard and settled all the suits filed by the Indians against other Indians and those brought by Spaniards against the natives (but not those filed by the Indians against Spaniards, which had to be heard by the *audiencia*). The role played by this court in the relationship between the viceroys and the indigenous population cannot be underestimated. Because the viceroys hardly ever left Mexico City during their term in office, it was only through their experience in this court that they could acquire any direct knowledge of the indigenous peoples of New Spain. Likewise, the repercussions that the court must have had on indigenous perceptions and views of the viceregal figure cannot be ignored.

As we saw in Chapter 2, it was the administration of justice that defined the essence of the Spanish monarchy. This principle was so fundamental that it would have been unthinkable, for example, to have denied the Indians their right to appeal to the *audiencias*. This, however, created a serious problem for the Spanish authorities, because, despite the insistence by the Spaniards on the Indians' lack of intellectual capacity, they understood early on that the authorities' decisions or transfers of land could be contested by appealing to the *audiencias*. As a consequence, the *audiencia* of Mexico had to deal, from very early on, with an avalanche of lawsuits and petitions by the natives.[16] It is paradoxical that this Indian skill for taking advantage of the Spanish judicial system was construed by the Spaniards as senseless litigiousness: The Indians, it was argued, did not understand what they were doing, nor what they were asking for, nor what it was best for them, with the result that a veritable army of *letrados*, clerks, and briefless lawyers had taken advantage of the "natural inclination" of the Indians to confront one another to fleece them.[17] The Indians liked to get entangled in lawsuits so much that they had almost lost "their weak and pusillanimous nature, becoming boisterous and litigious."[18] From the Spanish standpoint, the suits brought by the natives to the *audiencia* were about irrelevant things that were not worthy of the judges' time.[19] Martín Enríquez would advise his successor to take "these trivialities" of the Indians calmly, as, in any case, they had to deal with them because by so doing "the royal conscience of His Majesty was eased."[20] Likewise, Luis de Velasco II, speaking about the General Indian Court some years later, would observe that, because the Indians had a childish nature and were of little capacity, their affairs had to be of a similar character (i.e., childish things). Velasco added that the Indian Court should be maintained in spite of the opposition of some sectors of the population (lawyers, notaries, interpreters, etc.) because it was an institution that was concerned with "poor, wretched, and defenseless people."[21]

It would be, then, the infantilization of the indigenous population, along with the rhetoric of wretchedness, that would lead to the establishment of the General Indian Court. One of the privileges that had traditionally been granted to "poor and wretched" persons was the brevity of their lawsuits and legal proceedings, which were to be conducted summarily,[22] but it was also argued that, because of their own nature, Indians were unable to comprehend the transcendence of a formal process, which included sworn-in witnesses. As José de Acosta asked, if the law excluded children and infamous persons from testifying or taking oaths, because of the fragility of their judgment and the suspicion that they would commit perjury, why not exclude Indians from the oath, as they were more fickle than children, totally ignoring the truth? For that reason, Acosta advised the *corregidores* that they should resolve Indians' lawsuits more like a *paterfamilias* would than like a judge, as most of their cases were trifles, which resembled quarrels among children.[23] We have here what was, in fact, the ideological *raison d'etre* of the Indian court: If the viceroy was to be a father to the Indians, was it not logical that he administer justice to them in the way suggested by Acosta? Already in the 1560s, Mendieta, starting with his criticism of Indian litigiousness, had proposed that the *audiencia* should only deal with the most serious offenses committed by Indians, while civil lawsuits should be decided by the indigenous authorities or the *corregidores*. The trials should consist of summary proceedings, basically following an oral procedure, with no need for legalisms and proofs based on sworn-in witnesses; when the judge had heard all sides of the argument, he should resolve it according to his own judgment.[24]

In a very similar way, the principles upon which the General Indian Court would be founded were the reduction or elimination of judicial costs and a radical simplification of legal procedures. The first viceroy of New Spain, Antonio de Mendoza, had already established the custom that the viceroy himself should deal with the bulk of Indian complaints, hearing them and, in the majority of the cases, resolving them simply with an administrative order (by mandate, the lawsuits among Spaniards had to be decided through a judicial process); however, this procedure would not be regularized until the end of the sixteenth century with the establishment of the Indian court.[25] Until the year 1590, the viceroys tacitly continued to exercise judicial powers over the indigenous population through administrative decisions, but in that year Luis de Velasco II asked the Crown to grant the viceroys first-instance jurisdiction over all civil cases affecting the Indians. According to Velasco, this would expedite the Indians' lawsuits and eliminate the many expenses and abuses to which they were subjected by solicitors and lawyers; besides, the Indians would not oppose this type of procedure as they were already used to viceregal decisions expressed in brief orders.[26] The Crown quickly answer this petition and granted Velasco even more than he had asked for: Not only were the viceroys to act as first-instance judges in every lawsuit between Indians and between Spaniards and Indians (only when an Indian was sued by a Spaniard; in the opposite case, the Indians would have to turn to the town magistrates or the *audiencia*), but they were also granted jurisdictional power in criminal cases (the Indians could always appeal viceregal decisions to the *audiencia*). In addition, the viceroys were to have the power to investigate any subordinate authority (except for the *oidores*) without the intervention of the High Court.[27]

In his study of the Indian court, Woodrow Borah maintains that all this placed a powerful weapon in the hands of the viceroys, one that could curtail the abuses of the provincial authorities against the Indians, as the viceroy was to be able to impose administrative sanctions without needing the approval of the *audiencia*.[28] Though, no doubt, this was so, it is also very likely that, when approving these measures, Philip II had in mind not only the welfare of his poor and wretched vassals, but also the authority of his "living image" across the ocean, as those measures fostered a considerable increase in viceregal power, placing at the viceroys' disposal an effective instrument for receiving information about and controlling all the kings' officials (and even the priests who attended the Indian *doctrinas*). In this manner and in the name of justice, the king's authority ended up being strengthened. It is for this reason that, in all likelihood, Velasco II, when speaking of the Indians and how beneficial this special court was for them, observed that, although it was true that most of their cases appeared to be trivialities, he considered they were not, because, by trying them it was possible to learn quite a lot about the state of affairs of the viceroyalty. Similarly, Velasco's successor would notice that a viceroy, through his hearings at the Indian Court, was kept informed of the affairs of each province.[29] In this way, the Indian court would become an invaluable instrument of power for the viceroys.

Of course, the symbolism conveyed by the court to the indigenous population cannot be ignored. The thousands of orders and decrees signed by the viceroys as presidents of the Indian court, with relative rapidity by the standards of the period, must have served to communicate a powerful image of the viceroy as the fountain of Indian justice in the viceroyalty, even though, after the rule of the count of Monterrey, the viceroys would tend to leave everything in the hands of their *asesor letrado* (legal advisor), who really was the one who ran the court, the viceroy limiting himself to signing the court decrees.[30] Independently of the real efficacy of the court to solve the conflicts and the offenses done to the Indians, all this would contribute to solidify the image of the Spanish monarch as a just ruler, preoccupied with the well-being of his American vassals (to be sure, a degree of effectiveness had to exist; otherwise, that image could not have been established). This is what, no doubt, the count of Monterrey was referring to when he affirmed that the Indians, even when being ordered to do something that went against their interests, "comfort themselves and calm down more than other people when they are persuaded and think that [the order] comes from the will and by decree of the king himself, or of he who is in his place, and not from some official's judgment."[31] Nonetheless, as shall be shown next, this image of the viceroy as fountain of justice would be much more difficult to solidify among the subaltern groups of Mexico City, where the presence of the "king's living image" was felt in a more concrete and visible way.

A Republic Without Rhyme or Reason

The rhetoric of wretchedness, which, as has been seen, dominated viceregal discourse on the Indian, changes and becomes much more negative when it refers to the Indians who lived in Mexico City. This will become much more obvious in the course of the seventeenth century, when the population of the capital augmented considerably, culminating with the disturbances of 1692, which would confirm the worst fears of the elite.[32] In these years, we already find perfectly delineated two discursive practices that will persist, to a great extent, until the present. On the one hand was an idealization of the "Indian," with its main axis the rhetoric of misery, which continued with hardly any changes; on the other, the development of a completely negative view of the hybrid elements which infiltrated the interstices of the two republics of Indians and Spaniards — the mestizos, mulattos, and blacks, to whom the urbanized Indians and even some poor Spaniards would be added — all of them forming part of what was known at the time as the *plebe* (plebs) of the city.

These segments of the population were highly visible in the streets of Mexico City, and the viceroys would have much more direct contact with them than with the Indians of the rural communities. This multi-ethnic *plebe* would be the target of the harshest invectives on the part of the authorities and the elite, largely because they were seen as a security risk. Neither the Creoles nor the Indians were perceived as a threat to imperial security and stability. As Palafox, acting as viceroy, would tell his successor, the Creoles were very loyal and willing to serve the king, and if they were governed in a gentle way they would always be prompt to obey royal orders.[33] In the 1670s, the marquis of Mancera would express very similar ideas. To him, the Creole nobility was, by and large, "docile, reverent, and easy to rule; ... they love and venerate the majesty and name of their king, ... honoring with obliging respect and observance the image of the prince in their viceroys and magistrates."[34]

In the case of the indigenous people, the rhetoric of wretchedness excluded by definition the construction of the Indian as a threat to the security of the Spaniards. That was the view from the two sides of the Atlantic. In Spain, Alamos de Barrientos, for instance, pointed out in 1598 to the just-proclaimed Philip III that, "There is little to fear from the native Indians, because they have neither weapons nor leaders, are in a sorry state, and having experienced such a long servitude plus their natural weakness and vicious inclination, they do not have any determination, nor any memory of their former state and dominion."[35] In New Spain, Palafox would point out to his successor that, "The Indians are people so miserable that they will not give Your Excellency any more worry than protecting them, because from their sweat and upon their backs all the excesses of the alcaldes mayores, doctrineros, caciques, and gobernadores are manufactured."[36] In the case of Mancera, his views on the native were more pessimistic; the Indians were "a melancholic and pusillanimous people, though atrocious, vindictive, superstitious, and mendacious."[37] Their "obscenities, thefts, and barbarities" showed that teaching them Christianity had been of little use; nevertheless, concluded the viceroy, "amid these vices, their dejection deserves great compassion and pity for being the object of the greed of the Spaniards." Mancera did not miss the opportunity to criticize the clergy, wondering whether the "vices" of the Indians would not be the result of the "negligence and avarice" of the Indian parish priests. According to Mancera, experience showed that the "errors and vices of the gentility" still persisted among the natives, and "sacrifices, sorcery, and obscenities" were discovered every day. However, in order to explain the persistence of these practices, Mancera did not resort to the traditional explanation (the Indians' lack of intelligence or their barbarism that hindered their understanding of the mysteries of Christianity), blaming instead the "moral ailments" of the Church (i.e., the lack of capacity or the scant interest of the clergy in carrying out their evangelizing duties).[38]

When judging the *plebe* of Mexico City (mostly blacks, mulattos, and mestizos), however, no excuses were made for them, and they were mercilessly condemned. This harsh attitude buried its roots in what was seen as the "original sin" of these segments of the population. In the racial discourse of the period, it was assumed that mestizos and mulattos were usually the by-product of, in the words of Juan de Solórzano, adultery or "other illicit and punishable copulations," because there were very few "honest Spaniards" who would be willing to marry Indian or black women. These vile origins, to which the "stain of an indeterminate color" (that is, not pure) was added, determined their character, as it predisposed mestizos and mulattos to all sorts of vices, which in them were "like natural and suckled in the milk."[39] The congenital imperfection and vileness of the mixed-blood population make them unreliable elements. To begin with, they were seen as a security threat. While Martín Enríquez believed that the large numbers of mestizos, mulattos, and free blacks who lived in New Spain constituted the only risk of sedition in the viceroyalty, Luis de Velasco affirmed that they should not be trusted.[40] Decades later, Palafox would contend that they put the white population of noble origin at risk with "so many diverse colors, nations, and conditions, all of them with little reason and no shame whatsoever."[41] Speaking of the *plebe* of the capital, "whose variety of colors and large numbers" were obvious to any observer, viceroy Mancera, for his part, pointed out that the "imperfection of their nature, the excess of victuals, their idleness, freedom, and drunkenness throw them into all kinds of laxity and vice." It was necessary to be especially careful with the mulattos and blacks, as they were "haughty, audacious, and given to novelties," without, however, showing distrust toward them or putting too much pressure upon them regarding the payment of tribute.[42] Finally, the mestizos, though "equally presumptuous," deserved a more positive opinion, as they were the ones who most resembled the Spaniards.[43] The multiracial character of Mexico City's inhabitants thus becomes, in the eyes of the authorities, a potential agent of disorder, and the confusing racial mix, which in Mexico City replaces the perfect order of the two republics of Indians and Spaniards, is perceived as the consummate representation of the political disorder that, according to the ruling elite, the city is always heading for.

This perception would have important implications in Mexico City's theater of power. As we saw in Chapter 4, the Spanish rulers tried to create in New Spain a ritual culture very similar to the one that existed in Spain. What differentiated this culture from its peninsular original was not the creation of new ritual forms but an intensification of the importance of the physical presence of power. This was so because the Mexican territory, as metonymically represented by its capital city, was constructed as a place where order and authority were more difficult to maintain due to, at least in the opinion of many viceroys, the presence there of a populace upon whom the inculcation of the principle of authority was highly ineffective, and this failure was largely due to the very racial and ethnic disorder of the city. Spanish political writers usually saw the *vulgo* (the common people) as a social group characterized by fickleness, easily shaken by the slightest accident and driven by blind impulses rather than reason. When a tumult had broken out, the physical presence of the ruler was a highly effective remedy for putting it down, because, in the words of Saavedra Fajardo, the people "relent or are filled with fear when they see the calm face of their natural lord." To him, that was the power of majesty: It easily captured the hearts of the people, because nature had given it a certain secret force that worked marvelous effects.[44] In the case of Mexico, the fickle and capricious nature of the *vulgo* was aggravated, so it was thought, by the racial hodgepodge that characterized the city. Speaking of the multitude of peoples "of all kinds of conditions, capacities, and colors" that constituted the population of Mexico City, the count of Baños declared: "There is no action of their superiors, especially in public, which is not news to them or does not surprise them ... because the common people of this city are comprised of Spaniards, Indians, mestizos, blacks, mulattos, and Chinese, and others similar to these," which according to the viceroy always made it possible for a public disturbance to break out.[45] In the view of the rulers of New Spain, this lack of internalization of the principle of authority on the part of the populace made the rulers' correct presence in public of crucial importance, as it was believed that the slightest alteration in the most insignificant sign of the semiology of power could have unpredictable consequences. Because the public ceremonies of colonial authorities were constitutive of their power, and it was through their participation in public rituals that they were endowed with their identity as such, the correct representation of their respective roles on the stage of the streets and churches of Mexico City would become of the utmost significance in the maintenance of their power.

One of the most negative views of Mexico City's lower class is presented, however, by a prominent Creole intellectual, Carlos de Sigüenza y Góngora, who in his description of the 1692 riot, influenced, no doubt, by the profound agitation that such an occurrence had caused in him, referred to the common people of the city in these terms:

> Being this plebs so extremely plebeian, to the point that it can only be reputed as being the most infamous of all plebs, since it is comprised of Indians, Creole and bozal blacks from various nations, Chinese, mulattos, moriscos, mestizos, zambaigos, lobos, and also Spaniards who, in declaring themselves zaramullos (which is the same as rascals, pimps, and cape-snatchers) and abandoning their obligations, are the worst among such a vile rabble.[46,47]

For Sigüenza, it is the very racial diversity of the populace that transforms it into the worst of all plebs, but it is the indigenous people of the city who receive his greatest invectives. He accuses the Indians of being ungrateful, as the many privileges awarded to them do not prevent them from committing all kinds of outrages. Sigüenza is convinced that the Indians hate the Spaniards and wish them all sorts of evil. He had found proof of this when, during the cleaning up of an irrigation ditch he had been in charge of, he discovered several little figures made of clay representing Spaniards pierced with spears or knives. According to Sigüenza, these figures had been put in exactly the same place where Hernán Cortés had been defeated when fleeing from Tenochtitlán. Furthermore, during the riot the Indians had yelled "Death to the Spaniards ... who eat our maize!" while telling one another there was nothing to fear because a Cortés was no longer around to keep them in check.[48] Almost 200 years after the conquest, Sigüenza invokes the spirit of Cortés as if he were trying to make up for the affront performed by the Indians against Spanish authority on the night of June 8, 1692. Persuaded that the Indians had a plan not only to kill the viceroy and burn the viceregal palace down, but also to take possession of the entire city, he wonders how it had been possible for the Spaniards to live all this time with such a lack of concern, surrounded as they were by such a populace.[49] Sigüenza had already shown this concern in a report on the different Indian barrios of Mexico City written a few weeks after the break of the tumult at the request of the viceroy. In it Sigüenza reminded the ruler that after the conquest the city aldermen did not think it was enough to keep the Indians "far from themselves" in separate barrios, but they had requested of the king and the first viceroys that the city be walled so as to protect themselves from the "innate malice" of the Indians and their hatred of the Spaniards, as the Indians were the ones who had always given substance to every city commotion, something that had been clearly seen during the riot of January 15, 1624.[50]

It is something of a paradox for someone such as Sigüenza to have so negative a view of the indigenous population and to convey such a sense of siege and danger, as he is usually presented as the prototype of Creole patriotism. Furthermore, as we saw in the first chapter, he was the first one to utilize images of Aztec rulers on a viceregal arch and he also concerned himself with recovering Aztec civilization, or at least some parts of it. Of course, the fact that he wrote the above opinions only two months after the riot took place when he was, no doubt, still deeply disturbed by the events of the ominous night of June 8 should not be dismissed; however, we have also seen that extremely negative images of the Mexican populace had originated much earlier.[51] Sigüenza, in reality, is engaging in one of the most common discursive strategies utilized by the Creole elite in its attempt to create a separate identity: the radical separation of indigenous history into a glorious past and a wretched present. The Creole elite of European descent will claim for itself the glories of the pre-Hispanic civilizations while radically separating itself from the descendants of those same indigenous cultures. This is what Mary Louise Pratt has defined as the "archeological perspective," wherein the links that obviously exist between the society that is being "archeologized" (that whose history is being reconstructed through the monuments and ruins recently "discovered") and its contemporary descendants are completely ignored. This strategy, moreover, denies the latter the possibility of establishing any kind of relationship with a "glorious" past which might be utilized to present all sorts of claims in the present. In other words, "To revive indigenous history and culture as archaeology is to revive them *as dead*."[52]

At any rate, it is quite likely that, in his harsh judgments on the indigenous population, Sigüenza had in mind only the urban elements of that population. The Indians of Mexico City occupied a place apart in colonial rhetoric, as they were not represented as poor and miserable but as cunning, drunkards, thieves, and with no respect whatsoever for authority.[53] This was due, it was contended, to their constant contact with blacks and mestizos, from which nothing good could be expected, but this "degeneration" of the urban Indian was also and paradoxically due, to a great extent, to their high degree of hispanization or *ladinización*. From this perspective, their contact with the Spaniards could only bring negative consequences to the Indians.[54] It was this notion that, in the last analysis, was at the base of the system of the two republics. Although at the beginning of the colonization the emphasis was on the commingling of the two communities as a way to foster the natives' Christianization and Europeanization, numerous *cédulas* since the time of Philip II had forbidden Spaniards, mestizos, mulattos, and blacks from living in Indian towns to avoid their teaching the natives "their bad habits and idleness, and also some errors and vices."[55] To many observers, the 1692 riot would simply confirm the harmful effects of the mixing of the two communities, but now there is an insistence upon the negative aspects of the Indians who, due to their bad inclinations, were only able to learn bad and sinful things from the Spaniards, but none of their good ones.[56]

Indeed, one of the viceroy's first reactions after the tumult was to order all the Indians who lived in the center of the city, mingling with Spaniards, blacks, and mestizos, to return to their original Indian barrios in the outskirts, because in the city the Indians lived with an "insolent liberty," filling the republic with "idle, vagrant, useless, disrespectful, and criminal people, ready to execute the most execrable and enormous crimes."[57] In the presence of the more or less hispaniziced Indian, the rhetoric of wretchedness vanishes to be substituted with a rhetoric of contempt. The hispaniziced Indians are an aberration, as they are neither Indian nor Spaniard, and, like the mestizos whom they resemble, they are impossible to ascribe to one of the two republics. By abandoning their communities and mixing with Spaniards, mestizos, and blacks, they learn the Spanish language, something that has consequences of great relevance, as this "is the first step in their insolence, because while they speak their language they are more humble."[58] It is not only language but clothing as well that serves to transmute the Indian from obedient vassal into insolent plebeian. When they move to the city center, the Indians start dressing in the Spanish style, "wearing stockings and shoes, and some, Vandyke collars, growing their hair, and the women put on skirts." The consequences cannot be but most negative: "Upon putting on a capote, shoes, and stockings, and growing his hair, the Indian transforms himself into a mestizo, and in a few days into a Spaniard, free from tribute and an enemy of God, his Church, and his king."[59] That makes it necessary to force the indigenous population to dress like "Indians"; above all, it is necessary to forbid them to wear capes, "because it seems that this instills in them arrogance, and with their blankets they are more humble and obedient," nor do they resemble mestizos.[60] In opposition to the perfect order of the two republics, then, we have the disorder of Mexico City, where everything is mixed together, and nothing is what it seems; thus, it is necessary to force the "blacks and mulattos to leave the [Indian] barrios and make them occupy the place that the Indians occupy in the city, and the Indians to occupy the place left in the barrios by the blacks, mulattos, and mestizos."[61]

It was, without a doubt, the very dynamics of colonial society that contributed to breaking down the system of the two republics. In a series of reports sent to the viceroy at his request, all the priests of the Indian parishes pointed out how difficult it would be to remove the Indians from the city center, as the majority of them could count on the protection of the Spaniards they served or worked for, and their houses had plenty of hiding places where the Indians were allowed to live. Many of them, moreover, had established relationships of *compadrazgo* (ritual practice of coparenting or fictive kinship) with Spaniards, who also opposed the attempts of the priests to take the Indians back to the *doctrinas*.[62] By the end of the seventeenth century, a dense network of patron–client relationships had developed that closely bound the elite of European origin to the lower classes, these relationships being responsible, to a great measure, for the "disorder" of the city.[63] From this supposed disorder, both the elite and the indigenous population benefited, because, thanks to it, the former could satisfy its need for a cheap and abundant labor force, whereas it allowed the latter to escape from the numerous obligations to which it was subjected as a member of the republic of Indians. Upon moving to the city center, the Indians, by hispanizing, mixed with the mestizo population, thus avoiding the payment of tribute, the forced labor draft, and the close control of the priests. The Indian thereby came to inhabit an interstitial, hybrid world, wherein the borders of the two republics became blurred to the point of disappearing, hence the insistence by the Crown, in the last third of the seventeenth century, that the "Indians" abandon the center and return to live in their barrios.[64] This insistence notwithstanding, the viceregal authorities thought that it was best not to force the Indians to leave, as it was feared that, if they were expelled from the center, they might decide to abandon the city altogether (this would cause an even greater problem, as Spaniards and Creoles both depended completely on indigenous labor). Thus, it was recommended that the "gentleness, caress, and warmth of the doctrineros" be utilized to convince the indigenous population to move back to Tlatelolco or the other Indian barrios of the city.[65]

For many observers, one factor that had enormously contributed to an increase in the confusion and disarray which, in their opinion, engulfed Mexico City was the free sale of alcohol, especially *pulque*, the favorite drink of the indigenous population. That was precisely what the count of Galve tried to make clear in the report he sent to the Court after the riot of 1692. Citing the opinions of the experts, the viceroy attributed the tumult to the drunkenness of the common people caused by their unlimited consumption of *pulque*. Only because they were inebriated, assured the viceroy, had they been able to commit such a contemptuous act.[66] The perpetual drunkenness of the Indians had become, since very early on, one of the most enduring stereotypes of the native population (we have already seen how Mendieta thought excessive drinking was one of two defects the

Indians possessed). Hence, the communal celebrations associated with the ritual ingestion of alcohol would be represented as bacchanals and orgies during which the unbridled consumption of liquor induced the participants to engage in all sorts of deviant behavior, starting with adultery and finishing with incest and sodomy. Added to this was the aggravating circumstance, Acosta would say, that the Indian bacchanals did not happen annually, like those of the ancients, but occurred monthly or even daily.[67]

If celebrations in the towns were labeled as bacchanals, the taverns of Mexico City frequented by urban Indians, known as *pulquerías*, places of socialization for the lower classes of the city, were no more than dens of vice, where all kinds of criminals were safe from prosecution, as the authorities could not enter their premises to make arrests (that was one of the clauses of the *asiento* or contract under which *pulque* was sold legally). This would make Agustín de Vetancourt, a Franciscan friar who was the parish priest of San Juan Tlatelolco, exclaim: "Where have we seen among Catholics that a synagogue of vagabonds and drunkards be granted church immunity?"[68] The drinking of *pulque* also fostered, according to its critics, the return of the Indians to their idolatrous practices. Both the growth of maguey (the plant from which *pulque* was produced) and the gatherings in which this drink was imbibed were surrounded by "superstitions" and even "formal idolatry," as *pulque* very often was offered to certain pre-Hispanic deities associated with it. In truth, *pulque* in and of itself was not perceived as a problem; rather, it was a kind of "adulterated" *pulque* (mixed with roots and other products in order to augment its fermentation and, consequently, its intoxicating effects) that the Indians and the rest of the populace who frequented the *pulquerías* were keen on.[69] In that sense, there was a close relation, in the eyes of the elite, between the mixed-race *plebe* (to whom the disorders of June 1692 would be attributed) and the equally mixed *pulque* (which would be blamed for sparking off the riot). As "mixed," adulterated, and non-pure, both possessed a degraded nature that conjured up images of degeneration and disorder impossible to control.

In the face of dominant images like these, it comes as no surprise that one of the first measures implemented by the count of Galve after the disturbances of 1692 was the prohibition of the sale of *pulque*.[70] Such a decision, however, was not an easy one for a viceroy, as the sale of *pulque*, which had been brought under the control of the Crown at the end of the 1660s, regularly brought fat profits to the royal treasury.[71] To lend more weight to his decision, then, Galve requested a series of reports on the effects of the consumption of *pulque* from practically all the ruling institutions. Given the dominant discourse on drinking and the native and the fact that the majority of those who wrote the reports were members of the clergy (who had always harshly criticized the sale of alcohol), it cannot be surprising that the overwhelming majority of the reports presented numerous arguments to justify the prohibition.

The main ideas that shaped all these reports were summarized in the one issued by the faculty of the University of Mexico, which would be printed.[72] To the professors, the wantonness of the Indians had transformed New Spain into a huge *magueyal*, as they had spent their time substituting maguey plants for necessary crops such as maize or wheat so they could satisfy their insatiable demand for *pulque*. Their drinking was always associated with aberrant behavior and the perpetration of crimes; nevertheless, the perpetual intoxication of the Indians did not prevent them from being aware that their inebriation could be used as an extenuating circumstance should they commit crimes. So, averred the professors, someone who wanted, for example, to commit incest prepared himself for executing the crime by getting drunk first. Also, the Indians spent all their earnings in the *pulquerías*, while their wives had to make a living by selling tortillas and other products in the public squares. *Pulquerías* were worse than brothels, because the only sin being committed in the latter was that of lasciviousness, whereas in the *pulquerías* not only was "abominable lasciviousness" rampant but thefts and murders happened all the time.[73] The authors of the report ask themselves whether it would be proper to prohibit the sale of *pulque*, as the consumption of wine by the Spaniards was legal. The answer for them was very simple, as a qualitative difference existed between each substance: While the Spaniards drank for pleasure, the Indians drank to get drunk; that is, drunkenness was something innate to the Indians, "a consubstantial defect," as Acosta had already observed one century before.[74] Because it was quite obvious that the drinking of *pulque* caused the ruin, both physical and spiritual, of the Indians, the viceroy should not worry about the loss of revenue by the royal treasury if its sale were prohibited, because it was clear that the Spanish monarch would always prefer the preservation of his vassals to the money that the sale of *pulque* might bring him. For all these reasons, the professors concluded, the prohibition of the sale of *pulque* should be maintained.[75] Because the rest of reports presented to the viceroy were unanimous in recommending the prohibition, its sale continued to be illegal but only for a few more years (until 1697, when the ban was lifted). As is usually the case with this type of measure, it was quickly realized that people kept consuming *pulque*, legal or not, while the Crown was losing thousands of pesos in revenues.[76] Thus, and despite the opposition of the clergy (Vetancourt published his "Manifiesto" one year after the prohibition was lifted), the consumption of *pulque* would become legal again.[77]

The Return of the Wretched Indian

As we have seen so far, it is evident that the rhetoric of power radicalizes itself in moments of crisis. This may help explain, in part, the extremely negative view of the urban Indian that has just been discussed, but we must ask whether the same radicalization took effect in relation to the rural

Indian. Likewise, we should ask to what extent the close association that the authorities of the capital established between Indian rebellion and drunkenness was also extended to the revolts that happened in rural areas. In this regard, an analysis of what was probably the most serious disturbance that occurred in New Spain outside the capital in the period under study, the already mentioned Tehuantepec rebellion (see Chapter 5), would be highly illustrative. The revolt, which started in March 1660 with the killing of the *alcalde mayor* of Tehuantepec at the hands of the Indians, would spread some months later to the districts of Nejapa and Ixtepeji, all of them located in the bishopric of Oaxaca. The rebellion was not excessively violent. The only fatal victims of indigenous violence were the aforementioned *alcalde mayor* of Tehuantepec, an Indian *cacique* who was with the *alcalde*, and two servants of the latter (one black and the other Spanish). More violence would come from the *oidor* of the *audiencia* of Mexico who was sent to reestablish order.[78] When analyzing the disturbances, the ruling elite put forward two opposing discourses. In the case of the 1692 tumult, the unanimity in condemning an allegedly intoxicated populace was almost complete, but it was very different with the Tehuantepec occurrence. Here, elite discourse will be dominated, in a large measure, by the traditional rhetoric of wretchedness and, as a result, by the absence of unanimous condemnation of the rebellious Indians, nor was a generalized attempt made to blame the drinking of *pulque* for what had happened. In this sense, the difference from the urban revolt of 1692 could not be any greater. In this occurrence, any type of explanation that tried to take into account the exploitation or misery of the city's lower class was not allowed; in the case of Tehuantepec, to the contrary, practically everyone, including the supporters of a more repressive approach, would recognize that the exploitation of the indigenous people by the *alcaldes mayores* was at the root of their uprising.

It would not be by coincidence, then, that the *alcaldes mayores* were the ones who adopted the most bellicose language and the most hostile attitude toward the Indians. After all, it was they who occupied the trenches of colonial exploitation, and it was precisely an *alcalde mayor* who was the only one, in all of the profuse documentation that has been preserved, to make some type of connection between drunkenness and rebellion. For Juan de Torres Castillo, a Creole in search of employment who would be appointed *alcalde mayor* of Nejapa after the disturbances, with their revolt the Indians only sought to gain the necessary freedom to give themselves over to their drunkenness and idolatry; if they were not kept under control, they would commit all kinds of excesses and cruelties. In his view, all the Indians were equally characterized by their evil intentions and their aversion and loathing of the Spaniards, for all of which punishing the rebellious Indians was mandatory; otherwise, "the fire of disobedience" would quickly spread throughout New Spain.[79] In a similar vein, Cristóbal Manso de Contreras, a *regidor* of the city of Antequera (the most important city in the bishopric of Oaxaca) who was appointed *alcalde mayor* of

Tehuantepec after the rebellion, asserted that the Indians were enraged, blood-thirsty barbarians. They were also traitors for revolting against their king. In his attacks on the Indians, Manso, in fact, articulated a counter-discourse that negates the official rhetoric of the wretched Indian, as he contended that the incapacity that was generally attributed to them should not have been an excuse for their behavior; on the contrary, the Indians took advantage of this alleged deficiency to commit their excesses (here, Manso is indirectly criticizing the bishop of Oaxaca who, as we shall see below, sided with the Indians). Finally, Manso, like Torres, articulates an alarmist discourse wherein the events of Tehuantepec are compared to the various grave crises that had shaken the Spanish monarchy in previous decades: Because those rebellions were not stopped in time, it cost much money and many lives to reestablish order later.[80]

All of these opinions greatly contrast with the language and attitude adopted by the duke of Alburquerque, the viceroy at the time of the uprising. It may appear quite surprising that, when the Spanish residents of Tehuantepec wrote to the viceroy to inform him that the natives had revolted against their *alcalde mayor*, he responded to them in these terms:

> I have received the letter … in which you inform me that, in a *scuffle* (*refriega*) that happened in that place, the alcalde mayor, don Juan de Avellán, *died* from some blows he received from stones; and *I much regret the vexations and troubles* that the natives experienced with said alcalde mayor. …And I shall be sending you a *worthy* (*benemérito*) alcalde mayor, whom I shall instruct to govern with the observance of the laws and royal decrees for the relief and benefit of that land.[81]

This passage is especially remarkable for the way in which the viceroy juxtaposes, in the same sentence, the rebellion of the Indians, which for him is no more than a "scuffle," with the acknowledgment of the abuses committed by the dead magistrate. Other than that, not a single word is expressed to lament the death of the *alcalde*, who after all had been appointed by the viceroy (note, also, that Alburquerque says that the *alcalde* "died," not that he was killed or murdered). Similarly, when the viceroy was informed that the municipal council of Antequera had decided to send troops to help Juan de Espejo, *alcalde mayor* of Nejapa, who was alleged to be surrounded by the Indians in the Dominican convent of that town where he had been forced to take refuge, his answer was to say he had been most surprised:

> … because without any orders from me such a resolution cannot be taken; to take arms in your hands and disturb the provinces which I have ruled and preserved in this post with so much peace and quietude is against the service of His Majesty. Because the vassals of His

> Majesty should not be risked for the help of an individual … I will care little about don Juan de Espejo if he dies at the hands of the Indians, should he give them the occasion, and much about the restlessness of the Indians because of how much I love serving His Majesty.[82]

Apparently, the viceroy did not have much appreciation for his underlings, even when their heads were at stake. In his study of the rebellion, Héctor Díaz-Polanco has pointed out that what preoccupied the viceroy at that moment was his responsibility to preserve law and order, and he was little concerned about the fate of the officials in disgrace; the emergency had placed private interests in the background, bringing out the public man, the statesman.[83] This certainly seems true because the viceroy, above all, seeks to appear as a ruler who is perfectly aware of his duties, especially at a moment when the end of his term and his return to Spain were near (as well as his *residencia*). In Alburquerque's comments, we find encapsulated many of the principles by which the viceroys, as we have seen, were expected to rule: first, the good treatment of the natives, which would explain why he apparently regretted their oppression more than the death of the *alcalde mayor*; second, the distribution of offices to the worthy, hence his adding right away that he will appoint a new *alcalde* who meets this requirement;[84] third, given the "wretched" nature of the Indians, the fact that they should be governed with a gentle hand, with no need for big displays of force (among other reasons, because the Indians were not perceived as a threat), which is why Alburquerque disapproved of using troops, accusing them, ironically, of increasing the disorder. Of course, the revolt could not have been more inopportune for him. Perhaps, it was this factor that made him appear so dismissive and unconcerned regarding his subordinates (and, of course, the certainty that the abuses of the *alcaldes mayores*, who happened to be his own appointees, were quite real).[85]

The duke was certain of all this because of the letters he had received (even before the revolt) from Alonso de Cuevas Dávalos, bishop of Oaxaca. He would play a crucial role in the uprising. The first measure taken by the viceroy after the outbreak of the rebellion was to request the bishop to go personally to the town of Tehuantepec to try to calm down the Indians.[86] As opposed to the language used by the *alcaldes mayores*, the many letters and reports sent by the bishop to the viceroy and the *audiencia* to inform them of his actions are dominated by the rhetoric of wretchedness. The Indians were "poor and miserable people," constantly vexed and troubled by the *alcaldes mayores* because they forced the distribution of goods upon the natives. The *alcaldes* were, in fact, the ones to be blamed for what had happened, and, in consequence, the bishop requested that the viceroy dismiss the abusive *alcaldes* (such as the one from Nejapa), as it was better for one individual to lose "four reales than for His Majesty to lose his vassals and royal tributes." Cuevas is also totally against sending troops to punish the rebels. The "docility and humble nature" of the Indians were such that he alone, without "military clatter" and expense to the royal treasury, would be able to restore peace. For these reasons, he appealed to the viceroy's clemency to grant, as "His Majesty's image," a pardon to those "wretched Indians."[87] The Dominican provincial was of the same opinion. Not wanting to abuse the bishop's good will and cooperative attitude, the viceroy had asked the provincial to go and try to appease the Indians from Nejapa. The provincial reported that, through their actions, the Indians, in truth, were not attacking royal authority but rather the forced distribution of goods. That was why all their rage was directed at the *alcaldes mayores*. For the provincial, the only problem with the Indians was that, because they were inept, they had erred in the method they had chosen and, instead of turning to the viceroy for help in putting a stop to their vexations, they had decided to take justice into their own hands.[88]

This was the state of things when a new viceroy, the count of Baños, took office in September 1660. The main consequence of this change would be a shift in the rhetoric of the civil authorities in the capital. The change, in fact, was facilitated by Alburquerque himself, who eagerly reminded the new viceroy that divine and human law, as well as the principles of good government, required that the four or five most significant leaders of the revolt be punished, something he had not been able to do because he had not found yet the right opportunity; unless the Indians were caught unawares, it would be impossible to put down the rebellion. Besides, upon learning of the appointment of a new viceroy, he had decided to leave the execution of the punishment to the new ruler.[89] In accordance with this new, more repressive approach, the events of Tehuantepec no longer were referred to as a "scuffle" but as a "riot" or as the "excesses of the natives," and it was requested that the leaders of the revolt be punished in a severe and exemplary way as a warning to the rest. Nevertheless, in this discourse of repression, the rhetoric of wretchedness never completely fades away. At the same time that severe punishment for the guilty is being sought, it is being requested that the abuses of the *alcaldes mayores* be punished, because it has been these very abuses that had irremediably pushed "these wretched ones" to a rebellion.[90] When, in September 1660, a resolution was approved to dispatch an *oidor* of the *audiencia* of Mexico to Tehuantepec, the alleged reason was that he was being sent to investigate and prosecute the vexations and the ill treatment of the Indians.[91] It was precisely to emphasize that the magistrate was being sent to do justice and redress the grievances of the natives, not to punish those responsible for the disturbances, that it was decided to dispatch an *oidor* rather than an *alcalde del crimen*, which would have been the logical thing given the nature of the affair,[92] but the repressive intentions of the mission were made quite evident when the *oidor* Juan Francisco de Montemayor de Cuenca, who before arriving in Mexico had distinguished himself by his military deeds in Catalonia and the island of Hispaniola, was commissioned to go to Tehuantepec invested with full powers as "lieutenant of the viceroy."[93] Of course, dispatching a judge from the *audiencia* rather than a military detachment was also part of the strategy of deception of the Indians followed by the authorities in Mexico City, seen as the best way to execute an exemplary punishment of the rebels.[94]

Montemayor's repressive approach was not approved by the Crown, not because it thought the leaders of the revolt should not be punished but because of its severity.[95] The image of the wretched Indian had taken hold of the Spanish monarchy in such a way that it was not possible to escape from it, not even when judging an indigenous uprising. A look at the deliberations of the Council of the Indies makes clear that the councilors, up to a certain point, saw as legitimate that the Indians had rebelled against the abuses of the *alcaldes mayores*; otherwise, it is difficult to understand the apparent lack of concern of the councilors or the monarch himself in regard to the events of Tehuantepec and Nejapa. After notifying the king about what had happened in those places, the only comment made by the councilors was to ask the king to read all the reports received by the Council, "so that Your Majesty will be aware of the manner in which the Indies are ruled and the way how those poor vassals of Your Majesty are mistreated." The king's answer to the Council would be in the same vein: to instruct the Council "to make sure the excesses and violence committed by the *alcaldes mayores* are remedied, since the revolts and restlessness of the Indians originate from this."[96] Evidently, the councilors gave more credit to the letters from Alburquerque and the bishop of Oaxaca than to the alarmist reports of the *alcaldes mayores*; thus, when the Council was informed of the repressive violence unleashed by the actions of the *oidor* Montemayor, its response would be to remind the count of Baños that he had been ordered to try to pacify the Indians "with much gentleness, without afflicting them with harsh punishments." Furthermore, viceroys and governors, he was told, should try "to pacify rather than conquer and wage war," for which reasons Montemayor should drop all the criminal proceedings initiated against the Indians and return immediately to serve his post of *oidor* in Mexico City.[97]

Yet, the Council did show great concern when it learned that some Indians had appointed one of their own as king. The Council described this incident as a "terrible excess" and asserted that, should this be true, this Indian king did not deserve the pardon that the viceroy, in the name of the king, had granted to all the participants in the rebellion. No worse crime, apart from heresy and apostasy, could be committed against him, the councilors let the king know. Furthermore, the penalties incurred by such a transgression passed to the descendants of the offenders, and the law condemned even imagining such a thing when it was expressed publicly, no matter how small the offense might have been.[98] The councilors' great concerns notwithstanding, they were quite willing to exculpate the Indians by questioning the veracity of the report sent to them by the viceroy with a fascinating argument. It seemed the viceroy had gotten this information from three Indians from Tehuantepec who had come to Mexico City to have their offices confirmed by the viceroy. For the councilors, although the three Indian officials had appeared to be confused (*turbados*) in the presence of the viceroy, and "the confusion (*turbación*) of the defendant in the judges' presence is usually an indication or suspicion of guilt," this argument could not be applied to this case, for one simple reason: These were three Indians who probably had never before seen the viceroy. When they saw him, he was in his chambers, surrounded by the "grandeur and retinue which those who represent the great person of His Majesty usually command," for which reason, the councilors concluded, the confusion of the Indians could be attributed to the "natural action of showing great respect and veneration."[99] To the councilors, it was, in a way, predictable that the Indians revolted against their *alcaldes mayores*, because their condition as "wretched people" made them easy targets of abuse. Thus, although Montemayor tried to present the revolt as an uprising against the king, it is clear that was not the way the Crown read it, but when the Indians dared to supplant the sacrosanct person of the king with one of their own then the councilors got exceedingly alarmed. For the councilors, however, it was easier to question the veracity of the viceroy's report than to accept the fact that the Indians had been capable of such transgression, for the simple reason that the Indian the official discourse had constructed was incapable of such an act of independence, one that questioned the ideas, images, and representations upon which the Spanish Empire in America had been built.

Conclusion: The Power of the King's Image

In 1747, Jorge Juan and Antonio de Ulloa, two Spanish navy officers, traveled to the viceroyalty of Peru as members of an international scientific mission led by Charles Marie de la Condamine. Following the instructions of the marquis of the Ensenada, the Spanish Secretary of State at the time, they wrote a confidential report on the general situation of the viceroyalty. In it they referred to the viceroy of Peru in the following terms:

> From the moment a viceroy is received in Peru and takes possession of his office, *he begins to be mistaken with royalty*. If one examines the ceremonies of his public entry into Lima …, it shall be seen that every aspect of this function shall make him imagine it. Thus, the city magistrates serve as his equerries, one walking on each side holding the reins of [the viceroy's] horse, while he is paraded under a magnificent canopy carried by the regidores of the city. Leaving aside many other ceremonies and attentions, could the honor and majestic pomp with which the true prince would be received by his most loyal and beloved vassals be any greater? Consider, therefore, the position of a viceroy so filled with acclaim, obsequiousness, and veneration in a land so far removed from his sovereign. One shall be forced to agree with us that he is bound to consider himself as just another sovereign, the only difference being the dependency and limited duration of this majesty.[1]

This description of the "majesty" of the viceroy of Peru served as an introduction to the authors' denunciation of what was, in their opinion, the excessive power of the viceroys. They concluded that in view of the almost sovereign power of the viceroys, it came as no surprise that instead of obeying the monarch's orders with exactitude, they interpreted royal commands or put them into execution only with tepidity.[2] That these criticisms came from two royal envoys is clear proof of a certain ambiguity that always surrounded the viceregal figure. It could also be argued, of course, that Antonio de Ulloa and Jorge Juan were the harbingers of the spirit of the Enlightenment and the Bourbon reforms which were to spread throughout the Spanish monarchy in the second half of the eighteenth century, but their views were not all that novel. They were not very different, for instance, from the attacks, one century before, of Juan de Palafox against the viceroys' excessive independence. In reality, as we have seen in the course of this study, denouncing viceregal power forms part of an "antiviceregal tradition" that goes back to the sixteenth century, a tradition that has strongly contributed to shaping the popular image of the viceroys' power as absolute and despotic; yet, this clearly is an image that needs to be revised. As has been shown in this study, the viceroys found their power limited by the rights and liberties of different social bodies. In New Spain, the autonomy of the ecclesiastic arm probably constituted the greatest limit to viceregal authority, although the *oidores* also represented an important check on the "absolutist" impulses of the viceroys. Even the *cabildo* of Mexico City had sufficient power to thwart the projects of the king's living images, if it considered it necessary.

Despite the many denunciations of the Crown's official envoys, we must ask if it was not precisely the aim of the Spanish monarchy in appointing viceroys to have them "mistaken for royalty" or if it was not in exactly this way that the viceroys were conceived of by the inhabitants of the New World. Writing in the 1620s, Matías de Caravantes, canon of the cathedral of Trujillo in Peru, declared that, "We may appropriately say that the viceroy is not different from the royal person, since [the king] lives in him by transmission and as a copy with such union and equality that the same honor and reverence which is owed to His Majesty is owed to His Excellency; both are due the same fidelity and vassalage, and, when one of them is offended, both are offended." Caravantes goes on to assert that, if the sovereign can be considered to be God's viceroy, His animate image, His simulacrum, His vicar general, and His companion in governing, "all these excellences befit the viceroy as someone who sheds his own person in order to take on the king's, with the same power although limited in part, for His Majesty, as a sign of his supreme dominion (*señorío*), has reserved to his Crown some royal prerogatives (*regalías*)."[3]

Expressed with great concision, this passage encapsulates the conception of power that the Spanish Crown tried to impose in its American territories. Because the rule of "only one" (that is, monarchical government) was accepted by everyone as the best and the most useful, with the appointment of viceroys the Crown attempted to transplant a system of monarchical rule to its American dominions. In a society in which power was conceived of in a personal manner and the concept of the state as a sovereign and impersonal entity to which we owe our loyalty was practically nonexistent, the benefits of the viceregal solution were clear to all. One of the characteristic elements of personalized power is the importance attributed to direct contact with the person in whom power resides. Because the great distances that separated the different territories of the monarchy from the seat of royal power made it almost impossible for the monarch to be physically present in them, the ideal solution was to send to them a representative of the sovereign vested with all the attributes of majesty. In this envoy, the inhabitants of the different provinces would see a surrogate monarch or even confuse him with the monarch himself, hence the usual description of the viceroy as *la viva imagen del rey* (the king's living image), as, in him, the subjects of the Spanish monarch would see not only a powerful governor but also the king himself.

As the king's living images, the viceroys were bound to replicate the gestures and behavior of their original, and if the sovereign should always look at the Heavens to learn how to best rule his realm, it made perfect sense that, among the many inhabitants of the celestial kingdom, one could be found who could be a model for the viceroys. In this regard, the cult of the archangel St. Michael, which became immensely popular in seventeenth-century New Spain, helped create a special connection between viceregal power and divine power: Just as the monarch of Heaven had at His disposal the archangels — images of the divinity and the most sublime of all the denizens of the heavenly court — to take care of the most important affairs in the government of the world, the monarch of Spain sent his living images — the viceroys — to rule the dominions of his "universal" monarchy. This conceptualization of the viceroy as the king's image sets him apart, in a very radical way, from the conventional view of the viceroy as the head of a colonial bureaucracy. In reality, a great gap exists between the way the figure of the viceroy was conceptualized and the modern bureaucratic ideal of professionalism and administrative efficiency. Instead of following a set of rigorously established administrative principles, his conduct was guided by a series of political and moral principles shaped by those virtues that reportedly should characterize every ruler. Each new viceroy was invariably reminded of these principles through the triumphal arches erected to welcome him ceremonially. The triumphal arch, in fact, functioned as a bigger-than-life political treatise, visible, though not totally intelligible, to all, on which were inscribed all the "constitutional" principles that governed the political life of New Spain. On the viceregal arches, the key terms were always religion, justice, prudence, liberality, and clemency. It is this language, in short, that allows us to understand the political practices of the Spanish monarchy in its American viceroyalties.[5]

To fully comprehend the viceregal figure we need to remember that the monarch was conceptualized as God's image and His vicar on earth, as Caravantes duly reminded us (while the viceroy, in turn, was seen as the king's image and his lieutenant in New Spain). Although the assimilation of the monarch to God endowed him with a majesty and power as incomprehensible to the human mind as God's majesty and power, bestowing on the king apparently unlimited power, at the same time it imposed upon him the heavy burden of having to ensure both the material and the spiritual well-being of his subjects. Paradoxically, this "divine" way of conceiving the monarch's authority imposed severe limits on his power, as his actions always had to focus on the public weal and not on his private interests. Although the absolute monarch has traditionally been depicted as ruling arbitrarily because he was not bound to obey his own laws, in reality very little was arbitrary in this system of government, much in the same way as God, though possessing unlimited power, does not rule the universe in an arbitrary manner. The fact that the king was God's vicar actually meant that he had to be God's imitator. Furthermore, this assimilation of the Spanish monarch to the divine should not be mistaken with the theory known as the Divine Right of Kings. The monarch's interests were not above those of the community; therefore, the king had the inescapable obligation of ruling for the benefit of the people. In other words, the king's chief mission was to administer justice, procuring the security and well-being of his subjects. Diego de Avendaño, a commentator on the government of the Indies, was worried about the many problems that the enormous distance that separated the monarch from his New World possessions created for their good administration and the welfare of the indigenous population, and he observed that, just as God, although separated from human beings by a great distance, "is present everywhere, touches everything with His hand, and looks carefully after that which seems very remote," the Catholic monarch should imitate God and conduct himself in the same manner.[4]

This way of conceiving royal power explains the endless succession of royal letters and decrees ordering the good treatment of the Indians, but this persistent concern, although it was certainly rooted in the awareness of the many abuses committed against the native population, was also greatly compounded by the fact that the Crown's own discourse had constructed the Indian as a wretched and destitute being, unable to defend himself (although, as we have seen, this image did not include the urban Indian). This essential wretchedness of the American native became so firmly engraved in the consciousness of the Spanish rulers that not even a revolt or a rebellion was able to alter it. The problem was that the Spanish Crown was never able to acknowledge that its colonial enterprise, with its civilizing mission and its exploitation of the riches of the New World, made the preservation of the welfare of the native population a very difficult task. In that sense, a basic contradiction always existed in the practices of the Spanish monarchy in relation to the indigenous populations of the New World. To begin with, in theory the natives were to remain separated from the population of European descent, living in their own república de indios, because this was seen as the best way to protect them from the abuses of the Spaniards (both *peninsulares* and *criollos*), but at the same time the push for assimilation was strong (in many ways, the inevitable effect of the Christianization of the Indians, which was the ultimate reason for Spanish rule). The result was that, in practice, the Indians were incorporated into the polity as legitimate, but subordinate, members, quickly acquiring a status similar to that of the Castilian peasants and commoners (in the organicist language of the time, they came to be the feet of the monarchy's mystical body), but the forced labor imposed upon the indigenous population, whose necessity the Crown's civilizing discourse would rationalize and justify, radically separated the New World natives from their Castilian counterparts. As we saw, this dissimilarity would be poignantly highlighted by Gerónimo de Mendieta in one of his numerous invectives against the Indian labor draft, when he wondered why New Spain's indigenous inhabitants should be forced to carry out certain kinds of work if the peasants of Spain were subjected to nothing like it, the former being as free as the latter. It was this difference in particular that contributed to the separation of the American natives from the rest of the subaltern populations of the monarchy, bestowing upon them their typical colonial status. In this sense, the viceroys contributed to the consolidation of this status in decisive ways by shaping and justifying the forced labor of the Indians with their discursive practices and actions. This is the great paradox embedded in the viceroys' relations with the indigenous population of New Spain: If, on the one hand, their position as the head of the Indian court made the viceregal figure into the great symbol of justice for the natives of New Spain, on the other those same viceroys would play a decisive role in consolidating the colonial condition of the Indian.

Despite the anti-viceregal denunciations, it appears that the monarchs were never completely convinced of the reality of the danger of the excessively independent power of the viceroys; they never doubted the fidelity of their "living images." In this regard, the idea, so widespread among certain historians, that the monarchs deeply distrusted initiatives taken by their American officials and public servants should be qualified. In fact, two harsh critics of viceregal power, the aforementioned Antonio de Ulloa and Jorge Juan, asserted exactly the opposite. As they wonder in their confidential report, "Who can be surprised that [the viceroy] directs everything according to his will, if *he has the monarch's trust* on his side, and he is assured that his reports will prevail over all those with opposing views?"[6]

That the viceroys always had the royal trust does not mean, of course, that the monarchs did not try to make sure they always had the necessary means to keep the viceroys under their control. There is a moment in the early seventeenth century when the Crown reveals with great clarity how it felt as regards its American viceroys. In the year 1629, due to the confrontations between the viceroy of New Spain and the archbishop of Mexico, already discussed in Chapter 3, the king asked the Council of the Indies to consider whether it would be advisable that the viceroys of New Spain be appointed for only three years instead of the six that had been the norm heretofore. In their answer to the king, a majority of the councilors concluded that it was not desirable that the viceroys of the Indies be appointed for only a three-year term. In a comment on the councilors' awareness of colonial realities, they argued that any viceroy who would want to honestly serve the king and his American subjects would reject the appointment on the grounds that he would not have enough time to accomplish anything in just three years. On the other hand, should a viceroy accept the post for his own material and personal benefit, knowing that his term was going to be so brief, he would try to fleece his subjects as fast and as much as he could. Besides, the councilors argued, because viceroys were "another Your Majesty" and their authority was essentially based on the representation they had of the royal person, it would be undeniable that a viceroy appointed for life would be far more respected and would possess far more authority than one commissioned for a short period, and this was even more so in the Indies, where viceroys were allowed to provide "very honorable offices and posts, which allowed them to keep their subjects more dependent on them." If viceroys were to be appointed for just three years, they would have time to distribute offices only once during their rule, and this would diminish viceregal authority, as the viceroys would not be able to maintain their rule with the promise of future distributions of offices; however, three members of the Council disagreed with the majority and pointed out a great advantage in appointing viceroys for only three years: If a viceroy proved to be a good ruler, the king could easily reward him by renewing his term of office, but should a viceroy be guilty of misrule, it would be easy for the monarch to punish him simply by not renewing his appointment. This had the great advantage of allowing the king to change the governor of the province "without discrediting the person or the post." Moreover, when appointments to remote provinces were made for long periods, the public good was neglected and attention to one's own interests increased greatly. The monarch seemed to be convinced by these arguments, and, consequently, he resolved that the American viceroys should thenceforth be appointed for a period of three years "more or less according to my will," as was usually stated in the letter of appointment given to each viceroy.[7]

Perhaps this is the best example of the Crown's careful approach when dealing with its most prominent representatives, but being careful is not the same as being distrustful. As a matter of fact, it would have been impossible to rule such remote lands if the Crown had not trusted its own officials. In connection with this, the old idea that the existence of political conflict in colonial Spanish America came about because the Spanish Crown allowed and even encouraged overlapping agencies to compete with and check one another needs also to be revised. The jurisdictional conflicts that opposed one institution of colonial rule to another did not happen as a consequence of a deliberate attempt of the Crown to bring individuals or institutions face to face, as the best way to prevent any one of them from becoming too powerful. It occurred because each social body, as the holder of certain rights and privileges, was obliged to defend the rights it was entitled to. In this sense, conflicts of jurisdiction and competence constituted real limitations on the effectiveness of royal authority, although they have nothing to do with the concept of a system of checks and balances, which is merely a projection of modern political theory onto an utterly different world. My argument has been that the level of antagonism between the members of the ruling elite in New Spain was the "natural" product of the political system itself. The local and circumstantial factors may help explain the greater or lesser intensity of the conflicts but not its existence, as conflict was embedded in the very nature of the system.

The existence of conflicting political views among the members of the New Spanish ruling elite manifested itself with great force in the theater of colonial politics. The ritual activities of the inhabitants of New Spain constituted a crucial stage on which was developed not only the process of creation of legitimizing discourses but also those processes of cooperation and contestation that characterize every political system. In this sense, the public ceremonies of New Spain's rulers were constitutive of their power. It was through their participation in public rituals that they were endowed with their identity as such. At the same time, these rituals were representative of colonial power. The apparently irrelevant disputes to decide the exact place that the different colonial actors should occupy at these ceremonies or the controversies that arose over matters of cushions, armchairs, stairways, or corridors were much more than quaint aspects of "Old Mexico's Baroque times," lacking in importance or meaning. They were clear indicators of the existence of different political views and of the struggles that went on among the members of the ruling elite in an effort to impose a particular political vision. This is the reason why, in the theater of New Spanish politics, one of its main protagonists, the archbishop of Mexico, very often confronted the viceroys to deny, with gestures sometimes explicit and sometimes subtle, the supremacy of viceregal power over ecclesiastical authority. Similarly, the Justices of the Mexican *audiencia* resisted those ritual gestures of the viceroys that meant an assertion of an undisputed viceregal supremacy over them. Confronting this public stripping of their authority, the *oidores* repeatedly tried to reaffirm ritually their belief that the New Spanish republic would always be better governed if the viceroys ruled with the cooperation of the *audiencia*. The members of the tribunal of the Inquisition, for their part, always insisted that, on the public stage, that institution ought to appear as independent from both secular and ecclesiastical power. Finally, the *regidores* of Mexico City, in competition with other institutions of colonial rule, attempted to assert at every public ceremony that, in the structure of colonial power, they occupied a special place as representatives not only of the residents of Mexico City but of all the inhabitants of the kingdom of New Spain as well.

At the apex of the system of colonial rule was the Spanish monarch who constituted such a powerful figure and created such strong bonds of loyalty that the mere idea of severing these bonds could not be taken seriously by almost anyone. Anyone except for Francisco de Seijas y Lobera, a peculiar character and harsh critic of viceregal power. A peninsular appointed by the king as *alcalde mayor* of Tacuba in 1693, Seijas got involved in constant clashes with the viceroy, the count of Galve, who imprisoned him several times. Seijas eventually renounced his *alcaldía mayor* to avoid further problems. After traveling around the continent and also antagonizing the count of La Monclova, the viceroy of Peru, he decided to move to France, where he offered his services and knowledge of the New World to Louis XIV. The French monarch granted him a pension so he could write about his American experiences. This allowed Seijas to write a voluminous treatise (published only recently) on the government of the Spanish Indies, in which he offered all kinds of advice to the new Spanish monarch (and grandson of Louis XIV), Philip V, on how to keep his dominion over his American possessions. In his writings, Seijas always contended that his problems with Galve had originated in the viceroys' hostility toward all those who were appointed in Spain — either directly by the king as a reward or because they had bought a post — to fill any of the offices whose appointment had usually corresponded to the viceroys of New Spain. What makes the opinions of Seijas interesting is his assertion that the main danger threatening the security of the Indies was not exterior (i.e., the possibility that the European enemies of Spain would grab her American territories) but interior insofar as the viceroys and other governors did not obey the monarch's orders, doing instead exactly as they pleased. In the view of Seijas, viceregal patronage, instead of working as a mechanism that served to reinforce the monarch's power, had turned into something that put at risk his dominion over his overseas possessions.[8] Moreover, he argued that if grandees of Spain or their brothers continued to be sent to the New World as viceroys, these lands would become separated from the monarchy, because the ultimate goal of the viceroys would always be to crown themselves as kings of New Spain. He went as far as to accuse the count of Galve of being the main instigator of the 1692 riot, because he aspired to crown himself king of New Spain.[9]

Although it is not clear whether the opinions of Seijas ever reached the Spanish monarch, most of his views, in reality, were not very original. As in the case of Antonio de Ulloa and Jorge Juan, they were not very different from the denunciations of Juan de Palafox against the viceroys' excessive independence and their corruption of the system of royal patronage (Seijas also proposed the elimination of the *alcaldes mayores* and their substitution with *alcaldes ordinarios*[10]). As for Seijas' accusation against the viceroys regarding their desire to sever New Spain from the rest of the monarchy, this is clearly an exaggeration provoked by the resentment of a disgruntled official, as no evidence whatsoever exists to sustain it. On the contrary, all evidence seems to indicate that the effect produced by the extreme geographical distance that separated the members of New Spain's ruling class — both *peninsulares* and *criollos* — from the center of the monarchy was an intensification rather than a weakening of their loyalty to the king. While Spanish political writers of the period usually established a distinction between the king and the republic, often stressing the idea of service to the republic (which in time would contribute to the creation of the abstract and impersonal entity of the state), in the political practice of New Spain this concept almost completely disappeared. All the emphasis was placed on the ties of personal service that united its inhabitants to the king and that were the foundation of their loyalty and fidelity toward the sovereign, especially in "lands so remote," an expression which became a trope of political rhetoric on both sides of the Atlantic.[11] Proof of this intense loyalty was that during the 13 long years of the succession crisis inaugurated in 1700, hardly any incidents happened in New Spain to put in doubt the fidelity of its inhabitants to the new monarch. Although he belonged to a different dynasty, he had been chosen by Carlos II, who had been the legitimate ruler of the people of New Spain for 35 years.[12] Something very different, however, would happen a century later with the new crisis of succession provoked by the Napoleonic invasion of Spain. But that's another century and another story.

Appendix

The Viceroys of New Spain in the 16th and 17th Centuries

1535–1550	Antonio de Mendoza
1550–1564	Luis de Velasco I
1564–1566	Rule of the *audiencia* of Mexico
1566–1567	Gastón de Peralta, marqués de Falces
1568–1580	Martín Enríquez de Almansa
1580–1583	Lorenzo Suárez de Mendoza, conde de La Coruña
1584–1585	Pedro Moya de Contreras, archbishop of Mexico (acting viceroy)
1585–1590	Alvaro Manríquez de Zúñiga, marqués de Villamanrique
1590–1595	Luis de Velasco II
1595–1603	Gaspar de Zúñiga y Acevedo, conde de Monterrey
1603–1607	Juan de Mendoza y Luna, marqués de Montesclaros
1607–1611	Luis de Velasco II, marqués de Salinas
1611–1612	Francisco García Guerra, archbishop of Mexico (acting viceroy)
February 1612–October 1612	Rule of the *audiencia* of Mexico
1612–1621	Diego Fernández de Córdoba, marqués de Guadalcázar
March 1621–September 1621	Rule of the *audiencia* of Mexico

1621–1624	Diego Carrillo de Mendoza y Pimentel, conde de Priego, marqués de Gelves
1624–1635	Rodrigo Pacheco y Osorio, marqués de Cerralvo
1635–1640	Lope Díez de Armendáriz, marqués de Cadereita
1640–1642	Diego López Pacheco, marqués de Villena, duque de Escalona
June 1642–November 1642	Juan de Palafox y Mendoza, bishop of Puebla (acting viceroy)
1642–1648	García Sarmiento de Sotomayor, conde de Salvatierra
1648–1649	Marcos de Torres y Rueda, bishop of Yucatán (held the title of bishop–governor)
1649–1650	Rule of the *audiencia* of Mexico
1650–1653	Luis Enríquez de Guzmán, conde de Alba de Liste
1653–1660	Francisco Fernández de la Cueva, duque de Alburquerque
1660–1664	Juan de Leiva y de la Cerda, marqués de Leiva, conde de Baños
June 1664–October 1664	Diego Osorio de Escobar, bishop of Puebla (acting viceroy)
1664–1673	Antonio Sebastián de Toledo Molina y Salazar, marqués de Mancera.
November 1673–December 1673	Pedro Nuño Colón de Portugal, duque de Veragua
1673–1680	Payo Enríquez de Rivera, archbishop of Mexico (acting viceroy)
1680–1686	Tomás Antonio de la Cerda, conde de Paredes, marqués de La Laguna
1686–1688	Melchor Portocarrero Laso de la Vega, conde de la Monclova
1688–1696	Gaspar de la Cerda Sandoval Silva y Mendoza, conde de Galve
February 1696–November 1696	Juan de Ortega y Montañés, bishop of Michoacán (acting viceroy)
1696–1701	José Sarmiento de Valladares, conde de Moctezuma

The Archbishops of Mexico in the 16th and 17th Centuries

1527–1547	Fray Juan de Zumárraga, first bishop of Mexico
1547–1548	Fray Juan de Zumárraga, first archbishop (died in Spain)
1551–1569	Fray Alonso de Montúfar (died in Mexico)
1573–1591	Pedro Moya de Contreras (appointed president of the Council of the Indies)
1592	Alonso Fernández de Bonilla (died in Peru)
1600–1606	Fray García de Santa María y Mendoza (died in Mexico)
1607–1612	Fray Francisco García Guerra (died in Mexico)
1613–1625	Juan Pérez de la Serna (transferred to Spain)
1628–1635	Francisco Manso y Zúñiga (transferred to Spain)
1636	Francisco Verdugo (died in Mexico)
1639–1640	Feliciano de la Vega (died in Mexico)
1640	Juan de Palafox y Mendoza (renounced)
1643–1650	Juan de Mañozca (died in Mexico)
1653	Marcelo López de Azcona (died in Mexico)
1655–1661	Mateo Sagade Bugueiro (transferred to Spain)
1663–1664	Diego Osorio de Escobar (renounced)
1664–1665	Alonso de Cuevas y Dávalos (died in Mexico)
1666–1667	Fray Marcos Ramírez de Prado (died in Mexico)
1670–1681	Fray Payo Enríquez de Rivera (returned to Spain)
1681–1698	Francisco de Aguiar y Seijas (died in Mexico)
1701–1710	Juan de Ortega y Montañés (died in Mexico)

Glossary of Spanish Terms

Acuerdo — Periodical sessions held jointly by the viceroy and the *oidores* to discuss matters of political administration.

Alcabala — Sales tax.

Alcalde de corte — Same as *alcalde del crimen*.

Alcalde del crimen — Judge of the criminal division of the *audiencia*.

Alcalde mayor — Chief Spanish magistrate of a district; also known as *corregidor*.

Alcalde ordinario — City magistrate, having jurisdiction in both civil and criminal cases; usually two per municipality.

Alcaldía mayor — The district ruled by an *alcalde mayor*.

Alférez real — The member of a *cabildo* in charge of bearing the city standard.

Alguacil — A bailiff or constable, appointed by both secular and ecclesiastical authorities.

Alguacil mayor — Chief constable.

Altepetl — Pre-Hispanic indigenous territorial units or, in an approximate translation, city-states or local ethnic states, which would become the *pueblos de indios* of the colonial era.

Asesor — The viceroy's legal advisor.

Audiencia — The highest royal court of appeals within a jurisdiction, serving at the same time as an advisory council to the viceroy or governor; the term was also applied to the area or district under the jurisdiction of the *audiencia*.

251

Auto de fe — Public ceremony at which the sentences of the Inquisition were pronounced.

Beneficio — Benefice, an office granted to an ecclesiastic that guaranteed a fixed amount of income.

Beneméritos de Indias — Those American subjects of the Spanish monarch worthy of royal favors and rewards.

Cabildo eclesiástico — Ecclesiastical or cathedral chapter.

Cabildo secular — Municipal council.

Capitán General — Title granted to the viceroy in his capacity as commander in chief of the viceroyalty.

Cédula — Royal decree or letter.

Colación — Conferral of an ecclesiastical office.

Concordia — Written agreement established between the civil authorities and the Inquisition to solve conflicts of jurisdiction.

Consulta — A written opinion of the royal councils and *audiencias*; a consultative meeting.

Corregidor — A city's chief magistrate; Spanish official in charge of a province or district.

Corregimiento — The district of jurisdiction of a *corregidor*.

Cortes — Castilian parliament; its deputies were elected by the eighteen cities that had the right to send representatives to the *Cortes*.

Criollo — A person of Spanish blood born in the New World.

Cura — A parish priest.

Doctrina — Indian parish, usually administered by regular clergy.

Doctrinero — Friar or priest in charge of a *doctrina*.

Dosel — Baldachin, a canopy placed above a chair or throne.

Encomendero — Holder of an *encomienda*.

Encomienda — Grant of Indians as tribute payers and laborers.

Familia — The retinue of any person of rank, especially viceroys and bishops.

Familiar — Lay deputy of the Inquisition.

Fiestas de tabla — Feast days on which it was mandatory for the viceroy and the *audiencia* to participate in the processions and celebrations in the cathedral.

Fiscal — Crown attorney; while in civil cases he represented the royal interests, in criminal cases he was the prosecutor.

Fuero — Charter of privileges or legal code.

Gobernador — Governor; here, specifically, governor of an Indian head town.

Letrado — Holder of a law degree, usually a royal official.

Oficiales Reales — Royal treasury officials.

Oidor — Justice of the *audiencia*.

Palio — Canopy, a covering of fabric, supported on poles and suspended above an exalted personage or sacred object.

Pallium or palio — Woolen religious insignia worn only by archbishops.

Pase Regio — Previous approval by the Council of the Indies of all the documents issued by the Holy See directed to the American territories.

Patronato Real — The body of rights and privileges that regulated the ecclesiastical patronage of the Spanish monarchs.

Peninsular — A person born in Spain who lived in the New World.

Plebe — The common people; here, the ethnically and racially diverse lower classes of Mexico City, very often having the connotation of rabble.

Policía — The good government and "civilized" life made possible by the laws and ordinances of a well-ordered community; civic order; civility; urbanity, refinement, and manners.

Pueblos de indios — Legally recognized Indian towns.

Pulque — Fermented juice of the maguey plant.

Pulquería — Tavern for the sale of pulque.

Real Provisión — Writ issued by the *audiencias* as if given by the king himself.

Recurso de fuerza — Legal process whereby the decisions of the ecclesiastical judges could be appealed to the royal courts.

Regidor — Alderman.

Regimiento — Office of alderman; synonymous with *cabildo secular*.

Reino — Kingdom, realm; in Spanish constitutional tradition, it was usually identified with the Cortes.

Repartimiento — Indian labor draft.

Repartimiento de mercancías — Forced sale of goods.

República de españoles — In the New World, the political community formed by the people of European descent.

República de indios — Here, the indigenous population seen as an entity separate from the rest of the population; also, the voting body of an Indian political community.

Residencia — Judicial review of an official's conduct in office at the conclusion of his term.

Visita — General or specific investigation of governmental operation; tour of inspection made by an *oidor* or a bishop.

Visitador — A judge conducting a general or specific *visita*.

Vulgo — The common people.

List of Abbreviations

Archives and Libraries

AGI	Archivo General de Indias, Seville
AGN	Archivo General de la Nación, Mexico City
AGN, RCD	Reales Cédulas Duplicados
AGN, RCO	Reales Cédulas Originales
AHCM	Archivo Histórico de la Ciudad de México
AHN	Archivo Histórico Nacional, Madrid
BNM	Biblioteca Nacional, Madrid
BNMex	Biblioteca Nacional, Mexico City
BPR	Biblioteca del Palacio Real, Madrid
RAH	Real Academia de la Historia, Madrid

Other Abbreviations

BAE	*Biblioteca de Autores Españoles*
cap.	*capítulo*
CDHH	*Colección de Documentos para la Historia de la Formación Social de Hispanoamérica, 1493–1810*
exp.	*expediente*
leg.	*legajo*
lib.	*libro*
núm.	*número*
Recopilación	*Recopilación de leyes de los reinos de las Indias*
tít.	*título*

Endnotes

Introduction*

1. Antonio García de León, ed., *EZLN: Documentos y comunicados* (México, 1994), pp. 49–66.
2. Enrique Krauze, "Will Mexico Break Free?," *The New York Times*, 5 July 1997, p. 23. Here, Krauze is simply repeating those same ideas that Octavio Paz had expressed, in forceful and poetic terms, some 25 years ago. For Paz, "The Spanish viceroys and the Mexican presidents are the successors of the Aztec rulers. … [T]here is a bridge that reaches from *tlatoani* to viceroy, viceroy to president." See his "Critique of the Pyramid" in *The Labyrinth of Solitude and Other Writings* (New York, 1985), pp. 298, 315, 324. Like Marcos, both Paz and Krauze interpret the history of Mexico as a continuum that, in their case, goes back to the remote times of the Aztec empire.
3. Irving A. Leonard, *Baroque Times in Old Mexico: Seventeenth-Century Persons, Places, and Practices* (Westport, CN, 1959), p. 220.
4. Among these biographical studies are Arthur S. Aiton, *Antonio de Mendoza, First Viceroy of New Spain* (Durham, NC, 1927); Roberto Levillier, *Don Francisco de Toledo, supremo organizador del Perú* (Madrid, 1935); Arthur F. Zimmerman, *Francisco de Toledo, Fifth Viceroy of Peru, 1569–1581* (New York, 1938); Justina Sarabia Viejo, *Don Luis de Velasco, virrey de Nueva España, 1550–1564* (Sevilla, 1978); Antonio F. García-Abasolo, *Martín Enríquez y la reforma de 1568 en Nueva España* (Sevilla, 1983); María Pilar Gutiérrez Lorenzo, *De la corte de Castilla al virreinato de México: el conde de Galve (1653–1697)* (Guadalajara, Spain, 1993); Pilar Latasa Vassallo, *Administración virreinal en el Perú: Gobierno del marqués de Montesclaros (1607–1615)* (Madrid, 1997). The most complete biographical and institutional study of New Spain's viceroys is, no doubt, José Ignacio Rubio Mañé, *El virreinato*, 3 vols. (México, [1955] 1992). The most exhaustive institutional studies of the

---

*Spanish spellings have been modernized throughout the book. All translations are the author's unless otherwise indicated.

257

viceregal figure within the Spanish monarchy are those of Jesús Lalinde Abadía, *La institución virreinal en Cataluña (1471–1716)* (Barcelona, 1964) and "El régimen virreino-senatorial en Indias," *Anuario de Historia del Derecho Español* (Madrid, 1967). A recent study of a Spanish viceroy oriented more toward social history is Carlos José Hernando Sánchez, *Castilla y Nápoles en el siglo XVI: el virrey Pedro de Toledo: linaje, estado y cultura (1532–1553)* (Valladolid, 1994).

5. Charles Gibson, *Spain in America* (New York, 1966); Richard E. Boyer, "Absolutism vs. Corporatism in New Spain: The Administration of the Marqués de Gelves, 1621–1624," *The International History Review* IV, no. 4 (1982): 475–503.

6. John H. Elliott, "Spain and Its Empire in the Sixteenth and Seventeenth Centuries," in *Spain and Its World, 1500–1700: Selected Essays* (New Haven, CT, 1989), pp. 7–26; "Spain and America before 1700," in *Colonial Spanish America*, edited by Leslie Bethell (Cambridge, U.K., 1984), p. 63.

7. John Leddy Phelan, "Authority and Flexibility in the Spanish Imperial Bureaucracy," *Administrative Science Quarterly* 5 (1960): 47–65; Peggy K. Liss, *Mexico Under Spain, 1521–1556: Society and the Origins of Nationality* (Chicago, 1975), pp. 56–68.

8. John Leddy Phelan, *The Kingdom of Quito in the Seventeenth Century: Bureaucratic Politics in the Spanish Empire* (Madison, 1967), p. 126; Mario Góngora, *Studies in the Colonial History of Spanish America* (Cambridge, U.K., 1975), p. 98.

9. The historian who has no doubt presented these ideas in a most elaborate way with regard to Spain is José Antonio Maravall in his *Estado moderno y mentalidad social, siglos XV a XVII* (Madrid, 1972), especially vol. I, pp. 13–86. Similarly, Immanuel Wallerstein is also the author of a highly influential, though controversial, study that emphasizes the protagonism of the state from the sixteenth century onward. He contends that the rise of the state and absolutism as its ideology were essential components of the development of modern capitalism. Thus, the emergence of a transnational economic system found its political strength in the creation of strong state machineries, the "core" states being the most centralized. See his *The Modern World-System: Capitalist Agriculture and the Origins of the European World-Economy in the Sixteenth Century* (New York, 1974), pp. 133–162. For a critique of Wallerstein's "Eurocentrism," though not of his "statism," see Steve J. Stern, "Feudalism, Capitalism, and the World-System in the Perspective of Latin America and the Caribbean," *American Historical Review* 93 (Oct. 1988): 829–872.

10. Francisco Tomás y Valiente is perhaps the historian who has presented these ideas in the most straightforward way. See his "La España de Felipe IV. El gobierno de la monarquía y la administración de los reinos en la España del siglo XVII," in *Historia de España Menéndez Pidal*, 2nd ed., edited by F. Tomás y Valiente (Madrid, 1990), vol. XXIII, pp. 3–19. Among the English-speaking historians, Perry Anderson is the author of a highly influential book on the

emergence of the "absolutist state" in the sixteenth century. Using a Marxist approach, he explains the absolutist state as a modernized instrument for the maintenance of noble domination over the rural masses in the epoch of transition to capitalism. See his *Lineages of the Absolutist State* (London, 1974), especially pp. 15–42.

11. See, for example, Horst Pietschmann, *El Estado y su evolución al principio de la colonización española de América* (México, 1989), pp. 161–163; John Leddy Phelan, *The Kingdom of Quito*, pp. 321–337; Enrique Semo, *Historia del capitalismo en México. Los orígenes, 1521–1763* (México, 1973), pp. 65–70; Charles Gibson, *Spain in America*, pp. 90–91; J.M. Ots Capdequí, *El Estado español en las Indias* (México, 1941), pp. 44–45.

12. John Lynch, "The Institutional Framework of Colonial Spanish America," *Journal of Latin American Studies* 24 (1992): 69–77. Speaking more specifically of the colonial state in Peru, Kenneth J. Andrien has argued that, though the Spanish government was able to create a powerful state apparatus in colonial Peru thanks to the reforms of viceroy Toledo in the 1560s, this was a passing phenomenon, as many of the Toledan reforms were undermined by local interests, both Spanish and Andean. By the mid-seventeenth century, the colonial state had become weak, corrupt, and inefficient. See his "Spaniards, Andeans, and the Early Colonial State in Peru," in *Transatlantic Encounters: Europeans and Andeans in the Sixteenth Century*, edited by K. J. Andrien and R. Adorno (Berkeley, 1991), pp. 121–148. This is basically the same conclusion previously reached by John H. Coatsworth in his analysis of the colonial state in the eighteenth century. For him, the colonial state was effective only in extracting resources, regulating economic activity, and discouraging economic growth. In everything else, the colonial state was extremely weak by European standards of the time; it was just "an empty Pandora's Box." See J.H. Coatsworth, "The Limits of Colonial Absolutism: The State in Eighteenth Century Mexico," in *Essays in the Political, Economic and Social History of Colonial Latin America*, edited by Karen Spalding (Newark, 1982), pp. 25–41.

13. Among the most influential works of the *dependentista* approach are Fernando Henrique Cardoso and Enzo Faletto, *Dependencia y desarrollo en América Latina* (México City, 1969); Andre Gunder Frank, *Capitalism and Underdevelopment in Latin America: Historical Studies of Chile and Brazil* (New York, 1969); and Stanley J. Stein and Barbara H. Stein, *The Colonial Heritage of Latin America: Essays on Economic Dependence in Perspective* (New York, 1970).

14. William B. Taylor, "Between Global Process and Local Knowledge: An Inquiry into Early Latin American Social History, 1500–1900," in *Reliving the Past: The Worlds of Social History*, edited by O. Zunz (Chapel Hill, 1985), pp. 115–190.

15. Ibid., p. 141.

16. This is so much so that it is common to argue that, once the population of a limited area is subject to government, it is reasonable to speak of the existence of a state. Thus, Bernard Guenée has contended that, even if the political organizations that existed in Europe in the late Middle Ages did not look very much like "states," that does not mean that no states existed in Europe at that

time. According to him, we should avoid the trap of enclosing the concept of the "state" in a definition that is too exact or too modern. See his *States and Rulers in Later Medieval Europe*, translated by Juliet Vale (Oxford, 1985), p. 6. Similarly, Charles Tilly contends that, "States have been the world's largest and most powerful organizations for more than five thousand years." He defines the state as a coercion-wielding organization that is distinct from household and kinship groups and which exercises "clear priority in some respects over all other organizations within substantial territories." See *Coercion, Capital, and European States, AD 990–1990* (Oxford, 1990), p. 1. While in these definitions the state has been completely objectified and naturalized, becoming an entity outside of history, I believe that the "state" has a history and belongs to a very specific historical moment.

17. Philip Abrams, "Notes on the Difficulty of Studying the State (1977)," *Journal of Historical Sociology* 1, no. 1 (1988): 58–89.

18. For a critique of this approach, see Dietrich Gerhard, *Old Europe: A Study of Continuity, 1000–1800* (New York, 1981), pp. 2–3; António M. Hespanha, *Vísperas del Leviatán. Instituciones y poder político (Portugal, siglo XVII)*, translated by F.J. Bouza Álvarez (Madrid, 1989), pp. 19–37.

19. An example of this kind of approach is Philip Corrigan and Derek Sayer's *The Great Arch: English State Formation as Cultural Revolution* (Oxford, 1985). Theirs is a study of the growth of the state in England since the Middle Ages, their main argument being that the state emerges through a cultural revolution and that state formation is an essential aspect of capitalist civilization. The problem with their study is that they write, as one critic has put it, as if they were looking back down the tunnels of history, identifying all the continuities in this seemingly unstoppable process of state formation with the benefit of hindsight. Here, all roads lead to the capitalist state, even those of the remote Middle Ages. The fact is that the more one favors a diachronic model for explaining change, the more one tends to presume the presence of an order or structure in historical reality that exerts an independent influence on the behavior of human agents. See H.V. Emy's review of *The Great Arch*, in *History and Theory* 26, no. 2 (1987): 213–222.

20. For an influential study that implicitly made this assumption, see Charles Tilly, ed., *The Formation of National States in Western Europe* (Princeton, 1975). More recently, Tilly has criticized his own approach for assuming that Europe's genuine experiences of state formation belonged to France, Great Britain, and a few other countries, while other national experiences constituted failures, deviations, or derivative cases. See his *Coercion, Capital, and European States*, chaps. 1 and 2; also, "The Long Run of European State Formation," in *Visions sur le développement des États européens. Théories et historiographies de l'État moderne*, edited by W. Blockmans and J.-Ph. Genet (Rome, 1993), pp. 137–150.

21. See Pablo Fernández Albaladejo's critique of this approach in his "Epílogo" to the Spanish edition of Helmut G. Koenigsberger, *La práctica del Imperio*, translated by Graciela Soriano (Madrid, 1989), pp. 245–258. This is also

probably one of the main reasons why so many historians are so prone to emphasize the "medieval" aspects of colonial Latin America as a way to explain its "failure" to modernize. No one has expressed this idea in a more flamboyant manner than Irving A. Leonard, who contends that, in America, Spain created a "neomedieval regime" that was "already an anachronism." He concurs with the opinion that argues the Spaniards "never emerged from the imaginative period, they never developed the economic type, and in consequence they never centralized as the English centralized." See his *Baroque Times in Old Mexico: Seventeenth-Century Persons, Places, and Practices* (Westport, CT, 1959), pp. 10, 32, 35, 219. Richard M. Morse is another author who has emphasized the "medieval" aspects of colonial Spanish America. See his influential article "The Heritage of Colonial Latin America," in *The Founding of New Societies: Studies in the History of the United States, Latin America, South Africa, Canada and Australia*, edited by L. Hartz (New York, 1964), pp. 123–177. The most complete study of the "medieval" traits of colonial Mexico can be found in Luis Weckmann, *La herencia medieval de México* (Mexico, 1983). Weckmann, however, does not present, at least explicitly, this "medieval heritage" as an unsurmountable obstacle for the modernization of Mexico.

22. Quentin Skinner, "The State," in *Political Innovation and Conceptual Change*, edited by T. Ball et al. (Cambridge, U.K., 1989), pp. 90–131. The fundamental conceptual shift to a relatively impersonal idea of the "state" first took place in France and England, where it slowly began to take shape in the course of the sixteenth century. See Quentin Skinner's *The Foundations of Modern Political Thought*, vol. 2: *The Age of Reformation* (Cambridge, U.K., 1978), pp. 354–358. But, even seventeenth-century English republican writers such as John Milton or James Harrington hardly ever use the term "state" when speaking of the institutions of civil government. They almost always prefer the term "commonwealth" to signify the body of citizens or the forms of political authority. Similarly, opponents of absolutism such as François Hotman or John Locke assume that the apparatus of government amounts to nothing more than a reflection of, and a device for upholding, the sovereignty of the people. No effective contrast is drawn between the power of the people and the power of the state, and they continue to invoke the terms *civitas* or *respublica* to refer to the apparatus of civil government (translated as "city" or "commonwealth"). See Skinner, "The State," pp. 113–116.

23. "En otra manera se toma por el gobierno de la persona real y de su reino, para su conservación, reputación y aumento." See Sebastián de Covarrubias Orozco, *Tesoro de la lengua castellana o española* (Madrid, [1611] 1979).

24. "Es todo lo que pertenece al gobierno, conservación, aumento y reputación del estado del reino y príncipe," in *Diccionario de Autoridades (1726–1739)*, facsimile ed. (Madrid, 1963). In relation to this, John Elliott has pointed out that the word "state" was generally absent from the vocabulary of seventeenth-century Spanish rulers. Even though they might have used terms such as "matters of state" or "reason of state," they did not employ the word "state" to designate

a transcendent entity. See his *Richelieu and Olivares* (Cambridge, U.K., 1984), pp. 42–48. For a discussion of the meanings and uses of the word *Estado* in sixteenth- and seventeenth-century Spain, see Jesús Lalinde Abadía, "España y la monarquía universal (en torno al concepto de 'Estado moderno')," *Quaderni Fiorentini per la Storia del Pensiero Giuridico Moderno*, vol. 15 (1986): 109–138. For a critique of Maravall's ideas on the modern state, see Bartolomé Clavero, "Institución política y derecho: acerca del concepto historiográfico de "Estado moderno,'" *Revista de Estudios Políticos* 19 (1981): 43–57.

25. For these arguments, see Bartolomé Clavero, *Tantas personas como estados: Por una antropología política de la historia europea* (Madrid, 1986), pp. 53–105; *Razón de Estado, razón de individuo, razón de historia* (Madrid, 1991), pp. 39–45.

26. Gerhard, *Old Europe*, pp. 80–95, 108; Julius Kirshner, "Introduction: The State Is "Back In,'" in *The Origins of the State in Italy, 1300–1600*, edited by J. Kirshner (Chicago, 1996), pp. 1–10.

27. See Frances A. Yates, *Astraea: The Imperial Theme in the Sixteenth Century* (London, 1975), especially pp. 1–28; Roy Strong, *Art and Power: Renaissance Festivals, 1450–1650* (Berkeley, 1973), pp. 65–97; David Armitage, ed., *Theories of Empire, 1450–1800* (Aldershot, 1998), chaps. 2–5; Anthony Pagden, *Lords of All the World: Ideologies of Empire in Spain, Britain and France, c. 1500–1800* (New Haven, CT, 1995), pp. 29–62; James Muldoon, *Empire and Order: The Concept of Empire, 800–1800* (New York, 1999), especially the Introduction and chap. 6; J.G.A. Pocock, "States, Republics, and Empires: The American Founding in Early Modern Perspective," in *Conceptual Change and the Constitution*, edited by T. Ball and J.G.A. Pocock (Lawrence, KS, 1988), pp. 55–77.

28. Juan de Solórzano Pereira, *Política indiana*, edited by M.A. Ochoa Brun (Madrid, [1647] 1972), lib. IV, cap. IV, no. 10. One of the most straightforward expressions of this providential destiny can be found in Fray Juan de Salazar, *Política española (1619)*, edited by M. Herrero García (Madrid, 1997), pp. 41–46, 185–188, 199–231. On this subject, see Pablo Fernández Albaladejo, "'Imperio de por sí': la reformulación del poder universal en la temprana Edad Moderna," in his *Fragmentos de Monarquía. Trabajos de historia política* (Madrid, 1992), pp. 168–184; idem, ""Rey Católico': Gestación y metamorfosis de un título," in *Repubblica e virtù: pensiero politico e monarchia cattolica fra XVI e XVII secolo*, edited by Ch. Continisio and C. Mozzarelli (Roma, 1995), pp. 109–120; James Muldoon, *The Americas in the Spanish World Order: The Justification for Conquest in the Seventeenth Century* (Philadelphia, 1994), pp. 143–164; David Brading, "La monarquía católica," in *De los imperios a las naciones: Iberoamérica*, edited by A. Annino et al. (Zaragoza, 1994), pp. 19–28.

29. John H. Elliott, "A Europe of Composite Monarchies," *Past & Present* 137 (Nov. 1992): 48–71; also, "The Spanish Monarchy and the Kingdom of Portugal, 1580–1640," in *Conquest and Coalescence: The Shaping of the State in Early Modern Europe*, edited by M. Greengrass (London, 1991), pp. 48–67;

also, Gerhard, *Old Europe*, p. 75. This logic would explain the resounding failure of attempts, such as that of the count-duke of Olivares, at a greater integration of the different territories of the monarchy.

30. Here I am paraphrasing Dale Hoak's ideas in his introduction to *Tudor Political Culture* (Cambridge, U.K., 1995), p. 2.

31. I follow here Keith Baker's understanding of the concept of political culture as the set of discourses and symbolic practices characterizing the political activity of any given community, this activity being understood as the articulation, negotiation, implementation, and enforcement of the competing claims that individuals and groups make one upon another. See Keith M. Baker, ed., *The French Revolution and the Creation of Modern Political Culture*, vol. 1: *The Political Culture of the Old Regime* (Oxford, 1987), pp. xi–xiii.

32. Skinner, "The State," pp. 124–126.

33. Michel Foucault, *Power/Knowledge: Selected Interviews and Other Writings, 1972–1977*, translated by Colin Gordon et al. (New York, 1980), pp. 104–105, 119. Obviously, I cannot agree with Charles Tilly's argument, as presented in *Coercion, Capital, and European States*, according to which coercion (understood as the permanent presence of an armed force that constitutes the largest single branch of government) was the central element of the premodern state. This argument can hardly be applied to colonial Spanish America, where there was never a standing army or regular police force. This is not to deny that coercion existed, as it indeed did, but permanent coercion was not a central aspect of the Spanish colonial regime, at least until the second half of the eighteenth century.

34. These are William Beik's arguments in his *Absolutism and Society in Seventeenth-Century France: State Power and Provincial Aristocracy in Languedoc* (Cambridge, U.K., 1985), pp. 179–187. Although both Foucault's and Beik's comments refer to France, I believe that they very well apply to New Spain, too.

35. Giorgio Chittolini, "The 'Private,' the 'Public,' the 'State,'" in *The Origins of the State in Italy*, edited by J. Kirshner (Chicago, 1996), pp. 34–61.

36. A large literature on the concept of colonial discourse is available. I have found especially useful Edward Said, *Orientalism* (London, 1978) and *Culture and Imperialism* (New York, 1993); Peter Hulme, *Colonial Encounters: Europe and the Native Caribbean, 1492–1797* (London, 1986); Patricia Seed, "Colonial and Postcolonial Discourse," *Latin American Research Review* 26, no. 3 (1991): 181–200; Mary Louise Pratt, *Imperial Eyes: Travel Writing and Transculturation* (London, 1992); David Spurr, *The Rhetoric of Empire: Colonial Discourse in Journalism, Travel Writing and Imperial Administration* (Durham, 1993); José Rabasa, *Inventing America: Spanish Historiography and the Formation of Eurocentrism* (London, 1993); Nicholas Thomas, *Colonialism's Culture: Anthropology, Travel and Government* (Princeton, 1994).

37. Rolena Adorno, "Reconsidering Colonial Discourse for Sixteenth- and Seventeenth-Century Spanish America," *Latin American Research Review* 28, no. 3 (1993): 139–145.

38. John H. Elliott, "Empire and State in British and Spanish America," in *Le Nouveau Monde, Mondes Nouveaux: L'expérience américaine*, edited by S. Gruzinski and N. Wachtel (Paris, 1996), pp. 370–371. See also Elliott's comments in *Itinerario* 19, no. 2 (1995): 20.

39. This is what J. Jorge Klor de Alva contends in "The Postcolonization of the (Latin) American Experience: A Reconsideration of 'Colonialism,' 'Postcolonialism,' and 'Mestizaje,'" in *After Colonialism: Imperial Histories and Postcolonial Displacements*, edited by Gyan Prakash (Princeton, 1995), pp. 241–275. Klor de Alva also includes the mestizos among the population of European descent, thus characterizing them as a sector to which the term "colonialism" should not be applied. I think, however, that he is simplifying the position of the mestizos excessively. As we will see, the place they occupied in the colonial polity was as ambiguous as their ethnic and racial identities. Though in theory forming part of the Spanish community, colonial discourse would very often conceptualize them in the same ways as the indigenous population.

40. Consulta of the Council of Castile of 24 May 1641, quoted in María José del Río Barredo, *Madrid, Urbs Regia. La capital ceremonial de la Monarquía Católica* (Madrid, 2000), p. 211. Interestingly, Juan de Solórzano would use the same argument to contend that the Council of the Indies should have precedence over that of Flanders. Because the American territories had been united to Castile *accesoriamente*, reasoned Solórzano, the "Empire of the Indies" and the Council that ruled it could be considered as being part of the Council of Castile, thus it should have the same preeminence and prerogatives. See his *Memorial y discurso de las razones que se ofrecen para que el Real y Supremo Consejo de las Indias deba preceder en todos los actos públicos al que llaman de Flandes* (Madrid, 1629), fos. 20v–21v.

41. Mark Thurner, "After Spanish Rule: Writing Another After," in *After Spanish Rule: Postcolonial Predicaments of the Americas*, edited by Mark Thurner and Andrés Guerrero (Durham, 2003), p. 43. For Klor de Alva, the term "colonialism" should be applied only to those sectors of the population that, under Spanish rule, continued to live as "Indians." See his "The Postcolonization of the (Latin) American Experience," pp. 255–256. See also Gustavo Verdesio, "Colonialism Now and Then: Colonial Latin American Studies in the Light of the Predicament of Latin Americanism," in *Colonialism Past and Present: Reading and Writing about Colonial Latin America Today*, edited by A.F. Bolaños and G. Verdesio (Albany, 2002), p. 6.

42. José Rabasa, *Writing Violence on the Northern Frontier: The Historiography of Sixteenth-Century New Mexico and Florida and the Legacy of Conquest* (Durham, 2000), pp. 16–20.

Chapter 1

1. Juan de Solórzano y Pereira, *Política indiana*, edited by M.A. Ochoa Brun (Madrid, [1647] 1972), lib. V, cap. XIII, nos. 2–5. Similarly, in the *Recopilación de leyes de los reinos de las Indias* (Madrid, 1680; I have used the 1791

edition), lib. III, tít. III, ley ii, it is stated that the viceroys of New Spain and Peru "shall provide all that We could do and provide of any quality or condition in the provinces under their charge as if they were governed by Our person in all that they are not specifically prohibited from doing." This law concludes by asserting that "all that [the viceroys] shall do, order and command in Our name and under Our power and authority, We shall consider as firm, permanent, and valid forever and ever."

2. Throughout this study, I use the term "Spanish monarchy" rather than "Spanish empire," as officially a "Spanish Empire" never existed (in the early modern period, the only legally recognized empire was the Holy Roman Empire).

3. *Recopilación*, lib. III, tít. III, leyes iii, iiii, v; José Ignacio Rubio Mañé, *El virreinato I* (México, [1955] 1992), chaps. VI and VIII.

4. *Recopilación*, lib. III, tít. III, ley lxxi. See also Rubio Mañé, *El virreinato I*, pp. 199–201.

5. *Recopilación*, lib. III, tít. III, ley ii. For Juan de Palafox y Mendoza, who was appointed bishop of Puebla in the mid-seventeenth century and served as acting viceroy for a year, the office of viceroy of New Spain (because the viceroy did not need to worry about neighboring kingdoms) was basically about keeping those provinces in peace and justice, taking good care of the king's treasury, protecting the Indians, promptly dispatching the fleets, defending the coastline from enemy invasions, and preventing the outbreak of tumults. "Relación de Juan de Palafox y Mendoza" [1642?], in *Los virreyes españoles en América durante el gobierno de la Casa de Austria, México IV*, BAE, vol. CCLXXVI, p. 39.

6. Solórzano, *Política indiana*, lib. V, cap. XIII: "De las cosas que pueden y no pueden hacer los virreyes de las Indias, conforme a los títulos, poderes e instrucciones que llevan para estos cargos."

7. Ibid., nos. 12–15, 19, 22, 26–29, 41. As something specific to the American territories, Solórzano observes that the orders, decrees, and sentences (in the case of the Mexican Indian court) of the viceroys can be appealed to the audiencias. Ibid., no. 40.

8. Ibid., nos. 30–31.

9. Quoted in James Tully, "The Pen Is a Mighty Sword: Quentin Skinner's Analysis of Politics," in *Meaning and Context: Quentin Skinner and His Critics*, edited by James Tully (Princeton, 1988), p. 9.

10. Quentin Skinner, *The Foundations of Modern Political Thought*, vol. 1: *The Renaissance* (Cambridge, U.K., 1978), p. xiii. Ibid., "Meaning and Understanding in the History of Ideas," in *Meaning and Context: Quentin Skinner and His Critics*, p. 48.

11. For an account of the events and political context that led to this killing, see John Day, Bruno Anatra, and Lucetta Scaraffia, *La Sardegna medioevale e moderna* (Torino, 1984), pp. 623–637; Antonello Mattone, "Le istituzione e le forme di governo," in *Storia dei sardi e della Sardegna*, vol. 3: *L'Età Moderna: dagli aragonesi alla fine del dominio spagnolo*, edited by B. Anatra, A. Mattone, and R. Turtas (Milan, 1987), pp. 217–252; Luis Antonio Ribot García, "La

España de Carlos II," in *Historia de España Menéndez Pidal*, edited by P. Molas Ribalta (Madrid, 1993), vol. XXVIII, pp. 179–203.

12. Rafael de Vilosa, *Disertación jurídica y política sobre si es delito de lesa majestad in primo capite matar a un virrey* (Madrid, 1670), pp. 2, 29, 31–32, 35.

13. In the royal decrees specifically addressed to the viceroys, the king always calls the viceroy "my cousin" or "my relative." This was also a prerogative of the grandees.

14. Vilosa, *Disertación jurídica y política*, pp. 104–128.

15. The fundamental study from which I have drawn these ideas is Ernest Kantorowicz, *The King's Two Bodies: A Study in Medieval Theology* (Princeton, 1957), especially chap. V. For the medieval origins of the concept in Spain, see also José Antonio Maravall, *Estudios de historia del pensamiento español* (Madrid, 1983), pp. 181–199.

16. Kantorowicz, *The King's Two Bodies*, pp. 270–271.

17. Michael Walzer, "On the Role of Symbolism in Political Thought," *Political Science Quarterly* 82, no. 2 (June 1967): 193–196.

18. *Las Siete Partidas del sabio rey don Alonso el Nono, nuevamente glosadas por el licenciado Gregorio López del Consejo Real de Indias de Su Majestad*, 7 vols., facsimile ed. ([Salamanca, 1555] Madrid, 1974), Segunda Partida, tít. I, ley V.

19. See Alonso Ordóñez, *Tratado del gobierno de los príncipes del angélico doctor Santo Tomás de Aquino* (Madrid, 1625), fos. 1–6, 103v–105. I have used the seventeenth-century Spanish translation of *De Regimine Principum*, although I am aware of the possible inexactitudes and misreadings of the translation; however, I am more concerned here with discerning the way Aquinas was read and understood in early modern Spain than with establishing an accurate translation of the original.

20. For a discussion of the classical and medieval origins of these beliefs, see Quentin Skinner, *The Foundations of Modern Political Thought*, vol. 1: *The Renaissance*, chap. 3.

21. Juan de Santa María, *Tratado de república y policía cristiana para reyes y príncipes, y para los que en el gobierno tienen sus veces* (Madrid, 1615), pp. 7–8. Further references will be given in the text.

22. On the similarities between political government and the human body, see also Jerónimo de Cevallos, *Arte real para el buen gobierno de los reyes y príncipes y de sus vasallos, en el cual se refieren las obligaciones de cada uno, con los principales documentos para el buen gobierno* (Toledo, 1623), fos. 1–5. On the king as head of the body politic, see Andrés Mendo, *Príncipe perfecto y ministros ajustados: documentos políticos y morales en emblemas* (Madrid, 1656?), documento LX, pp. 47–51.

23. The author of the manuscript explicitly states that the "present circumstances" do not allow him to reveal his name. On this debate, see António de Oliveira, *Poder e oposição política em Portugal no período filipino (1580–1640)* (Lisboa, 1990), pp. 20–27.

24. BNM ms. 904 (*Apología del gobierno por virreyes para el reino de Portugal*) (n.d.), fos. 268–270.

25. Solórzano, *Política indiana*, lib. V, cap. XII, nos. 1–9. On the power and authority a viceroy possessed as the king's image, see also Vilosa, *Disertación jurídica y política*, pp. 76–94; Sebastián de Cortiada, *Discurso sobre la jurisdicción del Exmo. Sr. Virrey y del Exmo. Sr. Capitán General del principado de Cataluña* (Barcelona, 1676), pp. 1–8, 11–19, 49–51, 180–187.

26. Arches were also built in other cities, such as Tlaxcala or Puebla, but I limit my study to only those of Mexico City, which, as the center of the viceroyalty, always displayed the most impressive structures. For a study of the Puebla arches, see Nancy H. Fee, "La Entrada Angelopolitana: Ritual and Myth in the Viceregal Entry in Puebla de los Angeles," *The Americas* 52, no. 3 (Jan. 1996): 283–320. The first known printed description of a viceregal arch was published in 1625 to welcome the marquis of Cerralvo. The reasons why the descriptions of viceregal arches began to be printed are not clear. Magdalena Chocano has argued that showing to the world the loyalty and nobility of Mexico City was a way to recover the tarnished image of the city after the tumult of 1624. See Magdalena Chocano Mena, *La fortaleza docta. Elite letrada y dominación social en México colonial (siglos XVI–XVII)* (Barcelona, 2000), pp. 270–271.

27. In his analysis of the *Neptuno alegórico*, the arch that Sor Juana designed in 1680, Octavio Paz describes it as a "perfect example of the admirable and abominable baroque prose," and a "work done to order and an example of court adulation." Nevertheless, Paz acknowledges that the work is valuable as a "document for the history of ideas in the Hispanic world." See his *Sor Juana Inés de la Cruz o las trampas de la fe* (México, 1982), pp. 215 and 240.

28. A recent study of the Mexico City arches is Linda A. Curcio-Nagy, *The Great Festivals of Colonial Mexico City: Performing Power and Identity* (Albuquerque, 2004). For an iconographical description of those same arches, see José Miguel Morales y Folguera, *Cultura simbólica y arte efímero en Nueva España* (Granada, 1991).

29. On the royal entry arch as "mirror of princes," see Roy Strong, *Art and Power: Renaissance Festivals, 1450–1650* (Berkeley, 1984), pp. 7–11.

30. Alonso de Medina, *Espejo de príncipes católicos y gobernadores políticos. Erigióle en arco triunfal la Santa Iglesia Metropolitana de México a la entrada del … conde de Salvatierra … en el cual se ven copiadas sus virtudes, heroicos hechos y prudencial gobierno* (México, 1642).

31. Ibid., p. 3. In the political literature of the period, it was quite common to present the figure of Joseph as a "mirror of viceroys." See, for example, Vilosa, *Disertación jurídica y política*, pp. 77, 95; Diego de Avendaño, *Thesaurus Indicus*, edited by A. Muñoz García ([Antwerp, 1668] Pamplona, 2001), pp. 383, 387.

32. See, for example, Matías de Bocanegra, *Teatro jerárquico de la luz, pira cristiano política del gobierno que … la imperial ciudad de México erigió en la real portada que dedicó al … conde de Salvatierra … en su feliz venida por virrey gobernador y capitán general de esta Nueva España* (México, 1642), fo. 1v; Carlos de Sigüenza y Góngora, *Teatro de virtudes políticas que constituyen a*

un príncipe, advertidas en los monarcas antiguos del mexicano imperio (México, [1680] 1928), p. 13; Sor Juana Inés de la Cruz, *Neptuno alegórico, océano de colores, simulacro político que erigió la ... Iglesia Metropolitana de Méjico en las lucidas alegóricas ideas de un arco triunfal que consagró obsequiosa y dedicó amante a la feliz entrada del ... conde de Paredes, marqués de la Laguna ...* (México, [1680] 1992), p. 779.

33. "Un claro espejo (Señor / Excelentísimo) intenta / presentar a vuestros ojos / aquesta príncipe iglesia / en que vea a sus umbrales / retratada su grandeza, / copiada su majestad, / bosquejada su excelencia, ... / Contémplese en este vidrio, / en este cristal se vea, / no para enmendar defectos, / para mirar, sí, perfecta / la imagen que le retrata, / la historia que le compendia, / los hechos que le acreditan, / y de su forma la idea." Medina, *Espejo de príncipes católicos*, pp. 21–22. This is also the meaning of the title — "Portada alegórica, espejo político" — given by its anonymous author to the description of the arch that the cathedral chapter erected to receive the count of Alba de Liste in 1650. The author, while acknowledging that the theme of the arch is an "allegorical fable" (that of Hercules), declares that his main objective is to describe the qualities that constitute the perfect prince. See *Portada alegórica, espejo político, que la augusta y muy esclarecida Iglesia Metropolitana de México dedicó al ... conde de Alba de Liste ...* (México, 1650), fo. 2.

34. See the introduction in Frederick Goldin, *The Mirror of Narcissus in the Courtly Love Lyric* (Ithaca, 1967). Also, Marianne Shapiro, "Mirror and Portrait: The Structure of Il Libro del Cortegiano," *The Journal of Medieval and Renaissance Studies* 5 (1975): 41–44.

35. Goldin, *The Mirror of Narcissus*, pp. 14–15.

36. Sor Juana, *Neptuno alegórico*, p. 779. See also the Dedication of *Portada alegórica*.

37. On the viceroy as prince of the province he rules, see Vilosa, *Disertación jurídica y política*, pp. 94–103. On the viceroy as minister, see *Conclusiones políticas de los ministros* (Madrid, 1636), pp. 4, 6, 15–16.

38. This is the definition given by the *Diccionario de Autoridades (1726–1739)*, facsimile ed. (Madrid, 1963).

39. This is precisely what, in a rather blunt way, the marquis of Villamanrique was told by the rector of the Dominican school of Puebla. The cleric accused the viceroy of pretending to be feared as if he were God, while he was but a servant of the king and his lieutenant who could be removed and replaced at any time. "Carta del padre fray Francisco Ximénez ... al virrey marqués de Villamanrique," in *Cartas de religiosos de Nueva España*, edited by J. García Icazbalceta (México, 1886), p. 162.

40. See, for example, *Espejo de príncipes católicos*, p. 1, where the author asserts that the reason why the cathedral erected a triumphal arch was to show the "jubilation and joy with which it received its new viceroy and patron." Also, the anonymous author of the arch commissioned by the ecclesiastical chapter to receive the duke of Alburquerque at the cathedral doors claims that, with his rule, the duke brings "moral fertility and joy to all the empire." See *Marte*

católico, astro político, planeta de héroes y ascendiente de príncipes, que en las lucidas sombras de una triunfal portada ofrece, representa, dedica la ... Iglesia Metropolitana de México al Exmo. Señor Don Francisco Fernández de la Cueva, duque de Alburquerque ... (México, 1653), fo. 9, no. 2.

41. E.H. Gombrich, *Gombrich on the Renaissance*, vol. 2: *Symbolic Images* (London, 1985), pp. 13–14. On how Neoplatonic ideas shaped the art of emblematics, see ibid., pp. 145–150, 158–160, 177–178. In Neoplatonic thought, an image of something is not viewed as a mere sign that stands for an abstract concept; the essence of that concept is somehow embodied in the mysterious shape. An allegory was a revelation of a higher reality whose very presence exerted its mysterious effects. The allegorical image, then, neither symbolizes nor represents the Platonic Idea. It is the Idea itself.

42. Sigüenza y Góngora, *Teatro de virtudes políticas*, p. 61. On Kircher's thought and intellectual significance, see R.J.W. Evans, *The Making of the Habsburg Monarchy, 1550–1700* (Oxford, 1979), pp. 433–442; Frances A. Yates, *Giordano Bruno and the Hermetic Tradition* (Chicago, 1964), pp. 416–423. On Kircher's influence in New Spain, see Ignacio Romero Osorio, *La luz imaginaria: epistolario de Athanasius Kircher con los novohispanos* (México, 1993).

43. When the disciples asked Jesus why he spoke in parables, he answered: "Because it is given unto you to know the mysteries of the kingdom of heaven, but to them it is not given. ...Because they seeing see not; and hearing they hear not, neither do they understand" (St. Mathew, 13, 10–13).

44. Sor Juana, *Neptuno alegórico*, pp. 777–778. On Sor Juana's Neoplatonic ideas, see Octavio Paz, *Sor Juana Inés de la Cruz*, pp. 220–228. In the case of viceregal arches, in fact, it is doubtful that contemporaries (let alone we) could have found their meaning without the aid of the printed descriptions. As Sigmund Jádmar Méndez Bañuelos has argued in "Ingenio y construcción alegórica en dos arcos triunfales novohispanos," in *Carlos de Sigüenza y Góngora. Homenaje 1700–2000*, edited by A. Meyer (México, 2000), p. 45, the images painted on the viceregal arches had an intention both esoteric and exoteric. While their ultimate meaning was only intelligible to a selected few, it was assumed that the common people would be seduced by their magnificent appearance, stirring up in them a sense of wonder and awe at a superior power.

45. See, for example, Octavio Paz, *Sor Juana Inés de la Cruz* (México, 1982), pp. 203–211; Anthony Pagden, *Spanish Imperialism and the Political Imagination* (New Haven, CT, 1990), pp. 93–97; David Brading, *The First America: The Spanish Monarchy, Creole Patriots and the Liberal State, 1492–1867* (Cambridge, U.K., 1991), pp. 362–372.

46. Pagden, *Spanish Imperialism*, p. 96. For a study of Sigüenza's and Sor Juana's arches, see Méndez Bañuelos, "Ingenio y construcción alegórica," pp. 35–65.

47. Sigüenza, *Teatro de virtudes políticas*, pp. 5–11 and 60–62. For his part, Alonso de Alavés Pinelo, who had been commissioned to design the arch erected by Mexico's municipal council to welcome the count of Alba de Liste in 1650, asserted in the printed account that the main subject matter of the

arch was "to express the most important concerns which are the duty of a great prince and governor." According to the author, these duties are vigilance and diligence, the preservation of dignity and decorum, maintaining the abundance of the kingdom, the care of boats and fleets and the security of the coast, punctuality in holding audiences, the preservation of the republic's status quo, observance of the laws, the administration of justice, and giving relief and pleasure to the people. See Alonso de Alavés Pinelo, *Astro mitológico político que en la entrada y recibimiento del ... conde de Alba de Liste ... consagró la ... ciudad de México, metrópoli del imperio occidental, en el arco triunfal que erigió por trofeo a la inmortalidad de su memoria* (México, 1650), fo. 20v.

48. For a study of the sixteenth-century humanist version of the "mirrors for princes" literature, see Skinner, *The Foundations of Modern Political Thought*, vol. 1, pp. 118–128 and 213–243. On the concept of kingship in early modern Spain, especially after the reign of Philip II, see Fernando Bouza Alvarez, "La majestad de Felipe II. Construcción del mito real," in *La corte de Felipe II*, edited by José Martínez Millán (Madrid, 1994), pp. 37–72; Antonio Feros, *Kingship and Favoritism in the Spain of Philip III, 1598–1621* (Cambridge, U.K., 2000), chaps. 1 and 4.

49. Matías de Bocanegra, *Teatro jerárquico de la luz*, fo. 13v. Bocanegra was also the author of *The comedia de San Francisco de Borja*, a play performed in 1640 on the occasion of the visit to the Jesuit school by the recently arrived viceroy the marquis of Villena. This work can also be understood as a variation of the genre of "mirror for princes" literature, though here the embodiment of the idea of the good ruler, in which the new viceroy should see his own image reflected, was a historical figure, Saint Francis Borgia, who, before serving as the third Vicar General of the Society of Jesus, had held the position of viceroy of Catalonia by appointment of the Emperor Charles V. For an analysis of the political content of this work, see Frederick Luciani, "The Comedia de San Francisco de Borja (1640): The Mexican Jesuits and the Education of the Prince," *Colonial Latin American Review* 2 (1993): 121–141.

50. Alavés Pinelo, *Astro mitológico político*, pp. 21, 26.

51. *Elogio panegírico y aclamación festiva, diseño triunfal y pompa laudatoria de Ulises verdadero. Conságrala al Exmo. Señor Don Francisco Fernández de la Cueva, duque de Alburquerque ... la ... imperial ciudad de México ...* (México, 1653), fos. 5v, 6, 14, 18v, 19.

52. Bocanegra, *Teatro jerárquico de la luz*, fo. 18v.

53. On anti-Machiavellian thought, which deeply shaped Spanish political ideas, see J.A. Fernández-Santamaría, *Reason of State and Statecraft in Spanish Political Thought, 1595–1640* (Lanham, MD, 1983), chap. 1; Robert Bireley, *The Counter-Reformation Prince: Anti-Machiavellianism or Catholic Statecraft in Early Modern Europe* (Chapel Hill, 1990).

54. Sor Juana, *Neptuno alegórico*, p. 784; also, pp. 796–798.

55. Sigüenza, *Teatro de virtudes políticas*, pp. 102–107.

56. Bocanegra, *Teatro jerárquico de la luz*, fo. 14.

57. Ibid., fo. 5; *Portada alegórica*, fo. 9.
58. Sor Juana, *Neptuno alegórico*, p. 793.
59. Sigüenza, *Teatro de virtudes políticas*, pp. 85–93. Clemency is the complement of justice, as the anonymous author of the arch erected by the city council to welcome the marquis of Villena made it clear. In the middle of the arch gates, he painted an imperial crown that was being held by Justice on one side and by Mercy on the other. See *Descripción y explicación de la fábrica y empresas del sumptuoso arco que la … ciudad de México, cabeza del occidental imperio, erigió a la feliz entrada y gozoso recibimiento del Exmo. Sr. Don Diego López Pacheco … duque de Escalona, marqués de Villena* (México, 1640), fo. 11r.
60. Sigüenza, *Teatro de virtudes políticas*, p. 133.
61. *Portada alegórica*, fos. 3v, 4, 9.
62. Sor Juana, *Neptuno alegórico*, p. 802.
63. Sigüenza, *Teatro de virtudes políticas*, pp. 70, 73.
64. Counsel to the prince was perhaps the most important subject in the works of early modern political writers. See Skinner, *The Foundations of Modern Political Thought*, vol. 1, pp. 219–220; Feros, *Kingship and Favoritism*, pp. 24–27. In the next chapter, I will elaborate on the theme of a ruler's need for advice and, more specifically, on the very important role played by the *oidores* as viceregal counselors.
65. Alavés Pinelo, *Astro mitológico político*, p. 13.
66. *Elogio panegírico y aclamación festiva*, fos. 12–13.
67. Sigüenza, *Teatro de virtudes políticas*, pp. 124–128.
68. This is Octavio Paz's opinion. See his *Sor Juana Inés de la Cruz*, p. 206.
69. Frederick Luciani has already shown how this is also the role Sor Juana played when she wrote *Amor es más laberinto*, a comedy written in 1689 and performed in the viceregal palace as part of a larger court spectacle to commemorate the birthday of the viceroy, the count of Galve. While the comedy itself can be viewed as a mirror in which the count looks and sees his image reflected in the mythological figure of Teseo (the personification of the idea of the perfect prince), Sor Juana, in the act of showing the mirror to the count, is acting out the counselor's role. See his "Sor Juana's *Amor es más laberinto* as Mythological *Speculum*," in *Estudios sobre escritoras hispánicas en honor de Georgina Sabat-Rivers*, edited by Lou Charnon-Deutsch (Madrid, 1992).
70. Bocanegra, *Teatro jerárquico de la luz*, fo. 7.
71. Medina, *Espejo de príncipes católicos*, pp. 12–13. For a study of the binary images king–viceroy–sun/queen–vicereine–moon, see Víctor Mínguez, *Los reyes solares. Iconografía astral de la monarquía hispánica* (Castelló de la Plana, 2001), chap. 11.
72. *Marte católico*, fos. 3v, 5v, 10. Very little is known of the role played by the vicereines in the social and political life of New Spain, although we know enough as to be able to assert that their role was certainly not a negligible one. As in the case of the Spanish queens, the vicereines created a court parallel to that of the viceroys which wielded considerable power and influence. Perhaps no better example of the significance of this influence is the literary career of

Sor Juana, which always depended upon the favor and the close relationship established between her and several vicereines. See Paz, *Sor Juana Inés de la Cruz*, pp. 248–272; Alessandra Luiselli, "Sobre el peligroso arte de tirar el guante: la ironía de Sor Juana hacia los virreyes de Galve," in *Los empeños: Ensayos en homenaje a Sor Juana Inés de la Cruz* (México, 1995), pp. 93–144. Antonio Rubial García has argued, in fact, that court life in New Spain was shaped, to a great extent, by the vicereines. See his *La plaza, el palacio y el convento: La ciudad de México en el siglo XVII* (México, 1998), p. 86.

73. As Diego de Saavedra Fajardo put it, "*La presencia de los príncipes es fecunda, como la del sol. Todo florece delante della, y todo se marchita y seca en su ausencia*"; see *Empresas políticas*, edited by S. López ([Munich, 1640] Madrid, 1999), empresa 23, p. 385. On the ruler as "political sun" of his subjects, see also Fradrique Moles, *Audiencia de príncipes* (Madrid, 1637), fos. 36v–37r. A late but consummate example of the use of sun imagery to describe Spanish kingship was the catafalque erected in the cathedral of Mexico City for the royal obsequies of Charles II. His designer contended that he had chosen the sun to signify a great ruler because the "sun is the monarch of light, the prince of the stars, and the president of the entire republic of the heavens." See Agustín de Mora, *El sol eclipsado antes de llegar al cenit. Real pira que encendió a la apagada luz del rey N.S.D. Carlos II el … conde de Moctezuma …* (México, 1700), fo. 16r. For a study of these images, see Fernando Checa, "Arquitectura efímera e imagen del poder," in *Sor Juana y su mundo. Una mirada actual*, edited by Sara Poot Herrera (México, 1995), pp. 276–280; Mínguez, *Los reyes solares*, chap. 14.

74. Sigüenza, *Teatro de virtudes políticas*, pp. 56–57.

75. Strong, *Art and Power*, p. 26. See also Mínguez, *Los reyes solares*, chap. 3. At the same time, it should be noted that the allegory created by the author of *Marte católico* only worked in a geocentric world. It is not clear whether the author was simply making use of traditional classical mythology for the purposes of his argument or whether he was still thinking within a geocentric paradigm.

76. Peter Burke, *The Fabrication of Louis XIV* (New Haven, CT, 1992), pp. 127–128.

77. AGN, *Reales Cédulas Originales*, vol. 11, exp. 78, fos. 239–241, the queen regent to the marquis of Mancera, 29 June 1670.

78. For a discussion of this matter, see Feros, *Kingship and Favoritism*, pp. 81–86. The typical invisibility of the Spanish Habsburgs has been recently qualified in relation to Philip III and Philip IV by María José del Río Barredo. She has argued that the frequent appearances of the monarchs in the streets of Madrid to participate in processions, rogations, and other public rituals contradict the idea of a totally invisible king. In reality, she maintains, it was more a matter of discerning when it was the best moment to either hide or publicly manifest the royal person; of finding the right balance between the need for the monarch to be accessible to his subjects and the need to avoid that an excessive informality might cause a diminution of the veneration due

the royal figure. See María José del Río Barredo, *Madrid, Urbs Regia. La capital ceremonial de la Monarquía Católica* (Madrid, 2000), pp. 44–54, 171, 199–204. For different opinions on the advantages and disadvantages of the ruler's invisibility expressed by seventeenth-century writers, see Juan Márquez, *El gobernador cristiano, deducido de las vidas de Moisén y Josué, príncipes del pueblo de Dios* ([Salamanca, 1612] Brussels, 1664), pp. 107, 111, 358–359; Moles, *Audiencia de príncipes*, fos. 17–19, 35; Mendo, *Príncipe perfecto*, documentos LVIII, LXI.

79. BNM, R/19809 (*Pragmática de Felipe II sobre el tratamiento de palabra y por escrito*, 1586).

80. In the 1586 edict, the king had ordered that archbishops and bishops, the grandees and members of the titled nobility, and the capital cities of the different kingdoms that comprised the monarchy all were to be addressed as *Señoría* (Lordship). This also included viceroys and presidents of *audiencias*; however, in the seventeenth century much more elaborate tittles were used, probably because of the need to differentiate the secular from the ecclesiastical authorities and as a way to enhance the symbolic status of the viceregal figure. Thus, from the beginning of the seventeenth century onward, viceroys would be addressed as *Excelentísimo Señor* (Most Excellent Lord), while bishops would be called *Ilustrísimo Señor* (Most Illustrious Lord) or *Señoría Ilustrísima* (Most Illustrious Lordship). For their part, tribunals such as the *audiencias* or *chancillerías* were addressed as *Muy Poderoso Señor* (Very Powerful Lord) when taken as a corporate body, while individual judges were called *Vuestra Merced* (Your Grace or Your Worship). See BNM, R/19809 (*Pragmática de Felipe II sobre el tratamiento de palabra y por escrito*, 1586); BNM, R/22472, *Premáticas que han salido este año de 1600*. On the problems created by the usage of different forms of addressing the viceroys before the consolidation of the title of *Excelentísimo Señor*, see AGI, Mexico 23, no. 53, and Mexico 24, no. 17, the count of Monterrey to the king, 21 April 1596 and 20 December 1598, respectively; AGI, Mexico 25, no. 52, the marquis of Montesclaros to the king, 20 November 1603.

81. In the words of Jerónimo Castillo de Bobadilla, "This attribute and honorific word *señor* is the greatest of all and belongs only to God, who is universal and omnipotent Lord, and to kings, who are His vicars on earth." See his *Política para corregidores y señores de vasallos, en tiempo de paz y de guerra, y para jueces eclesiásticos y seglares, y de sacas, aduanas y de residencias, y sus oficiales, y para regidores y abogados, y del valor de los corregimientos y gobiernos realengos, y de las órdenes* (Amberes, 1704; the treatise was originally published in Madrid in 1597), lib. II, cap. XVI, no. 23.

82. In fact, this was not a Spanish peculiarity but something common in the European world of the time. See, for instance, Michael C. Schoenfeldt, *Prayer and Power: George Herbert and Renaissance Courtship* (Chicago, 1991), where the author analyzes how Herbert turned the language of this world into the medium for his worship of God, especially by constructing his religious poems from conventions used in the secular world to seek rewards from superiors.

83. Jerónimo de Saona, *Jerarquía celestial y terrena y símbolo de los nueve estados de la iglesia militante, con los nueve coros de la triunfante* (Cuenca, 1603), p. 2. For similar ideas, see also the work by the Jesuit Martín de Roa, *Beneficios del Santo Angel de Nuestra Guarda* (Córdoba, 1632), fos. 6v–8r.

84. Saona, *Jerarquía celestial y terrena*, p. 3.

85. Ibid., p. 27. Martín de Roa describes the angels as the "servants of God's household"; see *Beneficios del Santo Angel*, fo. 14v. Angels are divided into three hierarchies, and in each hierarchy are three choirs or orders of angels. From superior to inferior, the names of the nine choirs of angels are seraphs, cherubs, and thrones, who form the first hierarchy (those closest to God); dominions, virtues, and powers, who constitute the second hierarchy; and principalities, archangels, and angels, who comprise the lowest hierarchy and thus are closest to men. According to Saona, this division into three groups has its *raison d'etre*. First of all, it shows a correspondence with the three divine persons, but also, if the "supreme oneness who is God, in whom all angels end up," is added to these nine orders, "it amounts to the number ten, which is most perfect," because if the beginning of all numbers is one, the end is ten, where all the numbers end up. See Saona, *Jerarquía celestial y terrena*, pp. 16, 18–19; Roa, *Beneficios del Santo Angel*, fos. 6v–10v.

86. Saona, *Jerarquía celestial y terrena*, pp. 31–32.

87. In the early modern period, a perfect transliteration of signs takes place between political discourse and religious discourse. On the one hand, the monarch is assimilated to God and he is expected to rule his dominions in the same manner as God rules the world (by rewarding the good and punishing the bad). As Sigüenza y Góngora put it, "*Los príncipes no son tanto vicarios de Dios ... sino una viviente imagen suya, o un Dios terreno.*" What makes this view still more revealing is that he was not talking about kings, but about viceroys. See his *Teatro de virtudes políticas*, p. 14. See also Cevallos, *Arte real*, fo. 159v, for whom the ruler is "a simulacrum of God on earth, whose actions he must follow and imitate." But, at the same time, the figure of God is constructed in the monarch's image and likeness. For contemporaries, it was clear that God ruled from Heaven as the king did from his palace: He was the "monarch" of the universe and was surrounded by the "queen" of Heaven and a celestial "court" inhabited by angels and saints, who enjoyed the singular privilege of their closeness to the divinity. Martín de Roa, for example, refers to the angels as "these courtiers of Heaven"; see *Beneficios del Santo Angel*, fo. 9r.

88. The gentlemen of the chamber (*gentileshombres de la cámara*) were the only ones allowed to enter the king's rooms without knocking, as they were in possession of the key that granted them access to the *retrete*, the king's *Sancta Sanctorum*. For a description of the offices and etiquette of the royal palace, see BPR, ms. II/2642, "Etiquetas generales que han de observar los criados de la casa de Su Majestad en el uso y ejercicio de sus oficios." For two illuminating studies of palace etiquette, see John H. Elliott, "The Court of the Spanish Habsburgs: A Peculiar Institution?" in *Spain and Its World, 1500–1700:*

Selected Essays (New Haven, CT, 1989); Feros, *Kingship and Favoritism*, pp. 82–86, 91–98.

89. Saona, *Jerarquía celestial y terrena*, pp. 71–73.

90. Ibid., pp. 375–383.

91. See, for example, Saavedra Fajardo, *Empresas políticas*, empresa 38, pp. 485–492; Cevallos, *Arte real*, fos. 158, 160; Diego de Tovar Valderrama, *Instituciones políticas* ([Alcalá de Henares, 1645] Madrid, 1995), pp. 189–190.

92. Medina, *Espejo de príncipes católicos*, pp. 14–15; Bocanegra, *Teatro jerárquico de la luz*, fo. 6.

93. Saona, *Jerarquía celestial y terrena*, p. 36.

94. Ibid., pp. 3–6.

95. See, for example, Castillo de Bobadilla, *Política para corregidores*, lib. I, cap. III, nos. 57–63; Cevallos, *Arte real*, fos. 135–138; Tovar Valderrama, *Instituciones políticas*, pp. 162–163; Mendo, *Príncipe perfecto*, pp. 42–46; Juan de Matienzo, *Gobierno del Perú (1567)* (París, 1967), pp. 201–202. The author of one of the descriptions of the duke of Alburquerque's entry noted that the prince, as the soul of his vassals, communicated to them an inclination toward goodness and virtuosity. See *Elogio panegírico y aclamación festiva*, fo. 3v.

96. On the conciliar character of the Spanish monarchy, see Fernández Albaladejo, *Fragmentos de monarquía*, pp. 88–140. For the mechanism of the *consulta*, see John H. Elliott, *Imperial Spain* (London, 1963), pp. 160–172, especially page 167.

97. Saona, *Jerarquía celestial y terrena*, pp. 76–83.

98. Juan Eusebio Nieremberg, *De la devoción y patrocinio de San Miguel, príncipe de los ángeles, antiguo tutelar de los godos y protector de España, en que se proponen sus grandes excelencias y títulos que hay para implorar su patrocinio* (México, 1643), pp. 46, 50. Further references will be given in the text. On the popularity of the cult of St. Michael in New Spain, see Eduardo Báez Macías, *El arcángel San Miguel: su patrocinio, la ermita en el Santo Desierto de Cuajimalpa y el Santuario de Tlaxcala* (México, 1979); Juana Gutiérrez Haces et al., *Cristóbal de Villalpando, ca. 1649–1714* (México, 1997), pp. 38, 88, 177, 206–207, 209, 226–228, 241, 269–272, 322–325, 332–333.

99. See Solórzano, *Política indiana*, lib. V, cap. XII, no. 5; Vilosa, *Disertación jurídica y política*, pp. 135–139; Cortiada, *Discurso sobre la jurisdicción del Exmo. Sr. Virrey*, pp. 2–5.

100. One of the functions of the viceroys in New Spain was to "present" (to choose), from a list of three candidates nominated by either the bishops or the provincials of the religious orders, a cleric to fill the ecclesiastical benefices or one of the Indian parishes. On the procedure for the selection, see AGI, México 2707, Royal Order of 3 June 1634; Avendaño, *Thesaurus Indicus*, pp. 430–432.

101. As shall be shown in Chapter 5, one of the most important and troubling tasks of New Spain's viceroys, and what most defined them as viceroys, was the distribution of the offices of *alcaldes mayores* and *corregidores* (local magistrates). This was a prerogative that belonged to them as the king's "vicars."

102. The appropriation of angels for political purposes did not end with the figure of St. Michael. A variant that became extremely popular in the viceroyalty of Peru was that of the *ángeles arcabuceros*. Ramón Mujica Pinilla has argued that these figures, richly dressed as military commanders and always carrying a harquebus, were a reflection of a political theology that imagined the angels as the warrior-like defenders of the Spanish monarchy in its struggle against heresy and idolatry. See his *Ángeles apócrifos en la América virreinal* (Lima, 1996), chap. IV.

103. *Sermón en la festividad del glorioso arcángel San Miguel, patrón del reino de La Galicia, predicado el día 29 de septiembre del año 66 por el bachiller D. Bernardo de Frías, canónigo de la Santa Iglesia Catedral de Guadalajara* ... (México, 1667), dedication to Pedro de Medina Rico, *visitador general* of the Mexican Inquisition. Further references will be given in the text.

104. Nieremberg, *De la devoción y patrocinio de San Miguel*, pp. 41–42.

105. Alavés Pinelo, *Astro mitológico político*, p. 24. Compare this with what Jerónimo de Cevallos affirmed in his treatise on royal government. For him, royal majesty, sovereignty, and power are so great that they can be neither explained with words nor comprehended by human understanding. That is why, adds Cevallos, some say royal majesty is a virtue of God and an emanation of the "rays and lights of his divine majesty," while others call kings "angels and God's ministers." See *Arte real*, fo. 112. It should be noted here that Cevallos made these assertions to uphold his vision of an "absolute" monarch, in opposition to those who sustained a more "constitutionalist" approach to the figure of the king. For a discussion of the different positions regarding this matter in the seventeenth century, see Chapter 2.

106. Vilosa, *Disertación jurídica y política*, pp. 51–75.

107. *Sermón en la solemnidad que anualmente consagra al Santísimo Sacramento del altar el Rey Nuestro Señor* ... *Predicólo el bachiller Juan de Gárate en la Santa Iglesia Catedral* ... (México, 1677), fo. 3. Perhaps, no one represented this association between the Catholic monarchy and the Sacred Host better than the playwright Pedro Calderón de la Barca in his allegorical religious drama *El nuevo palacio del Retiro*, written for performance at the new royal palace of the Buen Retiro during the feast of Corpus Christi of 1634. The play, which depicted the new palace as a symbol of the heavenly kingdom, equating God with the king and the Church with the queen, culminated with the enactment of the mystery of the Eucharist. See Jonathan Brown and J.H. Elliott, *A Palace for a King: The Buen Retiro and the Court of Philip IV* (New Haven, CT, 1980), p. 230.

108. See *Sermón al Santísimo Sacramento por el feliz viaje y milagroso escape de la armada real de España el año de 25, predicado el año de 75 en la Santa Iglesia Catedral de la Puebla por el bachiller D. José Valero Caballero* ... (México, 1677), fo. 12. For a study of the association of the Habsburg dynasty with the Holy Eucharist and the different versions of archduke Rudolf's legend, see Antonio Alvarez-Ossorio, "Virtud coronada: Carlos II y la piedad de la casa de Austria," in *Política, Religión e Inquisición en la España Moderna*, edited by

P. Fernández Albaladejo, J. Martínez Millán, and V. Pinto Crespo (Madrid, 1996), pp. 29–57.

109. See, for example, Juan de Salazar, in *Política Española (1619)*, edited by M. Herrero García (Madrid, 1997), pp. 67–70; Mora, *El sol eclipsado*, fos. 29r–30r. It comes as no surprise, then, that the viceroys, as the king's living images, should imitate this royal devotion to the Sacred Host with gestures that closely followed those performed by the Habsburg monarchs. For example, we are told by a Mexican chronicler that, one day in 1688 when the count of Galve encountered a priest who was carrying the Sacrament on foot, the viceroy without hesitation asked the cleric into his carriage while he walked alongside. See Antonio de Robles, *Diario de sucesos notables (1665–1703)*, edited by A. Castro Leal (México, 1972), vol. II, p. 171.

110. In his decree, the king adopts the same language of humility and patronage in his relation with God as his subjects do when they petition the monarch. The rescue of the fleet was an "extraordinary favor" that God granted him. This deserved his greatest gratitude, which is why he went to "prostrate himself at Our Lord's feet" in order to thank Him "with the greatest humility of heart and resignation." In any case, as the king himself added to the decree in his own handwriting, he would have thanked God anyway, even if the fleet had been lost, as he was convinced that "whatever His Divine Majesty did, it would be the most appropriate" (which is very much the same as saying "Your Majesty will order as he likes"). AGN, *Reales Cédulas Originales*, vol. 1, exp. 13, fos. 35–37, the king to the marquis of Cerralvo, 21 March 1626. See also, *Recopilación*, lib. I, tít. I, leyes xxii and xxvi. For the cult of the Holy Sacrament as imperial cult, see Chocano Mena, *La fortaleza docta*, pp. 292–296.

111. Gregorio Martín de Guijo, *Diario, 1648–1664*, edited by M. Romero de Terreros (México, 1952), vol. I, p. 264; vol. II, p. 9.

112. Jacinto de la Serna, *Sermón en la fiesta de los tres días al Santísimo Sacramento en la capilla del Sagrario de la Santa Iglesia Metropolitana de México, que sus rectores y curas celebraron en 3 de febrero de 1655 años …* (México, 1655), p. 19.

113. For a description of these monstrances, see Manuel Trens, *Las custodias españolas* (Barcelona, 1952); Carl Hernmarck, *Custodias procesionales en España* (Madrid, 1987). On the relation between solar imagery, Spanish kingship, and the Holy Sacrament, see Mínguez, *Los reyes solares*, chap. 17.

114. De la Serna, *Sermón en la fiesta de los tres días*, p. 28.

115. On this subject, see Moles, *Audiencia de príncipes*, especially fos. 3–4, 26v–28v.

116. De la Serna, *Sermón en la fiesta de los tres días*, pp. 19–20.

117. Ibid., p. 21.

Chapter 2

1. For a thorough account of these conflicts, see Jonathan I. Israel, *Race, Class and Politics in Colonial Mexico, 1610–1670* (London, 1975), pp. 135–160, 217–240.

2. Jonathan I. Israel, "Mexico and the 'General Crisis' of the Seventeenth Century," *Past & Present* 63 (1974): 33–57.

3. See, for example, the descriptions in RAH, *Colección Salazar y Castro*, F-20, "Relación de la entrada que hizo en la ciudad de México ... el Señor Arzobispo don Fray García Guerra ... a tomar la posesión del oficio de virrey y capitán general de aquel reino por Su Majestad...," fo. 113; Cristóbal Gutiérrez de Medina, *Viaje del virrey marqués de Villena* (México, [1640] 1947), pp. 70–73.

4. Kevin Sharpe and Steven N. Zwicker, *Politicis of Discourse: The Literature and History of Seventeenth-Century England* (Berkeley, 1987), pp. 7–8.

5. Pierre Bourdieu, *Language and Symbolic Power* (Cambridge, MA, 1991), pp. 106–116. See also Keith M. Baker, *Inventing the French Revolution: Essays on French Political Culture in the Eighteenth Century* (Cambridge, U.K., 1990), pp. 4–5.

6. C.H. Haring, *The Spanish Empire in America* (New York, 1947), pp. 110–113. These ideas are somewhat repeated by John Elliott in his study of imperial Spain. To him, it is clear that royal authority was vested not in the viceroys alone, but "in the twin institutions of audiencias and viceroyalties." Viceroys were primarily governors, whose enormous power was more a result of their remoteness from the metropolis than of any deliberate policy on the part of the Spanish Crown, as they were closely tied to the government in Spain through the Council of the Indies. This would explain why the task of administering justice did not belong to them, but to the *audiencias*. It also explains why the *audiencias*, unlike those in Spain, had political and administrative functions in addition to their regular judicial ones. This system of checks and balances was, according to Elliott, the best, or the only one, that allowed the Spanish monarchy to preserve its authority in such remote territories. See John Elliott, *Imperial Spain, 1469–1716* (London, 1963), pp. 165–166; see also "Spain and America Before 1700," in *Colonial Spanish America*, edited by Leslie Bethell (Cambridge, U.K., 1984), pp. 64–69.

7. José Ignacio Rubio Mañé, *El Virreinato I* (México, [1955] 1992), p. 51; Haring, *The Spanish Empire in America*, p. 124.

8. As he points out, "There was no authority in the Indies which could be sure of obedience, no jurisdiction which could not be inhibited, and no decision which could not be reversed on appeal to Spain." See John H. Parry, *The Audiencia of New Galicia in the Sixteenth Century: A Study in Spanish Colonial Government* (Cambridge, U.K., 1948), pp. 167–168.

9. Diego Felipe de Albornoz, *Cartilla política y cristiana* (Madrid, 1666). In his work, Albornoz also included the words *religión* for the letter "r" (which he placed before any other letter), *dadivoso* (generous) for the letter "d," and *magnanimidad* for the letter "m." These concepts will be discussed in further chapters.

10. For a discussion of the meaning of "absolute monarchy" (an expression used by early modern writers) as opposed to the word "absolutism" (a concept created by modern historians), see Roger Mettam, *Power and Faction in Louis XIV's France* (Oxford, 1988), p. 34; Richard Bonney, "Absolutism: What's in a Name?" *French History* 1, no. 1 (1987): 93–99.

11. Magali Sarfatti, *Spanish Bureaucratic–Patrimonialism in America* (Berkeley, 1966), p. 14. Similarly, J.H. Parry contended that the government of the American territories was "based upon the formal assumption that the Indies were the private estate of the rulers of Castile" and that all the "important institutions there, judicial, ecclesiastical, economic, and local, became converted into one vast centralised civil service, designed to enforce arbitrary legislation." See his *The Spanish Theory of Empire in the Sixteenth Century* (Cambridge, U.K., 1940), pp. 71–72.

12. The theory of the Divine Right of Kings was best argued by the supporters of English absolutism, especially in the first half of the seventeenth century. See J.P. Sommerville, *Politics and Ideology in England, 1603–1640* (London, 1986), pp. 9–56.

13. Juan de Santa María, *Tratado de república y policía cristiana para reyes y príncipes, y para los que en el gobierno tienen sus veces* (Madrid, 1615), pp. 220–221. On the theory of the origins of political society in Thomist thought as reinterpreted by Spanish thinkers in the sixteenth and seventeenth centuries, see Skinner, *The Foundations*, vol. 2, pp. 148–166.

14. This argument was put forward in the most explicit way by the Jesuit Francisco Suárez in his *Defensio Fidei*, written to contradict the arguments of James I. See his *Defensio Fidei III. Principatus politicus o la soberanía popular*, edited by E. Elorduy and L. Pereña ([Coimbra, 1613] Madrid, 1965), especially chaps. II and III. Also, in the case of the Spanish monarchs, two other important differences existed that set them apart from the strict absolutism of the English kings. First, the English monarchs, especially James I, took an active role in the promotion of the Divine Right of Kings theory, something that the Spanish kings never did. Second, the English monarchs were anointed, thus proving their special connection and relationship with God. This ceremony, however, was never performed with the Spanish kings, at least in the early modern period. In this regard, it is simply wrong to affirm, as Ramón Gutiérrez does when discussing seventeenth-century Spanish politics in *When Jesus Came, the Corn Mothers Went Away*, p. 99, that "inspired by medieval theories of divine kingship, since the Iberian reconquest Spain's monarchs had insisted on episcopal consecration and anointment to authenticate their authority as divinely derived." On the almost total lack of the sacral dimension in the Spanish monarchy, see I.A.A. Thompson, "Absolutism in Castile," in *Crown and Cortes: Government, Institutions and Representation in Early Modern Castile* (Aldershot, 1993), p. V:74.

15. For a concise explanation of this, see Tovar Valderrama, *Instituciones políticas*, pp. 137–146. For the application of these ideas to the American lands, see Juan de Silva, in *Los memoriales del Padre Silva sobre predicación pacífica y repartimientos (1618)*, edited by P. Castañeda Delgado (Madrid, 1983).

16. Francisco Suárez is a good example of the view that tended to emphasize the king's power. See his *Defensio Fidei III*, pp. 34–36. Another Jesuit, Juan de Mariana, was one of the most prominent representatives of the political current that stressed the power of the kingdom over that of the monarch. See his

La dignidad real y la educación del rey (De rege et regis institutione), edited by L. Sánchez Agesta (Madrid, [1599] 1981), pp. 92–105. In the early modern period, the "constitution" of a given commonwealth was a set of historically established, even fundamental, laws that imposed limits upon royal power. In "constitutionalist" thought, the community was the immediate source of the ruler's authority, and only limited power was transferred to him. This meant, therefore, that royal power had to be exercised within institutionally determined limits. For a study of the meaning of constitutionalism in the early modern period, see Howell A. Lloyd, "Constitutionalism," in *The Cambridge History of Political Thought, 1450–1700*, edited by J.H. Burns (Cambridge, U.K., 1991), pp. 254–297. For a brief but illuminating discussion of what it meant for a Spanish monarch to be "absolute," see Thompson, "Absolutism in Castile," in *Crown and Cortes*, pp. V:71–74.

17. On Bodin's theory of absolutism, see Skinner, *The Foundations*, vol. 2, pp. 284–301; Julian H. Franklin, "Sovereignty and the Mixed Constitution: Bodin and His Critics," in *The Cambridge History of Political Thought*, edited by J.H. Burns, pp. 298–309.

18. Santa María, *Tratado de república y policía cristiana*, pp. 224–228. For similar ideas, see also Pedro de Rivadeneira, "Tratado de la religión y virtudes que debe tener el príncipe cristiano para gobernar y conservar sus estados, contra lo que Nicolás Maquiavelo y los políticos deste tiempo enseñan," in *Obras escogidas del Padre Pedro de Rivadeneira*, edited by V. de la Fuente (Madrid, [1595] 1952), pp. 526–527; Juan de Salazar, *Política Española* (1619), edited by M. Herrero García (Madrid, 1997), pp. 91–93; Jerónimo de Cevallos, *Arte real para el buen gobierno de los reyes y príncipes y de sus vasallos, en el cual se refieren las obligaciones de cada uno, con los principales documentos para el buen gobierno ...* (Toledo, 1623), fos. 59–66; Diego Saavedra Fajardo, *Empresas políticas*, edited by S. López ([Munich, 1640] Madrid, 1999), empresas 21 and 22, pp. 356–377. For his part, Juan de Mariana would contend that "*princeps non est solutus legibus*"; that is, the king is not exempted from observing the law, because this is the best way to ensure that he administers justice as an honest and just ruler. See *La dignidad real*, pp. 106–114, 383–392. The idea that the main obligation of monarchs was to administer justice still appears in a treatise on monarchical government written at the very end of the seventeenth century by Pedro Portocarrero, the king's chaplain and Patriarch of the Indies. Following Saavedra, he asserts the virtue of justice had been the "foundation of the great Spanish Monarchy." See Pedro Portocarrero y Guzmán, *Teatro Monárquico de España*, edited by C. Sanz Ayán (Madrid, [1700] 1998), pp. 91–105. Although Portocarrero's views are not very original, the work is nonetheless of great interest as a middle-of-the-road compendium of the fundamental political ideas on which the Habsburg monarchy had been built. This treatise was to serve as the model to be followed by the new foreign king who was to succeed the dying Charles II. In his work, Portocarrero mainly follows three writers — Rivadeneira, Mariana, and Saavedra Fajardo — who were among the most influential representatives of the different approaches to

government prevalent in early modern Spain. For a discussion of these political currents, see this chapter, below.

19. In *The Spanish Empire in America*, pp. 113–114, Haring argues that this disobedience of the laws was not something unique to Hispanic societies but was a characteristic of frontier societies in general; however, to define New Spain in the seventeenth century as a frontier society does not seem adequate, at least for the central areas of Mexico.

20. For two royal orders in which this is explicitly stated, see *Recopilación*, lib. II, tít. I, leyes xxii and xxiiii.

21. Castillo de Bobadilla, *Política para corregidores*, lib. II, cap. X. See also, Mario Góngora, *El Estado en el derecho indiano. Época de fundación (1492–1570)* (Santiago de Chile, 1951), pp. 282–285. John Leddy Phelan has explained this formula as the result of the constant need of colonial bureaucrats to strike a delicate balance between the orders of their superiors in Spain and the dictates of local pressures. See his "Authority and Flexibility in the Spanish Imperial Bureaucracy," *Administrative Science Quarterly* 5 (1960): 57–60. However, as Antonio Annino has argued, this principle was not invented in the colonies in order to "corrupt" any legal practices, as it had been part of Castilian law for at least two centuries before 1492. Besides, no evidence suggests that this principle was practiced more widely in the New World than in Castile. See Antonio Annino, "Some Reflections on Spanish American Constitutional and Political History," *Itinerario* 19, no. 2 (1995): 36. For its use in Castile, see Thompson, "Absolutism in Castile," in *Crown and Cortes*, p. V:77.

22. Juan de Madariaga, *Del senado y su príncipe* (Valencia, 1617), p. 49.

23. Juan de Solórzano y Pereira, *Política indiana*, edited by M.A. Ochoa Brun (Madrid, [1647] 1972), lib. V, cap. III, núms. 7, 8.

24. Quoted in Solórzano, *Política indiana*, lib. V, cap. III, núm. 8.

25. In the seventeenth century, the *audiencia* of Mexico City had twelve judges divided into two chambers, a civil chamber of eight *oidores* and a criminal chamber of four *alcaldes del crimen*, in addition to two *fiscales* or crown attorneys, one for civil and the other for criminal cases. The *fiscales*, although not very visible figures, played an important role. They were appointed to protect the royal interests, especially those affecting the treasury and the rights of the Indians. They also offered legal advice to the viceroy in political and administrative matters. For the composition of the Mexican *audiencia*, see AGI, Mexico 41, no. 48e, 27 November 1667. For a description of all the officials that comprised the Mexican High Court, see AGI, Mexico 22, no. 47bis, Luis de Velasco to the king, May 1591; AGI, Mexico 27, no. 50c, "Memoria de los oidores, alcaldes de corte, fiscales …," 23 June 1608. For a description of the general functioning, competencies, and procedures of a Spanish–American *audiencia*, see Parry, *The Audiencia of New Galicia*, pp. 150–166; Haring, *The Spanish Empire in America*, pp. 120–122.

26. Solórzano wondered whether it was better to appoint *togados* (gentlemen of the robe) or *caballeros de capa y espada y señores de título* (members of the nobility) as viceroys; however, he does not seem to have a definite opinion on

this matter. See his *Política indiana*, lib. V, cap. XII, núms. 12 and 13. In any case, the viceroys appointed in the seventeenth century were all members of the hereditary nobility.

27. This mission is clearly reflected in a decree directed to the count of Baños due to complaints that had arrived at the Council of the Indies concerning the bad administration of justice. Apart from charging him with convoking the judges and *fiscales* of the *audiencia* to "reprimand them severely," the monarch reminds the viceroy that, if the *oidores* and *alcaldes del crimen* had not complied with their obligations, it was still his fault, because, in his capacity as president of the *audiencia*, it was his obligation to be certain that justice was imparted appropriately. See AGN, RCO, vol. 7, exp. 18, fo. 46, the king to the count of Baños, 30 June 1661.

28. With respect to this, the policy of the Crown was to a certain extent ambivalent. In the times of Philip III, a decree was issued authorizing the viceroys of the Indies to pardon all those crimes that the monarch himself was permitted to pardon. This decree was included in the *Recopilación* of 1680 (lib. III, tít. III, ley xxvii). Nevertheless, in 1662, the fiscal of the Council of the Indies was of the opinion that the right to grant pardons belonged exclusively to the monarch or to whomever this particular power was conceded. In the case of the viceroy of Mexico, this concession did not exist, which is why, at least in theory, he was not able to pardon prisoners convicted by the alcaldes del crimen. See AGI, Mexico 77, no. 4, the criminal chamber to the king, 20 November 1662. Solórzano is also of the same opinion because, according to him, pardoning crimes is a royal prerogative; see his *Política indiana*, lib. V, cap. XIII, núm. 36.

29. See, for example, AGI, Mexico 27, no. 52, the *oidor* Landeras de Velasco to the king, 20 May 1607; ibid., the viceroy Luis de Velasco to the king, 23 June 1608.

30. Madariaga, *Del senado y su príncipe*, pp. 1–26, 125. Similar arguments had already been advanced by Rivadeneira in his "Tratado de la religión y virtudes," pp. 552–555, and by Juan de Santa María in *Tratado de república y policía cristiana*, pp. 58–82. See also Cevallos, *Arte Real*, fos. 45–54.

31. Salazar, *Política Española*, pp. 117–128.

32. Madariaga, *Del senado y su príncipe*, dedication to the count of Lemos (emphasis added).

33. This had already been noted by Solórzano in his *Política indiana*, lib. V, cap. III, núm 10.

34. In the opinion of Jesús LaLinde, the New World *audiencia* became an autonomous body, due to the special circumstances of the overseas territories. In Lalinde's view, in Catalonia, for instance, the monarch had to stress, as much as he could, the viceroy's power, because of the many norms and privileges that limited his authority there, while in his American possessions he did not have such constraints; therefore, he was bound to limit rather than accentuate viceregal power by increasing the political power of the *audiencias*. Although it is certainly true that the Spanish kings did not have to deal with constitutional restrictions in Peru or New Spain in the Catalan or Sicilian

way, still an "implied" constitution, as I showed above, put many constraints on the king's power. In any case, a few pages later Lalinde asserts that, by the seventeenth century, all the viceroys of the Spanish monarchy were very similar in that none of them intervened in the administration of justice, although some of them had judicial powers. See Lalinde Abadía, "El régimen virreino-senatorial en Indias," pp. 106–108.

35. This also seems to have been the case in other territories of the monarchy. The situation in the kingdom of Valencia was in some ways similar to that of the American viceroyalties. There, the supreme ruler was also a "foreign" (i.e., Castilian) viceroy, who in theory was in possession of judicial authority, although in practice this power was exercised by the *audiencia*. See Teresa Canet Aparisi, *La Audiencia valenciana en la época foral moderna* (Valencia, 1986). The author, however, concludes that the *audiencia* constituted a "parallel power" to that of the viceroy and was "an instrument of monarchical absolutism." See pp. 65–69, 100–104, and 190. It would be more appropriate instead to see the *audiencia,* on the one hand, as "complementing" viceregal power and, on the other, as a "constitutional constraint" of the royal power embodied by the viceroy.

36. Fernández Albaladejo, *Fragmentos de monarquía,* p. 293. On the conciliar structure of the Spanish monarchy, see ibid., pp. 88–140; J.M. Batista i Roca, "Foreword," in *The Practice of Empire,* edited by Helmut G. Koenigsberger (Ithaca, 1969), pp. 9–35.

37. Diego Pérez de Mesa, *Política o razón de Estado,* edited by L. Pereña and C. Baciero (Madrid, 1980), p. 319.

38. AGI, Mexico 77, no. 38c, consulta of the bishop of Puebla to the *audiencia,* 4 June 1664.

39. On the privilege of the *audiencias* to issue decrees bearing the king's name and his seal, see *Recopilación,* lib. II, tít. XV, ley cxvi. On the royal order prohibiting viceroys to issue *provisiones* on their own with the king's name and seal, see *Recopilación,* lib. III, tít. III, ley xxxxii. This order, however, refers only to judicial cases. In Solórzano's opinion, it was customary for viceroys to issue decrees bearing the king's name and seal in matters of great importance and when granting offices, benefices, and *encomiendas.* See *Política indiana,* lib. V, cap. XII, núm. 54.

40. One of the basic principles of good government of the Spanish monarchy was the right of vassals to write directly to the king or to his councils to let him know about some matter or some injustice they had suffered. In the political theory of the period, this was a basic principle of civility as well as its opposite, a sign of oppression and violence, which was why in a well-ordered Christian republic it was not possible for this right not to exist. See *Recopilación,* lib. III, tít. XVI, leyes vi and vii; AGI, Mexico 76, no. 80b, "Consulta que hizo la Real Audiencia de México al Señor Virrey Conde de Baños" (n.d.); AGI, Mexico 6, Ramo 2, consulta of the Council, 14 May 1661; AGN, RCO, vol. 7, exp. 9, fos. 33–34, the king to the *audiencia,* 19 June 1661; AGI, Mexico 6, Ramo 4, Francisco Calderón and Manuel de Escalante to the king, 3 June 1663.

41. The most common "methods of punishment" that the Crown was wont to use against any *oidores* whom the Council of the Indies found guilty of some crime generally consisted of the imposition of a fine or their transferral to another *audiencia* or, more commonly, of a "severe reprimand" by the viceroy in the name of the king, which, in order to increase its disciplinary effect, could be given in the presence of the other *oidores*. See, for instance, AGN, RCO, vol. 1, exp. 227, fo. 440, the king to the marquis of Cadereita, 22 February 1638.

42. "Carta de la Audiencia de México a S.M., 10.I.1620," in *Los virreyes españoles en América durante el gobierno de la casa de Austria, México III*, edited by Lewis Hanke, BAE, vol. CCLXXV, pp. 71–96.

43. For these two *cédulas*, see *Recopilación*, lib. II, tít. XVI, ley xxxxiii; lib. II, tít. XV, ley xxxvi; lib. III, tít. III, ley xxxiiii.

44. "Carta de la Audiencia de México a S.M., 10.I.1620," in *Los virreyes, México III*, BAE, vol. CCLXXV, pp. 92–94.

45. See *Recopilación*, lib. II, tít. XVI, ley xxxxiiii. In relation to this, see also AGN, RCO, vol. 7, exp. 78, fo. 143, the king to the count of Baños, 28 February 1663; vol. 9, exp. 76, fos. 196–199, the queen to the marquis of Mancera, 28 November 1666; vol. 27, exp. 119, fo. 258, the king to the count of Moctezuma, 22 May 1697. Logically, the *oidores* could not proceed legally against the viceroys. See *Recopilación*, lib. II, tít. XVI, ley xxxxv.

46. AGN, RCO, vol. 2, exp. 13, fo. 22, the king to the marquis of Guadalcázar, 5 September 1620. This *cédula* was included in the *Recopilación*, lib. III, tít. XV, ley lvii. Years later, in 1643, due to the lack of unity and harmony between the members of the *audiencia* and their "head," this order was reissued and sent to the viceroy in office at that time. See AGN, RCO, vol. 2, exp. 13, fo. 23, the king to the count of Salvatierra, 4 August, 1643.

47. See António M. Hespanha, *La gracia del derecho. Economía de la cultura en la Edad Moderna*, translated by A. Cañellas (Madrid, 1993), pp. 156–159. On how the idea of friendship shaped all aspects of society, including the economy, see Bartolomé Clavero, *Antidora. Antropología católica de la economía moderna* (Milan, 1991), pp. 187–198. For the political uses of the language of friendship in early modern Spain, see Feros, *Kingship and Favoritism*, pp. 120–124. Aristotle's ideas on friendship are introduced in books VIII and IX of *Nicomachean Ethics* and in book VII of *Eudemian Ethics*. Cicero's ideas on this subject can be found in his *Laelius: De amicitia* (On Friendship). For a detailed description of how friendship worked in an urban environment, see Richard Trexler, *Public Life in Renaissance Florence* (Ithaca, 1980), pp. 131–158.

48. Madariaga, *Del senado y de su príncipe*, dedication and pp. 131–132.

49. In the "Instructions" that each viceroy received before departing for New Spain, the king always asked them to try to keep "peace and conformity" with the *oidores*, avoiding provoking their enmity and making sure there was no friction among the judges. Also, he was reminded that the viceroys, in spite of holding the title of president of the *audiencia*, did not vote on judicial decisions. In the Instructions it is clearly specified that, if, on the one

hand, the viceroy does not intervene in the administration of justice, on the other, all government affairs are his exclusive concern, although he is advised (without being obliged) to consult with the *oidores* on all matters of importance. See "Instrucción al conde de Monterrey, 20.III.1596," in *Los virreyes, México II*. BAE, vol. CCLXXIV, p. 136. This *Instrucción* was the model for most of the Instructions given to the viceroys in the seventeenth century. Cf. "Instrucción al marqués de Cerralvo, 18.VI.1624," in *Los virreyes, México III*, BAE, vol. CCLXXV, p. 259; "Instrucción al conde de Alba de Liste, 28.V.1649" and "Instrucción al duque de Alburquerque, 1653 (?)," in *Los virreyes, México IV*, BAE, vol. CCLXXVI, pp. 136–137 and p. 156; "Instrucción al conde de Moctezuma, 10.V.1696," in *Los virreyes, México V*, BAE, vol. CCLXXVII, pp. 196–197.

50. Solórzano, *Política indiana*, lib. V, cap. XII, núms. 29–30. For similar ideas, see also Diego de Avendaño, *Thesaurus Indicus*, edited by A. Muñoz García ([Antwerp, 1668] Pamplona, 2001), pp 419–422.

51. "Relación de Juan de Palafox y Mendoza, 1642 (?)," in *Los virreyes, México IV*, BAE, vol. CCLXXVI, pp. 40–42 and 62–63 (emphasis added).

52. Fernández Albaladejo, *Fragmentos de monarquía*, p. 294. For an analysis of these two main currents, which dominated Spanish political thought in the late sixteenth and seventeenth centuries, see José A. Fernández-Santamaría, "Reason of State and Statecraft in Spain (1595–1640)," *Journal of the History of Ideas* 41 (1980): 355–379; see also from the same author, the "Estudio preliminar," in Baltasar Alamos de Barrientos, *Aforismos al Tácito español* (Madrid, 1987), vol. I, pp. cxliii–cxlvii; Joan Pau Rubiés, "La idea del gobierno mixto y su significado en la crisis de la Monarquía Hispánica," *Historia Social* 24 (1996): 57–81; Feros, *Kingship and Favoritism*, pp. 19–27, 221–225. The existence of this ideological debate makes it necessary to revise the image of the Spanish monarchy as a monolithic structure, where all ideological dissent had been crushed — with a little help from the Inquisition.

53. The viceroys usually defended their position by advancing the "rule of one" argument. The marquis of Cerralvo, for example, contended that, even though it was stipulated that when a vacancy occurred in the office of the viceroy the *audiencia* was to take charge of the government, this created great difficulties "because government by many is always cumbersome," and, besides, when offices and rewards were handed out, dissension broke out and political factions were created. See "Relación del estado en que dejó el gobierno el marqués de Cerralvo, 17.III.1636," in *Los virreyes, México III*, BAE, vol. CCLXXV, p. 276. The *audiencia* view was succinctly presented by one of its *fiscales*, for whom it was clear that if the will of the king had been to confide public affairs to the free will of a single person (the viceroy), the *audiencias* would have been superfluous. See AGN, RCO, vol. 1, exp. 153, fo. 289, the king to the marquis of Cadereita, 5 November 1635. It was probably not a coincidence that, among the very few political works published in New Spain in the seventeenth century, it stands out a treatise in defense of the Catholic reason of state and against the followers of Machiavelli and Tacitus, written by

an official of the royal treasury who was at odds with the viceroy. See Juan Blázquez Mayoralgo, *Perfecta razón de estado, deducida de los hechos de el señor rey don Fernando el Católico, quinto de este nombre en Castilla y segundo en Aragón, contra los políticos ateístas* (México, 1646). On Blázquez Mayoralgo, see Magdalena Chocano Mena, *La fortaleza docta. Elite letrada y dominación social en México colonial (siglos XVI–XVII)* (Barcelona, 2000), pp. 263–269.

54. AGI, Patronato 221, ramo 12, "Los puntos que la Real Audiencia comunicó a VE …," 8 November 1621; the *audiencia* to the king, 11 November 1621; Gelves to the king, 26 February 1622. One year later, Gelves would complain that the *oidores* expected him not to take any measures without first consulting them and getting their approval. See AGI, Mexico 30, no. 1, Gelves to the king, 23 February 1623.

55. RAH, Colección Jesuitas, vol. CXLII, 4, "Justifícase por razón, por derecho divino y humano el acuerdo que tomó la Real Audiencia de México en retener en sí el gobierno de la Nueva España y no volverlo al marqués de Gelves" (n.d.).

56. Israel, *Race, Class and Politics in Colonial Mexico*, pp. 267–273.

57. Municipal authority was vested in two kinds of officers, *regidores* or councilors and *alcaldes ordinarios* or magistrates. The king's representative in the city council was the *corregidor*, the city's chief magistrate. He sat on the *cabildo*, presiding over it, although he was not, in a strict sense, a member of it. In the seventeenth century, Mexico City usually had sixteen *regidores* and two *alcaldes*, who were elected by the *regidores* every year on New Year's day. See María Luisa J. Pazos Pazos, *El ayuntamiento de la ciudad de México en el siglo XVII: Continuidad institucional y cambio social* (Sevilla, 1999), pp. 43–113, 269–290.

58. Roger B. Merriman, *The Rise of the Spanish Empire in the Old World and in the New* (New York [1918, 1925, 1934] 1962), vol. I, pp. 183–197; vol. II, pp. 144–152; vol. III, pp. 637–639; J.M. Ots Capdequí, *El estado español en las Indias* (México, 1941), pp. 61–63; Haring, *The Spanish Empire in America*, pp. 147–155; John H. Parry, *The Sale of Public Office in the Spanish Indies Under the Habsburgs* (Berkeley, 1953), pp. 33–47; O. Carlos Stoetzer, *The Scholastic Roots of the Spanish American Revolution* (New York, 1979), pp. 6–13.

59. Haring, *The Spanish Empire in America*, p. 163.

60. Israel, *Race, Class and Politics*, pp. 94–98.

61. J.A. Maravall, *Las comunidades de Castilla. Una primera revolución moderna* (Madrid, 1963) and *Estado moderno y mentalidad social, siglos XVI a XVII* (Madrid, 1972), pp. 356–364. For his part, Perry Anderson, who bases his arguments on Maravall's work, contends in *Lineages of the Absolutist State* (London, 1974), p. 68, that "the crushing of the *comunero* rebellion effectively eliminated the last vestiges of a contractual constitution in Castile, and doomed the Cortes … to nullity henceforward."

62. Charles Jago, "Habsburg Absolutism and the Cortes of Castile," *American Historical Review* 86 (1981): 307–326; Thompson, "Crown and Cortes in Castile, 1590–1665," in *Crown and Cortes*, pp. VI: 29–45; Fernández Albaladejo,

Fragmentos de monarquía, pp. 241–349. For a detailed description of the mechanisms used by Philip IV and his ministers to try to convince the *Cortes* and the cities to vote new subsidies and the staunch opposition they had to face, see John Elliott, *The Count-Duke of Olivares: The Statesman in an Age of Decline* (New Haven, CT, 1986), pp. 146–162.

63. Charles Jago, in a recent article, has refined his previous assertions about the role of the *Cortes* by arguing that, although the *Cortes* (through the establishment of a contractual relation between the Crown and the realm) tried to assert its autonomy from the Crown, resisting royal interference, it did not succeed. See Ch. Jago, "Fiscalidad y cambio constitucional en Castilla, 1601–1621," in *Política y hacienda en el Antiguo Régimen*, edited by J.I. Fortea López and C.M. Cremades Griñán (Murcia, 1993), vol. I, pp. 117–132.

64. To Madariaga, for example, a senate is any "council, consistory, court, town council, chapter, or university senate because all mean the same thing." See the prologue in his *Del senado y de su príncipe*.

65. Fernández Albaladejo, *Fragmentos de monarquía*, pp. 291–294, 335–336, 348. For an analysis of the relationships between the Spanish cities and the monarchy in the early modern period, see also Pablo Fernández Albaladejo, "Cities and the State in Spain," in *Cities and the Rise of States in Europe, A.D. 1000 to 1800*, edited by Ch. Tilly and W.P. Blockmans (Boulder, 1994), pp. 168–183.

66. Similarly, the quintessential "democratic" parliament — the English parliament — was summoned to cooperate with the monarch, not to oppose him, its obligation being to provide advice when the king requested it. See John Guy, "The Rhetoric of Counsel in Early Modern England," in *Tudor Political Culture*, edited by Dale Hoak (Cambridge, U.K., 1995), pp. 292–310; see also Fernández Albaladejo, *Fragmentos de monarquía*, pp. 305–310.

67. Thompson, "Absolutism in Castile," in *Crown and Cortes*, p. V:75.

68. Charles Gibson, in his study of the structure of Spanish American colonial government, had already observed this, although he mentioned it only in passing. See his *Spain in America* (New York, 1966), p. 97.

69. Castillo de Bobadilla, *Política para corregidores*, vol. II, pp. 109, 161–162.

70. Ibid., pp. 121–122.

71. Ibid., p. 153.

72. Ibid., p. 142. For that reason, Bobadilla believes that town criers should not be allowed to say "by order of the corregidor and regidores" because to execute the city council resolutions, ordering them to be cried out, and to impose penalties, "is an act that belongs to the *corregidor*'s power to command (*mero y mixto imperio*) (p. 143). For the same reason, Bobadilla thinks that the *regidores* have no authority to impose corporal punishments because this power is particular to the *mero imperio* that resides only in the royal person (pp. 142, 156). Here, Bobadilla is clearly identifying the *corregidor* with the monarch. Not only does the *imperio* or power to command reside in the *corregidor*, but also the power to do justice, an unmistakable sign of royalty (the *corregidor*, as judge of first instance, did have the power to impose such punishments).

73. Ibid., pp. 153–154.

74. For a description of the hierarchy that, in a harmonious way, ordered all the officials and magistrates of the Spanish monarchy, which, in turn, was a reflection of the perfect hierarchy and order that existed in the heavenly republic, see Martín de Roa, *Beneficios del Santo Angel de Nuestra Guarda* (Córdoba, 1632), fos. 8, 16.

75. In the municipal bylaws of the city of Mexico, approved by a *cédula* of 11 May 1687, the following is declared: "In conformity with the cédula issued by the emperor Charles V and the queen Juana, his mother, in Valladolid in 24 July 1548, this most noble city of Mexico is to be called and titled The Very Noble, Distinguished and Very Loyal and Imperial City of Mexico, and is to enjoy the privileges and preeminences of a grandee, as metropolis of this New Spain." See AHCM, Ordenanzas 2981, no. 1. See also AGI, Mexico 319, decree of 24 July 1648. In this regard, a previous *cédula*, dated 25 June 1530, was included in the *Recopilación*, in which the emperor declared that "taking into consideration the greatness and nobility of the city of Mexico, that the viceroy, the government and *audiencia* of New Spain reside there, and that it was the first city peopled with Christians, it is our grace and wish and command that it should have the first vote of the cities and towns of New Spain, in the same way as the city of Burgos has it in our kingdoms, and the first place, after the chief magistrate, in those congresses summoned by our mandate, because it is not our intention or will to allow the cities and towns of the Indies to gather together without our mandate." *Recopilación*, lib. IIII, tít. VIII, ley ii.

76. AGI, Mexico 319, the crown attorney to the council, 16 November 1690.

77. On the Union of Arms scheme, see Elliott, *The Count-Duke of Olivares*, pp. 244–266; Thompson, "The Government of Spain in the Reign of Philip IV," in *Crown and Cortes*, pp. IV:17–20.

78. AGI. Mexico 30, no. 10c, "Razonamiento que el Exmo. Sr. marqués de Cerralvo, virrey desta Nueva España, hizo al cabildo de México sobre la Unión de las Armas en 19 de octubre de 1628."

79. AGI, Mexico 30, no. 10, the marquis of Cerralvo to the king, 9 May 1628; AGI, Mexico 30, no. 10, fos. 16–24, *cabildos* of 11 and 14 November 1628; AGI, Mexico 30, no. 10, fos. 24v–26r, the marquis of Cerralvo to the *cabildo*, 15 November 1628.

80. The attitude of Cerralvo contrasts with that of one of his predecessors, the marquis of Falces, who had suggested in 1567 that the convocation of the *Cortes* in New Spain would be the best way to ensure the approval of subsidies for the Crown. See *Los virreyes, México I*, BAE, vol. CCLXXIII, pp. 173–174. In fact, the Crown was never completely opposed to the summoning of *Cortes* in the Indies. In 1609, for example, it asked the viceroy of Peru (the marquis of Montesclaros, who had previously served as viceroy of New Spain) to consider the possibility of summoning the assembly every three years, but after Montesclaros rejected that possibility categorically the idea was shelved. It was in reality the determined opposition of the viceroys, who always feared that the convocation of *Cortes* would mean a curbing of their powers, that prevented

altogether the establishment of that institution in the New World. See Pilar Latasa Vasallo, *Administración virreinal en el Perú: Gobierno del marqués de Montesclaros (1607–1615)* (Madrid, 1997), pp. 122–124. On the different proposals presented in the sixteenth and seventeenth centuries to summon the *Cortes* in the American territories, see Guillermo Lohmann Villena, "Las Cortes en Indias," *Anuario de Historia del Derecho Español* XVIII (1947): 655–662; "Notas sobre la presencia de la Nueva España en las Cortes metropolitanas y de Cortes en la Nueva España en los siglos XVI y XVII," *Historia Mexicana* XXXIX (1989): 33–40.

81. AGI, Mexico 30, no. 10, fo. 27, *cabildo* of 18 November 1628. To obtain an extension of the Union of Arms contribution was not something that could be taken for granted at all, as the duke of Alburquerque would observe years later when informing the king of how he had been able to convince Mexico City's aldermen to extend the subsidy for another fifteen years. See AGI, Mexico 38, no. 45, Alburquerque to the king, 8 May 1658. On the difficulties collecting the money approved for the Union of Arms contribution, including the continuous resistance of Mexico City's *regidores*, see Louisa S. Hoberman, *Mexico's Merchant Elite, 1590–1660* (Durham, 1991), pp. 196–200.

82. AGI, Mexico 31, no. 49, fo. 58, the marquis of Cadereita to the *cabildo*, 23 February 1636.

83. Ibid., fos. 58v–60r, the *cabildo* to Cadereita, 11 March 1636.

84. Ibid., fos. 65r–67v, *cabildo* of 2 May 1636. For a detailed description of all the rewards requested by the Mexican *cabildo*, see Manuel Alvarado Morales, *La ciudad de México ante la fundación de la Armada de Barlovento: Historia de una encrucijada (1635–1643)* (México, 1983), pp. 71–91.

85. Alvarado Morales, *La ciudad de México*, pp. 91–142.

86. Ibid., pp. 158–161. On the significance and importance of the commercial relations between Mexico and Peru, see ibid., pp. 55–70; Israel, *Race, Class and Politics*, pp. 193–198; Hoberman, *Mexico's Merchant Elite*, pp. 214–220.

87. Alvarado Morales, *La ciudad de México*, pp. 161–178, 206–210; Hoberman, *Mexico's Merchant Elite*, pp. 200–214.

88. This has been pointed out by I.A.A. Thompson for the Castilian case in *Crown and Cortes*, pp. VI:36–37, and by Hoberman in *Mexico's Merchant Elite*, pp. 220–222. For an example of a viceroy acting specifically as corregidor of Mexico City (in a moment when the post of corregidor was actually vacant), see AHN, Diversos-Documentos de Indias, no. 78, the marquis of Cadereita to the *cabildo*, 2 January 1639 (the viceroy writes to the *regidores* to recriminate them for having neglected their obligations in the government of the city). For many other instances of viceregal interference in the affairs of the *cabildo*, see Pazos Pazos, *El ayuntamiento de la ciudad de México*, pp. 213–250. To this, it should be added that the viceroys very often were able to control the post of *corregidor* by appointing members of their clientele as interim *corregidores*. Ibid., pp. 57–87.

89. "Relación del conde de Salvatierra, 26.II.1645," in *Los virreyes, México IV,* BAE, vol. CCLXXVI, pp. 99–101.

90. AGI, Mexico 31, no. 49, fo. 43, the city of Mexico to the king (n.d.); Mexico 34, no. 5, fos. 77r–79r, 164, the marquis of Cadereita to the king, 19 July 1638; Mexico 34, no. 5, fo. 80, *consulta* of the Council, 12 January 1639. In 1603, the *cabildo* had already requested the suppression of the post of *corregidor*, but the viceroy had strongly opposed such a measure by arguing that it would greatly harm the administration of justice (because the *alcaldes ordinarios*, as natives of the city, would be much too influenced by personal relations), the management of the public works, and the provisioning of the city. See AGI, Mexico 25, no. 36, the count of Monterrey to the king, 27 May 1603. Before Monterrey, two other viceroys had also manifested their hostility toward the *alcaldes ordinarios*, who, according to one of them, were a perpetual threat to the peace and concord of any commonwealth. See AGI, Mexico 21, no. 11, the marquis of Villamanrique to the king, 28 April 1587; AGI, Mexico 22, no. 101, Luis de Velasco to the king, 8 June 1592.

91. Alvarado Morales, *La ciudad de México*, pp. 213, 243.

92. On the *Cabildo*'s difficulties to meet this payment, see Alvarado Morales, *La ciudad de México*, pp. 222–238; Pazos Pazos, *El ayuntamiento de la ciudad de México*, pp. 66–74. On the interference of the Peruvian viceroys in the affairs of the *cabildo* of Lima, which did not have a *corregidor* for most of the colonial period, see Guillermo Lohmann Villena, "El Corregidor de Lima: estudio histórico–jurídico." *Revista Histórica* XX (1953): 153–180.

93. Thompson, "The Government of Spain," in *Crown and Cortes*, pp. IV:78–85. The same ideas are expressed in an even darker tone by John Lynch in *The Hispanic World in Crisis and Change, 1598–1700* (Oxford, 1992), pp. 348–360. For the idea that absolutism was essentially a "redeployed and recharged apparatus of feudal domination," see Anderson, *Lineages of the Absolutist State*, p. 18.

94. Enrique Florescano, "The Hacienda in New Spain," in *Colonial Spanish America*, edited by Leslie Bethell (Cambridge, U.K., 1987), p. 264.

95. Mark A. Burkholder and Douglas S. Chandler, *From Impotence to Authority: The Spanish Crown and the American Audiencias, 1687–1808* (Columbia, MS, 1977).

96. Lynch, *The Hispanic World*, pp. 344–347.

97. In his study of the Indian court, which was presided over by the viceroy, Woodrow Borah has uncovered many cases involving hacienda Indians, clearly contradicting Florescano's affirmation. See his *Justice by Insurance: The General Indian Court of Colonial Mexico and the Legal Aides of the Half-Real* (Berkeley, 1983), pp. 129–187.

98. See AGN, RCO, vol. 24, exp. 54, fo. 161, the king to the viceroy and the *audiencia*, 8 August 1691. In fact, Burkholder and Chandler show evidence of this in their own study; see *From Impotence to Authority*, pp. 18–22.

99. Jonathan Israel, "The Seventeenth-Century Crisis in New Spain: Myth or Reality?" *Past & Present* 97 (Nov. 1982): 150–156.

100. AGI, Mexico 81, no. 43, the *audiencia* to the queen regent, 18 July 1673; AGN, RCO, vol. 26, exp. 13, fo. 25, the king to the count of Galve, 20 May 1694; Pazos Pazos, *El ayuntamiento de la ciudad de México*, pp. 118–119, 269, 277–290.

101. See Albaladejo, *Fragmentos de monarquía*, pp. 241–247, 282–283; Charles Jago, "Taxation and Political Culture in Castile 1590–1640," in *Spain, Europe and the Atlantic World: Essays in Honour of John H. Elliott*, edited by R. Kagan and G. Parker (Cambridge, U.K., 1995), 56–67.

102. This discussion is informed by the ideas expressed by António M. Hespanha in *Vísperas del Leviatán: Instituciones y poder político (Portugal, siglo XVII)*, translated by F. Bouza Alvarez (Madrid, 1989), pp. 232–241, 437–442.

103. J. Vicens Vives, "The Administrative Structure of the State in the Sixteenth and Seventeenth Centuries," in *Government in Reformation Europe, 1520–1560*, edited by Henry J. Cohn (Bloomington, 1979), p. 64. See also Gerhard Oestreich, *Neostoicism and the Early Modern State* (Cambridge, U.K., 1982), pp. 263–264; Thompson, "Absolutism in Castile," in *Crown and Cortes*, pp. V:95–98. In this regard, most of the traits of the supposed process of "degeneration" of the Spanish monarchy in the seventeenth century can be equally found in the rest of the European monarchies, not least the absolute regime of Louis XIV in France, which is not exactly considered a regime in decline. William Beik has convincingly shown this for the French case in *Absolutism and Society in Seventeenth-Century France: State Power and Provincial Aristocracy in Languedoc* (Cambridge, U.K., 1985); see also Mettam, *Power and Faction*, especially chap. 1.

Chapter 3

1. "Una certificación dada por el escribano Diego de Torres, de orden del virrey marqués de Gelves, del medio que tomó el Sr. Arzobispo, D. Juan de la Serna, para resistir que le sacasen de San Juan Teotihuacan para Veracruz," in *Documentos para la historia de México*, 2a. serie, tomo III (México, 1855), pp. 5–8. For a version of this incident sympathetic to the archbishop, see Cristóbal Ruiz de Cabrera, *Algunos singulares y extraordinarios sucesos del gobierno de D. Diego Pimentel, marqués de Gelves, virrey desta Nueva España, por su excesivo rigor, ayudado de sus consejeros* (México, 1624), fos. 6v–7v. On the confrontation between Gelves and Pérez de la Serna, see Jonathan I. Israel, *Race, Class and Politics in Colonial Mexico, 1610–1670* (London, 1975), pp. 135–160.

2. Not long ago, Frederick P. Bowser observed that, "Though perhaps unparalleled among historical developments in the range and significance of its import for the region, the rise and decline of the Middle American Church has thus far received only sporadic and patchy attention from historians." See his "The Church in Colonial Middle America," *Latin American Research Review* 25, no. 1 (1990): 138. Some of the most relevant works dealing with the Church in colonial Mexico are Nancy M. Farriss, *Crown and Clergy in Colonial Mexico, 1759–1821: The Crisis of Ecclesiastical Privilege* (London, 1968); Stafford Poole, *Pedro Moya de Contreras: Catholic Reform and Royal Power in New Spain, 1571–1591* (Berkeley, 1987); David A. Brading, *Church and State in Bourbon Mexico: The Diocese of Michoacán 1749–1810* (Cambridge, U.K., 1994). For the local level, the following is indispensable: William

B. Taylor's monumental *Magistrates of the Sacred: Priests and Parishioners in Eighteenth-Century Mexico* (Stanford, 1996). A notable recent study of the colonial Church from the perspective of the cathedral chapters is Oscar Mazín Gómez, *El cabildo catedral de Valladolid de Michoacán* (Zamora, MI, 1996).

3. See, for example, C.H. Haring, *The Spanish Empire in America* (New York, 1947), pp. 167–169; Farriss, *Crown and Clergy*, pp. 10, 15, 32, 89; Poole, *Pedro Moya de Contreras*, pp. 211–212.

4. Patricia Seed, "The Colonial Church as an Ideological State Apparatus," in *Intellectuals and Power in Mexico*, edited by R. Camp et al. (Los Angeles, 1981), pp. 397–415. For his part, José Antonio Maravall has argued that a progressive nationalization of the Spanish Church took place in the early modern period, which helped the process of formation of the absolutist state. This process was characterized by increasing incorporation of the Church into the structures of the state and by utilization of the Church by the state. Thus, religion as a "means of domination, used to keep the masses in submission," became a matter of state. See his *Estado Moderno y Mentalidad Social (Siglos XV a XVII)* (Madrid, 1972), vol. I, pp. 215–245.

5. That is exactly what happened in 1571 to fray Alonso de Molina, a well-known Franciscan author of Nahuatl grammars and translations, when he dedicated one of his works to viceroy Martín Enríquez. In the dedication, the enthusiastic friar affirmed that the great solicitude and care with which the king ruled his dominions had moved him to appoint such an excellent prince — the ruling viceroy — as the "supreme head of this Church of New Spain." Needless to say, Molina was denounced to the Inquisition and forced to correct his affirmation. See AHN, Diversos-Documentos de Indias, no. 209, "Epístola nuncupatoria al muy excelente señor don Martín Enríquez"; ibid., no. 247, the archbishop Moya de Contreras to the president of the Council of the Indies (n.d.). In this regard, nothing could be more wrong than to affirm, as Ramón A. Gutiérrez has done, that the "legal reality was that Spain's sovereign was both *rex et sacerdos*, king and high priest over the Indies." See his *When Jesus Came, the Corn Mothers Went Away: Marriage, Sexuality, and Power in New Mexico, 1500–1846* (Stanford, 1991), p. 99.

6. On the conflicts between the ecclesiastical hierarchy and the religious orders in New Spain, see Robert C. Padden, "The *Ordenanza del Patronazgo*, 1574: An Interpretative Essay," *The Americas* 12 (1956): 333–354; Poole, *Pedro Moya de Contreras*, pp. 66–87; Antonio Rubial García, "La mitra y la cogulla. La secularización palafoxiana y su impacto en el siglo XVII." *Relaciones* 73 (Winter 1998): 239–272.

7. Here, I follow Pablo Fernández Albaladejo's arguments as presented in "Iglesia y configuración del poder en la monarquía católica (siglos XV–XVII). Algunas consideraciones," in *Etat et Eglise dans la genèse de l'Etat moderne* (Madrid, 1986), pp. 209–216.

8. Castillo de Bobadilla, *Política para corregidores*, lib. II, cap. XVII, no. 1 (my emphasis).

9. Francisco Ugarte de Hermosa y Salcedo *Origen de los dos gobiernos divino y humano y forma de su ejercicio en lo temporal* (Madrid, 1655), pp. 128–129.

10. António M. Hespanha, *Vísperas del Leviatán: Instituciones y poder político (Portugal, siglo XVII)*, translated by F. Bouza Alvarez (Madrid, 1989), pp. 235–238. *Iurisdictio* literally means the act of saying the law. The king's obligation to defend every one's rights is what made Bobadilla affirm that secular judges were obligated to help the clerics because "secular princes are the protectors of the ecclesiastical jurisdiction." See Bobadilla, *Política para corregidores*, lib. II, cap. XVII, no. 181.

11. Hespanha, *Vísperas del Leviatán*, pp. 256–274. See also I.A.A. Thompson, "Absolutism in Castile," in *Crown and Cortes: Government, Institutions and Representation in Early Modern Castile* (Aldershot, 1993), pp. V:82–84.

12. To better explain his arguments, Bobadilla refers to the incident that took place between Peter and the soldiers who were coming to seize Jesus Christ. When Peter unsheathed his sword to protect Jesus, He said to him: "Put your knife back into the sheath." To Bobadilla, this sentence means that, although the "material knife belongs to Saint Peter and is in the possession of Saint Peter and as a result in the possession of the Church, because the word 'your knife' denotes ownership," Christ did not want the Church, which must be "benign and gentle with the contumacious and malefactors," to utilize the methods of secular justice but rather those that are spiritual in nature (that is, interdicts and excommunications). See Bobadilla, *Política para corregidores*, lib. II, cap. XVII, nos. 2–7. All these ideas about the two knives or the two luminaries and about the superiority of the pope and ecclesiastical power over the monarch and secular power are equally advanced by Ugarte, for whom "to the greatness and highness of the sun corresponds the excellence of the soul and the superiority of the pontiff, and to the smallness and inferiority of the moon, the lowliness of the body and the inferiority of the king." His clerical status probably led Ugarte to emphasize still more the pope's power. The pope, according to him, "is the world's wonder and the greatest thing among all things, being neither God nor man." See his *Origen de los dos gobiernos*, pp. 100–117, 126–140. For an example of how the solar and lunar imagery was used in New Spain to criticize viceregal encroachment on ecclesiastical autonomy, see "Carta del padre fray Francisco Ximénez … al virrey marqués de Villamanrique," in *Cartas de religiosos de Nueva España*, edited by J. García Icazbalceta (México, 1886), p. 162.

13. Francisco Suárez, *Defensio Fidei III. Principatus politicus o la soberanía popular*, edited by E. Elorduy and L. Pereña ([Coimbra, 1613] Madrid, 1965), pp. 64–86.

14. Ugarte, probably reflecting the opinion of a majority of writers, affirms that, though the pope can be compared to the sun and the king to the moon, in order to highlight the superiority of the former this comparison is only of use when the pope meets the king or the emperor, because the "king is the emperor of his kingdom"; that is, within his kingdom the monarch does not recognize any superior power. See Ugarte, *Origen de los dos gobiernos*, pp.

208–209. For an account of the turbulent relations between the Spanish monarchy and the papacy in the seventeenth century, see Antonio Domínguez Ortiz, "Regalismo y relaciones Iglesia-Estado en el siglo XVII," in *Historia de la Iglesia en España*, edited by R. García-Villoslada (Madrid, 1979), vol. IV, pp. 73–89.

15. See Bobadilla, *Política para corregidores*, lib. II, cap. XVII, no. 5; Juan de Solórzano y Pereira, *Política indiana*, edited by M.A. Ochoa Brun (Madrid, [1647] 1972), lib. IV, cap. I, nos. 1–7; Ugarte, *Origen de los dos gobiernos*, pp. 113–114. For a detailed study of Solórzano's thought on this matter, see James Muldoon, *The Americas in the Spanish World Order: The Justification for Conquest in the Seventeenth Century* (Philadelphia, 1994), chaps. 5–8. On the sixteenth- and seventeenth-century debates and controversies over the Spanish possession of the Indies, see Anthony Pagden, *Spanish Imperialism and the Political Imagination* (New Haven, CT, 1990), pp. 13–36.

16. *Las Siete Partidas*, Primera Partida, tít. V, leyes XVII, XVIII.

17. On the ecclesiastical patronage established in Granada and its influence in America, see Antonio Garrido Aranda, *Organización de la Iglesia en el Reino de Granada y su proyección en Indias, Siglo XVI* (Sevilla, 1979).

18. Christian Hermann, "Le patronage royal espagnol: 1525–1750," in *Etat et Eglise dans la genèse de l'Etat moderne* (Madrid, 1986), pp. 257–266.

19. The royal Patronato in the American territories was established in its definitive form by a *cédula* issued by Philip II on 1 June 1574 and would not experience any great changes until the second half of the eighteenth century. Among many other things, it established the monarchs' right of presentation to all benefices in the Indies (although by a *cédula* of 1609 the presentation of the lesser benefices of parish priests was delegated to viceroys, presidents of *audiencias*, or governors); the *pase regio* (the control of all the documents issued by the Holy See and directed to the American territories, which had to be previously approved by the Council of the Indies); the *recursos de fuerza* (the right to appeal the decisions of the ecclesiastical judges to the royal courts); the control of the passage to the Indies of clerics; and the sending of episcopal reports on the state of the dioceses to the Council of the Indies instead of to Rome. The majority of the provisions of the 1574 *cédula* will be included subsequently in the *Recopilación*, lib. I, tít. VI. See also AGN, RCO, vol. 5, exp. 8, fos. 35–38, *cédula* of 1 June 1574; Padden, "The *Ordenanza del Patronazgo*," pp. 333–354; Farriss, *Crown and Clergy*, pp. 15–38; John F. Schwaller, "The *Ordenanza del Patronazgo* in New Spain, 1574–1600," *The Americas* 42 (1986): 253–274; Alberto de la Hera, "El patronato y el vicariato regio en Indias," in *Historia de la Iglesia en Hispanoamérica y Filipinas (siglos XV-XIX)*, edited by P. Borges (Madrid, 1992), vol. I, pp. 63–79.

20. Solórzano, *Política indiana*, lib. IV, cap. II.

21. Ibid., lib. IV, cap. III, nos. 14–17.

22. See Antonio de Egaña, *La teoría del Regio Vicariato Español en Indias* (Rome, 1958), pp. 126–156.

23. AGI, Mexico 41, no. 22a, the bishop of Oaxaca to Mancera, 8 December 1665; ibid., the Crown attorney to Mancera, 11 January 1666.
24. Solórzano, *Política indiana*, lib. IV, cap. III, no. 26. See also *Recopilación*, lib. I, tít. VI, leyes iii, iiii, xviiii, xxi.
25. Padden, "The *Ordenanza del Patronazgo*," pp. 333–334. For the same argument made in relation to the peninsular bishops, see Ignasi Fernández Terricabras, "Al servicio del rey y de la Iglesia. El control del episcopado castellano por la Corona en tiempos de Felipe II," in *Lo conflictivo y lo consensual en Castilla: Sociedad y poder político, 1521–1715*, edited by F.J. Guillamón and J.J. Ruiz (Murcia, 2001), pp. 205–232.
26. In the Instructions to the viceroys, a section was always included in which the monarch earnestly instructed every viceroy to take special care in the defense of the royal Patronato that belonged to the monarch, not allowing any prelate to take that royal prerogative away. See, for example, "Instrucción al conde de Monterrey, 20.III.1596," in *Los virreyes españoles en América durante el gobierno de la casa de Austria, México III*, edited by Lewis Hanke; BAE, vol. CCLXXIV, p. 130. The same section is reproduced by Solórzano in the chapter in which he discusses the *Patronato Real* in his *Política indiana*, lib. IV, cap. II, no. 6.
27. "Gran Memorial (Instrucción secreta dada al rey en 1624)," in *Memoriales y cartas del conde duque de Olivares*, edited by J.H. Elliott and J.F. de la Peña (Madrid, 1978), vol. I, pp. 50–51.
28. Solórzano, *Política indiana*, lib. IV, cap. IV, no. 37. In the final analysis, this system was part of the network of patronage created by the Crown to secure the fidelity of all vassals, both lay and religious. See Chapter 5 for a study of the system of patronage created by the viceroys in the name of the monarchs.
29. Suárez, *Defensio Fidei III*, pp. 108, 132, 144.
30. Pedro de Reina Maldonado, *Norte claro del perfecto prelado en su pastoral gobierno* (Madrid, 1653), vol I, pp. 28, 30–31, 35–36, 50–54, 126, 131.
31. Gaspar de Villarroel, *Gobierno eclesiástico pacífico y unión de los dos cuchillos, pontificio y regio* (Madrid, 1656), pp. 4, 6–8.
32. Villarroel, *Gobierno eclesiástico*, p. 10. For this same reason, when the king writes to the prelates he never says "We command" (*mandamos*) but "We request and ask" (*rogamos y encargamos*). Nevertheless, both Bobadilla and Villarroel maintain that the concept *rogamos y encargamos* has the value of a precept and not of a request when it comes from the prince. For that reason, if the ecclesiastics do not comply with what they are being requested and asked, they can be punished for being disobedient (Villarroel specifies that this refers only to those cases in which the monarch can order something to a prelate; Bobadilla specifically cites the case of the *recursos de fuerza*). See Bobadilla, *Política para corregidores*, lib. II, cap. X, nos. 63, 66; Villarroel, *Gobierno eclesiástico*, pp. 39, 44.
33. As argued by several authors, the bishop is the greatest ecclesiastical figure, as cardinals do not have greater authority than bishops, only a greater office. Bishops are individuals of such a high rank that the king rises to welcome

them and they all are regarded as the king's advisors; they have precedence over all the king's councilors and sit at the king's right. See Ugarte, *Origen de los dos gobiernos*, pp. 118–122; Bobadilla, *Política para corregidores*, lib. II, cap. XVII, nos. 12, 15.

34. In the early modern period the pope's figure is constructed like that of a monarch. For fray Juan de Pineda, for example, the Church is but an "ecclesiastical monarchy" with a supreme head, the Sovereign Pontiff. And, just as the monarch rules with the help of his councilors, the pope does so with the help of the cardinals and bishops, who illuminate him with their advice. See the preface in *Los treinta libros de la monarquía eclesiástica o historia universal del mundo* (Barcelona, 1620); also Suárez, *Defensio Fidei III*, p. 96; Ugarte, *Origen de los dos gobiernos*, pp. 124–125. On the pope as monarch, see Paolo Prodi, *The Papal Prince. One Body and Two Souls: The Papal Monarchy in Early Modern Europe*, translated by S. Haskins (Cambridge, U.K., 1987).

35. Villarroel, *Gobierno eclesiástico*, pp. 17–19. For his part, Solórzano points out that, because of the great distance of the American bishops from Rome, they had been granted authority over many matters which usually were reserved to the pope. See *Política indiana*, lib. IV, cap. VII, no. 9.

36. Villarroel, *Gobierno eclesiástico*, pp. 27–28.

37. *Esfera de Apolo y teatro del sol. Ejemplar de prelados en la suntuosa fábrica y portada triunfal que la … Iglesia Metropolitana de México erigió … a la venida del Ilmo. Sr. Don Marcelo López de Azcona … arzobispo de México* (México, 1653), fo. 3.

38. Alonso de la Peña Peralta and Pedro Fernández Osorio, *Pan místico, numen simbólico, simulacro político, que en la fábrica del arco triunfal, que erigió el amor y la obligación en las aras de su debido rendimiento la … Metropolitana Iglesia de México al felicísimo recibimiento y plausible ingreso del Ilustrismo. y Revermo. Señor M.D. Fr. Payo Enriques de Rivera, … su genialísimo pastor, prelado y esposo* (México, 1670). For his part, Francisco de Aguiar y Seijas, who succeeded Enríquez de Rivera as archbishop of Mexico, would appear on his arch as the sea god Proteus. See *Transformación teopolítica, idea mitológica de príncipe pastor, sagrado Proteo, alegorizada en imágenes, decifrada en números, que en el aparato magnífico del triunfal arco y padrón glorioso, en el fausto día de su plausible recibimiento, dispuso y consagró al Ilustmo. y Revmo. Señor D.D. Francisco de Aguiar Seijas y Ulloa … dignísimo arzobispo de esta metrópoli, la siempre augusta iglesia metropolitana de México* (México, 1683).

39. See the descriptions of the paintings of the episcopal arch in Peña Peralta and Fernández Osorio, *Pan místico*; also *Esfera de Apolo*, fos. 5v–8, 9v, 11v, and *Transformación teopolítica*, fos. 4v–19r. On the episcopal entry and its great similarity with the viceregal entry, see Chapter 4.

40. Villarroel, *Gobierno eclesiástico*, p. 278; Solórzano, *Política indiana*, lib. IV, cap. XIII, nos. 1–5; cap. XIV, no. 1. The cathedral chapter was usually comprised of five *dignidades* (dignitaries) — *deán* (dean), who acted as president whenever the see was vacant; *arcediano* (archdeacon); *chantre* (precentor or choirmaster); *maestrescuela* (schoolmaster); and *tesorero* (treasurer) — plus ten

canónigos (canons), six *racioneros* (prebendaries), and six *medio-racioneros* (junior prebendaries). They were all known as *prebendados*. See Solórzano, *Política indiana*, lib. IV, cap. IV, nos. 12–17; Brading, *Church and State*, pp. 175–187; Poole, *Pedro Moya de Contreras*, pp. 220–221. For the important role played by the cathedral chapters in the political life of New Spain since the beginnings of Spanish rule, see Mazín Gómez, *El cabildo catedral*, pp. 138–143, 186–192, 252–255.

41. Villarroel, *Gobierno eclesiástico*, pp. 215–230. For a description of the typical retinue of a bishop, see Juan de Palafox, "Direcciones pastorales. Instrucción de la forma con que se ha de gobernar el prelado en orden a Dios, a sí mismo, a su familia y súbditos," in *Obras del Ilmo., Exmo. y venerable siervo de Dios, don Juan de Palafox y Mendoza* (Madrid, 1762), vol. III, pp. 42–112. See also the list of the fifty persons with whom Palafox, appointed bishop of Puebla, traveled to Mexico in AGI, Contratación 5422, no. 39 (15 March 1640). On conspicuous consumption as a sign of power, see Chapter 4; on the role played by a viceroy's retinue, see Chapter 5.

42. Reina Maldonado, *Norte claro del perfecto prelado*, vol. II, pp. 1–31. See also Diego de Avendaño, *Thesaurus Indicus (1668)*, edited by A. Muñoz García (Pamplona, 2001), pp. 229–236.

43. Solórzano, *Política indiana*, lib. IV, cap. VI, nos. 1–29.

44. Specifically, the king orders bishops to swear before a notary public and witnesses that they "shall not contravene in any manner our royal Patronato, keeping it and complying with it in its entirety as it is contained in it, straightforwardly and without any impediment, and … they shall not impede or hinder the use of our royal jurisdiction and the collection of whatever royal duties and rents belonging to us, including that of the two-ninths which are reserved to us from the tithes of the churches of the Indies, and … they shall make the nominations, institutions, and collations that they are obliged to make in accordance with our said Patronato." See *Recopilación*, lib. I, tít. VII, ley i; AGN, RCO, vol. 9, exp. 140, fo. 373, *cédula* of 25 October 1667. For the oath taken, for instance, by Diego Osorio, bishop of Puebla, see AGI, Mexico 42, no. 71a, 9 December 1655.

45. Solórzano, *Política indiana*, lib. IV, cap. VI, nos. 30–35. On the difficulties found in making the bishops take this oath, see AGI, Mexico 41, no. 22, Mancera to the king, 1 April 1666; AGI, Mexico 42, no. 71, Mancera to the queen regent, 19 July 1668.

46. It was common to argue that the government of the household (*oeconomia*) was the best model for the government of the republic (*politia*), because the family constituted the best image of the republic, domestic authority being very similar to political authority. See Bobadilla, *Política para corregidores*, lib. I, cap. I, no. 29.

47. Villarroel, *Gobierno eclesiástico*, pp. 36–41. Bobadilla had already used this argument in his *Política para corregidores*, lib. II, cap. XVIII, no. 62. Solórzano similarly employs it to justify the view that the monarch may ban clerics from his kingdom or forbid the foundation of new churches and convents in

the Indies without the king's license. According to Solórzano, this is not against ecclesiastical immunity, as the sovereign may order such a thing because of the "political and economic government that he possesses and exercises over all of his realm," and "though clerics and other ecclesiastical persons are exempt from the king's jurisdiction, this does not mean that they are not his vassals or that they are not considered as such, nor are they released from the fidelity and obedience that all of us as such vassals owe him and swear to keep, especially as regards those commands and orders which are aimed at the public utility." See his *Política indiana*, lib. IV, cap. XXIII, no. 23; cap. XXVII, nos. 10–16. For his part, Avendaño argues that clerics should be removed from their posts — something that, he makes clear, goes against ecclesiastical immunity — only if they have committed some serious crime, but he thinks that bishops should not refuse to leave their dioceses if they are summoned by the king, as it always has to be assumed that the king would have made such a decision because of some grave reason. See Avendaño, *Thesaurus Indicus*, pp. 367–377.

48. Villarroel, *Gobierno eclesiástico*, pp. 42, 285.

49. While the duty to serve two powers was always present in the language of the clergy, this duty also appeared, though less frequently, among royal officials, who generally emphasized more the language of service to the king. As evidence, see the comment made by the *fiscal* of the Council of the Indies about the obligation of the ecclesiastical arm to cooperate with the secular one, which was what always had to be done for the greater "service of the divine and human majesties." See AGI, Mexico 45, no. 67a, "Respuesta del fiscal del Consejo," 24 March 1670.

50. This ideal constituted an important element in the rhetoric of the viceregal arch, especially in those erected by the Church. For instance, one of the paintings in the arch built in 1625 by the ecclesiastical chapter to welcome the marquis of Cerralvo depicted both the viceroy and the archbishop supporting a globe on their shoulders and above the globe a two-headed imperial eagle, one of its heads covered with the royal crown and the other with a miter. See Sebastián Gutiérrez, *Arco triunfal … con que la Iglesia Catedral Metropolitana de la ciudad de México hizo recibimiento al Exmo. Sr., D. Rodrigo Pacheco Osorio, marqués de Cerralvo, virrey de la Nueva España, con una alegoría al nuevo gobierno* (México, 1625), fos. 36v–37. Similarly, one of the panels of the arch erected in 1653, also by the ecclesiastical chapter, to receive the duke of Alburquerque showed a depiction of the temple of Janus, symbol of concord; on one side of the temple was an image of Mars, who represented the viceroy, and on the other side was the image of Mercury, as an allegory of the archbishop, who was offering his caduceus — symbol of friendship — to Mars. See *Marte católico, astro político*, fo. 8. Juan de Palafox, for his part, explained in detail how both powers were supposed to help each other: The spiritual should help the secular power by exhorting the subjects to reverence their rulers, by pacifying the people, and by inculcating in the faithful their loyalty to princes; while the temporal ought to support the spiritual power by

enforcing the obedience and veneration of ecclesiastical precepts and decrees and by setting an example for the subjects of obedience to and fear of the Church. See Juan de Palafox, "Injusticias que intervinieron en la muerte de Cristo," in *Tratados Mejicanos* (Madrid, 1968), vol. II, pp. 336–337.

51. Bobadilla, *Política para corregidores*, lib. II, cap. XVIII, nos. 1, 15, 16, 60.

52. Ibid., lib. II, cap. XVII, no. 87; cap. XIX, nos. 24, 30, 40, 48, 49. For the opposite view of how much rulers should fear excommunication, see Pedro de Rivadeneira, "Tratado de la religión y virtudes que debe tener el príncipe cristiano para gobernar y conservar sus estados, contra lo que Nicolás Maquiavelo y los políticos deste tiempo enseñan," in *Obras escogidas del Padre Pedro de Rivadeneira*, edited by V. de la Fuente (Madrid, [1595] 1952), pp. 507–511; Juan Márquez, *El gobernador cristiano, deducido de las vidas de Moisén y Josué, príncipes del pueblo de Dios* ([Salamanca, 1612] Brussels, 1664), pp. 270–271.

53. These are the words that the anonymous chronicler put in the mouth of Alonso de Cuevas Dávalos, archbishop of Mexico. See *Funeral lamento, clamor doloroso, y sentimiento triste que a la piadosa memoria del Ilustrísimo y Reverendísimo Señor Doctor D. Alonso de Cuevas Dávalos, obispo que fue de Oaxaca y arzobispo de México, … repite su Santa Iglesia Catedral … en las sepulcrales pompas de su muerte, para póstumo elogio de su vida* (México, 1666), fo. 6v.

54. Maldonado, *Norte claro del perfecto prelado*, vol. I, pp. 83–85.

55. Francisco Núñez de Cepeda, *Idea de el buen pastor, copiada por los SS. Doctores, representada en Empresas Sacras con avisos espirituales, morales políticos y económicos para el gobierno de un príncipe eclesiástico* (Lyon, 1682), p. 474. See also Juan de Palafox, "Memorial al rey por la inmunidad eclesiástica," in *Obras*, vol. III, pp. 472–516.

56. Núñez de Cepeda, *Idea de el buen pastor*, pp. 467–468, 580–582. For similar views, see Alonso de Andrade, *Idea del perfecto prelado, en la vida del eminentísimo cardenal don Baltasar de Moscoso y Sandoval, arzobispo de Toledo, primado de las Españas* (Madrid, 1668), pp. 444–449. The archbishop of Mexico, Enríquez de Rivera, had expressed himself in the very same terms in the course of the conflict that arose in 1669 between the ecclesiastical chapter and viceroy Mancera because the members of the chapter celebrated some public prayers without having first notified the viceroy of the motives for such prayers. The capitularies maintained that the chapter, exercising its liberty and right, could celebrate public prayers without having to notify the viceroy because that was an act peculiar to their ministry. Thus, when the viceroy issued a writ ordering the chapter not to celebrate any public prayers without informing him in advance, the archbishop made known to the viceroy that he was prepared to defend the liberty and jurisdiction of his church "spilling, if necessary, up to the last drop of [my] blood." See AGI, Mexico 45, no. 67a-2, the cathedral chapter to the king [*sic*], 6 August 1669; ibid., no. 67a, Mancera to the queen regent, 16 August 1669. At the beginning of the seventeenth century, another archbishop, Fray García de Santa María, arguing in defense of his right to sit under a baldachin in the cathedral, had also

let the viceroy know that he had sworn to defend ecclesiastical liberty with his life. See AGI, Mexico 278, "Copia de carta que escribió el arzobispo de México al conde de Monterrey, virrey de la Nueva España, en 2 de febrero, 1603."

57. Núñez de Cepeda, *Idea de el buen pastor*, pp. 639–643. Similarly, Avendaño would argue that laying an excommunication when its effectiveness was not assured was counterproductive. See Avendaño, *Thesaurus Indicus*, p. 477.

58. AGI, Mexico 38, no. 15, the duke of Alburquerque to the king, 20 July 1656. For a similar comment made by Alburquerque to Méndez de Haro, see Israel, *Race, Class and Politics*, p. 258.

59. AGI, Mexico 40, no. 4, the marquis of Mancera to the king, 24 January 1665. Ironically, Mancera was unaware at the time of his writing that he would also become embroiled in a bitter and protracted clash with archbishop Enríquez de Rivera, which would only serve to confirm his worst forebodings. See below and also Chapter 4.

60. In reality, this was not a problem specific to the viceroys but common to all royal authorities. So was it emphatically expressed by Gaspar de Villarroel in the dedication to the king of his aforementioned work, which has, as one may recall, the revealing title of *Gobierno eclesiástico pacífico y unión de los dos cuchillos*. As bishop of Santiago de Chile, his conflicts would have been not with a viceroy but with the *oidores* of the *audiencia* of Chile. Thus, Villarroel declares that the motive that had moved him to write the book had been "to make peace between bishops and magistrates and unite these two knives, which being together at the side of Christ, Our Lord, I find them in the Indies not only divided but opposed." This is so much so, adds Villarroel, that "because of its rarity it looks like a marvel that an *audiencia* and a bishop be on friendly terms."

61. AGI, Mexico 41, no. 49, Osorio to Mancera, 10 June 1666. Very similarly, in the previous century, the rector of the Dominican school in Puebla, in conflict with the marquis of Villamanrique, had written a blunt letter to the viceroy to make it clear that neither bishops nor archbishops were the lieutenants of the pope, like viceroys were of kings — they were the vicars of Christ Himself in their dioceses, and their authority and power came directly from Him. Moreover, he asserted, all clerics were exempt from royal jurisdiction, and very harsh censures were imposed upon those who dared to violate the immunity and liberty of the Church. "Carta del padre fray Francisco Ximénez … al virrey marqués de Villamanrique," in *Cartas de religiosos de Nueva España*, p. 163.

62. AGI, Mexico 41, no. 49, the crown attorney to Mancera, 17 September 1666; ibid., Mancera to the queen regent, 31 October 1666. The fiscal's opinions were but a confirmation of those of the Crown when it reminded Mancera that, because everyone was subject to him in "economic, political, and military matters," he should procure peaceful relations between ecclesiastical and secular officials through the use of gentle and prudent means. To this, the viceroy responded, referring to his problems with the bishop of Puebla, that

for his part he would always do everything possible to stay on good terms with that prelate, as it was fitting "to the service of both majesties." See AGN, RCO, vol. 9, exp. 23, fo. 86, the queen regent to Mancera, 30 June 1666; AGI, Mexico 42, no. 17, Mancera to the queen regent, 25 April 1667.

63. "Relación del marqués de Mancera, 22.X.1673," in *Los virreyes españoles en América*, BAE, vol. CCLXXVII, pp. 25–32, 45–50.

64. On Mancera's complaints about this matter and the arguments of archbishop Enríquez de Rivera to justify his behavior, see also AGI, Mexico 46, no. 13, Mancera to the queen regent, 2 April 1672; AGI, Mexico 116, no. 13, Enríquez de Rivera to the queen regent, 3 December 1671.

65. This allowed the bishops to appoint their retainers as priests of numerous parishes, thus eliminating any intervention of the viceroys in the process of appointment. In the 1630s, the marquis of Cerralvo had already accused archbishop Manso of doing this. See AGI, Mexico 31, no. 11, Cerralvo to the king, 20 November 1632; ibid., no. 20, Cerralvo to the king, 15 February 1634. Mancera also criticized the bishops for refusing to punish the many priests who were more interested in commercial transactions than in setting a good example for the Indians of their parishes. (AGI, Mexico 45, no. 25, Mancera to the queen regent, 24 April 1671). Compare these criticisms, for example, with those made by the bishops themselves that the viceroys, besides appointing their retainers as *alcaldes mayores*, did nothing to prevent the latter's abuses, equally devoted to exploiting the indigenous population. These criticisms will be examined in detail in Chapter 5.

66. Viceregal complaints about New Spain's ecclesiastical hierarchy had a long history. Almost a century before, the marquis of Villamanrique had already denounced the usurpation of the *Royal Patronato* by the prelates of that kingdom. See his "Advertimientos generales que el marqués de Villamanrique dio a Luis de Velasco. 14.II.1590," in *Los virreyes, México I*, BAE, vol. CCLXXIII, p. 282. In 1618, the marquis of Guadalcázar had written to the king that *Patronato* matters always were a cause for confrontation with the prelates. AGI, Mexico 29, no. 14, Gudalcázar to the king, 16 October 1618. In the 1630s, the marquis of Cerralvo had expressed very similar complaints to those of Mancera. See "Relación del estado en que dejó el gobierno del marqués de Cerralvo, 17.III.1636," in *Los virreyes, México III*, BAE, vol. CCLXXV, pp. 285–286; AGI, Mexico 30, no. 37, Cerralvo to the king, 21 August 1631. Years later, the duke of Alburquerque would inform the king that the "bishops' main intention is to encroach upon the Royal Patronato of Your Majesty." AGI, Mexico 38, no. 6, Alburquerque to the king, 5 May 1655. On the confrontations of the viceroys with the bishops on the public stage, see Chapter 4.

67. AGI, Mexico 25, nos. 41c, 41f, Monterrey to García de Santa María, 1 February 1603 and 21 February 1603; ibid., nos. 41e, 41g, García de Santa María to Monterrey, 2 February 1603 and 21 February 1603; AGI, Mexico 25, no. 25 and AGI, Mexico 26, no. 14, Monterrey to the king, March 1603 and 30 April 1604.

68. RAH, Col. Jesuitas, vol. CXVIII, 29, "Información en derecho en que se impugna el parecer que al marqués de Gelves, virrey de Nueva España, se le dio que no podía ser excomulgado por el arzobispo" (n.d.), fos., 1, 2, 4–6; Cabrera, *Algunos singulares y extraordinarios sucesos*, fo. 5r.

69. RAH, Jesuitas, vol. CXVIII, 29, "Información en derecho," fo. 1; Cabrera, *Algunos singulares y extraordinarios sucesos*, fo. 4r.

70. RAH, Jesuitas, vol. CXVIII, 29, "Información en derecho," fos. 3, 8, 9.

71. AGI, Patronato 221, ramo 12, "Apología hecha por el padre fray Bartolomé de Burgillos … confesor del Exmo. Señor marqués de Gelves" (n.d.); AGI, Patronato 223, ramo 2, "Parecer … del Dr. Agustín de Barrientos, catedrático de filosofía en propiedad en esta universidad de México" (n.d.).

72. RAH, Jesuitas, vol. CXVIII, 29, "Información en derecho," fos. 2, 12, 13.

73. Ibid., fo. 16. When discussing the question of whether viceroys should submit themselves to a prelate's censures, Avendaño would use the same arguments advanced by Pérez de la Serna, asserting that the viceroys could be excommunicated by the bishops, but because he was very much aware of the long history of conflict between the former and the latter he would conclude that, generally speaking, it was not licit to excommunicate a viceroy because of the ever-present risk of this act causing a riot, especially in the Indies. See his *Thesaurus Indicus*, pp. 475–476.

74. For an account of the confrontation between Cerralvo and Manso, see Israel, *Race, Class and Politics*, pp. 174–189.

75. AGI, Mexico 31, nos. 2, 6, 11, Cerralvo to the king, 20 March, 2 May, 20 November 1632. Not even when the king, when informed, ordered the archbishop to punish the prebendary did he receive any type of punishment. On the contrary, complained Cerralvo, the archbishop not only had entrusted him with the most important sermons but also had made a particular point of attending his preaching. See AGI, Mexico 31, no. 34, Cerralvo to the king, 11 April 1635.

76. AGI, Mexico 3, no. 133, Manso to the king, 7 and 8 November 1629, and 25 April 1630.

77. See, for example, the opinions of the bishop of Puebla in AGI, Mexico 345, fos. 81–82, Osorio to the king, 30 October 1666.

78. As the duke of Escalona wryly observed, a viceroy should always try to excuse himself from dealing with *visitadores*, and if he ever had to deal with a *visitador* who also was a councilor and a prelate, he would better excuse himself from the post of viceroy. See "Carta del duque de Escalona al conde de Salvatierra, su sucesor," in *Los virreyes, México IV*, BAE, vol. CCLXXVI, p. 33.

79. Indicative of the power vested on Francisco Manso as councilor of the Indies was that the fleet that brought him to New Spain had been under his command (this privilege was also awarded to the viceroys). See AGI, Mexico 3, no. 37, *consulta* of 23 June 1627.

80. AGI, Mexico 30, nos. 23, 26, 27, Cerralvo to the king, 19 July 1629, 24 January 1630, and 24 January 1630; AGI, Mexico 31, no. 37, Cerralvo to the king, 7 May 1635.

81. AGI, Mexico 30, nos. 24, 38, Cerralvo to the king, 24 August 1629 and 21 August 1631; AGI, Mexico 3, no. 140, Cerralvo to the king, 12 September 1630.

82. As proof of the serious consideration given by the Council to a prelate's opinions, see, for example, the Council's long discussion of the accusations of dishonesty made by Manso against Cerralvo in AGI, Mexico 3, no. 131, *consulta* of 18 September 1629.

83. As the marquis of Mancera would point out to the monarch years later, in the wake of his conflicts with the bishop of Puebla, the "attention, respect and obedience due to the viceroy increase and decrease in time with the indications of the good or bad place he occupies in Your Majesty's favor. Without your favor being well known to everyone and without knowledge of [the viceroy's] credit being well established among the superior ministers, his operations can have no vigor, spirit or effect … because being the subjects of these provinces naturally fickle, loose, and unruly, it is not possible to contain them in the appropriate subjection once the bridle of authority is overcome." See AGI, Mexico 42, no. 15b, Mancera to the queen regent, 31 March 1667.

84. AGI, Mexico 30, no. 27, Cerralvo to the king, 24 January 1630; ibid., no. 27a, "Copia de papel que el Marqués mi señor escribió a don Francisco del Castillo Albarado, oidor más antiguo de la Real Audiencia de México" (n.d.); ibid., no. 38bis, Cerralvo to the king, 21 August 1631; AGI, Mexico 3, no. 140, Cerralvo to the king, 12 September 1630.

85. For these arguments, see Palafox, "Respuesta y discurso sobre las frecuentes translaciones que se hacen de los señores obispos de unas a otras iglesias," in *Obras*, vol. III, pp. 417–469. One viceroy, the marquis of Guadalcázar, had made a direct reference to this when, in the course of his disputes with archbishop Pérez de la Serna (the same one who would bring the downfall of the count of Gelves in 1624), wrote to the king that the prelate knew very well how extremely difficult it was to remove him from his post. For that reason, the viceroy suggested Pérez de la Serna should be appointed to some bishopric in Spain, where he would be kept in check. AGI, Mexico 29, nos. 30, 54, Guadalcázar to the king, 27 September 1619 and 4 June 1621.

86. AGI, Mexico 3, no. 131, *consulta* of 18 September 1629.

87. AGI, Mexico 3, no. 82, *consulta* and royal answer of 30 May 1629; ibid., no. 117, *consulta* of 4 May 1630; AGN, RCO, vol. 1, exp. 44, fo. 78, the king to Cerralvo (n.d.). On the greater power of councils and tribunals when constituted as "bodies," in comparison to that of individuals, see Chapter 4.

88. AGI, Mexico 3, no. 140, *consulta* of 18 February 1631; AGN, RCO, vol. 1, exp. 68, fo. 124, the king to Cerralvo, 15 March 1631; AGI, Mexico 3, no. 215, Manso to the king, 18 September 1631, 29 March 1632, 25 January 1633, 6 March 1633.

89. AGI, Mexico 3, no. 215, the *audiencia* to the king, 17 May 1632; ibid., no. 232, Cerralvo to the king, 30 August 1633; the *audiencia* to the king, 1 September 1633.

90. AGI, Mexico 3, nos. 215, 259, 265, *consultas* of 19 August 1633, 18 January 1635, and 23 April 1635. See also Israel, *Race, Class and Politics*, pp. 187–188. Another problem that had to be taken into account when deciding to remove a prelate from his bishopric was the objections of the Holy See, which required the mobilization of the ambassadors in Rome to secure the papal consent. In reality, the only sure way to deprive a prelate of his bishopric permanently was by his renouncing it (this is what archbishop Manso eventually did before departing for Spain). In that case, the pope had to accept the renunciation, as it was he who had to issue an appointment for a new prelate. See AGI, Mexico 3, no. 252, Manso to the king, 20 July 1634; ibid., *consulta* of 14 November 1634.

91. The clashes in fact went back to the sixteenth century. For a description, for example, of the conflicts between archbishop Moya de Contreras (1573–1586) and several viceroys, see Poole, *Pedro Moya de Contreras*, pp. 59–65. In the seventeenth century, after the clash of Cerralvo with Manso, no conflicts occurred during the rule of Cerralvo's successor because the archbishopric remained vacant for several years. Then, in 1640 bishop Palafox arrived in New Spain and the strife continued without interruption until the 1670s. On Palafox's disputes with the duke of Escalona (1640–1642) and the count of Salvatierra (1642–1648), the continuous clashes of the duke of Alburquerque (1653–1660) with the archbishop Mateo Sagade Bugueiro (1655–1661), and the fight between the count of Baños (1660–1664) and Diego Osorio de Escobar, bishop of Puebla, see Israel, *Race, Class and Politics*, pp. 199–247, 257–259, and 260–265. Israel concludes his study in 1665. For the conflicts between the marquis of Mancera (1664–1673) and the archbishop Enríquez de Rivera (1670–1681), see AGI, Mexico 44, no. 79; Mexico 45, nos. 3, 9, 32; Mexico 79, nos. 2, 3; Mexico 338; AGN, RCO, vol. 11, exps. 55, 77, 111; vol. 12, exp. 96.

92. The prelates appointed as interim viceroys in the sixteenth and seventeenth centuries were Pedro Moya de Contreras (1584–1585), Francisco García Guerra (1611–1612), Juan de Palafox y Mendoza (1642), Marcos de Torres y Rueda (1648–1649), Diego Osorio de Escobar (1664), Payo Enríquez de Rivera (1673–1680), and Juan de Ortega y Montañés (1696). In comparison, the *audiencia* of Mexico only acted as "interim viceroy" from 1564 to 1566 and from 1649 to 1650 (on this last occasion, only because Marcos de Torres, bishop of Yucatan and the acting viceroy, had suddenly died).

93. In the words of the count-duke of Olivares, ecclesiastics were "good as visitadores because their greater independence and well-being make them freer." See *Memoriales y cartas del conde-duque de Olivares*, vol. I, p. 51. For Pedro Portocarrero, having clerics in the councils was highly beneficial, as they would help to set a good example to the other councillors. See Pedro Portocarrero y Guzmán, *Teatro Monárquico de España*, edited by C. Sanz Ayán (Madrid, [1700] 1998), pp. 283–292. Núñez de Cepeda, however, believed that it was not always wise for kings to turn to the bishops to make appointments for presidencies, governorships, ambassadorships, or viceroyalties

because if God "gave the bishops a superior intelligence, it was to rule souls, not wars or political affairs. ...Their principal study must be to keep vigil in the sanctuary at all times to placate the Lord." See Núñez de Cepeda, *Idea de el buen pastor*, pp. 437–439. This was also Andrés Mendo's view in his *Príncipe perfecto y ministros ajustados: documentos políticos y morales en emblemas* (Madrid, 1656?), documento LXVIII. As *visitadores*, councilors, or acting viceroys, the jurisdiction they exercised was temporal because it proceeded from a temporal prince. This, in theory, was easy to explain but, as we have seen, it presented great difficulties in practice. See Bobadilla, *Política para corregidores*, lib. II, cap. XVII, no. 31.

94. AGI, Mexico 7, ramo 4, *consulta* of 2 June 1674. The queen agreed with the opinion of the Council.

95. AGI, Mexico 7, ramo 4, *consulta* of 20 November 1672; AGI, Mexico 7, ramo 6, *consulta* of 1 April 1675. Although the queen regent responded to the Council that interim governments were not appropriate, asking it to propose candidates for viceroy of New Spain, it does not seem that the queen ever made a decision because the archbishop of Mexico continued at the head of New Spain's government until 1680 (perhaps the fact that her son Charles II took over the government of the monarchy that same year, 1675, could have some relation with the permanence of the archbishop in the post of viceroy). On the political bonds created by royal liberality, see Chapter 5.

96. On the political turmoil in Castile during Queen Mariana's regency and the reign of Charles II, see Henry Kamen, *Spain in the Later Seventeenth Century, 1665–1700* (London, 1980), pp. 328–345, 372–394; Luis Antonio Ribot García, "La España de Carlos II," in *Historia de España Menéndez Pidal*, edited by P. Molas Ribalta (Madrid, 1993), vol. XXVIII, pp. 71–144.

97. Throughout his mandate, the archbishop was especially active erecting new churches and other religious establishments. See Francisco Sosa, *El episcopado mexicano. Galería biográfica ilustrada de los Illmos. Señores Arzobispos de México desde la época colonial hasta nuestros días* (México, 1877), pp. 154–157. Seijas also distinguished himself for his asceticism and puritanism, showing a special distaste for all kinds of public entertainment. He was notorious for his aversion toward cockfights, which had become extremely popular in Mexico, and he did everything possible to eliminate them, going as far as to offer to pay to the royal treasury, from his own purse, the rent generated from this activity. Eventually, he would secure a royal *cédula* in 1688 that prohibited the game. See AGN, RCO, vol. 22, exp. 62, fos. 130–131, the king to the count of la Monclova, 15 June 1688; ibid., exp. 92, fo. 365, the count of Galve to the king, 30 December 1689; ibid., vol. 23, exp. 6, fos. 25–26, *cédula* of 3 February 1690.

98. Mazín Gómez, *El cabildo catedral*, pp. 252–255. Nelly Sigaut has argued that this consolidation of the power of the cathedrals had its artistic manifestation in the triumphal way in which the secular Church represented itself in a set of paintings commissioned by the ecclesiastical chapter in the last decades of the seventeenth century to decorate the sacristy of Mexico City's cathedral. See

her "La tradición de estos reinos," in *Barroco Iberoamericano. Territorio, arte, espacio y sociedad* (Seville, 2001), vol. I, pp. 477–498.

99. One of the arguments that Juan de Palafox, bishop of Puebla, used to decline his appointment as archbishop of Mexico in 1642 was that if he stayed in Puebla he would be able to live peacefully, but if he moved to Mexico City he would inevitably end up clashing with the viceroys. See BPR, ms. II/1982, fos. 8–12, Palafox to Saenz Navarrete, 25 July 1642.

100. One of the most powerful actions the tribunal could take to intimidate its enemies was to accuse them of obstructing the free exercise of the Holy Office, which brought a sentence of excommunication. This was the most formidable weapon that the Inquisition could wield in its innumerable conflicts with other authorities and could only be removed by the pope or by the Inquisition itself. The weapon was especially formidable against secular authorities, because they could not counterattack effectively and were left to appeal to the king for relief; however, only the Holy Office could lift the ban. See Henry Charles Lea, *A History of the Inquisition of Spain* (New York, 1988), vol. I, p. 355.

101. The *fuero inquisitorial* carried judicial privileges of royal origin under which no official of the Inquisition, including relatives and servants, could be tried in ordinary tribunals for civil or criminal matters; rather, they had to be tried by the Inquisition's own tribunal. The inquisitors themselves could only be tried by the pope, although in the case of the Spanish Inquisition this authority was delegated to the inquisitor general. See Roberto López Vela, "Las estructuras administrativas del Santo Oficio," in *Historia de la Inquisición en España y América*, edited by J. Pérez Villanueva and B. Escandell Bonet (Madrid, 1993), vol. II, pp. 215–220.

102. AGI, Mexico 278, the marquis of Mancera and the *audiencia* to the queen regent, 16 November 1666. The fiscal of the *audiencia* also sent a letter to Madrid a few months later, complaining about the same matter. The crown attorney was shocked at the audacity of the inquisitors' disgraceful treatment of the viceroys and the *oidores* — as though they were "aiding and abetting heretics." However, the *fiscal* said most of the inquisitorial invective was directed against him because they accused him of "ill will toward the tribunal of the Holy Inquisition." In response, the *fiscal* noted in his letter that he was a knight of the Order of Santiago, by reason of which the Inquisition had carried out sixteen investigations of his relatives, all with favorable results. The inquisitors had an aversion to him, he asserted, simply because his post always required him to defend royal interests, thus moving him to inquire whether a crown attorney could be excommunicated for defending the king's jurisdiction. See AGI, Mexico 278, the crown attorney to the king [*sic*], 15 April 1667.

103. Bartolomé Bennassar, "Por el Estado, contra el Estado," in *Inquisición española: poder político y control social*, edited by B. Bennassar (Barcelona, 1981), p. 322.

104. Jaime Contreras, *El Santo Oficio de la Inquisición de Galicia (poder, sociedad y cultura)* (Madrid, 1982), pp. 12–14.

105. Domínguez Ortiz, "Regalismo y relaciones Iglesia-Estado en el siglo XVII," in *Historia de la Iglesia en España*, edited by R. García-Villoslada (Madrid, 1979), vol. IV, pp. 113–121; "Inqusición y Estado en la España de los Austrias," in *État et Église dans la génése de l'État Moderne*, p. 157.
106. Henry Kamen, *The Spanish Inquisition. A Historical Revision* (New Haven, CT, 1997), pp. 165–170. This seems to contradict his previous assertion that, "The Inquisition was in every way an instrument of royal policy, and remained politically subject to the crown." Ibid., p. 137.
107. Thompson, "Absolutism in Castile," in *Crown and Cortes*, p. V:84.
108. For the concept of a mixed institution, see Francisco Tomás y Valiente, "Relaciones de la Inquisición con el aparato institucional del Estado," in *Gobierno e instituciones en la España del Antiguo Régimen* (Madrid, 1982), pp. 16–18. Lea had already pointed out that what distinguished the Spanish Inquisition from the medieval Inquisition was its dual nature (the medieval Inquisition was clearly ecclesiastic) and that its very duality gave it a considerable degree of autonomy. See Lea, *A History of the Inquisition*, vol. I, p. 289.
109. Kamen, *The Spanish Inqusition*, pp. 163–165. See also Francisco Bethencourt, *La Inquisición en la época moderna. España, Portugal, Italia, siglos XV–XIX* (Madrid, 1997), pp. 368–372.
110. See López Vela, "Las estructuras administrativas," pp. 78–79, 84–88, 100–101, 107; Bethencourt, *La Inquisición en la época moderna*, pp. 94–97, 147 152, 158–159.
111. The *familiar* was a lay servant of the Inquisition, always ready to perform duties in the service of the tribunal. In return, he enjoyed a number of privileges. For an analysis of this controversial figure in the history of the Spanish Inquisition, see Kamen, *The Spanish Inquisition*, pp. 145–148. For the role played by and the importance of the Mexican familiares, see Solange Alberro, *Inquisición y sociedad en México, 1571–1700* (México, 1988), pp. 53–60.
112. The *Concordia* of 1610 is reproduced by Solórzano in his *Política indiana*, lib. IV, cap. XXIV, no. 39. It was also included in the *Recopilación*, lib I, tít. XVIII, ley xxviiii. This *Concordia* would be supplemented with another one in 1633, because the problems and conflicts did not cease with the regulations of the previous one. The *Concordia* of 1633 can be found in AGN, RCO, vol. 1, exp. 108, fos. 204–209 and also in *Recopilación*, lib. I, tít. XVIIII, ley xxx.
113. See Solórzano, *Política indiana*, lib IV, cap. XXIV, nos. 40–46, for a chronological account of the conflict that is, not surprisingly, favorable to the claims of the *audiencia*.
114. This was emphatically expressed by the anonymous author of the account of the funeral celebrated by the Mexican Inquisition for the death of Philip IV, according to whom, the authority of the Inquisition was supreme, the "two arms of its power equally embracing the ecclesiastical and secular estates." Proof of this supreme authority was that none of the royal councils had jurisdiction over the Inquisition and that its officials were exclusively appointed by the inquisitor general or the Council of the Inquisition. See *Honorario túmulo, pompa exequial y imperial mausoleo que más fina Artemisa la fe*

romana, por su sacrosanto tribunal de Nueva España, erigió y celebró, llorosa Egeria, a su católico Numa y amante rey Philippo Quarto el Grande en su real convento de Santo Domingo de México ... (México, 1666), fo. 12r.

115. The fact that the inquisitor general was "presented" or nominated by the monarch but was appointed by the pope, while the members of the Council of the Inquisition were nominated by the inquisitor general and appointed by the king, might have contributed to a certain degree of confusion over the exact place where authority ultimately resided. This has been emphasized by López Vela in "Las estructuras administrativas," pp. 73–90.

116. Viceroy Monterrey had already complained in 1603 that the Mexican inquisitors received orders only from the Council of the Inquisition, and neither the viceroy nor the Council of the Indies was informed. See AGI, Mexico 25, no. 34, the count of Monterrey to the king, 25 May 1603.

117. AGI, Indiferente 3016, *consulta* of 20 September 1629.

118. AGI, Indiferente 756, *consulta* of 28 February 1630.

119. AGN, RCO, vol. 1, exp. 144, fo. 267, royal decree of 1 October 1635.

120. See royal order of 7 May 1640 in AGI, Indiferente 3016, and *cédula* of 30 May 1640 in AGN, RCO, vol. 1, exp. 238, fo. 467 and AGN, Inquisición, vol. 1477, exp. 59, fo. 122.

121. Solórzano, *Política indiana*, lib. IV, cap. XXIV, no. 46.

122. AGI, Indiferente 3016, the *audiencia* to the king, 26 February 1645. The *audiencia* also tries to justify its position with the same juridical arguments previously used by the Council of the Indies. In the reasoning of the members of the *audiencia*, the *oidores* were in possession of the "ordinary royal jurisdiction," which was always superior to the "delegated jurisdiction," the one possessed by the inquisitors and that could be used only in certain cases. See their letter (also signed by the viceroy) in AGI, Indiferente 3016, the *audiencia* to the king, 25 July 1651.

123. AGI, Mexico 278, the *audiencia* to the king, 10 December 1662.

124. The *cédula* can be found in AGN, RCD, vol. 180, fo. 24. It was also reproduced by Solórzano in his *Política indiana*, lib. IV, cap. XXIV, no. 12. See also the letter sent to the duke of Alburquerque in 1655 instructing him to favor and help not only the *visitador* of the Inquisition who was being sent to inspect the Mexican tribunal but also the inquisitors and officials of that tribunal, who, at least in theory, were going to be investigated. AGN, RCO, vol. 5, exp. 79, fo. 188.

125. Solórzano, *Política indiana*, lib. IV, cap. XXIV, nos. 1–3. See also Rivadeneira, "Tratado de la religión y virtudes," pp. 500–504 and Juan de Mariana, *La dignidad real y la educación del rey (De rege et regis institutione)*, edited by L. Sánchez Agesta (Madrid, [1599] 1981), pp. 439–462, for two eloquent expositions of the idea that religious diversity was always the source of tumults and upheavals in the commonwealth.

126. The documents made a reference to alleged embezzlement by the inquisitors. The prosecuted was Guillén de Lampart, an adventurer of Irish origin, whose case would become famous later on. See Alberro, *Inquisición y sociedad*, pp. 154–156.

127. Solórzano, however, contends that viceroys can be excommunicated, as their representation of the royal person does not grant them immunity. See *Política indiana*, lib. V, cap. XIII, no. 46.

128. AGN, RCO, vol. 4, exp. 60, fos. 141–142, the king to the count of Alba de Liste, 31 December 1651.

129. AGN, RCO, vol. 9, exp. 68, fo. 182, the queen regent to the marquis of Mancera, 26 November 1666.

130. López Vela, "Las estructuras administrativas," pp. 222–223. In 1696, the government in Madrid set up a special committee consisting of two members from each of the six leading councils in an almost desperate attempt to resist this trend. It was hoped that this measure would prevent the judges who confronted the Inquisition from being treated as its opponents, thus avoiding the fearful excommunications laid down by the tribunal, which nobody but the inquisitors themselves were able to remove. The result was a damning report on the abuses of jurisdiction committed by the Inquisition. Yet, its resolutions were not approved and things remained the same. See Kamen, *The Spanish Inquisition*, pp. 248–249; López Vela, "Las estructuras administrativas," pp. 167–168.

131. This privilege was established by a royal *cédula* in 1553, whereby the inquisitors' sentences were to be appealed only to the Council of the Inquisition (whose seat was in Madrid). This can be seen as one more proof of the autonomy of the Inquisition with regard to royal justice. The *cédula* was included in the *Recopilación*, lib. I, tít. XVIIII, ley iiii, and in Solórzano, *Política indiana*, lib. IV, cap. XXIV, no. 20.

132. Inquisitorial jurisdiction was not "ordinary" like that of bishops but was directly delegated by the Holy See, which had awarded the Inquisition exceptional and special powers to fight heresy, among others the power to inhibit any other ecclesiastical judge, including bishops and archbishops, from matters of faith. As a result of this, the Inquisition always claimed its superiority over episcopal authority. See López Vela, "Las estructuras administrativas," pp. 80–81.

133. BNM, mss. 7758, "Consulta del Consejo de Indias al rey N.S. Dn. Carlos 2o. sobre el exceso de la Inquisición de Méjico en el nombramiento de comisarios, calificadores, ..." (n.p., n.d.). The *consulta* was made in all likelihood between 1696 and 1700.

134. This competition for power did not preclude, of course, the collaboration between royal and inquisitorial authorities when it was considered necessary to safeguard colonial rule. This was the case with an alleged conspiracy of the black and mulatto population of Mexico City in 1665. On this occasion, the tribunal did not hesitate to communicate to the viceroy some information that had reached the inquisitors through a denunciation, The viceroy, in turn, asked the inquisitors to carry out the inquiry necessary to establish the veracity of the allegations, because, in the viceroy's opinion, the secrecy of the inquisitorial procedure would make the inquiry much more effective. See Alberro, *Inquisición y sociedad*, pp. 156–159. For Alberro, this case shows

clearly how, in fundamental matters, the inquisitors were more than willing to cooperate with the political power of the viceroyalty. It could be added, besides, that nothing was as effective in colonial society as the specter of a black rebellion to unite the white elite — even though blacks in Mexico were always a minority. For a study of the relations of the black population with the Mexican Inquisition, see Alberro, *Inquisición y sociedad*, pp. 455–485.

135. This conclusion has also been reached by Fernández Albaladejo in relation to the Sicilian Inquisition, which, in his view, became an independent power in constant conflict with the viceroys, without contributing much to the effectiveness of imperial administration. See his "Epílogo" in Helmut G. Koenigsberger, *La práctica del Imperio*, translated by Graciela Soriano (Madrid, 1989), pp. 255–257.

136. Speaking of the peninsular Inquisition, Bartolomé Bennassar, for example, asserts that it was a tribunal more efficient than the rest. For him, the "almost complete occupation of the territory, the network of collaborators and informers, guaranteed, at least for two centuries, a social control without fissures, reinforced, moreover, by the prestige of the institution and the sacred terror that it inspired." See Bennassar, *Inquisición española*, p. 337.

137. Kamen, for instance, affirms, in a recent analysis of the Catalan Inquisition, that the tribunal never developed into a tool of repression, ready to be used by Church or state for their own ends. Furthermore, he contends that the vast majority of Catalans never saw an inquisitor in their lives nor had any contact with the Holy Office. See his *The Phoenix and the Flame: Catalonia and the Counter Reformation* (New Haven, CT, 1993), pp. 245, 250, 265. See also his *The Spanish Inquisition*, pp. 280–282. In the case of the tribunal in Santiago that kept the northwestern part of Spain under its control, it has been similarly argued that the Galician villages and countryside never saw the Inquisition. See Contreras, *El Santo Oficio*, pp. 481–491. Jean-Pierre Dedieu, in his study of the tribunal of Toledo, speaks of the "failure of the Inquisition," as it was unable to impose its will upon a reticent population while at the same time it was dominated by local interests. See Jean-Pierre Dedieu, *L'administration de la foi. L'Inquisition de Tolède, XVIe–XVIIIe siècle* (Madrid, 1989), pp. 355–359.

138. After the creation of the Mexican tribunal in 1571, the indigenous population was formally removed from the jurisdiction of the Holy Office. The Indians' religious offenses were punished by the bishops through an episcopal court known as the *provisorato*. See Richard E. Greenleaf, "The Inquisition and the Indians of New Spain: A Study in Jurisdictional Confusion," *The Americas* 22, no. 2 (Oct. 1965): 138–166; Roberto Moreno de los Arcos, "New Spain's Inquisition for Indians from the Sixteenth to the Nineteenth Century," in *Cultural Encounters: The Impact of the Inquisition in Spain and the New World*, edited by M.E. Perry and A.J. Cruz (Berkeley, 1991), pp. 23–36.

139. This is the conclusion reached by two main experts on the Mexican Inquisition. Richard Greenleaf, for instance, maintains that the tribunal and its agents were never able to effect thought control over either the white or the

Indian population. See Richard E. Greenleaf, "The Inquisition in Colonial Mexico: Heretical Thoughts on the Spiritual Conquest," in *Religion in Latin American Life and Literature*, edited by L.C. Brown and W. Cooper (Waco, 1980), p. 80. Alberro, for her part, gives us a portrait of the Mexican Inquisition in which the tribunal appears as a highly inefficient and sloppy institution of social control, asserting that in repressive matters the figures were almost ridiculous. See Alberro, *Inquisición y sociedad*, pp. 23–29, 589–593.

Chapter 4

1. "Carta de la *audiencia* de México a S.M., 10.I.1620," in *Los virreyes españoles en América durante el gobierno de la casa de Austria, México III*, edited by L. Hanke (Madrid, 1977), BAE, vol. CCLXXV, pp. 72–73, 76–78, 80–84. For the viceroy's version, see AGI, Mexico 29, nos. 26, 31, the marquis of Guadalcázar to the king, 27 September and 19 October 1619; AGI, Mexico 29, no. 31, "Papeles y autos para que [la audiencia] excusase hacer o introducir novedades en los actos públicos a que asiste," 9 August 1619.

2. AGI, Mexico 35, no. 42, the count of Salvatierra to the king, 20 February 1645. The meetings of the viceroy with the oidores in the *Sala del Acuerdo*, on the second floor of the viceregal palace, were highly ritualized. The *Sala*, where the most important matters of government were debated and voted upon, represented the *Sancta Sanctorum* of the palace and it was decorated in a highly symbolic way. There, on an elevated platform covered with a rug, the viceroy would sit at a long table and on a chair under a canopy or baldachin with the royal coat of arms and the portrait of the king presiding over the room. At the sides of the table were twelve more chairs on which the *oidores* and any other persons attending the meetings sat according to their seniority and rank. On the walls, in addition to the portraits of Charles V and Hernán Cortés, hung half-length portrait paintings of all the viceroys of New Spain. For a description of the *Sala*, see Isidro Sariñana, *Llanto del Occidente en el ocaso del más claro sol de las Españas. Fúnebres demostraciones que hizo, pira real que erigió en las exequias del rey, N. Señor, D. Felipe IIII el Grande el … marqués de Mancera, virrey de la Nueva España* (México, 1666), fo. 14.

3. In his study of the Mexican viceroys, José Ignacio Rubio Mañé, for example, notes that today the thousands of letters written by the viceroys on "insignificant matters" would make any serious administrator laugh. See his *El Virreinato* (1955) (Mexico, 1992), vol. 1, p. 85. For his part, Irving A. Leonard argues in *Baroque Times in Old Mexico: Seventeenth-Century Persons, Places, and Practices* (Westport, CT, 1959), pp. 32–33, that to win favors, the Creole "was obliged to cloak his bitter resentment in a hypocritical adulation of the more privileged class, the European-born Spaniard, and, in an unsatisfying dilettantism, he often frittered away his talents on pageant-like ceremonies."

4. Edward Muir, for instance, argues in *Ritual in Early Modern Europe* (Cambridge, U.K., 1997), p. 231, that states require rituals in order to mask or legitimize hegemony, because they make coercion less evident.

5. Clifford Geertz has argued that presenting ritual as legitimating the exercise of political power casts rituals as mere artifice, designed to disguise the brute exercise of "real" power. For him, rituals do not refer to politics; they are politics, they are power itself. See his *Negara: The Theatre-State in Nineteenth-Century Bali* (Princeton, N.J., 1980), pp. 121–136. For an elaboration of these ideas, see also Catherine Bell, *Ritual Theory, Ritual Practice* (New York, 1992), pp. 182–196; David Cannadine, "Introduction: Divine Rights of Kings," in *Rituals of Royalty: Power and Ceremonial in Traditional Societies*, edited by D. Cannadine and S. Price (Cambridge, U.K., 1987), pp. 1–19.

6. For these ideas, see Robert A. Schneider, *The Ceremonial City: Toulouse Observed, 1738–1780* (Princeton, 1995), pp. 10–12; Clifford Geertz, "Religion as a Cultural System," in his *The Interpretation of Cultures* (New York, 1973), pp. 87–125.

7. Muir, *Ritual in Early Modern Europe*, p. 7.

8. See *Recopilación*, lib. II, tít. XXI, ley i; AGI, Mexico 41, no. 54, the marquis of Mancera to the queen regent, 30 November 1666.

9. Michel Foucault, *Discipline and Punish: The Birth of the Prison*, translated by Alan Sheridan (New York, 1977), pp. 47–57, 187.

10. For many instances of these public rituals of punishment, see Gregorio Martín de Guijo, *Diario, 1648–1664*, 2 vols., edited by M. Romero de Terreros (México, 1952); Antonio de Robles, *Diario de sucesos notables (1665–1703)*, 3 vols., edited by A. Castro Leal (México, 1972).

11. "Instrucción dada al marqués de Montesclaros por Pablo de la Laguna, presidente del Consejo de Indias, 14.I.1603," in *Los virreyes, México II*, BAE, vol. CCLXXIV, pp. 267–270.

12. See John Elliott, "The Court of the Spanish Habsburgs: A Peculiar Institution?," in his *Spain and Its World, 1500–1700* (New Haven, CT, 1989), p. 150.

13. On the relation between power and body language, see, for instance, Castillo de Bobadilla, *Política para corregidores*, lib. I, cap. VIII; Juan de Madariaga, *Del senado y su príncipe* (Valencia, 1617), pp. 303–305.

14. One of the functions of servants dressed in splendid liveries was to accompany their masters as walking signs of wealth and power. On "conspicuous consumption" as a symbol of status and power, see Peter Burke, *The Historical Anthropology of Early Modern Italy* (Cambridge, U.K., 1987), pp. 132–149.

15. Bobadilla, *Política para corregidores*, lib. I, cap. III, nos. 44–47. For a similar argument, see Diego de Tovar Valderrama, *Instituciones políticas* ([Alcalá de Henares, 1645] Madrid, 1995), pp. 193–194. Part of the *instrucción* given by the president of the Council of the Indies to the marquis of Montesclaros was devoted to the viceroy's "adornment," something that, in the president's words, would give "honor and credit" to the viceroy. See "Instrucción dada al marqués de Montesclaros," in *Los virreyes, México II*, BAE, vol. CCLXXIV, pp. 271–272. On the extraordinary importance given by the *regidores* of Mexico to the clothing they had to wear for the viceregal entry, see Linda A. Curcio-Nagy, *The Great Festivals of Colonial Mexico City: Performing Power and Identity* (Albuquerque, 2004), p. 20.

16. This idea has been advanced by Pierre Bourdieu in his *The Logic of Practice*, translated by Richard Nice (Stanford, 1990), pp. 117–120.

17. Pedro de Reina Maldonado, *Norte claro del perfecto prelado en su pastoral gobierno* (Madrid, 1653), vol I, pp. 8, 10. These ideas were accepted by everybody. Even the Franciscan Juan de Torquemada would maintain that it was a universal custom for kings and rulers to be adorned magnificently and to inhabit great and beautiful palaces, because such "excess and majesty cause reverence and admiration." For that reason, he thought that the churches in the Indian towns should always be splendidly adorned, because it was through their adornment and the solemnity of the ceremonies that the Indians would learn to know and revere God. "Relaciones informativas que las tres órdenes mendicantes … dan por donde no les conviene subjectar sus religiosos al examen de los obispos … Recopiladas por Fray Juan de Torquemada," in *Códice Mendieta. Documentos franciscanos, siglos XVI y XVII. Tomo Segundo*, edited by J. García Icazbalceta (México, 1892), pp. 174–176.

18. The idea that to define itself and advance its claims political authority requires a "cultural frame" or "master fiction" that has a central authority with sacred status was first proposed by Clifford Geertz in "Centers, Kings, and Charisma: Reflections on the Symbolics of Power," in *Culture and Its Creators: Essays in Honor of E. Shils*, edited by J. Ben-David and T.N. Clark (Chicago, 1977), pp. 13–38. However, as will be shown below, the viceroy was not only the manifest center of political action and colonial power in New Spain but of resistance as well.

19. Orest Ranum, "Courtesy, Absolutism, and the Rise of the French State, 1630–1660," *Journal of Modern History* 52 (Sept. 1980): 426–451.

20. On how the Spanish kings' power was constructed through ritual, see Carmelo Lisón Tolosana, *La imagen del rey. Monarquía, realeza y poder ritual en la Casa de los Austrias* (Madrid, 1991), pp. 115–170. On the constitutive power of etiquette and ceremonial, see Norbert Elias, *The Court Society*, translated by E. Jephcott (New York, 1983), pp. 78–116. Further on in his study, Elias, however, argues that etiquette was used by the king as an instrument to dominate his subjects, especially the nobility; see ibid., pp. 117–118, 130–131, 137–138.

21. Geertz, "Centers, Kings, and Charisma," p. 16.

22. Octavio Paz, *Sor Juana Inés de la Cruz o los trampas de la fe* (México, 1982), pp. 193–195.

23. The formalities of the entry constituted a ritual defense of the city, because cities were physically and symbolically vulnerable at their gates. The entry can also be understood as a liminal rite during which the body of the prince entered the "closed" space of the city. See Muir, *Ritual in Early Modern Europe*, p. 241.

24. This description is based on Cristóbal Gutiérrez de Medina, *Viaje del virrey marqués de Villena* (1640) (México, 1947), pp. 85–87; RAH, Col. Salazar y Castro, F-20, "Relación de la entrada que hizo en la ciudad de México … el Sr. Arzobispo Don Fray García Guerra, de la orden de predicadores, a tomar

la posesión del oficio de virrey y capitán general de aquel reino por Su Majestad .., año 1610," fos. 113–116; also in Mateo Alemán, *Sucesos de D. Fray García Guerra, arzobispo de México, a cuyo cargo estuvo el gobierno de la Nueva España* (México, 1613), pp. 27–30; Martín de Guijo, *Diario*, vol. I, pp. 107–108, 233–235. For an almost identical way of receiving the king, see BNM, ms. 11260 (17), "Ceremonial que suele guardarse en el recibimiento del rey cuando entra en las ciudades" (n.d.). A very similar procession, but without the arches, was staged every time a viceroy left the city after his term in office had ended. See, for example, RAH, Col. Salazar y Castro, M-15, "Relación sumaria del viaje que el marqués de Montesclaros mi señor virrey de la Nueva España hizo desde la ciudad de México hasta el puerto de Acapulco para embarcar a los reinos del Perú, adonde Su Majestad se sirvió de promover a Su Excelencia por su virrey" (1607), fos. 291r–292v.

25. For a discussion of the meaning of processions in general, see Schneider, *The Ceremonial City*, pp. 138–147. Interestingly enough, although plenty of evidence is available with regard to the disputes that the processional order provoked, I have not found any evidence that these squabbles ever happened during a viceregal entry. See below for an analysis of these tensions.

26. R. Malcolm Smuts, "Public Ceremony and Royal Charisma: The English Royal Entry in London, 1485–1642," in *The First Modern Society: Essays in English History in Honour of Lawrence Stone*, edited by A.L. Beier et al. (Cambridge, U.K., 1989), pp. 68–73.

27. In the late Middle Ages, the royal entry was conceived above all as an "advent," after Jesus' entry in Jerusalem on Palm Sunday, in which worldly government was presented as a mirror of the heavenly one, but starting in the sixteenth century the notion of the entry as "triumph" gained currency, and monarchs began to be represented as heroes in the fashion of the triumphal entries celebrated by Roman generals and emperors after some victory. As a result, the entry gradually lost its character as a dialog between the rulers and the ruled and became instead an assertion of absolute power. See Roy Strong, *Art and Power: Renaissance Festivals, 1450–1650* (Berkeley, 1984), pp. 7–11, 44–50.

28. On the role played by the natives in the viceregal entry, see Curcio-Nagy, *The Great Festivals*, pp. 44–58.

29. Teófilo Ruiz, "Unsacred Monarchy: The Kings of Castile in the Late Middle Ages," in *Rites of Power: Symbolism, Ritual, and Politics Since the Middle Ages*, edited by S. Wilentz (Philadelphia, 1985), p. 125.

30. See Solórzano, *Política indiana*, lib. V, cap. XII, nos. 49–50; *Recopilación*, lib. III, tít. XV, leyes i, x; AGI, Mexico 21, no. 49f, "Las ceremonias que se hacen con el rey Nro. Sr., así en su capilla como fuera de ella por sus capellanes y prelados, 14 March 1588" (also in AGI, Mexico 82, no. 2b). On the *Te Deum* as a triumphal ritual of thanksgiving, reserved primarily for kings, their families, and military victories, see Schneider, *The Ceremonial City*, pp. 161–165.

31. On the absence of a coronation ceremony of the Spanish monarchs and the importance instead of the ceremony of proclamation carried out through the raising of the banner of Castile, see Ruiz, "Unsacred Monarchy." On the royal

proclamation in Mexico during the Habsburg period, see Linda A. Curcio, "Saints, Sovereignty and Spectacle in Colonial Mexico," Ph.D. dissertation (Tulane University, 1993), pp. 141–154. For the medieval origins of the royal canopy, see J.M. Nieto Soria, *Ceremonias de la realeza. Propaganda y legitimación en la Castilla Trastámara* (Madrid, 1993), p. 195.

32. Nevertheless, it should be noted that the use of the canopy was not specific to the Spanish monarchy. In the case of France, for example, where the canopy was also associated with royalty, an interesting parallelism could be established between the use of the canopy by the Spanish viceroys and the French provincial governors. See Robert R. Harding, *Anatomy of a Power Elite: The Provincial Governors of Early Modern France* (New Haven, CT, 1978), pp. 11–17.

33. AGI, Mexico 29, no. 57a, *cédula* of 7 June 1620.

34. AGI, Indiferente 760, *consulta* of 3 April 1632. Jonathan Israel has argued that Gelves was a puritan reformer who did not allow being received in New Spain in the lavish way that was customary because he saw "such effusions as a waste of time and money." See Israel's *Race, Class and Politics in Colonial Mexico, 1610–1670* (London, 1975), pp. 136–137. However, this does not seem to be the real reason at all in light of a letter Gelves wrote to the king after taking possession of the viceroyalty, in which he asserted that if he had not allowed any celebrations and expenses for his entry it had been only to obey the 1620 *cédula*. But, in his letter he strongly requested that viceroys be permitted to be received under the *palio* and that the cities and towns through which they passed in their progress toward Mexico City also be allowed to spend the money necessary to appropriately welcome the person who directly represented the king. He went on to contend vigorously that the elimination of these ceremonies would contribute to the discredit and loss of authority of the viceroys. See AGI, Mexico 29, no. 57, Gelves to the king, 4 November 1622.

35. Although the king acceded to Escalona's petition, he never had a chance to put it into practice as he died before taking possession of his post. The king's decision, however, appears to be solely based on the duke's status as a grandee. When, three years later, the marquis of Cadereita asked that he also be allowed to use the *palio*, the monarch, following the opinion of the president of the Council of the Indies, rejected his petition with the arguments that the causes that had brought the prohibition were still in force and that that privilege had been awarded to the duke of Escalona only on account of his being a grandee and of the many services that he and his predecessors had performed for the Crown. See AGI, Indiferente 760, *consulta* of 23 March 1635. The king's attitude could indicate the existence of an unresolved tension in the conceptualization of the viceregal figure, who, while always representing the king, also represented himself and his "class."

36. AGI, Indiferente 760, *consulta*s of 9 November and 17 November 1638. See also Juan de Solórzano y Pereira, *Política indiana*, edited by M.A. Ochoa Brun (Madrid, [1647] 1972), lib. V, cap. XII, nos. 47–48.

37. AGN, RCD, vol. 40, fos. 487–488r, *cédula* of 24 December 1638.

38. AGI, Indiferente 760, *consulta* of 28 May 1649; AGI, Mexico 38, no. 15, the duke of Alburquerque to the king, 25 July 1656; AGI, Mexico 77, ramo 1, no. 8, *consulta* of 26 May 1663; AGI, Mexico 41, no. 20, the marquis of Mancera to the king, 31 March 1666; AGN, RCD, vol. 40, fo. 498, *cédulas* of 6 May 1688.

39. Smuts, "Public Ceremony and Royal Charisma," pp. 89–93.

40. AGI, Mexico 21, no. 49, Villamanrique to the king, 29 November 1588.

41. This was the case, above all, of Louis XIV, as Ralph Giesey has argued in "Models of Rulership in French Royal Ceremonial," in *Rites of Power: Symbolism, Ritual, and Politics Since the Middle Ages*, edited by S. Wilentz (Philadelphia, 1985), pp. 58–62.

42. On the declining importance of the viceregal entry as a public ceremony and its replacement with private in-palace entertainment in the course of the eighteenth century, see Curcio-Nagy, *The Great Festivals*, pp. 79–83.

43. Malcom Smuts has also noted that, by the mid-seventeenth century, the English royal entry had become both prohibitively expensive and increasingly out of step with changing attitudes toward conspicuous consumption among the aristocracy. See Smuts, "Public Ceremony and Royal Charisma," pp. 87–89. On the costs and willingness of the Mexican *cabildo* to incur debt in order to finance the viceregal entry in the first half of the seventeenth century, see Curcio-Nagy, *The Great Festivals*, pp. 35–37. By the end of the century, this attitude does not appear to have changed much, as attested by a petition to the king by one of the many creditors of the Mexican *cabildo* to limit the expenses of the viceregal entry, which entailed an expenditure of more than 20,000 pesos, way above the 8000 peso cap. See AGN, RCD, vol. 40, fos. 488–491, 498v–501, *cédulas* of 30 December 1690.

44. Colin M. MacLachlan, *Spain's Empire in the New World: The Role of Ideas in Institutional and Social Change* (Berkeley, 1988), p. 23.

45. For a description of this ritual, see, for instance, Baltasar Fernández de Castro, *Relación ajustada, diseño breve y montea sucinta de los festivos aplausos … en la … nueva del feliz nacimiento de nuestro deseado príncipe Felipe Próspero* (México, 1659), fos. 7–9; *Real mausoleo y funeral pompa, que erigió el Excelentísimo Señor conde de Salvatierra y la Real Audiencia desta ciudad de México a las memorias del Serenísimo Príncipe de España Don Baltasar Carlos* (México, 1647), fos. 2r–3v; Martín de Guijo, *Diario*, vol. I, p. 249, vol. II, pp. 13, 90–94, 110–111, 147, 181. In relation to the royal rites of passage as seen from Mexico, see also AGI, Mexico 36, no. 22, the count of Salvatierra to the king, 18 May 1647; AGI, Mexico 38, no. 44, the duke of Alburquerque to the king, 20 April 1658; AGI, Mexico 50, no. 23, the archbishop–viceroy Enríquez de Rivera to the king, 20 February 1678; AGI, Mexico 52, no. 25, the count of Paredes to the king, 8 July 1681.

46. See Carlos M.N. Eire, *From Madrid to Purgatory: The Art and Craft of Dying in Sixteenth-Century Spain* (Cambridge, U.K., 1995), pp. 255–368. On the exequies of the Spanish monarchs, see also Javier Varela, *La muerte del rey. El ceremonial funerario de la monarquía española (1500–1885)* (Madrid, 1990).

The funeral ceremonies for a viceroy's death were an almost exact replica of those for the king's, the most notable difference obviously being the presence of the viceroy's dead body, which in the ceremonies occupied the place that the royal insignia had in the king's funeral. The great picaresque writer Mateo Alemán has left us a detailed description of the obsequies for archbishop García Guerra, who died while serving as acting viceroy. See his *Sucesos de D. Fray García Guerra, arzobispo de México, a cuyo cargo estuvo el gobierno de la Nueva España* (México, 1613), reprinted in *The Sucesos of Mateo Alemán*, edited by Alice H. Bushee (New York, 1911), pp. 38–48.

47. As the designer of the ceremonies for the funeral of Charles II would assert, "To erect a catafalque to honor an august person is the same as erecting a triumphal arch to solemnize his heroic deeds." See Agustín de Mora, *El sol eclipsado antes de llegar al cenit. Real pira que encendió a la apagada luz del rey N.S.D. Carlos II el ... conde de Moctezuma ...* (México, 1700), fo. 15r. For a study of the catafalques erected in Mexico for the obsequies of Philip IV and Charles II, see Fernando Checa, "Arquitectura efímera e imagen del poder," in *Sor Juana y su mundo. Una mirada actual*, edited by Sara Poot Herrera (México, 1995), pp. 261–283. For a comparison with the catafalque erected in Madrid for the funeral of Philip IV, see Steven N. Orso, *Art and Death at the Spanish Habsburg Court: The Royal Exequies for Philip IV* (Columbia, MO, 1989).

48. See *Real mausoleo y funeral pompa*, fo. 25r.

49. For a description of the cortege, see Sariñana, *Llanto del Occidente*, fos. 108v–111v. For similar funeral processions in Mexico City, see also *Real mausoleo y funeral pompa*, fos. 22–25; Mora, *El sol eclipsado*, fos. 83v–85, 93–95. For a viceroy's funeral procession, see Alemán, *Sucesos de D. Fray García Guerra*, pp. 40–45.

50. On these ideas, see Solórzano, *Política indiana*, lib. II, cap. VI, nos. 5–11.

51. See *Honorario túmulo, pompa exequial y imperial mausoleo que más fina Artemisa la fe romana, por su sacrosanto tribunal de Nueva España, erigió y celebró, llorosa Egeria, a su católico Numa y amante rey Philippo Quarto el Grande en su real convento de Santo Domingo de México ...* (México, 1666). The Inquisition also celebrated its own funeral for Philip III. See AHN, Diversos-Colecciones 26, no. 33, "Honras que hizo el Sancto Oficio de la Inquisición de Nueva España a la majestad del rey Philipo Tercero, Nuestro Señor," 16 and 17 September 1621.

52. Edward Muir, *Civic Ritual in Renaissance Venice* (Princeton, 1981), pp. 189–190.

53. So it was believed at least by the anonymous author of the account of Prince Baltasar Carlos' funeral. He was pleased by the harmony that existed at that moment between the two "princes," which increased the splendor of the obsequies. See *Real mausoleo y funeral pompa*, fo. 4.

54. For a description of an archbishop's entry, see Alemán, *Sucesos de D. Fray García Guerra*, pp. 23–25.

55. Among the privileges of those cities that were "head of the kingdom" was that of having to go to meet only royal persons, although an exception was made

with archbishops and bishops the first time they entered their dioceses. This clearly put archbishops on a symbolic level very similar to that of viceroys, who were the only persons the Mexico City *cabildo* received ceremonially. See Bobadilla, *Política para corregidores*, lib. III, cap. VIII, no. 21; Villarroel, *Gobierno eclesiástico*, pp. 28–29; AHCM, Ordenanzas 2981, nos. 16, 17, 22. On the archbishop's entry, see, for example, AHCM, Actas de *Cabildo*, vol. 365-A, *cabildo*s of 29 and 31 August 1628; vol. 369-A, *cabildo*s of 31 December 1640, and 3, 8, and 9 January 1641; AGI, Mexico 44, no. 73, the *corregidor* of Mexico City to the viceroy, 30 November 1670.

56. On the arches erected to welcome the archbishops, see Chapter 3, notes 37 and 38.

57. See, for instance, Alonso Fernández Osorio, *Breve relación de las solemnísimas exequias, que en la Santa Iglesia Metropolitana de el Arzobispado de México se hicieron, en la translación y entierro del venerable cuerpo de el ilustrísimo señor D. Feliciano de Vega, obispo de la Paz y Popayán, y arzobispo de México* (México, 1642); *Funeral lamento, clamor doloroso, y sentimiento triste que a la piadosa memoria del Ilustrísimo y Reverendísimo Señor Doctor D. Alonso de Cuevas Dávalos, obispo que fue de Oaxaca y arzobispo de México, ... repite su Santa Iglesia Catedral ... en las sepulcrales pompas de su muerte, para póstumo elogio de su vida* (México, 1666).

58. In the first two decades of the seventeenth century the archbishops of Mexico were still customarily received under the *palio*. For García de Santa María's entry in Mexico City in 1600, see AGI, Mexico 278 (n.d); Alemán, *Sucesos de D. Fray García Guerra*, p. 24. For García Guerra's entry in 1607, see AGI, Mexico 27, no. 60, Luis de Velasco to the king, 17 December 1608.

59. AGN, RCD, vol. 180, fo. 20, *cédula* of 2 July 1596; AGN, RCO, vol. 6, exp. 33, *cédula*s of 29 August and 20 November 1608. This prohibition would be later included in the *Recopilación*, lib. III, tít. XV, ley iiii.

60. See AGI, Mexico 38, no. 15b, *cabildo* of 17 July 1640.

61. AGI, Mexico 38, no. 15a, the duke of Alburquerque to the king, 20 July 1656; ibid., no. 15, the duke of Alburquerque to the king, 26 July 1656; ibid., no. 15b, "Copia de las diligencias fechas sobre la consulta que la ciudad de la Puebla de los Angeles hizo al duque de Alburquerque ... sobre si se había de recebir con palio por dicha ciudad al obispo della," 20 July 1656; ibid., no. 15c, the *alcalde mayor* of Puebla to the duke of Alburquerque, 24 July 1656; ibid., no.15d, "Testimonio que remitió la ciudad de la Puebla sobre haber entrado el obispo della debajo de palio...," 25 July 1656. As a result of this incident, the Council of the Indies resolved to send a *cédula* to every viceroy and district governor where there was a bishop, reiterating the prohibition from using the *palio*. See AGI, Mexico 6, ramo 1, *consulta* of 17 May 1658; AGN, RCO, vol. 6, exp. 33, *cédula* of 23 July 1658.

62. This was probably one of the reasons for his strained relations with the archbishop. For the prelate's complaints about the viceroy's assertion of authority, see AHN, Documentos de Indias, no. 29, Moya de Contreras to the president of the Council of the Indies, 24 January 1575.

63. AGI, Mexico 278, Monterrey to the king, 20 March 1603; ibid., Santa María to the king, 20 March 1603; ibid., *consultas* of the Council, 27 June and 12 July 1603; ibid., Santa María to the Council, 4 May 1604.

64. See AGI, Mexico 39, no. 13b, the king to the count of Baños, 9 March 1660; ibid., no. 13, the count of Baños to the king, 20 November 1663; the fiscal of the Council, 18 August 1664; *Recopilación*, lib. III, tít. XV, ley iii.

65. The political–religious career of Diego Osorio was very similar to that of Juan de Palafox, another controversial figure of seventeenth-century New Spain. Both were bishops of Puebla, both were appointed archbishops of Mexico, both renounced the archbishopric in order to remain in the diocese of Puebla, both were appointed acting viceroys, and last, but not least, their clashes with the viceroys were among the most virulent of the entire century.

66. AGI, Mexico 39, no. 13b, Montemayor to the count of Baños, 11 October 1663.

67. AGI, Mexico 39, no. 13b, Acuerdo of 22 October 1663.

68. AGI, Mexico 39, no. 13b, bishop Osorio to the count of Baños, 6 and 29 October 1663; AGI, Mexico 344, bishop Osorio to the king, 18 January 1664.

69. On the importance and significance of Corpus Christi in Mexico City, see Linda Curcio-Nagy, "Giants and Gypsies: Corpus Christi in Colonial Mexico City," in *Rituals of Rule, Rituals of Resistance: Popular Celebrations and Popular Culture in Mexico*, edited by W.H. Beezley et al. (Wilmington, 1994), pp. 1–26.

70. The procession in Madrid was not completely exempt from controversies, though the conflicts usually arose between secular institutions (the different councils, for example), rather than between secular and religious bodies. The main reason for this lack of controversy between the civil and religious authorities was, no doubt, the fact that in Madrid there was no powerful center of religious authority, as the city lacked both a bishop and a cathedral. For an analysis of the Corpus procession in Madrid, see María José del Río Barredo, *Madrid, Urbs Regia. La capital ceremonial de la Monarquía Católica* (Madrid, 2000), chap. VI.

71. AGI, Mexico 39, no. 10, the count of Baños to the king, 2 June 1663; ibid., no. 10f, autos hechos por orden del virrey, 30 June 1663; Martín de Guijo, *Diario*, vol. II, pp. 208–209.

72. AGI, Mexico 39, no. 10e, Diego Osorio to the king, 26 May 1663; ibid., no.10d, the ecclesiastical chapter to the king, 26 May 1663; ibid., no.10a, autos hechos por orden del arzobispo, 23 May 1663.

73. On Corpus Christi as a feast of concord and unity, which nonetheless brought about conflict because of the competition for "honor," see Mervyn James, "Ritual, Drama and Social Body in the Late Medieval English Town," *Past & Present* 98 (1983): 3–29.

74. This has already been noted by Curcio-Nagy in "Giants and Gypsies," pp. 8–10. See also James, "Ritual, Drama and Social Body," p. 5.

75. The function of the viceregal pages was to illuminate the monstrance with their torches. The controversy over the viceroy's pages was an old one. See, for example, AGN, Historia, vol. 36, exp. 3, fos. 198–277, "Testimonios sobre

haber hecho injurias el marqués de Cerralvo en público con palabras pesadas, prefiriéndoles mis pajes, el día de la octava del Corpus" (1626).

76. AGI, Mexico 36, no. 58, the count of Alba de Liste to the king, 31 July 1651; ibid., no. 58c, the *audiencia* to the king, 11 July 1651; ibid., no. 58b, the ecclesiastical chapter to the king, 8 August 1651; ibid., no. 58d, the dean of the ecclesiastical chapter to the king, 14 July 1651; ibid., no. 58e, "Testimonio de los autos fechos en razón de que el *cabildo* eclesiástico de la santa iglesia catedral de esta ciudad guarde la costumbre en el modo de llevar las hachas los pajes de Su Excelencia el día del Corpus Christi" (1651); Martín de Guijo, *Diario*, vol. I, pp. 159–161.

77. *Recopilación*, lib. III, tít. XV, ley xxxvi.

78. *Recopilación*, lib. III, tít. XV, leyes xxxviiii, xxxx; AGI, Mexico 44, no. 15e-1, decree of the marquis of Mancera, 12 September 1669.

79. For a description of the viceregal palace in Mexico City and how it could be seen as a replica of the royal palace in Madrid, see Checa, "Arquitectura efímera e imagen del poder," pp. 256–261.

80. This liturgy of space is the same as that which took place in the royal palace in Madrid, the only difference being that the number of "referential space signs" (i.e., rooms) was probably much greater. See Lisón Tolosana, *La imagen del rey*, pp. 141–145.

81. This has been pointed out by Richard Trexler in *Public Life in Renaissance Florence* (Ithaca, 1980), pp. 319–321.

82. An early example of this is the many ritual gestures performed by viceroy Martín Enríquez on the public stage of the cathedral to show the preeminence of his power and his displeasure toward archbishop Moya de Contreras (for example, he would wait at his seat for the archbishop to come give him the ashes instead of the viceroy going to the altar to receive them from the prelate, as was the custom). See AHN, Documentos de Indias, no. 247, Moya de Contreras to the president of the Council of the Indies (n.d.).

83. AGI, Mexico 44, no. 15e-3, Enríquez de Rivera to the marquis of Mancera, 9 October 1669. See also AGI, Mexico 338, Enríquez de Rivera to the queen regent, 26 January 1670; Antonio Rubial García, "La mitra y la cogulla. La secularización palafoxiana y su impacto en el siglo XVII." *Relaciones* 73 (Winter 1998): 252–255.

84. AGI, Mexico 44, no. 15e, the marquis of Mancera to the king, 29 October 1669.

85. AGI, Mexico 44, no. 15a, testimonio, 12 June 1670. The notary, always close to the viceroy, was an indispensable figure in any ceremony or procession, as his duty was to put on record any kind of incident that might happen during the celebration. On the importance of the physical proximity of viceregal notaries to the viceroy on all ceremonial occasions, see AGN, RCD, vol. 14, fos. 437–438, petition of the viceregal secretaries to the count of Salvatierra, 15 May 1647.

86. The archbishop maintained that "in the presence of the consecrated Divine Majesty, this ceremony should not be performed with the temporal magistrates,

not even with the sovereign princes." To this, Mancera responded that no text or ecclesiastical authority justified such an opinion; see AGI, Mexico 44, no. 15, the marquis of Mancera to the queen regent, 17 July 1670. The dispute between archbishops and viceroys over the prelates' cape train was an old one — as early as 1586, the marquis of Villamanrique and archbishop Moya de Contreras were already arguing about this matter; see AGI, Mexico 20, no. 124, Villamanrique to the king, 20 May 1586. On the occasions when bishops had to release the cape train in the viceroy's presence, see *Recopilación*, lib. III, tít. XV, ley xxxviiii.

87. AGI, Mexico 338, "Dos testimonios…," 1670 (emphasis added). In the face of what in the viceroy's eyes were constant insults aimed at him by the archbishop, Mancera communicated to the king his decision to no longer attend any celebrations that took place in the cathedral. To this decision the monarch reacted by asking Mancera not to suspend his attendance at those festivities, as the viceroy's absence would set a bad example to the republic. The archbishop, on the other hand, was asked not to be disrespectful toward the viceroy and to show him all due respect. See AGI, Mexico 44, no. 15f, *consulta* of 31 January 1671; AGN, RCO, vol. 12, exp. 16, fos. 56–57, the queen regent to the marquis of Mancera, 9 February 1671; ibid., fo. 58, the queen regent to the archbishop Enríquez de Rivera, 9 February 1671.

88. AGI, Mexico 44, no. 15e-1, "Consulta del virrey marqués de Mancera al Acuerdo," 6 September 1669.

89. AGI, Mexico 44, no. 15e-1, "Respuesta del fiscal," 8 September 1669.

90. William Beik, *Absolutism and Society in Seventeenth-Century France: State Power and Provincial Aristocracy in Languedoc* (Cambridge, U.K., 1985), pp. 179, 336–337. On privately owned authority, see also Pierre Bourdieu, *The Logic of Practice*, translated by Richard Nice (Stanford, 1990), pp. 128–131.

91. On the meaning and importance of the concept of personal "credit" in the early modern world, see Kristen B. Neuschel, *Word of Honor: Interpreting Noble Culture in Sixteenth-Century France* (Ithaca, 1989), pp. 72–77; Jonathan Dewald, *Aristocratic Experience and the Origins of Modern Culture. France, 1570–1715* (Berkeley, 1993), pp. 157–158; and Jay M. Smith, "No More Language Games: Words, Beliefs, and the Political Culture of Early Modern France," *The American Historical Review* 102, no. 5 (Dec. 1997): 1427–1438.

92. AGI, Mexico 75, no. 61, Gaspar Fernández de Castro to the king, 8 August 1643; AGI, Mexico 75, no. 61a bis, decree of the Council, March 1644.

93. "La autoridad es el crédito de la Majestad: con ella hace más en sus súbditos que con el poder, armas y suplicios. […] Asímismo se toma por crédito, estimación, fe, verdad y aprecio. […] Significa también ostentación, aparato, fausto, magestad, señorío, gravedad, así en el modo de obrar como en el decoro y representación de alguno," in *Diccionario de Autoridades (1726–1739)*, facsimile ed. (Madrid, 1963).

94. AGI, Mexico 47, no. 11b, Fernández de Madrigal to the count of Baños, 4 June 1674; AGI, Mexico 47, no. 11a, the duke of Alburquerque to Fernández de Madrigal, 12 June 1674.

95. AGI, Mexico 47, no. 11, the marquis of Mancera to the queen regent, 11 January 1674; AGI, Mexico 47, no. 1, archbishop Enríquez to the queen regent, 31 January 1674.

96. For the testimonies of the witnesses presented by the *oidores* and the *cabildo*, see AGI, Mexico 39, nos. 15a and 15b.

97. As Juan de Madariaga argued, for a Senate to be legitimately constituted, it is essential and indispensable that the senators meet "as one." As he explains, "Just as the human body when it is dismembered and divided into many parts loses the shape that it had and ceases to be an organic physical body, being stripped of those ties that united and tied together its parts, so the Senate loses its shape as a mystical body when it is stripped of that tie that unites all its parts, which said tie is the desire to deliberate among themselves by common consent in a common place." See Juan de Madariaga, *Del Senado y de su príncipe* (Valencia, 1617), pp. 96, 102.

98. See, for instance, AGI, Mexico 24, nos. 9 and 38, the count of Monterrey to the king, 1 May 1598 and 3 March 1600.

99. "Carta de la audiencia de México a S.M., 10.I.1620," in *Los virreyes, México III*, pp. 72–73. Since the late sixteenth century it had been established that four or six prebendaries would always meet the viceroy at the cathedral doors and then accompany him to his seat, as a way to acknowledge that they were beneficiaries of the king's patronage. See AGI, Mexico 22, no. 116, Luis de Velasco to the king, 5 October 1593; ibid., no. 116a, "Información sobre el recibimiento que los capitulares de la catedral desta ciudad hacen al virrey," 23 September 1593. In 1665, the marquis of Mancera would contend that it should not be allowed for the archbishop to be met by the entire ecclesiastical chapter outside the cathedral while only four prebendaries met the viceroy inside the cathedral. The Council, however, rejected Mancera's proposal. See AGI Mexico 40, no. 67, Mancera to the king, 3 December 1665.

100. For a very similar complain regarding fiestas de tabla, see AGI, Mexico 76, no. 80d bis, the *audiencia* of Mexico to the king, 12 October 1660. On *fiestas de tabla*, see AGN, RCO, vol. 8, exp. 15, fo. 51, the king to the marquis of Mancera, 8 March 1665; vol. 9, exp. 27, fo. 94, the queen regent to the marquis of Mancera, 30 June 1666; vol. 27, exp. 52, fo. 123–124, the king to the count of Moctezuma, 21 August 1696.

101. AGI, Mexico 82, no. 2, the *audiencia* of Mexico to the queen regent, 12 January 1674. The queen agreed with the arguments of the *oidores* and ordered the viceroys not to force the *oidores* to escort them when they were not obligated to do so. See AGI, Mexico 82, no. 2, Fernando Paniagua to the Council, 14 June 1674; AGN, RCO, vol. 14, fos. 88, 90, 92, 93, 94, 95, the queen regent to the archbishop–viceroy Enríquez de Rivera, 6 July 1674 (also in AGI, Mexico 48, nos. 23, 27, 29, 30, 31).

102. See, for example, AGN, RCO, vol. 4, exp. 114, fos. 243–244, the king to the *oidores*, 9 March 1653.

103. Solórzano, *Política indiana*, lib. V, cap. XII, núms. 30–32. On the secrecy with which a viceroy's reprimands to the *oidores* should be carried out, see

Recopilación, lib. II, tít. XVI, ley li. For a detailed instruction on how a viceroy must act without impairing the *oidores'* authority whenever he thought they were not complying with their obligations, see AGN, RCD, vol. 61, fos. 152–154, the king to the count of Galve, 30 December 1694. In conflicts between the viceroy and other members of New Spanish society (the bishops, for example), it was expected that the *oidores* would stay on the sidelines or, at least, support the viceroy. See, for example, AGN, RCO, vol. 1, exp. 67, fo. 122, the king to Herrera Campuzano and Villabona Cubiaurri, 15 March 1631.

104. It is certainly ironic that Juan de Palafox — Salvatierra's great rival and critic of the excessive power of the viceroys — in trying to defend episcopal authority against what he thought was a lack of respect by the *alcaldes mayores*, would argue exactly the same. For him, royal power resided entirely only in the person of the king, while royal officials had a measure of the king's power in proportion with the quality and importance of their offices. For him, viceroys possessed the greatest amount of royal power, though they did not have all, while the presidents of the *audiencias* had less, and less still the *oidores*, the *alcaldes mayores*, the constables, and so on. For Palafox, the "farther away from the original, the less power, brilliance, honor, and representation a royal official should have." See Juan de Palafox, "Razón que da a Vuestra Majestad Don Juan de Palafox de los acontecimientos del año de 1647," in his *Tratados mejicanos II*, edited by F. Sánchez Castañer (Madrid, 1968), p. 83. For very similar arguments, see also Pedro de Reina Maldonado, *Norte claro del perfecto prelado en su pastoral gobierno* (Madrid, 1653), p. 93.

105. AGI, Mexico 35, no. 42, the count of Salvatierra to the king, 20 February 1645. The following year, a royal order was issued upholding the viceroy's arguments. See AGN, RCO, vol. 2, exp. 94, fo. 192, the king to the count of Salvatierra, 18 February 1646. Similarly, only when the *audiencia* had taken over the government because of the absence of a viceroy was the senior *oidor* allowed to use a cushion in public ceremonies. See AGI, Mexico 29, no. 95, decree of the Council of the Indies (n.d.); *Recopilación*, lib. III, tít. XV, ley xxvi.

106. On the symbolism that surrounded the way in which the *Sala* was furnished and decorated, see Michael J. Schreffler, "Art and Allegiance in Baroque New Spain," Ph.D. dissertation (University of Chicago, 2000), chap. 3. As Schreffler observes, "The Sala del Acuerdo was a place in which the viceroy and the audiencia convened symbolically with the Crown. ...While written communication made the king's voice present, his portrait made him visibly there" (pp. 71–72).

107. AGI, Mexico 29, no. 40b, the *oidor* Galdós de Valencia to the king, 27 May 1619; "Carta de la audiencia de México a S.M., 10.I.1620," in *Los virreyes, México III*, BAE, vol. CCLXXV, pp. 81–84; AGI, Mexico 29, no. 40h, decrees of the Council, 7 December 1619 and 13 January 1621; ibid., no. 40, "Pedro de Toro en nombre del marqués de Guadalcázar ...," 14 October 1620.

108. While Paredes had based his petition on the "authority and reverence" owed to his post, the monarch, for instance, justified the order given to the *oidores*

to always accompany the viceroy from his private residence to the viceregal palace (viceroys usually moved out of the palace in the weeks before their successors took office) with the argument that it was precisely at that time when, more than ever, the viceroy's authority needed to be reinforced, as it was a period of transition in which his power was weaker. See AGN, RCO, vol. 19, exp. 5, fos. 7–12r, the king to the *audiencia* of Mexico, 31 December 1681.

109. The inspection of the jails was one of the most important rituals of justice in New Spain. Its objective was to make sure that all the prisoners in both the royal and the city prisons had been jailed for fair reasons. Thus, it was mandated that two *oidores*, accompanied by the *alcaldes del crimen*, "visit" or inspect these prisons every Saturday afternoon, plus on Christmas, Easter and Whitsuntide. During their visits, the judges could release any prisoners they saw fit. See *Recopilación*, lib. VII, tít. VII. On the inspection of the Indian jail, see Woodrow Borah, *Justice by Insurance: The General Indian Court of Colonial Mexico and the Legal Aides of the Half-Real* (Berkeley, 1983), pp. 231–233.

110. On the arguments of the *oidores*, see AGI, Mexico 46, no. 39a, *consulta* of the *oidores* to the viceroy, 19 October 1672; AGI, Mexico 81, ramo 2, no. 21a, "Informe que hicieron los oidores que fueron de visita de cárcel de la de México," 26 November 1672; AGI, Mexico 81, ramo 2, no. 21, the *audiencia* to the queen regent, 17 June 1673.

111. BNMex, ms. R/850/LAF, "Consulta de la Real Sala del Crimen sobre concurrir a la visita de cárcel los sábados con los oidores," 26 October 1672. On the arguments made by the *alcaldes*, see also AGI, Mexico 81, ramo 2, no. 21b, "Apuntamientos que esta Real Sala del Crimen ha hecho...," 7 September 1672; AGI, Mexico 46, no. 39a, and Mexico 81, ramo 1, no. 1c, "Informe de los sres. alcaldes," 26 October 1672; AGI, Mexico 81, ramo 1, no. 21c, the *alcaldes* to the queen regent, 30 November 1672; AGI, Mexico 81, ramo 1, no. 1, the *alcaldes* to the queen regent, 8 April 1673.

112. AGI, Mexico 46, no. 34b, Informe del fiscal del Consejo, 6 June 1673; see also ibid., nos. 34, 39, the marquis of Mancera to the queen regent, 26 August 1672, 2 February 1673; AGN, RCO, vol. 13, exp. 171, fos. 408–410, the queen regent to the marquis of Mancera, 22 June 1673; AGN, RCO, vol. 14, fos. 42–44r, the queen regent to the viceroy and the *oidores*, 3 March 1674.

113. To highlight the importance of the ceremony, the *alférez mayor* was to ride at the viceroy's left side while the senior *oidor* was at his right. See *Recopilación*, lib. III, tít. XV, ley lvi; AHCM, Ordenanzas 2981, Alférez Real, nos. 2 and 3.

114. AGI, Mexico 76, ramo 15, no. 80o, the *audiencia* to the king, 19 October 1660; ibid., no. 80p, the *oidores* to the viceroy, 22 May 1660.

115. AGI, Mexico 39, no. 14e, the city of Mexico to the king, 29 November 1663. The monarch had already agreed with the *regidores*' position, letting the *oidores* know that the feast should continue to be celebrated as it had always been because it was very fitting to celebrate the day when the city "was reduced to the knowledge of the Catholic faith and to the [king's] obedience." See AGI, Mexico 39, nos. 14a and 14e, *cédula* of 19 June 1661. The transcendental quality attributed to the splendor of public ceremonies can be appreciated in the

petition presented to the viceroy by the Mexican *cabildo* in 1663 to postpone the celebration of San Hipólito, because all the *oidores* had asked to be excused from attending because of poor health. For the *regidores*, it was better to cancel the parade rather than to allow its celebration without the necessary "decorum and authority." See AGI, Mexico 39, no. 14e, the city of Mexico to the king, 29 November 1663.

116. The prohibition to which the *oidores* were referring can be found in *Recopilación*, lib. III, tít. XV, ley vi. That law consolidated several *cédulas* of 1579, 1618, and 1621, whereby all the members of the *audiencia* were ordered to escort the viceroy at all the *fiestas de tabla*. The senior *oidor* was to march on the viceroy's left side and, on their way back to the viceregal palace, they were to remain mounted at the entrance of the palace while the viceroy would pass through their midst.

117. AGI, Mexico 82, ramo 3, no. 88a "Respuesta del sr. fiscal," 19 August 1676; *consulta* of Juan de Gárate to the *audiencia,* 17 August 1676; *consulta* of the city of Mexico to the viceroy, 12 August 1676; ibid., no. 88, the *audiencia* to the queen regent, 24 August 1676. This time the king would agree with the *audiencia,* issuing a *cédula* ordering that the *oidores* ought not to go up to the *alférez*'s chamber. See AGI, Mexico 82, ramo 3, no. 88, informe del fiscal del Consejo, 29 June 1677; AGI, Mexico 319, the king to the *audiencia,* 16 December 1677. However, in 1696, the city still requested of the king that the "custom" of the *oidores* going up to the *alférez*'s chamber be kept, although the Council again rejected the request. See AGI, Mexico 319, Juan Diego Serrano to the king, n.d.; *consejo* of 13 October 1696.

118. See AHCM, Ordenanzas 2981, no. 24; AGI, Mexico 278, *cédulas* of 5 October 1630 and 6 November 1648.

119. AGI, Mexico 318, the city of Mexico to the king, 30 June 1663.

120. See *Recopilación*, lib. III, tít. XV, ley xxv.

121. For that same reason, the marquis of Gelves had requested that only viceroys be allowed to sit on chairs in public functions while the *oidores* should sit on benches. In his view, it was not permissible that in so remote a kingdom the viceroy's authority be diminished by raising that of the *oidores*. His request, however, did not prosper. See AGI, Mexico 29, no. 95, Gelves to the king, 8 November 1622; ibid., decree of the Council (n.d.).

122. AGN, RCO, vol. 4, exp. 78, fo. 168, *cédula* of 26 June 1652. See also *Recopilación*, lib. III, tít. XV, ley xxviii. On the symbolism of the chair as a marker of power, see AGN, RCO, vol. 24, exp. 37, fo. 85, the king to the count of Galve, 22 June 1691 (also in AHCM, Cédulas y Reales Ordenes, vol. 2977, exp. 12).

123. See, for example, AGN, RCO, vol. 16, exp. 84, fos. 168–169, *cédula* of 13 September 1678; AGI, Mexico 319, the city of Mexico to the king, 13 July 1689; AGI, Mexico 318, informes del fiscal, 29 August and 16 November 1690; AGN, RCO, vol. 23, exp. 111, fo. 428, the king to the count of Galve, 30 December 1690; AGN, RCD, vol. 39, fo. 47v, the king to the count of Galve, 30 December 1692.

124. AGI, Mexico 318, the city of Mexico to the king, 21 November 1625. The city always resented having to sit on a bench instead of chairs. See, for instance, AGI, Mexico 33, L. 2, F. 5–12, the marquis of Cadereita to the king, 22 July 1637. Another way of defending the preeminence of the city was by ceremonially strengthening the figure of the *corregidor*, because all the honors bestowed upon the "head" were likewise reflected on the rest of the "body." This was the reason for the request of Mexico City's *cabildo* to allow the *corregidor* to sit on a chair in his visits to the viceroy. See AGN, RCD, vol. 180, fo. 67v, *cédula* of 27 August 1614; AGI, Mexico 28, no. 45, the marquis of Guadalcázar to the king, 15 February 1617.

125. Francisco Bethencourt, *La Inquisición en la época moderna. España, Portugal, Italia, siglos XV–XIX* (Madrid, 1997), pp. 133–144, 379.

126. See AGI, Mexico 278, the count of Monterrey to the king, 23 April 1596; AGI, Mexico 25, nos. 34b and 34d, Monterrey to inquisitor Peralta, 23 and 24 May 1603; AGI, Mexico 26, no. 44, the marquis of Montesclaros to the king, 31 March 1605. For the inquisitors' arguments, see AGI, Mexico 278, Peralta to Monterrey, 24 May 1603; ibid., Peralta to the king, 20 October 1604. In theory, the bishops had no precedence over the inquisitors. See *Recopilación*, lib. I, tít. XVIII, ley v. Because of this, the bishops rarely appeared in the public ceremonies of the Inquisition to avoid being seen in a position of inferiority in relation to the inquisitors.

127. AGI, Indiferente 3016, "Petición del fiscal de la audiencia," 9 April 1649; AGN, Inquisición, vol. 1510, exp. 19, fo. 174, *Real Provisión* of 9 April 1649.

128. AGI, Indiferente 3016, the *audiencia* of Mexico to the king, 19 May 1649 (also in AGI, Mexico 278); "Respuesta de los inquisidores…," 9 April 1649.

129. AGI, Indiferente 3016, informe del fiscal, 17 February 1652.

130. AGI, Indiferente 3016, Solórzano to the Council, 1653.

131. AGI, Mexico 278, "Proposición del señor corregidor," *cabildo* of 17 March 1650; see also *cabildo* of 18 February 1650; "Protesta del corregidor, 12 March 1650; "Protesta de la ciudad," 13 March 1650.

132. Solórzano himself had reasoned in a very similar way when defending the preeminence of the Council of the Indies. For him, questions of precedence were not vain or frivolous matters, as both distributive justice and the preservation of natural and divine order depended upon it. For that reason, the defense of these rights deserved to be praised, every magistrate being obliged not only to preserve but also augment the dignity, authority, and preeminence of his office. Furthermore, a magistrate could not renounce to his honors and preeminence even if he wished to do so, because they were inextricably linked to the office. See his *Memorial y discurso de las razones que se ofrecen para que el Real y Supremo Consejo de las Indias deba preceder en todos los actos públicos al que llaman de Flandes* (Madrid, 1629), fos. 6v–8v, 32, 33r.

133. AGI, Mexico 278, "Petición del procurador mayor de la ciudad," 25 February 1655; "Noticia que se dio al tribunal de la Real Cédula y respuesta suya," 26 February 1655; the city of Mexico to the king, May 1655; the duke of Alburquerque to the king, 15 May 1655.

134. On the etiquette that regulated the relations of the viceroys with the inquisitors, see AGN, Inquisición, vol. 1513, fos. 370–373, "Declaración de Don Pedro Serrano," 22 December 1626; "Declaración de Cristóbal de Molina," 24 December 1626; fo. 233, "Recebimiento de los virreyes al tribunal," 1635. On how the Inquisition should be received by the viceroys, see also AGN, Inquisición, vol. 1513, fos. 10–13, the *comisario* of Puebla to the inquisitors of Mexico, 17 June 1650.
135. AGN, Inquisición, vol. 1513, fo. 64, the inquisitors to the *audiencia*, 19 May 1696 (emphasis added).
136. AGN, Inquisición, vol. 1513, fos. 83–86, autos de la Inquisición of 17 and 20 December 1696.
137. Elias, *The Court Society*, p. 94.

Chapter 5

1. Carlos de Sigüenza y Góngora, *Teatro de virtudes políticas que constituyen a un príncipe, advertidas en los monarcas antiguos del mexicano imperio (1680)* (México, 1986), pp. 128–134; Sor Juana Inés de la Cruz, *Neptuno alegórico, océano de colores, simulacro político que erigió la … Iglesia Metropolitana de Méjico en las lucidas alegóricas ideas de un arco triunfal que consagró obsequiosa y dedicó amante a la feliz entrada del … conde de Paredes, marqués de la Laguna … (1680)* (México, 1992), pp. 795–796.
2. On the need for viceroys to be liberal, see Pedro de Avilés, *Advertencias de un político a su príncipe observadas en el feliz gobierno del Excelentísimo Señor … marqués de Astorga, virrey y capitán general del reino de Nápoles* (Nápoles, 1673), pp. 170–183.
3. For an analysis of the relations between patronage and monarchical power in early modern Spain, see Antonio Feros, "Clientelismo y poder monárquico en la España de los siglos XVI y XVII," *Relaciones* 73 (1998): 15–49.
4. John Elliott has recently called our attention to this fact by observing that the workings of the patronage system in the Spanish empire still await systematic study. See his "Empire and State in British and Spanish America," in *Le Nouveau Monde, Mondes Nouveaux: l'expérience américaine*, edited by S. Gruzinski and N. Wachtel (Paris, 1996), p. 379.
5. Mario Biagioli, *Galileo Courtier: The Practice of Science in the Culture of Absolutism* (Chicago, 1993), pp. 4, 13, note 7.
6. On the importance of personal ties in seventeenth-century government, see Sharon Kettering, *Patrons, Brokers, and Clients in Seventeenth-Century France* (New York, 1986); William Beik, *Absolutism and Society in Seventeenth-Century France: State Power and Provincial Aristocracy in Languedoc* (Cambridge, U.K., 1985), pp. 15–16, 223–244; Linda Levy Peck, *Court Patronage and Corruption in Early Stuart England* (London, 1990); Robert Shepard, "Court Factions in Early Modern England," *Journal of Modern History* 64 (1992): 721–745; Antonio Feros, *Kingship and Favoritism in the Spain of Philip III, 1598–1621* (Cambridge, 2000), 91–98, 128–134, 184–188.

7. "Papel que el Conde Duque puso en manos de su Majd. sobre que se ajustase a hacer incomunicable su hacienda con todo lo que no fuese necesidad de su corona, religión, armas y autoridad," in *Memoriales y cartas del conde-duque de Olivares, edited by* John H. Elliott and José F. de la Peña (Madrid, 1978), vol. I, p. 7.

8. Juan de Solórzano y Pereira, *Política indiana*, edited by M.A. Ochoa Brun (Madrid, [1647] 1972), lib. III, cap. III, nos. 46–48.

9. Feros, "Clientelismo y poder monárquico," p. 39.

10. See Jerónimo de Cevallos, *Arte real para el buen gobierno de los reyes y príncipes y de sus vasallos* (Toledo, 1623), fo. 81; "Papel que el Conde Duque puso en manos de su Majd.," p. 9.

11. Juan Pablo Mártir Rizo, *Norte de príncipes*, edited by J.A. Maravall (Madrid, [1626] 1988), pp. 59, 61; Diego Saavedra Fajardo, *Empresas políticas*, edited by S. López ([Munich, 1640] Madrid, 1999), empresa 40, pp. 501–502.

12. Pedro Fernández Osorio, *Júpiter benévolo, astro ético político, idea simbólica de príncipes, que en la sumptuosa fábrica de un arco triunfal dedica obsequiosa y consagra festiva la Ilustrísima Iglesia Metropolitana de México al Exmo. Señor D. Juan de la Cerda y Leyba, conde de Baños, …* (México, 1660), fo. 8r.

13. Pedro de Rivadeneira, "Tratado de la religión y virtudes que debe tener el príncipe cristiano para gobernar y conservar sus estados, contra lo que Nicolás Maquiavelo y los políticos deste tiempo enseñan," in *Obras escogidas del Padre Pedro de Rivadeneira*, edited by V. de la Fuente (Madrid, [1595] 1952), pp. 527, 531. This is a common idea, expressed by many authors. See, for example, Juan de Mariana, *La dignidad real y la educación del rey (De rege et regis institutione)*, edited by L. Sánchez Agesta (Madrid, [1599] 1981), pp. 300–308, 413–414; Cevallos, *Arte real*, fo. 15; Saavedra Fajardo, *Empresas políticas*, empresa 23, pp. 381–382; Diego de Tovar Valderrama, *Instituciones políticas* ([Alcalá de Henares, 1645] Madrid, 1995), pp. 180, 183, 191–192; Andrés Mendo, *Príncipe perfecto y ministros ajustados* (Madrid, 1656?), pp. 169–170; Pedro Portocarrero y Guzmán, *Teatro Monárquico de España*, edited by C. Sanz Ayán (Madrid, [1700] 1998), pp. 328–332.

14. Juan de Santa María, *Tratado de república y policía cristiana* (Madrid, 1615), p. 256; Cevallos, *Arte real*, fo. 50. Justice is divided into three types: vindicatory, which punishes crimes (criminal justice); commutative, which gives everyone that which is theirs (civil justice); and distributive, which is the type that, as the term itself indicates, distributes rewards according to the merits of each and every subject. See *Conclusiones políticas del príncipe y sus virtudes* (Madrid, 1638), fos. 12–14. The appointments for public offices made by the viceroys, like those of the monarch, had to be informed always, at least in the political writers' views, by the principles of distributive justice. See, for example, Avilés, *Advertencias de un político a su príncipe*, pp. 49–55; Diego de Avendaño, *Thesaurus Indicus*, edited by A. Muñoz García ([Antwerp, 1668] Pamplona, 2001), pp. 425–430. The importance of this concept at the time merited the publication, in 1609, of a treatise entirely devoted to discuss it. That this discussion was especially relevant in the New World is shown by the

fact that its author was an Augustinian friar from Mexico who dedicated his work to the president of the Council of the Indies. See Juan Zapata y Sandoval, *Disceptación sobre justicia distributiva y sobre la acepción de personas a ella opuesta*, edited by A.E. Ramírez Trejo (México, 1994). (This is a partial translation of the Latin original published in Valladolid, Spain).

15. Seneca, "On Favors" [*De Beneficiis*], in *Moral and Political Essays*, edited and translated by J.M. Cooper and J.F. Procopé (Cambridge, U.K., 1995), p. 200.

16. Miguel de Cervantes, *The Ingenious Gentleman Don Quixote de la Mancha*, translated by S. Putnam (New York, 1949), p. 175.

17. Alonso de Contreras, *Vida, nacimiento, padres y crianza del capitán Alonso de Contreras* (Madrid, 1967), pp. 238–239. Similarly, Seneca considered ingratitude as the worst form of human depravity. See "On Favors," pp. 204–206, 242–245. See also Mendo, *Príncipe perfecto*, pp. 171, 173, 182–183. On the political implications of ingratitude, see Arthur L. Herman, "The Language of Fidelity in Early Modern France," *Journal of Modern History* 67 (1995): 20–21.

18. As Sor Juana contended, the reward given by the prince must always be greater than the service received. See her *Neptuno alegórico*, p. 795.

19. António M. Hespanha, *La gracia del derecho. Economía de la cultura en la Edad Moderna*, translated by A. Cañellas (Madrid, 1993), pp. 151–156; Bartolomé Clavero, *Antidora. Antropología católica de la economía moderna* (Milan, 1991), pp. 100, 104 105, 211. For that same reason, Seneca believed that ingratitude could not be made subject to legal prosecution, because a favor cannot be treated as a business transaction without ruining it. See "On Favors," pp. 245–255.

20. Pierre Bourdieu, *The Logic of Practice*, translated by Richard Nice (Stanford, 1990), pp. 123–128. Similarly, in his analysis of the politics of gift-giving in pre-modern societies, Marcel Mauss asserts that "to give is to show one's superiority, to show that one is something more and higher. …To accept without returning or repaying more is to face subordination, to become a client and subservient." See *The Gift: Forms and Functions of Exchange in Archaic Societies*, translated by I. Cunnison (New York, 1967), p. 72.

21. Because family relationships were among a man's oldest ties, they tended to be the core of any clientele he later built. Moreover, the natural emulation of fathers and the need to live up to the family name were common justifications for nepotism, which was, in this age, unquestionably an accepted norm in appointments and awards. See Robert Harding, "Corruption and the Moral Boundaries of Patronage in the Renaissance," in *Patronage in the Renaissance*, edited by G. F. Lytle and S. Orgel (Princeton, 1981), p. 55; Kettering, *Patrons, Brokers, and Clients*, p. 73.

22. For example, the count of Chinchón, appointed viceroy of Peru in 1628, was asked by the president of the Council of the Indies "not to receive retainers by recommendation of the members of this Council or any other persons, and to take with him only those necessary for his service." See AGI, Indiferente 756, *consulta* of 7 February 1628. It should be noted that a viceroy, besides being a patron, could be the client of a higher noble, something not uncommon if we

bear in mind that most of the viceroys appointed to rule New Spain belonged to the lesser nobility or were the younger sons of the great noble houses.

23. See, for instance, AGI, Contratación 5422, no. 34, and AGI, Contratación 5430, no. 3, ramo 31, for a detailed listing of the retainers of the duke of Escalona and the duke of Alburquerque, respectively. For the retinue of the count of Galve, see María Pilar Gutiérrez Lorenzo, *De la corte de Castilla al virreinato de México: el conde de Galve (1653–1697)* (Guadalajara, Spain, 1993), pp. 145–148. On the composition and functions of the king's household, see BPR, ms. II/2642, "Etiquetas generales que han de observar los criados de la Casa de S.M. en el uso y exercicio de sus oficios"; Antonio Rodríguez Villa, *Etiquetas de la Casa de Austria* (Madrid, 1913).

24. Xavier Gil Pujol, "Una cultura cortesana provincial. Patria, comunicación y lenguaje en la Monarquía Hispánica de los Austrias," in *Monarquía, imperio y pueblos en la España moderna*, edited by P. Fernández Albaladejo (Alicante, 1997), pp. 225–257.

25. Ibid., pp. 235–236.

26. *Los virreyes españoles en América durante el gobierno de la casa de Austria, México I*, edited by L. Hanke and C. Rodríguez (Madrid, 1976), BAE, vol. CCLXXIII, p. 129. The same opinion would be expressed some years later by the viceroy Martín Enríquez and, at the beginning of the seventeenth century, by Velasco's own son. See "Advertimientos de Martín Enríquez al conde de La Coruña, su sucesor, 25.IX.1580," in ibid., p. 211; AGI, Mexico 27, no. 32, Velasco to the king, 30 August 1607.

27. In New Spain, the chief magistrates of local government were usually known as *alcaldes mayores*, while in other parts of colonial Spanish America, as well as in Spain, they received the title of *corregidores*. Most of the *alcaldes mayores* and *corregidores* were appointed (usually for one or two years) by the viceroy or the presidents of the *audiencias*. The term of office of those *corregidores* appointed by the king was of either five years (if they were in Spain) or three (if they were already in the Indies). On the provincial administration of the Spanish American possessions, see C.H. Haring, *The Spanish Empire in America* (New York, 1947), pp. 128–138; Alberto Yalí Román, "Sobre alcaldías mayores y corregimientos en Indias. Un ensayo de interpretación," *Jahrbuch für Geschichte von Staat, Wirtschaft und Gesellschaft Lateinamerikas* 9 (1972): 1–39; Woodrow Borah, ed., *El gobierno provincial en la Nueva España, 1570–1787* (México, 1985).

28. *Recopilación*, lib. III, tít. II, ley primera. At the beginning of the seventeenth century, the monarch only appointed five *alcaldes mayores*, all of them in places of little importance: Tabasco, Cuautla de Amilpas, Tacuba, Metepec-Ixtlahuac, and Tlanepantla. See Yalí Román, "Sobre alcaldías mayores," p. 13. For all the places where the viceroys appointed *alcaldes mayores* and *corregidores* at the beginning of the seventeenth century, see Antonio Vázquez de Espinosa, *Compendio y descripción de las Indias Occidentales*, edited by B. Velasco Bayón (Madrid, 1969), pp. 115, 121–122, 124.

29. Enríquez de Rivera, archbishop of Mexico and acting viceroy between 1673 and 1680, argued that the intervention of the *oidores* in the distribution of offices was not advisable because of the discords that could arise between viceroy and *oidores* and also because it would be a great inconvenience for the candidates, as they had to petition not only the viceroy but also all the *oidores* in order to assert their claims. See AGI, Mexico 47, no. 2, archbishop Enríquez to the queen regent, 31 January 1674. It is not difficult to imagine that most viceroys would have agreed with the words of the archbishop–viceroy.

30. "Instrucción al conde de Monterrey, 20.III.1596," in *Los virreyes, México II*, BAE, vol. CCLXXIV, pp. 136, 144. This *Instrucción* was the model for the Instructions given to all the viceroys in the seventeenth century. See also Solórzano, *Política indiana*, lib. III, cap. III, no. 38. For a definition of *beneméritos* as those to whom the monarch owes gratitude for something just, which makes them worthy of his rewards, see Diego Felipe de Albornoz, *Cartilla política y cristiana* (Madrid, 1666), fo. 31v.

31. See AGI, Mexico 22, no. 2, the king to the marquis of Villamanrique, 18 June 1588; *Recopilación*, lib. III, tít. II, leyes xiii, xiiii. On this subject, see Silvio A. Zavala, *Las instituciones jurídicas en la conquista de América* (México, 1988), pp. 197–211.

32. Fernando Pizarro y Orellana, *Discurso legal y político de la obligación que tienen los reyes a premiar los servicios de sus vasallos, o en ellos o en sus descendientes* (Madrid, 1639), pp. 7–53.

33. It should be noted that Gómez de Cervantes made these claims to justify his request that the *encomiendas* be granted in perpetuity. See "Memorial de Gonzalo Gómez de Cervantes para el doctor Eugenio Salazar, oidor del Real Consejo de las Indias," printed in *La vida económica y social de Nueva España al finalizar el siglo XVI*, edited by A.M. Carreño (México, 1944), pp. 75–92. Writers such as Solórzano and Avendaño generally agreed with these claims. To Solórzano, for example, one of the reasons for the creation of the *encomiendas* was to reward the services of the *conquistadores* and their descendants. See Solórzano, *Política indiana*, lib. III, cap. II, nos. 14–30; cap. III, nos. 40–48; also, Avendaño, *Thesaurus Indicus*, pp. 219–227.

34. AGI, Mexico 21, no. 49, the marquis of Villamanrique to the king, 29 November 1588; AGI, Mexico 22, no. 14, Luis de Velasco to the king, 2 June 1590; AGI, Mexico 24, no. 8, the count of Monterrey to the king, 22 April 1598; AGI, Mexico 27, no. 57, Luis de Velasco to the king, 17 December 1608. It is interesting to note that Avendaño, writing in the 1660s, thought that granting offices to the descendants should not be a problem for the viceroys because there were few of them left, whereas the posts to distribute were many. See his *Thesaurus Indicus*, p. 429.

35. On Spanish racial prejudices and stereotypes with regard to the mixed-blood population of New Spain, see Chapter 7.

36. Before undertaking the duties of their office, *corregidores* and *alcaldes mayores* were required to deposit a bond to guarantee the payment of any fines that might result from their *residencia*. See Haring, *The Spanish Empire*, p. 130.

37. "Relación del marqués de Montesclaros, 2.VIII.1607," in *Los virreyes, México II*, BAE, vol. CCLXXIV, pp. 280–282. For similar arguments, see AGI, Mexico 22, no. 87 and Mexico 27, no. 32, Luis de Velasco to the king, 24 May 1592 and 30 August 1607. For the complaints of the conquistadors' descendants, see AGI, Mexico 27, no. 32a, "Petición que los hijos y nietos de conquistadores dieron en el Acuerdo contra el marqués de Montesclaros" (n.d.).

38. For these opinions, see Rivadeneira, "Tratado de la religión y virtudes," p. 528; Mendo, *Príncipe perfecto*, documento LXVI; Avilés, *Advertencias de un político a su príncipe*, pp. 49–55. For a study of the political uses made by the Spanish nobility of the concepts of royal liberality and distributive justice during the reign of Charles II, see Antonio Alvarez-Ossorio, "El favor real: liberalidad del príncipe y jerarquía de la república (1665–1700)," in Ch. Continisio and C. Mozzarelli, *Repubblica e virtù: pensiero politico e monarchia cattolica fra XVI e XVII secolo* (Roma, 1995), pp. 393–453. On the privileged position of the nobility in general, see Hespanha, *Vísperas del Leviatán*, pp. 242–256.

39. AGI, Mexico 22, no. 87 and Mexico 27, no. 32, Luis de Velasco to the king, 24 May 1592 and 30 August 1607.

40. "Carta del duque de Escalona al conde de Salvatierra, 13.XI.1642," in *Los virreyes, México IV*, BAE, vol. CCLXXVI, p. 34.

41. Juan de Palafox, "Diversos dictámenes espirituales, morales y políticos," in *Obras del Ilmo., Exmo. y venerable siervo de Dios, don Juan de Palafox y Mendoza* (Madrid, 1762), vol. X, nos. xcii–xciii. He also expressed similar views in "Razón que da a Vuestra Majestad Don Juan de Palafox de los acontecimientos del año de 1647," in his *Tratados Mejicanos II*, pp. 64–65.

42. AGN, RCD, vol. 180, fo. 78v, the king to the marquis of Guadalcázar, 19 December 1618. Around this time, it was also prohibited that the viceroys extend at their will the term of office of the *alcaldes mayores*. See AGN, RCD, vol. 180, fo. 77, the king to the marquis of Guadalcázar, 1618.

43. AGN, RCD, vol. 30, fos. 98–99v, *cédula* of 12 December 1619. See also, AGN, RCD, vol. 180, fo. 83v, the king to the marquis of Guadalcázar, 12 December 1619; AGI, Mexico 29, no. 36, decreto del Consejo, 7 November 1620; *Recopilación*, lib III, tít. II, ley xxvii. For a definition of the term *criados* as meaning all those who received a salary or stipend from the viceroy, see ibid., ley xxviii.

44. AGI, Mexico 600, fo. 1, Palafox to the king, 24 June 1641.

45. Referring to the provincial magistrates appointed by the viceroys, Thomas Gage, the seventeenth-century English traveler, observed around the same time that "most of the governours about the country being the viceroy his creatures, placed by him, doe contribute great gifts and bribes for their preferment." See Thomas Gage, *The English-American, His Travail by Sea and Land, or A New Survey of the West-Indias* (London, 1648), p. 61.

46. According to one of viceroy Salvatierra's supporters, these commercial activities were "an original sin in every alcalde mayor ever since the Indies were taken and something *necessary* in those who accept offices with salaries of

scarcely two hundred and fifty pesos." See BPR, ms. II/1984, fo. 88v, Fr. Juan de la Madre de Dios to the king, 28 November 1646 (emphasis added).

47. AGI, Mexico 600, fos. 1–4, Palafox to the king, 24 June 1641. In the 1680s, Gabriel Fernández de Villalobos, the marquis of Varinas, a courtier who had lived in Spanish America for twenty years, would express very similar criticisms about all the American viceroys, *alcaldes mayores*, and *corregidores*. See *Estado eclesiástico, político y militar de la América (o grandeza de Indias)*, edited by J. Falcón Ramírez (Madrid, 1990), pp. 605–639.

48. Jonathan I. Israel, *Race, Class and Politics in Colonial Mexico, 1610–1670* (London, 1975), pp. 202, 215–218. All this notwithstanding, Israel recognizes at some point that Mexican reality was more complicated than the mere division into two parties (p. 108).

49. D.A. Brading, *The First America: The Spanish Monarchy, Creole Patriots and the Liberal State, 1492–1867* (Cambridge, U.K., 1991), pp. 228–251.

50. AGI, Mexico 600, fos. 56, 60v, 61v, *consulta* of 31 May 1647. This is also the opinion of Pedro de Gálvez, the new *visitador* sent in 1650 to finish Palafox's visit. He also had decided not to hear any cases of *alcaldes mayores* to avoid muddling the good relations that existed between him and the new viceroy, the count of Alba de Liste. The following year, the Council would order Gálvez not to intervene in any cases of *alcaldes mayores*. See AGI, Patronato 244, ramo 23, Gálvez to the king, 22 July 1650; AGI, Mexico 600, fos. 95–99, *consejo* of 6 June 1651.

51. BPR, ms. II/1983, fos. 197v–205v, decrees of Palafox, 9 and 16 November 1646.

52. It is interesting to note here that, at the time when he transferred power to Salvatierra, Palafox advised him that, while trying to be on good terms with the *visitadores*, since both viceroys and *visitadores* were servants of the same king, the viceroys should also try to preserve their power and jurisdiction, not allowing the *visitadores* to go beyond their responsibilities, since a viceroy had to be "father of all jurisdictions, and he must help everyone, as he represents the person of His Majesty, from whom all [jurisdictions] are derived." See "Relación de Juan de Palafox y Mendoza 1642(?)," in *Los virreyes, Mexico IV*, BAE, vol. CCLXXVI, p. 41.

53. BPR, ms. II/1983, fos. 51–52r, the Dominican superior to Salvatierra, 18 November 1646; ibid., fos. 52v–55r, the Mercedarian superior to Salvatierra, 20 November 1646. Similar arguments in defense of the viceroy's position were presented by the archbishop of Mexico, the bishop of Michoacan, and the inquisitors. See ibid., fos. 55v–60v, 139–140.

54. AGI, Mexico 600, fos. 57v–58r, 60, *consulta* of 31 May 1647. The monarch also rejected Palafox's proposal to eliminate the post of *alcalde mayor* and its substitution with *alcaldes ordinarios*. See "R. Respuesta al obispo de la Puebla de los Angeles sobre reducir los alcaldes mayores de algunos lugares de la Nueva España a alcaldes ordinarios, 30 December 1647," in *Colección de Documentos para la Historia de la Formación Social de Hispanoamérica, 1493–1810*, edited by R. Konetzke (Madrid, 1958), vol. II, pp. 429–430. On the "detailed instructions"

given to the successor of Salvatierra about the abuses of the *alcaldes mayores*, see AGN, RCO, vol. 3, exp. 77, fos. 142–143, the king to the count of Alba de Liste, 12 August 1649.

55. AGI, Mexico 600, fo. 64, royal answer, 9 July 1647; AGI, Mexico 5, no. 11, the king to the bishop of Yucatan, 10 July 1647; AGI, Mexico 600, fos. 95–99, informes del Consejo, 24 May and 6 June 1651. The bishop of Yucatan did not, however, abide by his instructions, and, besides getting involved in numerous conflicts with different sectors of Mexican society, he appointed many *alcaldes mayores* and *corregidores*. See Israel, *Race, Class and Politics*, pp. 240–242. Interestingly, Palafox had a very positive opinion of the bishop–governor regarding this matter. According to him, the bishop had distributed all the offices that had vacated to "worthy conquistadores," thus satisfying their "thirst of distributive justice," something that had not happened in the six previous years. See AGI, Mexico 5, no. 56, Palafox to the king, 12 December 1648.

56. AGN, RCO, vol. 2, exp. 81, fo. 165, the king to the count of Salvatierra, 11 October 1645; "Consulta de la Cámara de Indias para proveer cinco oficios que el virrey de la Nueva España tiene dados a hijos y hermanos y deudos de los oidores y ministros de la audiencia (7 January 1646)," in CDHH, vol. II, pp. 393–396.

57. This had already been pointed out almost twenty years before by Francisco Manso, the archbishop of Mexico, who, in the course of his many clashes with viceroy Cerralvo, had argued that the "biggest drain that Your Majesty's treasury suffers in this kingdom occurs in the two ports of entry and exit of New Veracruz and Acapulco, with all the frauds being committed in them …, as both the governors of the fortresses and the alcaldes mayores happen to be servants of the viceroys." See AGI, Mexico 3, no. 126, Manso to the king, 26 May 1628. See also ibid., no. 133, *consulta* of 16 September 1630.

58. AGI, Mexico 5, nos. 62 and 105, *consultas* of 7 January and 31 December 1649.

59. In the case of San Luis Potosí, the Crown apparently never made a definitive decision, and for many years the *alcalde mayor* sometimes was appointed by the viceroys and sometimes by the king (it seems that in those occasions when the monarch appointed the *alcalde mayor* it was only because the post had been sold). See AGI, Mexico 4, no. 53, the king to the marquis of Cerralvo, 21 August 1625; AGI, Mexico 4, no. 53, *consulta* of 1638; AGI, Mexico 36, no. 24, the count of Salvatierra to the king, 26 May 1647; AGI, Mexico 36, no. 24, informe del consejo, 7 October 1647.

60. AGI, Mexico 5, no. 105, Alba de Liste to the king, 10 December 1649. At the beginning of the seventeenth century, the marquis of Montesclaros had pointed out to the king (and the king seemed to have agreed) that the provision of several offices by the Council of the Indies would affect the authority of the viceroy in a negative way. See AGI, Mexico 25, Montesclaros to the king, 28 June 1603. For his part, the marquis of Guadalcázar informed the

king in 1620 that, out of 120 offices of district magistrate he had distributed, only three which were involved in the security of ports and borders had been granted to his retainers, because those posts were always given to persons who could be entirely trusted by the viceroys. See AGI, Mexico 29, no. 36, Guadal-cázar to the king, 27 May 1620. In the 1630s, viceroy Cerralvo had presented similar arguments when referring to the hardships he had to face in trying to impose his authority over the two treasury officials of Veracruz, who had become supporters of archbishop Manso (treasury officials were usually appointed by the king). See AGI, Mexico 31, nos. 36, 37, Cerralvo to the king, 1 May 1635 and 7 May 1635. In relation to this, see also AGI, Mexico 3, no. 117, *consulta* of 4 May 1630.

61. It has been argued that government through patron–client ties was character-istic of incompletely centralized states. This was the case, for example, of France in the sixteenth and seventeenth centuries, where the king in faraway Paris had less authority in the provinces than did provincial officials. There, the Crown, of course, used royal officials to govern, but institutional proce-dures alone were insufficient because royal authority was too uncertain and its enforcement too weak. Patron–client ties were used to manipulate politi-cal institutions from within and to act in place of institutions. They were "interstitial, supplementary, and parallel structures." See Kettering, *Patrons, Brokers, and Clients*, p. 5. Something similar has been argued for Spain in the case of the viceroys appointed to rule the kingdom of Valencia. Many viceroys there were appointed because of their local connections, as these links were expected to facilitate the passage of the king's business through the Estates. See James Casey, "Some Considerations on State Formation and Patronage in Early Modern Spain," in *Patronages et Clientélismes, 1550–1750 (France, Angl-eterre, Espagne, Italie)*, edited by Ch. Giry-Deloison and R. Mettam (Lille, n.d.), pp. 103–115.

62. This Indian uprising will be examined in more detail in the last section of Chapter 7.

63. Accordingly, a royal order was issued once more to remind the viceroys of the prohibitions of the 1619 *cédula*; however, this order would not materialize until two years later. See AGN, RCD, vol. 30, fo. 99, *cédula* of 20 March 1662 (also in CDHH, vol. II, p. 490).

64. AGI, Mexico 600, fos. 531–533v, *consulta* of 29 May 1660 (emphasis added).

65. Ibid., fo. 535v; CDHH, vol. II, pp. 494–495, the king to the bishop of Micho-acán, 23 June 1662. Gil de Castejón, one of the councilors, however, believed that to request more information about a problem that had been under dis-cussion for over twenty years was "to make the harm eternal," the only solu-tion being the substitution of *alcaldes ordinarios* for *alcaldes mayores* without any further delay. See ibid., fos. 535v–539.

66. AGI, Mexico 600, fos. 567–574, López de Solís to the king, 3 October 1662; ibid., fos. 553–561, bishop Osorio to the king, 25 October 1662; ibid., fos. 585–602, Medina Rico to the king, 2 December 1662; ibid., fos. 689–692, bishop Ramírez to the king, 16 July 1664.

67. AGI, Mexico 600, fos. 685–686, informe del fiscal, 24 November 1663. This was not the first time that such a measure was proposed. In 1638, the president of the Council of the Indies had already suggested that the Council should discuss whether it would be advisable that all the offices being granted by the viceroys should be provided instead by the king. See AGI, Mexico 4, no. 53, *consulta* of 1638.

68. On the administration of the count of Baños, see Israel, *Race, Class and Politics*, pp. 260–266. On the distribution of offices by the viceroy and the many complaints it prompted, see AGI, Mexico 600, fos. 604–671, "Información fecha ... sobre diferentes cosas tocantes al gobierno del conde de Baños," 1662–1663; CDHH, vol. II, pp. 498–499, the king to the count of Baños, 30 August 1662.

69. AGI, Mexico 39, no. 16, bishop Osorio to the king, 20 July 1664; auto del virrey, 5 August 1664; "R.C. al virrey de la Nueva España para que en la provisión de los oficios sean premiados los beneméritos, 17 March 1665," in CDHH, vol. II, pp. 525–526.

70. AGI, Mexico 39, no. 16, resolución del Consejo, 29 April 1665; AGI, Mexico 40, no. 56, the marquis of Mancera to the king, 18 November 1665; ibid., *cédula* of 20 May 1665.

71. AGN, RCO, vol. 16, exp. 26, fo. 52, the king to the viceroy of New Spain, 28 February 1678. Similarly, a *cédula* of 24 May 1678 established that the monarch thenceforth would appoint all the *corregidores* who until that moment had been appointed by the presidents of the *audiencias* and the governors. See AGN, RCO, vol. 18, exp. 8, fos. 16–17, *cédula* of 22 February 1680.

72. See CDHH, vol. II, pp. 648–649, the king to the count of Castellar, 1 February 1678; ibid., pp. 650–653, *consulta* of 4 February 1678; ibid., pp. 688–689, the king to the archbishop of Lima, 6 December 1679. See also Guillermo Lohmann Villena, *El corregidor de indios en el Perú bajo los Austrias* (Madrid, 1957), pp. 125–127; Yalí Román, "Sobre alcaldías mayores," p. 29.

73. It appears that the excesses committed by the son of viceroy Baños moved the Crown to forbid "for ever and ever" the viceroys bringing their sons and daughters to New Spain or Peru, although it does not seem that this order was strictly enforced. See CDHH, vol. II, pp. 501–502, *cédula* of 22 November 1662; ibid., pp. 582–583, *consulta* of 14 June 1672.

74. AGI, Mexico 7, ramo 6, *consulta* of 30 April 1676.

75. AGI, Mexico 600, fos. 694–696, "Relación muy por menor de todos los oficios que proveen los virreyes de Nueva España en su distrito," 17 May 1676.

76. AGN, RCO, vol. 18, exp. 8, fos. 16–17, *cédula* of 22 February 1680. Interestingly enough, this was also the opinion of one of the critics of viceregal patronage. Fernández de Villalobos, in his *Estado eclesiástico, político y militar*, pp. 641–642, argues that "as long as a viceroy has [offices] to distribute, he will be respected and feared by his inferiors, being able to keep the kingdom in peace and tranquillity and in devotion to Your Majesty. Because should the subjects, especially the Creoles, realize that the viceroy has not the necessary authority to both give and punish, they will belittle him and

procure for themselves a much greater authority and easily go on to scorn his orders and even those of Your Majesty."

77. AGI, Mexico 52, no. 3, the count of Paredes to the king, 16 February 1681. Although it is not clear, it is rather likely that the count of Paredes, given his high-level connections at the court, played a decisive role in the monarch's change of mind in regard to the 1678 *cédula*. In his response to Paredes' letter, the Council made clear that the offices ought to be distributed not only among the natives of New Spain, but also among all those *beneméritos* who lived in New Spain, even if they had not been born there (as long as they were not retainers of the viceroy). See AGI, Mexico 52, no. 3, Cámara de Indias, 23 July 1681; CDHH, vol. II, pp. 726–728, "R.C. sobre la forma en que los virreyes, presidentes y gobernadores de las Indias han de proveer los oficios de su provisión (2 August 1681)." In 1623, a *cédula* had been issued to make clear that the prohibition to give offices to the members of the viceroy's household did not include those descendants of *conquistadores* who might be serving the viceroy in his retinue. See AGN, RCO, vol. 8, exp. 25, fo. 70, the king to the marquis of Mancera, 17 May 1665.

78. "Consulta del Consejo de las Indias sobre un papel de don Melchor de Navarra, virrey del Perú," 8 October 1680, in CDHH, vol. II, pp. 709–712.

79. AGN, RCO, vol. 18, exp. 26, fo. 50, *cédula* of 14 May 1680; ibid., exp. 67, fos. 143–144, *cédula* of 23 November 1680. On the three or four different categories into which the *alcaldías mayores* were divided, according to their economic worth, see AGI, Mexico 600, fos. 698–702, "Memoria de todos los oficios que provee S.E. en esta gobernación como en los demás obispados de su gobierno," 1663. For the twelve offices assigned to the viceroy of Peru, see CDHH, vol. II, pp. 716–717, *cédula* of 19 November 1680.

80. AGN, RCO, vol. 22, exp. 24, fo. 46, *cédula* of 6 May 1688; ibid., exp. 46, fo. 86, *cédula* of 9 June 1688. On these sales of offices, see also Yalí Román, "Sobre alcaldías mayores," pp. 31–35; Fernando Muro Romero, "El 'beneficio' de oficios públicos con jurisdicción en Indias. Notas sobre sus orígenes," *Anuario de Estudios Americanos* 35 (1978): 1–67.

81. The count of Galve to the duke of the Infantado, 10 January 1693 and 4 June 1693, in Gutiérrez Lorenzo, *De la corte de Castilla al virreinato de México*, pp. 155–158, 167–170. His predecessor, the count of la Monclova (who went from Mexico to the viceroyalty of Peru, which he ruled until 1705) likewise refused to hand over their posts to those appointed by the Crown. In view of this attitude, the Council would simply instruct the *audiencias* that they would be in charge of handing over the posts, should the viceroys refuse to do it. See Yalí Román, "Sobre alcaldías mayores," p. 30.

82. See "Consulta del consejo de las Indias sobre los inconvenientes que resultan en beneficiar los oficios en Indias, y especialmente los puestos de justicia y gobierno (9 November 1693)," in *CDHH*, vol. III, pp. 34–39.

83. See, for example, John H. Parry, *The Sale of Public Office in the Spanish Indies Under the Hapsburgs* (Berkeley, 1953); Mark A. Burkholder and Douglas S. Chandler, *From Impotence to Authority: The Spanish Crown and the*

American Audiencias, 1687–1808 (Columbia, MS, 1977); Kenneth J. Andrien, "The Sale of Fiscal Offices and the Decline of Royal Authority in the Viceroyalty of Peru, 1633–1700," *Hispanic American Historical Review* 62, no. 1 (1982): 49–71; "Corruption, Inefficiency, and Imperial Decline in the Seventeenth-Century Viceroyalty of Peru," *The Americas* 41, no. 1 (1984): 1–20.

84. John Leddy Phelan, *The Kingdom of Quito in the Seventeenth Century: Bureaucratic Politics in the Spanish Empire* (Madison, 1967), pp. 147–176.

85. Horst Pietschmann, *El Estado y su evolución al principio de la colonización española de América* (México, 1989), pp. 163–182.

86. Ibid., pp. 161–163. As could be expected, Pietschmann criticizes Phelan for exaggerating the "patrimonial" features of the Spanish empire. For the idea of a "centralized bureaucratic empire," see S.N. Eisendstadt, *The Political System of Empires* (New York, 1963), pp. 11, 22–24. Alternatively, a Weberian intermediate approach is the one taken by Magali Sarfatti, who argues that the "first colonizing nation of Europe embodied a political conception the content of which was both modern (being part of the rise of national states in Western Europe) and traditional (deriving its patrimonial structure from the medieval body of political thought)." See her *Spanish Bureaucratic-Patrimonialism in America* (Berkeley, 1966), p. 6. Max Weber's ideas on "bureaucratism," on which the idea of the modern state is based, as opposed to the "patrimonial" state can be found in his *Economy and Society: An Outline of Interpretive Sociology* (Berkeley, 1978), pp. 212–241.

87. Roger Mettam, *Power and Faction in Louis XIV's France* (Oxford, 1988), pp. 7, 12.

88. Kettering, *Patrons, Brokers, and Clients,* p. 192.

89. See, for example, Avendaño's long discussion in his treatise on the government of the Indies on whether viceroys may receive gifts (*Thesaurus Indicus,* pp. 399–407). See also the uneasiness manifested by Juan de Palafox in his capacity as *visitador* of New Spain for certain gifts given to him by the viceroy, in BPR, II/1981, fos. 130–132, 138, Palafox to the king, 20 October and 13 November 1640. Octavio Paz has described the exchange of gifts between Sor Juana and the viceroys as an expression of the relations of patronage that united the former with the latter. See his *Sor Juana Inés de la Cruz o las trampas de la fe* (México, 1982), pp. 248–272. On the gift culture in early modern Europe, see Sharon Kettering, "Gift-Giving and Patronage in Early Modern France," *French History* 2 (1988): 131–151; Peck, *Court Patronage and Corruption,* pp. 12–20; Biagioli, *Galileo Courtier,* pp. 36–54.

90. This has been pointed out by Jean-Claude Waquet in his study of corruption in early modern Florence. See the Introduction in *Corruption: Ethics and Power in Florence, 1600–1770,* translated by Linda McCall (University Park, PA, 1991).

91. On the sales of offices debate, see Francisco Tomás y Valiente, "Opiniones de algunos juristas clásicos españoles sobre la venta de oficios públicos," in *Filosofía y derecho: Estudios en honor del profesor José Corts Grau* (Valencia,

1977), vol. II, pp. 627–645. For opinions against the sales, see Cevallos, *Arte real*, fos. 176–182; Mendo, *Príncipe perfecto*, documento LXVI. For the reasons advanced by the Council of the Indies to justify the sale of non-judicial offices, see "Consulta del Consejo de las Indias sobre los inconvenientes ... de venderse los oficios de contadores y otros oficiales de la Real Hacienda de V.M. en las Indias, 27 April 1633," in CDHH, vol. II, pp. 340–344. On the arguments to justify the sale of *alcaldías mayores*, see Yalí Román, "Sobre alcaldías mayores," pp. 33–34.

92. Portocarrero y Guzmán, *Teatro Monárquico de España*, pp. 449–467.
93. Avilés, *Advertencias de un político*, pp. 109–131. Mendoza's opinions were originally published in Naples in 1602 under the title *Tres tratados compuestos ... para el ... conde de Lemos, virrey de Nápoles*. Avilés reproduced in his book the first two tracts, "De las gracias" and "De los oficios vendibles." For similar ideas, see Avendaño, *Thesaurus Indicus*, pp. 409–413. The Council of the Indies used the same arguments to strongly oppose the king's decision to sell the *alcaldía mayor* of San Luis Potosí, one of the most lucrative in New Spain. See "Consulta del Consejo de las Indias sobre que no se vendan los oficios de alcaldes mayores, 9 December 1638," in CDHH, vol. II, pp. 368–370.
94. In fact, at the very end of the sixteenth century, the viceroy of New Spain himself had proposed to the Crown the raise of the salaries of the *corregidores* as a way to prevent the exactions to which the Indians were subjected by these officials because of their low salaries. See AGI, Mexico 24, no. 6, the count of Monterrey to the king, 15 April 1598. Among contemporaries, some voices contended that the solution to this problem was to raise not the *corregidores'* but the viceroys' salaries. See Fernández de Villalobos, *Estado eclesiástico, político y militar*, pp. 651–652.
95. The count of Galve to the duchess of the Infantado, 12 January 1693, in Gutiérrez Lorenzo, *De la corte de Castilla al virreinato de México*, pp. 159–161.
96. Colin M. MacLachlan, *Spain's Empire in the New World: The Role of Ideas in Institutional and Social Change* (Berkeley, 1988), p. 36.
97. These prohibitions had been issued uninterruptedly from as early as 1530, when the instructions for *corregidores* were issued, including the oath that all appointees had to swear not to engage in commercial transactions in their offices (neither directly nor through intermediaries), until the end of the seventeenth century, when, once more, a *cédula* was issued in which the viceroys were ordered to punish those *alcaldes mayores* and *corregidores* who had broken their oath. See, for example, *Recopilación*, lib. V, tít. II, ley vii; "Instrucción a los alcaldes y corregidores de Nueva España, 1561," in *Documentos inéditos del siglo XVI para la historia de México*, edited by M. Cuevas (México, 1975), p. 248; "R.C. al virrey de la Nueva España que guarde y cumpla las *cédulas* y órdenes que estuvieren dadas sobre los tratos y contratos de las justicias con los indios (19 August 1631)," in CDHH, vol. II, p. 332; AGN, RCO, vol. 22, exp. 2, fo. 3, *cédula* of 16 February 1688.

98. Cicero, *On Duties (De Officiis)*, edited and translated by M.T. Griffin and E.M. Atkins (Cambridge, U.K., 1991), pp. 33–34, 93–95.

99. Santa María, *Tratado de república*, pp. 37–44. See also Cevallos, *Arte real*, fo. 63.

100. AGN, RCD, vol. 180, fo. 78v, the king to the marquis of Guadalcázar, 19 December 1618.

101. Not until 1751 can any significant changes be appreciated. In this year, after two and a half centuries of prohibitions, the commercial activities of *alcaldes mayores* and *corregidores* would be legalized. See Yalí Román, "Sobre alcaldías mayores," p. 37. This decision could be seen as an indicator of the important changes that were beginning to take form in the political culture of the Spanish monarchy.

102. Avendaño, *Thesaurus Indicus*, pp. 291–295.

103. Not surprisingly, in his "Weberian analysis of the Spanish bureaucracy," Phelan could not avoid concluding that, "The Spanish bureaucracy contained both patrimonial and legal features in a bewildering combination." For him, the Spanish imperial bureaucracy was midway between a patrimonial bureaucracy in which officials were paid in kind, in tips, and in graft and a modern administration with regular, monetary salaries paid by the state. See Phelan, *The Kingdom of Quito*, pp. 320–337.

104. See Tamar Herzog, *La administración como un fenómeno social: La justicia penal de la ciudad de Quito (1650–1750)*, especially pp. 124–150, a study that shows how colonial institutions functioned through networks of patronage and personal ties and loyalties, even in the act of administering justice, rather than through the use of coercive or legal means. It should be noted that this was not specific to the Spanish monarchy. See, for instance, Kettering's discussion of the workings of the French bureaucracy of intendants in the seventeenth century in her *Patrons, Brokers, and Clients*, pp. 224–231.

105. In Avilés, *Advertencias de un político*, pp. 84–96. A frequent and effective argument used by the viceroys to justify the granting of offices to their retainers and relatives or to those of the *oidores* and other royal officials was that these individuals had been appointed, not because of their personal connections, but because they were *beneméritos* whose services or those of their progenitors deserved to be rewarded. See AGI, Escribanía 227A, cuaderno 3º, fos. 22r–28r, *residencia* of the marquis of Mancera, 1674; AGI, Escribanía 229B, fos. 26r–31r, residencia of the count of Paredes, 1688.

106. Pietschmann, *El Estado y su evolución*, pp. 168–169; Gregorio Martín de Guijo, *Diario, 1648–1664* (México, 1952), especially vol. I.

107. Pietschmann, who is, no doubt, the historian of colonial Spanish America who has shown the greatest interest in the study of corruption, more recently and to some extent has revised some of his ideas about the "modernity" of the political system established by the Spaniards in the New World and has pointed out that corruption, while forming part of the system, played an important political role, as it helped balance the interests of the Crown with those of colonial society. He has also acknowledged the extreme importance

of personal relationships in colonial society and has gone as far as to wonder whether the concept of corruption is a useful category of analysis, given the high degree of tolerance shown toward it by that society. See his "Corrupción en las Indias españolas: Revisión de un debate en la historiografía sobre Hispanoamérica colonial," in *Instituciones y corrupción en la historia*, edited by M. González Jiménez et al. (Valladolid, Spain, 1998), pp. 31–52.

108. AGI, México 5, no. 167, *consulta* of 3 March 1653; no. 175, *consulta* of 30 June 1653. For the business deals of the viceroys, see Louisa S. Hoberman, *Mexico's Merchant Elite, 1590–1660* (Durham, 1991), pp. 176–180.

109. Avendaño, for one, thought it licit that viceroys profited from commercial transactions done in their name through third persons, as long as these persons were not relatives or retainers. See *Thesaurus Indicus*, pp. 395–397.

110. Michel Foucault, *Discipline and Punish: the Birth of the Prison*, translated by Alan Sheridan (New York, 1977), pp. 82, 88.

111. A good example of this balancing game can be found in the arguments used by the marquis of Mancera during his *residencia* to justify the granting of offices to some of his retainers, or by the count of Paredes to justify his appointment of relatives of the *oidores* and members of his own retinue. See AGI, Escribanía 227A, cuaderno 3º, fos. 22r–28r, 21 February 1674; AGI, Escribanía 229B, fos. 26r–31r, 28 February 1688.

112. Even Palafox admitted that a "moderate profit" obtained from their offices by the *alcaldes mayores* was an acceptable thing. See "Relación de Juan de Palafox y Mendoza, 1642," in *Los virreyes, México IV*, BAE vol. CCLXXVI, p. 60. Likewise, Alonso de Cuevas Dávalos, the bishop of Oaxaca, who, as we will see in Chapter 7, would blame the Tehuantepec rebellion of 1660 on the excesses of the *alcaldes mayores*, made a distinction between the "licit profits" of the *alcaldes mayores*, even if they were forbidden by the king, and the "exorbitant and excessive gains" that they usually obtained by subjecting the Indians to all kinds of harshness and abuse. See *Documentos sobre las rebeliones indias de Tehuantepec y Nexapa (1660–1661)*, edited by H. Díaz-Polanco and C. Manzo (México, 1992), p. 138. See also AGI, Mexico 346, fo. 26, the bishop of Puebla to the king, 22 February 1681. The same view was voiced by Fernández de Villalobos in *Estado eclesiástico, político y militar*, pp. 644–645. For a similar opinion, this time expressed by a viceroy, see "Relación del estado en que dejó el gobierno del Marqués de Cerralvo, 17.III.1636," in *Los virreyes, México III*, BAE, vol. CCLXXV, pp. 277–278.

Chapter 6

1. As Anthony Pagden has shown, despite the apparent novelty of the sixteenth-century imperial projects, it was the Roman Empire, in reality, that furnished the ideologues of the Spanish, British, and French imperial systems with the necessary language and political models. See his *Lords of All the World: Ideologies of Empire in Spain, Britain and France, c. 1500–c.1800* (New Haven, CT, 1995), chap. 1.

2. See, for example, Lewis Hanke, *Aristotle and the American Indians* (Bloomington, 1959) and *The Spanish Struggle for Justice in the Conquest of America* (Boston, 1965); Anthony Pagden, *The Fall of Natural Man: The American Indian and the Origins of Comparative Ethnology* (Cambridge, U.K., 1982) and *Spanish Imperialism and the Political Imagination* (New Haven, CT, 1990), chap. 1.

3. AGN, RCD, vol. 180, fos. 80v–81v, the king to the marquis of Guadalcázar, 8 June 1619.

4. *Recopilación*, lib. VI, tít. X, ley ii. This double emphasis on the good treatment of the Indians, on the one hand, and on their forced labor, on the other, and its apparently contradictory nature are analyzed in the last section of this chapter.

5. *Recopilación*, lib. I, tít. VII, ley xiii.

6. It should be pointed out that the concept of a "wretched person" was not invented to be applied to the American Indian but originated in Roman and medieval law. See Paulino Castañeda Delgado, "La condición miserable del indio y sus privilegios," *Anuario de Estudios Americanos* XXVIII (1971): 245–258.

7. On the Franciscan vision of the providential mission of the Spanish monarchy, see "Carta de fray Toribio de Motolinía al emperador Carlos V, enero 2 de 1555," in fray Toribio de Benavente, *Historia de los indios de la Nueva España*, edited by E. O'Gorman (México, 1969), pp. 211–212; "Carta de fray Gerónimo de Mendieta a Felipe II, 15 de abril de 1587," in *Documentos inéditos del siglo XVI para la historia de México*, edited by M. Cuevas (México, 1975), pp. 415–417; Fray Juan de Silva, "Memorial Tercero (1618)," in *Los memoriales del Padre Silva sobre predicación pacífica y repartimientos*, edited by P. Castañeda Delgado (Madrid, 1983), pp. 371–386. For similar arguments advanced by a strong supporter of the Franciscan views, see "Parecer del Dr. Alonso Zorita acerca de la doctrina y administración de los sacramentos a los naturales, 1 de marzo de 1584," in *Documentos inéditos del siglo XVI*, especially pp. 347–353. See also John Leddy Phelan, *The Millennial Kingdom of the Franciscans in the New World* (Berkeley, 1970), pp. 11–14.

8. Gerónimo de Mendieta, "Memorial de algunas cosas que conviene representar al rey D. Felipe, Nuestro Señor, para descargo de su real conciencia," in *Códice Mendieta. Documentos franciscanos. Siglos XVI y XVII. Tomo Segundo*, edited by J. García Icazbalceta (México, 1892), pp. 7–10. For the ways in which the infantilization of the indigenous inhabitants of the New World had been elaborated and rationalized in the Spanish universities in the first half of the sixteenth century, especially by the Dominican Francisco de Vitoria and his disciples of the "School of Salamanca," see Pagden, *The Fall of Natural Man*, pp. 104–108.

9. Mendieta, "Memorial," in *Códice Mendieta II*, p. 11 (the emphasis is mine). The Indians, however, are not perfect, having two main defects: The first one is the "vice of drinking until they pass out"; the other defect is "their

natural laziness and sluggishness" (Mendieta, ibid., p. 10). These images of the drunk and idle Indian will persist throughout the entire colonial period and beyond and will have, as we shall see later, important social and political consequences.

10. On the ideas of Mendieta and the Franciscans about the New World, see José Antonio Maravall, *Utopía y reformismo en la España de los Austrias* (Madrid, 1982), pp. 79–110; Phelan, *The Millennial Kingdom*; Georges Baudot, *Utopia and History in Mexico: The First Chroniclers of Mexican Civilization (1520–1569)* (Niwot, CO, 1993); Carlos Sempat Assadourian, "Memoriales de fray Gerónimo de Mendieta." *Historia Mexicana* XXXVII, no. 3 (1988): 357–422; David A. Brading, *The First America: The Spanish Monarchy, Creole Patriots, and the Liberal State, 1492–1867* (Cambridge, U.K., 1991), pp. 110–116. For a critique of the idea that the Franciscan project was a millenarian one, see Elsa Cecilia Frost, "A New Millenarian: Georges Baudot," *The Americas* 36, no. 4 (April 1980): 515–526. The political aspects of Mendieta's project will be discussed in more detail in the next chapter.

11. Mendieta, "Memorial," in *Códice Mendieta II*, pp. 11–12.

12. "Consideraciones cerca de los indios de la Nueva España," in *Códice Mendieta II*, pp. 28–36. Mendieta included all these ideas in his magnum opus, *Historia eclesiástica indiana* (México, 1997), lib. I, caps. II, IV, V; lib. IV, caps. XXI, XXXIX. The *Historia* was written at the end of his life, in the last years of the sixteenth century, although it would not be published until 1870. Mendieta was highly influenced by the ideas of Friar Toribio de Benavente Motolinía, whose disciple he considered himself. This influence can be seen in the similarity of the images and concepts used by both to describe the Indians. Cf. Fray Toribio de Motolinía, *Historia de los indios de la Nueva España*, edited by Georges Baudot (Madrid, 1985), pp. 188–189, 233.

13. Georges Baudot, "Amerindian Image and Utopian Project: Motolinía and Millenarian Discourse," in *Amerindian Images and the Legacy of Columbus*, edited by R. Jara and N. Spadaccini (Minneapolis, 1992), pp. 375–400.

14. Juan de Matienzo, *Gobierno del Perú (1567)* (París, 1967), pp. 16, 18.

15. "Decretos del III Concilio Provincial Mexicano," in José A. Llaguno, *La personalidad jurídica del indio y el III Concilio Provincial Mexicano (1585)* (México, 1963), pp. 271–273, 277, 285. On the Third Council and the Indian, see Pilar Gonzalbo Aizpuru, *Historia de la educación en la época colonial. El mundo indígena* (México, 1990), pp. 100–109. On the social and racial meaning of corporal punishment in Mexico, see my "Theater of Power: Writing and Representing the Auto de Fe in Colonial Mexico," *The Americas* 52, no. 3 (Jan. 1996): 332–333.

16. "Memorial al rey, por Don Juan de Palafox y Mendoza. De la naturaleza y virtudes del indio," in Juan de Palafox, *Tratados mejicanos II*, edited by F. Sánchez-Castañer (Madrid, 1968), p. 96.

17. Ibid., pp. 101, 103–106.

18. Ibid., pp. 108–109. On the process of resettlement of Indian towns, see below.

19. Ibid., p. 100.

20. It is important to point out that a majority of the concepts and images used to describe the "wretched Indian" were similarly utilized to refer to the "rustic persons" who lived in Castile and the other peninsular kingdoms. Rustics were those who lived outside of the cities and were characterized by their "ignorance and brutality" and their lack of a written literary culture. As in the case of the Indians, the condition of rustic, with all its discriminatory burden, was based, in theory, on the notion of protection, due to the simplicity and lack of capacity of the rustics. See Antonio M. Hespanha, *La gracia del derecho. Economía de la cultura en la Edad Moderna*, translated by A. Cañellas Haurie (Madrid, 1993), pp. 32–38, 52–60. On the frequent comparison of American Indians to European peasants in the sixteenth century, see Pagden, *The Fall of Natural Man*, pp. 97–99. On the Indians' assumed lack of intellectual capacity, see Magdalena Chocano Mena, *La fortaleza docta. Elite letrada y dominación social en México colonial (siglos XVI–XVII)* (Barcelona, 2000), chap. 1.

21. Juan de Solórzano y Pereira, *Política indiana*, edited by M.A. Ochoa Brun (Madrid, [1647] 1972), lib. II, cap. XXVIII, núms. 6–7, 24–31. All these ideas would be incorporated, some years later, by Alonso de la Peña Montenengro, bishop of Quito, in his influential *Itinerario para párrocos de indios* (Madrid, [1668] 1995), pp. 249–255, 383–403. This manual for priests in charge of Indian parishes would become the text of reference in matters of Indian evangelization.

22. Solórzano, *Política indiana*, lib. II, cap. XXVIII, núm. 46.

23. See, for example, Castañeda Delgado, "La condición miserable del indio" pp. 263–267, 273, 281–282.

24. Solórzano, *Política indiana*, lib. II, cap. XXVIII, núms. 6, 7.

25. On the civilizing discourse of the nineteenth- and twentieth-century colonial endeavors, see David Spurr, *The Rhetoric of Empire: Colonial Discourse in Journalism, Travel Writing and Imperial Administration* (Durham, 1993) chap. 7; Robert J.C. Young, *Postcolonialism: An Historical Introduction* (Oxford, 2001), pp. 29–30, 88–89.

26. Matienzo, *Gobierno del Perú*, pp. 43, 46, 60. In any case, it should be pointed out that it was generally argued that the tribute all Indians between the ages of 18 and 50 had to pay annually was a royal prerogative due to the king (or to the *encomenderos* in his name) to acknowledge his suzerainty over the inhabitants of the Indies who, after the conquest, had become his vassals and subjects. See *Recopilación*, lib. VI, tít. V, ley i; Solórzano, *Política indiana*, lib. II, cap. XIX, núms. 1–12; cap XX, núm. 2. Matienzo himself also espouses this view in his *Gobierno del Perú*, p. 42. On the Indian tribute, see José Miranda, *El tributo indígena en la Nueva España durante el siglo XVI* (México, 1952), especially pp. 144–164, 176–185; Charles Gibson, *The Aztecs Under Spanish Rule: A History of the Indians of the Valley of Mexico, 1519–1810* (Stanford, 1964), chap. VIII.

27. José de Acosta, *De procuranda indorum salute*, Spanish version by L. Pereña et al. ([Salamanca, 1588] Madrid, 1984), p. 433.

28. Ibid., pp. 441, 459.
29. Ibid., pp. 443, 445, 447. Solórzano will agree with Acosta's arguments. For him, the only beneficial tributes are those that the tribute payers can pay. He points out, in addition, that the tributes the Indians pay have been reduced so much that they can pay them with ease, unless they are lazy and want to be idle. See his *Política indiana*, lib. II, cap. XIX, núms. 18, 34; cap. XX, núm. 26; cap. XXI, núm. 2.
30. Solórzano, *Política indiana*, lib. II, cap. XXII, núm. 2.
31. "Respuesta que los religiosos de las tres órdenes de la Nueva España dieron en el año de 1557, siendo preguntados por S.M. del parecer y sentimiento que tenían acerca de los diezmos, si era bien y convenía que estos naturales indios los pagasen," in *Códice Mendieta. Documentos franciscanos, Siglos XVI y XVII, Tomo Primero*, edited by J. García Icazbalceta (México, 1892), pp. 1–18. See also la "Relación de Fray Domingo de la Anunciación acerca del tributar de los indios (1554)," in *Documentos inéditos del siglo XVI*, pp. 235–242. On the controversy that took place around the middle of the sixteenth century between the religious orders and the archbishop of Mexico because of the question of the tithes, see Georges Baudot, *La pugna franciscana por México* (México, 1990), chap. III.
32. This is what the former *oidor* of the *audiencia* of Mexico and great supporter of the Franciscans, Alonso de Zorita, had proposed. See his *Relación de los señores de la Nueva España*, edited by G. Vázquez (Madrid, 1992), pp. 192–193. See also Solórzano, *Política indiana*, lib. II, cap. XXIII.
33. "Relación de Antonio de Mendoza a Luis de Velasco … c. 1550," in *Los virreyes, México I*, BAE, vol. CCLXXIII, p. 52.
34. See, for example, "Instrucción a Luis de Velasco, 16.IV.1550," in *Los virreyes, México I*, BAE, vol. CCLXXIII, pp. 142–143; "Memorial del obispo de Chiapa don fray Pedro de Feria para el Sínodo Provincial que se celebra en México este presente año de 1585," in Llaguno, *La personalidad jurídica del indio*, pp. 191–192; AGI, Mexico 20, n. 122, the marquis of Villamanrique to the king, 10 May 1586.
35. Francisco Antonio Lorenzana, *Concilios provinciales primero y segundo, celebrados en la Muy Noble y Muy Leal ciudad de México, presidiendo el Illmo. y Rmo. Señor D. Fr. Alonso de Montúfar, en los años de 1555 y 1565* (México, 1769), pp. 147–148.
36. The Aristotelian origins of these ideas are quite obvious. On the classical roots of the concept of "barbarian" and its relation to the Roman Empire and to Christianity, see Pagden, *The Fall of Natural Man*, pp. 15–26; Pagden, *Lords of all the World*, pp. 19–24. For a discussion of the term "policía," see Richard L. Kagan, *Urban Images of the Hispanic World, 1493–1793* (New Haven, CT, 2000), pp. 26–28.
37. Lorenzana, *Concilios provinciales*, p. 148. Speaking of the Indians, the III Concilio Limense, celebrated in 1583, will similarly proclaim that "hardly can they be taught how to be Christians if we do not teach them first how to learn to be men and live as such." Quoted in Solórzano, *Política indiana*, lib. II, cap.

XXV, núm. 4. Acosta uses a similar argument in his *De procuranda*, p. 539, just like Matienzo in *Gobierno del Perú*, p. 48. For his part, Solórzano will draw from Aristotle and Cicero to argue that man is not only defined as a rational animal, but also as sociable, political, or civil. According to him, Aristotle and Cicero define the city as "a perfect congregation of men who, being previously scattered in huts throughout forests or woods," came together as one in order to help and defend one another. A civil or political life is, therefore, much better than a solitary one, as the solitary person, asserts Solórzano, can only be either God or a beast. *Política indiana*, lib. II, cap. XXIV, núms. 2, 5, 7, 9.

38. III Concilio Limense, quoted in Solórzano, *Política indiana*, lib. II, cap. XXV, núm. 4. See also Matienzo, *Gobierno del Perú*, p. 53. It is necessary to observe that this emphasis on the transformation of manners and human behavior is not specific to the New World, but it developed in Europe, starting in the sixteenth century, as part of the "civilizing process" of these societies. This process and its close relation to mechanisms of power and domination has been studied by Norbert Elias in *The Civilizing Process: Sociogenetic and Psychogenetic Investigations*, translated by E. Jephcott (Oxford, 2000), in particular pp. 45–182. In this regard, it could be argued with Foucault, as John Sullivan has done, that the congregation program, with its distribution of bodies and spatial rearrangements, was one of the first formulations of the disciplinary techniques which, in later centuries, would characterize capitalist societies, and whose main purpose was the production of obedient subjects. The congregation of the Indians was then an indispensable mechanism for the establishment and maintenance of royal authority in the New World. See John Sullivan, "La congregación como tecnología disciplinaria en el siglo XVI," *Estudios de Historia Novohispana* 16 (1996): 35–55.

39. Solórzano, *Política indiana*, lib. II, cap. XXV.

40. AGI, Mexico 24, no. 8, the count of Monterrey to the king, 25 April 1598.

41. Solórzano, *Politica indiana*, lib. II, cap. XXIV, núms. 10, 11, 17, 18, 33. Solórzano goes on to add that, although the Indians are free vassals, their freedom is conditional because they are obligated to pay tributes and perform certain services. Ibid., núm. 32. For similar arguments, see Peña Montenengro, *Itinerario*, pp. 403–404.

42. Quoted in Solange Alberro, "La aculturación de los españoles en la América colonial," in *Descubrimiento, conquista y colonización de América a quinientos años*, edited by C. Bernand (México, 1994), p. 253, note 5. The New World experience would also strongly influence the civilizing discourse directed at the lower classes (both rural and urban) of places such as southern Italy — a dominion of the Spanish monarchy that was often pejoratively compared to the Indies. See Jennifer D. Selwyn, "Procur[ing] in the Common People These Better Behaviors: The Jesuits' Civilizing Mission in Early Modern Naples 1550–1620," *Radical History Review* 67 (1997): 4–34.

43. Nicholas Thomas, *Colonialism's Culture: Anthropology, Travel and Government* (Princeton, 1994), pp. 53–54, 71–72.

44. See, for example, the instructions given between the years 1550 and 1590 to Luis de Velasco I, Martín Enríquez, the count of la Coruña, and the marquis of Villamanrique. See *Los virreyes, México I*, BAE, vol. CCLXXIII, pp. 142, 199, 240, 263.

45. James Lockhart, *The Nahuas after the Conquest* (Stanford, 1992), pp. 44–45; Rik Hoekstra, *Two Worlds Merging: The Transformation of Society in the Valley of Puebla, 1570–1640* (Amsterdam, 1993), pp. 68–70.

46. AGI, Mexico 22, nos. 64, 74, 148, Velasco to the king, 9 November 1591, 20 March 1592, 25 October 1594; "Advertimientos," in *Los virreyes, México II*, BAE, vol. CCLXXIV, p. 105.

47. Mendieta, "Carta para Don Pedro Moya," in *Códice Mendieta II*, pp. 90–94. Mendieta offered a detailed plan on how the congregations should be carried out and the new towns designed. Ibid., pp. 86–89, 94–98.

48. Llaguno, *La personalidad jurídica del indio*, p. 286, 310–311.

49. "Advertimientos," in *Los virreyes, México II*, BAE, vol. CCLXXIV, p. 105.

50. AGI, Mexico 25, no. 48a, the king to Luis de Velasco, 13 July 1594.

51. Lockhart, *The Nahuas*, p. 45. Hoekstra has argued that the most important goal of the congregations was not to resettle the Indian population, but rather to facilitate the recording of the new division of land between Spaniards and Indians. See *Two Worlds Merging*, pp. 116–117.

52. That *cédula* was specifically mentioned in Monterrey's Instructions. See "Instrucción al conde de Monterrey, 20.III.1596," in *Los virreyes, México II*, BAE, vol. CCLXXIV, p. 141.

53. AGI, Mexico 24, no. 8, the count of Monterrey to the king, 25 April 1598; "Papel del conde de Monterrey sobre las congregaciones de los indios, 14 de enero de 1604," in *Los virreyes, México II*, BAE, vol. CCLXXIV, pp. 157–160.

54. Most of the money would come from the Indians themselves, as the Crown resolved that part of the tributes paid by the Indians were to be used for their resettlement. See AGI, Mexico 25, no. 48a, the king to Luis de Velasco, 13 July 1594; "Consulta del Consejo de las Indias sobre reducir los indios a poblaciones (19 October 1598)" and "R.C. al virrey de la Nueva España, conde de Monterrey, sobre asuntos de gobierno temporal (20 October 1598)," in CDHH, vol. II, pp. 55–57.

55. For a description of the resettlement procedure, see Howard F. Cline, "Civil Congregations of the Indians in New Spain, 1598–1606," *The Hispanic American Historical Review* XXIX (1949): 349–369; Bernardo García Martínez, *Los pueblos de la sierra. El poder y el espacio entre los indios del norte de Puebla hasta 1700* (México, 1987), pp. 163–174.

56. For an analysis of the political symbolism embedded in the regular and geometric design of the cities and towns of colonial Spanish America, see Kagan, *Urban Images*, pp. 31–39.

57. AGI, Mexico 25, no. 48m, "Copia de la instrucción que se dio a los jueces de la ejecución de congregaciones..." (n.d.). See also "Instrucción que vos Don Fernando de Villegas, alcalde mayor de la provincia de Mechoacán, habéis de guardar en las congregaciones que de esa provincia os están cometidas," in

Ernesto de la Torre Villar, *Las congregaciones de los pueblos de indios. Fase terminal: aprobaciones y rectificaciones* (México, 1995), pp. 315–316.

58. Lockhart argues that the congregation project, although not without any impact, failed to alter the sociopolitical structure of indigenous communities. The only tangible effect on the structure of the *altepetl* would have been the relocation of the inhabitants of some of the smaller units to the central settlement, with the resulting disappearance of those units. In that way, the process would have contributed to a greater identification between the *altepetl* central settlement and the Spanish concept of *cabecera* (head town). See *The Nahuas*, pp. 45–46. To the contrary, García Martínez, although recognizing that they had extremely variable consequences, concludes that the congregations as a whole were successful and permanent, as there was never a return to the spatial ordering of the pre-Hispanic period. See *Los pueblos de la sierra*, p. 179. It should be pointed out that Lockhart concentrated his analysis on the central valley of Mexico, whereas García Martínez's study is based on Puebla's northern sierra. These are two very different regions, which could help explain the different conclusions reached by these two authors, although one would have expected greater change in the central valley, where the Spanish presence was much more pronounced.

59. See, for instance, AGI, Mexico 22, no. 148, Velasco to the king, 25 October 1594; AGI, Mexico 24, no. 56, Monterrey to the king, 20 May 1601; AGI, Mexico 25, nos. 36 and 48, Monterrey to the king, 27 May and 18 November 1603. To expedite the process, Monterrey requested, and the Crown granted, that any appellations by either Indians or Spaniards of the decisions made by the viceroy in relation to the congregations should be sent directly to the Council of the Indies instead of going to the *audiencia*; meanwhile, the process should not be stopped. AGI, Mexico 23, no. 98, Monterrey to Juan de Ibarra, 29 November 1597; AGI, Mexico 25, no. 48c, the king to Monterrey, 20 October 1598.

60. Fray Juan de Torquemada, *Monarquía indiana* (1645), edited by M. León-Portilla (México, 1975), lib V, cap. XLIII. Another influential Franciscan, Juan de Silva, also was very critical of the relocation of the indigenous population. See *Memoriales del Padre Silva*, pp. 284–285. For the collective, critical view of the Franciscans, see AGI, Mexico 26, no. 80a, the order of Saint Francis to the marquis of Montesclaros, 30 January 1606. For a critique by the Dominicans, see the letter written to the king in 1610 by Antonio de la Serna, provincial of the order in the district of Oaxaca, included in Francisco de Burgoa's *Palestra historial de virtudes y ejemplares apostólicos, fundada del celo de insignes héroes de la sagrada Orden de Predicadores en este Nuevo Mundo de la América en las Indias Occidentales* (México, [1670] 1989), pp. 190–195. The count of Monterrey himself would acknowledge that, although he had made use of the parish priests to convince the Indians to relocate, the process of resettlement around Mexico and Puebla had been put off until the last moment because the majority of the parish priests were opposed to any kind of relocation, as they considered them unnecessary. See AGI, Mexico 24, no. 21, Monterrey to the king, 11 June 1599; "Papel del conde de Monterrey," pp. 170–171.

61. Monterrey was well-aware of this. He knew that, as soon as the officials in charge of the removal left the new towns, no one would be able to prevent the Indians from returning to their old settlements, as the district magistrates would not be willing to take over this task without a monetary compensation. See AGI, Mexico 25, no. 48g, "Consulta que hizo el conde mi Sr. a la Real Audiencia en razón de la provisión de los oficios con las congregaciones" (n.d.); AGI, Mexico 24, no. 46, Monterrey to the king, 18 December 1600.

62. Evidence of how numerous Indians had abandoned the new settlements to return to the places where they used to live can be found, for example, in AGN, Congregaciones, vol. 1, fos. 130–134, 136v–137, 141. The examples are from the years 1613, 1614, 1616, and 1625. Torquemada also mentions these flights in his *Monarquía indiana*, lib. V, cap. XLIII, p. 471. For a discussion of the many difficulties the authorities faced in the implementation of the congregations program, see Hoekstra, *Two Worlds Merging*, pp. 108–118.

63. In 1604, due to their numerous complains, the Indians had already been allowed to return to their old homes if they wanted to. See AGI, Mexico 27, no. 16a, the king to the marquis of Montesclaros, 3 December 1604. Although Montesclaros insisted that the resettlement should continue, because otherwise the Indians would undo what it had already been done, the Crown did not change its mind, in this way unofficially putting an end to the congregation process. See AGI, Mexico 26, no. 80a, Montesclaros to the religious orders, 26 January 1606; AGI, Mexico 26, no. 80 and Mexico 27, no. 16, Montesclaros to the king, 17 February 1606 and 26 May 1607.

64. "Instrucción al conde de Moctezuma, 10.V.1696," in *Los virreyes, México V*, BAE, vol. CCLXXVII, p. 201.

65. For him, of course, the model in matters of language could be no other than imperial Rome. See his *Política indiana*, lib. II, cap. XXVI, núms. 33, 34. On the subject of language and the Spanish empire, see Walter D. Mignolo, *The Darker Side of the Renaissance: Literacy, Territoriality, and Colonization* (Ann Arbor, 1995), chap. 1.

66. Mignolo, *The Darker Side of the Renaissance*, pp. 48–52.

67. On the relationships between indigenous languages and Christian religion, see Chocano Mena, *La fortaleza docta*, chap. 2.

68. "R.C. que a los indios se les enseñe la lengua castellana, 7 de junio de 1550," in CDHH, vol. I, pp. 272–273; "Carta de Tomás López Medel, oidor de Guatemala al rey, 9 de junio de 1550," in *Documentos sobre política lingüística en Hispanoamérica (1492–1800)*, edited by F. de Solano (Madrid, 1991), pp. 52–55; "Consulta del Consejo de las Indias sobre las causas porque pareció se debía ordenar que los indios hablasen la lengua castellana, 20 de junio de 1596," in CDHH, vol. II, pp. 38–40; Silvio Zavala, *Poder y lenguaje desde el siglo XVI* (México, 1996), pp. 43–45.

69. The authors of grammars and manuals for the learning of indigenous languages, though always assuming the barbaric nature of these languages, tended to have a more positive view of them, especially Nahuatl, which sometimes was compared to classical Greek. See Ignacio Guzmán Betancourt,

"Policía y 'barbarie' de las lenguas indígenas de México, según la opinión de gramáticos e historiadores novohispanos," *Estudios de Cultura Náhuatl* 21 (1991): 179–218.

70. Gonzalbo Aizpuru, *Historia de la educación*, pp. 185–186. On the insistence on spreading the Nahuatl language throughout New Spain in preference to Spanish as part of the millenarian project of the Franciscans and the difficulties and opposition they had to face, see Baudot, *Utopia and History in Mexico*, pp. 91–104.

71. "Consulta de 20 de junio de 1596" and "R.C. que se ordene poner maestros para los indios que voluntariamente quieran aprender el castellano, 3 de julio de 1596," in CDHH, vol. II, pp. 38–41. See also Gonzalbo Aizpuru, *Historia de la educación*, pp. 188–189; Zavala, *Poder y lenguaje*, pp. 56–57, 66–76.

72. On the lack of resources and the Crown's determination not to assign funds from the royal treasury to cover for the expenses of teaching Spanish to the Indians, see AGI, Mexico 24, no. 8, the count of Monterrey to the king, 25 April 1598; AGN, RCD, vol. 180, fo. 47v, *cédula* of 16 August 1599.

73. For an analysis of these tracts and the concept of "idolatry" in general, see Carmen Bernand and Serge Gruzinski, *De la idolatría. Una arqueología de las ciencias religiosas* (México, 1992), chap. VI; Chocano Mena, *La fortaleza docta*, chap. 3. It should be pointed out that, in the mid-1600s, Solórzano showed himself to be a determined supporter of Indian Castilianization, in which he saw not only religious but political advantages as well. "Not only as a way to expand Christ's faith — he argued — is it advisable that Spaniards and Indians use the same language, … but also because, in that way, [the Indians] will love us and like us more, and become closer to us." See *Política indiana*, lib. II, cap. XXVI, núm. 30.

74. AGN, RCD, vol. 60, *cédula* of 6 April 1691. See also AGN, RCD, vol. 30, fo. 189, *cédula* of 20 June 1686; AGI, México 346, fos. 1015, 1038–1039r, the bishop of Puebla to the king, 12 August 1687 and 30 December 1688; "R.C. al obispo de Puebla, 10 de noviembre de 1689," in CDHH, vol. II, pp. 817–819; AGN, RCD, vol. 30, fos. 262–269, *cédula* of 25 June 1690; AGI, México 346, fos. 1230–1231, the bishop of Puebla to the king, 30 December 1692; AGN, RCO, vol. 24, exp. 134, fo. 524, *cédula* of 30 December 1693.

75. On the program of Castilianization undertaken at the end of the seventeenth century, see Gonzalbo Aizpuru, *Historia de la educación*, pp. 189–191; Chocano Mena, *La fortaleza docta*, pp. 119–121. On the efforts at Castilianization in the eighteenth century, see Zavala, *Poder y lenguaje*, pp. 25–26, 84–101, 118–127, 145–154, and the studies by Dorothy Tanck de Estrada, "Castellanización, política y escuelas de indios en el arzobispado de México a mediados del siglo XVIII," *Historia Mexicana* 152 (1989): 701–741; *Pueblos de indios y educación en el México colonial, 1750–1821* (México, 1999), pp. 168–189, 426–438.

76. See Gibson, *The Aztecs*, pp. 58–81.

77. "R. Instrucción sobre el trabajo de los indios (24 November 1601)," "R.C. que se haga guardar lo proveído sobre los servicios personales de los indios (21 May 1605)," "R.C. sobre los servicios personales y repartimientos de indios (26

May 1609)," in CDHH, vol. II, pp. 71–73, 113–114, 165; "Testimonio del auto de esta Real Audiencia en que mandó cesar los repartimientos de indios que se daban a obras públicas y personas particulares… (18 March 1624)," in *Fuentes para la historia del trabajo en Nueva España*, 8 vols., edited by S. Zavala and M. Castelo (México, 1980), vol. VI, pp. 394–397; *Recopilación*, lib. VI, tít. XII, leyes i, xxxxii, xxxxiii, xxxxviiii.

78. Solórzano, *Política indiana*, lib. II, cap. V, núm. 1.
79. For a description of how the *repartimiento* functioned, see Gibson, *The Aztecs*, pp. 220–231; Hoekstra, *Two Worlds Merging*, pp. 126–141; Rebecca Horn, *Postconquest Coyoacan: Nahua–Spanish Relations in Central Mexico, 1519–1650* (Stanford, 1997), pp. 100–104.
80. Gibson, *The Aztecs*, pp. 231–233; Horn, *Postconquest Coyoacan*, pp. 104–108. On the epidemics that decimated the indigenous population, see Hanns J. Prem, "Disease Outbreaks in Central Mexico during the Sixteenth Century," in N.D. Cook and W.G. Lovell, *Secret Judgments of God: Old World Disease in Colonial Spanish America* (London, 1992), pp. 20–48; N.D. Cook, *Born To Die: Disease and New World Conquest, 1492–1650* (Cambridge, U.K., 1998), pp. 120–122, 137–139.
81. Mendieta, *Historia*, lib. IV, cap. XXXVII, p. 203.
82. "Parecer del P. Provincial y otros religiosos teólogos de la orden de S. Francisco, dado en México a 8 de marzo de 1594, acerca de los indios que se dan en repartimiento a los españoles," in *Cartas de religiosos de Nueva España*, edited by J. García Icazbalceta (México, 1886), pp. 170–173.
83. "Tratado del servicio personal y repartimiento de los indios de Nueva España, escrito por fray Gaspar de Recarte, terminado el 3 de octubre de 1584," en *Documentos inéditos del siglo XVI*, pp. 354–360, 362–363. When the Third Mexican Provincial Council discussed, in 1585, the lawfulness of the labor draft, the Franciscans presented expert advice that followed very closely the arguments advanced by Recarte in his treatise. See "Consulta sobre los repartimientos," in Llaguno, *La personalidad jurídica del indio*, pp. 239–258.
84. Mendieta, *Historia*, lib. IV, cap. XXXVII, pp. 204–205.
85. *Memoriales del Padre Silva*, pp. 270, 273.
86. *Memoriales del Padre Silva*, pp. 271–274. This argument is very similar to the one that was usually made in Spain regarding the peasants. As Jerónimo de Cevallos wrote, "The majesty and power of the princes would be useless if there were no ploughmen … because although they are the feet of the republic, the head cannot move without them." Indeed, in a remark highly revealing of the image that early seventeenth-century Spain had of the New World's native population, Cevallos observed that the Castilian peasants were the "Indians and vassals of the constables and magistrates." For him, they, like the New World natives, were subject to their abuses and at the mercy of those officials. See his *Arte real para el buen gobierno de los reyes y príncipes y de sus vasallos* (Toledo, 1623), fos. 171–175. On the equilibrium that should exist among all the members of the body politic, see José Antonio Maravall, *Estudios de historia del pensamiento español* (Madrid, 1983), pp. 183, 194.

87. "Tratado del servicio personal," in *Documentos inéditos del siglo XVI*, pp. 360–361, 381.
88. "Consulta sobre los repartimientos," p. 239; *Memoriales del Padre Silva*, p. 280.
89. Mendieta reserves his greatest invectives against the draft for the mines, a punishment that, according to him, even the pagans reserved for the most serious crimes. In his view, the mines should be worked by black slaves and captive Chichimec Indians, and not by the free Indians who paid their tributes to the king and were the ones who supported the republic. "Carta para el padre fray Gaspar de Ricarte, que fue a España, contra el repartimiento de los indios, 1587," in *Códice Mendieta II*, pp. 3–6; "Carta para el virrey Don Luis de Velasco, sobre el alzamiento de unos chichimecos, 14 de mayo de 1592," in *Códice Mendieta II*, pp. 114–115. The Chichimec war took place intermittently throughout the second half of the sixteenth century on the northern frontier (which at that time corresponded approximately to the region around Zacatecas). This war and the treatment that should be awarded to the rebel Indians also generated vigorous debates. See Philip W. Powell, *La guerra chichimeca (1550–1600)* (México, 1977); Alberto Carrillo Cazares, *El debate sobre la guerra chichimeca, 1531–1585. Derecho y política en la Nueva España*, 2 vols. (Zamora, MI, 2000).
90. Mendieta, "Memorial de 1587," in *Códice Mendieta II*, pp. 20–28. See also "Parecer del P. Provincial (1594)," in *Cartas de religiosos*, pp. 173–175; *Memoriales del Padre Silva*, p. 344.
91. "Consulta sobre los repartimientos," pp. 258–269.
92. It is important to note that in the months during which the Council took place, Moya de Contreras also held the post of acting viceroy, in addition to those of inspector general and inquisitor general. On both the religious and political careers of this personage, see Stafford Poole, *Pedro Moya de Contreras: Catholic Reform and Royal Power in New Spain, 1571–1591* (Berkeley, 1987).
93. "Consulta sobre los repartimientos," p. 269.
94. "Ampliación de la Instrucción a Antonio de Mendoza, 14.VII.1536," in *Los virreyes, México I*, BAE, vol. CCLXXIII, pp. 35–36.
95. "Instrucción a Martín Enríquez, 7.VI.1568," in *Los virreyes, México I*, BAE, vol. CCLXXIII, pp. 193–194.
96. "Consulta sobre los repartimientos," p. 239; *Memoriales del Padre Silva*, pp. 317–321, 348–349. Mendieta, on the other hand, denies the justification utilized by the supporters of the draft — that if the Indians are not forced they will not work voluntarily — because the Indians have no other alternative but to work for the Spaniards to be able to pay their tribute. *Historia*, lib. IV, cap. XXXVIII, p. 208. Against the idea of the idle Indian, see also *Memoriales del Padre Silva*, pp. 277–278; "Vejaciones que sufren los naturales de la Nueva España," in Silvio Zavala, *El servicio personal de los indios en la Nueva España, 1576–1599* (México, 1987), vol. III, p. 86. Although anonymous, this account might have been written by Torquemada.
97. The Dominicans adopted, in general, a position that was very similar to that of the Franciscans, condemning straightforwardly any type of forced labor.

See the memorials written by Fray Juan Ramírez, "Advertencia sobre el servicio personal al cual son forzados y compelidos los indios de la Nueva España por los visorreyes que en nombre de Su Majestad la gobiernan (1595)" and "Parecer sobre el servicio personal y repartimiento de los indios" (n.d.), both in *Cuerpo de documentos del siglo XVI*, edited by Lewis Hanke (México, 1943), pp. 271–282, 283–292 (a summary of these memorials has been published by Silvio Zavala in *El servicio personal*, vol. III, pp. 135–142).

98. Acosta, *De procuranda*, cap. XVII. See also "Parecer de los PP. Antonio Rubio y Pedro de Hortigosa, S.J., acerca del repartimiento de los indios," in *Documentos inéditos del siglo XVI*, pp. 478–481. This opinion was given in 1596 and is, by and large, a summary of the ideas advanced by Acosta a decade before. For these two Jesuits, it is necessary to force the Indians to work; otherwise, they won't — first of all, because that is the way they had been governed since before the conquest; second, because their proclivity to idleness so requires it; and, finally, because they are not greedy and are not moved by any personal interest to work to make money. The draft, therefore, does not deprive the Indians of their liberty and, if they are paid that which is just, it serves "to make them use well their liberty as required for the good of the republic."

99. Acosta, *De procuranda*, cap. XVIII.

100. See the comments made by the count of Monterrey and Luis de Velasco II regarding this matter in AGI, Mexico 24, no. 6, Monterrey to the king, 15 April 1598 and AGI, Mexico 27, no. 68, Velasco to the king, 24 May 1609. See also Zavala, *El servicio personal*, vol. V, p. 821.

101. "Consulta sobre los repartimientos," p. 260; Ramírez, "Advertencias," p. 273; *Memoriales del Padre Silva*, pp. 261, 266.

102. *Los virreyes, México I*, BAE, vol. CCLXXIII, p. 273. See also the remarks by Luis de Velasco II on the importance of the miners in *Los virreyes, México II*, BAE, vol. CCLXXIV, p. 106. For the count of Monterrey, the entire question of Indian forced labor was "an odious government affair" and "one of the most difficult and encumbering matters a viceroy has to deal with in this kingdom." See AGI, Mexico 25, nos. 19 and 47, Monterrey to the king, 8 December 1602 and 18 November 1603; AGI, Mexico 26, no. 17, Monterrey to Montesclaros, 15 February 1604.

103. In the time of Luis de Velasco II, for example, the daily wage the drafted Indians received was increased from one half to one *real*, which, according to the viceroy, was a "considerable and great amount." See *Los virreyes, México II*, BAE, vol. CCLXXIV, pp. 95, 102. All the viceroys also point out that the labor problem in the mines would be solved by importing more black slaves (up to 3000 were requested by Villamanrique) or by forcing the free blacks and mulattos who lived in New Spain to serve in the mines. See *Los virreyes, México I*, BAE, vol. CCLXXIII, pp. 274, 279, 294–295; *Los virreyes, México II*, BAE, vol. CCLXXIV, p. 94. It was even suggested that the labor problem would be solved by following the example of Potosí (i.e., by establishing a year-long labor draft). See AGI, Mexico 24, no. 6, Monterrey to the king, 15 April 1598.

On the debates over replacing forced Indian labor with black slaves in the Potosí mines, see Frederick P. Bowser, *The African Slave in Colonial Peru, 1524–1650* (Stanford, 1974), chap. 5.

104. "Luis de Velasco II to Mendieta, 1 August 1592," in *Códice Mendieta II*, p. 119.

105. "Advertimientos que Luis de Velasco dejó al conde de Monterrey, 1596," in *Los virreyes, México II*, BAE, vol. CCLXXIV, pp. 101–102. See also the letter sent by Velasco to the king on 6 April 1594 in Zavala, *El servicio personal*, vol. III, pp. 59–60.

106. Ironically, Mendieta himself would not have completely disagreed with this assessment — one more proof of the inherently contradictory nature of his project — as he believed that the Indians were not "good at commanding or ruling, but at being commanded and ruled." See *Historia*, lib. IV, cap. XXIII, p. 119.

107. Solórzano, *Política indiana*, lib II, caps. II, III. This seems to be the only question about which the author has not hesitations. Although he mentions that both Matienzo and Acosta — whom, on the other hand, he follows and cites profusely — contend that these personal services to private individuals are necessary, Solórzano rejects these opinions by arguing no law admits using forced labor for the benefit of private individuals. These services, moreover, had been repeatedly prohibited.

108. Solórzano, *Política indiana*, lib II, cap. VI, núm. 32.

109. Ibid., lib. II, cap. VII, núm. 1.

110. "Consulta del consejo de las Indias sobre los servicios personales de los indios (15 August 1596)"; "R. Instrucción sobre el trabajo de los indios (24 November 1601)," in CDHH, vol. II, pp. 43–47, 71–85.

111. "R.C. sobre los servicios personales y repartimientos de indios (26 May 1609)," in CDHH, vol. II, pp. 154–168. Excerpts from these *cédulas* were incorporated into the *Recopilación*, lib. VI, tít. XII, leyes i, xviiii; tít. XIII, ley i. See also Solórzano, *Política indiana*, lib. II, cap. VI, núms. 55 and 56; Zavala, *El servicio personal*, vol. V, pp. 13–53. After the *cédula* of 1601 was received in México, viceroy Monterrey informed the king that the Indians hated and feared the new system as much as the old one, that only a scant number of them offered themselves for hire, and that there seemed to be no remedy for this problem "because of the natives' short and weak intellect and a nature which is not easily brought to discipline." AGI, Mexico 25, nos. 19 and 26, Monterrey to the king, 8 December 1602 and March 1603.

112. AGI, Mexico 31, nos. 14 and 14a, Cerralvo to the king, 25 January 1633; vice-regal decree of 31 December 1632. See also *Fuentes para la historia del trabajo en Nueva España*, vol. VI, pp. 615–624. For an account of the different opinions and royal orders that, between 1609 and 1632, led to Cerralvo's resolution, see Zavala, *El servicio personal*, vol. V, pp. 53–96. It should be pointed out that the *cabildo* of Mexico City had informed the viceroy that same year that no benefit resulted from the Indian labor draft and that the largest haciendas and mines did not use it, for which reason the *regidores* thought that the draft should be abolished. See AGI, Mexico 31, no. 14c, "Copia de parecer

de la ciudad de México sobre el repartimiento de indios," 15 November 1632. However, a few years later, the *cabildo* would present a petition to the viceroy in which it was contended that, because of the abolition of the *repartimiento*, farmers were not able to grow enough wheat to supply the city of Mexico for lack of enough laborers to harvest it. See AGI, Mexico 33, L. 2, fos. 5–11, "Consulta de la ciudad de México al Excelentísimo Señor Virrey Marqués de Cadereita sobre cuatro puntos que miran a la conservación deste reino," 24 May 1636. In any event, this prohibition did not mean the complete end of forced labor in agriculture or public works. In reality, during the seventeenth century different systems of coercive and non-coercive labor would coexist in New Spain. See Gibson, *The Aztecs*, pp. 235–256; Hoekstra, *Two Worlds Merging*, p. 141; *Fuentes para la historia del trabajo en Nueva España*, vol. VIII, pp. x-xi.

113. Solórzano, *Política indiana*, lib. II, cap. XVII.
114. *Los virreyes, México V*, BAE, vol. CCLXXVII, p. 116 (my emphasis).

Chapter 7

1. "Advertimientos de Martín Enríquez al Conde de la Coruña, su sucesor, 25.IX.1580," in *Los virreyes españoles en América, México I*, edited by Lewis Hanke, BAE, vol. CCLXXIII (Madrid, 1976), p. 204. For viceroy Enríquez, the Indians are also "so pusillanimous that a six-year-old child is powerful enough to do them wrong." See *Cartas de Indias I*, BAE, vol. CCLXIV (Madrid, 1974), p. 306.
2. "Relación del estado en que dejó el gobierno el marqués de Cadereita, 6.XII.1641," in *Los virreyes, México IV*, BAE, vol. CCLXXVI, p. 12.
3. "Instrucción al Conde de Monterrey, 20.III.1596," in *Los virreyes, México II*, BAE, vol. CCLXXIV, pp. 133–134. Compare, for example, with the Instruction given to the count of Moctezuma one century later, in 1696 (*Los virreyes, México V*, BAE, vol. CCLXXVII, p. 194).
4. "Carta del padre fray Jerónimo de Mendieta al rey Don Felipe II (8 October 1565)," in *Cartas de religiosos de Nueva España*, edited by J. García Icazbalceta (México, 1886), p. 41.
5. "Carta del padre fray Jerónimo de Mendieta al padre Comisario General fray Francisco de Bustamante (1 January 1562)," in *Cartas de religiosos*, pp. 18–19.
6. Ibid., p. 18.
7. Ibid., pp. 13, 18–20.
8. The struggle between the orders and the royal authorities that took place in the 1560s is well reflected, for example, in the remarks about the discontent of the mendicants expressed by the viceroy, the marquis of Falces, in a memorial sent to the king in 1567 (*Los virreyes, México I*, BAE, vol. CCLXXIII, p. 176) and in the letters written in 1565 by the provincial of the Franciscans to the king and the Council of the Indies to denounce the civil authorities' attempts to discredit the *mendicants* (*Códice Mendieta I*, pp. 35–45). Carlos Sempat Assadourian has examined this tension between the religious orders and the

Crown, showing how the most radical ideas of the Franciscans could make one friar, with opinions very similar to those of Mendieta but with a less discreet tongue, pay a visit to the Inquisition's jail ("Fray Alonso de Maldonado: la política indiana, el estado de damnación del rey católico y la Inquisición," *Historia Mexicana* XXXVIII, no. 4 (1989): 623–661.

9. Fray Juan de Torquemada, *Monarquía indiana*, edited by M. León-Portilla ([Sevilla, 1615] México, 1975), lib. V, cap. XXIV, p. 414.

10. See "Carta de Fray Gerónimo de Mendieta a un Ilustrísimo Señor, 8 de septiembre de 1574," in *Documentos inéditos del siglo XVI*, pp. 300–304; "Carta para Don Pedro Moya de Contreras, arzobispo de México … 25 de mayo de 1589" and "Carta para el virrey D. Luis de Velasco II, 20 de junio de 1590," in *Códice Mendieta II*, pp. 83–84, 107–109; *Historia eclesiástica indiana*, lib. IV, cap. XLVI, pp. 248–249. For his part, Martín Enríquez would tell his successor that religious affairs in New Spain were very different from those in Spain, because in the peninsula the members of the religious orders complied with their obligations by staying in their convents and only occasionally doing some charitable work, whereas in Mexico the friars were a source of trouble, as they insisted on keeping control of both the spiritual and temporal affairs of the Indian towns. See "Advertimientos," in *Los virreyes, México I*, BAE, vol. CCLXXIII, pp. 205–206.

11. Juan de Palafox, "De la naturaleza y virtudes del indio," in his *Tratados mejicanos II*, edited by F. Sánchez-Castañer (Madrid, 1968), p. 91.

12. It was not by coincidence that the marquis of Villamanrique, who ruled the viceroyalty between 1585 and 1590, began the *relación* he wrote for his successor in the last year of his government by asserting that, "One of the most important things to which the viceroys of New Spain must attend is looking after the Royal Treasury of His Majesty and its proper collection and administration." See *Los virreyes, México I*, BAE, vol. CCLXXIII, p. 266. The Franciscan Juan de Silva would observe in the 1620s that a viceroy was expected to send back as much silver as or more than any of his predecessors, and that this was the main responsibility he was entrusted with. He would wryly add that it was well known that the more silver a viceroy sent from the Indies, the better his affairs and concerns at the court would go. See Fray Juan de Silva, "Memorial Tercero (1618)," in *Los memoriales del Padre Silva sobre predicación pacífica y repartimientos*, edited by P. Castañeda Delgado (Madrid, 1983), p. 340.

13. Recall the importance of personal credit and the fact that the higher one individual was situated in the sociopolitical hierarchy, the more credit that person was given at the Court and the easier it was for him to harm a viceroy's reputation. On the political implications of personal credit, see Chapter 4.

14. BPR, ms. II/1983, fos. 4v–5v, the *alcalde mayor* of Cuicatlan to the count of Salvatierra, 22 October 1646. See also ibid., fos. 2v–4v.

15. "Relación del estado en que dejó el gobierno el marqués de Cerralvo, 17.III.1636," in *Los virreyes, México III*, BAE, vol. CCLXXV, pp. 273–274.

16. Viceroy Enríquez observed in 1580 that the majority of the Indians' legal suits were challenges to the grants of land awarded by the viceroys. See

"Advertimientos," in *Los virreyes, México I*, BAE, vol. CCLXXIII, p. 205. For a study of the many cases brought by the indigenous people before the *audiencia* of Mexico, see Susan Kellogg, *Law and the Transformation of Aztec Culture, 1500–1700* (London, 1995), especially chaps. 1 and 2.

17. Two of the harshest critics of this early Indian litigiousness happened to be two of their greatest defenders. One was Gerónimo de Mendieta, whose ideas on the natives and the Spanish justice system have already been mentioned; the other was Alonso de Zorita, *oidor* of the *audiencia* of Mexico between 1556 and 1565. On the former, see the letters to Bustamante of 1 January 1562 and to Philip II of 8 October 1565, both in *Cartas de religiosos*, pp. 20–24 and 43; also, "Carta para el virrey D. Luis de Velasco, sobre que no se dé lugar para que los indios revoltosos levanten pleitos, 20 de febrero de 1591," in *Códice Mendieta II*, pp. 109–111. On the latter, see his *Relación de los Señores de la Nueva España*, edited by G. Vázquez (Madrid, 1992), p. 79.

18. "Advertimientos de Martín Enríquez," in *Los virreyes, México I*, BAE, vol. CCLXXIII, p. 205.

19. See Gerónimo de Mendieta's views in *Cartas de religiosos*, p. 21.

20. "Advertimientos de Martín Enríquez," in *Los virreyes, México I*, BAE, vol. CCLXXIII, pp. 204–205.

21. "Advertimientos que Luis de Velasco dejó al conde de Monterrey (1596)," in *Los virreyes, México II*, BAE, vol. CCLXXIV, pp. 103–104. See also AGI, Mexico 22, nos. 58, 93, 115, Velasco to the king, 28 October 1591, 2 June 1592, and 1 October 1593.

22. Juan de Solórzano y Pereira, *Política indiana*, edited by M.A. Ochoa Brun (Madrid, 1972), lib. II, cap. XXVIII, núm. 26.

23. José de Acosta, *De procuranda indorum salute*, Spanish version by L. Pereña et al. ([Salamanca, 1588] Madrid, 1984), pp. 583, 585, 587. See also Solórzano, *Política indiana*, lib. II, cap. XXVIII, núms. 33, 34.

24. *Cartas de religiosos*, pp. 20–24. In an early example of Indian appropriation of the rhetoric of wretchedness, the native authorities of Mexico City wrote a letter to the king in 1574 in which they requested that "our lawsuits be summarily concluded and determined whether the case is civil or criminal because we are poor and ignorant"; quoted in Susan Kellogg, "Hegemony Out of Conquest: The First Two Centuries of Spanish Rule in Central Mexico," *Radical History Review* 53 (1992), p. 38. Kellogg has observed that the image of ignorance used by the Indians was belied by the legalistic arguments contained in the letter. In fact, the language and rhetoric are so similar to the ideas we have examined so far that the letter was most likely inspired by the hand of Mendieta or other like-minded Spaniards.

25. For a study of the historical evolution that led to the establishment of this court, see Woodrow Borah, *Justice by Insurance: The General Indian Court of Colonial Mexico and the Legal Aides of the Half-Real* (Berkeley, 1983), chaps. III and IV.

26. AGI, Mexico 22, no. 23, Velasco to the king, 8 October 1590.

27. *Recopilación*, lib. III, tít. III, ley lxv; lib. V, tít. X, ley xii; Borah, *Justice by Insurance*, pp. 91–95. The court and its officials was to be financed with a contribution of a half *real* taken from the two *reales* that each tributary had to pay to their community treasury. This would make it unnecessary for court officials to charge the Indians for their services. See Borah, *Justice by Insurance*, pp. 104–105.

28. Borah, *Justice by Insurance*, p. 95.

29. "Advertimientos que Luis de Velasco dejó al conde de Monterrey," in *Los virreyes, México II*, BAE, vol. CCLXXIV, pp. 104; AGI, Mexico 24, no. 6, the count of Monterrey to the king, 15 April 1598; "Parecer del conde de Monterrey sobre el Juzgado General de Indios (April 1604)," in *Los virreyes, México II*, BAE, vol. CCLXXIV, p. 239.

30. On the figure of the *asesor*, see the comments made by the count of Monterrey in AGI, Mexico 24, no. 6, "Relación que me ha parecido enviar a V. M. sobre el despacho de las causas de los indios en el juzgado general (15 April 1598)"; "Parecer del conde de Monterrey," pp. 240–241; Borah, *Justice by Insurance*, pp. 96–97, 248–250, 267–269. From the last third of the seventeenth century onward, the post of *asesor* was always filled by an *oidor* or *alcalde del crimen* of the *audiencia*.

31. "Papel del conde de Monterrey sobre las congregaciones de los indios (14 January 1604)," in *Los virreyes, México II*, BAE, vol. CCLXXIV, pp. 161, 163. This close identification, or even the confusion, between the two equally distant figures of the king and his viceroy can be best appreciated in the "primordial titles" of many Indian communities, a series of anonymous documents written in Nahuatl in the late seventeenth and eighteenth centuries in order to establish and protect the territorial rights of the pueblos. See James Lockhart, *Nahuas and Spaniards: Postconquest Central Mexican History and Philology* (Stanford, 1991), chap. 3; Serge Gruzinski, *The Conquest of Mexico* (Cambridge, U.K., 1993), chap. 3.

32. On the development of Mexico City in the seventeenth century, see Charles Gibson, *The Aztecs Under Spanish Rule: A History of the Indians of the Valley of Mexico, 1519–1810* (Stanford, 1964), chap. XIII; R. Douglas Cope, *The Limits of Racial Domination: Plebeian Society in Colonial Mexico City, 1660–1720* (Madison, 1994), chap. 1; Natalia Silva Prada, "La política de una rebelión. Los indígenas frente al tumulto de 1692 en la ciudad de México," Ph.D. dissertation (El Colegio de México, 2000), chaps. I and II.

33. "Relación de Juan de Palafox y Mendoza (1642?)," in *Los virreyes, México IV*, BAE, vol. CCLXXVI, p. 39.

34. "Relación del marqués de Mancera, 22.X.1673," in *Los virreyes, México V*, BAE, vol. CCLXXVII, p. 12.

35. Baltasar Alamos de Barrientos, *Discurso político al rey Felipe III al comienzo de su reinado* (Barcelona, 1990), p. 15. In an attempt to convince the Crown of the impossibility of an Indian rebellion, the Franciscan Juan de Silva had asserted that the Indians were so cowardly that just one Spaniard with a harquebus could put many of them to flight. See *Memoriales del Padre Silva*, p.

282. It should be added that Silva used these arguments to attack the idea that the reason of state advised that the labor draft should be preserved as an adequate means to maintain the Spanish dominion over the Indians.

36. "Relación," in *Los virreyes, México IV*, BAE, vol. CCLXXVI, p. 39.

37. In his perception of the indigenous population, the viceroy appears to be echoing the pessimism and negative views about the Indians that, as already mentioned, had become widespread in New Spain since the mid-seventeenth century.

38. "Relación," in *Los virreyes, México V*, BAE, vol. CCLXXVII, pp. 13–14, 49–50. As we saw in Chapter 4, this emphasis on the shortcomings of the clergy was very likely the result of Mancera's clashes with the archbishop of Mexico.

39. Solórzano, *Política indiana*, lib. II, cap. XXX, núms. 18–21. Despite this very negative view, Solórzano thought that mestizos and mulattos, as long as they were not the product of an illegitimate union, should have their merits and services and those of their progenitors rewarded by the king like the rest of Spaniards (thus, they should not be excluded from receiving *encomiendas* or being granted offices or benefices). If their origins were legitimate, Solórzano contended, it would be too "harsh and inhuman to exclude them just because of their mixed blood." See *Política indiana*, lib. III, cap. VI, núms. 15–21.

40. "Advertimientos de Martín Enríquez," in *Los virreyes, México I*, BAE, vol. CCLXXIII, p. 210; AGI, Mexico 27, nos. 52 and 63, Velasco to the king, 23 June 1608 and 13 February 1609.

41. "Relación," in *Los virreyes, México IV*, BAE, vol. CCLXXVI, pp. 39–40. Palafox's adversary, the viceroy Salvatierra, equally thought that this racially mixed plebe was the one sector of the population that usually presented a security risk. See BPR, ms. II/1989, fos.100–101r, the count of Salvatierra to the king, 24 August 1647. See also very similar opinions expressed by one of Salvatierra's supporters in BPR, ms. II/1984, fos. 86–92, Fray Juan de la Madre de Dios to the king, 28 November 1646.

42. Colonial society always displayed a particular distrust toward the population of African descent, there existing a widespread belief that blacks and mulattos, both free and slave, were especially prone to insurrection. Viceroy Enríquez had already warned the king in 1574 about this danger because of the large number of blacks and mulattos in New Spain. See *Cartas de Indias I*, BAE, vol. CCLXIV, pp. 298–300. A reflection of this fear was the numerous orders that forbade them to bear arms. See, for example, CDHH, vol. I, pp. 167, 239, 299, 386, 420, 433; vol. II, pp. 182, 427, 510, 513, 707. On this topic, see Colin A. Palmer, *Slaves of the White God: Blacks in Mexico, 1570–1650* (Cambridge, MA, 1976), chap. 5; Carmen Bernand, *Negros esclavos y libres en las ciudades hispanoamericanas* (Madrid, 2001), pp. 46–47, 55–57, 79–80.

43. "Relación," in *Los virreyes, México V*, BAE, vol. CCLXXVII, pp. 1–14, 49–50. Juan de Ortega y Montañés, bishop of Michoacán, espoused similar opinions in the long *Relación* he wrote for his successor after holding the post of acting viceroy in 1696. He thought the nobility, both peninsular and Creole, was of great fidelity to the king and the viceroys, just like the rest of the population

of European descent; the Indians were of a "poor and wretched nature" and whether as viceroy or as prelate, he had devoted himself to helping and favoring them, while the multitude of the *plebe* had always required a lot of dedication on the part of the viceroys in order to keep them in check. See "Relación de Juan de Ortega y Montañés, 4.III.1697," in *Los virreyes, México V*, BAE, vol. CCLXXVII, pp. 112–115.

44. Diego Saavedra Fajardo, *Empresas políticas (1640)*, edited by S. López (Madrid, 1999), empresa 73, pp. 819–823. In the words of Jerónimo de Cevallos, the *vulgo* is an "untamed and fierce horse which has to be treated with craftiness." See his *Arte real para el buen gobierno de los reyes y príncipes y de sus vasallos, en el cual se refieren las obligaciones de cada uno, con los principales documentos para el buen gobierno...* (Toledo, 1623), fos. 65, 118–119. Similar opinions were espoused by Juan Blázquez Mayoralgo in *Perfecta razón de estado, deducida de los hechos de el señor rey don Fernando el Católico, quinto de este nombre en Castilla y segundo en Aragón, contra los políticos ateístas* (México, 1646), fos. 59v, 155.

45. AGI, México 39, no. 15, the count of Baños to the king, 25 November 1663. For very similar comments, see BPR, ms. II/1989, fos. 100–101r, the count of Salvatierra to the king, 24 August 1647; AGI, Mexico 707, the duke of Alburquerque to the king, 20 December 1657 and 17 May 1658.

46. The tumult broke on the evening of 8 June 1692 and had its focal point on the main square; its most visible consequence was the burning by the rioters of the city hall and most of the viceregal palace. Sigüenza was an eye witness to the disturbances, participating actively, according to his own account, in the rescue from the fire of many files and documents from the municipal archive. See Carlos de Sigüenza y Góngora, *Alboroto y motín de los indios de México*, edited by I.A. Leonard (México, 1986), pp. 208–209, 213. Sigüenza's account is also a defense of the viceroy, the count of Galve, who had been accused by some sectors of the elite of having provoked the riot for not having sufficiently secured the city's supply of wheat and maize and also for having ruled in a tyrannical way. See "Los vasallos leales del reino de México dan cuenta a V.M. del tumulto que sucedió en México a 8 de junio de este año," printed in *Alboroto y motín de México del 8 de junio de 1692*, edited by I.A. Leonard (México, 1932), pp. 131–138. For a detailed analysis of the tumult, see Cope, *The Limits of Racial Domination*, chap. 7.

47. Sigüenza, *Alboroto y motín de los indios*, p. 81. For an explanation of the system of *castas* and the terms used by Sigüenza to describe the ethnic and racial composition of the plebe, see Ilona Katzew, "Casta Painting: Identity and Social Stratification in Colonial Mexico," in *New World Orders: Casta Painting and Colonial Latin America*, edited by I. Katzew (New York, 1996), pp. 8–29. For an analysis of the racial, ethnic, and class divisions among the city's populace and their effects on the different groups, see Cope, *The Limits of Racial Domination*, chaps. 3 and 4.

48. Sigüenza, *Alboroto y motín de los indios*, pp. 184, 186–187, 197–198.

49. Ibid., p. 191.

50. The report is in AGN, Historia, vol. 413, fos. 4–5r. This siege mentality was not exclusive to Sigüenza. According to the priest of one of the city's Indian parishes, the city was undermined by Indian huts, which was the same as having "within ourselves many Greek horses to throw fire at us, putting at risk the permanence of this most faithful city." See AGN, Historia, vol. 413, fos. 18–19r, "Informe del padre ministro de Santa Cruz, 9 July 1692."

51. The *cabildo* of Mexico City also used extremely harsh terms to condemn the Indians and the other ethnic groups that comprised the lower classes of the city. See AGI, Mexico 333, fos. 321r–323r, "Informe de la Nobilísima y Muy Leal Ciudad de México," 1692. It should be noted that the majority of the *regidores* that comprised the *cabildo* at this time had been appointed by viceroy Galve. See María Luisa J. Pazos Pazos, *El ayuntamiento de la ciudad de México en el siglo XVII: Continuidad institucional y cambio social* (Sevilla, 1999), p. 250.

52. Mary Louise Pratt, *Imperial Eyes: Travel Writing and Transculturation* (London, 1992), pp. 132–135. See also José Rabasa, "Pre-Columbian Pasts and Indian Presents in Mexican History," in A.F. Bolaños and G. Verdesio, *Colonialism Past and Present: Reading and Writing about Colonial Latin America Today* (Albany, 2002), especially pp. 64–72. On Sigüenza's Creole patriotism and his interest in the splendors of the Aztec past, see David Brading, *The First America: The Spanish Monarchy, Creole Patriots, and the Liberal State, 1492–1867* (Cambridge University Press, London), pp. 362–372.

53. Already in the early seventeenth century, Juan de Torquemada had denounced those natives who were not registered as members of the *república de indios* and therefore were free from the control of their *doctrineros*, as "big thieves" and "great drunkards." See "Relaciones informativas que las tres órdenes mendicantes … dan por donde no les conviene subjectar sus religiosos al examen de los obispos … Recopiladas por Fray Juan de Torquemada," in *Códice Mendieta II*, pp. 178–179. Some years later, Francisco de Ugarte, drawing on Palafox's authority, would argue that the Indians who stayed in their native towns, lacking all ambition, lived good, healthy, and happy lives, obediently attending to all their obligations. In contrast, those who left their villages, besides living in sin and being prey to illnesses, became thieves and homicides and were never content. See Francisco de Ugarte de Hermosa y Salcedo, *Origen de los dos gobiernos divino y humano y forma de su ejercicio en lo temporal* (Madrid, 1655), pp. 382–385.

54. Mendieta asserted that the main reason why the customs of the entire New Spain were so "depraved" was the "cohabitation of Spaniards among the Indians." See his "Carta para el virrey Don Luis de Velasco… (11 January 1590)," in *Códice Mendieta II*, p. 103. A few years later, it would be a viceroy, the count of Monterrey, who asserted that, although at the beginning it had been quite a positive thing that the Spaniards lived among the Indians to serve as their model, it was no longer necessary; on the contrary, argued the viceroy, the Indians learned many bad and wrong things from their contact with the Spaniards. See *Los virreyes, México II*, BAE, vol. CCLXXIV, p. 197.

55. See, for example, "R.C. que manda que ningún vagamundo español no casado no viva ni esté en los pueblos de indios (2 May 1563)" and "R.C. que no habiten con los indios negros, mulatos, ni mestizos (25 November 1578)," in CDHH, vol I, pp. 400, 513. See also ley xxi, tít. III, lib. VI of the *Recopilación*. For a study of the ideas, debates, and many laws that were promulgated regarding the separation of the two communities, see Magnus Mörner, *La Corona española y los foráneos en los pueblos de indios de América* (Stockholm, 1970); Borah, *Justice by Insurance*, pp. 27–34. Felipe Castro has recently argued that, although the policy of separation was to a large measure successful because the native population was always in support of it, not all the Indians were in favor of expelling the Spaniards and *castas* from their villages, as they very often were indispensable intermediaries and mediators between the indigenous and Spanish worlds. See Felipe Castro Gutiérrez, "Indeseables e indispensables: los vecinos españoles, mestizos y mulatos en los pueblos de indios de Michoacán," *Estudios de Historia Novohispana* 25 (July–Dec. 2001): 59–80.

56. AGN, Historia, vol. 413, fo. 17, "Informe [al virrey] del ministro de doctrina de Santiago Tlatelolco" (n.d.).

57. AGI, Patronato 226, no. 1, ramo 17, fos. 4r–11r; AGN, Historia, vol. 413, fo. 1. Before proceeding with the expulsion of the indigenous population from the city center, the viceroy had requested the opinion of all the priests of the Indian parishes of the capital. All were unanimous in asserting that, when the Indians of their respective parishes moved to the center, it was very difficult to keep them under control. See AGN, Historia, vol. 413, fols. 10–19.

58. AGN, Historia, vol. 413, fo. 10r, "Informe del padre ministro de San Pablo acerca de la jurisdicción y distrito de su doctrina (4 July 1692)." This remark belies the official discourse on the learning of the Spanish language by the Indians that was in circulation at the end of the seventeenth century and that was examined in the previous chapter. Although I do not know whether this kind of thinking was common, it might well be that the Castilianization of the Indian in an urban context was seen as something that would contribute to increasing the confusion which allegedly characterized the capital.

59. AGN, Historia, vol. 413, fos. 14, 63 ("Informe del párroco de Santa María a la Redonda," 1 July 1692).

60. AGN, Historia, vol. 413, fo. 13r, "Informe del padre ministro de San Pablo." Neither Matienzo nor Solórzano saw anything wrong in the use of the Spanish dress, especially by the *caciques* and the members of the Indian elite, as it would serve as a mechanism of acculturation; besides, in doing so, the Indians would begin to have "some humanity." Matienzo, always a pragmatic, also saw an economic benefit in the fostering of the Spanish dress among the Indians, as that would increase the sales of Spanish products and the revenues of the Crown. See, respectively, *Gobierno del Perú*, pp. 69–70, and *Política indiana*, lib. II, cap. XXVI, núms. 40–42. Undoubtedly, both Matienzo and Solórzano could allow themselves to be much more optimistic than those writing at the end of the seventeenth century, after the outbreak

of a very grave riot. As theorists of the imperial system, they had to make explicit that the civilizing mission of the Spanish monarchy required that the natives be made into perfect replicas, obedient and subordinate, of the Spaniards, but this kind of idea could also indicate the existence of an unresolved tension between the need to maintain the dualism of the two republics and the push for a total assimilation of the indigenous population.

61. AGN, Historia, vol. 413, fo. 16, "[Informe de] Fr. Agustín de Vetancourt, maestro de doctrina y cura por S.M. de la parte de San Juan y San Francisco (1 July 1692)."

62. AGN, Historia, vol. 413, fos. 11v, 14, 17r, 18v.

63. On the patron–client relationships established between the elite and the lower class of Mexico City, see Cope, *The Limits of Racial Domination*, chap. 5.

64. On the orders given to make the Indians who lived in the city center go back to the Indian neighborhood of Tlatelolco, see AGN, RCD, vol. 26, fo. 233, Fr. Hernando de la Rúa to the queen, 1 August 1670; AGN, RCD, vol. 26, fo. 232v, the queen regent to the marquis of Mancera, 9 March 1671; AGN, RCD, vol. 30, fo. 27, the queen regent to the viceroy and *oidores* of the *audiencia* of Mexico, 30 July 1672. See also "R.C. al virrey de la Nueva España encargándole el cuidado de que los indios no vivan fuera de sus barrios (2 April 1676)," in CDHH, vol. II, p. 629.

65. AGI, México 45, no. 84a, the Crown attorney to the marquis of Mancera, 2 November 1671; ibid., "Parecer de los señores del Real Acuerdo (5 November 1671)"; AGI, México 45, no. 84, the marquis of Mancera to the queen regent, 25 November 1671.

66. AGI, Patronato 226, no. 1, ramo 1, the count of Galve to the king, 30 June 1692 (also in AGI, Escribanía 230B, fo. 83; this letter has been published in *Alboroto y motín de México*, pp. 121–126). Galve's views are repeated in "Relación de Juan de Ortega y Montañés, 4.III.1697," in *Los virreyes, México V*, BAE, vol. CCLXXVII, pp. 119–120. Both the *audiencia* and the *cabildo* also argued that it was only because the crowd was drunk that they dared to riot. See AGI, Patronato 226, no. 1, ramo 1 (3), the *audiencia* to the king, 16 August 1692; AGI, Mexico 333, fos. 322v–323r, "Informe de la Nobilísima y Muy Leal Ciudad de México (1692)." Sigüenza, likewise, manifests that the drinking of *pulque* contributed to inflame the spirits of the crowd. See his *Alboroto y motín de los indios*, pp. 185, 195, 215. It is also mentioned by Antonio Robles in his *Diario de sucesos notables (1665–1703)* (México, 1972), vol. II, p. 257. Not everyone, however, made the drinking of *pulque* responsible for the riot. The authors of several anonymous letters sent to the king as well as Gerónimo Chacón, *alcalde del crimen* of the *audiencia* of México, contended that *pulque* had always existed without provoking tumults. To them, the cause of the revolt had been the tyrannical government of the viceroy. See "Los vasallos leales del reino de México," pp. 135–136; Silva Prada, "La política de una rebelión," pp. 335–341. Silva Prada maintains that the author of the anonymous letters was Gerónimo Chacón. It should be mentioned that Chacón was at odds with the viceroy, who had even banished the *alcalde* from the city.

67. Acosta, *De procuranda*, pp. 559, 561. On the ritual and social function of drinking in the indigenous communities, see William B. Taylor, *Drinking, Homicide, and Rebellion in Colonial Mexican Villages* (Stanford, 1979), chap. 2.

68. Agustín de Vetancourt, "Manifiesto del celo de un religioso ministro de los naturales, acerca de el estado de la república de los indios con el pulque que beben y la perdición que tienen," included in his *Teatro mexicano. Descripción breve de los sucesos ejemplares, históricos, políticos, militares y religiosos del Nuevo Mundo Occidental de las Indias* (México, [1698] 1971), p. 95. On *pulquerías* as places of sociability, see Sonia Corcuera de Mancera, *Del amor al temor. Borrachez, catequesis y control en la Nueva España (1555–1771)* (México, 1994), pp. 210–220; Cope, *The Limits of Racial Domination*, pp. 34–35; Silva Prada, "La política de una rebelión," pp. 469–484.

69. On the different kinds of *pulque* and their methods of production, see José Jesús Hernández Palomo, *La renta del pulque en Nueva España, 1663–1810* (Sevilla, 1979), chap. I.

70. AGI, Patronato 226, no. 1, ramo 17, fos. 2r–4r; AGI, Escribanía 230B, fos 83v–84r; Sigüenza, *Alboroto y motín de los indios*, pp. 215–216. In theory, *pulque* with mixtures had always been illegal. See ley xxxvii, tít. I, lib. VI, of the *Recopilación*. Now, all kinds of *pulque* were prohibited.

71. See the remarks by the marquis of Mancera in this regard in *Los virreyes, México V*, BAE, vol. CCLXXVII, pp. 14–15. On the *pulque asiento*, see Hernández Palomo, *La renta del pulque*, pp. 31–67.

72. *Informe que la Real Universidad y Claustro Pleno de ella de la ciudad de México de esta Nueva España hace a el Exmo. Sr. virrey de ella, en conformidad de orden de Su Excelencia de 3 de julio de este año de 1692, sobre los inconvenientes de la bebida de el pulque*. The rest of the reports came from the municipal council, the archbishop, the ecclesiastical chapter, the Inquisition, the religious orders, the priests of the Indian parishes, and the city physician. For an analysis of these reports, see Hernández Palomo, *La renta del pulque*, pp. 67–80.

73. *Informe que la Real Universidad* ..., fos. 3v, 8, 9v–10v.

74. Ibid., fo. 11r; Acosta, *De procuranda*, p. 545.

75. *Informe que la Real Universidad* ..., fo. 7v.

76. See the *consulta* of 21 February 1694 in AGI, Patronato 226, no. 1, ramo 27. For the arguments advanced by the Council of the Indies to legalize the drinking of *pulque* again, see AGI, Mexico 333, fos. 609r–610r, informe del fiscal, 21 February 1697; fos. 589r–597v, *consulta* of 11 May 1697.

77. AGI, Mexico 333, fos. 629r–630v, the count of Moctezuma to the king, 24 April 1698; Hernández Palomo, *La renta del pulque*, pp. 80–84. Vetancourt will reproduce most of the ideas and images that appeared in the 1692 report from the university in his "Manifiesto." To him, there are numerous "politic and Christian reasons" to prohibit the sale of *pulque*: "It is neither useful to the republic, since the *pulquería* is a synagogue of vice, nor to the Indian, who is left naked, nor to His Majesty, since his predecessors put God's service before profit by not permitting the Jews in Spain, who paid so many tributes,

and expelling the *moriscos*, who were so useful for the cultivation of the land." See *Teatro mexicano*, p. 99.

78. For a description and analysis of these revolts, see the collection of essays in *El fuego de la inobediencia. Autonomía y rebelión india en el obispado de Oaxaca*, edited by Héctor Díaz-Polanco (Oaxaca, 1996).

79. Juan de Torres Castillo, "Relación de lo sucedido en las provincias de Nejapa, Ixtepeji y la Villa Alta …," in *Documentos inéditos o muy raros para la historia de México*, edited by Genaro García (México, 1982), pp. 277, 278, 283, 286, 295. See also *Documentos sobre las rebeliones indias de Tehuantepec y Nexapa (1660–1661)*, edited by H. Díaz-Polanco and C. Manzo (México, 1992), pp. 39, 167–169.

80. Cristóbal Manso de Contreras, "Relación cierta y verdadera de lo que sucedió y ha sucedido en esta villa de Guadalcázar, provincia de Tehuantepec, desde los 22 de marzo de 1660 hasta los 4 de julio de 1661 …," in *Documentos inéditos o muy raros*, pp. 316, 321, 331, 333, 334. Although he does not mention it in an explicit way, Manso in all likelihood was referring to the rebellions of the 1640s, which shook the Spanish monarchy profoundly.

81. Manso de Contreras, "Relación," p. 324 (the emphasis is mine). See also ibid., p. 325, and *Documentos de Tehuantepec*, p. 110.

82. *Documentos de Tehuantepec*, pp. 66–67. Alburquerque, however, changed his mind a few days later, allowing the troops gathered in Antequera to reach Nejapa and cooperate with the Dominican provincial in his mission of pacification, although they should avoid, at all costs, clashing with the Indians. Ibid., pp. 68–71.

83. Héctor Díaz-Polanco and Araceli Burguete, "Sociedad colonial y rebelión indígena en el Obispado de Oaxaca (1660)," in *El fuego de la inobediencia*, p. 41.

84. For that same reason, Alburquerque tried hard to prove that the *alcalde mayor* of Tehuantepec and the *alcalde mayor* of Nejapa deserved their appointments, reporting in a very detailed way all the merits accumulated by both individuals, which supposedly made them worthy of the viceroy's favor. See AGI, Mexico 600, fos. 128, 131, the duke of Alburquerque to the count of Baños, 4 October 1660; ibid., fo. 126, Alburquerque to the king, 6 November 1660.

85. It was not only the viceroy but the members of the *audiencia* as well who followed a similar line. For the *oidores*, the disturbances in Oaxaca were the result of the many vexations and oppressions experienced by the Indians at the hands of the *alcaldes mayores*. When the Justices of the *audiencia* wrote their report, Alburquerque was no longer the viceroy, so they had no problem in stressing that all of these *alcaldes* had been retainers of the former viceroy. See AGI, Mexico 600, fos. 141–145v, *consulta* of the *audiencia* to the count of Baños, 27 September 1660.

86. For a description by the bishop himself of his journey and the many ritual gestures he used to convince the Indians to change their attitude, see *Documentos de Tehuantepec*, pp. 108–124. See also Manso de Contreras, "Relación," pp. 327–330; "Viaje que hizo el Ilustrísimo Señor Doctor Don Alonso de

Cuevas Dávalos, obispo de Oaxaca, a pacificar la provincia de Tehuantepec," in *Documentos inéditos o muy raros*, pp. 305–310; Héctor Díaz-Polanco and Consuelo Sánchez, "El vigor de la espada restauradora. La represión de las rebeliones indias en Oaxaca (1660–1661)," in *El fuego de la inobediencia*, pp. 54–57.

87. *Documentos de Tehuantepec*, pp. 41–43, 118–124, 128–129, 137–139; Manso de Contreras, "Relación," p. 330. For Alburquerque, it was not possible to accede to the petition of a general pardon, because, although neither divine nor human law allowed the punishment of all the people involved in the uprising, these same laws and good government required that the leaders of the revolt be punished. See AGI, Mexico 600, fos. 129v–130r, the duke of Alburquerque to the count of Baños, 4 October 1660.

88. *Documentos de Tehuantepec*, p. 100. For a description (and denunciation) of the forced distribution of goods (*repartimiento de mercancías*) to the indigenous population by the *alcaldes mayores*, see AGI, Mexico 600, 109–111v, the bishop of Puebla to the king, 29 October 1660. On this topic, see Rodolfo Pastor, "El repartimiento de mercancías y los alcaldes mayores novohispanos: un sistema de explotación, de sus orígenes a la crisis de 1810," in *El gobierno provincial en la Nueva España, 1570–1787*, edited by W. Borah (México, 1985), pp. 201–236. Although the majority of historians have accepted the view of the coerced nature of the *repartimientos*, more recently Jeremy Baskes has argued, quite convincingly, that Indian participation in the *alcaldes mayores' repartimientos de mercancías* was voluntary and that the *repartimiento* should be understood instead as a system of consumer and producer credit designed to operate under conditions of high risk. This would explain why accusations by Indians of force in the distribution of goods were uncommon, the majority of these accusations coming from clerics who condemned the *repartimientos de mercancías* as usury. See his *Indians, Merchants, and Markets: A Reinterpretation of the Repartimiento and Spanish-Indian Economic Relations in Colonial Oaxaca, 1750–1821* (Stanford, 2000), especially chap. 4.

89. AGI, Mexico 600, fos. 128–134, the duke of Alburquerque to the count of Baños, 4 October 1660. Alburquerque's ideas regarding this matter were, in fact, not very different from those espoused by many political writers. See, for example, Saavedra Fajardo, *Empresas políticas*, empresa 73, pp. 826–829.

90. AGI, Mexico 600, fos. 106–108r, "Parecer y voto de don Juan Francisco de Montemayor de Cuenca, oidor de la Real Audiencia de México ... sobre el alboroto que tuvieron las provincias de Tehuantepec y Nejapa, ocasionado de los malos tratamientos de sus alcaldes mayores (27 September 1660)"; "Petición del fiscal de la Audiencia de México (20 October 1660)," in *Documentos de Tehuantepec*, pp. 148–150. See also the letter of 12 October 1660 sent to the count of Baños by Alonso Ramírez, *alcalde mayor* of Tehuantepec, and the petition presented to the *audiencia* on 18 November 1660 by Juan de Torres, *alcalde* of Nejapa, both in *Documentos de Tehuantepec*, pp. 146–147, 167–169.

91. *Documentos de Tehuantepec*, pp. 143–144.

92. AGI, Mexico 600, fos. 150–151r, the count of Baños to the king, 18 December 1660. See also ibid., fos. 147–148v, the *alcaldes del crimen* to the king, 28 November 1660.

93. AGI, Mexico 78, "Relación de méritos y servicios de D. Francisco de Montemayor de Cuenca (14 October 1665)." On the repressive strategy Montemayor followed once he arrived in Tehuantepec, see Manso de Contreras, "Relación," pp. 337–368; Díaz-Polanco and Sánchez, "El vigor de la espada restauradora," pp. 57–62.

94. AGI, Mexico 600, fos. 107v–108r, "Parecer y voto de don Juan Francisco de Montemayor."

95. Montemayor imposed five death penalties, condemned two women to have one hand each cut off (although he later suspended the execution of this part of their sentence), and sentenced another woman to have her ear cut off, besides sentencing many to serve in the mines for periods of up to ten years. See Manso de Contreras, "Relación," pp. 352–355. A mention should be made of Montemayor's remarks regarding the Indians' dress, which, as we saw, acquires a sudden relevance in moments of crisis. If a well-ruled and obedient commonwealth is one in which everyone occupies his or her place, we should not be surprised by Montemayor's observation that the Hispanicized Indians of Tehuantepec, especially those who wore Spanish garments, were the most prone to revolt. According to the *oidor*, "having shed their Indian dress, their spirits get stirred up because of the new clothes they wear," and they are always the ones who lead every feud or riot. See *Documentos de Tehuantepec*, p. 188.

96. *Documentos de Tehuantepec*, pp. 173, 178.

97. AGN, RCD, vol. 25, fo. 227v, the king to the viceroy and *oidores*, 30 August 1662. See also the petition by the *fiscal* of the Council of the Indies on 26 July 1662 and the Council's *consulta* on 14 August 1662, in *Documentos de Tehuantepec*, pp. 197–204; AGN, RCO, vol. 7, exp. 20, fos. 49–50, the king to the count of Baños, 1 July 1661.

98. AGI, Mexico 600, fos. 154–155r, the count of Baños to the king, 28 December 1660; *Documentos de Tehuantepec*, pp. 177–179.

99. *Documentos de Tehuantepec*, p. 179.

Conclusion

1. Jorge Juan and Antonio de Ulloa, *Noticias Secretas de América*, edited by L.J. Ramos Gómez (Madrid, 1991), p. 463 (the emphasis is mine).

2. Ibid., pp. 463–464.

3. Matías de Caravantes, "Poder ordinario del virrey del Pirú sacadas de las cédulas que se han despachado en el Real Consejo de las Indias," edited by Pilar Aguirre Zamorano, *Historiografía y bibliografía americanistas* XXIX, no. 2 (1985), p.15. Of course, not everybody seemed to agree on this. In the late sixteenth century, the rector of the Dominican school in Puebla would contend that the honor owed to the king was not owed to the person who was in his place, although he certainly was owed some. See "Carta del padre fray

Francisco Ximénez ... al virrey marqués de Villamanrique," in *Cartas de religiosos de Nueva España*, edited by J. García Icazbalceta (México, 1886), p. 162. See also Palafox's comments in Chapter 4, note 106, p. 321.

4. Diego de Avendaño. *Thesaurus Indicus*, edited by A. Muñoz García ([Antwerp, 1668] Pamplona, 2001), pp. 238–239.

5. These principles, or at least the two fundamental ones, still formed the cornerstone of good government around the middle of the eighteenth century. As was observed by Antonio de Ulloa and Jorge Juan in the prolog of their confidential report, the "two main duties of princes" were "religion and justice, to which and to the means that guarantee their preservation they must direct their fatherly aspirations and pious solicitude." See *Noticias secretas*, p. 119.

6. Juan and Ulloa, *Noticias secretas*, p. 464 (the emphasis is mine).

7. AGI, Indiferente 756, *consulta* of the Council, 4 December 1629. See also *Recopilación*, lib. III, tít. III, ley lxxi; Rubio Mañé, *Introducción al estudio de los virreyes*, vol. 1, pp. 199–200. Usually, the three-year appointment would be extended for another three years. The Council had already discussed this matter the year before on account of a request by the count of Chinchón, who had been appointed viceroy of Peru for the usual term of six years, that he be appointed for ten to twelve years. See AGI, Indiferente 756, *consulta* of the Council, 14 January 1628. For a typical letter of appointment, see the one given to the marquis of Cadereita in the year 1635 in AGI, Mexico 34, no. 21, fos. 339–340.

8. Francisco de Seijas y Lobera, *Gobierno militar y político del reino imperial de la Nueva España (1702)*, edited by P.E. Pérez-Mallaína Bueno (México, 1986), pp. 271–282, 304–324.

9. Ibid., pp. 200, 214–216, 271–272, 312. As already mentioned in Chapter 5, the count of Galve was the younger brother of the duke of El Infantado, one of the Spanish grandees.

10. See Seijas, *Gobierno militar y político*, pp. 265–270.

11. I find it difficult to understand what may have made Ruggiero Romano and Marcello Carmagnani recently assert that, while for the peninsular Spaniards the idea of the "king" was undoubtedly clear, for the Creole Spaniards (let alone the Indians), that image was "confused and unreal." See their essay "Componentes sociales" in M. Carmagnani, A. Hernández Chávez, and R. Romano, *Para una historia de América. I. Las estructuras* (México, 1999), p. 341. I cannot find any reasons for this confusion on the part of the Creole population, especially because Romano and Carmagnani do not specify whether they are referring to the population as a whole, the ruling elite, or the lower classes. And, even if what they had in mind was the lower strata, there is no reason to believe that the inhabitants of the peninsular kingdoms might have had an image of the king more clear or less confused than their counterparts from across the ocean.

12. See, for example, the account by Antonio de Robles of the years 1700 through 1703 in his *Diario de sucesos notables (1665–1703)*, edited by A. Castro Leal

(México, 1972). For the entire period of the War of Succession, see Manuel Rivera Cambas, *Los gobernantes de México* (México, 1872), vol. I, pp. 290–294, 301–315; Vicente Riva Palacio, *México a través de los siglos* (Barcelona, 1888–1889), vol. II, pp. 751–767.

Bibliography

Manuscript Sources

Archivo General de Indias, Seville

Audiencia de México: legs. 3, 5, 6, 7, 30, 31, 33, 34, 35, 36, 38, 39, 40, 41, 42, 44, 45, 46, 47, 48, 50, 52, 75, 76, 77, 78, 79, 81, 82, 116, 278, 318, 319, 333, 338, 344, 345, 346, 600, 2707
Contratación: legs. 5422, 5430
Escribanía: legs. 227A, 229B, 230B, 252A
Indiferente: legs. 756, 760, 765, 3016
Patronato: legs. 221, 223, 226, 244

Archivo General de la Nación, Mexico

Historia: vols. 36, 413
Inquisición: vols. 1477, 1510, 1513
Reales Cédulas Duplicados: vols. 14, 25, 26, 30, 40, 61, 180,
Reales Cédulas Originales: vols. 1, 2, 3, 4, 5, 6, 7, 8, 9, 11, 12, 13, 14, 16, 18, 19, 22, 23, 24, 27, 39

Archivo Histórico de la Ciudad de México

Actas de Cabildo: vols. 365-A, 369-A
Cédulas y Reales Ordenes: vol. 2977
Ordenanzas: vol. 2981

Archivo Histórico Nacional, Madrid

Diversos-Colecciones 26, no. 33
Diversos-Documentos de Indias, nos. 29, 78, 209, 247

371

Biblioteca Nacional, Madrid

Mss. 904, 7758, 11260 (17)
R/19809, R/22472

Biblioteca Nacional, Mexico

Ms. R/850/LAF

Biblioteca del Palacio Real, Madrid

Mss. II/1981, II/1982, II/1983, II/1984, II/1989, II/2642

Real Academia de la Historia, Madrid

Colección Jesuitas: vols. CXVIII, CXLII
Colección Salazar y Castro: vols. F-20, M-15

Printed Sources

Acosta, José de. *De procuranda indorum salute (1588)*. Spanish version by L. Pereña et al., Madrid, 1984.

Alamos de Barrientos, Baltasar. *Discurso político al rey Felipe III al comienzo de su reinado (1598)*, edited by M. Santos. Barcelona, 1990.

Albornoz, Diego Felipe de. *Cartilla política y cristiana*. Madrid, 1666.

Alboroto y motín de México del 8 de junio de 1692, edited by I.A. Leonard. México, 1932.

Alemán, Mateo. *Sucesos de D. Fray García Guerra, arzobispo de México, a cuyo cargo estuvo el gobierno de la Nueva España* (Mexico, 1613). Reprinted in *The Sucesos of Mateo Alemán*, edited by Alice H. Bushee. New York, 1911.

Andrade, Alonso de. *Idea del perfecto prelado, en la vida del eminentísimo cardenal don Baltasar de Moscoso y Sandoval, arzobispo de Toledo, primado de las Españas*. Madrid, 1668.

Aristotle, *Nicomachean Ethics*, edited by J. Barnes. Princeton, 1984.

_____. *Eudemian Ethics*, edited by J. Barnes. Princeton, 1984.

Avendaño, Diego de. *Thesaurus Indicus* (1668), edited by A. Muñoz García. Pamplona, 2001.

Avilés, Pedro de. *Advertencias de un político a su príncipe observadas en el feliz gobierno del Excelentísimo Señor … marqués de Astorga, virrey y capitán general del reino de Nápoles*. Nápoles, 1673.

Benavente, Fray Toribio de. *Historia de los indios de la Nueva España*, edited by E.O'Gorman. México, 1969.

_____. Motolinía, Fray Toribio de. *Historia de los indios de la Nueva España*, edited by Georges Baudot. Madrid, 1985.

Blázquez Mayoralgo, Juan. *Perfecta razón de estado, deducida de los hechos de el señor rey don Fernando el Católico, quinto de este nombre en Castilla y segundo en Aragón, contra los políticos ateístas.* México, 1646.

Bocanegra, Matías de. *Teatro jerárquico de la luz, pira cristiano política del gobierno que … la imperial ciudad de México erigió en la real portada que dedicó al … conde de Salvatierra … en su feliz venida por virrey gobernador y capitán general de esta Nueva España.* México, 1642.

Burgoa, Francisco de. *Palestra historial de virtudes y ejemplares apostólicos, fundada del celo de insignes héroes de la sagrada Orden de Predicadores en este Nuevo Mundo de la América en las Indias Occidentales (1670).* México, 1989.

Caravantes, Matías de. "Poder ordinario del virrey del Pirú sacadas de las cédulas que se han despachado en el Real Consejo de las Indias." In *Historiografía y bibliografía americanistas,* vol. XXIX:2, edited by Pilar Aguirre Zamorano. Seville, 1985, pp. 15–97.

Cartas de Indias I. Biblioteca de Autores Españoles, vol. CCLXIV. Madrid, 1974.

Cartas de religiosos de Nueva España, edited by J. García Icazbalceta, Mexico, 1886.

Castillo de Bobadilla, Jerónimo. *Política para corregidores y señores de vasallos, en tiempo de paz y de guerra, y para jueces eclesiásticos y seglares, y de sacas, aduanas y de residencias, y sus oficiales, y para regidores y abogados, y del valor de los corregimientos y gobiernos realengos, y de las órdenes (1597).* Antwerp, 1704.

Cervantes, Miguel de. *The Ingenious Gentleman Don Quixote de la Mancha,* translated by S. Putnam. New York, 1949.

Cevallos, Jerónimo de. *Arte real para el buen gobierno de los reyes y príncipes y de sus vasallos, en el cual se refieren las obligaciones de cada uno, con los principales documentos para el buen gobierno ….* Toledo, 1623.

Cicero. *On Duties (De Officiis),* edited by M.T. Griffin and E.M. Atkins. Cambridge, 1991.

———. "Laelius: De amicitia." In *De senectute, de amicitia, de divinatione,* translated by W.A. Falconer. Cambridge, MA, 1988.

Códice Mendieta. Documentos franciscanos (siglos XVI y XVII), edited by J. García Icazbalceta. México, 1892.

Colección de Documentos para la Historia de la Formación Social de Hispanoamérica, 1493–1810, 3 vols., edited by R. Konetzke. Madrid, 1958.

Conclusiones políticas de los ministros. Madrid, 1636.

Conclusiones políticas del príncipe y sus virtudes. Madrid, 1638.

"Consulta sobre los repartimientos." In José A. Llaguno, *La personalidad jurídica del indio y el III Concilio Provincial Mexicano (1585).* México, 1963.

Contreras, Alonso de. *Vida, nacimiento, padres y crianza del capitán Alonso de Contreras (1630).* Madrid, 1967.

Cortiada, Sebastián de. *Discurso sobre la jurisdicción del Exmo. Sr. Virrey y del Exmo. Sr. Capitán General del principado de Cataluña.* Barcelona, 1676.

Covarrubias Orozco, Sebastián de. *Tesoro de la lengua castellana o española (1611).* Madrid, 1979.

Cruz, Sor Juana Inés de la. *Neptuno alegórico, océano de colores, simulacro político que erigió la ... Iglesia Metropolitana de Méjico en las lucidas alegóricas ideas de un arco triunfal que consagró obsequiosa y dedicó amante a la feliz entrada del ... conde de Paredes, marqués de la Laguna ... (1680).* México, 1992.

Cuerpo de documentos del siglo XVI, edited by Lewis Hanke. México, 1943.

Descripción y explicación de la fábrica y empresas del sumptuoso arco que la ... ciudad de México, cabeza del occidental imperio, erigió a la feliz entrada y gozoso recibimiento del Exmo. Sr. Don Diego López Pacheco ... duque de Escalona, marqués de Villena. México, 1640.

Diccionario de Autoridades (1726–1739). Facsimile ed. Madrid, 1963.

Documentos inéditos del siglo XVI para la historia de México, edited by M. Cuevas. México, 1975.

Documentos inéditos o muy raros para la historia de México, edited by G. García. México, 1982.

Documentos para la historia de México, 2a. serie, tomo III. México, 1855.

Documentos sobre las rebeliones indias de Tehuantepec y Nexapa (1660–1661), edited by H. Díaz-Polanco and C. Manzo. México, 1992.

Documentos sobre política lingüística en Hispanoamérica (1492–1800), edited by F. de Solano. Madrid, 1991.

Elogio panegírico y aclamación festiva, diseño triunfal y pompa laudatoria de Ulises verdadero. Conságrala al Exmo. Señor Don Francisco Fernández de la Cueva, duque de Alburquerque, ... la ... imperial ciudad de México.... México, 1653.

Esfera de Apolo y teatro del sol. Ejemplar de prelados en la suntuosa fábrica y portada triunfal que la ... Iglesia Metropolitana de México erigió ... a la venida del Ilmo. Sr. Don Marcelo López de Azcona ... arzobispo de México. México, 1653.

EZLN: Documentos y comunicados, edited by A. García de León. México, 1994.

Fernández de Castro, Baltasar. *Relación ajustada, diseño breve y montea sucinta de los festivos aplausos ... en la ... nueva del feliz nacimiento de nuestro deseado príncipe Felipe Próspero.* México, 1659.

Fernández de Villalobos, Gabriel. *Estado eclesiástico, político y militar de la América (o grandeza de Indias),* edited by J.F. Ramírez. Madrid, 1990.

Fernández Osorio, Alonso. *Breve relación de las solemnísimas exequias, que en la Santa Iglesia Metropolitana de el Arzobispado de México se hicieron, en la translación y entierro del venerable cuerpo de el ilustrísimo señor d. Feliciano de Vega, obispo de la Paz y Popayán, y arzobispo de México.* México, 1642.

Fernández Osorio, Pedro. *Júpiter benévolo, astro etico político, idea simbólica de príncipes, que en la sumptuosa fábrica de un arco triunfal dedica obsequiosa y consagra festiva la Ilustrísima Iglesia Metropolitana de México al Exmo. Señor D. Juan de la Cerda y Leiva, conde de Baños, ...* México, 1660.

Frías, Bernardo de. *Sermón en la festividad del glorioso arcángel San Miguel, patrón del reino de La Galicia, predicado el día 29 de septiembre del año 66 por el bachiller D. Bernardo de Frías, canónigo de la Santa Iglesia Catedral de Guadalajara....* México, 1667.

Fuentes para la historia del trabajo en Nueva España, 8 vols., edited by S. Zavala and M. Castelo. México, 1980.

Funeral lamento, clamor doloroso, y sentimiento triste que a la piadosa memoria del Ilustrísimo y Reverendísimo Señor Doctor D. Alonso de Cuevas Dávalos, obispo que fue de Oaxaca y arzobispo de México, … repite su Santa Iglesia Catedral … en las sepulcrales pompas de su muerte, para póstumo elogio de su vida. México, 1666.

Gárate, Juan de. *Sermón en la solemnidad que anualmente consagra al Santísimo Sacramento del altar el Rey Nuestro Señor… Predícolo el bachiller Juan de Gárate en la Santa Iglesia Catedral….* México, 1677.

Gage, Thomas. *The English-American, His Travail by Sea and Land, or A New Survey of the West-Indias, Containing a Journall of Three Thousand and Three Hundred Miles within the Main Land of America.* London, 1648.

Gómez de Cervantes, Gonzalo. "Memorial de Gonzalo Gómez de Cervantes para el doctor Eugenio Salazar, oidor del Real Consejo de las Indias." Printed in *La vida económica y social de Nueva España al finalizar el siglo XVI*, edited by A.M. Carreño. México, 1944.

Gutiérrez, Sebastián. *Arco triunfal … con que la Iglesia Catedral Metropolitana de la ciudad de México hizo recibimiento al Exmo. Sr. D. Rodrigo Pacheco Osorio, marqués de Cerralvo, virrey de la Nueva España, con una alegoría al nuevo gobierno.* México, 1625.

Gutiérrez de Medina, Cristóbal. *Viaje del virrey marqués de Villena (1640).* México, 1947,

Honorario túmulo, pompa exequial y imperial mausoleo que más jina Artemisa lu fe romana, por su sacrosanto tribunal de Nueva España, erigió y celebró, llorosa Egeria, a su católico Numa y amante rey Philippo Quarto el Grande en su real convento de Santo Domingo de México…. México, 1666.

Informe que la Real Universidad y Claustro Pleno de ella de la ciudad de México de esta Nueva España hace a el Exmo. Sr. virrey de ella, en conformidad de orden de Su Excelencia de 3 de julio de este año de 1692, sobre los inconvenientes de la bebida de el pulque. Mexico, 1692.

Juan, Jorge and Antonio de Ulloa, *Noticias Secretas de América*, edited by L.J. Ramos Gómez. Madrid, 1991.

Las Siete Partidas del sabio rey don Alonso el Nono, nuevamente glosadas por el licenciado Gregorio López del Consejo Real de Indias de Su Majestad (1555), 7 vols. Facsimile ed. Madrid, 1974.

Lorenzana, Francisco Antonio. *Concilios provinciales primero y segundo, celebrados en la Muy Noble y Muy Leal ciudad de México, presidiendo el Illmo. y Rmo. Señor D. Fr. Alonso de Montúfar, en los años de 1555 y 1565.* México, 1769.

Los virreyes españoles en América durante el gobierno de la casa de Austria: México, Biblioteca de Autores Españoles, vols. CCLXXIII–CCLXXVII, edited by L. Hanke and C. Rodríguez. Madrid, 1976–1978.

Machiavelli, *The Prince*, edited by Q. Skinner and R. Price. Cambridge, 1988.

Madariaga, Juan de. *Del senado y su príncipe.* Valencia, 1617.

Mariana, Juan de. *La dignidad real y la educación del rey (De rege et regis institutione) (1599)*, edited by L.S. Agesta. Madrid, 1981.

Márquez, Juan. *El gobernador cristiano, deducido de las vidas de Moisén y Josué, príncipes del pueblo de Dios (1612).* Brussels, 1664.

Marte católico, astro político, planeta de héroes y ascendiente de príncipes, que en las lucidas sombras de una triunfal portada ofrece, representa, dedica la … Iglesia Metropolitana de México al Exmo. Señor Don Francisco Fernández de la Cueva, duque de Alburquerque …. México, 1653.

Martín de Guijo, Gregorio. *Diario, 1648–1664*, 2 vols., edited by M.R. de Terreros. México, 1952.

Mártir Rizo, Juan Pablo. *Norte de príncipes y vida de Rómulo (1626)*, edited by J.A. Maravall. Madrid, 1988.

Matienzo, Juan de. *Gobierno del Perú (1567)*. Paris/Lima, 1967.

Medina, Alonso de. *Espejo de príncipes católicos y gobernadores políticos. Erigióle en arco triunfal la Santa Iglesia Metropolitana de México a la entrada del … conde de Salvatierra … en el cual se ven copiadas sus virtudes, heroicos hechos y prudencial gobierno*. México, 1642.

Memoriales y cartas del conde-duque de Olivares, 2 vols., edited by J.H. Elliott and J.F. de la Peña. Madrid, 1978–1981.

Mendieta, Gerónimo. *Historia eclesiástica indiana*. México, 1997.

Mendo, Andrés. *Príncipe perfecto y ministros ajustados. Documentos políticos y morales en emblemas*. Madrid, 1656.

Moles, Fadrique. *Audiencia de príncipes*. Madrid, 1637.

Mora, Agustín de. *El sol eclipsado antes de llegar al cenit. Real pira que encendió a la apagada luz del rey N.S.D. Carlos II el … conde de Moctezuma …*. México, 1700.

Nieremberg, Juan Eusebio. *De la devoción y patrocinio de San Miguel, príncipe de los ángeles, antiguo tutelar de los godos y protector de España, en que se proponen sus grandes excelencias y títulos que hay para implorar su patrocinio*. México, 1643.

Núñez de Cepeda, Francisco. *Idea de el buen pastor, copiada por los SS. Doctores, representada en Empresas Sacras con avisos espirituales, morales políticos y económicos para el gobierno de un príncipe eclesiástico*. Lyon, 1682.

Ordóñez, Alonso. *Tratado del gobierno de los príncipes del angélico doctor Santo Tomás de Aquino*. Madrid, 1625.

Palafox, Juan de. "Diversos dictámenes espirituales, morales y políticos." In *Obras del Ilmo., Exmo. y venerable siervo de Dios, don Juan de Palafox y Mendoza*, vol. X. Madrid, 1762.

_____. *Tratados Mejicanos*, 2 vols., edited by F. Sánchez-Castañer. Madrid, 1968.

Peña Montenengro, Alonso de la. *Itinerario para párrocos de indios (1668)*. Madrid, 1995.

Peña Peralta, Alonso de la, and Pedro Fernández Osorio, *Pan místico, numen simbólico, simulacro político, que en la fábrica del arco triunfal, que erigió el amor y la obligación en las aras de su debido rendimiento la … Metropolitana Iglesia de México al felicísimo recibimiento y plausible ingreso del Ilustrismo. y Revermo. Señor M. D. Fr. Payo Enriques de Rivera, … su genialísimo pastor, prelado y esposo*. México, 1670.

Pérez de Mesa, Diego. *Política o razón de Estado*, edited by L. Pereña and C. Baciero. Madrid, 1980.

Pineda, Juan de. *Los treinta libros de la monarquía eclesiástica o historia universal del mundo* Barcelona, 1620.

Pinelo, Alavés. *Astro mitológico político que en la entrada y recibimiento del ... conde de Alba de Liste ... consagró la ... ciudad de México, metrópoli del imperio occidental, en el arco triunfal que erigió por trofeo a la inmortalidad de su memoria.* México, 1650.

Pizarro y Orellana, Fernando. *Discurso legal y político de la obligación que tienen los reyes a premiar los servicios de sus vasallos, o en ellos o en sus descendientes.* Madrid, 1639.

Portada alegórica, espejo político, que la augusta y muy esclarecida Iglesia Metropolitana de México dedicó al ... conde de Alba de Liste .... México, 1650.

Portocarrero y Guzmán, Pedro. *Teatro Monárquico de España (1700)*, edited by C. Sanz Ayán. Madrid, 1998.

Real mausoleo y funeral pompa, que erigió el Excelentísimo Señor conde de Salvatierra y la Real Audiencia desta ciudad de México a las memorias del Serenísimo Príncipe de España Don Baltasar Carlos. México, 1647.

Recopilación de leyes de los reinos de las Indias (1681). Madrid, 1943.

Reina Maldonado, Pedro de. *Norte claro del perfecto prelado en su pastoral gobierno.* Madrid, 1653.

Rivadeneira, Pedro de. "Tratado de la religión y virtudes que debe tener el príncipe cristiano para gobernar y conservar sus estados, contra lo que Nicolás Maquiavelo y los políticos deste tiempo enseñan." In *Obras escogidas del Padre Pedro de Rivadeneira (1595)*, edited by Vicente de la Fuente. Madrid, 1952.

Roa, Martín de. *Beneficios del Santo Angel de Nuestra Guarda.* Córdoba, 1632.

Robles, Antonio de. *Diario de sucesos notables (1665–1703)*, 3 vols., edited by A. Castro Leal. México, 1972.

Ruiz de Cabrera, Cristóbal. *Algunos singulares y extraordinarios sucesos del gobierno de D. Diego Pimentel, marqués de Gelves, virrey desta Nueva España, por su excesivo rigor, ayudado de sus consejeros.* México, 1624.

Saavedra Fajardo, Diego. *Empresas políticas (1640)*, edited by S. López. Madrid, 1999.

Salazar, Juan de. *Política Española (1619)*, edited by M. Herrero García. Madrid, 1997.

Santa María, Juan de. *Tratado de república y policía cristiana para reyes y príncipes, y para los que en el gobierno tienen sus veces.* Madrid, 1615.

Saona, Jerónimo de. *Jerarquía celestial y terrena y símbolo de los nueve estados de la iglesia militante, con los nueve coros de la triunfante.* Cuenca, 1603.

Sariñana, Isidro. *Llanto del Occidente en el ocaso del más claro sol de las Españas. Fúnebres demostraciones que hizo, pira real que erigió en las exequias del rey, N. Señor, D. Felipe IIII el Grande el ... marqués de Mancera, virrey de la Nueva España.* México, 1666.

Seijas y Lobera, Francisco de. *Gobierno militar y político del reino imperial de la Nueva España (1702)*, edited by P.E. Pérez-Mallaína Bueno. México, 1986.

Seneca, "On Favors" [*De Beneficiis*]. In *Seneca: Moral and Political Essays*, edited by J.M. Cooper and J.F. Procopé. Cambridge, U.K., 1995.

Serna, Jacinto de la. *Sermón en la fiesta de los tres días al Santísimo Sacramento en la capilla del Sagrario de la Santa Iglesia Metropolitana de México, que sus rectores y curas celebraron en 3 de febrero de 1655 años....* México, 1655.

Sigüenza y Góngora, Carlos de. *Alboroto y motín de los indios de México (1692),* edited by I.A. Leonard. México, 1986.

____. *Teatro de virtudes políticas que constituyen a un príncipe, advertidas en los monarcas antiguos del mexicano imperio (1680).* México, 1986.

Silva, Juan de. *Los memoriales del Padre Silva sobre predicación pacífica y repartimientos (1618),* edited by P. Castañeda Delgado. Madrid, 1983.

Solórzano Pereira, Juan de. *Memorial y discurso de las razones que se ofrecen para que el Real y Supremo Consejo de las Indias deba preceder en todos los actos públicos al que llaman de Flandes.* Madrid, 1629.

____. *Política indiana (1647),* 5 vols. 252–256, edited by M.A. Ochoa Brun. Madrid, 1972.

Suárez, Francisco. *Defensio Fidei III. Principatus politicus o la soberanía popular (1613),* edited by E. Elorduy and L. Pereña. Madrid, 1965.

Torquemada, Fray Juan de. *Monarquía indiana (1615),* edited by M. León-Portilla. México, 1975.

Tovar Valderrama, Diego de. *Instituciones políticas (1645),* edited by J.L. Bermejo Cabrero. Madrid, 1995.

Transformación teopolítica, idea mitológica de príncipe pastor, sagrado Proteo, alegorizada en imágenes, decifrada en números, que en el aparato magnífico del triunfal arco y padrón glorioso, en el fausto día de su plausible recebimiento, dispuso y consagró al Ilustmo. y Revmo. Señor D. D. Francisco de Aguiar Seijas y Ulloa ... dignísimo arzobispo de esta metrópoli, la siempre augusta iglesia metropolitana de México. México, 1683.

Ugarte de Hermosa y Salcedo, Francisco. *Origen de los dos gobiernos divino y humano y forma de su ejercicio en lo temporal.* Madrid, 1655.

Valero Caballero, José. *Sermón al Santísimo Sacramento por el feliz viaje y milagroso escape de la armada real de España el año de 25, predicado el año de 75 en la Santa Iglesia Catedral de la Puebla por el bachiller D. José Valero Caballero....* México, 1677.

Vázquez de Espinosa, Antonio. *Compendio y descripción de las Indias Occidentales,* edited by B. Velasco Bayón. Madrid, 1969.

Vetancourt, Agustín de. *Teatro mexicano. Descripción breve de los sucesos ejemplares, históricos, políticos, militares y religiosos del Nuevo Mundo Occidental de las Indias (1698).* Facsimile ed. México, 1971.

Villarroel, Gaspar de. *Gobierno eclesiástico pacífico y unión de los dos cuchillos, pontificio y regio.* Madrid, 1656.

Vilosa, Rafael de. *Disertación jurídica y política sobre si es delito de lesa majestad in primo capite matar a un virrey.* Madrid, 1670.

Zapata y Sandoval, Juan. *Disceptación sobre justicia distributiva y sobre la acepción de personas a ella opuesta (1609),* edited by A.E. Ramírez Trejo. México, 1994.

Zorita, Alonso de. *Relación de los señores de la Nueva España,* edited by G. Vázquez. Madrid, 1992.

Secondary Sources

Abrams, Philip. "Notes on the Difficulty of Studying the State." *Journal of Historical Sociology* 1, no. 1 (1988): 58–89.

Adorno, Rolena. "Reconsidering Colonial Discourse for Sixteenth- and Seventeenth-Century Spanish America." *Latin American Research Review* 28, no. 3 (1993): 139–145.

Aiton, Arthur S. *Antonio de Mendoza: First Viceroy of New Spain*. Durham, NC, 1927.

Alberro, Solange. *Inquisición y sociedad en México, 1571–1700*. México, 1988.

———. "La aculturación de los españoles en la América colonial." In *Descubrimiento, conquista y colonización de América a quinientos años*, edited by C. Bernand. México, 1994.

Alvarado Morales, Manuel. *La ciudad de México ante la fundación de la Armada de Barlovento: Historia de una encrucijada (1635–1643)*. México, 1983.

Alvarez-Ossorio, Antonio. "El favor real: liberalidad del príncipe y jerarquía de la república (1665–1700)." In *Repubblica e virtù: pensiero politico e monarchia cattolica fra XVI e XVII secolo*, edited by Ch. Continisio and C. Mozzarelli. Roma, 1995.

———. "Virtud coronada: Carlos II y la piedad de la casa de Austria." In *Política, Religión e Inquisición en la España Moderna. Homenaje a J. Pérez Villanueva*, edited by P.F. Albaladejo, J.M. Millán, and V.P. Crespo. Madrid, 1996.

Anderson, Perry. *Lineages of the Absolutist State*. London, 1974.

Andrien, Kenneth J. "The Sale of Fiscal Offices and the Decline of Royal Authority in the Viceroyalty of Peru, 1633–1700." *Hispanic American Historical Review* 62, no. 1 (1982): 49–71.

———. "Corruption, Inefficiency, and Imperial Decline in the Seventeenth-Century Viceroyalty of Peru." *The Americas* 41, no. 1 (1984): 1–20.

———. "Spaniards, Andeans, and the Early Colonial State in Peru." In *Transatlantic Encounters: Europeans and Andeans in the Sixteenth Century*, edited by K.J. Andrien and R. Adorno. Berkeley, 1991.

Annino, Antonio. "Some Reflections on Spanish American Constitutional and Political History." *Itinerario* 19, no. 2 (1995).

Armitage, David, ed. *Theories of Empire, 1450–1800*. Aldershot, 1998.

Báez Macías, Eduardo. *El arcángel San Miguel: su patrocinio, la ermita en el Santo Desierto de Cuajimalpa y el Santuario de Tlaxcala*. México, 1979.

Baker, Keith M. *Inventing the French Revolution: Essays on French Political Culture in the Eighteenth Century*. Cambridge, U.K., 1990.

———, ed., *The French Revolution and the Creation of Modern Political Culture*. Vol. 1. *The Political Culture of the Old Regime*. Oxford, 1987.

Baskes, Jeremy. *Indians, Merchants, and Markets: A Reinterpretation of the Repartimiento and Spanish–Indian Economic Relations in Colonial Oaxaca, 1750–1821*. Stanford, 2000.

Batista i Roca, J.M. "Foreword." In *The Practice of Empire*, edited by H.G. Koenigsberger. Ithaca, 1969.

Baudot, Georges. *La pugna franciscana por México*. México, 1990.

_____. "Amerindian Image and Utopian Project: Motolinía and Millenarian Discourse." In *Amerindian Images and the Legacy of Columbus*, edited by R. Jara and N. Spadaccini. Minneapolis, 1992.

_____. *Utopia and History in Mexico: The First Chroniclers of Mexican Civilization (1520–1569)*. Niwot, CO, 1993.

Beik, William. *Absolutism and Society in Seventeenth-Century France: State Power and Provincial Aristocracy in Languedoc*. Cambridge, U.K., 1985.

Bell, Catherine. *Ritual Theory, Ritual Practice*. New York, 1992.

Bennassar, Bartolomé. "Por el Estado, contra el Estado." In *Inquisición española. Poder político y control social*, edited by B. Bennassar. Barcelona, 1981.

_____. "El reino del conformismo." In *Inquisición española. Poder político y control social*, edited by B. Bennassar. Barcelona, 1981.

Bernand, Carmen. *Negros esclavos y libres en las ciudades hispanoamericanas*. Madrid, 2001.

_____, and Serge Gruzinski. *De la idolatría. Una arqueología de las ciencias religiosas*. México, 1992.

Biagioli, Mario. *Galileo Courtier: The Practice of Science in the Culture of Absolutism*. Chicago, 1993.

Bireley, Robert. *The Counter-Reformation Prince: Anti-Machiavellianism or Catholic Statecraft in Early Modern Europe*. Chapel Hill, 1990.

Borah, Woodrow. *Justice by Insurance: The General Indian Court of Colonial Mexico and the Legal Aides of the Half-Real*. Berkeley, 1983.

_____, ed. *El gobierno provincial en la Nueva España, 1570-1787*. México, 1985.

Bourdieu, Pierre. *The Logic of Practice*, translated by Richard Nice. Stanford, 1990.

_____. *Language and Symbolic Power*. Cambridge, MA, 1991.

Bouza Alvarez, Fernando. "La majestad de Felipe II. Construcción del mito real." In *La corte de Felipe II*, edited by J. Martínez Millán. Madrid, 1994.

Bowser, Frederick P. *The African Slave in Colonial Peru, 1524–1650*. Stanford, 1974.

_____. "The Church in Colonial Middle America." *Latin American Research Review* 25, no. 1 (1990): 137–156.

Boyer, Richard E. "Absolutism vs. Corporatism in New Spain: The Administration of the Marqués de Gelves, 1621–1624." *The International History Review* IV, no. 4 (1982): 475–503.

Brading, David. *The First America: The Spanish Monarchy, Creole Patriots and the Liberal State, 1492–1867*. Cambridge, U.K., 1991.

_____. *Church and State in Bourbon Mexico: The Diocese of Michoacán 1749–1810*. Cambridge, U.K. 1994.

_____. "La monarquía católica." In *De los imperios a las naciones. Iberoamérica*, edited by A. Annino et al. Zaragoza, 1994.

Burke, Peter. *The Historical Anthropology of Early Modern Italy*. Cambridge, U.K. 1987.

_____. *The Fabrication of Louis XIV*. New Haven, 1992.

Brown, Jonathan and J.H. Elliott. *A Palace for a King: The Buen Retiro and the Court of Philip IV*. New Haven, 1980.

Burkholder, Mark A. and Douglas S. Chandler, *From Impotence to Authority: The Spanish Crown and the American Audiencias, 1687–1808*. Columbia, MS, 1977.

Canet Aparisi, Teresa. *La Audiencia valenciana en la época foral moderna*. Valencia, 1986.

Cannadine, David and Simon Price, eds., *Rituals of Royalty: Power and Ceremonial in Traditional Societies*. Cambridge, U.K., 1987.

Cañeque, Alejandro. "Theater of Power: Writing and Representing the Auto de Fe in Colonial Mexico." *The Americas* 52, no. 3 (1996): 321–343.

Cardoso, Fernando Henrique and Enzo Faletto, *Dependencia y desarrollo en América Latina*. México, 1969.

Carmagnani, M., A. Hernández Chávez, and R. Romano, eds., *Para una historia de América. I. Las estructuras*. México, 1999.

Carrillo Cazares, Alberto. *El debate sobre la guerra chichimeca, 1531–1585. Derecho y política en la Nueva España*, 2 vols. Zamora, MI, 2000.

Casey, James. "Some Considerations on State Formation and Patronage in Early Modern Spain." In *Patronages et Clientélismes, 1550–1750 (France, Angleterre, Espagne, Italie)*, edited by Ch. Giry-Deloison and R. Mettam. Lille, n.d.

Castañeda Delgado, Paulino. "La condición miserable del indio y sus privilegios." *Anuario de Estudios Americanos* XXVIII (1971): 245–258.

Castro Gutiérrez, Felipe. "Indeseables e indispensables: los vecinos españoles, mestizos y mulatos en los pueblos de indios de Michoacán." *Estudios de Historia Novohispana* 25 (July–Dec. 2001): 59–80.

Checa, Fernando. "Arquitectura efímera e imagen del poder." In *Sor Juana y su mundo. Una mirada actual*, edited by S. Poot Herrera. México, 1995.

Chittolini, Giorgio. "The 'Private,' the 'Public,' the 'State.'" In *The Origins of the State in Italy*, edited by J. Kirshner. Chicago, 1996.

Chocano Mena, Magdalena. *La fortaleza docta. Elite letrada y dominación social en México colonial (siglos XVI–XVII)*. Barcelona, 2000.

Clavero, Bartolomé. "Institución política y derecho: acerca del concepto historiográfico de 'Estado moderno.'" *Revista de Estudios Políticos* 19 (1981): 43–57.

_____. *Tantas personas como estados. Por una antropología política de la historia europea*. Madrid, 1986.

_____. *Razón de Estado, razón de individuo, razón de historia*. Madrid, 1991.

_____. *Antidora. Antropología católica de la economía moderna*. Milan, 1991.

Cline, Howard F. "Civil Congregations of the Indians in New Spain, 1598–1606." *The Hispanic American Historical Review* XXIX (1949): 349–369.

Coatsworth, John H. "The Limits of Colonial Absolutism: The State in Eighteenth Century Mexico." In *Essays in the Political, Economic and Social History of Colonial Latin America*, edited by K. Spalding. Newark, 1982.

Contreras, Jaime. *El Santo Oficio de la Inquisición de Galicia (poder, sociedad y cultura)*. Madrid, 1982.

Cook, N.D. *Born To Die: Disease and New World Conquest, 1492–1650*. Cambridge, U.K., 1998.

Cope, R. Douglas. *The Limits of Racial Domination: Plebeian Society in Colonial Mexico City, 1660–1720*. Madison, 1994.

Corcuera de Mancera, Sonia. *Del amor al temor. Borrachez, catequesis y control en la Nueva España (1555–1771)*. México, 1994.

Corrigan, Philip and Derek Sayer. *The Great Arch: English State Formation as Cultural Revolution*. Oxford, 1985.

Curcio, Linda Ann. "Saints, Sovereignty and Spectacle in Colonial Mexico." Ph.D. dissertation, Tulane University, 1993.

Curcio-Nagy, Linda. "Giants and Gypsies: Corpus Christi in Colonial Mexico City." In *Rituals of Rule, Rituals of Resistance: Popular Celebrations and Popular Culture in Mexico*, edited by W.H. Beezley et al. Wilmington, 1994.

_____. *The Great Festivals of Colonial Mexico City: Performing Power and Identity*. Albuquerque, 2004.

Day, John, Bruno Anatra, and Lucetta Scaraffia, *La Sardegna medioevale e moderna*. Torino, 1984.

Dedieu, Jean-Pierre. *L'administration de la foi. L'Inquisition de Tolède, XVIe–XVIIIe siècle*. Madrid, 1989.

Dewald, Jonathan *Aristocratic Experience and the Origins of Modern Culture. France, 1570–1715*. Berkeley, 1993.

Díaz-Polanco, Héctor, ed. *El fuego de la inobediencia. Autonomía y rebelión india en el obispado de Oaxaca*. Oaxaca, 1996.

Domínguez Ortiz, Antonio. "Regalismo y relaciones Iglesia–Estado en el siglo XVII." In *Historia de la Iglesia en España*, vol. IV, edited by R. García-Villoslada. Madrid, 1979.

_____. "Inquisición y Estado en la España de los Austrias." In *État et Église dans la génése de l'État Moderne*. Madrid, 1986.

Egaña, Antonio de. *La teoría del Regio Vicariato Español en Indias*. Rome, 1958.

Eire, Carlos M.N. *From Madrid to Purgatory: The Art and Craft of Dying in Sixteenth-Century Spain*. Cambridge, U.K., 1995.

Eisendstadt, S.N. *The Political System of Empires*. New York, 1963.

Elias, Norbert. *The Court Society*, translated by E. Jephcott. New York, 1983.

_____. *The Civilizing Process: Sociogenetic and Psychogenetic Investigations*, translated by E. Jephcott. Oxford, 2000.

Elliott, John H. *Imperial Spain, 1469–1716*. London, 1963.

_____. "Spain and America before 1700." In *Colonial Spanish America*, edited by Leslie Bethell. Cambridge, U.K., 1984.

_____. *Richelieu and Olivares*. Cambridge, U.K., 1984.

_____. *The Count-Duke of Olivares: The Statesman in an Age of Decline*. New Haven, 1986.

_____. *Spain and Its World, 1500–1700: Selected Essays*. New Haven, 1989.

_____. "The Spanish Monarchy and the Kingdom of Portugal, 1580–1640." In *Conquest and Coalescence: The Shaping of the State in Early Modern Europe*, edited by M. Greengrass. London, 1991.

_____. "A Europe of Composite Monarchies." *Past & Present* 137 (Nov. 1992): 48–71.

_____. "Empire and State in British and Spanish America." In *Le Nouveau Monde, Mondes Nouveaux: L'expérience américaine*, edited by S. Gruzinski and N. Wachtel. Paris, 1996.

Evans, R.J.W. *The Making of the Habsburg Monarchy, 1550–1700.* Oxford, 1979.

Farriss, Nancy M. *Crown and Clergy in Colonial Mexico, 1759–1821: The Crisis of Ecclesiastical Privilege.* London, 1968.

Fee, Nancy H. "La Entrada Angelopolitana: Ritual and Myth in the Viceregal Entry in Puebla de los Angeles," *The Americas* 52:3 (Jan. 1996): 283–320.

Fernández Albaladejo, Pablo. "Epílogo." In Koenigsberger, H.G., *La práctica del Imperio*, translated by G. Soriano. Madrid, 1989.

_____. *Fragmentos de Monarquía. Trabajos de historia política.* Madrid, 1992.

_____. "Cities and the State in Spain." In *Cities and the Rise of States in Europe, A.D. 1000 to 1800*, edited by Ch. Tilly and W.P. Blockmans. Boulder, 1994.

_____. "'Rey Católico': Gestación y metamorfosis de un título." In *Repubblica e virtù: pensiero politico e monarchia cattolica fra XVI e XVII secolo*, edited by Ch. Continisio and C. Mozzarelli. Roma, 1995.

_____. "Iglesia y configuración del poder en la monarquía católica (siglos XV–XVII). Algunas consideraciones." In *Etat et Eglise dans la genèse de l'Etat moderne.* Madrid, 1986.

Fernández-Santamaría, José A. "Reason of State and Statecraft in Spain (1595–1640)." *Journal of the History of Ideas* 41 (1980): 355–379.

_____. *Reason of State and Statecraft in Spanish Political Thought, 1595–1640.* Lanham, 1983.

_____. "Estudio preliminar." In de Barrientos, B.A., *Aforismos al Tácito español*, 2 vols., edited by J.A. Fernández-Santamaría. Madrid, 1987.

Fernández Terricabras, Ignasi. "Al servicio del rey y de la Iglesia. El control del episcopado castellano por la Corona en tiempos de Felipe II." In *Lo conflictivo y lo consensual en Castilla. Sociedad y poder político, 1521–1715*, edited by F.J. Guillamón and J.J. Ruiz. Murcia, 2001.

Feros, Antonio. "Clientelismo y poder monárquico en la España de los siglos XVI y XVII." *Relaciones* 73 (1998): 15–49.

_____. *Kingship and Favoritism in the Spain of Philip III, 1598–1621.* Cambridge, U.K., 2000.

Florescano, Enrique. "The Hacienda in New Spain." In *Colonial Spanish America*, edited by L. Bethell. Cambridge, U.K., 1987.

Foucault, Michel. *Discipline and Punish: The Birth of the Prison*, translated by A. Sheridan. New York, 1977.

_____. *Power/Knowledge: Selected Interviews and Other Writings, 1972–1977*, translated by C. Gordon et al. New York, 1980.

Frank, Andre Gunder. *Capitalism and Underdevelopment in Latin America: Historical Studies of Chile and Brazil.* New York, 1969.

Frost, Elsa Cecilia. "A New Millenarian: Georges Baudot." *The Americas* 36, no. 4 (1980): 515–526.

García-Abasolo, Antonio F. *Martín Enríquez y la reforma de 1568 en Nueva España.* Sevilla, 1983.

García Martínez, Bernardo. *Los pueblos de la sierra. El poder y el espacio entre los indios del norte de Puebla hasta 1700.* México, 1987.

Garrido Aranda, Antonio. *Organización de la Iglesia en el Reino de Granada y su proyección en Indias, siglo XVI.* Sevilla, 1979.

Geertz, Clifford. *The Interpretation of Cultures.* New York, 1973.

_____. "Centers, Kings, and Charisma: Reflections on the Symbolics of Power." In *Culture and Its Creators: Essays in Honor of E. Shils,* edited by J. Ben-David and T.N. Clark. Chicago, 1977.

_____. *Negara: The Theatre State in Nineteenth-Century Bali.* Princeton, 1980.

Gerhard, Dietrich. *Old Europe: A Study of Continuity, 1000–1800.* New York, 1981.

Gibson, Charles. *The Aztecs Under Spanish Rule: A History of the Indians of the Valley of Mexico, 1519–1810.* Stanford, 1964.

_____. *Spain in America.* New York, 1966.

Giesey, Ralph. "Models of Rulership in French Royal Ceremonial." In *Rites of Power: Symbolism, Ritual, and Politics Since the Middle Ages,* edited by S. Wilentz. Philadelphia, 1985.

Gil Pujol, Xavier. "Una cultura cortesana provincial. Patria, comunicación y lenguaje en la Monarquía Hispánica de los Austrias." In *Monarquía, imperio y pueblos en la España moderna,* edited by P.F. Albaladejo. Alicante, 1997.

Goldin, Frederick. *The Mirror of Narcissus in the Courtly Love Lyric.* Ithaca, 1967.

Gombrich, E.H. *Gombrich on the Renaissance.* Vol. 2. *Symbolic Images.* London, 1985.

Góngora, Mario. *El Estado en el derecho indiano. Época de fundación (1492–1570).* Santiago de Chile, 1951.

_____. *Studies in the Colonial History of Spanish America.* Cambridge, U.K., 1975.

Gonzalbo Aizpuru, Pilar. *Historia de la educación en la época colonial. El mundo indígena.* México, 1990.

Greenleaf, Richard E. "The Inquisition and the Indians of New Spain: A Study in Jurisdictional Confusion." *The Americas* 22, no. 2 (Oct. 1965): 138–166.

_____. "The Inquisition in Colonial Mexico: Heretical Thoughts on the Spiritual Conquest." In *Religion in Latin American Life and Literature,* edited by L.C. Brown and W. Cooper. Waco, 1980.

Gruzinski, Serge. *The Conquest of Mexico.* Cambridge, U.K., 1993.

_____, and Nathan Wachtel, eds. *Le Nouveau Monde, Mondes Nouveaux: l'expérience américaine.* Paris, 1996.

Guenée, Bernard. *States and Rulers in Later Medieval Europe,* translated by J. Vale. Oxford, 1985.

Gutiérrez, Ramón A. *When Jesus Came, the Corn Mothers Went Away: Marriage, Sexuality, and Power in New Mexico, 1500–1846.* Stanford, 1991.

Gutiérrez Haces, Juana et al., *Cristóbal de Villalpando, ca. 1649–1714.* México, 1997.

Gutiérrez Lorenzo, María Pilar. *De la corte de Castilla al virreinato de México: el conde de Galve (1653-1697).* Guadalajara, Spain, 1993.

Guy, John. "The Rhetoric of Counsel in Early Modern England." In *Tudor Political Culture*, edited by D. Hoak. Cambridge, U.K., 1995.

Guzmán Betancourt, Ignacio. "'Policía' y 'barbarie' de las lenguas indígenas de México, según la opinión de gramáticos e historiadores novohispanos." *Estudios de Cultura Náhuatl* 21 (1991): 179–218.

Hanke, Lewis. *Aristotle and the American Indians*. Bloomington, 1959.

———. *The Spanish Struggle for Justice in the Conquest of America*. Boston, 1965.

Harding, Robert. *Anatomy of a Power Elite: The Provincial Governors of Early Modern France*. New Haven, 1978.

———. "Corruption and the Moral Boundaries of Patronage in the Renaissance." In *Patronage in the Renaissance*, edited by G.F. Lytle and S. Orgel. Princeton, 1981.

Haring, Clarence H. *The Spanish Empire in America*. New York, 1947.

Hera, Alberto de la. "El patronato y el vicariato regio en Indias." In *Historia de la Iglesia en Hispanoamérica y Filipinas (siglos XV–XIX)*, vol. I., edited by P. Borges. Madrid, 1992.

Herman, Arthur L. "The Language of Fidelity in Early Modern France." *Journal of Modern History* 67 (1995): 1–24.

Hermann, Christian. "Le patronage royal espagnol: 1525–1750." In *Etat et Eglise dans la genèse de l'Etat moderne*. Madrid, 1986.

Hernández Palomo, José Jesús. *La renta del pulque en Nueva España, 1663–1810*. Sevilla, 1979.

Hernando Sánchez, Carlos José. *Castilla y Nápoles en el siglo XVI: el virrey Pedro de Toledo: linaje, estado y cultura (1532–1553)*. Valladolid, 1994.

Hernmarck, Carl. *Custodias procesionales en España*. Madrid, 1987.

Herzog, Tamar. *La administración como un fenómeno social: La justicia penal de la ciudad de Quito (1650–1750)*. Madrid, 1995.

Hespanha, António M. *Vísperas del Leviatán. Instituciones y poder político (Portugal, siglo XVII)*, translated by F.J. Bouza. Madrid, 1989.

———. *La gracia del derecho. Economía de la cultura en la Edad Moderna*, translated by A. Cañellas. Madrid, 1993.

Hoak, Dale, ed. *Tudor Political Culture*. Cambridge, U.K., 1995.

Hoberman, Louisa S. *México's Merchant Elite, 1590–1660*. Durham, 1991.

Hoekstra, Rik. *Two Worlds Merging: The Transformation of Society in the Valley of Puebla, 1570–1640*. Amsterdam, 1993.

Horn, Rebecca. *Postconquest Coyoacan: Nahua–Spanish Relations in Central Mexico, 1519–1650*. Stanford, 1997.

Israel, Jonathan I. "Mexico and the 'General Crisis' of the Seventeenth Century." *Past & Present* 63 (1974): 33–57.

———. *Race, Class and Politics in Colonial Mexico, 1610–1670*. London, 1975.

———. "The Seventeenth-Century Crisis in New Spain: Myth or Reality?" *Past & Present* 97 (1982): 150–156.

Jago, Charles. "Habsburg Absolutism and the Cortes of Castile." *American Historical Review* 86 (1981): 307–326.

_____. "Fiscalidad y cambio constitucional en Castilla, 1601–1621." In *Política y hacienda en el Antiguo Régimen*, edited by J.I. Fortea López and C.M. Cremades Griñán. Murcia, 1993.

_____. "Taxation and Political Culture in Castile 1590–1640." In *Spain, Europe and the Atlantic World: Essays in Honour of John H. Elliott*, edited by R. Kagan and G. Parker. Cambridge, U.K., 1995.

James, Mervyn. "Ritual, Drama and Social Body in the Late Medieval English Town." *Past & Present* 98 (1983): 3–29.

Kagan, Richard L. *Urban Images of the Hispanic World, 1493–1793*. New Haven, 2000.

Kamen, Henry. *Spain in the Later Seventeenth Century, 1665–1700*. London, 1980.

_____. *The Phoenix and the Flame: Catalonia and the Counter Reformation*. New Haven, 1993.

_____. *The Spanish Inquisition. A Historical Revision*. New Haven, 1997.

Kantorowiz, Ernest. *The King's Two Bodies: A Study in Medieval Theology*. Princeton, 1957.

Katzew, I., ed. *New World Orders: Casta Painting and Colonial Latin America*. New York, 1996.

Kellogg, Susan. "Hegemony Out of Conquest: The First Two Centuries of Spanish Rule in Central Mexico." *Radical History Review* 53 (1992): 27–46.

_____. *Law and the Transformation of Aztec Culture, 1500–1700*. London, 1995.

Kirshner, Julius. "Introduction: The State Is 'Back In.'" In *The Origins of the State in Italy, 1300–1600*, edited by J. Kirshner. Chicago, 1996.

Kettering, Sharon. *Patrons, Brokers, and Clients in Seventeenth-Century France*. New York, 1986.

_____. "Gift-Giving and Patronage in Early Modern France." *French History* 2 (1988): 131–151.

Klor de Alva, Jorge. "The Postcolonization of the (Latin) American Experience: A Reconsideration of 'Colonialism,' 'Postcolonialism,' and 'Mestizaje.'" In *After Colonialism: Imperial Histories and Postcolonial Displacements*, edited by G. Prakash. Princeton, 1995.

Koenigsberger, Helmut G. *La práctica del Imperio*, translated by G. Soriano. Madrid, 1989.

Lalinde Abadía, Jesús. *La institución virreinal en Cataluña (1471–1716)*. Barcelona, 1964.

_____. "El régimen virreino-senatorial en Indias." *Anuario de Historia del Derecho Español*. Madrid, 1967.

_____. "España y la monarquía universal (en torno al concepto de 'Estado moderno')." *Quaderni Fiorentini per la Storia del Pensiero Giuridico Moderno*, 15 (1986): 109–138.

Latasa Vassallo, Pilar. *Administración virreinal en el Perú: Gobierno del marqués de Montesclaros (1607–1615)*. Madrid, 1997.

Lea, Henry Charles. *A History of the Inquisition of Spain*. New York, 1988.

Leonard, Irving A. *Baroque Times in Old Mexico: Seventeenth-Century Persons, Places, and Practices*. Westport, 1959.

Levillier, Roberto. *Don Francisco de Toledo, supremo organizador del Perú.* Madrid, 1935.

Lisón Tolosana, Carmelo. *La imagen del rey. Monarquía, realeza y poder ritual en la Casa de los Austrias.* Madrid, 1991.

Liss, Peggy K. *México under Spain, 1521–1556: Society and the Origins of Nationality.* Chicago, 1975.

Llaguno, José A. *La personalidad jurídica del indio y el III Concilio Provincial Mexicano (1585).* México, 1963.

Lloyd, Howell A. "Constitutionalism." In *The Cambridge History of Political Thought, 1450–1700,* edited by J.H. Burns. Cambridge, 1991.

Lockhart, James. *Nahuas and Spaniards: Postconquest Central Mexican History and Philology.* Stanford, 1991.

_____. *The Nahuas after the Conquest.* Stanford, 1992.

Lohmann Villena, Guillermo. "Las Cortes en Indias." *Anuario de Historia del Derecho Español* XVIII (1947): 655–662.

_____. *El corregidor de indios en el Perú bajo los Austrias.* Madrid, 1957.

_____. "Notas sobre la presencia de la Nueva España en las Cortes metropolitanas y de Cortes en la Nueva España en los siglos XVI y XVII." *Historia Mexicana* XXXIX (1989): 33–40.

López Vela, Roberto. "Las estructuras administrativas del Santo Oficio." In *Historia de la Inquisición en España y América,* 2 vols., edited by J. Pérez Villanueva and B. Escandell Bonet. Madrid, 1993.

Luciani, Frederick. "Sor Juana's *Amor es más laberinto* as Mythological *Speculum.*" In *Estudios sobre escritoras hispánicas en honor de Georgina Sabat-Rivers,* edited by Lou Charnon-Deutsch. Madrid, 1992.

_____. "The Comedia de San Francisco de Borja (1640): The Mexican Jesuits and the Education of the Prince." *Colonial Latin American Review* 2 (1993): 121–141.

Luiselli, Alessandra. "Sobre el peligroso arte de tirar el guante: la ironía de Sor Juana hacia los virreyes de Galve." In *Los empeños. Ensayos en homenaje a Sor Juana Inés de la Cruz.* México, 1995.

Lynch, John. *The Hispanic World in Crisis and Change, 1598–1700.* Oxford, 1992.

_____. "The Institutional Framework of Colonial Spanish America." *Journal of Latin American Studies* 24 (1992): 69–77.

MacLachlan, Colin M. *Spain's Empire in the New World: The Role of Ideas in Institutional and Social Change.* Berkeley, 1988.

Maravall, José Antonio. *Las comunidades de Castilla. Una primera revolución moderna.* Madrid, 1963.

_____. *Estado moderno y mentalidad social, siglos XV a XVII.* Madrid, 1972.

_____. *Utopía y reformismo en la España de los Austrias.* Madrid, 1982.

_____. *Estudios de historia del pensamiento español.* Madrid, 1983.

Mattone, Antonello. "Le istituzione e le forme di governo." In *Storia dei sardi e della Sardegna.* Vol. 3. *L'Età Moderna: dagli aragonesi alla fine del dominio spagnolo,* edited by B. Anatra, A. Mattone, and R. Turtas. Milan, 1987.

Mauss, Marcel. *The Gift: Forms and Functions of Exchange in Archaic Societies,* translated by I. Cunnison. New York, 1967.

Mazín Gómez, Oscar. *El cabildo catedral de Valladolid de Michoacán*. Zamora, 1996.

Merriman, Roger B. *The Rise of the Spanish Empire in the Old World and in the New*, 4 vols. (1918, 1925, 1934). New York, 1962.

Mettam, Roger. *Power and Faction in Louis XIV's France*. Oxford, 1988.

Mignolo, Walter D. *The Darker Side of the Renaissance: Literacy, Territoriality, and Colonization*. Ann Arbor, 1995.

Mínguez, Víctor. *Los reyes solares. Iconografía astral de la monarquía hispánica*. Castelló de la Plana, 2001.

Miranda, José. *El tributo indígena en la Nueva España durante el siglo XVI*. México, 1952.

Morales y Folguera, José Miguel. *Cultura simbólica y arte efímero en Nueva España*. Granada, 1991.

Moreno de los Arcos, Roberto. "New Spain's Inquisition for Indians from the Sixteenth to the Nineteenth Century." In *Cultural Encounters: The Impact of the Inquisition in Spain and the New World*, edited by M.E. Perry, and A.J. Cruz. Berkeley, 1991.

Mörner, Magnus. *La Corona española y los foráneos en los pueblos de indios de América*. Stockholm, 1970.

Morse, Richard M. "The Heritage of Colonial Latin America." In *The Founding of New Societies: Studies in the History of the United States, Latin America, South Africa, Canada and Australia*, edited by L. Hartz. New York, 1964.

Mujica Pinilla, Ramón. *Ángeles apócrifos en la América virreinal*. Lima, 1996.

Muir, Edward. *Civic Ritual in Renaissance Venice*. Princeton, 1981.

_____. *Ritual in Early Modern Europe*. Cambridge, U.K., 1997.

Muldoon, James. *The Americas in the Spanish World Order: The Justification for Conquest in the Seventeenth Century*. Philadelphia, 1994.

_____. *Empire and Order: The Concept of Empire, 800–1800*. New York, 1999.

Muro Romero, Fernando. "El 'beneficio' de oficios públicos con jurisdicción en Indias. Notas sobre sus orígenes." *Anuario de Estudios Americanos* 35 (1978): 1–67.

Neuschel, Kristen B. *Word of Honor: Interpreting Noble Culture in Sixteenth-Century France*. Ithaca, 1989.

Nieto Soria, J.M. *Ceremonias de la realeza. Propaganda y legitimación en la Castilla Trastámara*. Madrid, 1993.

Oestreich, Gerhard. *Neostoicism and the Early Modern State*. Cambridge, U.K., 1982.

Orso, Steven N. *Art and Death at the Spanish Habsburg Court: The Royal Exequies for Philip IV*. Columbia, MO, 1989.

Ots Capdequí, J.M. *El Estado español en las Indias*. México, 1941.

Padden, Robert C. "The *Ordenanza del Patronazgo*, 1574: An Interpretative Essay." *The Americas* 12 (1956): 333–354.

Pagden, Anthony. *The Fall of Natural Man: The American Indian and the Origins of Comparative Ethnology*. Cambridge, U.K., 1982.

_____. *Spanish Imperialism and the Political Imagination*. New Haven, 1990.

_____. *Lords of All the World: Ideologies of Empire in Spain, Britain and France, c. 1500–1800*. New Haven, 1995.

Palmer, Colin A. *Slaves of the White God: Blacks in Mexico, 1570–1650.* Cambridge, MA, 1976.

Parry, J.H. *The Spanish Theory of Empire in the Sixteenth Century.* Cambridge, U.K., 1940.

____. *The Audiencia of New Galicia in the Sixteenth Century: A Study in Spanish Colonial Government.* Cambridge, U.K., 1948.

____. *The Sale of Public Office in the Spanish Indies Under the Habsburgs.* Berkeley, 1953.

Pastor, Rodolfo. "El repartimiento de mercancías y los alcaldes mayores novohispanos: un sistema de explotación, de sus orígenes a la crisis de 1810." In *El gobierno provincial en la Nueva España, 1570–1787,* edited by W. Borah. México, 1985.

Paz, Octavio. *Sor Juana Inés de la Cruz o las trampas de la fe.* México, 1982.

____. *The Labyrinth of Solitude and Other Writings.* New York, 1985.

Pazos Pazos, María Luisa J. *El ayuntamiento de la ciudad de México en el siglo XVII: continuidad institucional y cambio social.* Sevilla, 1999.

Peck, Linda Levy. *Court Patronage and Corruption in Early Stuart England.* London, 1990.

Phelan, John Leddy. "Authority and Flexibility in the Spanish Imperial Bureaucracy." *Administrative Science Quarterly* 5 (1960): 47–65.

____. *The Kingdom of Quito in the Seventeenth Century: Bureaucratic Politics in the Spanish Empire.* Madison, 1967.

____. *The Millennial Kingdom of the Franciscans in the New World.* Berkeley, 1970.

Pietschmann, Horst. *El Estado y su evolución al principio de la colonización española de América.* México, 1989.

____. "Corrupción en las Indias españolas: Revisión de un debate en la historiografía sobre Hispanoamérica colonial." In *Instituciones y corrupción en la historia,* edited by M. González Jiménez et al. Valladolid, 1998.

Pocock, J.G.A. "States, Republics, and Empires: The American Founding in Early Modern Perspective." In *Conceptual Change and the Constitution,* edited by T. Ball and J.G.A. Pocock. Lawrence, 1988.

Poole, Stafford. *Pedro Moya de Contreras: Catholic Reform and Royal Power in New Spain, 1571–1591.* Berkeley, 1987.

Powell, Philip W. *La guerra chichimeca (1550–1600).* México, 1977.

Pratt, Mary Louise. *Imperial Eyes: Travel Writing and Transculturation.* London, 1992.

Prem, Hanns J. "Disease Outbreaks in Central Mexico during the Sixteenth Century." In *"Secret Judgments of God": Old World Disease in Colonial Spanish America,* edited by N.D. Cook and W.G. Lovell. London, 1992.

Prodi, Paolo. *The Papal Prince. One Body and Two Souls: The Papal Monarchy in Early Modern Europe,* translated by S. Haskins. Cambridge, U.K., 1987.

Rabasa, José. *Writing Violence on the Northern Frontier: The Historiography of Sixteenth-Century New Mexico and Florida and the Legacy of Conquest.* Durham, 2000.

_____. "Pre-Columbian Pasts and Indian Presents in Mexican History." In *Colonialism Past and Present: Reading and Writing about Colonial Latin America Today*, edited by A.F. Bolaños and G. Verdesio. Albany, 2002.

Ranum, Orest. "Courtesy, Absolutism, and the Rise of the French State, 1630–1660." *Journal of Modern History* 52 (Sept. 1980): 426–451.

Ribot García, Luis Antonio. "La España de Carlos II." In *Historia de España Menéndez Pidal*, vol. XXVIII, edited by P. Molas Ribalta. Madrid, 1993.

Río Barredo, María José del. *Madrid, Urbs Regia. La capital ceremonial de la Monarquía Católica*. Madrid, 2000.

Riva Palacio, Vicente. *México a través de los siglos*, 5 vols. Barcelona, 1888–1889.

Rivera Cambas, Manuel. *Los gobernantes de México*, 2 vols. México, 1872.

Rodríguez Villa, Antonio. *Etiquetas de la Casa de Austria*. Madrid, 1913.

Romero Osorio, Ignacio. *La luz imaginaria: epistolario de Athanasius Kircher con los novohispanos*. México, 1993.

Rubiés, Joan Pau. "La idea del gobierno mixto y su significado en la crisis de la Monarquía Hispánica." *Historia Social* 24 (1996): 57–81.

Rubial García, Antonio. *La plaza, el palacio y el convento. La ciudad de México en el siglo XVII*. México, 1998.

_____. "La mitra y la cogulla. La secularización palafoxiana y su impacto en el siglo XVII." *Relaciones* 73 (Winter 1998): 239–272.

Rubio Mañé, José Ignacio. *El virreinato* (1955), 3 vols. México, 1992.

Ruiz, Teófilo. "Unsacred Monarchy: The Kings of Castile in the Late Middle Ages." In *Rites of Power: Symbolism, Ritual, and Politics Since the Middle Ages*, edited by S. Wilentz. Philadelphia, 1985.

Sarabia Viejo, Justina. *Don Luis de Velasco, virrey de Nueva España, 1550–1564*. Sevilla, 1978.

Sarfatti, Magali. *Spanish Bureaucratic Patrimonialism in America*. Berkeley, 1966.

Schneider, Robert A. *The Ceremonial City: Toulouse Observed, 1738–1780*. Princeton, 1995.

Schoenfeldt, Michael C. *Prayer and Power: George Herbert and Renaissance Courtship*. Chicago, 1991.

Schreffler, Michael J. "Art and Allegiance in Baroque New Spain." Ph.D. dissertation, University of Chicago, 2000.

Schwaller, John F. "The *Ordenanza del Patronazgo* in New Spain, 1574–1600." *The Americas* 42 (1986): 253–274.

Seed, Patricia. "The Colonial Church as an Ideological State Apparatus." In *Intellectuals and Power in Mexico*, edited by R. Camp et al. Los Angeles, 1981.

_____. "Colonial and Postcolonial Discourse." *Latin American Research Review* 26, no. 3 (1991): 181–200.

Selwyn, Jennifer D. "Procur[ing] in the Common People These Better Behaviors: The Jesuits' Civilizing Mission in Early Modern Naples 1550–1620." *Radical History Review* 67 (1997): 4–34.

Semo, Enrique. *Historia del capitalismo en México. Los orígenes, 1521–1763*. México, 1973.

Sempat Assadourian, Carlos. "Memoriales de fray Gerónimo de Mendieta." *Historia Mexicana* XXXVII, no. 3 (1988): 357–422.

_____. "Fray Alonso de Maldonado: la política indiana, el estado de damnación del rey católico y la Inquisición." *Historia Mexicana* XXXVIII, no. 4 (1989): 623–661.

Shapiro, Marianne. "Mirror and Portrait: The Structure of Il libro del Cortegiano." *The Journal of Medieval and Renaissance Studies* 5 (1975).

Sharpe, Kevin and Steven N. Zwicker, eds., *Politicis of Discourse: The Literature and History of Seventeenth-Century England.* Berkeley, 1987.

Shepard, Robert. "Court Factions in Early Modern England." *Journal of Modern History* 64 (1992): 721–745.

Sigaut, Nelly. "La tradición de estos reinos." In *Barroco Iberoamericano. Territorio, arte, espacio y sociedad.* Seville, 2001.

Silva Prada, Natalia. "La política de una rebelión. Los indígenas frente al tumulto de 1692 en la ciudad de México." Ph.D. dissertation, El Colegio de México, 2000.

Skinner, Quentin. *The Foundations of Modern Political Thought,* 2 vols. Cambridge, U.K., 1978.

_____. "Meaning and Understanding in the History of Ideas." In *Meaning and Context: Quentin Skinner and His Critics,* edited by J. Tully. Princeton, 1988.

_____. "The State." In *Political Innovation and Conceptual Change,* edited by T. Ball et al. Cambridge, U.K., 1989.

Smith, Jay M. "No More Language Games: Words, Beliefs, and the Political Culture of Early Modern France." *The American Historical Review* 102, no. 5 (Dec. 1997): 1413–1440.

Smuts, R. Malcolm. "Public Ceremony and Royal Charisma: The English Royal Entry in London, 1485–1642." In *The First Modern Society: Essays in English History in Honour of Lawrence Stone,* edited by A.L. Beier et al. Cambridge, U.K., 1989.

Sommerville, J.P. *Politics and Ideology in England, 1603–1640.* London, 1986.

Sosa, Francisco. *El episcopado mexicano. Galería biográfica ilustrada de los Illmos. Señores Arzobispos de México desde la época colonial hasta nuestros días.* México, 1877.

Spurr, David. *The Rhetoric of Empire: Colonial Discourse in Journalism, Travel Writing and Imperial Administration.* Durham, 1993.

Stein, Stanley J. and Barbara H. Stein, *The Colonial Heritage of Latin America: Essays on Economic Dependence in Perspective.* New York, 1970.

Stern, Steve J. "Feudalism, Capitalism, and the World System in the Perspective of Latin America and the Caribbean." *American Historical Review* 93 (Oct. 1988): 829–872.

Stoetzer, O. Carlos. *The Scholastic Roots of the Spanish American Revolution.* New York, 1979.

Strong, Roy. *Art and Power: Renaissance Festivals, 1450–1650.* Berkeley, 1973.

Sullivan, John. "La congregación como tecnología disciplinaria en el siglo XVI." *Estudios de Historia Novohispana* 16 (1996): 35–55.

Tanck de Estrada, Dorothy. "Castellanización, política y escuelas de indios en el arzobispado de México a mediados del siglo XVIII." *Historia Mexicana* 152 (1989): 701–741.

_____. *Pueblos de indios y educación en el México colonial, 1750–1821.* México, 1999.

Taylor, William B. *Drinking, Homicide, and Rebellion in Colonial Mexican Villages.* Stanford, 1979.

_____. "Between Global Process and Local Knowledge: An Inquiry into Early Latin American Social History, 1500–1900." In *Reliving the Past: The Worlds of Social History,* edited by O. Zunz. Chapel Hill, 1985.

_____. *Magistrates of the Sacred: Priests and Parishioners in Eighteenth-Century Mexico.* Stanford, 1996.

Thompson, I.A.A. *Crown and Cortes: Government, Institutions and Representation in Early Modern Castile.* Aldershot, 1993.

Tilly, Charles. *Coercion, Capital, and European States, AD 990–1990.* Oxford, 1990.

_____. "The Long Run of European State Formation." In *Visions sur le développement des États européens. Théories et historiographies de l'État moderne,* edited by W. Blockmans and J.-Ph. Genet. Rome, 1993.

_____, ed. *The Formation of National States in Western Europe.* Princeton, 1975.

Tomás y Valiente, Francisco. "Opiniones de algunos juristas clásicos españoles sobre la venta de oficios públicos." In *Filosofía y derecho: Estudios en honor del profesor José Corts Grau.* Valencia, 1977.

_____. *Gobierno e instituciones en la España del Antiguo Régimen.* Madrid, 1982.

_____. "La España de Felipe IV. El gobierno de la monarquía y la administración de los reinos en la España del siglo XVII." In *Historia de España Menéndez Pidal,* vol. XXIII, 2nd ed., edited by F. Tomás y Valiente. Madrid, 1990.

Torre Villar, Ernesto de la. *Las congregaciones de los pueblos de indios. Fase terminal: aprobaciones y rectificaciones.* México, 1995.

Trens, Manuel. *Las custodias españolas.* Barcelona, 1952.

Trexler, Richard. *Public Life in Renaissance Florence.* Ithaca, 1980.

Tully, James. "The Pen Is a Mighty Sword: Quentin Skinner's Analysis of Politics." In *Meaning and Context: Quentin Skinner and His Critics,* edited by J. Tully. Princeton, 1988.

Varela, Javier. *La muerte del rey. El ceremonial funerario de la monarquía española (1500–1885).* Madrid, 1990.

Verdesio, Gustavo. "Colonialism Now and Then: Colonial Latin American Studies in the Light of the Predicament of Latin Americanism." In *Colonialism Past and Present: Reading and Writing About Colonial Latin America Today,* edited by A.F. Bolaños and G. Verdesio. Albany, 2002.

Vicens Vives, Jaime. "The Administrative Structure of the State in the Sixteenth and Seventeenth Centuries." In *Government in Reformation Europe, 1520–1560,* edited by Henry J. Cohn. Bloomington, 1979.

Wallerstein, Immanuel. *The Modern World-System: Capitalist Agriculture and the Origins of the European World Economy in the Sixteenth Century.* New York, 1974.

Walzer, Michael. "On the Role of Symbolism in Political Thought." *Political Science Quarterly* 82, no. 2 (June 1967): 193–196.

Waquet, Jean-Claude. *Corruption: Ethics and Power in Florence, 1600–1770*, translated by L. McCall. University Park, 1991.

Weber, Max. *Economy and Society: An Outline of Interpretive Sociology.* Berkeley, 1978.

Weckmann, Luis. *La herencia medieval de México.* México, 1983.

Yalí Román, Alberto. "Sobre alcaldías mayores y corregimientos en Indias. Un ensayo de interpretación." *Jahrbuch für Geschichte von Staat, Wirtschaft und Gesellschaft Lateinamerikas* 9 (1972): 1–39.

Yates, Frances A. *Giordano Bruno and the Hermetic Tradition.* Chicago, 1964.

_____. *Astraea: The Imperial Theme in the Sixteenth Century.* London, 1975.

Young, Robert J.C. *Postcolonialism: An Historical Introduction.* Oxford, 2001.

Zavala, Silvio A. *El servicio personal de los indios en la Nueva España*, 5 vols. México, 1984.

_____. *Las instituciones jurídicas en la conquista de América.* México, 1988.

_____. *Poder y lenguaje desde el siglo XVI.* México, 1996.

Zimmerman, Arthur F. *Francisco de Toledo, Fifth Viceroy of Peru, 1569–1581.* New York, 1938.

Index

A

Abrams, Philip, 7
Acosta, José de, 193–194, 207–208, 220, 230
Acuerdo, 57, 61, 62, 69
Aeolus, 31
Aguiar y Seijas, Francisco de, 104–105
Ahuitzotl, 34
Alavés Pinelo, Alonso de, 31, 34, 44
Alba de Liste, count of, 113–114, 136–137, 170
Alburquerque, duke of, 31, 34, 46, 48, 93, 171, 232–233, 234, 235
alcabala, 218
alcalde del crimen, 79, 234
alcaldes, 61, 72, 217
   de corte, 73
   del crimen, 18, 124, 137
     vs. *oidores*, 145–146
   mayores, 24, 72, 89, 166–183, 218, 231, 233, 234, 236, 244
     corruption, and, 176
     patronage, and, 158
   ordinarios, 66, 73, 124, 167, 171, 172, 244
alcaldía mayor, 163, 173, 174, 177, 244
alcohol, *see pulque*
alférez mayor, 146–148
alguaciles, 217
allegados, 166
altepetl, 197

Alter Nos, 25
ancien régime, 13, 121, 175, 177, 182
angels, 39–44, 136
Antequera, 231
Aquinas, Thomas, 22, 45
archangels, 38, 41–44, 239
archbishops, 86–106, 150, 243
   as councilors, 101
   as viceroys, 104
   characteristics of, 88–89
   Corpus Christi procession, and, 137
   entries of, 88
   inquisitors, and, 154
   patronage, and, 159
   public image of, 132–133
   use of *dosel*, and, 134–135
   visits by viceroys, 137–138
   vs. viceroys, 79–117
archeological perspective, 226
arches, viceregal, 26–36, 124, 157, 239
   allegories in, 29
   archepiscopal, 88
   as mirrors, 26, 30
   Aztec mythology in, 29
   count of Paredes, marquis of La Laguna, 29
   count of Salvatierra, 27
   duke of Alburquerque, *see* Alburquerque, duke of
   heroes in, 27

armada de Barlovento, 71–73
asesor letrado, 18, 221
asiento, 229
audiencias, 17, 24, 25, 51, 52, 53, 54, 56,
    57–65, 67, 68, 75, 79, 85, 87, 92,
    102, 106–107, 109, 110, 112, 115,
    119, 120, 122, 124, 131, 132, 134,
    137, 139, 140, 141, 142, 144, 145,
    148, 149, 150, 151, 152, 153, 166,
    167, 182, 190, 214, 219, 220, 221,
    231, 233, 234, 235, 243
autos de fe, 121, 150–151
Avendaño, Diego de, 180, 240
Aztec emperors, virtues of, 32

B

baldachin, 125, 134
Baños, count of, 94, 134, 135, 160,
    172–173, 224, 234, 235
Barrientos, Alamos de, 223
barrios, 226–228
benefit vs. sale, 174–175
beneméritos de Indias, 163, 170
bishops, 85–106, 215, 218
    accusations of sedition, 101
    as equals of viceroys, 86
    as governors of dioceses, 88
    characteristics of, 87
    confrontations with viceroys, 138
    entourage of, 89
    obligation to obey monarch, 90
    patronage, and, 159
    power to command and execute, 89
    public display of power, 122
    removal of, 100
    symbols of, 88
    use of *dosel*, and, 134
    use of *palio*, and, 133–134
blacks, 205, 206, 210, 222, 223, 224, 226,
    227
Bobadilla, Castillo de, 56, 68, 81–82, 83,
    91–92, 122
Bocanegra, Matías de, 30–31, 32, 35, 40
Bodin, Jean, 55, 63
body politic, 20, 21, 36, 76, 77, 83, 124,
    131, 159, 186

C

caballerizo mayor, 162
cabildo, 24, 53, 65–77, 120, 125, 129, 137,
    141, 142, 148–149, 152, 238
    eclesiástico, 52, 136
    secular, 12, 52
cacique, 200, 231
Cadereita, marquis of, 71, 102, 213
calpolli, 197
canon law, 83
canopy, 125; *see also palio*
capitanes generales, 17
Caravantes, Matías de, 238, 239
Caribbean naval squadron, 71
Carlos II, 245
Castellar, count of, 173
Castile, Council of, 15
Castilianization, 200, 201
Castrillo, count of, 101–102
catafalque, 48, 49, 129, 130, 133, 144, 160,
    188
Catholic ruler, fundamental virtues of, 31
cédula, 61, 90, 109–110, 111, 112, 127,
    145, 153, 166, 170, 173, 201, 210,
    213, 227
    real, 36
Cerralvo, marquis of, 70, 73, 98, 99, 102,
    210, 218–219
chairs as signs of power, 149–150
Chalco, 174
chancillerías, 57, 67, 110
Charles II, 5, 46, 49, 54, 105, 115, 160,
    178, 199
Charles V, 57, 66
Chiapas, Mexico, 1–3
city-states, 197
clientelism, 13
colateral, 20
colonialism, political culture of, 185–212
compadrazgo, 228
concordia, 109, 111
conquistadores, 163–165, 166, 174
Consulado, 131
consulta, 40, 41, 110
Contreras, Alonso de, 161
Contreras, Moya de, 134, 207

Corpus Christi, 135–138
corpus iuridicum/mysticum, 20
corregidores, 66, 68, 69, 73, 74, 76, 89, 92,
    108, 124, 137, 141, 149, 152–153,
    164, 170, 171, 173, 179, 187, 218,
    220
    corruption, and, 176
    elimination of post of, 72, 73, 74
    patronage, and, 158
corregimientos, 163, 174
corruption, 175–183
Cortes, 66–76
Cortés, Hernán, 225
Council of Trent, 135
courtesy calls, 138
Covarrubias, Sebastian de, 9
crédito, 140
Creoles, 65, 66, 72, 73, 75, 165, 166, 167,
    168, 172, 174, 183, 185, 214, 222,
    226, 228
criados, 65
    y familiares, 166
criollos, 214, 241, 245
Crown, the, 9, 13, 14, 15, 17, 54, 67, 69,
    70, 72, 73, 74, 81, 83, 84, 85, 102,
    108, 109, 111, 113, 115, 116, 127,
    133, 143, 144, 158, 162, 163,
    165–175, 178, 193, 194, 196, 197,
    198, 199, 200, 201, 204, 210, 216,
    220, 221, 228, 229, 235, 236, 238,
    240, 241, 242
cuerpo de audiencia, 142
Cuevas Dávalos, Alonso de, 233–234

D

de la Serna, Jacinto, 48, 49–50
dependency approach, 6
desagüe, 210
Diego Rivera, mural of, 1, 2
Divine Right, 54, 55, 240
doctrinas, 89, 221, 228
dosel, 125, 133, 134, 135

E

El Escorial, 129
encomenderos, 193, 194, 201

encomienda, 18, 72, 201
Enríquez, Martín, 15, 134, 207, 213, 216,
    219, 223
Enríquez de Rivera, Payo, 88, 102–104,
    138, 139, 140–141, 144–145, 173
entourage, 162
epidemics, 204
Escalona, duke of, 125–127
Escobar, Diego Osorio de, 133
Espejo, Juan de, 232
estados, vs. *Estado*, 9
estates, social, 9
excommunication, 97–98

F

familia, 162
familiares, 109, 115
favors
    economy of, 157–183
    rewards, and, 159–165
fiestas de tabla, 142
First Mexican Council, 195
fiscal, 60, 61, 69, 72, 85, 95, 139, 148, 150,
    151, 172
Foucault, Michel, 12, 121, 182
Franciscans, 187, 188, 189, 190, 191, 192,
    194, 204, 205, 206, 207, 208
Frías, Bernardo de, 43
friendship, language of, 62
fuero, 96
    inquisitorial, 107
funerals, 129–131, 133

G

Galve, count of, 174–175, 179, 228, 229,
    244
Gelves, marquis of, 51, 52, 64–65, 79–80,
    96, 100, 101, 125, 127
    vs. *audiencia* of Mexico, 64–65
General Indian Court, 219–222
gentileshombres de la cámara, 162
Gómez de Cervantes, Gonzalo, 164
grandee, 125
gratitude vs. ingratitude, 161
Guadalcázar, marquis of, 142, 144, 186
Guanajuato, 174

H

Habsburg dynasty, 3, 14, 48, 66, 67, 125, 199
 end of, 15
 Holy Sacrament, and, 46
hats, of *oidores*, 141
Heaven, structure of, 38, 40
hierarchy of universe, 38
Holy Eucharist, 45, 46, 50
Holy Sacrament, 37, 46, 48, 49, 125, 135, 139
Huancavélica, 210
Huatulco, 174
human body, comparison of state to, 21–24

I

ideology, defined, 19
imperio, 34
Indians; *see also* "rhetoric of wretchedness"; viceroys: personal services of Indians, and
 alcohol, and, 228–231
 appointment of a king, 235–236
 as characterized by José de Acosta, 193–194
 as characterized by Juan de Matienzo, 193
 as characterized by Juan de Palafox, 191–192
 as characterized by Juan de Solórzano, 192
 as described by Alamos de Barrientos, 223
 as described by the marquis of Mancera, 223, 224
 as described by Carlos de Sigüenza, 225
 as feet of monarchy's body, 241
 as ideal Franciscan friars, 189
 as labor force, 194
 Castilianization of, 200, 201
 civilization of, 201–212
 congregation of in towns, 195, 196, 197, 198, 218
 epidemics of, 204
 forced labor in mines, 208
 General Indian Court, 219–222
 hybrid world of, 228
 judicial system, and, 219
 laziness of, 211
 mission to civilize, 192–201
 need for viceroy, 214–216
 perception of by the Crown, 187
 politicization of, 195
 protection of, 190
 punishment of, 191
 resettlement program, 198–199, 204
 service of to Spaniards, 201–212
 Spanish language, and, 200
 transition from obedient to insolent, 227
 viewed as children, 188–190, 192, 215–216, 220
 vs. *plebes*, 223
Indies, Council of the, 15, 24, 39, 95–96, 100–104, 115, 127, 140, 146, 168, 169, 170, 171, 172, 173, 175, 182, 187, 191, 200, 235, 241–242
Inquisition, 1, 15, 52, 72, 81, 106–117, 150–155, 243
 council, 110
 funeral processions, and, 131–132
 mission of, 112
 power of, 111
 tribunal of, 142
inquisitors, 150, 154, 218
Ixtepeji, 231

J

jail inspections, 145
Juan, Jorge, 241, 242, 244

K

king; *see also* Crown, the
 as absolute monarch, 54
 as head of a body, 21, 23
 invisibility of, 37
 mission of, 55
 vs. God, 37
Kircher, Athanasius, 29

L

La Monclova, count of, 244
La Palata, duke of, 174
ladinización, 226
Las Siete Partidas, 84
lawsuits, Indians and, 219
lese majesty, 19, 44
letrados, 4, 59, 181, 219
liberality, 161
Liñán, Melchor de, 173
Louis XIV, 177, 244

M

maceros, 149
Machiavelli, 8, 63
Madariaga, Juan de, 56–57, 58, 62
Madrid, 173
    celebration of Corpus Christi, 135,
        136
maguey, 229
Mancera, marquis of, 36, 93–94, 95, 103,
    106, 114, 138, 139, 140–141, 222,
    223, 224
Manso de Contreras, Cristóbal, 231
Manso, Francisco de, 98–99, 100–102
Mars, 35
Martín de Guijo, Gregorio, 182
Matienzo, Juan de, 190, 193
Medina, Alonso de, 26–27, 35, 40
Mendieta, Gerónimo de, 188–190, 191,
    197, 204, 205, 206, 209, 214–216,
    220, 228, 241
Mendoza, Antonio de, 216, 220
Mendoza, Hernando de, 178, 181
Mestitlan, 174
mestizos, 164, 205, 206, 210, 222, 223,
    224, 226, 227, 228
Mexico City, 132, 133
    as head of New Spain, 69
    audiencia, 57–58
    auto de fe, 150–151
    cabildo, 66, 69, 148–149, 152; *see also*
        cabildo
    cathedral of, 36, 44
    Indian barrios, 226, 227, 228
    Indians living in, 222
    Inquisition, and, 152
    multiracial character of, 224–225
    use of *palio* for arrival in, 127
    viceroy arrival in, 123
Mexico City riot of 1624, 51, 64, 80, 99,
    100, 125, 226
Mexico City riot of 1692, 14, 100, 225,
    227, 228, 229, 231, 244
Miaguatlan, 174
ministro superior, 20, 28
Moctezuma, count of, 126, 147, 154, 199
Monarquía Hispánica, 17
monstrance, 48, 50, 106, 136, 137
Montemayor, Juan Francisco de,
    134–135, 234, 236
Monterrey, count of, 95–96, 134, 198,
    221, 222
Montesclaros, marquis of, 164, 165, 198
Motecohçuma Xocoyotzin, 157
Moya de Contreras, Pedro, 207
mulattos, 164, 205, 206, 222, 223, 224, 227
mystical body, 20, 21, 62

N

Nahuatl, 200, 203, 217
Nejapa, 231, 232, 233, 235
Neptune, 32, 33, 157
Nieremberg, Juan Eusebio, 41–43, 44
Núñez de Cepeda, Francisco, 92–93

O

Oaxaca, 85, 173, 174, 232, 233, 235
obligaciones, 162
oficial real, 106
oidores, 18, 58, 60–65, 72, 75, 80, 94,
    106–107, 109, 110, 111, 112, 119,
    120, 124, 129, 131, 132, 134, 135,
    136, 140–152, 166, 173, 176, 190,
    201, 214, 218, 221, 231, 234, 238,
    243
    as king's representatives, 142
    viceroys, and, 142–152
    vs. *alcaldes*, 145
Olivares, count-duke of, 52, 67, 70, 159
Ortega y Montañés, Juan de, 105, 211
Osorio, Diego, 94, 103, 133, 134, 135, 172

P

Palafox, Juan de, 51, 52, 62, 103, 119, 127, 133, 165, 166, 167, 168, 169, 170, 179, 191, 216, 218, 222, 223, 238, 244
palio, 124–128, 133–134
Paredes, count of, 36, 104, 157, 174
parish priests, appointment of, 95
Partidas, 21
paterfamilias, 220
patronage, 13, 84, 89, 158–160, 162–163, 165–166, 174–176, 178–179, 181, 183, 244
Patronato Real, 16, 84, 85, 86, 90, 95, 97, 104
patron–client relationships, 4, 159, 162, 171, 177, 228
Peace of Westphalia, 81
Pegasus, 31
peninsulares, 65, 214, 241, 245
Pérez de la Serna, Juan, 79–80, 96–97, 101
Pérez de Mesa, Diego, 59
Perseus, 31
persona miserable, 187
personae fictae, 9
Philip II, 15, 37, 46, 52, 187, 207, 214, 216, 221, 227
Philip III, 112, 223
Philip IV, 46, 67, 75, 86, 159, 187, 188
    funeral procession for, 131
Philip V,, 244
Pizarro, Fernando, 163
plebe, 222, 223, 224, 229
Política indiana, 18, 24, 33, 62, 209–210; *see also* Solórzano, Juan de
pope, 116, 133, 187
    power of, 81–88
Portocarrero, Pedro, 178
power, 175
    duality of, 82, 105; *see also* "two-knives" doctrine
    inquisitorial, dual nature of, 108
    mystery of, 36–50
    papal, 81–88
    patronage, and, 158
    prelate vs. viceroy, 79–117
    rituals of, 119–155

    secular vs. ecclesiastical, 132, 139
    symbolic representations of, 12
    transmission of by God, 83
    viceregal vs. royal, 174
    viceregal, limitations of, 238
    viceroy's vs. *oidores*, 143
praetor, 41
primus inter pares, 87
prince
    qualities of, 31–32
    symbols of, 88
princeps legibus solutus, 55
processions
    Corpus Christi, 135–138
    funeral, 129–131, 133
    Madrid Corpus Christi, 135
    official viceroy welcome, 123–124
    proclamation of Edict of Faith, 152
    to Mexico City by viceroys, 123–125
    to triumphal arch, 129
    viceroy's body, and, 121
    welcome vs. funeral, 131
procuradores, 67
proreges, 25
Protomedicato, 131
prudence, 31, 32, 54, 63, 87, 103, 239
Puebla, 123, 133, 165, 170, 172, 191
pueblos de indios, 197
pulque, 228–231
pulquerías, 229

R

Ramírez de Arellano, Juan, 207
real provisión, 120, 137
rebellion, 213–236
Reconquista, 84
regalía, 85
regidores, 64, 66, 67, 68, 69, 70, 71, 72, 73, 74, 77, 124, 129, 141, 146–149, 231, 243
Reina Maldonado, Pedro de, 87, 89, 92, 122
Reino, 67
Renaissance, 10
repartimiento, 204–206, 208–210, 218
república de españoles, 215
república de indios, 215, 240

residencias, 169
"rhetoric of wretchedness", 14, 186–192,
   197, 211, 213, 220, 222, 227,
   230–236, 240
rituals of power, 119–155, 243
   challenges to, 132–141
   reception of royal seal, 120
Rivadeneira, Pedro de, 160
Roman Index, 85
Royal patronato, 135, 137
royal seal, 120
Rudolf I, 46
rule of one, 19–26, 102, 106, 238

S

Saavedra Fajardo, Diego, 224
Sala del Acuerdo, 143
Salazar, Juan de, 58
Salvatierra, count of, 27, 35, 40, 51, 73,
   119, 143–144, 165, 167, 168, 169,
   170, 218
San Luis Potosí, 170
Santa María, García de, 95, 134
Santa María, Juan de, 23, 56, 180
Santísimo Sacramento, 45
Saona, Jerónimo de, 38, 39, 40, 41
sedition, 101
Seijas y Lobera, Francisco de, 244
selling of offices, 175–183
Seneca, patronage and, 161
senses, human, and correspondence to
   qualities of a good ruler, 23
separation of king and state, 21
seraphim, 38, 39, 40
Sigüenza, Carlos de, 29, 30, 32, 34, 36,
   157, 225
Silva, Juan de, 205
Skinner, Quentin, 12, 19
Society of Jesus, 15, 36, 51, 131
solar imagery, viceregal power and, 36
Solórzano, Juan de, 10, 17, 24–26, 57, 62,
   85, 86, 90, 111–112, 113, 143,
   152, 159, 192, 196, 200, 201,
   209–210, 223
Sor Juana Inés de la Cruz, 26, 28, 29, 32,
   157
St. Michael, 41–44, 106, 239

state
   absolutist, 4–5
   as collective body of the prince, 21
   as political organization, 4
   as vehicle of coercion, 6
   colonial, 159, 176
   consensus, 5–6
   introduction of term by Hobbes, 8
   invention of, 7–11
   modern, 4, 5, 76, 176
   true, 4
   vs. Church, 80–93
   vs. *status*, 8
statist paradigm, 8, 76, 81
Suárez, Francisco, 83, 87
Sultepec, 174
superintendente de propios, 149

T

Tacuba, 244
Taylor, William B., 6
Tehuacan, 174
Tehuantepec, 171, 231–236
   uprising of 1660, 14, 183
Tenochtitlán, 225
   conquest of, 147
   flood of, 34
Teotihuacán, 79–80
terms of office, for viceroys, 18, 242
Third Mexican Provincial Council, 190,
   197, 206
Thomist political theory, 21
tithes, 91, 167, 194
Tlatelolco, 228
tlatoanis, 3
Tlaxcala, 123
Toledo, Francisco de, 15, 216
Tonalá, 174
Torquemada, Juan de, 199, 216
Torres Castillo, Juan de, 231
Torres, Marcos de, 103
"two-knives" doctrine, 80–93

U

Ugarte, Francisco, 82
Ulloa, Antonio de, 241, 242, 244

Ulysses, 31, 34
University of Mexico professors, 230

V

Velasco I, Luis de, 163, 202, 203, 216, 217
Velasco II, Luis de, 165, 197, 198, 209,
    219–220, 221
Veracruz, 123, 170, 171
Veracruz Vieja, 174
Veragua, duke of, 104, 140
Vetancourt, Agustín de, 229
viceregal courts, 162–163
vicereine, 35, 135, 136, 137, 142, 144, 166
viceroy
    ambiguous nature of power of, 28
    appointment of parish priests by, 95
    as *capitán general*, 62
    as defined by Mendieta, 215
    as depicted in Diego Rivera mural, 1
    as king's image, 25–26, 143, 218,
        221, 239
    as praetor, 41
    as prince, 30
    as source of patronage, 158
    as symbol of royalty, 121
    audiencias, and, 57–59
    bishops as, 102
    canopy, and; *see palio*
    companions of, 53–65
    compelling Indians to offer
        themselves for hire, 207
    conquistadores, and, 164–165
    control over subordinates by, 53
    Corpus Christi, and, 136
    duties of, 18
    entourages of, 162
    entry into Mexico City, 52
    excessive power of, 237
    excommunication, and, 97
    Indian justice, and, 221
    Indian relations, 220, 241
    Indian resettlement, and, 199
    Inquisition, and, 106–117
    inquisitors, and, 150, 154
    itinerary from Veracruz to Mexico
        City, 123
    justice, and, 58; *see also audiencias*

king's servant vs. supreme ruler, 28
labor draft, and, 208–209
Mexico City riot of 1692, and, 227
mission of, 40, 50
obeying monarch's orders, 244
official welcome procession, 123–124
oidores, and, 61–65, 142–152
order to obey in Indies, 25
orders of, vs. those of the king, 168
personal services of Indians, and,
    201–204
politics of, 120–132
power, limitations of, 238
preservation of power of, 100
privileged position of, 17
processions; *see* processions
public image of, 122–123, 132–133
relationship with archbishops, 94
responsibility to preserve law, 233
ritual power of, 119–155
seeing, 11–16
selling of offices by, 168, 174, 175,
    178
social distance from indigenous
        population, 216–217
St. Michael, and, 42
symbols of royalty, 125, 131
term of office, 18, 242
two republics of, 214–222
use of *dosel*, and, 134
virtues of, 32, 62
visibility of, 13
visits by archbishops, 137–138vs.
        archangels, 42
vs. *audiencia*, 53
vs. prelates, 12, 79–117
welcome of, 52
Villamanrique, marquis of, 128, 209
Villarroel, Gaspar de, 87–88, 89, 90–91,
    94
Vilosa, Rafael de, 19–20, 45
virtue, 31–32, 103
visita, 101, 166, 169, 202
visitador, 99, 119, 150, 169*visitador*
    general, 51, 165, 168, 218
visitas de cárcel, 145
vulgo, 224

W

Weberian idea of the professional
    bureaucrat, 181
Weberian model of legal domination, 5

X

Xochimilco, 174
Xocoyotzin, Motecohçuma, 157

Y

Yo el Rey, 42
Yucatan, bishop of, 150, 169, 170

Z

Zacatecas, 106
Zapatista, 1
Zephyr, 31